INTEGRATING
RESEARCH

Applied Social Research Methods Series
Volume 2

APPLIED SOCIAL RESEARCH METHODS SERIES

Series Editors
LEONARD BICKMAN, Peabody College, Vanderbilt University, Nashville
DEBRA J. ROG, Vanderbilt University, Washington, DC

Other volumes in this series are listed at the end of the book

INTEGRATING RESEARCH

A Guide for Literature Reviews

Second Edition

Harris M. Cooper

Applied Social Research Methods Series
Volume 2

SAGE PUBLICATIONS
The International Professional Publishers
Newbury Park   London   New Delhi

To Elizabeth

For information address:

SAGE Publications, Inc.
2455 Teller Road
Newbury Park, California 91320
E-mail: order@sagepub.com

SAGE Publications Ltd.
6 Bonhill Street
London EC2A 4PU
United Kingdom

SAGE Publications India Pvt. Ltd.
M-32 Market
Greater Kailash I
New Delhi 110 048 India

Printed in the United States of America

Library of Congress Cataloging-in-Publication Data

Cooper, Harris M.
  Integrating research.

  (Applied social research methods series ; v. 2)
  Rev. ed. of: The integrative research review /
Harris M. Cooper. c1984.
  Bibliography: p.
  Includes indexes.
  1. Social sciences—Research. I. Cooper, Harris M.
Integrative research review. II. Title. III. Title:
Literature reviews. IV Series.
H62.C5859 1989   300′72   88-36233
  ISBN 0-8039-3430-0
  ISBN 0-8039-3431-9 (pbk.)

97 98 99 00 01 15 14 13 12 11

CONTENTS

PREFACE TO THE FIRST EDITION

Every research project in the social sciences should involve the inquirer searching out previous, related investigations. Without this step, an integrated, comprehensive picture of the world cannot be built. Researchers working in isolation repeat past mistakes and rarely achieve a sense of progress. Progress in social science comes from building on the efforts of those who have worked before.

Yet, the novice researcher has little guidance for how to conduct an integrative research review—how to find, evaluate, and synthesize previous research on the topic of interest. This book attempts to fill that void. It is intended for use by social science students with some background in basic research methods and statistics.

The approach to research reviewing espoused in this book represents a significant departure from how research reviews have been conducted in the past. Instead of the intuitive, subjective, narrative style that has been the traditional approach to research reviewing, this book presents a systematic, objective alternative. This approach is rapidly gaining acceptance in many social science fields. The reader learns how to carry out problem formulations, literature searches, research evaluations, and research syntheses according to rules based on scientific principles. The intended result is a replicable review that can create consensus among scholars and focus debate in a constructive fashion. Most important, users of this approach should finish their reviews feeling knowledgeable about the research area and confident that their future primary research can make a contribution to the field.

Several institutions and individuals were instrumental in the preparation of this book. First, the National Institute of Education provided research support while the manuscript was prepared. The grant, entitled "A systematic examination of the literature review and knowledge synthesis activities," was overseen by Spencer Ward of the NIE's Dissemination in Practice Program.

Special thanks go to four former graduate students: Maureen Findley, Ken Ottenbacher, David Tom, and Julie Yu. Each performed a research review in his or her own area of interest under my supervision. Their efforts have been used throughout the book to illustrate abstract points. While they were becoming expert in their fields, I was learning about problems in reviewing that transcend topic areas as well as about many more unique reviewing difficulties.

Jeanmarie Fraser, a librarian at the University of Missouri's Elmer Ellis Library, spent many hours conducting computerized literature searches for me and my students. She also graciously gave me a crash course in library science.

The first draft of this volume was read and critiqued by twelve people: Len Bickman, Ruth Haber, Larry Hedges, Ken Ottenbacher, Jolene Pettis, Ronald Ribble, Debra Rog, Robert Rosenthal, David Schumann, David Tom, Tedra

Walden, and Julie Yu. Each made comments that helped improve the final product.

Finally, the Center for Research in Social Behavior and especially its staff deserve my thanks. Patricia Shanks, Janice Meiburger, Terry Brown, and Diane Chappell transcribed, typed, and proofread the manuscript while tolerating a frenetic author. No simple task.

—Harris Cooper

PREFACE TO THE SECOND EDITION

In the years between editions of this book, scientific research reviewing changed from a controversial to an accepted practice. Its application is now found in every area of the social sciences; in some areas it is required.

The years have also brought improvements in integrative research reviewing techniques. Especially, the technology surrounding literature searching has improved. Also, the theoretical underpinnings of meta-analysis have been comprehensively described and the application of these procedures has been made more accessible.

This second edition incorporates these changes. In addition, two of the illustrations have been replaced with more up-to-date examples. Material on coding sheets and on the identification of independent hypothesis tests has been expanded. Finally, the tables needed to perform meta-analysis have been included in the text.

Even revisions require the help of others. Pamela Hazelrigg, a student of mine, coauthored one of the new illustrative reviews. Kathleen Connors, a reference librarian at the University of Oregon Library, helped update the sections on abstracting and indexing services. Larry Hedges again examined my exposition of statistical techniques. Cathy Luebbering typed, retyped, and proofread the manuscript. My thanks to these friends and colleagues.

—Harris Cooper

1

Introduction

This chapter presents a definition of the term *integrative research review*, a justification for critical attention to research reviews, and a five-stage research model for the reviewing process. The chapter also introduces four research reviews that serve as practical examples in the chapters that follow.

The pursuit of knowledge with the tools of science is a cooperative, interdependent process. The dozens or hundreds of hours spent conducting a scientific study ultimately contribute just one piece to an enormous puzzle. The value of any single study is derived as much from how it fits with and expands on previous work as from the study's intrinsic properties. Although it is true that some studies receive more attention than others, this is typically because the pieces of the puzzle they solve (or the puzzles they introduce) are extremely important, not because the studies are solutions in and of themselves.

THE NEED FOR ATTENTION TO
RESEARCH REVIEWS

Given the cumulative nature of science, trustworthy accounts of past research form a necessary condition for orderly knowledge building. Yet, research methods textbooks in the social sciences show a remarkable lack of attention to how an inquirer finds, evaluates, and integrates past research. This inattention is especially troubling today because the social sciences have recently undergone a huge increase in the amount of research being conducted. To accommodate the expanding demand for communication, the number of outlets for theoretical and research reports has burgeoned.

The ability to gain access to social science information has also changed dramatically in recent years. In particular, retrieval of past work has been facilitated by the computerized literature search. The computer's ability to scan abstracts rapidly has improved interested scientists' access to evidence, if they know how to use the technology.

Finally, the need for trustworthy accounts of past research is also strengthened by growing specialization within the social sciences. Time constraints make it impossible for most social scientists to keep abreast of primary research except within a few topic areas of special interest to them. Garvey and Griffith (1971) wrote about this situation in psychology:

The individual scientist is being overloaded with scientific information. Perhaps the alarm over an "information crisis" arose because sometime in the last information doubling period, the individual psychologist became overburdened and could no longer keep up with and assimilate all the information being produced that was related to his primary specialty. (p. 350)

GOALS AND PREMISES OF THE BOOK

The goal for this book is to compensate for the lack of attention given to the literature review in social science methods texts. It will apply the basic tenets of sound data gathering to a comprehensive synthesis of past research on a topic. The rules of rigorous, objective inquiry are the same whether the inquirer is conducting a primary study or a research review. The two types of inquiry, however, require techniques specific to their purpose, and the techniques for integrative research reviewing have largely been ignored in the past.

The underlying premise of this treatment is that *locating and integrating separate research projects involves inferences as central to the validity of knowledge as the inferences involved in primary data interpretation*. Due to the amount and diverse locations of social science information, the comprehensiveness and validity of review conclusions can no longer be taken for granted. A scientist performing a research review makes numerous decisions that affect the outcome of the review, and each choice may create threats to the outcome's trustworthiness. Therefore, if social science knowledge transmitted through research reviews is to be objective and believable, *research reviewers must be required to use the same rigorous methodology that is required of primary researchers*.

While substantial attention has been paid to validity issues in primary research (Bracht & Glass, 1968; Campbell, 1969; Campbell & Stanley, 1963; Cook & Campbell, 1979), the social sciences lack a conceptualization of the research review process that provides systematic guidelines for evaluating the validity of review outcomes. This book is an attempt to provide such an organizing scheme.

DEFINITIONS OF LITERATURE REVIEWS

Literature reviews typically appear as introductions to reports of new primary data or as more detailed independent works (e.g., Harper, Weins, & Matarazzo, 1978; Maccoby & Jacklin, 1974). The scope of a literature review that introduces new data is typically quite narrow. Research cited as an introduction to other primary research will be restricted to those studies pertinent to the specific issue addressed by the new data.

When a literature review appears independent of new data, it can serve decidedly broader purposes. A literature review can have numerous different focuses, goals, perspectives, coverage strategies, organizations, and audiences (Cooper, 1988). For instance, reviews can focus on research outcomes, research methods, theories, and/or applications. Reviews can attempt to integrate what others have done and said, to criticize previous scholarly works, to build bridges between related topic areas, and/or to identify the central issues in a field.

Reviews combining two sets of focuses and goals appear most frequently. The first type of literature review is the *integrative research review*. Integrative reviews summarize past research by drawing overall conclusions from many separate studies that are believed to address related or identical hypotheses. The integrative reviewer hopes to present the state of knowledge concerning the relation(s) of interest and to highlight important issues that research has left unresolved. From the reader's viewpoint, an integrative research review is intended to "replace those earlier papers that have been lost from sight behind the research front" (Price, 1965, p. 513), and to direct future research so that it yields a maximum amount of new information.

The second kind of literature review is a *theoretical review*. Here, the reviewer hopes to present the theories offered to explain a particular phenomenon and to compare them with regard to breadth, internal consistency, and the nature of their predictions. Theoretical reviews will typically contain descriptions of critical experiments already conducted or suggested, assessments of which theory is most powerful and consistent with known relations, and sometimes reformulations or integrations of abstract notions from different theories.

Often a comprehensive review will address several of these sets of issues. Integrative research reviews are most common, however, and theoretical reviews will typically contain some integrative review components. It is also not unusual for integrative reviews to address multiple, related hypotheses. For instance, a review might examine the relation between several different independent variables and a single dependent variable, or it might try to summarize research related to a series of temporally linked hypotheses.

The major emphasis of this book will be the integrative research review. Not only is this the most frequent kind of review, but it also contains all the decision points present in other reviews—and some unique points as well.

THE STAGES OF RESEARCH REVIEW

Most textbooks on research methodology suggest that scientific inquiry involves a temporally sequenced set of activities. Although methodologists differ in the subtlety of their definitions for research stages, the most important distinctions in stages can be identified with a gratifying degree of consensus. Methodologists also uniformly agree that the sequencing of stages is not fixed;

practicing researchers often skip over one or more stages and sometimes move backward as well as forward (Selltiz, Wrightsman, & Cook, 1976).

In this book, the process of integrative research reviewing will be conceptualized as containing five stages or phases: (1) problem formulation, (2) data collection, (3) evaluation of data points, (4) analysis and interpretation, and (5) presentation of results. Each stage of the review serves a function similar to the one it serves in primary data research. For example, in both primary research and research review the problem formulation stage involves the definition of variables, and the analysis and interpretation stage involves making a choice about what results are significant. Reviewers, like primary data collectors, can make different choices about how to carry out their inquiries. Differences in review methodologies will create variation in review conclusions. Most important, each methodological choice at each stage of a review may undermine the trustworthiness of the review's conclusion or, in more scientific terms, create a threat to the review's validity. (A more formal definition of *validity* appears in Chapter 4.)

The functions, sources of variance, and potential threats to validity associated with each stage of the review process are summarized in Figure 1.1. In the chapters that follow, each stage of the research review will be examined in greater detail.

Problem formulation stage. The first stage in the research process is the problem formulation stage. During problem formulation, the variables involved in the inquiry are given both abstract and concrete definitions. At this stage the researcher asks: "What operations are relevant to the concepts that concern the review?" More broadly, the researcher must decide what distinguishes relevant from irrelevant material.

In Chapter 2, the decision points encountered by a reviewer during the problem formulation stage are discussed. Included in this discussion will be answers to the following questions: (a) What affects a reviewer's decisions about the conceptual relevance of particular studies? (b) How should a reviewer handle hypotheses that involve the interaction of two or more independent variables? and (c) What role should past reviews play in formulating a problem? Chapter 2 will also present some concrete recommendations about what information a reviewer should collect from empirical studies that have been judged relevant to a problem area.

Data collection stage. The data collection stage of research involves making a choice about the population of elements that will be the focus of the study. Identifying populations for research reviews is complicated by the fact that the reviewer wants to make inferences about two targets. First, the reviewer wants the cumulative result of the review to be based on all previous research on the problem. Second, the reviewer hopes that the included studies will allow generalizations to the population of individuals (or other units) who are the focus of the topic area.

Stage Characteristics	Stage of Research				
	Problem Formulation	Data Collection	Data Evaluation	Analysis and Interpretation	Public Presentation
Research Question Asked	What evidence should be included in the review?	What procedures should be used to find relevant evidence?	What retrieved evidence should be included in the review?	What procedures should be used to make inferences about the literature as a whole?	What information should be included in the review report?
Primary Function in Review	Constructing definitions that distinguish relevant from irrelevant studies.	Determining which sources of potentially relevant studies to examine.	Applying criteria to separate "valid" from "invalid" studies.	Synthesizing valid retrieved studies.	Applying editorial criteria to separate important from unimportant information.
Procedural Differences That Create Variation in Review Conclusions	1. Differences in included operational definitions. 2. Differences in operational detail.	Differences in the research contained in sources of information.	1. Differences in quality criteria. 2. Differences in the influence of nonquality criteria.	Differences in rules of inference.	Differences in guidelines for editorial judgment.
Sources of Potential Invalidity in Review Conclusions	1. Narrow concepts might make review conclusions less definitive and robust. 2. Superficial operational detail might obscure interacting variables.	1. Accessed studies might be qualitatively different from the target population of studies. 2. People sampled in accessible studies might be different from target population of people.	1. Nonquality factors might cause improper weighting of study information. 2. Omissions in study reports might make conclusions unreliable.	1. Rules for distinguishing patterns from noise might be inappropriate. 2. Review-based evidence might be used to infer causality.	1. Omission of review procedures might make conclusions irreproducible. 2. Omission of review findings and study procedures might make conclusions obsolete.

Figure 1.1: The Integrative Review Conceptualized as a Research Project

SOURCE: Cooper, H., "Scientific guidelines for conducting integrative research reviews." *Review of Educational Research*, 1982, *52*, 291-302. Copyright 1982, American Educational Research Association, Washington, D.C. Reprinted by permission.

Chapter 3 presents a detailed discussion of methods for locating studies. The discussion includes a listing of the sources of studies available to social scientists, how to use the most important sources, and what biases may be present in the information contained in each source.

Data evaluation stage. After data are collected, the inquirer makes critical judgments about the quality of individual data points. Each data point is examined in light of surrounding evidence to determine whether it is contaminated by factors irrelevant to the problem under consideration.

Chapter 4 discusses how evaluations of research quality can be carried out and makes some suggestions concerning the assessment of interjudge reliability and where biases in judgments come from. Also, Chapter 4 contains some recommendations concerning unavailable research reports and reports that are incomplete.

Analysis and interpretation stage. During analysis and interpretation, the separate data points collected by the inquirer are synthesized into a unified statement about the research problem. Interpretation demands that the inquirer distinguish systematic data patterns from "noise" or chance fluctuation.

Chapter 5 contains an explanation of some methods for combining the results of separate studies and for estimating the size or magnitude of a relation. Some techniques for analyzing the difference in relation size found in different studies are also examined.

Public presentation stage. Creating a public document that describes the review is the task that completes a research endeavor. In Chapter 6, some concrete guidelines will be offered on how to report integrative research reviews.

FOUR ILLUSTRATIONS OF
RIGOROUS RESEARCH REVIEW

The best way to demonstrate both the feasibility and benefits of rigorous research reviewing is through example. For this reason, four research reviews have been chosen to illustrate the practical aspects of conducting rigorous integrative research reviews. The topics of the four reviews represent a broad spectrum of social science research, encompass qualitatively different kinds of research, and involve diverse conceptual and operational variables. Even though the topics are diverse, they are also general enough that readers in any discipline should find all four topics instructive and easy to follow without a large amount of background in the separate research areas. However, a brief introduction to each topic will be helpful.

The effect of homework on academic achievement (Cooper, 1989). Requiring students to carry out academic tasks during nonschool hours is a practice as old as formal schooling itself. However, the effectiveness of homework is still a source of controversy. Public opinion about homework has fluctuated throughout the twentieth century. Past summaries of the homework research have concluded that homework has positive effects or no effects, that the research was inconclusive, or that the effects of homework were mediated by too many circumstantial variables for any general conclusion to be drawn.

In examining the literature, this illustrative review uncovered ten different questions motivating homework research. Three dealt with the general issue of whether homework is effective and seven with variations in homework procedures (e.g., individualization, grading). The three hypotheses relating to homework's overall utility asked whether students doing homework outperformed students doing no homework or students doing in-class supervised study, or whether the amount of homework students do correlates with their achievement. For purposes of illustration, the results of research looking at only the first question will be examined: Do students doing homework achieve better than students receiving no homework and no alternative compensatory treatment?

Personality moderators of interpersonal expectancy effects in laboratory experiments (Cooper & Hazelrigg, 1988). One of the best established findings in social psychology is that the expectations one person holds for another can affect the other person's behavior. Empirical tests of interpersonal expectancy effects were first carried out in laboratory settings. Naive experimenters were led to believe photos of faces would receive either success or failure ratings from subjects when, in fact, identical photos were used in both conditions. Results revealed that experimenters who were expecting more successful ratings obtained more successful ratings from their subjects.

Realizing that not all people are equally susceptible to interpersonal expectancy effects, efforts were then undertaken to identify personality variables that might moderate the degree to which expectancies influence behavior. Five general hypotheses guided this research. Three hypotheses relate to the experimenter. They suggest that experimenters who have greater need to influence others, who are better encoders of nonverbal messages, and who make more favorable impressions on their subjects should produce more dramatic interpersonal expectancy effects. Two hypotheses relate to the subject. These suggest that subjects who are more acquiescent and who are better decoders of nonverbal messages ought to be more prone to behave in the way the experimenter expects. Cooper and Hazelrigg (1988) undertook the task of collecting and summarizing the research testing these five hypotheses.

Drug treatment of hyperactive children (Ottenbacher & Cooper, 1983). Hyperactivity, a disorder involving a deficit in attention, has been estimated to afflict between 4% and 20% of school-aged children. Due to its frequency, both educators and physicians have vigorously pursued effective treatments for hyperactivity. The proposed treatments range from dietary restrictions and supplements to behavior modification training. However, by far the most prevalent treatment of hyperactivity is pharmacological management; almost all children identified as hyperactive receive some form of drug therapy in the course of their treatment.

Although drug treatment of hyperactivity is so frequently prescribed, there is still substantial controversy over the advisability of its use. In addition, there has been some question about the relative effectiveness of different types of drugs (stimulants and nonstimulants) and about any drug's ability to affect behaviors beyond motor or perceptual performance (i.e., social adjustment and educational performance).

The research review undertaken by Ottenbacher and Cooper (1983) was intended to address three of these outstanding issues. Specifically, the primary questions the review was meant to answer were as follows: (a) What is the impact of the placebo effect on drug treatments of hyperactivity? (b) Do different drugs differ in their effect on hyperactivity? and (c) Is the effect of drug treatment generalizable to the social and educational behavior of hyperactive children?

Response rates to questionnaires (Yu & Cooper, 1983). One problem that plagues all the social sciences, and marketing research in particular, is nonresponse to survey questionnaires. When people are chosen for inclusion in a study but refuse or are unable to take part in it, the researcher must confront the possibility that the remaining sample is no longer representative of the target population.

Numerous techniques have been employed to maximize questionnaire response (Kanuk & Berensen, 1975), including preliminary notification that a questionnaire is coming, cover letters with different types of appeals, personalization of the request, inclusion of return envelopes and postage, monetary and nonmonetary incentives, and follow-up contacts. Past reviews of the effectiveness of these techniques have concluded that there was no strong support for the value of any technique other than the use of monetary incentives and follow-up contacts (Kanuk & Berensen, 1975). These reviews, however, were narrative syntheses of research.

Yu and Cooper (1983) attempted to go beyond past efforts by conducting a quantitative synthesis of the research literature. It was stated that because "response rates (or responses as a percent of the size of the contacted samples) are a universal measure of the effectiveness of a technique, the results [i.e., raw data] of studies which used the same technique [can be directly] arithmetically combined" (pp. 36-37). Conducting such an analysis was the purpose of this review.

EXERCISE

The best exercise to carry out while reading this book is to conduct an integrative research review in an area of interest to you. The review should attempt to apply the guidelines explicated in the chapters that follow. If such an exercise is not possible, try to conduct the more discrete exercises that appear at the end of each chapter. Often, these exercises can be further simplified by dividing the work among members of your class.

2

The Problem Formulation Stage

This chapter describes the process of formulating a hypothesis for guiding an integrative research review. Topics include the treatment of concepts and operations, the distinction between study-generated and review-generated evidence, the treatment of main effects and interactions, the role of previous reviews in new reviewing efforts, the development of coding sheets for primary research reports, and the threats to validity during problem formulation.

"No matter what problem you want to work on and no matter what method you will eventually use, your empirical work *must* begin with a careful consideration of the research problem" (Simon, 1978, p. 98). In its most basic form, the research problem includes the definition of variables and the rationale for relating the variables to one another. The rationale can be that a theory predicts a particular association between variables (as in confirmatory research) or that some other practical or intuitive consideration suggests that *any* discovered relation might be important (as in exploratory research). Either problem rationale can be used for undertaking primary research or a research review.

The choice of a relation to study in primary research is influenced by the interests of researchers and the social conditions that surround them (Selltiz et al., 1976). This holds true for the choice of a topic by prospective research reviewers as well, with an important restriction. Primary researchers are limited only by their imaginations, but research reviewers must study topics that already appear in the literature. In fact, a topic is probably not suitable for review unless it has appeared in the literature and has created appreciable interest within a discipline, either because the problem is of broad conceptual caliber or because it is surrounded by intense research activity.

The fact that reviews are tied to a finite universe of problems does not mean the activity of research synthesis is any less creative than primary research. Instead, the creativity in research review enters when reviewers are asked to make sense of many related but not identical theories or studies. More often than not, the cumulative results of studies are many times more complex than envisioned by the separate researchers who conducted them. The reviewer's instinct for uncovering variables that influence a relation and ability to generate divergent schemes are important ingredients in the research synthesis process.

DEFINITION OF VARIABLES
IN SCIENTIFIC INQUIRY

Similarities Between Primary Research and Research Review

The variables involved in a scientific inquiry must be defined in two ways. First, the variables must be given conceptual definitions. These describe qualities of the variables that are independent of time and space but that can be used to distinguish events that are and are not relevant to the concept (Carlsmith, Ellsworth, & Aronson, 1976). For instance, a conceptual definition of *achievement* might be "a person's level of academic functioning." Conceptual definitions can differ in abstractness, or in the number of events to which they refer. Thus if *achievement* is defined as "something gained through effort or exertion," the concept is more abstract than the first definition. The second definition would allow one to consider as achievement goals reached in social, physical, and political spheres, as well as academic ones. Both primary researchers and research reviewers must choose a conceptual definition and a degree of abstractness for their problem variables. Both must decide how likely it is that an event represents an instance of the variable of interest.

In order to relate concepts to concrete events, a variable must also be operationally defined. An operational definition is a set of instructions describing the observable events that allow one to determine if a concept is present in a particular situation (Reynolds, 1971). Thus an operational definition of an interpersonal expectancy effect might include "the difference between subjects' ratings of photos when the experimenter is expecting success ratings versus failure ratings." Again, both primary researchers and research reviewers must specify the operations included in their variable definitions.

Differences Between Primary Research and Research Review

Some differences between the two types of inquiry can also be found in variable definition. Primary researchers have little choice but to define their concepts operationally before the inquiry begins. Primary data collection cannot start until variables have been given some circumscribed empirical reality. An investigator of hyperactivity treatments must choose a drug and a dosage. Reviewers, on the other hand, need not be quite so theoretically rigorous. The literature search can begin with only a conceptual definition. The research reviewer has the comparative luxury of being able to evaluate the conceptual relevance of different operations as they appear in the literature (e.g., should after-school tutoring be considered homework?) or simultaneously with data collection. Of course, some a priori specification of operations is desirable and most reviewers do begin with empirical realizations in mind. It is not unusual, however, for reviewers to stumble upon operations that they did not initially consider but that, upon inspection, they decide are relevant to the construct. In sum, a primary researcher usually knows exactly what events constitute the domain to be sampled before data collection begins, but a reviewer may discover unanticipated samplings along the way.

A more significant distinction between the types of inquiry is that primary research typically involves only one (sometimes two) operational definition of the same construct. In contrast, research reviews usually involve many empirical realizations. Although no two participants are treated exactly alike in any single study, this variation will ordinarily be small compared to that introduced by the differences in laboratories, treatments, measurements, sampled population, and analysis techniques used in separate studies (see Light & Pillemer, 1984). The multiple operations contained in research reviews introduce a set of unique problems that need to be examined carefully.

MULTIPLE OPERATIONS IN
RESEARCH REVIEW

The "fit" between concepts and operations. Research reviewers undertaking the formulation of a problem must be aware of two potential incongruities that may arise because of the variety of operations in the literature. First, the reviewer anticipating multiple operations may begin a literature search with a broad problem definition but find that the operations used in previous relevant research have been quite narrow. For instance, the illustrative review of the relation between homework and achievement might have begun with a broad definition of achievement, including the academic, social, and physical spheres of behavior. If this were the case, the result would have been disappointing, since the vast majority of past research dealt only with achievement in academic matters. When such a circumstance arises, the reviewer must narrow the conceptual underpinnings of the review to be more congruent with operations. Otherwise, the conclusions of the review will appear more general than the data warrant.

The opposite problem, using narrow concepts defined by multiple broad measures, can also confront a reviewer. This would have occurred if the homework and achievement review had initially sought only academic measures of achievement but the literature search revealed many other types of achievement behavior. The reviewer then faces the choice of either broadening the concept or excluding many studies.

It is extremely important that a reviewer take care to reevaluate the correspondence between the level of abstractness of a concept definition and the representativeness of the operations that primary researchers have used to define it. While such redefinition of the problem as an inquiry proceeds is frowned upon in primary research, it appears that some flexibility may be necessary, if not beneficial, in research review.

Multiple operationism and concept-to-concept correspondence. Webb, Campbell, Schwartz, Sechrest, and Grove (1981) present strong arguments for the value of multiple operationism. They define *multiple operationism* as the use of many measures that supposedly share a theoretical concept "but have different patterns of irrelevant components" (p. 35). Multiple operationism has positive consequences because

> once a proposition has been confirmed by two or more independent measurement processes, the uncertainty of its interpretation is greatly reduced. . . . If a proposition can survive the onslaught of a series of imperfect measures, with all their irrelevant error, confidence should be placed in it. Of course, this confidence is increased by minimizing error in each instrument and by a reasonable belief in the different and divergent effects of the sources of error. (p. 35)

While Webb et al. (1981) hold out the potential for strengthened inferences due to multiple operations, their qualification must also be underscored. Multiple operationism can enhance concept-to-operation correspondence if all or most of the measures encompassed in the research review are of at least satisfactory validity. This reasoning is akin to the reasoning applied in classical measurement theory to the single items on a personality questionnaire. Small correlations between individual items (in this case operations) and a "true" score can add up to a reliable indicator *if* a sufficient number of minimally valid items (operations) are present. However, if the majority of operations bear no correspondence to the underlying concept or the operations share a different concept to a greater degree than they share the intended one, the conclusion of the review will be invalid regardless of how many items or operations are involved; this is also analogous to measurement theory.

The research reviewer also must examine research designs for threats to the correspondence of operations and concepts. If the research designs uncovered by a literature search contain the same invalidating procedures, then the correspondence between operations and concepts is threatened. The illustrative review of research concerning homework and achievement again provides a good example. Homework studies are conducted in naturally occurring classrooms. Because these studies are often conducted as theses or dissertations, they typically involve only a small sample of classrooms, with only one or two classrooms in the homework and no-homework conditions and with the teacher also being the experimenter. Therefore, the teacher can treat the students in the classes differently in ways other than whether or not he or she assigns homework. If all of the studies uncovered by the literature search were conducted by teachers teaching both conditions, then the rival hypothesis that differences in treatment other than homework might account for achievement differences could not be ruled out, no matter how many studies have been conducted. Luckily, studies were also conducted in which different teachers were randomly assigned to either homework or no-homework conditions or in which homework was manipulated within classrooms.

As another example, in the review of drug treatments of childhood hyperactivity, some studies were found that kept only physicians (those administering the treatment) blind as to whether they were giving a placebo or drug while other studies kept only recorders of the dependent variables blind. If results across both types of studies are similar, the possibility that expectancy effects explain the results is less plausible when the accumulated findings are examined.

In sum, then, the existence of multiple operations in research literatures presents the potential benefit of stronger inferences through "triangulation" of evidence. However, multiple operations do not ensure concept-to-operation correspondence if all or most of the measures lack minimal correspondence to the concept or if research designs all share a similar confounding of unintended influences with intended ones.

Substituting new concepts for old. Perhaps the most challenging circumstance in the social sciences occurs when a new concept is introduced to explain old findings. For example, in social psychology the notion of cognitive dissonance has been employed frequently to explain why an individual who was paid $1 to voice a counterattitudinal argument subsequently experiences greater attitude change than another person who was paid $25 to perform the same activity (Festinger & Carlsmith, 1959). Dissonance theory suggests that because the amount of money is not sufficient to justify the espousal of the counterattitudinal argument, the person feels discomfort that can be reduced only through a shift in attitude. However, Bem (1967) recast the results of these dissonance experiments by invoking a self-perception theory. Briefly, he speculated that participants who observe themselves espousing counterattitudinal arguments infer their opinions the same way an observer would. Participants who see themselves making an argument for $1 assume that because they are performing the behavior with little justification they must feel positive toward the attitude in question.

No matter how many replications of the $1/$25 experiment are uncovered, a research reviewer could not use the results to evaluate the correctness of the two theories. The research reviewer must take care to differentiate concepts and theories that predict similar and different results for the same set of operations. If predictions are different, the accumulated evidence can be used to evaluate the correctness of one theory or another, or the different circumstances in which each theory is correct. If, however, the theories make identical predictions, no comparative judgment based on research outcomes is possible.

The use of operations not originally related to the concept. Literature searches often uncover research that has been cast in a conceptual framework different from the reviewer's but that includes measures or manipulations relevant to the concepts the reviewer had in mind. For instance, there are several concepts similar to "hyperactivity" that appear in research. When relevant operations associated with different abstract constructs are identified, they most certainly should be considered for inclusion in the review. In fact, different concepts and theories behind similar operations can often be used to demonstrate the robustness of results. There is probably no better way to ensure that operations contain different patterns of irrelevant components than to have different researchers with different theoretical backgrounds perform related experiments.

The effects of multiple operations on review outcomes. Operational multiplicity does more than introduce potentially stronger inferences to conceptual variables. It is also the most important source of variance in the conclusions of different reviews meant to address the same topic. Operational multiplicity can affect review outcomes in two ways:

(1) *Variance in operational definitions.* The operational definitions used in two research reviews on the same topic can vary. As noted earlier, two reviewers using an identical label for an abstract concept can employ very different operational definitions or levels of abstraction. Each definition may contain some operations excluded by the other, or one reviewer's definition may completely contain the other.

(2) *Variance in operational detail.* Operational multiplicity also affects review outcomes by allowing reviewers to vary in their attention to methodological distinctions in the literature. This effect is attributable to differences in the way study operations are treated *after* the literature has been searched. Research reviewers, as Cook and Leviton (1981) note, "become detectives who use obtained data patterns as clues for generating potentially explanatory concepts that specify the conditions under which a positive, null, or negative relationship holds between two variables" (p. 462). Reviewers differ in how much detective work they undertake. Some reviewers may pay careful attention to study operations. They may decide to identify the operational and sample distinctions among retrieved studies meticulously. Other reviewers may feel that method- or participant-dependent relations are unlikely or they may simply use less care.

The illustrative reviews. Two of the four illustrative research reviews provide contrasting examples with regard to the broadness of their definitions, their fit between concepts and operations, and the impact of multiple operations on their findings.

The search for personality moderators of interpersonal expectancy effects uncovered 32 different scales used to measure experimenter personality and 27 scales used on subjects. There were 8 different scales used to measure the experimenter's need for social influence, 9 to measure expressiveness (encoding ability), and 11 to measure likability (4 measured constructs unrelated to the hypotheses). For subjects, 11 different scales were used to measure influenceability. Clearly, multiple operations have been used in this area. Thus, because multiple operations were used, it is fairly certain that other personality variables confounded with any single scale had little effect on the review's conclusions regarding these four hypotheses. However, while the broad hypotheses may appear to be covered by the multiple scales, nearly all of the measures were of the paper-and-pencil variety. Therefore, we must still entertain the possibility that confounds associated with paper-and-pencil tests in general (like the social desirability of answers and evaluation apprehension) may still be confounded in the review's results.

With regard to measures of the effect of interpersonal expectancies, four different operationalizations were used. The simplest was to use raw score photo ratings and enter the expectancy condition (success or failure) into an analysis of variance along with the personality dimension. Other procedures defined expectancy effects by looking at the discrepancy between the expected and obtained ratings. These measures differ not only in how they are calculated but also in whether they define an expectancy effect by the extremity of the obtained rating or by the accuracy with which the obtained rating reflects the expectation—two very different conceptualizations.

The review involving the effects of research design on questionnaire response rates presented the least difficulty with regard to problem formulation. The dependent variable, response rates to questionnaires, was identical across all studies. This is an instance in which very narrow conceptual and operational definitions are perfectly commensurate with the review's objectives. Similarly, the research designs covered by the review were all operationally defined. Thus, although about two dozen different research designs were examined (e.g., cover letters, monetary incentives), there was no need to propose an overarching conceptual variable to encompass them all (other than "research design," of course).

JUDGING THE
CONCEPTUAL RELEVANCE OF STUDIES

In presenting the operations included in two illustrative reviews and relating these to the reviewers' abstract notions, a more fundamental question was sidestepped: How were studies judged to be conceptually relevant in the first place? The rules the reviewer uses to distinguish relevant from irrelevant studies determine the degree of "fit" between concepts and operations.

Information scientists have closely scrutinized the question of what makes a study relevant to a research problem (Saracevic, 1970). Regrettably, the degree of concept abstractness that a reviewer employs has not been examined as an influence on the relevance judgment. It has been shown, however, that judgments about the relevance of studies to a literature search are related to a reviewer's open-mindedness and expertise in the area (Davidson, 1977), whether the decision is based on titles or abstracts (Cooper & Ribble, in press), and even the amount of time the reviewer has for making relevance decisions (Cuadra & Katter, 1967). Thus, while the conceptual definition and level of abstractness that a reviewer chooses for a problem are certainly two influences on the studies deemed relevant, a multitude of other factors also affect this screening of information.

The only general recommendation that can be made with regard to conceptual relevance is that the reviewer should begin the literature search with the broadest conceptual definition in mind. In determining the acceptability of operations for inclusion within the broad concept, the reviewer again should remain as open-minded as possible. At later stages in the review—notably, during data evaluation—it is possible for a reviewer to exclude particular operations due to their lack of relevance or impurity. In the problem formulation and search stages, however, the reviewer should err on the overly inclusive side, just as a primary researcher collects some data that might not be used in analysis. It is most distressing to find out *after* studies have been retrieved and catalogued that available pieces of the puzzle were passed over and that the search must be reconstituted.

The broader search also allows the reviewer to undertake a review with greater operational detail. The benefits of broad conceptualization are underscored many times in the chapters that follow.

The illustrative reviews. The review of the effectiveness of homework faced several problems concerning whether or not to include certain kinds of operations. Behavior therapists often assign their clients "homework," or exercises meant to help them overcome phobias. A broad conceptualization might include this type of homework. Closer to the usual school-related meaning, some students often receive tutoring after school hours. Others take study-at-home television or videocassette courses. Some ways to define the concept of homework might include all or any of these activities. Ultimately, the decision was made to exclude these types of activities by defining *homework* as "tasks assigned to students by schoolteachers that are meant to be carried out during nonschool hours."

The drug treatments and response rate reviews presented few cases in which studies were difficult to classify as relevant or irrelevant, because the narrow objectives of these reviews meant there was little variation in method from one relevant study to another.

RELATIONS BETWEEN DIFFERENT CONCEPTS
IN RESEARCH REVIEWS

The problems that motivate most research reviews initially involve relations between two variables. There is a simple explanation for this: Main effects have typically been tested more often than any given interaction involving the same three variables. Three of the four research reviews serving as illustrations took a bivariate relation as their initial focus. These reviews, however, also examined potential influences on the main effect relation. One review, looking at personality moderators of interpersonal expectancy effects, began by examining three-variable relations. The main effect involved the impact of expectancies on social judgments, but the relation of interest involved how this main effect was influenced by the personality of the expectant person and target.

While some specific interactional hypotheses in the social sciences have generated enough interest to require independent research review, for the vast majority of topics the initial problem formulation will involve a main effect question. Again, however, the initial undertaking of the review to establish the existence of a main effect should in no way diminish the reviewer's attention to the interactive or moderating influences that may be discovered. If main effect relations are found to be moderated by third variables, these findings have inferential priority. Even when an interaction is the primary focus, the search for higher-order interactions should continue. Thus the review of personality moderators looked at whether these interaction effects were more or less likely to appear under different circumstances, including the presence of incentives for the experimenter to obtain expectancy effects and the degree of ambiguity in the photos. More will be said on the relations between variables in Chapter 5, which discusses how main effects and interactions are interpreted in research reviews.

STUDY-GENERATED AND
REVIEW-GENERATED EVIDENCE

There are two different sources of evidence about relations contained in research reviews. The first type is called *study-generated evidence*. Specifically, study-generated evidence is present when a single study contains results that directly test the relation being considered. Research reviews also contain evidence that does not come from individual studies, but rather from the variations in procedures across studies. This type of evidence, called *review-generated evidence*, is present when the results of studies using different procedures to test the same hypothesis are compared to one another.

Any relation can be examined through either study- or review-generated evidence, but only study-generated evidence allows the reviewer to make statements concerning causality. An example will clarify the point. With regard to hyperactivity studies, suppose a reviewer is interested in whether stimulants and nonstimulants have different effects on hyperactivity. Suppose also that 16 studies are found that randomly assigned children to stimulant or nonstimulant experimental conditions. The accumulated results of these studies could then be interpreted as supporting or not supporting the idea that different drugs cause different effects on hyperactivity. Now assume that the reviewer uncovered 8 studies that employed only stimulant drugs tested against no-drug control groups and 8 other studies that compared only nonstimulant drugs with no-drug controls. If this review-generated evidence revealed a diminution in hyperactivity in the stimulant drug studies but not in the nonstimulant drug studies, then an association, but not a causal relation, could be inferred.

Why is this the case? Causal direction is not the problem with review-generated evidence. It would be foolish to argue that the amount of change in hyperactivity experienced by children caused the experimenters' choice of a drug. However, another ingredient of causality, the absence of potential third variables causing the relation, or nonspuriousness, is problematic. A multitude of third variables are potentially confounded with the original experimenter's choice of a stimulant or a nonstimulant drug. For instance, the experimenters who used nonstimulant drugs may also have employed different means for assessing hyperactivity. Or experimenters who are interested in studying children with different severities or types of hyperactivity may also choose to study different drugs. If the number of studies showing different results is large, it may be difficult to find other design characteristics confounded with the researchers' choice of what drug to use, but it is still possible. Therefore, review-generated evidence cannot legitimately rule out variables confounded with the study characteristic of interest as possible true causes. Spuriousness cannot be eliminated because the reviewer did not randomly assign drugs to experiments! In primary research it is this random assignment that allows us to assume third variables are represented equally in the experimental conditions.

The above example illustrates how review-generated evidence is typically used to examine potential moderators of relations. As in this example, most review-generated evidence examines interactional hypotheses, or the effect of a third variable on the strength or direction of a relation. It is often quite difficult to test main effect relations with review-generated evidence because social scientists use different scales to measure their dependent variables, even within a topic area. The problem of nonstandard measurements is circumvented when study characteristics are tested as *third* variables because the main effect relations *within* the studies can be transformed into standard effect size estimates, thus controlling for different scales (see Chapter 5).

One example of how main effect relations can be tested through review-generated evidence, however, is contained in the illustrative review of research design effects on response rates. In this review, studies were identified in which a particular design characteristic—say, the employment of a monetary incentive—was experimentally manipulated by the primary researchers. That is, in some studies a randomly chosen subsample of potential respondents was given a monetary incentive and another subsample was not give an incentive. This is study-generated evidence on a main effect hypothesis. However, the reviewers were also able to locate studies that explicitly stated that *all* respondents received a monetary incentive or that *no* respondents received a monetary incentive. Because the dependent variables used in these studies were identical (i.e., response rates), it was possible to compare the response rates in these separate studies with one another, thus testing a main effect relation with review-generated evidence. The study-generated evidence comparing monetary incentive and no-incentive conditions could tell whether monetary incentives caused a difference in response rates. Such information could then be supplemented by examining the response rates in studies without an incentive and studies with an incentive. The second source of evidence could not stand alone as the basis of causal inferences, however.

It is important, then, for reviewers to keep the distinction between study-generated and review-generated evidence in mind. Only evidence coming from experimental manipulations within a single study can support assertions concerning causality. But the lesser status of review-generated evidence with regard to causal inferences does not mean this evidential base should be ignored.

The use of review-generated evidence allows the reviewer to test relations that may have never been examined by primary researchers. Even though this evidence is equivocal, it is a major benefit of research reviewing and a source of potential hypotheses for future primary research.

THE ROLE OF PAST REVIEWS

If the topic of a review has a long history of interest within a discipline, it is likely that a reviewer attempting to use the guidelines set forth in this book will find that relevant reviews already exist. Obviously, these efforts need to be scrutinized carefully before the new review is undertaken. Past reviews can help establish the necessity of a new review. This assessment process is much like that used in primary research before a researcher undertakes a new study.

There are several things a new reviewer can look for in past reviews. First, past reviews can be employed to identify the positions of other scholars in the field. In particular, past reviews can be used to determine whether conflicting conclusions exist about the evidence and, if they do, what has caused the conflict.

Second, one can review past reviews to assess the earlier efforts' completeness and validity. As a demonstration of the benefits of using quantitative procedures in reviews, I compared a statistical review of research on gender differences in conformity to a traditional review (Maccoby & Jacklin, 1974). Using the same studies employed by the narrative reviewers, I was able to demonstrate that the narrative review's conclusions were somewhat conservative in light of the evidence the authors uncovered (see Cooper, 1979).

Past reviews can also be a significant help in identifying interacting variables that the new reviewer might wish to examine. Rather than restart the compilation of potential moderating variables, past reviewers will undoubtedly offer many suggestions based on previous efforts and their own intellect. If more than one review of an area has been conducted, the new review will be able to incorporate all of the suggestions.

Finally, past reviews allow the researcher to begin the compilation of a relevant bibliography. Most reviews have fairly lengthy bibliographies. If more than one review exists, the citations will usually overlap somewhat, but they may also be quite distinct. As an example, Findley and Cooper (1981) found that the research cited under the same chapter titles in introductory social psychology textbooks differed substantially. Along with the techniques described in the next chapter, the research cited in past reviews provides an excellent place for the new reviewer to start the literature search.

The illustrative reviews. Of the four illustrative reviews, the review of homework research is the one that best demonstrates the use of past reviews. Nine previous independent reviews were located that made statements about whether or not homework affected academic achievement. Given that nine past reviews existed, it was necessary to justify the need for yet a tenth review. First, it was shown that the nine reviews differed dramatically in their general conclusions concerning homework's effectiveness. Second, different reviews examined different sets of variables posited as moderators of homework's effects. Third, when the same moderators were examined, different reviewers sometimes drew opposite conclusions about their effects. Fourth, it was found that none of the past reviews was very comprehensive—no single review included more than 60% of the total research base uncovered by all the reviewers. Therefore, the new review could be used to resolve conflicts among previous reviews, to examine all at once the proposed moderators of homework's effects, and to include a more comprehensive research base. It was not claimed, however, that the past reviews were of no use—they helped in the development of a conceptual framework for describing the homework process, laid out issues that needed to be addressed when the effects of homework were assessed, and suggested a comprehensive catalog of contextual factors that might influence the utility of home study.

THE RESEARCH REVIEW CODING SHEET

Once the reviewer has formulated the problem and has an idea about what theorists, primary researchers, and past reviewers have said on the topic, the next step is to construct a coding sheet. The coding sheet is used to collect information from the primary research reports. If the number of studies involved in the research review is small, it may not be necessary for the reviewer to have a well-formulated idea about what information to extract from reports before the literature search begins. If only a dozen or so relevant articles exist, the reviewer can retrieve them in their entirety and read and reread them until he or she has gleaned the needed information. Small sets of studies allow the reviewer to follow up interesting ideas that emerge after he or she has read several studies by returning briefly to those previously scrutinized. However, if the reviewer expects to uncover a large amount of research, such a rereading of reports may be prohibitively time-consuming. In this instance, it is necessary for the reviewer to consider carefully what data will be retrieved from each research report before the formal search begins. It is important to pilot test this expectation against a few research reports and to modify the coding sheet so that a fairly standard and thorough examination of each research report can be conducted in a single reading. The rules for constructing a coding sheet are similar to those used in creating a coding frame and data matrix for a primary research effort (see Selltiz et al., 1976).

The first rule in constructing a review coding sheet is that any information that might have the remotest possibility of being considered relevant to the research review should be retrieved from the studies. Once the literature search has begun, it is exceedingly difficult to re-retrieve new information from studies that have already been coded. It is much less of a problem to include information that will not be used.

Information to include on the coding sheet. There are certain pieces of information about primary research that every reviewer will want to include on a research review coding sheet.

First, the reviewer will want to retrieve information concerning the background characteristics of the research report itself: the authors of the report, the source of the report, when the report was published, and what information channel led to the report's discovery.

The reviewer will also want to retrieve information concerning the research design of the primary studies. The particular design characteristics of interest will vary from topic to topic. A comprehensive discussion of research designs and their interpretation can be found in Cook and Campbell (1979). Most research designs, however, are covered by five categories: one-group pretest-posttest, correlational, nonequivalent control group (i.e., treatments are given to groups that existed before the research began), nonequivalent control group with matching or statistical control (i.e., some procedure was used to enhance the equivalence of intact groups), and random assignment to treatments. In some instances this categorization will suffice, but in others different designs will need to be added (e.g., time series) or finer distinctions made in the designs described above (e.g., distinctions between different matching or statistical control procedures).

Other features of research design may also be relevant. These might include whether or not repeated measures and/or counterbalancing of treatments was used, and the presence or absence of controls against experimenter bias.

In addition to basic research design issues, the reviewer will need to describe carefully the details that went into manipulating or measuring the independent variable. What was the nature of the treatment? Did it vary in intensity and duration from study to study? Were manipulation checks taken and, if so, what did they reveal?

Equally important are characteristics of how control or comparison groups were treated. Was there an alternate treatment? If so, what was it? If not, what did control groups do or how were they obtained? Differences among studies on any of these variables would be prime candidates for causes of differences in study outcomes.

For studies involving personality or other multi-item scales, the reviewer will want to retrieve information concerning the names of the tests, whether or not they were standardized, the number of items they included, and the tests' reliability, if this information is available. Similar information on the dependent variables used in experimental studies also needs to be cataloged carefully. While experimental dependent variables are often answers to single questions or discrete behaviors, they too can vary in important ways from study to study—for example, in their reactivity, sensitivity, or the length of delay before they are measured.

Another area of information needed in most reviews involves the characteristics of the participants included in the primary research. It is clearly important to retrieve the number of participants in each condition of the study. The reviewer will also want to retrieve information concerning the location and age of participants as well as any restrictions on participant populations that were employed.

Research review coding sheets should also contain information on the outcomes of the study. First and most important, the coding sheet needs to identify the direction of outcomes of comparisons. Was the hypothesis supported or refuted and what was the level of significance associated with the hypothesis test?

If a quantitative synthesis of results is envisioned, the reviewer will also need to record more precise information on the statistical outcomes of studies. Because reporting of results varies from article to article and can take several different forms, it is possible to list the statistical outcomes of studies in terms of how desirable they are for use in quantitative synthesis. Listed from most to least desirable, these would be as follows:

(1) the means, standard deviations, and sample sizes for each group in a comparison or hypothesis test;

(2) an estimate of the treatment's impact or the association between variables (e.g., correlation coefficient);

(3) the exact value of an inference test statistic and its associated degrees of freedom; and

(4) an inexact p-level and sample size.

Means and standard deviations allow the reviewer to calculate any effect sizes precisely for whatever comparisons he or she chooses. Effect sizes calculated by the primary researchers, while an excellent source of information, may contain unknown errors and may not be in the metric chosen by the reviewer. Values of inference test statistics and degrees of freedom allow the reviewer to estimate effect sizes, and inexact p-levels along with sample sizes allow the estimation of inference test values. The inference test values and p-levels also sometimes refer to analyses containing multiple factors (e.g., analysis of variance with more than one independent variable) and, unless these factors are the same across studies, this will add to the imprecision in estimates. Many issues involved in the extraction of statistical information from research reports will be discussed further in the chapters that follow.

Finally, each study report will also contain some miscellaneous but important design characteristics or results that the reviewer will want to note on the coding sheet. In many instances, the coding sheet will be standardized to accommodate information about the main effect comparison of interest, but the research report will contain evidence concerning interactions between the main effect and other variables. Therefore, the coding sheet should contain space for noting the number of variables employed in a design or analysis and the outcomes of any interaction tests that involved the relation of interest.

Low- and high-inference codings. The categories listed above might all be thought of as "low-inference" codings. That is, they require the coder only to locate the needed information in the research report and transfer it to the coding sheet. In other circumstances, coders might be asked to make some inferential judgments about the studies. These judgments often involve coders' attempts to infer how an experimental manipulation might have been interpreted by subjects.

A review by Carlson and Miller (1987) provides a good example. These authors were summarizing the literature on why negative mood states seem to enhance the likelihood that people will lend a helping hand. In order to test different interpretations of this research, they needed to estimate how sad, guilty, angry, or frustrated different experimental procedures might have made subjects. To do this, they asked coders to read excerpts from the methods sections of relevant articles. The coders then used a 1-to-9 scale to rate, for example, the "extent to which subjects feel specifically downcast, sad, or depressed as a result of the negative-mood induction" (p. 96).

These "high-inference" codings create a special set of problems for research reviewers. First, careful attention must be paid to the reliability of high-inference coder judgments. Also, in these situations, coders are being asked to play the role of a research subject, and the validity of role-playing methodologies has been the source of much controversy (Greenberg & Folger, 1988). However, high-inference codings potentially add a new dimension to research reviewers' ability to interpret literatures and resolve controversies. If reviewers feel they can validly extract high-inference codes from articles and persuasively explain their rationale for doing so, then this technique deserves a try.

Revising and pilot testing the coding sheet. When an area of research is large and complex, the construction of a coding sheet can be a difficult task. In the process of devising categories, reviewers makes crucial decisions about what the important issues are in a field. Often, reviewers find that ideas they have about a topic and its research are only vague impressions. The coding sheet forces them to be more precise in their thinking.

The first draft of a coding sheet should never be the last. Reviewers need to show a first draft to knowledgeable colleagues for their input, and then code a few randomly selected studies using the coding sheet. They can then add categories and define category descriptors more precisely. Finally, they should have different coders pilot test the coding sheet to uncover any remaining ambiguities. This process shouldn't be viewed as a nuisance, but as an intrinsic part of problem formulation. The development of a coding sheet should be viewed as no less important to the success of a research review than the construction of a questionnaire is to survey research or an observation scheme to a study of naturalistic behavior.

Finally, a general coding sheet will never capture the unique aspects of all studies. Completed coding sheets often contain many blank spaces and notes in the margins. Perfection is never achieved. The reviewer can view these occurrences as failures (which they are not) or as targets for opportunity, highlighting the diversity of research in the topic area.

The illustrative reviews. The coding sheet for the review on the effects of homework is reproduced in Figure 2.1. The rationale behind most of the categories is self-evident, but an explanation concerning some decisions about what information to retrieve may prove instructive.

The section on research design contains no category for correlational studies, even though such a category was recommended above. This is because studies that used correlational designs invariably examined the amount of time students reported spending on homework as a continuous variable. An entirely different coding sheet was devised for these studies. They engendered a unique set of issues, including how samples of students were drawn from larger populations and whether teachers, students, or parents reported how much time the student spent on homework. There were also several of the categories in Figure 2.1 that were irrelevant to time-on-homework studies, such as the sections on research design and on the reporting of means and standard deviations.

There is no section in Figure 2.1 for delineating how the control group was treated. This is because all control groups used in these comparisons were treated identically—they received no treatment at all.

The homework coding sheet asked for a bit more detail regarding nonequivalent control group and random assignment designs than was suggested above. When a nonequivalent control group was used with a matching procedure, coders were asked to distinguish between matching based on (a) a pretest using the same measure as the dependent variable or (b) other variables related but not identical to the dependent variable. It was felt that the two procedures might differ in their ability to produce equivalent groups and therefore might explain differences in the outcomes of studies. For a similar reason a distinction was made among studies randomly assigning individual students or whole classrooms to homework and no-homework treatments.

It should be pointed out that much of the information asked for on the coding sheet was never actually examined in the completed review. This was true of all the information about students other than grade level. In these cases either too few studies reported information about the variable of interest (e.g., socioeconomic status of the students) or it was found that studies did not vary enough to allow valid inferences (e.g., comparing studies done in public and private schools).

Each of the coding sheets was designed to contain information concerning a single comparison. However, in some studies comparisons were reported for, say, more than one grade level or more than one dependent variable. When such a study was uncovered, the coder would fill out separate sheets for each two-group comparison. For example, a study with both standardized achievement and class grade measures reported separately for students in fifth and seventh grades would have four coding sheets associated with it. A more detailed discussion of how to handle multiple comparisons from the same study will be presented in Chapter 4.

VALIDITY ISSUES IN PROBLEM FORMULATION

Although, as has been noted, several decisions made during problem formulation can affect the validity of a research review, the two most central involve the notions of conceptual breadth and operational detail.

```
Author(s)_____

Title_____

Journal_____

Year_____ Volume_____ Pages_____

Source of Reference

Design (check one):

        One group pretest-posttest___      Random assignment___
        Nonequivalent control group___         of students___
           no matching___                       of classrooms___
           matching on pretest___
           statistical control___

Other Design Features:

        Repeated measures  yes___ no___
        Counterbalancing   yes___ no___
        Teacher as experimenter yes___ no___

Sample Size:

        # of schools_____
        # of classrooms_____
        # of students_____

School Variables:

        Location _____ (use state abbreviations)
        Source of funding: public___ private___

Student Variables:

        Grade level(s)___
        SES: lower___ middle___ upper___
        Race: white___ black___ other___ random sample or mixed___
        Ability level: low___ average___ high___

Subject Matter (check all that apply):

        Math___                          Social Studies___
           computation___                Science___
           problem solving___            Other (specify)_____
           concept formation___
        Reading___
        Writing/Spelling___
        Language/Vocabulary___
```

Figure 2.1: Coding Sheet for Homework Versus No-Treatment Studies

---

First, reviewers who use only a few operational definitions in their reviews typically do so to ensure consensus about how their concepts are related to operations. Such agreement is an attractive scientific goal. However, most methodologists agree that multiple realizations of concepts are desirable. As stated above, if multiple operations produce similar results, numerous rival interpretations for the findings may be ruled out. Also, narrow conceptualizations provide little information about the generality or robustness of results.

```
Homework Treatment:

    Weeks of treatment___
    Frequency of assignments per week___
    Average length of assignments___

Dependent Variable:

    Standard test (specify)_____
    Class grade_____
    Comprehensive tests (teacher-constructed)___
    Unit test___
    Attitude___

Statistical Outcome:

    Homework    M _____ sd _____ n _____
    No homework M _____ sd _____ n _____
    Type of inference test F___ t___ Chi___ Other _____
    Test value _____
    df _____
    p-level _____
    Effect size _____

Other Statistical Information:

    Other variables in analyses (list)
    _____

    _____
    _____


    Significant interactions involving homework
    variable _____ test value _____ df _____
    variable _____ test value _____ df _____
    variable _____ test value _____ df _____

Notes and comments:
```

Figure 2.1 continued

Therefore, the greater the conceptual breadth of a review, the greater its *potential* to produce conclusions that are more general than those from reviews using narrow definitions.

The word *potential* is emphasized because of the second threat to validity associated with the problem definition stage of review. If a reviewer details study operations only cursorily, the review conclusions may mask important distinctions in results. As Presby (1978) notes, "Differences [in studies] are cancelled in the use of very broad categories, which leads to the erroneous conclusion that research results indicate negligible differences in outcomes" (p. 514).

Of course, the most extreme attention to operational detail occurs when each study is treated as if it tested a completely different hypothesis. However, it is rare for a reviewer to conclude that no integration of the literature is possible due to the variation in methods across studies. Therefore, most reviews contain some threat to validity from ignoring methodological differences among studies, but the risk occurs in varying degrees in different reviews.

A lack of overlap in the operational definitions considered relevant by different reviews was not mentioned as a threat to validity, although it does create variance in review conclusions. This cannot be called a "threat," because it is impossible to say which of two reviews is more valid if the reviewers disagree about the operationalization of the same construct. Reviews that do not overlap in operations are not comparable on any level but the definitional one. On the other hand, it seems clear that a review that includes all the operations contained in another review plus additional operations is the more desirable review—if operational details receive appropriate treatment, of course. In practice, comparative evaluations will not be as clear-cut as these examples. Two reviews involving the same concept may share some operations while each also includes operations the other does not.

Protecting validity. Reviewers can use the following guidelines to protect their conclusions from threats to validity entering during problem formulation:

(1) Reviewers should undertake their literature searches with the broadest possible conceptual definition in mind. They should begin with a few central operations but remain completely open to the possibility that other relevant operations will be discovered in the literature. When operations of questionable relevance are encountered, the reviewer should err on the side of making overly inclusive decisions, at least in the early reviewing stages.

(2) To complement conceptual broadness, reviewers should be exhaustive in their attention to the distinctions in study procedures. The slightest suspicion that a difference in study results is associated with a distinction in study methods should receive some testing by the reviewer, if only in a preliminary analysis.

EXERCISES

1. Identify two integrative research reviews that claim to review the same or similar hypotheses. Which review employs the broader conceptual definition? On what other dimensions concerning problem definition do the two reviews differ? What aspect of problem definition in each review do you find most helpful? (If you cannot find two related reviews, use Bar-Tal & Bar Zohar, 1977, and Findley & Cooper, 1983.)

2. Identify a conceptual variable (e.g., "persistence" or "dogmatism") and list the operational definitions associated with it that are known to you now. Go to the library and find several reports that describe research relevant to your topic. How many new operational definitions did you find? Evaluate these with regard to their correspondence to the conceptual variable.

3. For studies on a topic of interest to you, draw up a preliminary coding sheet. Go to the library and find several reports that describe research relevant to the topic. How must you change the coding sheet to accommodate these studies? What did you leave out? (If you cannot think of a relation, use "gender differences in persistence.")

3

The Data Collection Stage

This chapter focuses on several methods for locating studies relevant to a review topic. Informal, primary, and secondary channels for obtaining research reports are described, along with the biases that may be present in each channel. Background material for using four abstracting services is also presented. This chapter concludes with a discussion of threats to validity encountered during data collection and ways to guard against them.

The major decision an inquirer makes during the data collection stage involves picking the *target population* that will be the referent for the inquiry (Williams, 1978). The target population includes those individuals, groups, or other elements that the inquirer hopes to represent in the study. A precise definition of a target population allows the researcher to list all of its constituent elements. Researchers are rarely required to generate such lists, but because the truth or falsity of so many social science hypotheses depends on the elements of interest, it is important that researchers present clear general definitions. The *accessible population* includes those individuals, groups, or elements the inquirer is able pragmatically to obtain (Bracht & Glass, 1968). In most instances, researchers will not be able to access all of a target population's elements because it would be too costly to do so or because some elements are hard to find.

POPULATION DISTINCTIONS
IN SCIENTIFIC INQUIRY

Similarities between primary research and research review. Both primary research and research review involve specifying target and accessible populations. In addition, both types of inquiry require that the researcher consider how the target and accessible populations may differ from each other. To the extent that the elements in the accessible population are not representative of the target population, the trustworthiness of any claims about the target will be compromised. Because it is easier to alter the target of an investigation than it is to access hard-to-find elements, both primary researchers and research reviewers may find they need to restrict or respecify their target population once an inquiry is complete.

Differences between primary research and research reviews. The most general target population for primary social science research can be characterized roughly as "all human beings." Most subdisciplines, of course, respecify the elements to include less grandiose clusters, like all schizophrenics, all Americans, or all schoolchildren. Topic areas delineate targeted people even more specifically.

Accessible populations in social science research are typically much more restricted than targets. Indeed, in 1946, McNemar (1946) called psychology "the science of the behavior of sophomores" and this characterization remains largely accurate today (e.g., Findley & Cooper, 1981). Most social scientists are aware of the gap between the diversity of people they hope their research encompasses and those people actually accessible to them. In fact, this problem is so pervasive that most research journals do not require repeated attention to the difficulty in every research report.

As noted in the introductory chapter, research reviews involve two targets. First, the reviewer hopes the review will cover "all previous research" on the problem. Reviewers can exert some control over this goal through their choice of information sources. The next several sections of this chapter are devoted to what these sources are and how they are used. Second, the reviewer wants the results of the review to pertain to all the elements of interest in the topic area. The reviewer's influence is constrained at this point by the types of individuals who were sampled by primary researchers. Research reviewing thus involves a peculiar process of sampling samplers. The primary researcher samples individuals and the reviewer retrieves researchers. This process is something akin to cluster sampling (Williams, 1978), with the clusters distinguishing people according to the research projects in which they participated. In reality, reviewers typically are *not* trying to draw representative samples of studies from the literature. Instead, they attempt to retrieve an *entire* population of studies. This formidable goal is rarely achieved, but it is certainly more feasible in a review than in primary research.

METHODS FOR LOCATING STUDIES

This section will present some background on the major channels for locating studies. In addition, an attempt will be made to evaluate the kind of information in each channel by comparing its contents to that of "all relevant work," or to the entire population of material the reviewer would find of interest. Regrettably, there are few empirical data on how the contents of different channels differ from each other or from all relevant work, so the comparisons will be speculative. The problem is complicated, of course, by the fact that the effect of the channel on its contents probably varies from topic to topic.

Informal Channels

The first informal source of information available to reviewers is their own research. The primary research that reviewers have conducted personally often has a strong, and perhaps overweighted, impact on their thinking (see Cooper, 1983).

Personal research will differ from all relevant research to the extent that the research outcomes are affected by the researcher's expectations. Individual researchers are also likely to repeat the same operations, causing many operational definitions relevant to a topic area to go unexamined in any particular laboratory.

The second informal source is the "invisible college" (Price, 1966). Invisible colleges, according to Crane (1969), are formed because "scientists working on similar problems are usually aware of each other and in some cases attempt to systematize their contacts by exchanging reprints with one another" (p. 335). Through a sociometric analysis, Crane found that most members of invisible colleges are not directly linked to one another but are linked to a small group of highly influential members. In terms of group communication, invisible colleges are structured like wheels—influential researchers are at the hub and less established researchers are on the rim, with lines of communication running mostly to the hub and less often among peripheral members.

Also, according to Crane (1969), invisible colleges are temporary units that deal with special problems and then vanish when the problem is solved or the focus of the discipline shifts. While estimates vary greatly from study to study, there is no doubt that researchers spend a significant amount of their time in informal exchanges through invisible colleges (Griffith & Mullins, 1972).

The structure of invisible colleges and the influence of prominent and active researchers over the information contained in them hints at the biases in the information transmitted through invisible college links. Relative to all of the research that might be ongoing in a topic area, information from an invisible college is probably more uniformly supportive of the findings of the central researchers than evidence based on more diverse sources. For instance, a fledgling researcher who produces a result somewhat in conflict with the hub of an invisible college network is not likely to find that transmitting the result to the central researcher will mean widespread dissemination throughout the network. Disconfirming findings may lead a researcher to leave the network. Also, because the participants in an invisible college use one another as a reference group, it is likely that the kinds of operations and measurements employed in the members' research will be more homogeneous than those employed by all researchers who might be interested in a given topic.

Other informal communications happen outside of invisible colleges. Students and their professors share ideas and pass on to one another papers and articles they find that are of mutual interest. Sometimes, a formal request soliciting recent work will be made of scholars in a field. Occasionally, readers or reviewers of a researcher's past work will suggest references they think are relevant to the topic that were not cited.

Another source of information, bridging the distinction between formal and informal channels, is that of attendance at professional meetings. A multitude of professional societies, structured both by career concerns and topic interests, exist within the social sciences; many of them hold yearly conventions at which papers are presented. By attending these meetings or requesting reprints of the papers delivered, researchers can discover what others in their topic area are doing and what research has recently been completed but has not yet entered the formal communication domain. In comparison to personal research and invisible colleges, the work found in convention programs is least likely to reveal a restricted sample of results or operations.

All of the informal channels share another important characteristic. Informal communications are more likely than formal ones to contain some inferior studies that have not been scrutinized carefully. Because of methodological flaws, these probably will not appear in more public systems. This is true of convention papers even though they do undergo evaluation, because they are typically selected for presentation on the basis of very short descriptions.

A research reviewer who relies solely on informal channels to collect relevant work would be similar to a survey researcher who decides to sample only his or her friends. Given their obvious biases, it is surprising to find how large a role informal channels play in the research retrieval process.

Primary Channels

Primary publications form the initial link between the reviewer and the formal communication system. There are essentially two methods through which a potential reviewer gains access to primary works. First, reviewers can learn of research done in a topic area through the use of their personal libraries or the journals they regularly follow that are carried by their institutional libraries. The Report of the National Enquiry into Scientific Communication found that the average scholar in the humanities and several social science disciplines scanned approximately seven journals and followed four or five other journals on a regular basis (*Scholarly Communication*, 1979). Most scholars said they spent between 10 and 12 hours per week reading scholarly books and journals and that this reading material came largely from their personal subscriptions.

The number of journals available and the amount of research being conducted probably introduces some serious biases if personal libraries are used as the sole or major source of work for research reviews. As Garvey and Griffith (1971) note, because of the amount of information being generated, individual scholars have lost the ability to keep abreast of all information relevant to their specialties through personal readings and journal subscriptions. This would not be a serious problem *if* the journals read by each researcher constituted a random sample of all journals available. However, researchers tend to operate within networks of journals. These journal networks, according to Xhignesse and Osgood (1967), involve a small number of journals that tend to cite other work available in the same journal and a small group of other outlets that also tend to cite one another. Xhignesse and Osgood found that about 30% of the citations in a given journal were to other work that appeared in the same journal and about 37% of citations were to other journals in the same network.

Given that personal libraries are likely to include journals in the same network, it would not be surprising to find some biases associated with the phenomenon. As with the more informal invisible colleges, we would expect greater homogeneity in both research findings and operations within a given journal network than in all the research available on a topic area. Again, however, the appeal of using the personal library and the journal network as a source of information lies in its ease of accessibility and its credibility to the reference group the reviewer hopes will read the review.

A second retrieval channel that uncovers primary publications is called the ancestry approach. Using this procedure, the reviewer retrieves information by tracking the research cited in already-obtained relevant research. Most reviewers are aware of several studies bearing on their topic before they formally begin the literature search. These studies provide bibliographies that cite earlier related research. The reviewer can examine these citations and judge them for their relevance to the problem. The reference lists of cited articles can also be scrutinized. Through reiteration, reviewers work their way back through a literature until either the important concepts disappear or the studies become so old that the reviewer judges their results to be obsolete.

Searching study bibliographies is also likely to overrepresent work that appears within the reviewer's primary network of journals. Researchers tend to cite other work available through the same outlet or a small group of other outlets. We should therefore expect more homogeneity among references found through reference tracking than would be present in all retrievable studies.

Both means for identifying studies through primary publications—personal libraries and the ancestry approach—share another bias. Obviously, published studies and studies found in their bibliographies are likely to overrepresent published research. However, the criteria for whether or not a study is published are not based solely on the scientific merit of the work. First, published research is probably biased toward statistically significant findings. This bias occurs primarily because of the practices and beliefs of researchers. Greenwald (1975) found that if a research project included a rejection of the null hypothesis the researcher intended to submit the result for publication about 60% of the time. On the other hand, if the study failed to reject the null hypothesis the researcher intended to submit the research for publication only 6% of the time. These intentions are probably based on the researcher's beliefs that nonsignificant findings are less interesting than significant ones and that journal editors are more likely to reject null results.

Also, Nunnally (1960) notes that researchers whose findings conflict with the prevailing beliefs of the day are less likely to submit their results for publication than researchers whose work confirms currently held beliefs. Likewise, journal reviewers appear to look less favorably on studies that conflict with conventional wisdom than studies that support it. Bradley (1981) reports that 76% of university professors answering a mail questionnaire said they had encountered some pressure to conform to the subjective preferences of the reviewers of their work.

Along similar lines, Lane and Dunlap (1978) noted that the significance criterion for publication ensures that the size of differences reported in published works will be larger than the actual differences in the population of interest. As an empirical test of this phenomenon, Smith (1980) found 10 instances of research reviews in which the average size of a relation from published studies could be compared with the average relation in unpublished theses and dissertations. In all 10 instances, the relations in the published articles were larger than those in the theses and dissertations.

Primary publications, then, should not be used as the sole source of information for a research review without convincing justification. The use of personal libraries introduces bias by overrepresenting the paradigms and results that are contained in the reviewer's chosen journal network reference group. This bias will also be contained in the exclusive use of the ancestry or reference-tracking approach. In addition, both techniques will overrepresent published research and therefore introduce the biases associated with the tendency for journals to contain only statistically significant results and the pressure to conform to previous findings.

Secondary Channels

The channels of information called secondary sources should form the backbone of any systematic, comprehensive literature search. This is because secondary sources probably contain the information most closely approximating all publicly available research. These sources have the least restrictive requirements for a study to gain entry into the system.

Bibliographies are nonevaluative listings of books and articles that are relevant to a particular topic area. Often the topic areas are quite broad. Bibliographies are often maintained by single scientists or groups of individuals within a particular area, rather than by a formal organization. For instance, Carl White's *Sources of Information in the Social Sciences* (1986) lists bibliographies on topics such as suicide, psychoanalysis, and experimental aesthetics in psychology. It is also possible to find bibliographies of bibliographies. The

Natural Research Council Research Information Service publishes a bibliography of bibliographies in psychology that lists over 2,000 publications.

The use of bibliographies prepared by others can be a tremendous time-saver for a potential reviewer. The problem, however, is that the bibliographies are likely to be of much greater breadth than the reviewer's interest and they may still contain some of the biases discussed above. Also, it is likely that most bibliographies will need updating for recent research. Even with these precautions, the use of bibliographies generated by others is strongly recommended because the compiler has spent many hours obtaining information and the biases involved in generating the bibliographies may obviate the biases that threaten the personal search of the reviewer.

The government system for publishing its own documents is a self-contained information retrieval system and might therefore be missed entirely by a researcher who does not decide to enter this system. Government documents fall into several categories, of which the most relevant to the present purpose is "research documents for specialists." Most government documents are printed by the U.S. Government Printing Office, which also issues a monthly catalogue that indexes the most recently published works. The novice entering the maze of government documents for the first time will probably find the *Guide to U.S. Government Publications* the best starting point. This work does not describe the documents themselves, but does describe the agencies that publish government documents. In addition to federal government documents, state and local governments have published works that should be available in major research libraries.

Finally, the sources of information most likely to prove fruitful to the potential reviewer are the indexing and abstracting services associated with the social sciences. An indexing or abstracting service will focus on a certain discipline or topic area and define its scope to be an explicit number of primary publication outlets. Each article that appears in the primary outlets will then be referenced in the system.

The limitation of indexing and abstracting services is the long time lag, often three or four years, between when a study is completed and when it appears in the system. Also, each service has certain restrictions on what is allowed to enter the system, based on topical or disciplinary guidelines. For instance, *Psychological Abstracts* will include only psychology-related journals (though certainly an exhaustive accounting of these), whereas the Educational Research Information Center indexes will exhaustively contain education journals. Thus a reviewer interested in an interdisciplinary topic needs to access more than one abstracting system. While secondary publications are least restrictive with regard to the studies within a discipline that will be contained in them, it is likely that more than one secondary source will be required for the literature search to be exhaustive.

ABSTRACTING AND INDEXING SERVICES

Two reasons were given above for why a single abstracting service probably cannot provide an exhaustive bibliography on many topics: (1) abstracting services tend to focus on particular disciplines, but research questions are often interdisciplinary; and (2) it typically takes from one to two years for a published report to appear in the abstracting services. A final limitation on the exhaustiveness of abstracting services derives not from their content but from how they are organized. Even though a service may cover exhaustively the journals that are relevant to a topic, a searcher may not necessarily be able to describe his or her topic in a manner that will ensure uncovering every relevant article, because the searcher must enter the abstracting service by specifying keywords associated with particular pieces of research. If a searcher is unaware of certain indexing terms that are applied to relevant articles, or if the indexers omit terms that the searcher employs, it is likely that the searcher will miss some relevant articles. This problem will become clearer when the particulars of several abstracting services are discussed.

What follows is a brief description of the four abstracting and indexing services most frequently employed in the social and behavioral sciences. In recent years, several full-length treatments of how social scientists can use libraries have appeared (e.g., Borchardt & Francis, 1984; Gover, 1983). Of special interest would be *Library Use: A Handbook for Psychology*, prepared under the auspices of the American Psychological Association (Reed & Baxter, 1983). This text covers in greater depth all of the issues in literature retrieval introduced below.

Psychological Abstracts. The most familiar and frequently used abstracting service in the behavioral sciences is *Psychological Abstracts*. This series covers literally every major journal in the world involved with psychology and related fields. *Psychological Abstracts* publishes monthly nonevaluative summaries of psychology articles along with author and subject indexes. Each monthly volume can include over 2,000 entries from journals and books (dissertations were included up to 1980 and foreign literature up to 1987). The abstracts are typically written by the authors of the articles themselves, but indexing terms are applied by *Psychological Abstracts* employees. An annual index is published, typically in two volumes for subjects and one for authors. Each volume is divided into 16 major classifications, including general psychology; psychometrics; developmental, social, and experimental psychology; physical and psychological disorders; and educational and applied psychology.

The broad classifications give searchers their first opportunity to screen out potentially irrelevant articles. The major screening, however, begins with the searcher's use of the *Psychological Abstracts' Thesaurus of Psychological Index Terms*. The *Thesaurus* is much like a dictionary. It compiles the most recent vocabulary used to define psychological terms of present and past interest. Thus before a searcher can enter the *Psychological Abstracts*, he or she needs to have at least one term known to be used frequently to describe research in the area of interest. The searcher locates this term in the "Relationship" section of the *Thesaurus*. The "Relationship" section displays the term the searcher is aware of and then lists other terms of either a broader or narrower range in the same or related fields that have been used by the indexers to categorize documents. Thus from a single term the searcher can expand the pool of potentially relevant terms into related areas. For instance, the illustrative review examining the relation between personality and interpersonal expectancy communication might have included the searcher going to the "Relationship" section in the *Thesaurus* and looking up the term "locus of control," a personality dimension commonly used in research. Figure 3.1 reproduces the *Thesaurus* entry for "internal-external locus of control."

With an appropriate set of terms in hand, the searcher then goes to the annual subject indexes. The searcher looks up each of the terms suggested by the *Thesaurus*. Under each term, the searcher finds a separate entry for each abstract to which it was assigned. Other terms that were used to index the abstract also appear, along with short phrases describing the content of the article—for example, the age, race, and sex of subjects. At the end of this string of descriptors appears an abstract number, which is used by the searcher to locate the full abstract in the separate monthly issues. Figure 3.1 also contains examples of an entry in the subject index and an abstract.

The abstract itself can be retrieved and this fuller (but still short) description used to judge whether the article is relevant. Finally, if the abstract proves interesting, its listing of the author(s), journal, and date of publication can be used to retrieve the full report.

The Educational Resources Information Center. The Educational Resources Information Center (ERIC) provides a multitude of information services for both practitioners and researchers. The ERIC system collects, screens, organizes, and disseminates any literature associated with educational practices or issues. ERIC maintains 16 clearinghouses throughout the country, each focusing on a different facet of education (e.g., adult education, reading, science education).

The ERIC system also has an associated dictionary called the *Thesaurus of ERIC Descriptors*. As in *Psychological Abstracts*, these descriptors are used to index and enter documents into the ERIC system and to assist users in retrieving documents relevant to their searches. In addition to the *Thesaurus*, ERIC publishes two monthly guides to its contents. The first is called the *Current Index to Journals in Education (CIJE)*. It presents a monthly listing of the periodical literature covering more than 700 major educational and education-related publications. The second is called *Resources in Education (RIE)*. It presents the abstracts to recently completed research reports and other documents of educational significance. These are indexed by subject, author, institutional source, and type of publication (e.g., book, convention paper). Most documents stored in *RIE* can be retrieved in their entirety through the system. The full documents

A. Relationship Section Entry for Internal-External Locus of Control in the *Thesaurus of Psychological Terms*

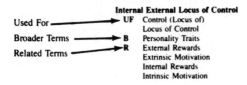

B. Subject Index Entry (partial) for Internal-External Locus of Control (July-Dec 1981)

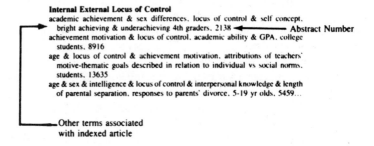

C. Abstract Entry for Abstract Number 2138 (July 1981)

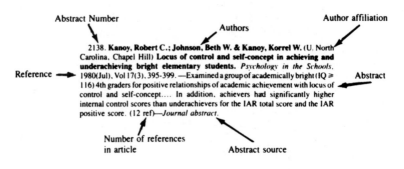

Figure 3.1: Examples of Entries in *Psychological Abstracts*

are typically contained in microfiche collections that can be found in major research libraries.

The steps involved in the use of *RIE* parallel those for the *Psychological Abstracts*. First, the searcher consults the *Thesaurus of ERIC Descriptors*, which is organized like the *Thesaurus of Psychological Terms*. That is, the searcher provides key descriptors relevant to the search and the *Thesaurus* then helps identify broader, narrower, and related terms that might be relevant. Figure 3.2 provides examples of *Thesaurus* and index entries for the term "locus of control." The searcher then consults the monthly issues of *Resources in Education* and the annual indexes for a listing of relevant documents that appear in the volumes associated with each index term. Following these brief article descriptions in the subject index, an accession number appears that can be used to find either the abstract or the full report. The *Current Index of Journals in Education* is entered in the same manner as *Resources in Education*, but the two guides need to be searched separately.

With the accession numbers in hand, the searcher goes to the "Resume" section in either of the guides to find the title, author, source, and abstract associated with the article. In *RIE*, if the article is still deemed potentially relevant the searcher proceeds to the microfiche collection. These contain transparencies that can be placed on microfiche reading machines to bring the document to full size. It is then possible in many libraries to photocopy the magnified microfiche documents to obtain a paper copy of the document. Or the searcher can contact the ERIC Document Reproduction Service to obtain a copy. In *CIJE*, the searcher finds the journal containing the complete document.

Dissertation Abstracts International. While many abstracting services also contain abstracts of dissertations, *Dissertation Abstracts International (DAI)* focuses exclusively on this type of document. However, *DAI* is broad in that all dissertations, regardless of discipline, are abstracted in it. Thus the first job of the searcher is to identify those disciplines and subdisciplines that are of interest.

The materials in *DAI* are indexed according to author and important keywords in the dissertation title. No indexer reads each dissertation in order to assign descriptive terms. Instead, a dissertation will appear in *DAI*'s subject indexes only under those important words that appear in the dissertation title. Also, *DAI* volumes contain only the abstracts associated with the dissertations. Most university libraries maintain microfilm copies of only those dissertations completed at that university and therefore, when an abstract appears relevant, the searcher usually must contact the university at which the dissertation was conducted through interlibrary loan to obtain a full-length copy. Alternatively, the searcher can purchase a copy from University Microfilms International in Ann Arbor, Michigan.

Obtaining dissertations is not only time-consuming; it can also be very expensive. If interlibrary loan fails, reviewers might consider writing to dissertation authors and asking to borrow theses or obtain copies of reprints or preprints of articles based on theses. Alternatively, the abstracts of dissertations

A. Alphabetic Descriptor Display Entry for Locus of Control in the *Thesaurus* of ERIC Descriptors

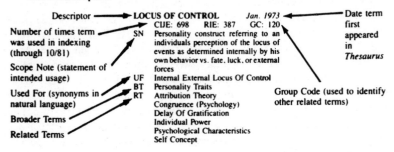

B. Subject Index Entry for Locus of Control in *Resources in Education* (July 1982)

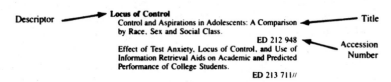

C. Document Resume (partial) for Accession Number ED 213 711 (July 1982)

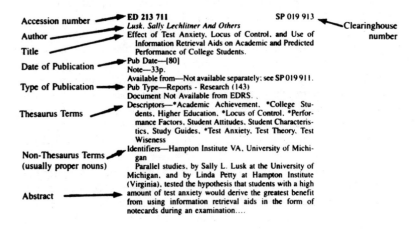

Figure 3.2: Examples of Entries in ERIC

are generally more detailed than abstracts published in *Psychological Abstracts* or by ERIC. Therefore, it is sometimes possible for a searcher to glean from the abstract itself the information needed to use the dissertation in the research review, if only in a cursory fashion. Figure 3.3 presents some of the features of *DAI*.

The Social Sciences Citation Index. The *Social Sciences Citation Index* (*SSCI*) is unique because it categorizes documents based on the work cited in them as well as their topical focus. According to the publishers of the *SSCI*, "a citation index for the journal literature identifies and groups together all newly published articles that have referenced (cited) the same earlier publication. The earlier publication becomes, in effect, an indexing term for current articles that deal with the same subject" (Institute for Scientific Information, 1980, p. 3). An example will make this strategy clear. At the beginning of a search for locus of control studies, a searcher might be aware of several standard measures of locus of control. One such measure, called the Intellectual Achievement Responsibility (IAR) Scale, was developed by Virginia C. Crandall (Crandall, Katkovsky, & Crandall, 1965). With this knowledge, the searcher could enter the *SSCI* by looking up "Crandall, V. C." in the "Citation Index" volumes, where he or she would find a listing of all articles for which "V. C. Crandall" was the first author that had been cited in other articles during the covered period. Each article that had cited a Crandall work would be listed by its author, source, and date of publication. Those articles citing Crandall et al.'s 1965 publication could have correlated the IAR scale with an interpersonal expectancy measure. A starting point for screening articles on this basis might be the *SSCI* Source Index, which lists publications making citations alphabetically and contains full titles and bibliographical references to the articles as well as summaries of the articles' citations. After using the Source Index, the searcher can go directly to the full report. Figure 3.4 presents an example of a citation index entry.

Citation indexes are most useful when particular researchers or research papers are closely associated with a problem area. The searcher can retrieve studies that cite central researchers in an area and then screen theses for topic relevance. Perhaps the most remarkable thing about the *SSCI* is the breadth of its social science coverage. The *SSCI* indexes every article in over 1,500 journals that cover 50 different social science disciplines, and selectively covers nearly 3,000 other journals that might or might not have social science information in them. Through this process the *SSCI* compiles more than 130,000 new journal articles every year.

The *SSCI* also contains a subject index, called the Permuterm Subject Index, that uses the significant words in article titles to index documents. Every significant title word is paired with every other significant title word, creating a two-level indexing system. Thus a searcher can take a single term and find it in the Permuterm Index and then examine the paired terms that might prove relevant to the relation under study. This feature of the *SSCI* is also illustrated in Figure 3.4.

A. Keyword Title Index Entry for "Locus" (partial) *(Humanities and Social Sciences, November 1981)*

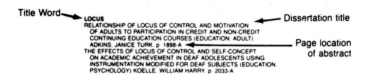

B. Dissertation Abstract (partial) from p. 2033-A *(Humanities and Social Sciences, November 1981)*

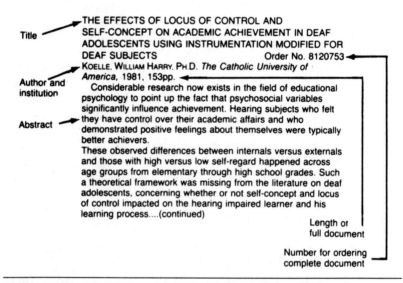

Figure 3.3: Examples of Entries in *Dissertation Abstracts International*

A. Citation Index Entry (partial) under Crandall, VC (1981, Annual)

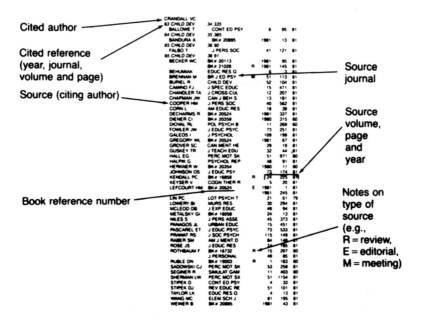

B. Permuterm Index Entry for Locus-of Control (1981, Annual)

Figure 3.4: Examples of Entries from *Social Sciences Citation Index*

Space limitations make it impossible to examine each of the hundreds of abstracting services available in the social sciences. As of late 1986, there were over 3,000 services available (Katz, 1987), most through the use of on-line computer searches. The content of these services varies from broad coverage of disciplines, as in the ERIC system, to highly specialized topic areas (e.g., alcohol and drug abuse, marriage and the family, exceptional children). Information on abstracting services can be obtained from your librarian or from the *Directory of Online Databases*.

Computer searches. The social science indexing and abstracting services allow the searcher to access thousands of documents from a wide variety of sources. These systems' exhaustiveness, coupled with the explosion in social science research, however, do not solve the problem of information overload so much as underscore it. The reader may have been struck by the time needed to conduct a comprehensive search of any of the four abstracting services, if a topic is broad. Without considerable time and money, it might appear that a thorough search of the abstracts is beyond the capability of a single searcher or even a search team.

Luckily, the computer revolution has touched the scientific communication system and has greatly reduced the effort needed to accomplish an exhaustive literature search. Instead of spending many hours manually searching the abstracting systems, a searcher can use a computer to access several abstracting services in just one or two hours. All major research libraries have on-line computer searches available. The services are also available to private users through telecommunication networks such as CompuServe. These can access the thousands of abstracting services that have been placed on computer tapes. The tapes are accessible through phone hookups to central computer storage facilities. For instance, the DIALOG/Information Retrieval Service has been in use since 1972. The DIALOG system stores more than 200 abstracting services and contains millions of records. Compact discs have also found use in this type of information storage. Universities can purchase subscriptions to discs that are updated periodically. For instance, Silver Platter Information, Inc., makes both *Psychological Abstracts* (called *PsychINFO* in its computer form) and ERIC indexes available on compact discs.

A searcher does not have to know how to operate computers to use the computer search services, though many universities make the hookups available for unsupervised use. Research libraries employ trained specialists who can conduct searches on behalf of searchers once they have the needed information. Typically, the searcher tells the librarian the topic of interest and, most important, what terms, synonyms, and related terms are involved in the search. The librarian and the searcher can browse through the thesauri to identify terms that the searcher might not have considered initially. Searchers are also often asked by the librarian to provide examples of documents they hope to retrieve, to give the librarian some concrete idea about the material desired.

Each of the four abstracting services described above has a slightly different technique for retrieval through the computer. For instance, *PsychINFO* can be accessed using several different computer retrieval techniques. First, the *Thesaurus* can be used to identify a "descriptor field." That is, as noted above, every document included in *PsychINFO* has been read by an indexer and assigned a series of terms (taken from the *Thesaurus*) that describe the document's contents. One can then retrieve documents by asking the computer to identify those that have been assigned the relevant descriptors. It takes the computer only seconds to tell how many documents have been assigned a descriptor and to print out examples of the documents covered.

A second technique is to use "natural language" or "free text" to identify terms that appear in the article title or abstract. The use of natural language descriptors frees the librarian and searcher from relying on the *Thesaurus* and the judgment of the indexer for identifying documents that might be relevant. This technique is especially useful if the searcher is interested in new terms that have not found their way into the *Thesaurus*.

A third method is to use the "identifier field." The identifier field contains, among other significant phrases, the proper nouns that appear in a document. For example, a searcher interested in examining the literature relevant to the Hawthorne effect would not find the term "Hawthorne effect" in the *Thesaurus*. However, because it is a proper noun, the identifier field can be used to search for all documents that mention the Hawthorne effect. The identifier field is also useful when a searcher wants to find research involving a particular test (e.g., the WISC or Strong Vocational Inventory).

Even more impressive, the computer can use Boolean algebra to retrieve abstracts based on the specified relations between sets of descriptions or terms. For example, a searcher might request the computer to identify all abstracts in which the term "homework" appears with the terms "achievement" or "grades" or "attitudes."

Finally, *PsychINFO* can be searched via the computer by using author names, journals, or institutions. For instance, if the searcher is interested in obtaining all of the research conducted at the Center for Research in Social Behavior, this institutional name could be used to locate relevant documents.

PsychINFO is available on computer tape from the present back to 1967. In some instances, the searcher may be interested in older documents, and these would have to be retrieved manually. Interestingly, however, the computerized abstracts are more up to date than the printed volumes available on the library shelves, because the process of abstracting and indexing articles is now done directly onto computer tape, which is then used to generate the printed volumes.

The computerized ERIC system is similar to *PsychINFO* although, of course, it has its own thesaurus. Also, the ERIC descriptor or index terms are divided into major and minor categories. Thus searchers have the option of retrieving only those studies in which the important terms are a major focus in the document or including those documents that treat their interest only tangentially. The other three means of accessing the system—use of free text, identifiers, and names of authors, journals, or institutions—are also available with ERIC. The ERIC data base is computerized back to 1966.

Dissertation Abstracts International has a much less sophisticated means for computerized retrieval. Documents can be located only through the use of free text terms that appear in dissertation titles. It is possible, however, to circumscribe the search somewhat by requesting that the computer access only a broad subject area. For instance, if the searcher is interested in psychological studies examining the Hawthorne effect, "Hawthorne effect" could be used as the keyword and the computer could be requested to retrieve only studies that appeared in the psychology subject category. It is also possible to search *Dissertation Abstracts International* through the use of the dissertation author or the institution granting the degree.

Dissertation abstracts (from *DAI, American Doctoral Dissertations*, and *Comprehensive Dissertation Index*) have been computerized back to the year 1861.

Subject searches of the *Social Science Citation Index* can be accomplished only through the use of free text terms from article titles. Subject searches can be specified to include only a specific type of document, such as journal articles or book reviews. In order to use the citation index component of *SSCI*, the searcher must provide the reference for which the citation history is of interest. A problem with the use of the citation indexes is that numerous errors are contained in the bibliographic information included in journal articles (Boyce & Banning, 1979). Apparently, authors and editors spend little time proofreading references, so it is often necessary for searchers to retrieve general information on a cited author and then sift through it to identify citations that are not listed accurately. Of course, this is a problem for the manual searcher of *SSCI* as well as for the computerized searcher. The *SSCI* has been computerized back to 1972.

The monetary cost of running a computer search is not prohibitive. In fact, approximately 90% of the searches run in my university's research library cost between $10 and $30, with ERIC searches the least expensive and *SSCI* searches the most expensive.

After meeting with the librarian and interacting with the computer, the searcher can request a printed bibliography that includes the authors, references, titles, and abstracts of every potentially relevant article. These bibliographies are sent through the mail by the computer services and usually arrive less than a week after the search. Bibliographies can also be printed on-line, but at greater expense.

It is impossible to overemphasize the value of the computer search to the research reviewer. Using computers, the reviewer can obtain an exhaustive listing of potentially relevant documents with phenomenal speed. Because of the amount of time saved and the convenience of having a hard copy of the search outcome, which can then be evaluated at the reviewer's convenience, the search can be much broader than if it were undertaken manually.

Computer searching is not without problems. In particular, when the computer is used, keywords must be completely specified before the search begins, eliminating the possibility of following up any promising leads that might arise during the search (Menzel, 1966; Stoan, 1982). If computerized searches precluded manual searches, the loss of accidental discoveries would be troubling indeed. However, the searcher is still free to browse, and browsing is recommended before the computer search begins. In browsing, the searcher can expand the keywords to be used in the computer search and identify relevant articles that should appear on the computer printout. Then, if those articles do not appear, he or she will know that something has gone awry. For a more detailed overview of on-line searches and services, see W. A. Katz's *Introduction to Reference Work* (Vol. 2) (1987).

Finally, there is empirical evidence that computer searching has some beneficial by-products. In an experimental study, Feinberg (1981) assigned students to either a "standard bibliographic skills" group or a computer search group for doing term papers. He found students in the computer search group received higher grades, believed the library was more adequate for literature reviews, and derived more satisfaction from the assignment than students who used standard bibliographic procedures.

DETERMINING THE ADEQUACY OF
LITERATURE SEARCHES

The question of which and how many sources of information to use has no general answer. The appropriate sources will be a function partly of the topic under consideration and partly of the resources of the reviewer. As a rule, however, I suggest that searchers should always employ multiple channels so that the chances of a strong unidentified bias distinguishing included from unincluded studies is small. If a reviewer has uncovered different studies through channels that do not share similar biases, then the overall conclusions of the review should be replicable by another reviewer using different, but also complementary, sources for primary research. This rule embodies the scientific criterion of replicability.

Informal sources revisited. Earlier in this chapter, it was noted that the information contained in informal channels is not likely to reflect information gleaned from all potential sources. This research, however, was also shown to complement that gained through formal channels because it is likely to be more recent. Therefore, searchers should not exclude it but should carefully examine the percentage of the total relevant literature that is made up of information retrieved through informal sources. If this percentage is large, the searcher should go to other, secondary, sources before terminating the search.

Published versus unpublished research. It was also mentioned earlier that concentrating only on published research will produce a set of studies that over-emphasize significant results. However, it may be counterargued that published research has undergone the most rigorous methodological appraisal by established researchers and probably is of the highest quality.

A focus on only published research might be legitimate in two circumstances. The first is when the published research contains several dozen, or in some cases several hundred, relevant works. In such an instance it is likely that while the published research may overestimate the magnitude of a relation, it probably will not incorrectly identify relation direction. The suggested magnitude of the relation can be cautiously interpreted. Also, enough instances of a hypothesis test will be covered to allow a legitimate examination of which study characteristics covary with study outcomes.

Second, there are many hypotheses that have multiple testings in the literature that were *not* the primary focus of the research. For instance, many psychological and educational studies include gender as a variable in the research design and report hypothesis tests of gender differences, although these are only an ancillary interest of the primary researchers. The bias toward significant results in publications probably does not extend much beyond the primary hypothesis. Therefore, a hypothesis that appears in many articles as a secondary interest of the researcher will be affected by the publication bias to a lesser degree than will the researcher's primary focus.

Generally speaking, however, focusing only on published studies is not advisable. In fact, as we shall see in Chapter 4, publication does not ensure that only studies of high quality will be included in the review. Faulty studies often make their way into print, and well-conducted studies may never be submitted for publication.

In addition, reviewers should not restrict their searches to published outlets even if they ultimately decide to include only published work in their reviews. To make well-informed choices about what to put in and what to leave out of a synthesis, and even to help them decide what the important issues are in a field, reviewers need to have a thorough grasp of the literature.

An empirical examination of search strategies. What searching techniques are actually used by research reviewers? Table 3.1 presents the results of a survey of 57 authors of research reviews published in journals and books covering psychology and education (Cooper, 1987). Authors indicated whether or not they used each of 15 different searching strategies, how useful they found each strategy, and how central or significant the references it yielded were.

On average, reviewers reported using six or seven different strategies. Three of the four most frequently used strategies were associated with the ancestry approach (i.e., examining the references in past reviews, books, and journal articles). Invisible college contacts were also a source of references for many reviewers, though these proved neither as useful nor as central. Some 61% of the reviewers conducted computer searches, and these yielded highly valued references. Searches of citation indexes were not used by many reviewers. However, among those who did use them the resulting references were rated very highly.

The illustrative reviews. To gather the homework literature, several complementary searching strategies were employed. First, four computerized

TABLE 3.1
Use, Utility, and Centrality of Different Sources of References

Use^a	$Utility^b$	Source of References	$Centrality^c$
35	2.6	computer search of abstract data bases (e.g., ERIC, *Psychological Abstracts*)	3.1
32	4.0	manual search of abstract data bases	4.5
5	4.5	computer search of citation index (e.g., *SSCI*)	3.7
8	4.0	manual search of citation index	3.1
53	2.7	references in review papers written by others	2.6
47	3.9	references in books written by others	3.4
40	3.3	references in nonreview papers from journals you subscribe to	3.4
31	4.0	references in nonreview papers you browsed through at the library	4.3
44	4.8	communication with people who typically share information with you	4.3
20	5.4	formal requests of scholars you knew were active in the field (e.g., solicitation letters)	4.5
22	6.1	informal conversations at conferences or with students	5.6
18	5.6	topical bibliographies compiled by others	5.6
15	6.3	browsing through library shelves	5.8
5	7.2	general requests to government agencies	5.2
9	7.3	comments from readers/reviewers of past work	5.5

SOURCE: Cooper (1987).
a. Use is the number of reviewers (out of 57) who said they used the source to locate references.
b. Utility is the average ranking of the source with regard to the number of references it yielded (only by authors who used the source).
c. Centrality is the average ranking of the source with regard to the "significance" or "centrality" of the references it yielded (only by authors who used the source).

research services were accessed: ERIC, *PsychINFO*, the Government Printing Office Monthly Catalog, and the National Technical Information Service. In all cases the natural language or free text keywords used to retrieve documents were "homework" or the word "home" adjacent to the word "work." If these appeared anywhere in the article abstract, the document was retrieved. ERIC included 346 homework citations, and *PsychINFO* included 249. The government services added an additional 48 citations. Obviously, not all of these were research reports.

Additional strategies were employed in order to retrieve studies of homework either too old or too new to be included in the on-line search services. To find older studies (and some missed by the computer because homework was not mentioned in the abstract), the reference lists of past reviews and relevant primary research reports were examined. To find newer studies, letters were sent to 13 researchers who had made recent contributions to the homework literature. Also, 25 requests for information were sent to the deans of education schools ranked as the most productive educational research institutions. The deans were asked to bring the homework review project to the attention of their faculties and to ask that relevant documents be sent. Finally, convention programs from the American Educational Research Association were examined for possible papers and symposia that included presentations on homework.

None of the strategies described so far helps to locate the "fugitive literature," reports that never become a part of the traditional channels of scientific communication. Homework is the kind of topic about which a large amount of fugitive literature might exist. Therefore, letters of inquiry were sent to the 53 state agencies that deal primarily with education, as listed in the *National Directory of State Agencies.* Finally, requests were sent to 110 directors of research and evaluation in selected North American school districts.

The literature search for the review of how research design affects response rates to questionnaires was quite different. *Psychological Abstracts, SSCI, BRS/Inform,* and *Management Contents* were used as parts of the computerized abstract search with the keywords "response rate," "inducement," "incentive," "survey," and "questionnaire." This search, as the descriptors indicate, was one for which the computer was least effective in uncovering relevant research. The reason, of course, was the difficulty in generating a list of descriptors that captured adequately the nature of the hypothesis under study. The computer uncovered 98 citations; of these, 25 were ultimately deemed relevant. Not surprisingly, however, a tracking of the references mentioned in these 25 articles (and past reviews) revealed an additional 68 relevant studies. Thus a total of 93 relevant articles were obtained that included 497 response rates that could be associated with different techniques. The literature search was also restricted to research that had been conducted after 1965. The age-of-research restriction was employed because it was felt that research previous to 1965 might not reflect accurately the response habits of present-day populations.

Without going into detail, the search for studies examining personality moderators of interpersonal expectancy effects on photo-rating tasks revealed 17 research reports that contained at least one relevant comparison. The drug-treatment-of-hyperactivity search found 61 relevant studies.

VALIDITY ISSUES IN STUDY RETRIEVAL

At the beginning of this chapter, it was mentioned that literature searches have two different targets—previous research and individuals or elements relevant to the topic area. It is necessary, therefore, for research reviewers to address the adequacy of their accessed studies with respect to each of the targets. The reviewer must ask (1) how the retrieved studies might differ from all studies and (2) how the elements contained in retrieved studies might differ from all elements of interest. Much of this chapter has dealt with how to answer the first of these questions. Every study does not have an equal chance of being retrieved by the reviewer. It is likely that studies contained in the reviewer's retrieval channels are different from studies that never become public or that can be accessed through other channels. Therefore, the reviewer must pay careful attention to what the inaccessible studies might have to say and how this might differ from what is contained in studies that have been retrieved.

The reviewer's second population of interest, referring to individuals or other basic units of analysis, injects a note of optimism into the discussion. There is some reason to believe that research reviews will pertain more directly to an area's target population than will the separate primary research efforts in the topic area. The overall literature can contain studies conducted at different times, on adults and children, and in different countries with varied racial and ethnic backgrounds (as well as under different testing conditions with different methods). For certain problem areas containing numerous replications, the population of referent individuals accessible to a reviewer may closely approximate the target population of the primary researcher. While a resignation to population restrictions in primary research is understandable, we need not be so acquiescent about the referent population of research reviews. We must bear in mind, of course, that the bias against null and contradictory findings may affect the available samples of elements as well as the sampled studies of the review. To the extent that more retrievable studies are associated with particular subpopulations of elements, the retrieval bias will restrict the accessible populations of individuals.

The first threat to validity associated with the data-gathering phase is that the studies in the review probably will not include all studies pertinent to the topic of interest. Again, reviewers should access as many information channels as needed to ensure that no obvious, avoidable bias exists, within the limits set by cost-effectiveness.

The second threat to validity occurring during study retrieval is that the individuals or elements in the retrieved studies may not represent all individuals or elements in the target population. Of course, the primary researcher's choice of units is beyond the control of the research reviewer, but the reviewer is obligated to describe the missing populations carefully and to qualify any conclusions based on missing or overrepresented samples.

Protecting Validity

(1) The most crucial protection against threats to validity caused by inadequate data collection comes from a broad and exhaustive search of the literature. While the law of diminishing returns does apply here, a complete literature

search has to include at least one major abstracting service, informal communications, and the bibliographies of past research or reviews. The more exhaustive a search, the more confident a reviewer can be that another reviewer using many but perhaps not identical sources of information will reach a similar conclusion.

(2) In their manuscripts, reviewers should be explicit about how studies were gathered, including information on sources, years, and keywords covered in the search. Without this information, the reader of the review has no way of comparing the validity of a particular review's conclusion with the conclusions that may be contained in other reviews.

(3) Reviewers should present whatever indices of potential retrieval bias are available to them. For instance, Rosenthal and Rubin (1982) distinguished published research from dissertations to determine if the evidence from the two sources differed. Cooper, Burger, and Good (1981) reviewed only published studies but speculated that little publication bias was present in their conclusions because the report titles rarely mentioned the hypothesis of interest (i.e., gender differences in locus of control).

(4) The research reviewer should summarize the sample characteristics of individuals used in the separate studies. Given the general gloom that accompanies most discussion of sample representativeness in the social sciences, many reviewers will find this practice reveals an unexpected strength rather than weakness in their research reviews.

EXERCISES

1. Count the number of abstracts indexed under the terms "cognitive dissonance" and "learned helplessness" in the yearly indexes to *Psychological Abstracts* from 1965 to the present. What does this tell you about research in these two areas? What does it tell you about the completeness of *Psychological Abstracts* listings on these two topics?

2. Define a topic area by specifying the keywords (and their crossings or intersections) that would guide a literature search. Pick a few years and do a manual search of an abstract service to locate relevant articles. Perform a parallel computer search. How are the two outcomes different? Which search was more useful and cost-effective?

3. For a topic of your choice, decide what channels you would use to search the literature and the order in which you would access them. For each step in the search, describe its strengths, limits, and cost-effectiveness.

4

The Data Evaluation Stage

This chapter details three approaches to judging methodological adequacy. Also discussed are problems encountered in retrieving data from studies and the procedures used to identify independent hypothesis tests when multiple tests or multiple studies are reported. The chapter concludes with a discussion of validity issues relevant to the data evaluation stage.

The data evaluation stage in a scientific endeavor involves making judgments about whether or not individual data points should be included in the inquiry. This activity must be carried out regardless of whether the data points are the scores of individuals or the outcomes of studies. Data evaluation requires the establishment of criteria for judging the procedural adequacy of how the data were generated. Inquirers must examine all of the potential influences on each data point that may make it irrelevant to the problem under consideration. Then they must determine whether or not these influences are substantial enough to require that the data point be dropped from the inquiry.

EVALUATIVE DECISIONS IN
SCIENTIFIC INQUIRY

Similarities between primary research and research review. Both primary researchers and research reviewers examine their data sets for wild values, errors in recording, or other unreliable measurements. In primary research, individual data points are compared to sample distributions to discover if they are so extreme as to be of questionable validity (that is, statistical outliers; see Barnett & Lewis, 1978). The search for statistical outliers in research reviews involves the examination of relationship magnitudes to determine if the strength of a relation in any study is too different from those in other studies to be considered reliable. Errors in recording are identified in both kinds of research through recalculation of results or the examination of wild values. A primary researcher may observe that a given individual's score is not on the scale of values employed for that particular variable. A research reviewer may recalculate the values of statistical tests presented in a study and find that the primary researcher's calculations were in error.

Differences between primary research and research review. Other means for identifying unreliable data are different for the two types of inquiry. In primary research, an individual's responses are sometimes discarded because surrounding evidence reveals that the individual did not attend to the appropriate stimuli or that the response instructions were misunderstood (see Carlsmith et al., 1976). If deception or some other form of misdirection was used in the research, individual data may be discarded because the participant did not believe the cover story or deduced the hidden hypothesis.

In research review there is only one potential criterion (beyond discordancy and error) for discarding data: the validity of the study's methods. Reviewers decide whether each study was conducted in a careful enough manner so that the result can be trusted. Reviewers can make either a discrete decision (to include the study or not) or a continuous one (to weight studies according to their relative degrees of trustworthiness). A large part of this chapter will be devoted to criteria for judging the methodological quality of a study.

Most social scientists agree that methodological quality should be the primary criterion for decisions about how much trust to place in a study's results. However, in practice the predispositions of reviewers about what the outcome of the review should be often have a strong impact on how studies are evaluated. It is important to examine the sources and effects of reviewers' prior beliefs.

PREDISPOSITIONS OF THE REVIEWER

Almost every primary researcher and research reviewer begins an inquiry with some idea about its outcome. In primary research, methodologists have constructed elaborate systems of controls to eliminate artifactual results created by experimenter expectancy effects (Rosenthal, 1976). In research reviews no such system of controls has been employed. Reviewers are fully aware of their biases *and* the outcomes of studies as the research is being evaluated. This leads to the possibility that the evaluation of research will be colored by its outcomes. The impact of predispositions on reviews has been so great that Gene Glass (1976) made the following remark about the process:

> A common method for integrating several studies with inconsistent findings is to carp on the design or analysis deficiencies of all but a few studies—those remaining frequently being one's own work or that of one's students or friends—and then advance the one or two "acceptable" studies as the truth of the matter. (p. 4)

Mahoney (1977) called this "confirmatory bias," and he performed an experiment that directly tested the impact of predispositions on the evaluation of research. He sampled guest editors for the *Journal of Applied Behavior Analysis* and asked them to rate several aspects of a controlled manuscript. Mahoney found that the methods, discussion, and contribution of the manuscript were evaluated more favorably if the study confirmed the reviewer's predisposition about the results. In a related study, Lord, Ross, and Lepper (1979) found that readers rated proattitudinal studies as better conducted than counterattitudinal studies. More strikingly, the undergraduates who participated in the Lord et al. study showed *polarization* in attitudes despite the fact that they all read the same research abstracts. That is, even though all participants read one study that supported their prior belief and one that refuted it, after reading the two studies participants saw more support for their initial positions.

It appears then that predispositions toward a review's results can influence the reviewer's judgment about the methodological quality of a piece of research. If a study disconfirms the reviewer's predisposition, the reviewer is more likely to attempt to find some aspect of the study that renders it irrelevant or methodologically unsound. On the other hand, studies that confirm the predisposition may be included although their relevance is questionable or their methods flawed.

JUDGING RESEARCH QUALITY

Problems with quality judgments may be even more extensive than those associated with reviewer predispositions. It may be the case that even "disinterested" judges of research could not agree on what is and is not a quality study.

Studies of evaluator agreement about research quality. Several studies have examined the reliability of judgments made about manuscripts submitted to journals in the field of psychology. These studies typically calculate the correlation between the recommendations made by manuscript readers concerning whether or not a manuscript should be accepted for publication. In many respects the judgments of manuscript evaluators are more complex than those of research synthesizers. The manuscript evaluator must consider several dimensions that do not interest the research synthesizer, including the clarity of writing and the interests of the journal's readership. Also, a journal editor will sometimes deliberately choose evaluators who represent different perspectives, while still hoping that the evaluators will agree on the disposition of the manuscript. And, of course, if perfectly objective criteria were available (and were employed), the evaluators would come to concurring decisions.

The interclass correlations reported in studies of manuscript evaluators' agreement on publication decisions range from $r = +.54$ (reported by Scarr & Weber, 1978) to $r = +.19$ (reported by Cicchetti & Eron, 1979). Marsh and Ball (1981) collected judgments on the "quality of research design and analysis" and found the interjudge reliability was $r = +.27$.

In an interesting demonstration, Peters and Ceci (1982) resubmitted 12 already-published research articles to the journals in which they initially appeared. The manuscripts were identical to the originals except that the names and institutions of the submitters were changed from "high status" to "low status." Only 3 of the 12 articles were detected as being resubmissions. Of the 9 articles that completed the re-review process, 8 were *not* accepted for publication. The journal in which the Peters and Ceci (1982) report appears, *The Behavioral and Brain Sciences*, contains open peer commentary on this study and peer review in general.

Some of the differences between judgments by manuscript evaluators and research synthesizers were controlled for in a study conducted by Gottfredson (1978). He removed much of the variability in judges' ratings that might be due to differing initial biases by asking authors to nominate experts competent to evaluate their work. Gottfredson was able to obtain at least two expert evaluations for each of the 121 articles. The experts evaluated the quality of the articles on a three-question scale that left the meaning of the term *quality* ambiguous. An interjudge agreement coefficient of r = +.41 was obtained. On a 36-item evaluation scale that tapped many explicit facets of research quality, an interjudge agreement coefficient of r = +.46 was obtained.

A judgment of the overall quality of a study requires the evaluator to assess and combine several dimensions along which studies can differ. It is therefore possible to locate two sources of variance in evaluators' decisions: (1) the relative importance they assign to different research design characteristics and (2) their judgments about how well a particular study met a design criterion. To demonstrate the first source of variance, I asked six experts in school desegregation research to rank order the importance of six design characteristics for establishing the "utility or information value" of a school desegregation study (Cooper, 1986). The six characteristics were (1) the experimental manipulation (or, in this case, the definition of desegregation), (2) the adequacy of the control group, (3) the validity of the outcome measure, (4) the representativeness of the sample, (5) the representativeness of the environmental conditions surrounding the study, and (6) the appropriateness of the statistical analyses. The intercorrelations of the rankings among the experts varied from r = +.77 to r = +.29, with the average correlation being r = +.47.

In sum, the studies of evaluator agreement are somewhat disheartening. It should be pointed out, however, that the intraclass correlation used to measure agreement has been criticized as being too conservative (Whitehurst, 1984). Also, the reliability of judgments can be enhanced by adding more judges. That is, a decision to accept or reject an article for publication based on ten evaluators' ratings will, on average, correspond more with the consensus of ten other evaluators than with any two evaluators' decisions. Rarely, however, are very large pools of evaluators used to make quality judgments about research by either journal editors or research synthesizers.

A priori exclusion of research versus a posteriori examination of research differences. The studies of agreement about research quality and the role of predispositions in the evaluation process demonstrate instances in which subjectivity intrudes on attempts to reach consensus about our world. The point is important because there is considerable disagreement about whether or not a priori judgments of research quality should be used to exclude studies from research reviews.

This debate was perhaps best captured in an exchange of views between Hans Eysenck (1978) and Gene Glass and Mary Smith (1978) concerning Smith and Glass's (1977) review of research on psychotherapy. Smith and Glass (1977) reviewed over 300 studies of psychotherapy with no a priori exclusion of studies due to poor methodology. Eysenck felt this strategy represented an abandonment of scholarship and critical judgment:

> A mass of reports—good, bad, and indifferent—are fed into the computer in the hope that people will cease caring about the quality of the material on which the conclusions are based. . . . "Garbage in-garbage out" is a well-known axiom of computer specialists; it applies here with equal force. (p. 517)

Eysenck concluded that "only better designed experiments than those in the literature can bring us a better understanding of the points raised" (p. 517).

In rebuttal, Glass and Smith (1978) made several points already mentioned in this chapter and earlier ones. First, as noted in Chapter 2, the poor design characteristics of different studies can "cancel" one another out, if the results of different studies are consistent. Second, the a priori quality judgments required to exclude studies are likely to vary from judge to judge and to be influenced by personal biases. Finally, Glass and Smith claimed they did not advocate the abandonment of quality standards. Instead, they regarded the impact of design quality on study results as "an empirical a posteriori question, not an a priori matter of opinion" (Glass, McGaw, & Smith, 1981, p. 222). They suggested that reviewers thoroughly code the design aspects, good and bad, of each study and then demonstrate if, in fact, the outcomes of studies are related to how the studies were conducted.

The position of Glass and his colleagues seems consistent with a rigorous approach to literature reviewing. The decision to include or exclude studies on an a priori basis requires the reviewer to make an overall judgment of quality that is often too subjective to be credible. Instead, a careful enumeration of study characteristics can be devised by a reviewer and study characteristics can be compared to study results to determine if they covary with one another. If it is empirically demonstrated that studies using "good" methods produce results different from those produced by "bad" studies, the results of the good studies can be believed. When no difference is found it is sensible to retain the "bad" studies because they contain other variations in methods (such as different samples and locations) that, by their inclusion, will help answer many other questions surrounding the problem area.

The only circumstance in which a priori exclusion of studies may be appropriate is when the criteria for excluding studies are defined before the literature is searched, so that the rules do not shift to suit the reviewer, and the number of acceptable studies is large enough to permit the reviewer to substantiate adequately any general conclusions that are drawn. In most cases, however, letting the data speak—that is, including all studies and examining empirically the differences in results associated with methods—substitutes a discovery process for the predispositions of the reviewer.

APPROACHES TO CATEGORIZING RESEARCH METHODS

The decision to take an empirical approach to the impact of research design does not relieve the reviewer of all evaluative responsibilities. The reviewer must still decide what methodological characteristics of studies need to be coded. Obviously, these decisions will depend on the nature of the question under scrutiny and the types of associated research. If a problem has been addressed mainly through experimental manipulations in laboratory settings, a different set of methodological characteristics may be important than if a correlational, field study, or some mix of the two types of research has been used. In the past, research reviewers have employed two approaches to coding methods so that potential differences between "good" and "bad" studies could be assessed. The first approach requires the reviewer to make judgments about the threats to validity that exist in a study. The second approach requires the detailing of the objective design characteristics of a study, as described by the primary researchers.

The Threats-to-Validity Approach

When Campbell and Stanley (1963) introduced the notion of "threats to validity," they literally transformed the social sciences. They suggested that an identifiable set of extraneous influences associated with each research design could be found that "might produce effects confounded with the experimental stimulus" (p. 5). Different research designs had different validity threats associated with them and designs could be compared according to their inferential capabilities. More important, less-than-optimal designs could be "triangulated" so that strong inferences could result from multiple studies when the single, "perfect" study could not be performed.

Campbell and Stanley's notion held the promise of increased sensitivity and objectivity in discussions of research quality. However, it was not long before some problems in the application of their scheme became apparent. The problems related to creating an exhaustive list of threats to validity and identifying what the implication of each threat might be.

Initially, Campbell and Stanley (1963) proposed two broad classes of validity threats. Threats to *internal* validity related to the direct correspondence between the experimental treatment and the experimental effect. To the extent that this correspondence was compromised by deficiencies in research design, the interpretability of a study's results would be called into question. Campbell and Stanley listed eight threats to internal validity. Threats to *external* validity related to the generalizability of research results. Evaluating external validity required assessing the representatives of a study's participants, settings, treatments, and measurement variables. While the external validity of a study could never be assessed definitively, Campbell and Stanley suggested four classes of threats to representativeness.

Next, Bracht and Glass (1968) offered an expanded list of threats to external validity. They felt that "external validity was not treated as comprehensively as internal validity in the Campbell-Stanley chapter" (p. 437). To rectify this omission, Bracht and Glass identified two broad classes of external validity: *population* validity, referring to generalization of persons not included in a study, and *ecological* validity, referring to nonsampled settings. Two specific threats to population validity were described, along with ten threats to ecological validity.

Later, Campbell (1969) added a ninth threat to internal validity, called "instability," defined as "unreliability of measures, fluctuations in sampling persons or components, autonomous instability of repeated or equivalent measures" (p. 411).

Finally, Cook and Campbell (1979) offered a list of 33 specific threats to validity grouped into four broad classifications. The notions of construct validity and statistical conclusion validity were added to internal and external validity. *Construct* validity referred to "the possibility that the operations which are meant to represent a particular cause or effect construct can be construed in terms of more than one construct" (p. 59). *Statistical conclusion* validity referred to the power and appropriateness of the data analysis technique.

From this brief history, the problems in using the threats-to-validity approach to assess the quality of empirical studies should be clear. First, different researchers may use different lists of threats. For instance, should the threat of "instability" offered by Campbell (1969) constitute one threat, as originally proposed, or three threats, as redefined by Cook and Campbell (1979)? Or should ecological validity constitute one threat or up to ten different threats? A second problem is the relative weighting of threats—is the threat involving historical confounds weighted equally with the threat involving restricted generalizability across constructs? Expert methodologists may even disagree on how a particular threat should be classified. For instance, Bracht and Glass (1968) listed "experimenter expectancy effects" as a threat to external validity, while Cook and Campbell (1979) listed it as a threat to the construct validity of causes.

All these problems aside, the threats-to-validity approach to the evaluation of research still represents an improvement in rigor, and is certainly preferable to the a priori single judgment of quality it replaces. Each successive list of threats represents an increase in precision and accumulation of knowledge. Also, the list of validity threats gives the reviewer an explicit set of criteria to apply or modify. In that sense, reviewers who use the threats-to-validity approach make their rules of judgment open to criticism and debate. This is a crucial step in making the research evaluation process more objective.

The Methods-Description Approach

In the second approach to study evaluation, the reviewer codes exhaustively the objective characteristics of each study's methods, as they are described by the primary researchers. This approach was discussed earlier in connection with the study coding sheet (see Chapter 2). Now a more detailed examination is in order.

In Campbell and Stanley's (1963) original work, three preexperimental designs, three true experimental designs, and ten quasi-experimental designs were examined. The list of designs was expanded by Cook and Campbell (1979). In most areas of research considerably fewer than all the available designs will be needed to describe exhaustively how independent and dependent variables have been paired in the relevant research.

As Campbell and Stanley (1963) noted, experimental designs relate mainly to eliminating threats to internal validity. They hold little information about the three other classes of threats to trustworthiness. Some of these were alluded to in Chapter 2, but a bit more detail should be added here. Examining the credibility of, say, experimental manipulations and measurements requires a description of the procedures that the primary researchers used to create independent variables and measure dependent variables. With regard to manipulated independent variables, reviewers can code the number and type of empirical realizations used: In how many ways was the independent variable manipulated? Was the manipulation accomplished through written instructions, films, or the creation of a live-action situation? Similarly, reviewers can record the presence or absence of controls to keep the experimenter blind to the treatment conditions and whether or not deception or misdirection was used to lead the participant away from guessing the hypothesis. Obviously, these considerations are relevant only when treatment manipulations were employed in the studies of interest.

Distinctions in measurement techniques can be codified by recording the number of measures used; whether they were verbal, written, behavioral, or interpersonal judgments; whether they were standardized, informal, or constructed for the particular study; and their relative reliability, if such assessments are available. Other measurement characteristics might be of interest to particular research areas.

As to the population and ecological generalizability of results, it has been suggested that the reviewer can record any restrictions on the types of individuals sampled in the primary studies, when and where the studies were conducted, and when the dependent variable measurements were taken in relation to the manipulation or measurement of the independent variables.

Finally, to assess a study's statistical power, reviewers should record the number of participants, whether a between- or within-subjects design was employed, the number of other factors (sources of variance) extracted by the analyses, and the statistical test used.

One problem with the methods-description approach to evaluating studies is shared with the threats-to-validity approach—different reviewers may choose to list different methodological characteristics. However, the methods-description approach has several advantages. First, when studies are being coded the methods-description approach does not require as much integration of material or inferential judgment. Making a judgment about the threat to validity called "low statistical power" provides a good example. The coder can judge whether a study has a good chance to reject a false null hypothesis only through a combination of several explicit study characteristics: size of the sample, between- or within-subjects design, inherent power of the statistical test (e.g., parametric versus nonparametric), and/or number of other sources of variance extracted in the analysis. Two coders of the same study might disagree on whether or not a study is low in power, but agree perfectly on a coding of the separate components that make up the decision. The objective design characteristics of studies can be coded with less ambiguity of meaning and, therefore, greater reliability. The question then becomes: Is the integration of methodological information when studies are first coded necessary to assess the presence or absence of a validity threat? For a majority of threats, the answer is no. If an analysis of study results shows that, say, only studies using within-subjects designs found significant results, then the reviewer can examine this design feature for all of its implications for validity. That is, between-subjects designs may have been too low in power to reveal an effect, or the premeasure in the within-subjects designs may have sensitized the participants to the independent variable manipulation. Thus, while it may be difficult to retrieve the particular aspect of a research design that created a threat to validity, the reviewer often can still examine validity threats when methodological distinctions are coded.

A Mixed-Criteria Approach

The optimal strategy for categorizing studies appears to be a mix of the two a posteriori approaches. First, the reviewer should code all potentially relevant, objective aspects of research design. However, there are threats to validity that may not be captured by this information alone. For instance, the threats to internal validity involving how a control group is treated—diffusion of treatments, compensatory rivalry, or resentful demoralization in the less desirable treatment—are probably best coded directly as threats to validity, though deciding whether they are present or absent still relies heavily on the description of the study presented by the primary researcher. While this mixed-criteria approach does not remove all problems from study evaluation, it is another step toward explicit objective decision making in an area previously rife with subjective and arbitrary judgments.

The illustrative reviews. Two of the four illustrative reviews provide good examples of how research evaluations can be conducted.

First, the review of the effects of homework included three codings related to the internal validity of studies: the type of experimental design (e.g., random assignment or nonequivalent control groups), whether or not treatments were counterbalanced, and whether or not the experimenter was also the teacher of the classes receiving the treatments. Other codings of the homework studies related to the measurement, external, and statistical validity of studies (see Table 2.1).

Note that the coders of homework studies made no inferences whatever about methods or their validity—they simply gathered information exactly as reported by the primary researchers. Studies that used random assignment, counter-balanced treatments, and nonexperimenter teachers were clearly preferable. However, studies that fell short of this ideal were also included in the review and the impact of the design factors on the actual outcomes of studies was examined. Only if important relations were found between design and outcome were the differences in study results weighted in regard to their relative trustworthiness.

In the review of drug treatments of hyperactivity the selection of studies was restricted to include only those that employed random assignment and double-bind procedures, the strongest possible design for causal inferences. Thus this review did exclude studies on an a priori basis. What was the rationale? A total of 61 studies were found that met very strict methodological requirements—a majority of all the studies identified as potentially relevant. This was a large enough pool of experiments to allow effective examination of the impact of other procedures on study results. That is, other aspects of studies related to other forms of validity varied considerably even within this restricted sample. It will be rare for this type of situation to prevail in the social sciences. When it does, the reviewer may be able to argue convincingly for a priori exclusion of studies. Certainly it would be difficult for a critic of the hyperactivity review to argue that the exclusion of studies was biased by the reviewers' predispositions.

PROBLEMS IN DATA RETRIEVAL

Thus far procedures have been discussed that allow reviewers to find and evaluate research in an exhaustive and rigorous fashion. Some deficiencies in both retrieval and evaluation procedures have been noted that will frustrate reviewers regardless of how thorough and careful they try to be. Some potentially relevant studies do not become public and defy the grasp of even the most conscientious search procedures. With regard to evaluating studies, it is impossible to remove subjectivity from the process completely. A third problem area spans both the retrieval and evaluation phases of literature reviewing. These problems, almost completely beyond the control of the reviewer, involve (1) the inability of libraries to ensure that all documents of potential relevance to the reviewer are on hand, (2) the careless or incomplete reporting of data by primary researchers, and (3) the less-than-perfect information-processing skills of the people who retrieve information from studies. Each of these three problems will be dealt with separately.

Problems in Library Retrieval

Every research reviewer will find that some articles of potential relevance (based on titles or abstracts) cannot be located in his or her personal or institutional library. To what lengths should the reviewer go to retrieve these articles? The use of interlibrary loans is a viable route for attempting to retrieve these studies. As noted earlier, interlibrary loan can even be used to obtain dissertations and master's theses, or dissertations can be purchased from University Microfilms International in Ann Arbor, Michigan. Contacting primary researchers directly is another possibility, although personal contact often results in only a low rate of response. Whether or not a primary researcher can be located and induced to send a reprint is influenced in part by the age of the article requested.

In general, when deciding how to retrieve articles that are difficult to obtain the searcher should consider (1) the percentage of the total of known articles that are difficult to find, (2) the cost involved in undertaking extraordinary retrieval procedures (e.g., interlibrary loan is cheap, buying dissertations is expensive), and (3) any time constraints under which he or she is operating.

Incomplete and Erroneous Results Sections

Perhaps the most frustrating occurrence in study retrieval is when the reviewer obtains a primary research report but the report is incomplete in its description of the results. For instance, in my review of research on gender differences in conformity, I found that 12 of 38 relevant research reports contained no description of the statistics that led to the conclusion (Cooper, 1979). Statistical data were most often omitted from a report when the results of the tests were nonsignificant. Most remarkable was the discovery of four studies that did report statistical data but neglected to mention the direction of the relation!

Obviously, incomplete reporting of statistical values will be of primary concern to research reviewers who intend to perform quantitative synthesis (discussed in the next chapter). What should the quantitative reviewer do about missing data? Several conventions can be suggested to handle the most common problems.

First, the reviewer can treat all studies that report hypothesis tests as "non-significant" without reporting the associated inference test value, p-levels, or effects sizes as having uncovered exactly null results. That is, for any statistical analysis involving these studies, a probability of .5 (in the one-tailed instance) and a relationship strength of zero is assumed. It is reasonable to expect that this convention has a conservative impact on any quantitative review results. In general, when this convention is used, cumulative p-levels should be higher and the average relationship strength closer to zero than if the exact results of these studies were known.

Another convention involves attempting to combine results when some primary researchers use parametric statistics and others use nonparametric statistics. In most cases one statistical paradigm will predominate greatly over the other across the entire set of studies. In this instance the different statistics can be aggregated as though they all shared the dominant set of assumptions without greatly distorting the results. If the split between parametric and nonparametric tests is roughly even, the two sets of studies should be examined separately.

Reviewers who want to perform statistical combinations sometimes find that separate studies are incommensurable because they employ different numbers of factors in their analysis. For instance, one study on drug treatments of hyperactive children might present a simple t-test comparison of a treated and control group. Another study might have employed the gender and age of children as additional factors in an analysis of variance design. All else being equal—and assuming some gender and age effects—the second experiment will produce a lower probability level and a larger treatment effect because the amount of error against which the treatment-control difference is compared will be smaller. Glass et al. (1981) have outlined procedures for equating statistical results from studies using different numbers of factors in their analytic design, but in practice primary researchers rarely report their results in enough detail for a reviewer to carry out the needed transformations. When this is the case, the reviewer should determine empirically whether the statistical results of a study are related to the number of factors in the analysis. If a relation is found, the reviewer should report separately the results obtained from analyses of studies that used only the single factor of interest.

In addition to incomplete reports, some reports are inexact in their statistical data. Many reports will describe statistical tests as reaching the $p < .05$ level of significance rather than describing the exact probability associated with the outcome of the inference test. In this case the reviewer can recalculate the p-levels to reflect their exact value.

Finally, there is the problem of errors in statistical analyses. As an empirical demonstration, Wolins (1962) contacted 37 psychologists who had recently published research reports and asked if he could see their raw data. Of these, 26 authors, or 70%, did not reply or claimed their data had been lost or inadvertently destroyed. Of 7 data sets Wolins was able to reanalyze, 3 were found to have large analytic errors.

While no one knows exactly how common errors are in statistical analyses, studies indicate they may be frequent enough to concern research reviewers. Whenever possible, the reviewer should cross-check the statistics presented in research reports to ensure that none of the results implies wild values and all of the results reported about a study are consistent with one another.

Unreliability in Coding Study Results

Just as researchers sometimes make errors in their data analysis, it is also the case that errors are made in the recording of data. Transcription errors are a problem for research reviewers when they extract information from research reports. Rosenthal (1978a) reviewed 21 studies that examined the frequency and distribution of recording errors. These studies uncovered error rates ranging from 0 to 4.2% of all the data recorded; 64% of the errors in recording were in a direction that tended to confirm the study's initial hypothesis.

Stock et al. (1982) empirically examined the number of unreliable codings made in a literature review. They had three coders (one statistician and two post-Ph.D. educational researchers) record data from 30 documents into 27 different coding categories. Stock et al. found that some variables, such as the means and standard deviations of the ages of participants, were coded with perfect or near perfect agreement. Only one judgment, concerning the type of sampling procedure employed by the researchers, did not reach an average coder agreement of 80%.

In sum, while coders of primary research are fairly reliable in their retrieval of information, it is good practice to monitor coder accuracy. This is especially true if the number of studies to be coded is large or if persons with limited research training are called upon to do the coding. In these instances the reviewer should treat the coding of studies as if it were a standard exercise in data gathering. Specifically, coding sheets should be accompanied by codebooks explaining the meaning of each entry. Prior to actual coding, discussions and practice examples should be worked on with coders. Assessments of reliability should be taken on controlled sets of studies. Coding should not begin until an acceptable level of intercoder reliability has been established.

The illustrative reviews. In the review of the effects of homework, fewer than a dozen potentially relevant manuscripts were identified in the literature search that could not be retrieved for examination. Most of these were very old, were published outside North America, or were unpublished. These documents represented less than 5% of all the documents actually judged potentially relevant.

The review of personality moderators of interpersonal expectancy effects had the most difficulty with missing data. This occurred because correlation coefficients were often reported as nonsignificant and the magnitude of the correlation was not given. One technique that helped fill in these missing data was to determine if a published journal article was a report of a dissertation. If it was, the full dissertation was obtained; this often contained more complete descriptions of data outcomes.

Finally, the homework review included a formal test of the reliability with which studies were coded. Kappa coefficients and percentages of agreement were calculated between two coders on thirteen categories. The reliability estimates indicated perfect agreement on seven of the categories. The poorest reliability, $k = .71$ and 79% agreement, occurred on the coders' retrieval of the number of assignments students did each week. Whenever disagreements occurred, the two coders examined the study together and resolved the difference.

IDENTIFYING INDEPENDENT HYPOTHESIS TESTS

Another important decision that must be made during the data evaluation stage involves how to identify independent hypothesis tests. Sometimes a single study may contain multiple tests of the same hypothesis. This can happen for two reasons. First, more than one measure of the same construct might be employed and each measure analyzed separately. For example, a hyperactivity researcher might measure school behavior problems through both teacher reports and classroom observation. Second, different samples of people might be used in the same study and their data analyzed separately. This would occur, for instance, if the hyperactivity researcher examined results for boys and girls separately. In both of these instances, the hypothesis tests are not completely independent—they share historical and situational influences, and in the former case they even share influences contributed by having been collected on the same subjects.

The problem of nonindependence of hypothesis tests can be taken further. Sometimes a single research report can describe more than one study. Sometimes multiple research reports describe studies conducted at the same laboratory. A reviewer might conclude that studies conducted at the same site, even if they appear in separate reports over a number of years, still contain certain constancies that imply the results are not completely independent. The same primary researcher with the same predispositions may be using the same laboratory rooms while drawing participants from the same population.

Especially in instances where the reviewer intends to perform a quantitative synthesis, a decision must be made about when hypothesis tests will be considered independent events. Several strategies can be suggested regarding how to decide on the unit of analysis in research reviews.

Laboratories as Units

The most conservative way to identify independent hypothesis tests employs the laboratory or researcher as the smallest unit of analysis. Advocates of this most conservative approach would suggest that the information value of repeated studies in the same laboratory is not as great as an equal number of studies reported from separate laboratories. (An intraclass r can be computed to assess the empirical degree of independence of studies from the same laboratory.) This approach requires the reviewer to gather all studies done at the same research laboratory and to come to some overall conclusion concerning the results at that particular site. One drawback, therefore, is that it requires the reviewer to conduct reviews within reviews, since decisions about how to synthesize results first must be made within laboratories and then again between laboratories.

This approach is rarely used in practice. It is generally considered too conservative and too wasteful of information obtained by examining the variations in results from study to study.

Studies as Units

Using the study as the unit of analysis requires the reviewer to make an overall decision about the results of comparisons reported in separate studies but not to aggregate results over more than one report.

If a single research report contains information on more than one test of the same hypothesis, the reviewer weights each discrete finding by the number of hypothesis tests in the report or study. This might be done by using the average or median result to represent the study. This procedure ensures that each study contributes equally to the overall review result. For example, a study of homework with two grade levels of students reporting results on five different measures of achievement (e.g., ten hypothesis tests) might be weighted so that a single result comes from the report and this result is given consideration equal to a report with one grade level and one measure.

Obviously, there will be some subjectivity in the reviewer's judgment of what constitutes a study. For instance, one reviewer might consider all results in a single journal article or manuscript as one study. Another reviewer might consider a report that divides results into separate studies as containing more than one study. Regrettably, the delineation is not as clear as we might like it to be.

Samples as Units

This approach permits a single study to contribute more than one hypothesis test, if the hypothesis tests are carried out on separate samples of people. Thus a hyperactivity reviewer would consider hypothesis tests on boys and girls within the same study as independent, but not tests that used alternate measures of the same construct given to the same children. The use of samples as units assumes that most of the variance shared by hypothesis tests in the same study comes from being collected on the same subjects.

Hypothesis Tests as Units

The least conservative approach to identifying comparisons is to use the individual hypothesis test or comparison as the unit of analysis. Each separate test of the hypothesis conducted by primary researchers is regarded as an independent test by the research reviewer. This technique's strength is that it does not lose any of the within-study information regarding potential moderators of the relation. Its weakness is that the assumption that hypothesis tests are independent, needed for most quantitative syntheses of results, will be violated. Also, the results of studies will not be weighted equally in any overall conclusion about results. Instead, studies will contribute to the overall finding in relation to the number of statistical tests contained in it. This is not necessarily a good weighting criterion.

Shifting Units

A compromise approach to identifying comparisons is to employ a shifting unit of analysis. Specifically, each statistical test is initially coded as if it were an independent event. Thus a single study that contained twelve statistical tests or comparisons would have twelve separate coding sheets filled out for it. Each coding sheet would be slightly different, depending on the aspects of the samples, measurements, or design characteristics used to distinguish the statistical test. However, when an overall cumulative result for the review is generated, statistical tests are weighted so that each *study* (all other weighting factors being equal) contributes equally to the general finding. Thus a study containing three correlations would have these averaged and then added as a single number into the analysis across all studies. However, when examining potential moderators of the overall relation, a study's results are aggregated only *within* the separate categories of the influencing variable. For example, if a homework and achievement study presented correlations for males and females separately, this study would contribute only one correlation to the overall analysis—the average of the male and female studies—but two correlations to the analysis of the impact of gender on the relation—one for the female group and one for the male group. To take the process one step further, if this study reported different correlations for class grades and standardized tests within each gender (i.e., four correlations in all), the two correlations for different measurements would be averaged within each gender group when the analysis for gender influence was conducted and the two gender group correlations would be averaged when the measurement moderator was examined. This means that for moderating hypotheses a single study can contribute one test to each of the categories distinguished by the third variable. This strategy is a compromise that allows studies to retain their maximum information value while keeping to a minimum any violation of the assumption of independence of hypothesis tests.

Statistical Adjustment

Raudenbush, Becker, and Kalain (1988) have proposed a statistical solution to the problem of nonindependent hypothesis tests. They have devised a procedure based on generalized least squares regression that statistically adjusts for interdependence among multiple outcomes within studies and for different numbers of outcomes across studies. The key to using their technique successfully lies in the reviewer having credible numerical estimates of the interdependence of hypothesis tests. For instance, assume a study of homework's effects includes both class grades and standard test scores as measures of achievement. In order to use the Raudenbush et al. technique, the reviewer must estimate the correlation between grades and achievement for the sample in this study. Data of this sort often are not provided by primary researchers. They might be estimated from other studies, however, or the analysis could be run with low and high estimates to generate a range of values.

The illustrative reviews. Three of the four illustrative research reviews employed the shifting unit of analysis procedure described above. The only exception was the review of research design effects on response rates to questionnaires. In this analysis, because the raw data from each study could be retrieved and aggregated, only the number of participants in a study determined its weighting. In instances where raw data can be retrieved, they should be used rather than sample statistics (see Chapter 5 for details).

VALIDITY ISSUES IN EVALUATING RESEARCH

The use of any evaluative criteria other than methodological quality introduces a potential threat to the validity of the review outcome. As Mahoney (1977) states, "To the extent that researchers display [confirmatory] bias our adequate understanding of the processes and parameters of human adaptation may be seriously jeopardized" (p. 162). It is safe to assume that evaluative bias has pernicious effects on our understanding.

A second threat to validity occurring during data evaluation involves the unreliability of data introduced by the incomplete reporting of primary researchers. We have seen that many research reports completely omit discussions of hypothesis tests or give only incomplete information on the tests that were mentioned. The greater the percentage of such incomplete reports within a research review, the wider are the confidence intervals that must be placed around the review's conclusion.

Finally, a third threat to the validity of a review involves the unreliability in coding of research results. In most instances coding can be done with fairly high reliability, especially if the strategy employed asks coders only to retrieve information directly as presented by the primary researchers, rather than to make inferences about research quality or the presence or absence of particular validity threats.

Protecting validity. In the course of this chapter several procedures have been described that are designed to increase the objectivity of research evaluation and related decisions:

(1) Reviewers should make every effort to ensure that *only* conceptual judgments influence the decision to include or exclude studies from a review.

(2) If studies are to be weighted differently, the weighting scheme should be explicit and justifiable. Personal involvement in a study is not a legitimate criterion for giving it added weight.

(3) The approach used to categorize study methods should exhaust as many design moderators as possible. The reviewer should detail each design distinction that was related to study results and tell the outcome of the analysis.

(4) More than one study coder should be employed, and intercoder agreement should be quantified and reported. Also, coding sheets should be filled out by coders who are blind to the results of the study.

(5) The reviewer should state explicitly what conventions were used when incomplete or erroneous research reports were encountered.

EXERCISES

1. List a set of criteria that you think distinguish good and bad research. Rank order the criteria with regard to their impact on research quality. Compare your criteria and rankings with those of a classmate. What is similar and different about your lists?

2. With your classmate, agree on a set of criteria and evaluative scales. Also, identify a set of ten studies on the same topic. Independently apply the criteria to the ten articles. Compare your ratings. How did they differ and what led to the differences? How might the criteria be revised to minimize differences in future use?

3. Using the same set of studies, and again in conjunction with a classmate, record the following information from each report: (a) sample size, (b) any restrictions on who was sampled, (c) the means of comparison groups (or other data) on the primary variable of interest, (d) whether or not the hypothesis was confirmed, and (e) the type and significance level of the inference test of primary interest. How many values did you agree and disagree on? Which values led to the most disagreement? Why?

5

The Analysis and Interpretation Stage

This chapter presents some statistical methods that can help reviewers summarize research results. Among the techniques discussed are those that generate cumulative probabilities, those that involve the calculation of an effect size, and those that help the reviewer examine the variability of effect sizes across studies. Finally, validity issues arising during data analysis and interpretation are outlined.

Data analysis and interpretation involve the synthesis of the separate data points collected by the inquirer into a unified statement about the research problem. According to Kerlinger (1973):

> *Analysis* means the categorization, ordering, manipulating and summarizing of data to obtain answers to research questions. The purpose of analysis is to reduce data to intelligible and interpretable form. . . . *Interpretation* takes the results of analysis, makes inferences pertinent to the research relations studied, and draws conclusions about these relations. (p. 134)

As noted in Chapter 1, data interpretation requires that decision rules be used to distinguish systematic data patterns from "noise" or chance fluctuation. Although different decision rules can be used, the rules typically involve assumptions about what noise looks like in the target populations (e.g., normally distributed errors).

INTEGRATING TECHNIQUES IN
THE TWO TYPES OF INQUIRY

Just as any scientific inquiry requires the leap from concrete operations to abstract concepts, both primary researchers and research reviewers must leap from samples of data to more general conclusions. Until the mid-1970s, however, there had been almost no similarity in the analysis and interpretation techniques used by primary researchers and reviewers. Primary researchers were obligated to present sample statistics and to substantiate any assertions about hypotheses with probability tests. Most frequently, primary researchers computed means and standard deviations descriptive of their samples, made the assumptions needed for statistical tests (e.g., normal distribution and independence of errors, homogeneity of variance), and reported the probabilities associated with whether potential sources of systematic variance could be distinguished from error.

Statistical aids to primary data interpretation have not gone uncriticized. Some have argued that significance tests are not very informative because they tell only whether or not the null hypothesis is true (e.g., Oakes, 1986). According to this argument, in a population of people the null hypothesis is almost never true and therefore the significance of a given test is mainly influenced by how many participants have been included in the study. Also, those skeptical about the value of significance test statistics point to limitations in the population of events referred to under parametric assumptions. No matter how statistically significant a relation may be, the results of a study are generalizable only to people like those who participated in that particular research effort.

Skepticism about the value of statistics helps those who use statistics to refine their skills and keep their output in proper perspective. Nonetheless, most primary researchers use statistics in their work and most would feel extremely uncomfortable about synthesizing data without some assistance (or credibility) supplied by statistical procedures.

In contrast to primary researchers, research reviewers were not obligated to apply any standard analysis and interpretation techniques in the synthesis process. Traditionally, reviewers interpreted data using rules of inference unknown even to them. Therefore, a description of the common rules of inference used in research reviews was not possible. Analysis and interpretation methods were idiosyncratic to the particular perspective of the individual reviewer. This subjectivity in analysis and interpretation led to skepticism about the conclusions of many reviews. To address the problem, critics introduced quantitative methods into the reviewing process. These methods build on the primary research statistics contained in the individual studies.

QUANTITATIVE SYNTHESIS OR META-ANALYSIS

It was suggested above that the two recent events that have had the strongest impact on research reviewing are the growth in research and the advent of the computerized literature search. A third strong impact was the introduction of quantitative procedures, called meta-analysis, into the reviewing process.

The explosion in social science research has focused considerable attention on the lack of standardization in how reviewers arrive at general conclusions from series of related studies. For some topic areas a separate verbal description of each relevant study will now be impossible. One traditional strategy, to focus on one or two studies chosen from dozens or hundreds, fails to portray accurately the accumulated state of knowledge. Most certainly, in areas where hundreds of studies exist, reviewers must describe "prototype" studies so that readers understand the methods primary researchers have used. However, relying on the *results* of prototype studies as representative of all studies may be seriously misleading. As we have seen, this type of selective attention is open to confirmatory bias: A particular reviewer may highlight only studies that support his or her initial position. Also, selective attention to evidence cannot give a good estimate of the strength of a relation. As evidence on a topic accumulates, researchers become more interested in the strength rather than the simple existence of a relation. Finally, selective attention to only a portion of all studies places little or imprecise weight on the volume of available testings. Presenting one or two studies without a cumulative analysis of the entire set of results gives the reader no estimate of the confidence that should be placed in a conclusion.

Reviewers also face problems when they consider the variations among the results of different studies. Reviewers will find distributions of results for studies sharing a particular procedural characteristic but varying on many other characteristics. They may not be able to conclude accurately whether a procedural variation affects study results because of the variability in results obtained by any single method or the likelihood that the distributions of results with different methods will overlap. It seems, then, that there are many situations in which reviewers must turn to quantitative reviewing techniques. Gene Glass (1977) has written, "The accumulated findings of . . . studies should be regarded as complex data points, no more comprehensible without statistical analysis than hundreds of data points in a single study" (p. 352).

The application of quantitative inference procedures to reviewing seems to be a necessary response to the expanding literature. If statistics are applied appropriately, they should enhance the validity of review conclusions. Quantitative reviewing is an extension of the same rules of inference required for rigorous synthesis in primary research. If primary researchers must specify quantitatively the relation of the data to their conclusions, the next users of the data should be required to do the same.

A Brief History of Meta-Analysis

Gene Glass (1976) introduced the term *meta-analysis* to stand for the statistical analysis of results from individual studies "for purposes of integrating the findings" (p. 3). Procedures for performing meta-analysis had existed long before 1976. Indeed, methods for combining results of independent studies date back to the 1930s (Fisher, 1932; Pearson, 1933), but instances of their application were rare. It took the expanding data base and the growing need for research reviews to provide impetus for the general use of meta-analysis.

Meta-analysis was not without its critics. The value of quantitative reviewing was questioned along lines similar to criticisms of primary data analysis (e.g., Mansfield & Bussey, 1977; Barber, 1978). However, much of the criticism stemmed less from issues in meta-analysis than from more general inappropriate reviewing procedures (such as a lack of operational detail) that were erroneously linked to it (see Cooper & Arkin, 1981).

Evidence indicates that meta-analysis is now an accepted procedure, and its application within the social sciences continues to grow. According to Guzzo, Jackson, and Katzell (1987), the number of articles and dissertations in *Psychological Abstracts* that were indexed under "meta-analysis" reached nearly 100 in 1985. Greenberg and Folger (1988) state that "if the current interest in meta-analysis is any indication, then meta-analysis is here to stay" (p. 191).

When Not to Use Statistics

Much of this chapter will examine the quantitative reviewing procedures that are available and how they are applied. It is important, however, to state explicitly some circumstances in which the use of quantitative procedures in reviews is *not* appropriate.

First, the basic premise behind the use of statistics in reviews is that *a series of studies have been identified that address an identical conceptual hypothesis.* If the premises of a review do not include this assertion, then there is no need for cumulative statistics. Quantitative procedures are applicable only to integrative research reviews, not to reviews with other focuses or goals (see Chapter 1). For instance, if a reviewer is interested in tracing the historical development of the concept of hyperactivity, it would not be necessary for him or her to do a quantitative review. However, if the reviewer also intends to make an inference about whether or not different definitions of hyperactivity (i.e., methods of diagnosis) lead to differing effectiveness for drug treatments, then a quantitative summary of relevant research would be appropriate.

The drug treatment of hyperactivity illustrative review points out a second limitation on quantitative syntheses. In this review, separate analyses were conducted on comparisons of drug treatment versus placebo control groups and drug treatment versus no-treatment control groups. Even though both comparisons assessed the effectiveness of drugs, it would not necessarily be informative to lump them together. When a hypothesis involves a comparison with controls, the reviewer might find that a distinction in the type of control is important enough not to be obscured by a quantitative analysis.

Third, a reviewer should not quantitatively combine studies at a broader conceptual level than readers would find useful. At an extreme, most social science research could be categorized as examining a single conceptual hypothesis—social stimuli affect human behavior. Indeed, for some purposes, such a hypothesis test might be very enlightening. However, this should not be used as an excuse to lump together concepts and hypotheses without attention to those distinctions that will be meaningful to the users of the review (see Kazdin,

Durac, & Agteros, 1979, for a humorous treatment of this issue). For instance, the review of personality moderators of interpersonal expectancy effects provides an example of when a quantitative combination of studies was possible but not profitable. A total of 33 studies were found that tested the broad conceptual hypothesis. Of those, 24 (contained in 17 reports) examined experimenter expectancy effects on photo-rating tasks, 6 used other laboratory settings, 1 used an instructional setting, and 2 used simulated therapeutic settings. Yet, rather than lump them all together, only the studies on photo-rating tasks were meta-analyzed. To have accumulated results at any broader conceptual level and to have claimed general ecological validity based on this cumulation would have been misleading, since over two-thirds of all comparisons were conducted in highly specific settings.

Integrating Techniques and Differences in Review Outcomes

While the relative validity of different inference strategies is difficult to assess, Cooper and Rosenthal (1980) did demonstrate some of the objective differences between quantitative and nonquantitative procedures in research reviews. Graduate students and faculty were asked to evaluate a literature on a simple question: Is gender related to task persistence? All reviewers evaluated the same set of studies, but half the reviewers used quantitative procedures and half used whatever criteria appealed to them. No reviewer in the latter condition chose quantitative techniques. Statistical reviewers reported more support for the hypothesis and a larger relationship between variables than did nonstatistical reviewers. Statistical reviewers also tended to view future replicative research as less necessary than did nonstatistical reviewers, although this finding did not reach statistical significance.

It is also likely that the different statistical tests employed by reviewers who adopt quantitative procedures will create variance in review conclusions. Several different paradigms have emerged for quantitatively reviewing social science research with a parametric model (Glass et al., 1981; Hedges & Olkin, 1985; Hunter, Schmidt, & Jackson, 1982; Rosenthal, 1984), and other paradigms can be used with a Bayesian perspective (Raudenbush & Bryk, 1985; Viana, 1980). There are numerous techniques available for combining the separate study probabilities to generate an overall probability for the run of studies (Rosenthal, 1984). The different techniques generate probability levels that vary somewhat. Thus the rules adopted to carry out quantitative analysis can differ from reviewer to reviewer, and this may create variance in how review results are interpreted. We can assume as well that the rules used by nonquantitative reviewers also vary, but their unexplicit nature makes them difficult to compare formally.

SYNTHESIZING MAIN EFFECTS AND INTERACTIONS

Before examining several of the quantitative techniques available to reviewers, it is important to take a closer look at some of the distinct features of accumulated tests of hypotheses. In the chapter on problem formulation, it was pointed out that at first most research reviews focus on tests of main effects. This is primarily because conceptually identical tests of main effects have occurred more frequently than tests of three or more interacting variables. Of course, once the reviewer has discerned whether or not a main effect is present, he or she next turns to potential moderators of the relation or to interaction hypotheses.

In research reviews the principal feature of both main effect and interaction tests is that the significance levels and relationship strengths associated with separate tests of the same hypothesis will vary from one testing to the next, and this variability is sometimes dramatic.

Variability in Main Effect Tests

Varying results for tests of main effects can be produced because of two classes of reasons. Perhaps the simplest cause is the one most often over-looked—sampling error. Taveggia (1974) made the point well:

> A methodological principle overlooked by writers of . . . reviews is that research results are *probabilistic*. What this principle suggests is that, in and of themselves, the findings of any single research are meaningless—they may have occurred simply by chance. It also follows that if a large enough number of researches has been done on a particular topic, chance alone dictates that studies will exist that report inconsistent and contradictory findings! Thus, what appears to be contradictory may simply be the positive and negative details of a distribution of findings. (pp. 397-398)

Taveggia highlights one of the implications of using probability theory and sampling techniques to make inferences about populations. As an example, suppose it were possible to measure the academic achievement of every American student. Also, suppose that if such a task were undertaken, it would be found that achievement was exactly equal for students who do homework and those who do not—that is, exactly equal group means existed for the two populations. Still, if 1,000 samples of 50 homeworkers and 50 no-homeworkers were taken and the sample means were compared using the $p < .05$ significance level (two-tailed), about 25 comparisons would show a significant difference favoring homeworkers while about 25 favored no-homeworkers. This variation in results is an unavoidable consequence of the fact that the means estimated by the samples will vary somewhat from the true population values. Therefore, just by chance some comparisons will pair sample estimates that vary from their true population values by large amounts and in opposite directions.

In the example given, it is unlikely that the reviewer would be fooled into thinking anything but chance caused the result—after all, 950 comparisons would reveal null effects and significant results would be distributed equally for both possible outcomes. In practical applications, however, the pattern of results is rarely this clear: First, as was pointed out in the chapter on study retrieval, the reviewer might not be aware of all null findings because they are hard to find. Also, even if an overall relation does exist between two variables (that is, the null hypothesis is false), some studies can still show significant results in a direction opposite to the overall conclusion. To continue the example, if the average achievement of homeworkers is greater than that of no-homeworkers, it is still possible that some samplings will favor no-homeworkers, depending on the size of the relation and the number of comparisons performed. In sum, one source of variance in the results of studies can be chance fluctuations due to the inexactness of sampled estimates.

A second source of variance in main effects is typically of more interest to reviewers: the differences in results created by variations in how studies are conducted and/or who participates in them. For instance, it might be that in the entire population, the difference between achievement among students who do and don't do homework is greater in high school than in elementary school. In Chapter 2, the notion of review-generated evidence for relations was introduced to describe the procedure of examining how study characteristics associate with variation in study results.

That two sources of variance in research results exist raises an interesting dilemma for the reviewer. When so-called contradictory findings occur, should the reviewer seek an explanation for them by attempting to identify differences among the methods used in studies? Or should the reviewer simply write off the contradictory findings as produced by chance variations due to sampling error? Some tests have been devised to help reviewers answer this question. In effect these tests use "sampling error" as the null hypothesis. If the variation in results across studies is too great to be explained by sampling error, then the reviewer knows to seek explanations elsewhere, that is, in methodological differences between studies. For now, however, it should simply be noted that these two distinct sources of variance in study results need to be considered by reviewers.

Variability in Interaction Tests

Obviously, the factors that create variability in main effects can also affect variability in tests of interaction. Interaction effects are as susceptible to sampling error and procedural variation as main effects. However, examining interactions in research reviews presents some unique problems. For ease of presentation, these will be discussed in regard to tests of two-way interactions, but the remarks generalize to higher-order interactions as well.

Figure 5.1 illustrates the results of two hypothetical studies demonstrating interactions. In Study I, the hyperactivity levels of two samples of children are examined. Drug intervention and control conditions are compared on the first day and the seventh day of treatment. On Day 1 children receiving drug treatment are less hyperactive than control children, but on Day 7 those children receiving drug treatment are considerably more hyperactive than those not receiving drug treatment. Thus the effect of the drug treatment on hyperactivity reverses itself over the course of the study.

In hypothetical Study II, on Day 1 children receiving the drug treatment are less hyperactive than children in the control group, but on Day 5 no difference between the drug and control group is found. Here the effect of the drug treatment "disappears" between the first and second measurement of hyperactivity.

A reviewer uncovering two studies with these findings might be tempted at first glance to conclude that they produced inconsistent results. Study I indicates that drug treatments are initially effective, but with the passage of time they actually become counterproductive. Study II evidences no counterproductive effect, just a vanishing of the desired result. A closer examination of the two figures, however, reveals why it might not be appropriate to conclude that the studies are inconsistent. The results of Study II probably would have been closely approximated by the researchers in Study I if they had taken a measurement of hyperactivity on Day 5. Likewise, had Study II contained a Day 7 measurement, these researchers probably would have produced results quite similar to the Day 7 results contained in Study I. In general, researchers who find the experimental effect appears at only one level of an interacting variable can only speculate about whether or not sampling from more extended levels of that variable would have led to a crisscrossing of the effects. Research reviewers, however, may have an opportunity to draw such conclusions more confidently.

As the example demonstrates, the research reviewer must not assume that different forms or strengths of interaction uncovered by different studies necessarily imply an inconsistency of results. Instead, research reviewers need to examine the differing levels of variables employed in different studies and if possible to chart results taking the different variable levels into account. In this manner one of the benefits of research reviewing is realized. While one study suggests that the effect of a drug on hyperactivity dissipates over time and another study suggests that the drug effect reverses itself over time, the research reviewer can find that the two results are in fact perfectly commensurate.

This possibility also underscores the importance of primary researchers presenting detailed information concerning the levels of variables used in their studies. Without specific information research reviewers may not be able to conduct an across-study analysis similar to the one presented above. If the primary researchers in Study I and Study II neglected to specify how long a delay was used between measurements, perhaps referring to the two measure-

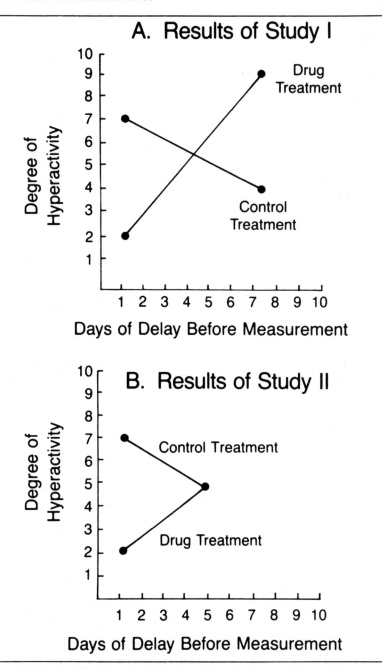

Figure 5.1: Results of Two Hypothetical Studies of Drug Treatment of Hyperactivity

ment intervals as, say, "short" and "long," the commensurability of the results would have been impossible to demonstrate.

Research reviewers must also carefully examine the statistical analyses that accompany reports of interactions. For instance, all else being equal, it is more likely that the researchers of Study I reported a significant interaction between time of measurement and treatment than did the researchers in Study II. In fact, assuming equal error terms, the F-value in Study I for the interaction should be several times greater than that in Study II.

In sum, it is extremely important that reviewers retrieve the most detailed data about interactions regardless of statistical significance. The problem, of course, is that unless the interaction was the chief concern of the primary researchers or the interaction proved significant, there is little likelihood that information detailed enough to perform the kind of analysis portrayed in Figure 5.1 will be contained in the report.

Interactions in Quantitative Reviews

The statistical combination of interactions in quantitative reviews is a very complex task. In fact, reviews rarely combine the statistical results of studies examining the same interaction (in the personality and experimenter expectancy study, a measure of expectancy effect was first devised and the main effect of personality on it was analyzed; see Zuckerman, DePaulo, & Rosenthal, 1981, for an interaction example). This is due partly to the infrequency with which studies have tested the same interaction and partly to the incomplete reporting of many tests of interaction.

There are two different ways that interactions could be statistically combined across studies. First, the separate p-levels and relationship strengths associated with each study's interaction test could be aggregated. An alternative strategy would be to aggregate separately the relation of two variables at each level of the third variable. For instance, a hyperactivity review could generate an estimate of the treatment effect by aggregating all measures taken with a one-day delay and compare this to an aggregation of all measures taken with a seven-day delay. This would probably be more useful and easily interpretable to readers than a direct estimate of the magnitude of the interaction effect. However, it is rare for primary research reports to contain the information needed to isolate the different simple main effects.

TECHNIQUES FOR COMBINING PROBABILITIES
OF INDEPENDENT STUDIES

In this section and several that follow, brief introductions to some of the quantitative techniques that are available to reviewers will be presented. The techniques were chosen because of their simplicity and broad applicability. The treatment of each technique will be conceptual and introductory. The reader who wants a fuller description of the techniques covered as well as many techniques not mentioned is advised to consult the primary sources cited in the text. For the discussion that follows, it is assumed the reader has a working knowledge of the basic statistical concepts and methods employed in the social sciences.

A major reason statistical techniques are used in research reviews is to combine the probability levels associated with separate comparisons to generate an overall probability relating to the existence of a relation. For instance, if three tests of a relation find statistically significant results and seven find null results, what is the reviewer to conclude? The techniques for combining probabilities allow the reviewer to synthesize the results of numerous tests so that overall conclusions can be drawn.

Three assumptions are crucial to the validity of a conclusion based on a cumulation of individual comparisons. First and most obviously, the individual comparisons that go into a cumulative analysis should all test the same conceptual hypothesis. Regardless of how conceptually broad or narrow the idea might be, the reviewer should be comfortable with the assertion that all the included comparisons address the same question.

Second, the separate comparisons that go into the cumulative analysis must be independent of one another. Identifying independent comparisons was discussed in the chapter on data evaluation. The quantitative reviewer must take care to identify comparisons so that it can be argued that each one contains unique information about the hypothesis.

Finally, the reviewer must believe that the initial assumptions made by the primary researchers to compute the results of the comparison were valid. Thus if the reviewer wishes to combine the probabilities associated with a series of t-test comparisons, he or she must assume that the observations, residuals, or errors of the two groups are independent and normally distributed and that the variances are roughly equal.

Vote Counting Methods

The simplest methods for combining results of independent comparisons are the vote counting methods. Vote counts can be done on the direction of the results of comparisons or on the frequency of statistically significant findings.

To do a vote count of directional results, the reviewer must first count the number of comparisons that report results in one direction (called *positive*, for presentation purposes) and compare this to the number of comparisons reporting results in the other direction (called *negative*). In this analysis the reviewer ignores the statistical significance of the separate findings. Once the number of results in each direction is counted, the reviewer performs a sign test to discover if the cumulative results suggest that one direction occurs more frequently than chance would suggest. If the null hypothesis is true—that is, if no relation between the variables under consideration exists in the population sampled by any study—we would expect the number of findings in each direction to be equal.

The formula for computing the sign test is as follows:

$$Z_{vc} = \frac{(N_p) - (\frac{1}{2} \times N_t)}{\frac{1}{2}\sqrt{N_t}}$$ [1]

where

Z_{vc} = the standard normal deviate, or Z-score, for the overall series of comparisons;

N_p = the number of positive findings; and

N_t = the total number of comparisons (positive plus negative findings).

The Z_{vc} can be referred to a table of standard normal deviates to discover the probability (one-tailed) associated with the cumulative set of directional findings. If a two-tailed p-level is desired, the tabled value should be doubled. The values of Z associated with different p-levels are presented in Table 5.1.

For example, if 25 of 36 comparisons find results in the positive direction, the probability that the positive and negative directions have an equal chance to occur in the population is $p < .02$ (two-tailed; $Z_{vc} = 2.33$). Therefore, this result would lead the reviewer to conclude that a positive relation was supported by the series of studies.

A practical problem with the directional vote count is that primary researchers frequently do not report the direction of results, especially if a comparison proves statistically nonsignificant. An alternative vote counting method is to perform a sign test on the frequency of only statistically significant results reported in the positive direction versus the frequency of significant results reported in the negative direction. In performing this procedure, the reviewer assumes that under the null hypothesis of no relation in the population of any study, the frequency of significant positive and that of negative results (in the null case, type I errors) are expected to be equal (Hedges & Olkin, 1980). The reviewer should bear in mind, however, that the number of nonsignificant findings under the null assumption is expected to be much greater than the number of either positive or negative significant findings. Therefore, it is *not* legitimate to test for equal frequencies across the three classes of outcomes (positive, negative, and nonsignificant findings). Hedges and Olkin (1980) have shown that if a reviewer makes the assumption that when no relation exists in the population the number of positive, negative, *and* null findings will be equal, then the vote count method is extremely conservative (that is, likely to miss relations that exist). For instance, assume that a correlation of $r = +.30$ exists between two variables in a population and 20 comparisons have been conducted,

TABLE 5.1
Standard Normal Deviate Distribution

γ	$\alpha'' = 1 - \gamma$	$\alpha' = \dfrac{1}{2}(1 - \gamma)$	z
.995	.005	.0025	2.807
.99	.01	.005	2.576
.985	.015	.0075	2.432
.98	.02	.01	2.326
.975	.025	.0125	2.241
.97	.03	.015	2.170
.965	.035	.0175	2.108
.96	.04	.02	2.054
.954	.046	.023	2.000
.95	.05	.025	1.960
.94	.06	.03	1.881
.92	.08	.04	1.751
.9	.1	.05	1.645
.85	.15	.075	1.440
.8	.2	.10	1.282
.75	.25	.125	1.150
.7	.3	.150	1.036
.6	.4	.20	0.842
.5	.5	.25	0.674
.4	.6	.30	0.524
.3	.7	.35	0.385
.2	.8	.40	0.253
.1	.9	.45	0.126

γ = area between $-z$ and z
   = confidence coefficient

$\alpha' = \dfrac{1}{2}(1 - \gamma)$

   = area above z
   = area above $-z$
   = significance level for one-sided test

$\alpha'' = 1 - \gamma = 2\alpha'$

   = area beyond $-z$ and z
   = significance level for two-sided test

SOURCE: Reprinted with permission from Noether (1971).

with 40 people in each comparison. The chance that the vote count associated with this series of studies will be significant if the assumption of equal numbers of each finding is used is only p = .059!

Adjusting the expected frequencies of the three findings so that the disproportionate number of expected nonsignificant findings is taken into account solves the theoretical problem but raises a practical one. We have seen that null results are less likely to be reported by researchers and thus are less likely to be retrieved by reviewers. Therefore, if the appropriate theoretical values are used in a vote count analysis, it should often occur that both positive and negative results appear *more* frequently than expected. Thus it seems that using the frequency of nonsignificant findings in a vote count procedure is of dubious value.

In sum, then, a reviewer can perform vote counts to aggregate results across individual studies by comparing the number of "raw" directional findings or the number of significant findings in the two directions. Both of these procedures will be conservative (i.e., will miss relations that exist) because much information will be lost—the raw direction of results will not appear in many research reports in one case and nonsignificant findings cannot contribute to the analysis in the other case. Vote counts should always be described in quantitative reviews but should be used to draw inferences only when the number of studies to be aggregated is large and should always be supplemented with more sensitive procedures.

Combining Significance Tests

Rosenthal (1978b) cataloged seven different methods for cumulating results that use as their basic data the precise probability values associated with each comparison. The simplest and most routinely applicable of the seven methods will be presented here. The method, called Adding Zs by Rosenthal, was first introduced by Stouffer in 1949.

The Adding Zs method uses the following formula:

$$Z_{st} = \frac{\sum_{i=1}^{N} Z_i}{\sqrt{N}} \qquad [2]$$

where

Z_{st} = the standard normal deviate, or Z-score, for the overall series of comparisons;

Z_i = the standard normal deviate for the ith comparison; and

N = the total number of comparisons in the series.

The steps for carrying out the analysis are simple. The reviewer must

(1) choose which direction for the hypothesis will be considered positive and which negative;

(2) record the probability associated with each comparison;

(3) if the reported probability is two-tailed, halve it;

(4) look up the Z-score associated with each probability;

(5) sum the Z-scores, remembering to place a minus sign before negative results; and
(6) divide this sum by the square root of the number of comparisons.

The resulting Z_{st} can then be referred to a table of standard normal deviates (see Table 5.1) to discover the probability associated with the cumulative set of individual probabilities. If a two-tailed probability is desired, the tabled p-level should be doubled. The probability describes the combined likelihood that the series of results included in the analysis could have been generated by chance if the null hypothesis were true for every study.

Table 5.2 presents a hypothetical application of the Adding Zs method. Note that hypothetical Studies 2 and 7 produced exact null results (probably due to inexact reporting). Studies 1 and 5 produced statistically significant results, and Study 4 produced a result opposite to that predicted.

The method of Adding Zs can be modified to allow the reviewer to weight the results of different comparisons differentially (see Mosteller & Bush, 1954; Rosenthal, 1978b). For instance, if several comparisons come from a single study, the reviewer might want to weight these less than another comparison that is the only contribution of another study. Or the reviewer might want to give added weight to studies based on larger sample sizes.

The formula for the Adding Weighted Zs method is:

$$Z_w = \frac{\sum_{i=1}^{N} W_i Z_i}{\sqrt{\sum_{i=1}^{N} W_i^2}} \qquad [3]$$

where

Z_w = the Z-score for the weighted combination of studies;
W_i = the weighting factor associated with each study; and all other terms are defined as before.

Table 5.2 presents a hypothetical example of the Adding Weighted Zs method, with the weighting factor being the sample size of the study.

The Fail-safe N

It has been mentioned several times that not all comparisons have an equal likelihood of being retrieved by the reviewer. Nonsignificant results are less likely to be retrieved than significant ones. This fact implies that the Adding Zs method may produce a probability level (chance of a type I error) that is an underestimate. Rosenthal (1979a) wrote, "The extreme view of this problem . . . is that the journals are filled with the 5% of studies that show Type I errors, while the file drawers back in the lab are filled with the 95% of studies that show

TABLE 5.2
Hypothetical Example of the Combination of Eight Comparisons

Study	Number of Participants (N)	N^2	One-Tailed p-Level	Associated Z-Score	NZ
1	48	2304	.025	1.96	94.08
2	28	784	.50	0	0
3	32	1024	.33	.44	14.08
4	24	576	.90	−1.28	−30.72
5	64	4096	.01	2.33	149.12
6	40	1600	.39	.28	11.20
7	20	400	.50	0	0
8	30	900	.15	1.04	31.20
Σ	286	11684		4.77	268.96

Adding Zs: $Z_{st} = \dfrac{4.77}{\sqrt{8}} = 1.69$, $p < .0461$, one-tailed

Adding Weighted Zs: $Z_w = \dfrac{268.96}{\sqrt{11684}} = 2.49$, $p < .0064$, one-tailed

$N_{FS.05} = \left(\dfrac{4.77}{1.645}\right)^2 - 8 = .41$ (or 1)

NOTE: The one-tailed p-level of .90 is from a study finding a direction opposite to that predicted (thus the associated Z-score is negative).

insignificant (e.g., p < .05) results" (p. 638). The problem is probably not this dramatic, but it does exist.

One of the advantages of the Adding Zs method is that it allows the calculation of a Fail-safe N (see Cooper, 1979; Rosenthal, 1979a). The Fail-safe N answers the question, "How many comparisons totaling to a null hypothesis confirmation (e.g., $Z_{st} = 0$) would have to be added to the results of the retrieved comparisons in order to change the conclusion that a relation exists?" Rosenthal (1979a) called this the "tolerance for future null results." The formula for calculating this number, when the chosen significance level is p < .05, is as follows:

$$N_{FS.05} = \left(\frac{\sum_{i=1}^{N} Z_i}{1.645} \right)^2 - N \qquad [4]$$

where

$N_{FS.05}$ = the number of additional null-summing comparisons needed to raise the combined probability of just above p < .05;

1.645 = the standard normal deviate associated with p < .05 (one-tailed); and all other quantities are defined as before.

Obviously, the Fail-safe N cannot be computed when studies are weighted unequally, unless the reviewer wishes to estimate what the average weight of unretrieved comparisons might be—a dubious estimate at best. A hypothetical example of a Fail-safe N is presented in Table 5.2.

The Fail-safe N is a valuable descriptive statistic. It allows the users of a review to evaluate the cumulative result of the review against their assessment of how exhaustively the reviewer has searched the literature. However, the Fail-safe N also contains an assumption that restricts its validity. That is, its user must find credible the proposition that the sum of the unretrieved studies is equal to an exact null result. It might be the case that unretrieved studies have a cumulative result opposite to that contained in the review—perhaps because primary researchers did not want to publish studies that contradicted studies already in print. Or unretrieved studies might cumulatively add support to the conclusion because the reviewer ignored information channels that paralleled those that were used. The plausibility of these alternatives should always be assessed when a Fail-safe N is interpreted.

When is a Fail-safe N large enough so that reviewers and readers can conclude a finding is resistant to unretrieved null results? Rosenthal (1979b) suggests that the resistance number equal 5 times the number of retrieved studies plus 10. No steadfast rule is intuitively obvious, so reviewers should argue anew for the resistance of their findings each time the formula is applied. The best argument for a resistant finding is a large Fail-safe N coupled with a comprehensive search strategy.

Combining Raw Data

The most desirable technique for combining results of independent studies is to integrate the raw data from each relevant comparison. The separate data points can be placed into an analysis of variance or multiple regression that employs the comparison that generated the data as a blocking variable. Obviously, instances in which the integration of raw data can be achieved are rare. Raw data are seldom included in research reports and attempts to obtain raw data from researchers often end in failure (see Chapter 4).

The benefits of integrating raw data can also be achieved, however, if the reviewer has access to the means and standard deviations associated with each comparison. A problem with the use of means and standard deviations is that the dependent variable measurements in the separate comparisons are often not commensurate with one another—that is, they use different instruments with different ranges of values. Of course, the reviewer can standardize the measurements in each comparison to make them commensurate. Again, however, the reporting of individual group means and standard deviations in primary research reports is infrequent, though certainly not as rare as the reporting of raw data.

In sum, analyzing raw data from separate comparisons is the optimum strategy for accumulating results. It is the level of analysis to which the reviewer should aspire and its feasibility should be assessed before other less adequate means for combining results are undertaken. In practice, however, the use of this technique is rare.

Combined Results and Study-Generated Evidence

In Chapter 2 the distinction between study-generated and review-generated evidence was discussed. It was pointed out that study-generated evidence is present when a single study contains results that directly test the relation being considered. The results of the cumulative analysis techniques presented thus far produce study-generated evidence. That is, each individual comparison being integrated has something to say about the hypothesis under consideration. Therefore, if the individual comparisons have used random assignment of participants to conditions in order to uncover causal mechanisms, the combined results of these comparisons relate to those causal mechanisms. Based on vote counts and combined probabilities, the reviewer can make assertions about causality if in fact the primary research included experimental manipulations. A similar assertion cannot be made about the evidence generated by an examination of research methods that covary with results, a topic to be pursued shortly.

The illustrative reviews. The review of personality moderators of interpersonal expectancy effects in laboratory experiments calculated five combined Z-scores and probabilities, one for each hypothesis. The study was used as the unit of analysis and each study was weighted equally. It was found that experimenters with a greater need for social influence were more likely to generate interpersonal expectancy effects. The combined Z-score, based on eight studies, was 2.94 with an associated p-level of .0032, two-tailed. The Fail-safe N, the number of null-summing studies needed to raise the combined probability to above $p = .05$ (two-tailed), was 10.02, or 11 (since 10 studies would be just below $p = .05$).

Tests of the expressiveness and likability of the experimenter indicated nonsignificant relations to experimenter bias, though in both cases the relation was positive (for expressiveness, $N = 3$, $Z = 1.79$. $p < .0734$, two-tailed; for likability, $N = 4$, $Z = 1.71$, $p < .0872$, two-tailed). The influenceability and decoding skills of the subject were both positively related to the appearance of expectancy effects (for influenceability, $N = 11$, $Z = 2.21$, $p < .027$, two-tailed; for decoding skill, $N = 7$, $Z = 2.60$, $p < .0094$, two-tailed).

The review of research design effects on response rates to questionnaires presented a rare opportunity to combine raw data. All of the 93 relevant studies reported their raw data. In this case, the raw data consisted of the number of persons contacted and the number who responded. In addition, in all studies the dependent variable, response or nonresponse, was identical. For instance, 8,577 people participated in studies that experimentally manipulated whether or not a monetary incentive was offered for responding to the questionnaire. Of these, 55.5% of participants who were offered a monetary incentive returned the questionnaire, while 35.2% of participants not offered an incentive returned the questionnaire. The chi-square value associated with these figures is 188.1, a highly significant value. The proportions used in these analyses were weighted by the number of persons contacted in each study. Thus those studies with larger samples contributed more to this overall result than studies that contained small samples.

MEASURING RELATIONSHIP STRENGTH

The primary function of the statistical procedures described above is to help the reviewer accept or reject the null hypothesis. The null hypothesis, of course, tests the "no relation in any study" hypothesis against all others. Most primary researchers have been content simply to identify hypotheses with some explanatory value—that is, to reject the null. The prevalence of this yes-or-no question is partly due to the relatively recent development of the social sciences. Social hypotheses are crudely stated first approximations to the truth. How potent variables are for explaining human behavior and how competing explanations compare with regard to relative potency are questions that have rarely been asked. As theoretical sophistication has increased, however, more social scientists are making inquiries about the size of relations.

Giving further impetus to the "How much?" question is a growing disenchantment with the null hypothesis significance test itself. Whether or not a null hypothesis can be rejected is tied closely to the particular research project under scrutiny. As mentioned earlier, if an ample number of participants are available or if a sensitive research design is employed, a rejection of the null hypothesis is not surprising. In research reviews this fact becomes even more apparent.

A null hypothesis rejection, then, does not guarantee that an important social insight has been achieved. This point was made by David Lykken (1968): "Statistical significance is perhaps the least important attribute of a good experiment. It is never a sufficient condition for claiming that a theory has been usefully corroborated, that a meaningful empirical fact has been established, or that an experimental report ought to be published" (p. 151). Answering the question "How much?" allows a considerably more informed judgment about explanatory value than does answering the question, "Is it different from zero?" And, as we shall see shortly, the latter question can be answered by placing a confidence interval around our "How much?" estimate, obviating the need for combined probabilities.

A Definition of Effect Size

In order to answer the "How much?" question meaningfully, a definition for the notion of relationship strength, or what is more often called the effect size (ES), must be agreed upon. Also, we need methods for quantitatively expressing the magnitude of a relation. Jacob Cohen, in *Statistical Power Analysis for the Behavioral Sciences* (1988), presents a very thorough and useful examination of the definition of effect sizes (also see Lipsey, in press). Cohen defines an effect size as follows:

> Without intending any necessary implication of causality, it is convenient to use the phrase "effect size" to mean "the *degree* to which the phenomenon is present in the population," or "the degree to which the null hypothesis is false." By the above route it can now readily be clear that when the null hypothesis is false, it is false to some specific degree, i.e., *the effect size (ES) is some specific non-zero value in the population*. The larger this value, the greater the *degree* to which the phenomenon under study is manifested. (pp. 9-10)

Figure 5.2 presents three hypothetical relationships that illustrate Cohen's definition. Suppose the illustrated results come from three experiments comparing a drug treatment of hyperactivity with a placebo. Figure 5.2A presents a null relationship. That is, the sampled children given the drug have a mean and distribution of hyperactivity scores identical to the placebo-treated children. In Figure 5.2B the treated children have a mean slightly higher than that of the placebo children, and in Figure 5.2C, the difference between treatments is even greater. A measure of effect size must express the three results so that greater departures from the null are associated with higher effect size values.

Cohen's book contains many different metrics for describing the strength of a relation. Each effect size index is associated with a particular research design in a manner similar to t-tests being associated with two-group comparisons, F-tests associated with multigroup designs, and chi-squares associated with frequency tables. The two primary metrics and one secondary metric for describing relationship strength will be presented below. These metrics are generally useful—almost any research outcome can be expressed using one of them. For more detailed information on these effect size metrics, as well as many others, the reader should consult Cohen (1988). However, it is strongly advised that both primary researchers and research reviewers not use effect estimates for multiple degree of freedom tests, even though Cohen lists several of them. All effect sizes should be expressed (1) as comparisons between two groups, (2) as measures of correlation between two continuous variables, or (3) as other single degree of freedom contrasts if multiple groups are involved. The reasoning behind this qualification is simple. In an analysis of variance a multiple degree of freedom F-test tells whether there is significant variability in the array of group means, but it does not tell which groups vary significantly from one another. Therefore, in all instances it is essential that multiple degree of freedom significance tests be followed by single degree of freedom comparisons. The same would be true for the effect sizes associated with these tests. If the primary researcher or research reviewer defines the problem precisely, he or she should be able to identify single degree of freedom inference tests and associated effect sizes for each comparison of interest. Thus the following discussion is restricted to metrics commensurate with single degree of freedom tests.

The d-Index

The d-index of an effect size is appropriate when the means of two groups are being compared. Thus the d-index is typically used in association with t-tests or F-tests based on a comparison of two conditions. The d-index expresses the distance between the two group means in terms of their common standard deviation. For example, if d = .40 it means 4/10 of a standard deviation separate the two means.

The hypothetical research results presented in Figure 5.2 will illustrate the d-index. For the research result that supports the null hypothesis (Figure 5.2A), the d-index equals zero. That is, there is no distance between the drug treatment and placebo group means. The second research result (Figure 5.2B) reveals a d-index of .40, that is, the mean of the drug treatment group lies 4/10 of a standard deviation above the placebo group's mean. In the third example, a d-index of .85 is portrayed. Here the group with the higher mean (drug treatment) has a mean that rests 85/100 of a standard deviation above the lower-meaned (placebo) group's mean.

Calculating the d-index is simple. The formula is as follows:

$$d = \frac{X_{1.} - X_{2.}}{SD} \qquad [5]$$

where

X_1 and X_2 = the two group means and
SD   = the average standard deviation of the two groups.

The formula for the d-index assumes that the two groups have equal (or roughly equal) standard deviations. In instances where the researcher does not wish to make the assumption that the standard deviations of the two groups are equal, the d-index can be calculated by using the standard deviation of one group or the other—typically the control group, if it is available.

The d-index is not only simple to compute, but it is also scale-free. That is, the standard deviation adjustment in the denominator of the formula means that studies using different measurement scales can be compared or combined.

In many instances reviewers will find that primary researchers do not report the means and standard deviations of the separate groups the reviewer wishes to compare. For such cases Friedman (1968) has provided a computation formula for the d-index that does not require the reviewer to have specific means and standard deviations. This formula is as follows:

$$d = \frac{2t}{\sqrt{df_{error}}} \qquad [6]$$

where

t   = the value of the t-test for the associated comparison and
df_{error} = the degrees of freedom associated with the t-test.

In instances where F-tests with single degrees of freedom in the numerator are reported, the t-value in the above formula can be substituted for by the square root of the F-value ($t = \sqrt{F}$), if the sign of the mean difference is known.

The d-index may leave something to be desired in terms of its intuitive appeal. For this reason, Cohen (1988) also presents a measure associated with the d-index called U_3. U_3 tells the percentage of the sample with the lower mean that was exceeded by 50% of the scores in the higher-meaned group. Put more informally, U_3 answers the question, "What percentage of the scores in the lower-meaned group was exceeded by the average score in the higher-meaned group?" Values for converting the d-index to U_3 are presented in Table 5.3. For example, the d-index of .40 presented in Figure 5.2B has an associated U_3 value of 65.5%. This means that 65.5% of the scores in the lower-meaned (placebo) group are exceeded by the average score in the higher-meaned (drug treatment) group. For Figure 5.2C, the d-index of .85 is associated with a U_3 of 80.2. Thus 80.2% of the scores in the lower-meaned (placebo) group are exceeded by the average score in the higher-meaned (drug treatment) group.

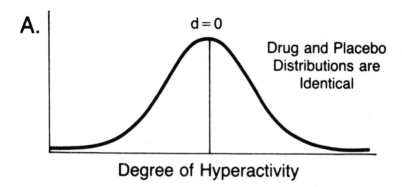

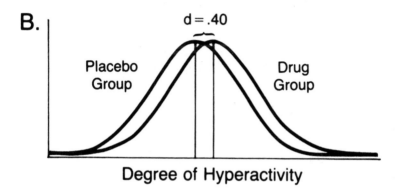

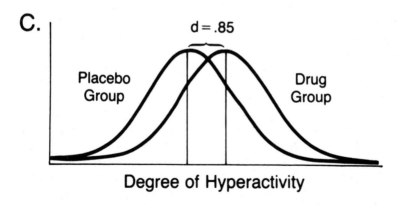

Figure 5.2: Three Hypothetical Relations Between Drug and Placebo Groups in Hyperactivity Experiments

Hedges (1980) has shown that the d-index may slightly overestimate the size of an effect in the entire population. However, the bias is minimal if the degrees of freedom associated with the t-test are more than 20. If a reviewer is calculating d-indexes from primary research based on samples smaller than 20, Hedges's (1980) correction factor should be applied.

The r-Index

A second effect size, the r-index, is simply the Pearson product-moment correlation coefficient. This index is familiar to most social scientists, but the formula for the r-index requires variances and covariances, so it can rarely be computed from information typically presented in primary research reports. Luckily, in most instances where r-indexes are applicable, primary researchers do report them. If only the t-test value associated with the r-index is given, the r-index value can be calculated using the following formula:

$$r = \sqrt{\frac{t^2}{t^2 + df_{error}}} \qquad [7]$$

Likewise, when a chi-square statistic associated with a 2×2 contingency table is given, the r-index can be estimated as follows:

$$r = \sqrt{\frac{\chi^2}{n.}} \qquad [8]$$

where

χ^2 = the chi-square value associated with the comparison and
n. = the total number of observations in the comparison.

Cohen distinguishes the effect size associated with chi-squares by calling it a w-index, but in fact it is identical to an r-index when df = 1.

Finally, one problem that may arise for the research reviewer is that different primary researchers may choose different metrics to study the same phenomena. For instance, in the review of the relation between personality and interpersonal expectancy effects, some primary researchers dichotomized personality variables into "high" and "low" groups and used a t-test to measure statistical significance. Other researchers left the personality scales in their continuous form and correlated them with continuous measures of expectancy effects. When this occurs the reviewer must convert one metric into the other so that a single metric can be used in the research review. Conveniently, the different effect size metrics are easily converted from one to the other. The r-index can be transformed into a d-index by the following formula:

$$d = \frac{2r}{\sqrt{1-r^2}} \qquad [9]$$

TABLE 5.3
Equivalents Among Several Measures of Effect

d	U_3	r	r^2
0	50.0%	.000	.000
.1	54.0	.050	.002
.2	57.9	.100	.010
.3	61.8	.148	.022
.4	65.5	.196	.038
.5	69.1	.243	.059
.6	72.6	.287	.083
.7	75.8	.330	.109
.8	78.8	.371	.138
.9	81.6	.410	.168
1.0	84.1	.447	.200
1.1	86.4	.482	.232
1.2	88.5	.514	.265
1.3	90.3	.545	.297
1.4	91.9	.573	.329
1.5	93.3	.600	.360
1.6	94.5	.625	.390
1.7	95.5	.648	.419
1.8	96.4	.669	.448
1.9	97.1	.689	.474
2.0	97.7	.707	.500
2.2	98.6	.740	.548
2.4	99.2	.768	.590
2.6	99.5	.793	.628
2.8	99.7	.814	.662
3.0	99.9	.832	.692
3.2	99.9	.848	.719
3.4	*	.862	.743
3.6	*	.874	.764
3.8	*	.885	.783
4.0	*	.894	.800

SOURCE: Reprinted with permission from Cohen (1988).
*Greater than 99.95.

or the d-index into the r-index by:

$$r = \frac{d}{\sqrt{d^2 + 4}}$$ [10]

Table 5.3 gives some of the equivalents among the measures of effect.

Statistical Factors Influencing the Size of Effects

In addition to the "true" impact one variable has on another, there are numerous influences on the magnitude of relations revealed in empirical research. Just a few of the more important statistical factors that may influence an effect size will be mentioned here. This introduction will largely be conceptual; for a detailed, technical discussion of these issues, the reader is advised to consult Glass et al. (1981).

The first statistical factor that will influence the magnitude of relations is the reliability of the measurements involved in the study. The less "pure" a measurement is, the less ability it has to detect relations involving the variable of interest. To estimate the impact that unreliability of measures may have on an effect size estimate in a research review, the reviewer might try to obtain the reliabilities (e.g., internal consistencies) of the various measures. These can then be used to see if effect sizes correlate with the reliability of the measures or to estimate what effect sizes would be if all measures were perfectly reliable (see Hunter et al., 1982, for details on how to perform this estimation).

A second statistical influence on effect size estimates is the choice of the standard deviation used to estimate the variance around group means. As noted above, most reviewers have no choice but to make the assumption that the two group standard deviations are equal to each other because the effect size must be estimated from an associated significance test, which also makes this assumption. However, in instances where information about standard deviations is available and they appear to be unequal, the reviewer should always choose one group's standard deviation to act as the estimate (e.g., the denominator in the d-index). If a treatment and control group are compared, the control group standard deviation should be used. For the U_3 index, this allows the reviewer to state the impact of the treatment in comparison to the untreated population, for example, "The average treated person scored higher than X% of the untreated population."

A third statistical influence on effect sizes, noted above, is the small sample bias. In addition to the bias in the effect size estimates, the reviewer should be cautious in interpreting any effect size based on small samples, for instance, when the sample size is smaller than 10. Especially when samples are small, a single extreme value can create an exceptionally large effect size estimate.

A fourth statistical influence on effect sizes is the number of factors employed in the research design. If factors other than the variable of interest are included in a research design, for instance, in an analysis of variance or a multiple regression, the reviewer is faced with the choice of employing a standard deviation estimate that has been reduced by the inclusion of the extra factors or attempting to retrieve the standard deviation that would have occurred had all the extraneous factors been ignored (i.e., been included in the error estimate). Whenever possible, the latter strategy should be employed by the reviewer; that is, an attempt should be made to calculate the effect size as though the comparison of interest were the sole comparison in the analysis. Practically speaking, however, it is often difficult for a reviewer to retrieve this overall standard deviation estimate. In such cases, the reviewer should examine whether or not the number of factors involved in the experiment is associated with the size of the experimental effect.

Combining Effect Sizes Across Studies

Once an effect size has been calculated for each study or comparison, the reviewer next averages the effects that test the same hypothesis. It is a generally accepted practice that these averages should weight the individual effect sizes based on the number of subjects in their respective samples. This is because, for example, a d-index or r-index based on 100 subjects will give a more precise and reliable estimate of the population effect size than will an estimate based on 10 subjects. The average effect size should reflect this fact.

One way to take account of sample size when calculating an average effect size is to multiply each effect by its sample size and then divide the sum of the multiplications by the sum of the sample sizes. However, there is a more precise procedure, described in detail by Hedges and Olkin (1985), that involves more complicated calculations but that has many advantages.

The d-index. For the d-index, this procedure first involves estimating a weighting factor, w_i, which is the inverse of the variance associated with each d-index estimate:

$$w_i = \frac{2(n_{i1} + n_{i2})n_{i1}n_{i2}}{2(n_{i1} + n_{i2})^2 + n_{i1}n_{i2}d_i^2} \qquad [11]$$

where

n_{i1} and n_{i2} = the number of data points in Group 1 and Group 2 of the comparison, and

d_i = the d-index of the comparison under consideration.

While the formula for w_i looks imposing, it is really a simple arithmetic manipulation of three numbers that should be available on the coding sheets. It is also easy to program a computer statistical package to perform the necessary calculation.

Table 5.4 presents the group sample sizes, d-indexes, and w's associated with seven study results. The example is drawn from actual data collected as part of the review of homework research. The seven studies each compared the effects on achievement of homework assignments that presented material only on the day the topic was covered in class with assignments that dispersed material over several days. All seven of the experiments produced results favoring dispersed homework assignments.

To demystify the weighting factor further, note that its values equal approximately half the average sample size in a group. It should not be surprising, then, that the next step in obtaining a weighted average effect size involves multiplying each d-index by its associated weight and dividing the sum of these multiplications by the sum of the weights. The formula is as follows:

$$d. = \frac{\sum\limits_{i=1}^{N} d_i w_i}{\sum\limits_{i=1}^{N} w_i} \qquad [12]$$

where all terms are defined as above. Table 5.4 shows that the average weighted d-index for the seven studies was found to be d = .115.

The advantage of using w_i over the sample sizes as weights is that w_i can be used to generate a precise confidence interval around the average effect size estimate. To do this, an estimated variance for the average effect size must be calculated. First, the inverse of the sum of the w_i's is found. Then, the square root of this variance is multiplied by the Z-score associated with the confidence interval of interest. Thus the formula for a 95% confidence interval would be as follows:

$$CId._{95\%} = d. \pm 1.96 \sqrt{\frac{1}{\sum\limits_{i=1}^{N} w_i}} \qquad [13]$$

where all terms are defined as above.

Table 5.4 reveals that the 95% confidence interval for the seven studies includes values .084 above and below the average d-index. Thus we can expect 95% of estimates of this effect to fall between d = .031 and d = .199. Note that this interval does not contain the value d = 0. It is this information that can be used to test the null hypothesis that no relation exists in the population, in place of the combined probability procedures discussed earlier. In the present instance, we would reject the null hypothesis that there was no difference in achievement between students who did current lesson only versus distributed homework.

The r-index. The procedure is simpler for finding the average weighted effect size and confidence interval when the r-index is used. Here, each r-index is first transformed to its corresponding z-score, z_i, and the following formula applied:

$$z. = \frac{\sum\limits_{i=1}^{N} (n_{i.} - 3)z_i}{\sum\limits_{i=1}^{N} (n_{i.} - 3)} \qquad [14]$$

TABLE 5.4
Example of d-Index Estimation and Tests of Homogeneity

Study	n_{i1}	n_{i2}	d_i	w_i	d_i^2/w_i	d_i/w_i	Q_b Grouping
1	259	265	.02	130.98	.052	2.619	A
2	57	62	.07	29.68	.145	2.078	A
3	43	50	.24	22.95	1.322	5.509	A
4	230	228	.11	114.32	1.383	12.576	A
5	296	291	.09	146.59	1.187	13.193	B
6	129	131	.32	64.17	6.571	20.536	B
7	69	74	.17	35.58	1.028	6.048	B
Σ	1083	1101	1.02	544.27	11.69	62.56	

$d = 62.56/544.27 = +.115$

$CI_{d.95\%} = .115 \pm 1.96\sqrt{\dfrac{1}{544.27}} = .115 \pm .084$

$Q_t = 11.69 - \dfrac{62.56^2}{544.27} = 4.5$

$Q_w = 1.16 + 2.36 = 3.52$

$Q_b = 4.5 - 3.52 = .98$

where n_i. = the total sample size for the ith comparison and all other terms are defined as above.

For the confidence interval, the formula is as follows:

$$CI_{z.95\%} = z. \pm \frac{1.96}{\sqrt{\sum_{i=1}^{N} (n_i. - 3)}} \qquad [15]$$

where all terms are defined as above.

Table 5.5 presents the r-to-z transformations needed to carry out the procedures. Once the confidence interval has been established, the reviewer can refer back to Table 5.5 to retrieve the corresponding r-indexes (the average r and the limits of the confidence interval).

Table 5.6 presents an example of how average r-indexes are calculated. The data are given for six comparisons correlating the amount of time a student reports spending on homework and the student's achievement level. These data are also a modification of an actual data set. The average z_i was .207, with the 95% confidence interval ranging from .195 to .219. Note that this confidence interval is quite narrow. This is because the sample sizes upon which the effect size estimates are based are large. Note also that the r-to-z transforms result in only minor changes in two of the r-index values. This would not be the case had the r-indexes been larger (e.g., an r-index of .60 is transformed to a z of .69; see Table 5.5). As with the earlier example, r = 0 is not contained in the confidence interval. Therefore, we can reject the null hypothesis that there is no relation between the amount of time students report spending on homework and their level of achievement.

The illustrative reviews. Both effect sizes presented above appeared in the illustrative reviews.

The review of drug treatments of hyperactivity revealed three separate general results. For comparisons between drug treatments and no placebo controls, the mean d-index equaled +1.21. A d-index of this magnitude indicates that the average child in the control group was more hyperactive than 88.5% of the children receiving drug treatment. The d-index for comparisons of drug treatments versus placebo controls was d = .84, or U_3 = 79.9%. For the placebo versus no-placebo control comparisons, the d-index was .32 and U_3 was 62.5%.

The r-index was used to measure effect size in the review of the relation between personality and interpersonal expectancy effects in laboratory experiments. The largest average correlation, r = +.15, was found between an experimenter's need for social influence and the generation of interpersonal expectancy effects.

Finally, the effect sizes uncovered in the review of research design effects on response rates to questionnaires were expressed using the r-index (or w-index, according to Cohen's terminology). In this case, however, the effect size was not computed by averaging the effects found in separate studies. Instead,

TABLE 5.5

Transformation of r to z

r	z	r	z	r	z	r	z	r	z
.000	.000	.200	.203	.400	.424	.600	.693	.800	1.099
.005	.005	.205	.208	.405	.430	.605	.701	.805	1.113
.010	.010	.210	.213	.410	.436	.610	.709	.810	1.127
.015	.015	.215	.218	.415	.442	.615	.717	.815	1.142
.020	.020	.220	.224	.420	.448	.620	.725	.820	1.157
.025	.025	.225	.229	.425	.454	.625	.733	.825	1.172
.030	.030	.230	.234	.430	.460	.630	.741	.830	1.188
.035	.035	.235	.239	.435	.466	.635	.750	.835	1.204
.040	.040	.240	.245	.440	.472	.640	.758	.840	1.221
.045	.045	.245	.250	.445	.478	.645	.767	.845	1.238
.050	.050	.250	.255	.450	.485	.650	.775	.850	1.256
.055	.055	.255	.261	.455	.491	.655	.784	.855	1.274
.060	.060	.260	.266	.460	.497	.660	.793	.860	1.293
.065	.065	.265	.271	.465	.504	.665	.802	.865	1.313
.070	.070	.270	.277	.470	.510	.670	.811	.870	1.333
.075	.075	.275	.282	.475	.517	.675	.820	.875	1.354
.080	.080	.280	.288	.480	.523	.680	.829	.880	1.376
.085	.085	.285	.293	.485	.530	.685	.838	.885	1.398
.090	.090	.290	.299	.490	.536	.690	.848	.890	1.422
.095	.095	.295	.304	.495	.543	.695	.858	.895	1.447
.100	.100	.300	.310	.500	.549	.700	.867	.900	1.472
.105	.105	.305	.315	.505	.556	.705	.877	.905	1.499
.110	.110	.310	.321	.510	.563	.710	.887	.910	1.528
.115	.116	.315	.326	.515	.570	.715	.897	.915	1.557
.120	.121	.320	.332	.520	.576	.720	.908	.920	1.589
.125	.126	.325	.337	.525	.583	.725	.918	.925	1.623
.130	.131	.330	.343	.530	.590	.730	.929	.930	1.658
.135	.136	.335	.348	.535	.597	.735	.940	.935	1.697
.140	.141	.340	.354	.540	.604	.740	.950	.940	1.738
.145	.146	.345	.360	.545	.611	.745	.962	.945	1.783
.150	.151	.350	.365	.550	.618	.750	.973	.950	1.832
.155	.156	.355	.371	.555	.626	.755	.984	.955	1.886
.160	.161	.360	.377	.560	.633	.760	.996	.960	1.946
.165	.167	.365	.383	.565	.640	.765	1.008	.965	2.014
.170	.172	.370	.388	.570	.648	.770	1.020	.970	2.092
.175	.177	.375	.394	.575	.655	.775	1.033	.975	2.185
.180	.182	.380	.400	.580	.662	.780	1.045	.980	2.298
.185	.187	.385	.406	.585	.670	.785	1.058	.985	2.443
.190	.192	.390	.412	.590	.678	.790	1.071	.990	2.647
.195	.198	.395	.418	.595	.685	.795	1.085	.995	2.994

SOURCE: Reprinted with permission from Edwards (1967).

because raw data could be retrieved, the overall effect size was based on the cumulation of raw data. For instance, the analysis of the presence versus absence of a monetary incentive on returning the questionnaire found incentives to be superior, with r = +.15.

TABLE 5.6
Example of r-Index Estimation and Tests of Homogeneity

Study	n_i	r_i	z_i	$n_i - 3$	$(n_i - 3)z_i$	$(n_i - 3)z_i^2$	Qb Grouping
1	1,021	.08	.08	1,018	81.44	6.52	A
2	1,955	.27	.28	1,952	546.56	153.04	A
3	12,146	.26	.27	12,143	3278.61	885.22	A
4	3,505	.06	.06	3,502	210.12	12.61	B
5	3,606	.12	.12	3,603	432.36	51.88	B
6	4,157	.22	.22	4,154	913.88	201.05	B
Σ	26,390	.85	.87	26,372	5464.97	1310.32	

$z = 5462.97/26,372 = .207$

$CI_{z.95\%} = .207 \pm \dfrac{1.96}{\sqrt{26,372}} = .207 \pm .012$

$Q_t = 1310.32 - \dfrac{(5462.97)^2}{26,372} = 178.66$

$Q_w = 34.95 + 50.40 = 85.35$

$Q_b = 178.66 - 85.35 = 93.31$

ANALYZING VARIANCE IN
EFFECT SIZES ACROSS STUDIES

The analytic procedures described thus far have illustrated how to combine the probabilistic results of separate studies and how to generate an estimate of the strength of relations. Another set of statistical techniques is helpful in discovering why effect sizes vary from one study to another. In these analyses the effect sizes found in the separate studies are the dependent variables and the varying characteristics of the studies are the predictor variables. Thus the reviewer asks whether the magnitude of relation between two variables in a study is affected by the way the study was designed or carried out.

One thing to note about the effect sizes in Tables 5.4 and 5.6 is that the sizes of the effects vary from comparison to comparison. An explanation for this variability is not only important, but it also represents the most unique contribution of the research review. By performing an analysis of differences in effect sizes, the reviewer can gain insight into the factors that affect relationship strengths even though these factors may have never been studied in a single experiment. Assume, for instance, that the first four studies listed in Table 5.4 were conducted in elementary school, and the last three studies were conducted in high school. Is the strength of relation between the two variables different for students at different grades? This question could be tentatively answered through the use of the analytic techniques described below, even though no single study employed both elementary and high school samples.

The techniques that follow are again only a few examples from many procedures for analyzing variance in effects. Their description is conceptual and brief. Those interested in applying the formulas are advised first to examine more detailed treatments, especially those in Hedges and Olkin (1985) or Rosenthal (1984).

Traditional Inference Statistics

The first means for analyzing the variance in effect sizes involves the application of the traditional inference procedures that are employed by primary researchers. Thus if a reviewer of drug treatments of hyperactivity wished to discover whether comparisons using boys revealed stronger or weaker effects than comparisons using girls, he or she might do a t-test on the difference between effect sizes found in comparisons using exclusively boys versus comparisons using exclusively girls. Or if the reviewer were interested in whether the effect size was influenced by the length of delay between treatment and the measurement of hyperactivity, he or she might correlate the length of delay in each comparison with its effect size. In this instance the predictor and dependent variables are continuous, so the significance test associated with the correlation coefficient is the appropriate inferential statistic. For more complex questions a reviewer might categorize effect sizes into multifactor groupings—for instance, according to the gender and age of participants—and perform an analysis of variance or multiple regression on effect sizes. For Table 5.4, if a one-way analysis of variance were conducted comparing the first four d-indexes with the last three d-indexes the result would be nonsignificant.

Standard inference procedures were the techniques initially used by quantitative reviewers for examining variance in effects. Glass et al. (1981) detail how this approach is carried out. However, at least two problems arise with the use of traditional inference procedures in research synthesis. The first is that these procedures do not test the hypothesis that the variability in effect sizes is due solely to sampling error (see the discussion of variability in main effects earlier in this chapter). Therefore, traditional inference procedures can reveal associations between design characteristics and study results without also indicating that the overall variance in effects is no greater than that expected by chance.

Finally, because effect sizes can be based on different numbers of data points (sample sizes), they can have different sampling variances associated with them. If this is the case, the effect sizes violate the assumption of homogeneity of variance that underlies traditional inference tests.

Homogeneity Analyses

A second set of techniques overcome the problems associated with the traditional procedures. Homogeneity statistics ask the question, Is the variance in effect sizes significantly different from that expected by sampling error? If the answer is no, then some methodologists suggest the reviewer might end the analysis there. After all, chance or sampling error is the simplest and most parsimonious explanation. If the answer is yes—that is, if the effect sizes display significantly greater variability than expected by chance—the reviewer then begins to examine other potential sources of variance.

An approach to homogeneity analysis will be described that was introduced simultaneously by Rosenthal and Rubin (1982) and Hedges (1982a). The formula presented by Hedges and Olkin (1985) will be given here and the procedures using d-indexes will be described first.

The d-index. In order to test whether a set of d-indexes is homogeneous, the reviewer must calculate a statistic that Hedges and Olkin (1985) call Q_t:

$$Q_t = \sum_{i=1}^{n} w_i d_i^2 - \left(\sum_{i=1}^{n} w_i d_i \right)^2 / \sum_{i=1}^{n} w_i \qquad [16]$$

where all terms are defined as above.

The Q-statistic has a chi-square distribution with $N - 1$ degrees of freedom, or one less than the number of comparisons. The reviewer refers the obtained value of Q_t to a table of (upper tail) chi-square values. If the obtained value is greater than the critical value for the upper tail of a chi-square at the chosen level of significance, the reviewer rejects the hypothesis that the variance in effect sizes was produced by sampling error alone. Table 5.7 presents the distribution of chi-square for selected probability levels.

For the set of comparisons given in Table 5.4 the value of Q_t equals 4.5. The critical value for chi-square at p < .05 based on 6 degrees of freedom is 12.59. Therefore, the hypothesis that sampling error explains the differences in these d-indexes cannot be rejected.

The procedures to test whether a methodological or conceptual distinction between comparisons explains variance in effect sizes involves three steps. First, a Q-statistic is calculated separately for each subgroup of comparisons. For instance, to compare the first four d-indexes in Table 5.4 with the last three, a separate Q-statistic is calculated for each grouping. Then, the values of these Q-statistics are summed to form a value called Q_w. This value is then subtracted from Q_t to obtain Q_b:

$$Q_b = Q_t - Q_w \qquad [17]$$

where all terms are defined as above.

The statistic Q_b is used to test whether the *average* effects of the groupings are homogeneous. It is referred to a chi-square table using as degrees of freedom one less than the number of groupings. If the average d-indexes are homogeneous, then the grouping factor does not explain variance in effects beyond that associated with sampling error. If Q_b exceeds the critical value, then the grouping factor is a significant contributor to variance in effect sizes.

In Table 5.4, the Q_b comparing the first four and last three d-indexes is .98. This result is not significant on 1 degree of freedom.

The r-index. The analogous procedures for performing a homogeneity analysis on r-indexes involves the following formula:

$$Q_t = \sum_{i=1}^{N} (n_{i.} - 3)z_i^2 - \left[\sum_{i=1}^{N} (n_{i.} - 3)z_i \right]^2 / \sum_{i=1}^{N} (n_{i.} - 3) \qquad [18]$$

where all terms are defined as above.

To compare groups of r-indexes, Formula 18 is applied to each grouping separately, and the sum of these results, Q_w, is subtracted from Q_t to obtain Q_b.

The results of a homogeneity analysis using the r-index are presented in Table 5.6. The Q_t value of 178.66 is highly significant, based on a chi-square test with 5 degrees of freedom. While it seems that a range of r-indexes from .08 to .27 is not terribly large, Q_t tells us that, given the sizes of the samples on which these estimates are based, the range is too great to be explained by sampling error alone. Something other than sampling error likely is contributing to the variance in r-indexes.

TABLE 5.7
Critical Values of Chi-Square for Given Probability Levels

df	\multicolumn{6}{c}{Upper Tail Probabilities}
	.500	.250	.100	.050	.025	.010
1	.455	1.32	2.71	3.84	5.02	6.63
2	1.39	2.77	4.61	5.99	7.38	9.21
3	2.37	4.11	6.25	7.81	9.35	11.3
4	3.36	5.39	7.78	9.49	11.1	13.3
5	4.35	6.63	9.24	11.1	12.8	15.1
6	5.35	7.84	10.6	12.6	14.4	16.8
7	6.35	9.04	12.0	14.1	16.0	18.5
8	7.34	10.2	13.4	15.5	17.5	20.1
9	8.34	11.4	14.7	16.9	19.0	21.7
10	9.34	12.5	16.0	18.3	20.5	23.2
11	10.3	13.7	17.3	19.7	21.9	24.7
12	11.3	14.8	18.5	21.0	23.3	26.2
13	12.3	16.0	19.8	22.4	24.7	27.7
14	13.3	17.1	21.1	23.7	26.1	29.1
15	14.3	18.2	22.3	25.0	27.5	30.6
16	15.3	19.4	23.5	26.3	28.8	32.0
17	16.3	20.5	24.8	27.6	30.2	33.4
18	17.3	21.6	26.0	28.9	31.5	34.8
19	18.3	22.7	27.2	30.1	32.9	36.2
20	19.3	23.8	28.4	31.4	34.2	37.6
21	20.3	24.9	29.6	32.7	35.5	33.9
22	21.3	26.0	30.8	33.9	36.8	40.3
23	22.3	27.1	32.0	35.2	38.1	41.6
24	23.3	28.2	33.2	36.4	39.4	43.0
25	24.3	29.3	34.4	37.7	40.6	44.3
26	25.3	30.4	35.6	38.9	41.9	45.6
27	26.3	31.5	36.7	40.1	43.2	47.0
28	27.3	32.6	37.9	41.3	44.5	48.3
29	28.3	33.7	39.1	42.6	45.7	49.6
30	29.3	34.8	40.3	43.8	47.0	50.9
40	49.3	45.6	51.8	55.8	59.3	63.7
60	59.3	67.0	74.4	79.1	83.3	88.4
	.500	.750	.900	.950	.975	.990

Lower Tail Probabilities

SOURCE: Reprinted with permission from Noether (1971).

Suppose we know that the first three correlations in Table 5.6 are from samples of high school students and the last three are from elementary school students. A homogeneity analysis testing the effect of grade level on the magnitude of r-indexes reveals a Q_b of 93.31. This value is highly significant, based on a chi-square test with 1 degree of freedom. For high school students, the average weighted r-index is .253, while for elementary school students it is

$r = .136$. Thus the grade level of the student is one potential explanation for why the r-indexes vary.

Using computer statistics packages. Calculating average weighted effect sizes and homogeneity statistics by hand is time-consuming and open to error. Conveniently, the major computer statistics packages can be used to do many of the calculations.

The weighting factors for the d-index (w_i) and the r-index ($n_i - 3$) can be generated by having the packages carry out the needed arithmetic calculations and defining these as new variables. The intermediate values can be obtained by further arithmetic definition of new variables and by summing these variables, and the sums can then be (1) used to create new data sets or (2) plugged into the final formulae by hand.

With regard to homogeneity analyses, Hedges and Olkin (1985) note that Q-statistics can be calculated using weighted least squares regression programs. For instance, in the Proc GLM procedure available in Version 5 of SAS, the reviewer simply requests that (1) a multiple regression be conducted using the d-indexes or z-transforms of r-indexes as the dependent variable, (2) the moderating variable of interest be used as the predictor variable, and (3) the appropriate weight be used as a weighting factor (SAS Institute, 1985).

The output of the regression analysis is interpreted as follows. The F-test associated with the model mean square is ignored. The total corrected sums of squares is Q_t. As above, the significance of Q can be found by referring this value to a table of chi-square values (Table 5.7). The model sums of squares is Q_b. It also must be referred to a chi-square table to establish its significance.

Problems in Homogeneity Analysis

The most important problem associated with the use of homogeneity statistics involves their practical application. In many instances the reviewer will be confronted with incomplete data reports, particularly when nonsignificant effects are found. It was suggested above that a conservative procedure was to set these effect sizes at zero. However, if the proportion of assumed zero effects is large but an effect actually exists in the population, greater variance in effect sizes may be estimated using this convention than would be the case if complete information on effect sizes were available. Thus while the assumption that researchers reporting null findings without statistics found effect sized equal to exactly zero will have a conservative impact on combined probabilities and estimates of average effect size, this assumption may lead to larger homogeneity statistics if relations actually exist.

A second problem with homogeneity statistics is that they appear to be low in power. If so, important relations may be missed when homogeneity statistics are used along with conventional levels of statistical significance.

Third, homogeneity statistics can become unreliable and difficult to interpret when the reviewer wishes to test more than one moderator of effect sizes at a time. Hedges and Olkin (1985) present a rigorous model for testing multiple moderators. The model uses sequential tests for homogeneity by removing one at a time variances in effects due to individual moderators. The procedure is often difficult to apply, however, because characteristics of studies are often correlated with one another. For example, suppose it is believed that the effect of homework on achievement is influenced by both the grade level of the student and the level of standardization of the dependent measure. In the comparisons to be analyzed, however, it is found that these two study characteristics are confounded—more studies of high school students used standardized tests, while more studies of elementary school students used class grades. Just as in traditional regression analyses, these intercorrelations make interpretation difficult. In particular, they make the order in which variables are entered into the analysis critical—different orders can result in dramatically different results.

One solution to intercorrelated study characteristics is to generate homogeneity statistics for each characteristic separately, by repeating the calculation of Q-statistics as described above. Then, when the results concerning moderators of effect are interpreted, the reviewer also examines a matrix of intercorrelations among the moderators. This way the reviewer can alert readers to study characteristics that may be confounded and draw inferences with these relations in mind.

A final problem is that the results of homogeneity statistics depend somewhat on the choice of the effect size metric. For instance, the same set of data can yield different results depending on whether d-indexes or r-indexes are used to express relations. This is because d-indexes and r-indexes are not related by a linear transform. The problem of nonequivalent results also appears in primary data analysis; that is, the same data analyzed with parametric and nonparametric statistics can yield different results. However, in primary statistical analyses the differences between one technique and another are well established and the relative appropriateness of one technique or another is fairly easy to evaluate. With the homogeneity statistics these ground rules are not yet clear.

In sum, the quantitative analysis of effect sizes is a new field. Problems in interpretation as well as the precise statistical properties of formulas are still being discovered. While it is clear that a formal analysis of effect sizes should be an integral part of any research review containing large numbers of comparisons, it is also clear that at present reviewers must take great care in the application of these statistics and in the description of how they were applied.

Raw Data Analysis

In instances where raw data from comparisons are available, the moderating hypotheses examined by the homogeneity statistics can be tested by the presence or absence of statistical interactions. That is, the reviewer can perform a mixed-model analysis of variance on the accumulated raw data, using comparison characteristics as between-groups factors and the within-study comparisons as the within-groups factor. If the influence of any within-comparison effect is dependent upon the moderator, it will appear as a significant interaction in the analysis. A significant main effect attributable to research characteristics (the between-groups factor) would indicate that the overall mean on the dependent variable varied from one group of studies to the other. For example, suppose 12 studies of drug treatment effects on children's hyperactivity were found and the raw data from each were available. In addition, assume that 6 of these studies were conducted on boys only and 6 conducted on girls only. The reviewer could conduct an analysis so that drug versus control groups was the within-groups factor and boys versus girls was the between-groups factor. A significant main effect for the drug versus control comparison would indicate study-generated evidence for a drug effect. A significant main effect for gender would indicate that comparisons using one gender revealed greater levels of hyperactivity than comparisons using the other gender. Finally, significant interaction between gender and treatment would indicate that the effect of the drug treatment depended on whether or not the sampled children were boys or girls.

As mentioned above, the practical utility of the raw data analysis is limited both by the infrequency with which raw data can be obtained and by the use of different measurement scales by different researchers.

Variance in Effect Sizes and Review-Generated Evidence

The evidence uncovered through an examination of variance in effect sizes is review-generated evidence, as discussed in Chapter 2. That is, relations between study characteristics and effect sizes cannot be interpreted by the reviewer as uncovering causal relations. As discussed in detail above, in many instances different characteristics of studies will be correlated with one another and it will be impossible to tell which of the correlated characteristics is the true causal agent. Therefore, while review-generated evidence is unique to the research review and represents an important addition to our information about and understanding of research topics, statements of causality based on review-generated evidence are very risky. Typically, when review-generated evidence indicates a relation exists, it is used by the reviewer to point out future fruitful directions for primary researchers.

The illustrative reviews. One of the illustrative reviews, on drug treatments of hyperactivity, employed traditional inference procedures for drawing distinctions in effect size magnitudes. Simple one-way analyses of variance and bivariate correlations were employed. In two of the reviews, on homework and on personality moderators of interpersonal expectancy effects, homogeneity statistics were used. Finally, the review of response rates to questionnaires accumulated raw data. Selected results from these analyses will be presented in the next chapter.

VALIDITY ISSUES IN RESEARCH SYNTHESIS

The first threat to validity arising during the analysis and interpretation stage is that the rules of inference a reviewer employs may be inappropriate. In nonquantitative reviews the appropriateness of inference rules is difficult to assess because the reviewer rarely makes them explicit. In quantitative reviews the suppositions underlying statistical tests are generally known and some statistical biases in reviews can be removed. A complete testing of inference rules may never be possible, but the users of quantitative reviews can decide at least informally whether the statistical assumptions have been met. Regardless of the strategy used, the possibility always exists that the reviewer has used an invalid rule for inferring a characteristic of the target population.

The second threat to validity introduced during analysis and interpretation is that review-generated evidence may be misinterpreted as supporting statements of causality. It has been noted several times in the text that any variable or relation within a review can be examined through either study- or review-generated evidence. However, the scientific status of conclusions based on the different types of evidence can be quite different. Specifically, study-generated evidence is capable of establishing causal precedence among variables, while review-generated evidence is always purely associational.

Protecting Validity

Recommendations about what assumptions are appropriate for reviewers to make about their data will depend on the purposes of a review and the peculiarities of a problem area. This is as true of quantitative procedures as of nonquantitative ones. The only sound general advice is that reviewers should open their rules of inference to public inspection.

(1) Reviewers should be as explicit as possible about their guiding assumptions when they convey their conclusions and inferences to readers.

(2) If there is any evidence bearing on the validity of the interpretation rules, it should be presented. Without this information the reader cannot evaluate the validity of conclusions. Review reports that do not address this issue ought to be considered incomplete.

(3) Reviewers should be careful to distinguish study- and review-generated evidence. Even if the number of studies using each design characteristic is large, the possibility exists that some other unknown methodological feature is correlated with the one involved in an uncovered relation. The more equivocal nature of review-generated inferences means that if this type of evidence indicates that a relation exists, the reviewer should call for the relation to be tested within a single study.

EXERCISES

Study	n_i	z-score (one-tailed)	d_i
1	366	−0.84	−.08
2	96	1.55	.35
3	280	3.29	.47
4	122	0	.00
5	154	1.96	.33
6	120	2.05	.41
7	144	−1.64	−.28

1. What is the combined Z-score and probability level of the seven studies listed above using the Adding Zs method? Using the Adding Weighted Zs method? What is the Fail-safe N?

2. What is the average weighted d-index?

3. Are the effect sizes of the seven studies homogeneous? Calculate your answer both by hand and by using a computer statistical package.

6

The Public Presentation Stage

It is proposed that reviews employ a reporting format similar to primary research reports, including introduction, methods, results, and discussion sections. Special attention is given to discussing how tabulated data can be used in reviews and how effect sizes can be substantively interpreted. Finally, the chapter describes threats to validity that arise from poor reporting and how to protect against them.

> Research is complete only when the results are shared with the scientific community. (American Psychological Association, 1983, p. 17)

The translation of an inquirer's notes, printouts, and remembrances into a public document describing the project is a task with profound implications for the accumulation of knowledge. The importance of the public presentation of results is readily acknowledged, but suggestions about how dissemination is best carried out are limited.

REPORT WRITING
IN THE TWO TYPES OF INQUIRY

The codified guidelines for reporting primary research focus mainly on the form of presentation. The American Psychological Association's *Publication Manual* (1983) is quite specific about the style and format of reports. Much less detailed assistance is provided for determining what specific aspects and conclusions of a study the researcher should deem important. For instance, the *Manual* tells researchers to report statistical data and to do so in the results section of the manuscript. However, most researchers perform more statistical tests than they think will interest readers. The *Manual* is much less explicit in guiding judgments about what makes a finding important to readers.

Obviously, the *Manual* is not to be faulted for this omission. Any guidelines for defining the scientific importance of information would need to be separately explicated for a huge array of different topic areas at specific junctures of problem development (Gallo, 1978). Statistical significance cannot be offered as a general guideline, because a null result may be of great interest in some topic areas.

The research reviewer's dilemma is similar in kind to that of the primary researcher, but the dilemma is more dramatic in degree. The reviewer has no formal guidelines similar to the *Publication Manual* that describe how to structure the final report. At best the reviewer follows informal guidelines provided by research reviews on the same or related topics. In most cases the reviewer chooses a format convenient for the particular review problem.

The lack of reporting guidelines for reviewers is a problem because differences in editorial judgments create variance in reviews. This variation is not found in the magnitude or direction of conclusions but in whether particular aspects and results of reviews are included in the report. One reviewer may believe that a methodological characteristic or result of the review would only clutter the manuscript. A second reviewer might think the same piece of information would be of interest to some readers and decide that the "clutter" was worthwhile.

A FORMAT FOR
INTEGRATIVE RESEARCH REVIEW REPORTS

Throughout this book rigorous and systematic rules for conducting primary research have been extended to integrative research reviews. It should not be surprising, then, to find that suggestions concerning the format of integrative review reports draw heavily upon how primary research is currently reported. The basic division of primary research reports into four sections—introduction, methods, results, and discussion—should serve nicely as a structure for integrative reviews. The division of reports into these four sections serves to highlight the types of information that need to be presented in order for readers to evaluate adequately the validity and utility of the review. In the paragraphs that follow, suggestions will be made about some of the information that should be included in integrative research review reports.

The Introduction Section

The introduction to a research review sets the stage for the empirical results that follow. It should contain a conceptual presentation of the research problem and a statement of the problem's significance. In primary research reports, introductions are typically short. Citations are restricted to only a few works closely related to the topic of primary interest. In research reviews introductions should be considerably more exhaustive. Reviewers should attempt to present a complete historical overview of the theoretical and methodological problems associated with the research question. Where do the concepts involved in the research problem come from? Are they grounded in theory, as with the notion of interpersonal expectancy effects, or in practical circumstance, as with the notion of hyperactivity? Are there theoretical debates surrounding the meaning or utility of the concepts? How do the existent theories predict the concepts will be related to one another, and are there conflicting predictions associated with different theories?

The introduction to an integrative research review must carefully contextualize the problem under consideration. Especially when the reviewer intends to apply statistics in the research integration, it is crucial that he or she pay ample attention to the qualitative and historical debates surrounding the research problem. Otherwise, the reviewer will be open to the criticism that numbers have been crunched together without suitable appreciation for the conceptual and theoretical underpinnings that give empirical data their meaning.

As mentioned in Chapter 2, the introduction to an integrative research review is also where the reviewer should discuss previous reviews of the research topic. This review of reviews points out the importance of the new effort and highlights the empirical controversies that the new review hopes to address and resolve.

In sum, the introduction to a research review should present an exhaustive overview of the theoretical and conceptual issues surrounding the research problem and present a general description of prior reviews and the controversies these reviews have created or left unresolved.

The Methods Section

The methods section of an integrative research review will be considerably different from that found in primary research reports, though its purpose is the same: to describe operationally how the inquiry was conducted. Although it is difficult to make general suggestions, most review methods sections will need to address six separate sets of questions.

First, the research reviewer should present the *details of the literature search* itself, including a description of the sources from which studies were retrieved. In addition, when abstract and indexing services and bibliographies are searched, the reviewer needs to report the years covered in them, the keywords that guided the search, and whether manual or computer searches were used, or both. If personal research is included in the review this should be noted as well. Information on the sources, keywords, and coverage of the literature search is perhaps the most crucial aspect of the methods section. It gives the reader the best indication of the extent of the search and therefore how much credibility to place in the conclusions of the review. The description of the literature search tells the reader how different his or her own search of the literature might be. In terms of attempted replication, it is the description of the literature search that is most closely examined when other scholars attempt to understand why different reviews on the same topic area have come to similar or conflicting conclusions.

The second topic that should be addressed in the methods section is the *criteria for relevance* that were applied to the studies uncovered by the literature search. What characteristics of studies were used to determine whether or not a particular effort was relevant to the topic of interest? How many relevance decisions were based on a reading of report titles? On abstracts? On full reports? What characteristics of studies led to exclusion? How many studies were excluded for any given reason? For instance, if a review included only studies that appeared in professional journals, how many potentially relevant but unpublished studies known to the reviewer were excluded?

Of equal importance to a description of excluded studies is a general, qualitative description of the studies that were deemed relevant. For instance, in the review of the effects of drug treatments on childhood hyperactivity, four criteria were met by every study included in the review: (1) the study investigated the effect of drug treatment on children diagnosed as hyperactive; (2) the study employed group comparisons between a drug treatment and control group, a drug and placebo group, and/or a placebo and control group; (3) random assignment was employed as part of the design; and (4) a double-blind procedure was used to administer the treatment and record the dependent variable.

When readers examine the relevance criteria section of a review, they will be critically evaluating the reviewer's notions about how concepts and operations fit together. Much theoretical debate surrounding the outcome of a particular review may focus on how these decisions were made. Some readers may find that relevance criteria were too broad—operational definitions of concepts were included that they feel were irrelevant. This contention can be addressed by employing these distinctions in analyzing potential moderators of research results. Other readers may find the operational definitions were too narrow. This may lead them to examine the results of excluded studies to determine if their results would affect the review's outcome. In general, however, the relevance criteria describe how the reviewer chose to leap from concepts to operations. A detailed description of this procedure will be central to constructive theoretical and conceptual debate concerning the review's outcome.

In addition to this general description of the included evidence, the methods section is a good place for reviewers to describe *prototypical methodologies*. This presentation of prototypes is necessary in research reviews that cover too many studies to examine each one individually. The reviewer should choose several studies that exemplify the methods used by many studies and present the specific details of these research efforts. In instances where only a few studies are found to be relevant, this process may not be necessary—the description of the methods used in a study can be combined with the description of the study's results.

A fourth important topic to be covered in the methods section involves the reviewer's choice of *how independent hypothesis tests were identified*. An explanation of the criteria used to determine whether multiple hypothesis tests from the same report or laboratory were treated as independent or dependent data points should be carefully spelled out.

A fifth subsection of methods should describe the *characteristics of primary research studies* that were retrieved and retained for examination as potential moderators of study outcome. Even if some of these characteristics are not formally tested and are not discussed later in the paper, they should be mentioned. This will alert the reader to characteristics the reviewer might be asked to test at a later date. In other words, the reviewer should fully describe the information about each study that was collected on the coding sheets. In the methods section it is not necessary to describe the frequency with which each retrieved characteristic occurred in the literature; this is best presented in the results section.

A final topic to be addressed in the methods section is that of the *conventions* the reviewer used to facilitate any quantitative analysis of results. Why was a particular effect size metric chosen? Was an adjustment to effect sizes used to remove bias? How were missing outcomes handled? What forms of analyses were chosen to combine results of separate studies and to examine the variability in results across studies? This section should contain a rationale for each choice of conventions and an analysis of what the impact of each choice might be upon the outcomes of the research review.

The Results Section

In the results section, the reviewer presents a summary description of the literature and the statistical basis for any cumulative findings. Thus the results section is where the synthesis of independent studies is described—the evidence that substantiates any inferences about the literature as a whole. While the results sections of reviews will vary considerably depending on the nature of the research topic and evidence, a general strategy for presenting results might divide the section into five subsections.

In the first subsection, the reviewer should tell readers the total number of independent relevant hypotheses tests, along with a breakdown of the sources of these hypotheses tests. For instance, the number of tests found in published versus unpublished reports is sometimes important, as is a description of particular journals that provided large numbers of hypotheses tests. Also, certain descriptive statistics about the literature should be reported. These would include the average or modal date and range of report appearance; the average or modal number of participants sampled in each study, as well as the range of sample sizes; the frequency of studies employing important participant characteristics, such as gender, age, or status differences; and the geographic locations for studies, if relevant. These are but a few of the potential descriptive statistics that might appear at the beginning of a results section.

In general, the first subsection should give the reader a broad quantitative overview of the literature that complements the qualitative overviews contained in the methods and introduction sections. In addition, it should give the reader a sense of the representativeness of the people, procedures, and circumstances contained in the studies. As mentioned in Chapter 3, there is reason to believe that research reviews will pertain more directly to a target population of all individuals and circumstances than will the separate research efforts in the area.

Whatever the outcome of this analysis, this subsection of results allows the reader to access the representativeness of the sampled people and circumstances and therefore the specificity of the review's conclusions.

The second subsection describing results should present the outcomes of combined probability tests covering the relations that were central to the research review. The related Fail-safe Ns should also appear. If any vote counts were done, these should be described.

A third subsection of results should present the effect size analysis. It should begin with a description of the magnitude of the overall effect, the distribution of effect sizes (perhaps presented in graphic form; see Light & Pillemer, 1984), and the 95% confidence interval. The result of the test for homogeneity of the entire set of related effects should also be presented.

A fourth subsection should describe the results of any analyses meant to uncover study characteristics that moderate the size of the effect. For each tested moderator, the reviewer should present the results on whether or not the study characteristic was a significant contributor to variance in effects. If the moderator proved significant, the reviewer should present an average effect size and confidence interval for each grouping of studies.

Finally, the reviewer should devote a subsection to interaction effects found in single studies, if such an analysis is relevant. For instance, Arkin, Cooper, and Kolditz (1980) were interested in summarizing the research on the self-serv-ing bias, that is, on whether individuals assume greater personal responsibility for successful outcomes than for failures. Arkin and colleagues summarized the tests of interactions contained in the covered studies. They found 59 tests for interaction, of which 14 proved significant. These 14 significant interactions were described in a table that contained p-levels and d-indexes associated with each interaction effect and a short description of the interacting third variable. In other reviews other detailed descriptions of the interactions might be war-ranted, along with quantitative syntheses of the interaction effects.

In sum, the results section should contain the reviewer's overall quantitative description of the covered literature and a report of the relations and moderators of relations that proved significant across studies. This lays the groundwork for the substantive discussion that follows.

The Discussion Section

The discussion section of a research review serves the same functions served by discussions in primary research. First, the reviewer should present a summary of the major results of the review. Then, the reviewer should describe the effect sizes found in the review and interpret their substantive meaning. Next, the reviewer should examine the results of the review in relation to the conclusions of past reviews. Particularly important would be a discussion of how the results of the present review differ from past reviews and why this difference may have occurred. The reviewer also needs to examine the results in relation to the theories and theoretical debates presented in the introduction. If not covered by one of the above suggestions, a discussion of the generality of any findings, as well as limiting conditions that restrict the applicability of any relations, should be included. For instance, if a relation was found between personality and interpersonal expectancy effects, does this hold true for both genders and all situations? Finally, the reviewer should include a discussion of research directions that would be fruitful for future primary research.

In general, then, the discussion section in both primary research and research review is used to make suggestions about the substantive interpretation of relations, the sources and resolution of past controversies, and fruitful directions for future research.

The illustrative reviews. Too much space would be needed to present adequate descriptions of the methods, results, and discussion sections of the illustrative reviews. Also, much of the material contained in the reports has already appeared scattered throughout the book. Selected results will be presented to demonstrate some of the uses of tabulated material in research reviews.

The results of the homework review were presented in a book (Cooper, 1989). Studies comparing homework with no treatment were discussed in one chapter, which began with narrative descriptions of eleven homework versus no-treatment studies conducted before 1962. Effect size estimates were calculated and presented for those studies containing the necessary data, but the effect sizes were not statistically combined.

A table was presented that gave for each study conducted since 1962 the first author, year of publication, and codings on thirteen characteristics. The text gave a summary of the characteristics of the set of studies. These studies were the ones used in the meta-analysis. The text also described one study not used in the meta-analysis because its results could not be transformed into a metric commensurate with the other studies.

A figure was presented that graphically illustrated the distribution of d-indexes. A total of 20 d-indexes were displayed. The text reported that the average d-index was +.21, meaning the average student doing homework had a higher achievement score than 54.7% of students not doing homework. The 95% confidence interval ranged from $d = +.13$ to $d = +.30$. Based on the confidence interval, rather than on a combined probability analysis, it was concluded that the difference between the homework and no-treatment conditions was statistically significant.

The significant results from the search for moderators of the homework effect were presented in a table (reproduced here as Table 6.1). Note that the number of comparisons that each test is based on varies for some moderators, due to the use of a shifting unit of analysis. In the text, these results were accompanied by a description of the interrelations among the moderator variables.

The text also contained sections on (1) the effect of homework with third variables controlled, (2) interactions between homework and other variables, and (3) the results of studies examining the effect of homework on attitudes.

TABLE 6.1
**Effect Sizes for Comparisons of Homework Versus No Homework on
Measures of Academic Achievement**

| | | 95% Confidence Interval | | |
| | | Low | | High |
	n	Estimate	Mean	Estimate
Overall ($\chi^2[19] = 57.41, p < .001$)	20	.13	.21	.30
Year ($\chi^2[1] = 8.00, p < .01$)				
1960s	6	.01	.16	.32
1970s	10	.06	.18	.30
1980s	4	.23	.48	.73
Counterbalancing and repeated				
measures ($\chi^2[1] = 4.68, p < .05$)				
present	4	−.35	−.08	.19
absent	16	.14	.24	.34
Experimenter ($\chi^2[1] = 9.52, p < .01$)				
teacher	8	.25	.41	.57
not teacher	12	.02	.12	.22
Duration of treatment ($\chi^2[1] = 3.89, p < .05$)				
10 weeks	12	.20	.32	.44
more than 10 weeks	8	−.03	.09	.21
Number of assignments($\chi^2[1] = 15.43, p < .001$)				
1-3 per week	14	−.01	.09	.19
4-5 per week	6	.30	.44	.58
Grade ($\chi^2[1] = 3.75, p < .06$)				
4-6	13	.05	.15	.25
7-9	5	.09	.31	.53
10-12	2	.33	.64	.95
Subject matter ($\chi^2[2] = 19.13, p < .001$)				
math	25	.10	.16	.22
reading and English	13	.18	.32	.46
science and social studies	10	.38	.56	.74
Math areas ($\chi^2[3] = 6.79, p < .01$)				
computation	9	.12	.24	.36
concepts	8	.07	.19	.31
problem solving	5	−.12	.02	.16
general or unspecified	3	−.01	.26	.53
Outcome measure ($\chi^2[1] = 6.49, p < .02$)				
class tests or grades	15	.18	.30	.42
standardized tests	5	−.07	.07	.21

SOURCE: Cooper, H. M. (1989). HOMEWORK. Copyright 1989 by Longman Inc. Reprinted by permission.

Finally, the chapter concluded with a summary of results. In a later chapter, the results of the review were compared to other reviews, and implications for policy and future research were discussed.

The results section of the review of personality moderators of interpersonal expectancy effects primarily described the meta-analysis of photo-rating studies. However, the review also contained a description of studies not using the photo-rating situations. In addition to a discussion in the text, a description of these nine studies was presented in tabular form. The table is reproduced here as Table 6.2.

The review of drug treatments of hyperactive children was presented in a very short report, but it still followed the guidelines presented above. The d-indexes from the 61 studies were presented in a figure called a stem-and-leaf display (Tukey, 1977). Figure 6.1 reproduces this display. In a stem-and-leaf display, all of the raw data can be presented in a simple graphic form. The data are first ordered according to magnitude and then the researcher chooses an appropriate number of digits to serve as the stems. The stem-and-leaf display is easier to demonstrate than to describe. For instance, the first column of Figure 6.1 displays the stems, or leading digits, for each of the d-indexes. The second column presents the leaves, or trailing digits, for each of the 16 d-indexes associated with drug versus control comparisons. In this instance, the stems are the first two digits of the d-index (units and tenths) and the leaves are the last digit (hundredths). Thus the smallest d-index uncovered by a drug versus control comparison was .34; the next smallest d-index was .36. A stem-and-leaf display is like a histogram where stems represent intervals and leaves are stacked up to express visually the frequency of intervals. So in the drug versus placebo comparisons (third column), d-indexes most frequently fell between values of .60 and .69, where seven d-indexes can be found. At the bottom of the stem-and-leaf display, information is presented on maximum and minimum values, quartile ranges, and means and standard deviations.

Table 6.3 presents the results of the analyses for the effect of monetary incentives from the review of techniques for increasing response rates to questionnaires. Four cumulative response rates are given. The first rate was called the *experimental* response rate. This was the average response rate for the technique in studies that experimentally manipulated the presence or absence of monetary incentives. The *control* response rate was the average of the control group (no technique) conditions in these experimental studies. The *without control* response rate included response rates from all studies that used monetary incentives but had no control condition. The *absent* response rate was for studies that specifically stated that participants did not receive monetary incentives.

A chi-square test of the frequency of questionnaire responding in studies that experimentally manipulated the presence versus absence of a monetary incentive (i.e., 50.5% for monetary rewards versus 35.2% for no monetary rewards) was highly significant ($\chi^2(1) = 188.1$, $p < .0001$). This result revealed an r-index

(text continued on page 136)

TABLE 6.2

Personality Moderators of Interpersonal Expectancy Effects: Nonphoto-Rating Studies

Authors	Expectancy Induction/Experimental Task	Personality Variable	Results
Laboratory settings			
Weiss (1969)	Es read instructions to Ss indicating that Ss could expect to overestimate or underestimate the number of dots on tachistoscopically presented slides. A third group of subjects received no expectancy instructions.	Ss' orality/anality	S personality × expectancy interaction *ns*.
Christensen and Rosenthal (1982)	Es led to believe they were about to interview an S of either high or low sociability.	Ss' audio decoding skill	Male Ss who were better decoders detected more bias. No difference for females.
Dusek (1972)	Es led to believe boys would outperform girls on a marble dropping task, or that girls would outperform boys. Ss retrieved marbles from one bin and dropped them through the holes of another bin.	Ss' test anxiety	S personality × bias condition interaction *ns*.
Dana and Dana (1969)	No information concerning expectancy induction. Es administered to Ss the Wechsler Adult Intelligence Scale.	Es' locus of control; Es' susceptibility to influence	E personality × bias interaction *ns* for both personality variables.

| Clark et al. (1976) | Es were led to believe that first 10 taps delivered to an S's Achille's tendon would be heavier or lighter than the next 10 taps. Ss were attached to EEG and EMG recording instruments. | Es' locus of control

Ss' locus of control | Significant expectancy × stimulus interval × E personality × S personality interaction for various measures of alpha activity (EEG). Significant expectancy × S personality interaction for a measure of muscle action potential—internal Ss showed effects in the direction of their experimenter's expectancy, external Ss showed effects in the direction opposite to their experimenter's expectancy. |
| Begum and Shams (1981) | Es were shown data suggesting that some Ss would provide positive color ratings and that other Ss would provide negative ratings. Es then showed colored papers to Ss and asked them to judge the richness of color in the papers. | Es' locus of control

Ss' locus of control | E Personality × Expectancy interaction *ns*.
S Personality × Expectancy interaction significant—External Ss confirmed their Es expectancies more than Internal Ss. |

TABLE 6.2 Continued

Authors	Expectancy Induction/Experimental Task	Personality Variable	Results
Instructional settings			
Babad et al. (1982)	Student teachers were led to believe that two of the students in their physical education classes were of "high potential." All students then ran races, performed sit-ups, push-ups, and distance jumps.	Teachers' susceptibility to bias	For sit-up and push-up performance, expectancy × T personality interaction significant—no expectancy effect for low-susceptible teachers, high-expectancy students of high-susceptible teachers outperformed objective expectations (as per an "expected value" for performance calculated by the authors). For distance jumps, expectancy × T personality interaction *ns*.
			For distance jumps, expectancy × T personality interaction significant—no expectancy effect for low-susceptible teachers, high-expectancy students of high-susceptible teachers outperformed objective expectations.

Therapeutic settings

Study			
Bednar and Parker (1969)	Students serving as clients were introduced to "personal growth" counseling by a high-prestige figure who presented information attesting to the validity of the counseling procedures or by a casually dressed research assistant who said nothing about treatment validity.	Clients' susceptibility to bias	Persuasibility and expectancy factors produced no significant effect on therapy-induced behavior change.
Harris and Rosenthal (1986)	Students serving as counselors were told their "clients" (other students) were either extroverted or introverted. Counselors and clients then role-played a peer-counseling session.	Counselors: 16 personality variables measured by the Jackson Personality Research Form; self-monitoring; dogmatism	Significant positive correlations between counselors' ability to bias their clients and counselors' dogmatism, nurturance, and social recognition; significant negative correlation between degree of bias and counselors' impulsivity.
		Clients: 16 personality variables measured by the Jackson Personality Research Form; self-monitoring; dogmatism	Significant positive correlations between clients' susceptibility to bias and clients' self-monitoring and social recognition. Significant negative correlation between degree of bias and clients' social recognition.

Stem	Drug vs Control	Drug vs Placebo	Placebo vs Control	Total[a]
2.1	5			5
2.0		8		8
1.9	4			4
1.8				
1.7	0	24		024
1.6		1		1
1.5	5	0688		05688
1.4	8	126	3	12368
1.3	2	02		022
1.2				
1.1	16	8		168
1.0		8	6	68
.9	39	12399	3	12333999
.8	4	05	9	0549
.7	9	5		59
.6		1125779		1125779
.5	09	07	0	00079
.4		2489		2489
.3	46	168	8	146688
.2		478		478
.1		56		56
.0		005	00000	00000005
Maximum	2.77	2.08	1.43	2.77
Q_3	1.55	1.30	.93	1.30
Median	1.10	.69	.19	.80
Q_1	.59	.42	.00	.38
Minimum	.34	.00	−1.30	−1.30
Mean	1.21	.84	.32	.84
SD	.67	.54	.72	.60

Figure 6.1: d-Indexes for Three Types of Comparisons

SOURCE: Ottenbacher, K. and Cooper, H. Drug treatments of hyperactive children. *Developmental Medicine and Child Neurology*, 1983, *25*, 353-357. Copyright 1983 by Spastics International Medical Publications. Reprinted by permission.

a. Two values, 2.77 and −1.30, are not included in the table.

equal to .15. Further, both prepaid and promised monetary incentives increased responding over no incentive at all (for prepaid, $\chi^2(1) = 145.8$, $p < .0001$, $r = .16$; for promised, $\chi^2(1) = 7.5$, $p < .01$, $r = .05$). Finally, the amount of the incentive paid appeared to have a strong positive relation to response rates. When the amount offered was correlated with the weighted average response rate, the resulting r-index equaled +.61. It was pointed out, of course, that

TABLE 6.3
Effect of Monetary Incentives on Response Rate

Monetary Incentive	Weighted Average Response Rate	Number of Contacts	Number of Response Rates	SD of Response Rates
Experimental	50.5	5,444	49	20.9
Control	35.2	3,133	30	20.2
Without control	52.2	2,382	15	18.6
Absent	20.1	961	3	21.8
Amount ($)				
0.10	41.6	1,484	17	9.5
0.25	53.9	2,399	10	25.1
0.50	34.7	1,035	9	12.9
1.00	35.9	697	5	19.9
2.00	41.0	200	1	0.0
3.00	40.5	200	1	0.0
5.00	62.1	1,012	13	14.6
10.00	82.0	314	2	5.9
25.00	54.1	205	2	22.5
50.00	75.0	83	1	0.0
Prepaid				
experimental	42.4	3,551	33	18.0
control	26.8	2,271	22	14.6
without control	54.8	1,614	4	29.0
Promised				
experimental	58.6	1,696	13	22.2
control	52.8	796	7	21.9
without control	46.8	768	11	15.1

SOURCE: Yu and Cooper (1983).

researchers should consider the cost/benefit ratio associated with paying extremely large sums of money for responses.

THE SUBSTANTIVE INTERPRETATION
OF EFFECT SIZE

In quantitative reviews, one function of a discussion section is the interpretation of the size of the relations. Once the reviewer has generated an effect size, how is he or she to know if it is large or small, meaningful or trivial? Since statistical significance cannot be used as a benchmark—that is, small effects can be statistically significant and large effects nonsignificant—a set of rules must be established for determining the explanatory or practical value of a given effect magnitude.

Cohen (1988) attempts to address the issue of interpreting effect size estimates, and suggests some general definitions for small, medium, and large effect sizes in the social sciences. However, Cohen chose these quantities to reflect the typical effect sizes encountered in the behavioral sciences as a whole—he warns against using his labels to interpret relationship magnitudes within particular social science disciplines or topic areas. His general labels, however, illustrate how to go about interpreting effects, and for this purpose they will be reviewed here.

Cohen labels an effect size small if $d = .20$ or $r = .10$. He writes, "Many effects sought in personality, social, and clinical-psychological research are likely to be small . . . because of the attenuation in validity of the measures employed and the subtlety of the issue frequently involved" (p. 13). Large effects, according to Cohen, are frequently "at issue in such fields as sociology, economics, and experimental and physiological psychology, fields characterized by the study of potent variables or the presence of good experimental control or both" (p. 13). Large magnitudes of effect are $d = .80$ or $r = .50$. Cohen places medium-sized effects between these two extremes, that is, $d = .50$ or $r = .30$.

Cohen's reasoning can be used to demonstrate the relative nature of effect sizes. Suppose the review of personality moderators of interpersonal expectancy effects revealed an average r-index of $+.30$. How should the relation's magnitude be interpreted? Clearly the interpretation depends on the other relations chosen as contrasting elements. According to Cohen, this is a medium-sized behavioral science effect. Thus, compared to other relations in the behavioral sciences in general, this would be an average effect size, not surprisingly large or small. However, compared to other personality effects, this effect size may best be described as large, if we accept Cohen's suggestion that personality relations are predominantly smaller than $r = .30$.

Comparing a specific effect to effect sizes found in other disciplines or a discipline in general may be interesting, but in most instances it is not very informative. The most informative interpretation occurs when the effect size is compared to other effects involving the same or similar variables. At the time Cohen offered his guidelines, holding an effect size in a specialized topic area up against a criterion as broad as "all behavioral science" might have been the best contrasting element available. Estimates of average effects for disciplines, subdisciplines, topic areas, or even single variables or operations were difficult to find. Today, these calculations are plentiful. Therefore, an effect size should be labeled "small" or "large" depending on its magnitude relative to a variety of related estimates. At least some of the contrasting effect sizes should be closely tied conceptually to the effect found in the specific topic area, involving the same variables contained in the relation of interest.

In addition to multiple and related choices of contrasting estimates, two other guides for effect size interpretation may be useful. First, reviewers can assess how much any relation might be valued by consumers of research. This assessment involves the difficult problem of making practical judgments about significance. A hypothetical example will illustrate the point. Suppose a study done in 1970 showed that motorists who regularly checked their tire pressure got 22 miles per gallon of gasoline, while motorists who did not check their tires got 20 miles per gallon. In each group, the standard deviation of the mean was 4 miles per gallon. This indicates that the average motorist driving 10,000 miles a year and buying gas at $.30 a gallon saved 45 gallons of gas and $13.50 annually by checking tire pressure. In terms of the d-index, the pressure checkers and noncheckers were separated by one-half a standard deviation (d = .50), or the average tire checker got better mileage than about 69% of the noncheckers. This effect might have been ignored in 1970. Practically speaking, it might have been considered inconsequential. The same results, however, produced in 1989 with gas costing $1.10 a gallon might elicit a much different reaction. Using 45 gallons less of a scarce resource and saving $49.50 annually would be appreciated by most motorists. Thus the researcher might argue convincingly that the result of the experiment had great practical significance.

If the pressure-checking effect is contrasted with other effects on automobile fuel economy (e.g., tune-ups, observing the speed limit), the comparison might still lead to a conclusion that the effect is small. The researcher, however, can argue that although the effect is of relatively small explanatory value, it may still have great practical significance. This judgment could be justified by arguing that small intervals on the gas usage scale represent large intervals on other, societally-valued indicators—for example, the amount of oil that needs to be imported. Or it might be argued that the cost of implementing a pressure-checking program is relatively inexpensive compared to other interventions. Levin and his colleagues (Levin, 1987; Levin, Glass, & Meister, 1987) have begun to lay out some ground rules for establishing the relative cost-effectiveness of social programs.

A final guide to effect size interpretation that involves research methodology has been alluded to several times in the text. When contrasting effect sizes are chosen, the relative size of effects will reflect not only the explanatory power of the relations but also differences in how data were collected. All else being equal, effect sizes based on studies with strict control over extraneous influences should produce larger effects than less controlled studies (i.e., should have smaller deviations around the mean). For example, a tire pressure-checking effect on gas mileage of d = .50 found in lab tests may be less impressive than a similar finding obtained under normal driving conditions. Effect sizes will also be a function of the strength of the manipulation (for example, the degree of tire underinflation in unchecked cars), the sensitivity of the measures (for example, counting the number of fill-ups versus the number of gallons used), and any restrictions on participant populations (for example, all cars versus only new cars). These illustrations point out only a few methodological considerations that can influence effect size interpretation.

Finally, it should be kept in mind that effect size estimates reported in research reviews are influenced not only by the methodology of the studies reviewed but also by the methodology of the review itself. As Cooper and Arkin (1981) point out:

> If an unbiased inference is to be made from the effect size estimate, it is that other literature reviews using similar retrieval procedures should expect to uncover similar ES's. Researchers . . . [and] policymakers . . . need to adjust ES estimates dependent upon whatever sources of bias (with whatever impact) they feel may have been present in the particular literature search. (p. 227)

Thus it may not be appropriate to assume that the effect size uncovered in a research review is equal to the effect found in the population. The reviewer must determine if the estimate is potentially inflated by an inability to uncover small effect sizes due to bias in the publication process or the literature search.

In sum, Cohen's (1988) labels give only the broadest interpretive yardstick for effect sizes. The most meaningful interpretation of an effect size comes from comparisons to other magnitudes of relation chosen because of their substantive relevance to the topic under study. Complementing this interpretation should be an assessment of the practical value of any explanation and the role of methodology in shaping the conclusion.

The illustrative reviews. The two best examples of how relationship strengths can be interpreted come from the reviews on homework and on questionnaire responding. For homework, it will be recalled that the average d-index of the difference in achievement between students doing homework and students doing no homework was d = +.21. Is this a small or large effect? To help answer this question, the results of other meta-analyses were examined. These were listed in a table, reproduced here as Table 6.4. The eleven meta-analyses contained in the table all examined the effect of instructional strategies or teaching skills on measures of achievement. They were taken from a chapter on research synthesis appearing in the *Handbook of Research on Teaching* (Walberg, 1986).

Based on a comparison with the entries in the table, it was concluded that the effect of homework on achievement can best be described as *above average.* The median effect size in the table is d = +.10, half the size of the homework effect. The relative quality of methods in the different topic areas was also considered. It was assumed that the trustworthiness of the measures of achievement used in the different areas and the soundness of the research designs were roughly equivalent. However, some of the assumptions on which effect size estimates were based were probably more conservative in the homework review than in other reviews. Finally, the practical value of homework was assessed by comparing the relative costs of implementing the different instructional and teaching treatments. Homework can be regarded as a low-cost treatment, especially in comparison with special-class placement and individualized and programmed instruction.

In the review of questionnaire responding, the relative effects of the dozen research design methods were evaluated in comparison to one another, instead

TABLE 6.4
Selected Effect Sizes from Meta-Analysis Examining
Influences on Achievement[a]

Authors (Year)	Independent Variable	Effect Size[b]
Bangert et al. (1981)	individualized versus conventional teaching	+.10
Carlberg and Kavale (1980)	special- versus regular-class placement	−.12
Johnson et al. (1981)	cooperative versus competitive learning	+.78
Kulik and Kulik (1981)	ability grouping	+.10
Kulik et al. (1982)	programmed instruction	+.08
Luiten, Ames, and Aerson (1980)	advance organizers	.23
Pflaum et al. (1980)	direct instruction	.60
Redfield and Rousseau (1981)	higher cognitive questions	.73
Wilkinson (1980)	praise	+.08
Williams et al. (1982)	amount of television watching	+.10
Willson and Putnam (1982)	pretests	+.17

SOURCE: Cooper, H. M. (1989). HOMEWORK. Copyright 1989 by Longman Inc. Reprinted by permission.
a. Topics are those listed by Walberg (1986) as involving achievement as the dependent variable.
b. Effect sizes are expressed in d-indexes.

of separately. Thus the contrasting elements were contained in the review itself. For instance, the r-index of +.16 associated with prepaid monetary incentives was compared with the r-index of +.05 for promised monetary incentives. This was done so that those administering the questionnaire in the future could determine which design characteristics would produce the greatest increase in responding relative to the cost involved in employing that procedure.

VALIDITY ISSUES IN REPORT WRITING

The two threats to validity accompanying report writing relate to the different target populations of the review. First, the omission of details about how the review was conducted is a potential threat to validity. As with primary research, an incomplete report reduces the replicability of the review conclusion. Jackson (1980) examined 36 reviews and found "complete" to be a far-from-accurate description of most reviews:

Only one of the 36 articles reported the indexes and information retrieval systems used to search for primary studies on the topic. Only three of the 36 reported the bibliographies used as a means of locating studies. Only seven indicated whether or not they analyzed the full set of located studies on the topic, instead of some subset. Only one-half of the 36 reported the direction and magnitude of the findings of any of the reviewed primary studies, and few did this for each finding. In addition, very few review articles systematically reported characteristics of the primary research that may have affected the findings. (pp. 456-457)

Without these details, the reader cannot ascertain whether or not a personal review of the literature would lead to similar findings.

The second validity threat in report writing involves the omission of evidence about moderators of relations that other inquirers may find important. Matheson, Bruce, and Beauchamp (1978) observe that "as research on a specific behavior progresses, more details concerning the experimental conditions are found to be relevant" (p. 265). Thus a review will lose its timeliness if the reviewer is not astute enough to identify the variables and moderators that are (or will be) important to an area. More complete reviews will take longer to be replaced by newer reviews, and will therefore have greater temporal generality.

Protecting validity. Recommendations about how reviewers can protect against these threats to validity are as difficult to offer as recommendations for how primary researchers should approach this stage of inquiry. This chapter is filled with suggestions that might provide a starting point. However, reviewers will never be able to predict perfectly which omitted characteristic or result of their reviews will eventually render their conclusions invalid or obsolete. On the positive side, reviewers certainly want their documents to have long lives. We can anticipate that reviewers give considerable thought to how to present the most exhaustive report in the most readable manner.

EXERCISES

1. Read two integrative research reviews. Outline what the authors tell about each of the following: (a) how the literature search was conducted, (b) what rules were used to decide if studies were relevant to the hypothesis, and (c) what rules were used to decide if cumulative relations existed.

2. Find two primary research reports on the same topic that vary in method. Calculate the effect size reported in each. Compare the effect sizes to one another, taking into account the influence of the different methods. Using other criteria, decide whether you consider each effect size large, medium, or small. Justify your decision.

7

Conclusion

This chapter presents general issues pertaining to how the notion of rigorous research reviewing is likely to evolve in the future as well as some considerations surrounding the feasibility of conducting reviews that meet rigorous criteria. Several issues concerning research reviewing and the philosophy of science are also discussed.

There are several issues related to research reviewing that cannot be placed easily into the packaging of events represented by the five-stage model. These overarching considerations deal with problems and promises in applying the guidelines set forth in the previous chapters.

VALIDITY ISSUES REVISITED

First, the five stages of reviewing contained eleven threats to validity. It is likely that other threats exist that have been overlooked in this treatment. Campbell and Stanley's (1963) list of validity threats to primary research was expanded by Campbell (1969), Bracht and Glass (1968), and Cook and Campbell (1979). This same expansion and respecification of threats to validity is also likely to occur in the area of research reviewing. It shows progress in the systematization of issues surrounding legitimate scientific inference.

Several of the threats to validity arising in the course of research reviewing are simply holdovers that represent pervasive problems in primary research. For instance, during data collection it was asserted that a threat to the validity of a review was that people contained in the covered studies might not be representative of the target population. This suggests that any threat associated with a particular primary research design is applicable to a review if the design represents a substantial portion of the covered research. In the examination of review-generated evidence, research designs should be carefully examined as potential moderators of study results. The creation of these "nomological nets" (Cronbach & Meehl, 1955) can be one of the research review's most valuable contributions. However, if an assortment of research designs is not contained in a review, then threats associated with the dominant designs also threaten the review's conclusions.

FEASIBILITY AND COST

It will be considerably more expensive for inquirers to undertake reviews using the guidelines set forth in this book than to conduct reviews in the traditional manner. Money is needed to conduct computer searches and to pay data collectors. Hours are needed to develop evaluative criteria and coding frames and to run analyses. Probably more than one person should be involved, at least in the data evaluation stage.

Should a potential reviewer with limited resources be discouraged from undertaking a project? Certainly not. Just as the perfect, irrefutable primary study has never been conducted, the perfect review remains an ideal. As much as the suggestions of this book have been presented as guidelines for conducting reviews, they are also presented as yardsticks for evaluating reviews. In fact, the reader should be aware of several instances in which the illustrative research reviews fell short of complete adherence to the abstract guidelines. Sacks, Berrier, Reitman, Ancona-Berk, and Chalmers (1987) surveyed 86 meta-analyses and concluded that there was an urgent need for improved methods. A potential reviewer should not hold the guidelines as absolute criteria that must be met, but rather as targets that help the reviewer refine the proposed procedures and breadth of a review until a good balance between rigor and feasibility is struck.

THE SCIENTIFIC METHOD AND DISCONFIRMATION

While the pragmatics of conducting research reviews may mean the inquirer must settle for a less-than-perfect product, this does not mean that the ideals of science need not be strictly applied to the research review process. The crucial scientific element that has been missing from traditional reviewing procedures has been the potential for the disconfirmation of the reviewer's prior beliefs. In most instances, primary researchers undertake their work with some recognition that the results of their study may alter their belief system. Not so the traditional reviewer. By extending the scientific method to research reviews, the reviewer accepts the potential for disconfirmation. Ross and Lepper (1980) state this position nicely:

> We know all too well that the scientific method is not immune to the diseases of biased assimilation, causal explanation, and a host of other nagging afflictions; scientists can be blind, sometimes deliberately so, to unanticipated or uncongenial interpretations of their data and recalcitrant in their theoretical allegiances. . . . Nevertheless, it is the scientific method . . . that has often been responsible for increasing human understanding of the natural and social world. Despite its flaws, it remains the best means of delivering us from the errors of intuitive beliefs and intuitive methods for testing those beliefs. (p. 33)

SCIENTIFIC RESEARCH REVIEWING
AND CREATIVITY

One objection to the introduction of systematic guidelines for research reviews is that such a systematization will stifle creativity. Critics who raise this issue think the rules for conducting and reporting primary research are a "straitjacket" on innovative thinking. I cannot disagree more. Rigorous criteria will not produce reviews that are mechanical and uncreative. The expertise and intuition of the reviewer will be challenged to capitalize on or create opportunities to obtain, evaluate, and analyze information unique to each problem area. I hope the illustrative reviews have demonstrated the diversity and complexity of issues that confront reviewers who adopt the scientific method. These challenges are *created* by scientific rules.

CONCLUSION

This book began with the supposition that research reviewing was a data-gathering exercise that needed to be evaluated against scientific criteria. Because of the growth in empirical research, the increased access to information, and the new techniques for research synthesis, the conclusions of research reviews will become less and less trustworthy unless something is done to systematize the process and make it more rigorous. It is hoped that the concepts presented here have convinced readers that it is feasible and desirable for social scientists to require more rigorous reviews, with greater potential for creating consensus among scholars and for focusing discussion on specific and testable areas of disagreement when conflict does exist. Because of the increasing role that research reviews play in our definition of knowledge, these adjustments in procedures are inevitable if social scientists hope to retain their claim to objectivity.

REFERENCES

American Psychological Association. (1983). *Publication manual* (3rd ed.). Washington, DC: Author.

Arkin, R., Cooper, H., & Kolditz, T. (1980). A statistical review of the literature concerning the self-serving attribution bias in interpersonal influence situations. *Journal of Personality, 48*, 435-448.

Barber, T. (1978). Expecting expectancy effects: Biased data analyses and failure to exclude alternative interpretations in experimenter expectancy research. *Behavioral and Brain Sciences, 3*, 388-390.

Barnett, V., & Lewis, T. (1978). *Outliers in statistical data.* New York: John Wiley.

Bar-Tal, D., & Bar Zohar, Y. (1977). The relationship between perception of locus of control and academic achievement. *Contemporary Educational Psychology, 2*, 181-199.

Bem, D. (1967). Self-perception: An alternative interpretation of cognitive dissonance phenomena. *Psychological Review, 74*, 183-200.

Borchardt, D., & Francis, R. (1984). *How to find out in psychology.* Oxford: Pergamon.

Boyce, B., & Banning, C. (1979). Data accuracy in citation studies. *RQ, 18*(4), 349-350.

Bracht, G., & Glass, G. (1968). The external validity of experiments. *American Educational Research Journal, 5*, 437-474.

Bradley, J. (1981). Pernicious publication practices. *Bulletin of Psychonomic Society, 18*, 31-34.

Campbell, D. (1969). Reforms as experiments. *American Psychologist, 24*, 409-429.

Campbell, D., & Stanley, J. (1963). *Experimental and quasi-experimental designs for research.* Chicago: Rand McNally.

Carlsmith, J., Ellsworth, P., & Aronson, E. (1976). *Methods of research in social psychology.* Reading, MA: Addison-Wesley.

Carlson, M., & Miller, N. (1987). Explanation of the relation between negative mood and helping. *Psychological Bulletin, 102*, 91-108.

Cicchetti, D., & Eron, L. (1979). The reliability of manuscript reviewing for the *Journal of Abnormal Psychology 1979. Proceedings of the American Statistical Association* (Social Statistics Section), *22*, 596-600.

Cohen, J. (1988). *Statistical power analysis for the behavioral sciences* (2nd ed.). Hillsdale, NJ: Lawrence Erlbaum.

Cook, T., & Campbell, D. (1979). *Quasi-experimentation.* Chicago: Rand McNally.

Cook, T., & Leviton, L. (1981). Reviewing the literature: A comparison of traditional methods with meta-analysis. *Journal of Personality, 48*, 449-471.

Cooper, H. (1979). Statistically combining independent studies: A meta-analysis of sex differences in conformity research. *Journal of Personality and Social Psychology, 37*, 131-146.

Cooper, H. (1983). Methodological determinants of outcomes of synthesis of research literature. In P. Wortman (Chair), *An analysis of methodologies used in synthesizing research on desegregation and student achievement.* Symposium conducted at the annual meeting of the American Educational Research Association, Montreal.

Cooper, H. (1986). On the social psychology of using research reviews: The case of desegregation and black achievement. In R. Feldman (Ed.), *The social psychology of education.* Cambridge: Cambridge University Press.

Cooper, H. (1987). Literature searching strategies of integrative research reviewers: A first survey. *Knowledge, 8*, 372-383.

Cooper, H. (1988). The structure of knowledge synthesis: A taxonomy of literature reviews. *Knowledge in Society, 1*, 104-126.

Cooper, H. (1989). *Homework.* New York: Longman.

Cooper, H., & Arkin, R. (1981). On quantitative reviewing. *Journal of Personality, 49,* 225-230.

Cooper, H., Burger, J., & Good, T. (1981). Gender differences in the academic locus of control beliefs of young children. *Journal of Personality and Social Psychology, 40,* 562-572.

Cooper, H., & Hazelrigg, P. (1988). Personality moderators of interpersonal expectancy effects: An integrative research review. *Journal of Personality and Social Psychology.*

Cooper, H., & Ribble, R. (in press). Influences on the outcome of literature searches for integrative research reviews. *Knowledge: Creation, Diffusion, Utilization.*

Cooper, H., & Rosenthal, R. (1980). Statistical versus traditional procedures for summarizing research findings. *Psychological Bulletin, 87,* 442-449.

Crandall, V., Katkovsky, W., & Crandall, V. (1965). Children's beliefs in their own control of reinforcement in intellectual-academic achievement situations. *Child Development, 36,* 91-109.

Crane, D. (1969). Social structure in a group of scientists: A test of the "invisible college" hypothesis. *American Sociological Review, 34,* 335-352.

Cronbach, H., & Meehl, P. (1955). Construct validity in psychological tests. *Psychological Bulletin, 52,* 281-302.

Cuadra, C., & Katter, R. (1967). Opening the black box of relevance. *Journal of Documentation, 23,* 291-303.

Davidson, D. (1977). The effects of individual differences of cognitive style on judgements of document relevance. *Journal of the American Society for Information Science, 8,* 273-284.

Edwards, A. L. (1967). *Statistical methods* (2nd ed.). New York: Holt, Rinehart & Winston.

Eysenck, H. (1978). An exercise in mega-silliness. *American Psychologist, 33,* 517.

Feinberg, R. (1981). Positive side effects of on-line information retrieval. *Teaching of Psychology, 8,* 51-52.

Festinger, L., & Carlsmith, B. (1959). Cognitive consequences of forced compliance. *Journal of Abnormal and Social Psychology, 58,* 203-210.

Findley, M., & Cooper, H. (1981). A comparison of introductory social psychology textbook citations in five research areas. *Personality and Social Psychology Bulletin, 7,* 173-176.

Findley, M., & Cooper, H. (1983). Locus of control and academic achievement: A literature review. *Journal of Personality and Social Psychology, 44,* 419-427.

Fisher, R. (1932). *Statistical methods for research workers.* London: Oliver & Boyd.

Friedman, H. (1968). Magnitude of experimental effect and a table for its rapid estimation. *Psychological Bulletin, 70,* 245-251.

Gallo, P. (1978). Meta-analysis: A mixed meta-phor? *American Psychologist, 33,* 515-517.

Garvey, W., & Griffith, B. (1971). Scientific communications: Its role in the conduct of research and creation of knowledge. *American Psychologist, 26,* 349-361.

Glass, G. (1976). Primary, secondary, and meta-analysis of research. *Educational Researcher, 5,* 3-8.

Glass, G. (1977). Integrating findings: The meta-analysis of research. In *Review of research in education* (Vol. 5). Itasca, IL: F. E. Peacock.

Glass, G., McGaw, B., & Smith, M. (1981). *Meta-analysis in social research.* Beverly Hills, CA: Sage.

Glass, G., & Smith, M. (1978). Reply to Eysenck. *American Psychologist, 33,* 517-518.

Gottfredson, S. (1978). Evaluating psychological research reports. *American Psychologist, 33,* 920-934.

Gover, H. (1983). *Keys to library research on the graduate level: A guide to guides.* Lanham, MD: University Press of America.

Greenberg, J., & Folger, R. (1988). *Controversial issues in social research methods.* New York: Springer-Verlag.

Greenwald, A. (1975). Consequences of prejudices against the null hypothesis. *Psychological Bulletin, 82,* 1-20.

Griffith, B., & Mullins, N. (1972). Coherent social groups in scientific change. *Science, 177,* 959-964.

Guzzo, R., Jackson, S., & Katzell, R. (1987). Meta-analysis analysis. In B. Staw & L. Cummings (Eds.), *Research in organizational behavior* (Vol. 9). Greenwich, CT: JAI.

Harper, R., Weins, A., & Matarazzo, J. (1978). *Nonverbal communication: The state of the art.* New York: John Wiley.

Hedges, L. (1980). Unbiased estimation of effect size. *Evaluation in Education: An International Review Series, 4,* 25-27.

Hedges, L. (1982a). Estimation of effect size from a series of independent experiments. *Psychological Bulletin, 92,* 490-499.

Hedges, L. (1982b). Fitting categorical models to effect sizes from a series of experiments. *Journal of Educational Statistics, 7*(2), 119-137.

Hedges, L., & Olkin, I. (1980). Vote-counting methods in research synthesis. *Psychological Bulletin, 88,* 359-369.

Hedges, L., & Olkin, I. (1985). *Statistical methods for meta-analysis.* Orlando, FL: Academic Press.

Hunter, J., Schmidt, F., & Jackson, G. (1982). *Meta-analysis: Cumulating research findings across studies.* Beverly Hills, CA: Sage.

Institute for Scientific Information. (1980). *Social Sciences Citation Index.* Philadelphia: Author.

Jackson, G. (1980). Methods for integrative reviews. *Review of Educational Research, 50,* 438-460.

Kanuk, L., & Berensen, C. (1975). Mail surveys and response rates: A literature review. *Journal of Marketing Research, 12,* 440-453.

Katz, W. (1987). *Introduction to reference work* (Vol. 2). New York: McGraw-Hill.

Kazdin, A., Durac, J., & Agteros, T. (1979). Meta-meta analysis: A new method for evaluating therapy outcome. *Behavioral Research and Therapy, 17,* 397-399.

Kerlinger, F. (1973). *Foundations of behavioral research* (2nd ed.). New York: Holt, Rinehart & Winston.

Lane, D., & Dunlap, W. (1978). Estimating effect sizes: Bias resulting from the significance criterion in editorial decisions. *British Journal of Mathematical and Statistical Psychology, 31,* 107-112.

Levin, H. (1987). Cost-benefit and cost-effectiveness analysis. *New Directions for Program Evaluation, 34,* 83-99.

Levin, H., Glass, G., & Meister, G. (1987). Cost-effectiveness and computer-assisted instruction. *Evaluation Review, 11,* 50-72.

Light, R., & Pillemer, D. (1984). *Summing up: The science of reviewing research.* Cambridge, MA: Harvard University.

Lipsey, H. (in press). *Design sensitivity: Statistical power for detecting the effects of interventions.* Newbury Park, CA: Sage.

Lord, C., Ross, L., & Lepper, M. (1979). Biased assimilation and attitude polarization: The effects of prior theories on subsequently considered evidence. *Journal of Personality and Social Psychology, 37,* 2098-2109.

Lykken, D. (1968). Statistical significance in psychological research. *Psychological Bulletin, 70,* 151-159.

Maccoby, E., & Jacklin, C. (1974). *The psychology of sex differences.* Stanford, CA: Stanford University Press.

Mahoney, M. (1977). Publication prejudices: An experimental study of confirmatory bias in the peer review system. *Cognitive Therapy and Research, 1,* 161-175.

Mansfield, R., & Bussey, T. (1977). Meta-analysis of research: A rejoinder to Glass. *Educational Researcher, 6,* 3.

Marsh, H., & Ball, S. (1981). Interjudgmental reliability of reviews for the *Journal of Educational Psychology. Journal of Educational Psychology, 73*, 872-880.

Matheson, D., Bruce, R., & Beauchamp, K. (1978). *Experimental psychology.* New York: Holt, Rinehart & Winston.

McClellend, C., Atkinson, J., Clark, R., & Lowel, E. (1953). *The achievement motive.* New York: Appleton-Century-Crofts.

McNemar, Q. (1946). Opinion-attitude methodology. *Psychological Bulletin, 43,* 289-374.

Menzel, H. (1966). Scientific communication: Five themes from sociology. *American Psychologist, 21,* 999-1004.

Mosteller, F., & Bush, R. (1954). Selected quantitative techniques. In G. Lindzey (Ed.), *Handbook of social psychology: Vol. 1. Theory and method.* Cambridge, MA: Addison-Wesley.

Noether, G. (1971). *Introduction to statistics: A fresh approach.* Boston: Houghton Mifflin.

Nunnally, J. (1960). The place of statistics in psychology. *Education and Psychological Measurement, 20,* 641-650.

Oakes, M. (1986). *Statistical inference: A commentary for the social and behavioural sciences.* Chichester: John Wiley.

Ottenbacher, K., & Cooper, H. (1983). Drug treatments of hyperactivity in children. *Developmental Medicine and Child Neurology, 25,* 353-357.

Pearson, K. (1933). On a method of determining whether a sample of size n supposed to have been drawn from a parent population having a known probability integral has probably been drawn at random. *Biometrika, 25,* 379-410.

Peters, D., & Ceci, S. (1982). Peer-review practices of psychological journals: The fate of published articles, submitted again. *Behavioral and Brain Sciences, 5,* 187-255.

Presby, S. (1978). Overly broad categories obscure important differences between therapies. *American Psychologist, 33,* 514-515.

Price, D. (1965). Networks of scientific papers. *Science, 149,* 510-515.

Price, D. (1966). Collaboration in an invisible college. *American Psychologist, 21,* 1011-1018.

Raudenbush, S., Becker, B., & Kalain, H. (1988). Modeling multivariate effect sizes. *Psychological Bulletin, 103,* 111-120.

Raudenbush, S., & Bryk, A. (1985). Empirical Bayes meta-analysis. *Journal of Educational Statistics, 10,* 75-98.

Reed, J., & Baxter, P. (1983). *Library use: A handbook for psychology.* Washington, DC: American Psychological Association.

Reynolds, P. (1971). *A primer in theory construction.* Indianapolis: Bobbs-Merrill.

Rosenthal, R. (1976). *Experimenter effects in behavioral research.* New York: Appleton-Century-Crofts.

Rosenthal, R. (1978a). How often are our numbers wrong? *American Psychologist, 33,* 1005-1008.

Rosenthal, R. (1978b). Combining results of independent studies. *Psychological Bulletin, 85,* 185-193.

Rosenthal, R. (1979a). The "file drawer problem" and tolerance for null results. *Psychological Bulletin, 86,* 638-641.

Rosenthal, R. (1979b). Replications and their relative utility. *Replications in Social Psychology, 1,* 15-23.

Rosenthal, R. (1980). Summarizing significance levels. *New Directions for Methodology of Social and Behavioral Science, 5,* 33-46.

Rosenthal, R. (1982). Valid interpretation of quantitative research results. *New Directions for Methodology of Social and Behavioral Science, 12,* 59-75.

Rosenthal, R. (1984). *Meta-analytic procedures for social research.* Beverly Hills, CA: Sage.

Rosenthal, R., & Rubin, D. (1982). Comparing effect sizes of independent studies. *Psychological Bulletin, 92,* 500-504.

Ross, L., & Lepper, R. (1980). The perseverance of beliefs: Empirical and normative considerations. *New Directions for Methodology of Social and Behavioral Science, 4,* 17-36.

Rotter, J. (1954). *Social learning and clinical psychology.* Englewood Cliffs, NJ: Prentice-Hall.

Sacks, H., Berrier, J., Reitman, D., Ancona-Berk, V., & Chalmers, T. (1987). Meta-analysis of randomized controlled trials. *New England Journal of Medicine, 316,* 450-455.

Saracevic, T. (1970). The concept of "relevance" in information science: A historical review. In T. Saracevic (Ed.), *Introduction to information science.* New York: Bowker.

SAS Institute. (1985). *SAS user's guide: Statistics* (Version 5). Cary, NC: Author.

Scarr, S., & Weber, B. (1978). The reliability of reviews for the *American Psychologist. American Psychologist, 33,* 935.

Scholarly communication: Report of the national enquiry. (1979). Baltimore: Johns Hopkins University Press.

Selltiz, C., Wrightsman, L., & Cook, S. (1976). *Research methods in social relations* (3rd ed.). New York: Holt, Rinehart & Winston.

Simon, J. (1978). *Basic research methods in social science* (2nd ed.). New York: Random House.

Smith, M. (1980). Publication bias and meta-analysis. *Evaluation in Education: An International Review Series, 4,* 22-24.

Smith, M., & Glass, G. (1977). Meta-analysis of psychotherapy outcome studies. *American Psychologist, 32,* 752-760.

Stoan, S. (1982). Computer searching: A primer for uninformed scholars. *Academe, 68,* 10-15.

Stock, W., Okun, M., Haring, M., Miller, W., Kinney, C., & Ceurvorst, R. (1982). Rigor and data synthesis: A case study of reliability in meta-analysis. *Educational Researcher, 11*(6), 10-14.

Taveggia, T. (1974). Resolving research controversy through empirical cumu.ation. *Sociological Methods and Research, 2,* 395-407.

Tukey, J. (1977). *Exploratory data analysis.* Reading, MA: Addison-Wesley.

Viana, M. (1980). Statistical methods for summarizing independent correlational results. *Journal of Educational Statistics, 5,* 83-104.

Walberg, H. (1986). Synthesis of research on teaching. In M. Wittrock (Ed.), *Handbook of research on teaching* (3rd ed.). New York: Macmillan.

Webb, E., Campbell, D., Schwartz, R., Sechrest, L., & Grove, J. (1981). *Nonreactive measures in the social sciences.* Boston: Houghton Mifflin.

White, C. (1986). *Sources of information in the social sciences.* Chicago: American Library Association.

Whitehurst, G. (1984). Interrater agreement for journal manuscript reviews. *American Psychologist, 39,* 22-28.

Williams, B. (1978). *A sampler on sampling.* New York: John Wiley.

Wolins, L. (1962). Responsibility for raw data. *American Psychologist, 22,* 657-658.

Xhignesse, L., & Osgood, C. (1967). Bibliographical citation characteristics of the psychological journal network in 1950 and 1960. *American Psychologist, 22,* 779-791.

Yu, J., & Cooper, H. (1983). A quantitative review of research design effects on response rates to questionnaires. *Journal of Marketing Research, 20,* 36-44.

Zuckerman, M., DePaulo, B., & Rosenthal, R. (1981). Verbal and nonverbal communication of deception. In *Advances in experimental social psychology* (Vol. 14). New York: Academic Press.

AUTHOR INDEX

153

SUBJECT INDEX

ABOUT THE AUTHOR

Harris M. Cooper is Professor of Psychology and Research Associate of the Center for Research in Social Behavior at the University of Missouri—Columbia. He has also taught at Colgate University, and has been a Postdoctoral Fellow at Harvard University, a Visiting Scholar at Stanford University, and a Visiting Professor at the University of Oregon. He has published articles on numerous facets of research reviewing and has conducted nearly two dozen substantive reviews. He is a member of the Advisory Committee of the Russell Sage Foundation's Program on Research Synthesis and an advising editor for four journals in psychology and education. He was the first recipient of the American Educational Research Association's Raymond B. Cattell Early Career Award for Programmatic Research.

NOTES

NOTES

APPLIED SOCIAL RESEARCH
METHODS SERIES

Series Editors

LEONARD BICKMAN, Peabody College, Vanderbilt University, Nashville
DEBRA J. ROG, Vanderbilt University, Washington, DC

Other volumes in this series are listed on the series page

Frommer's®

Nova Scotia, New Brunswick & Prince Edward Island

9th Edition

by Julie Watson

WILEY

John Wiley & Sons, Inc.

Published by:

JOHN WILEY & SONS, INC.

111 River St.
Hoboken, NJ 07030-5774

ISBN 978-1-118-13348-4 (paper); ISBN 978-1-118-22516-5 (ebk); ISBN 978-1-118-23743-4 (ebk);
ISBN 978-1-118-26325-9 (ebk)

Editor: Gene Shannon
Production Editor: Katie Robinson
Cartographer: Roberta Stockwell
Photo Editor: Richard Fox
Production by Wiley Indianapolis Composition Services

Front Cover Photo: Peggy's Cove Harbour, Peggy's Cove, Nova Scotia, Canada © Rubens Abboud / Alamy Images

Back Cover Photo: New Brunswick, Canada. Hopewell Rocks and The Ocean Tidal Exploration Site © Michael DeFreitas North America / Alamy Images

For information on our other products and services or to obtain technical support, please contact our Customer Care Department within the U.S. at 877/762-2974, outside the U.S. at 317/572-3993 or fax 317/572-4002.

Wiley also publishes its books in a variety of electronic formats. Some content that appears in print may not be available in electronic formats.

Manufactured in the United States of America

5 4 3 2 1

CONTENTS

4 NOVA SCOTIA 39

5 NEW BRUNSWICK 144

6 PRINCE EDWARD ISLAND 203

7 PLANNING YOUR TRIP TO THE MARITIME PROVINCES 252

Index 270

LIST OF MAPS

ABOUT THE AUTHOR

Julie V. Watson is a prolific writer based in Prince Edward Island with 28 books and numerous articles to her credit. Her writing focuses on Canada's Maritime Provinces, travel, food, lifestyles, seniors, and entrepreneurship. Julie and her husband travel extensively in the family RV writing along the way. The award winning writer shares her passion for writing, POD publishing, and scrapbooking through workshops across Canada, working with her son, Vancouver photographer, John Watson. "The best part of life as a writer is that it allows you to indulge in things that interest you. My favorite topics include my home region, the Maritimes, which have a fascinating history, rich culture, wonderful food, scenery, nature, and a lifestyle to be envied." For more go to www.seacroftpei.com.

HOW TO CONTACT US

In researching this book, we discovered many wonderful places—hotels, restaurants, shops, and more. We're sure you'll find others. Please tell us about them, so we can share the information with your fellow travelers in upcoming editions. If you were disappointed with a recommendation, we'd love to know that, too. Please write to:

Frommer's Nova Scotia, New Brunswick & Prince Edward Island, 9th Edition
John Wiley & Sons, Inc. • 111 River St. • Hoboken, NJ 07030-5774
frommersfeedback@wiley.com

ADVISORY & DISCLAIMER

Travel information can change quickly and unexpectedly, and we strongly advise you to confirm important details locally before traveling, including information on visas, health and safety, traffic and transport, accommodations, shopping, and eating out. We also encourage you to stay alert while traveling and to remain aware of your surroundings. Avoid civil disturbances, and keep a close eye on cameras, purses, wallets, and other valuables.

While we have endeavored to ensure that the information contained within this guide is accurate and up-to-date at the time of publication, we make no representations or warranties with respect to the accuracy or completeness of the contents of this work and specifically disclaim all warranties, including without limitation warranties of fitness for a particular purpose. We accept no responsibility or liability for any inaccuracy or errors or omissions, or for any inconvenience, loss, damage, costs, or expenses of any nature whatsoever incurred or suffered by anyone as a result of any advice or information contained in this guide.

The inclusion of a company, organization, or website in this guide as a service provider and/or potential source of further information does not mean that we endorse them or the information they provide. Be aware that information provided through some websites may be unreliable and can change without notice. Neither the publisher nor author shall be liable for any damages arising herefrom.

FROMMER'S STAR RATINGS, ICONS & ABBREVIATIONS

Every hotel, restaurant, and attraction listing in this guide has been ranked for quality, value, service, amenities, and special features using a **star-rating system.** In country, state, and regional guides, we also rate towns and regions to help you narrow down your choices and budget your time accordingly. Hotels and restaurants are rated on a scale of zero (recommended) to three stars (exceptional). Attractions, shopping, nightlife, towns, and regions are rated according to the following scale: zero stars (recommended), one star (highly recommended), two stars (very highly recommended), and three stars (must-see).

In addition to the star-rating system, we also use **seven feature icons** that point you to the great deals, in-the-know advice, and unique experiences that separate travelers from tourists. Throughout the book, look for:

special finds—those places only insiders know about

fun facts—details that make travelers more informed and their trips more fun

kids—best bets for kids and advice for the whole family

special moments—those experiences that memories are made of

overrated—places or experiences not worth your time or money

insider tips—great ways to save time and money

great values—where to get the best deals

The following abbreviations are used for credit cards:

AE   American Express   DISC   Discover   V   Visa

DC   Diners Club   MC   MasterCard

TRAVEL RESOURCES AT FROMMERS.COM

Frommer's travel resources don't end with this guide. Frommer's website, www.frommers.com, has travel information on more than 4,000 destinations. We update features regularly, giving you access to the most current trip-planning information and the best airfare, lodging, and car-rental bargains. You can also listen to podcasts, connect with other Frommers.com members through our active-reader forums, share your travel photos, read blogs from guidebook editors and fellow travelers, and much more.

THE BEST OF THE MARITIME PROVINCES

P lanning a trip to Atlantic Canada shouldn't be hard, yet the number of small towns, quaint inns, and potential driving routes makes it a bit complex. These are my suggestions for some of the best destinations and experiences.

THE best ACTIVE VACATIONS

- **Sea Kayaking in Nova Scotia:** The twisting, convoluted coastline of this province is custom-made for snooping around by sea kayak. Outfitters are scattered around the province. For expedition kayaking, contact outfitter **Coastal Adventures** (www.coastaladventures.com) about a current schedule of trips. See chapter 4.
- **Biking the Cabot Trail** (Nova Scotia): The long, strenuous loop around Cape Breton Highlands National Park is tough on the legs, but serious cyclists will come away with a head full of indelible memories. See "Cape Breton Island" in chapter 4.
- **Exploring Fundy National Park and Vicinity** (New Brunswick): You'll find swimming, hiking, and kayaking at this coastal national park. And don't overlook biking in the hills east of the park, or the outdoors center at Cape Enrage. See "Fundy National Park" in chapter 5.
- **Cycling Prince Edward Island:** This province sometimes seems like it was created specifically for bike touring. Villages are reasonably spaced apart, hills are virtually nonexistent, the coastal roads are picturesque in the extreme, and an island-wide bike path offers detours through marshes and quiet woodlands. See "The Great Outdoors" in chapter 6.

THE best SPOTS FOR OBSERVING NATURE

- **Digby Neck** (Nova Scotia): Choose from among the whale-watching outfitters located along this narrow peninsula of remote fishing villages. And simply getting to the tip of the peninsula is half the fun—it requires two ferries. See "Digby to Yarmouth" in chapter 4.

- **Cape Breton Highlands National Park** (Nova Scotia): The craggy geology on the west side of this headland is impressive enough, but don't let it overshadow the *rest* of the park, where you'll find bogs, moose, and plenty of quiet spots. See "Cape Breton Highlands National Park" in chapter 4.
- **Grand Manan Island** (New Brunswick): This big, geologically intriguing rock off the New Brunswick coast is a great base for learning about coastal ecology. Whale-tour operators search out the endangered right whale and dozens of birds roost and pass through. Boat tours from the island will also take you out to see puffins. See "Grand Manan Island" in chapter 5.
- **Hopewell Rocks** (New Brunswick): The force of Fundy's tremendous tides is most impressive at Hopewell Rocks, where great rock "sculptures" created by the winds and tides rise from the ocean floor at low tide. See "Fundy National Park" in chapter 5.

THE best SCENIC DRIVES

- **Cape Breton's Cabot Trail** (Nova Scotia): This 300km (185-mile) loop through the uplands of Cape Breton Highlands National Park is one of the world's great excursions. You'll see Acadian fishing ports, pristine valleys, and some of the most picturesque coastline anywhere. See "Cape Breton Island" in chapter 4.
- **Cobequid Bay** (Nova Scotia): When it comes to scenery, Cobequid Bay (near Truro) is one of the region's better-kept secrets. The bay is flanked by two roads: Route 2 runs from Parrsboro to Truro, Route 215 from South Maitland to Brooklyn. Take the time to savor the rocky cliffs, muddy flats, and rust-colored bays. See "Chignecto Bay, Minas Basin & Cobequid Bay" in chapter 4.
- **Fundy Trail Parkway** (New Brunswick): East of Saint John, you'll find this parkway winding along the contours of the coast. Get out and stretch your legs at any of the two dozen lookouts along the way for fantastic cliffside views. Or if the tides are out, clamber down to one of the stretches of sand nestled between the rocks. See "Saint John" in chapter 5.
- **St. John River Valley** (New Brunswick): Once the best way of traveling into the interior of New Brunswick, this 730km (454-mile) river is steeped in history. It finds its way almost to Québec, passing through fabulous bird-watching and boating areas, gorgeous gorges, lovely towns and villages, and the provincial capital, Fredericton. Follow the roads closest to the river for the best experience. See "Fredericton" in chapter 5.
- **Prince Edward Island National Park:** Much of the north central shore of PEI is part of a national park. The quiet park road tracks along the henna-tinted cliffs and grass-covered dunes. The coastal road is interrupted by inlets in spots, but each segment is still worth a leisurely drive, with frequent stops to explore the beaches and walkways. See "Prince Edward Island National Park" in chapter 6.

THE best HIKES & RAMBLES

- **Point Pleasant Park** (Nova Scotia): Overlooking the entrance to Halifax's harbor, Point Pleasant Park is a wonderful urban oasis, with wide trails for strolling along the water. Check out the Martello tower atop a wooded rise. See "Halifax" in chapter 4.

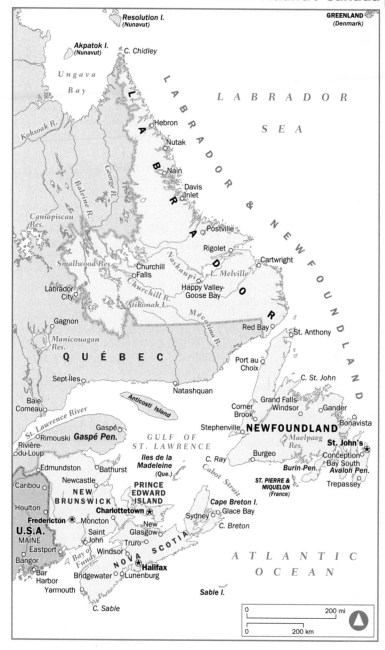

o **Cape Breton Highlands National Park** (Nova Scotia): There are certainly lots of quiet, contemplative walks on Cape Breton, but the best trails follow rugged cliffs along open ocean. The Skyline Trail is among the most dramatic walkways in Canada. See "Cape Breton Highlands National Park" in chapter 4.

o **Grand Manan Island** (New Brunswick): Grand Manan is laced with informal walking trails passing through forests and along the ocean's edge. This is a place for exploring; ask around locally for suggestions on the best hikes. See "Grand Manan Island" in chapter 5.

o **The Fundy Trail** (New Brunswick): Forward-thinking planners created this trail so that it can be walked, biked, or driven. Walking is best for the spectacular views of cliffs, waterfalls, and the Bay of Fundy, and the trail also offers lookouts, footpaths to beaches, foot bridges, and wildlife spotting. Accessed from St. Martins. See "Saint John" in chapter 5.

o **The Confederation Trail** (Prince Edward Island): This pathway across the island is best for long-distance cycling, but it's superb for a quiet stroll in spots along the path. See "Kings County" in chapter 6.

THE best FAMILY ACTIVITIES

o **Upper Clements Park** (Nova Scotia): About 5 minutes south of Annapolis Royal, this old-fashioned amusement park is full of low-key attractions that delight kids. Highlights include a flume ride (originally built for Expo '86 in Vancouver) and a wooden roller coaster that twists and winds through trees left standing during the coaster's construction. See "Annapolis Royal" in chapter 4.

o **Waterfront Walk** (Nova Scotia): Halifax's waterfront walk is filled with fun distractions, from the province's best museum to ships you can climb onto and explore. Also look for sweeping views of the bustling harbor. If you're here in early August during the internationally famous Busker Festival, lend an ear. See "Halifax" in chapter 4.

o **Kings Landing** (New Brunswick): At this living history museum, young kids are introduced to life in early Canada between 1790 and 1910. Ask about the week-long sessions designed to immerse kids in the past. See chapter 5.

o **Prince Edward Island's Beaches:** Choose between the red-sand beaches of the south shore or the white sand of the north. It's hard to beat a day or three splashing around these lukewarm waters while admiring the pastoral island landscapes. There are great beaches both within the national park and all around the coast. See "The Great Outdoors" in chapter 6.

THE best PLACES FOR HISTORY

o **Annapolis Royal** (Nova Scotia): The cradle of Canadian civilization can be found in this broad green valley, where early French settlers first put down roots. Visit Fort Anne and Port Royal, and walk some of the first streets on the continent. See "Annapolis Royal" in chapter 4.

o **Maritime Museum of the Atlantic** (Nova Scotia): Nova Scotia's history *is* the history of the sea, and no place better depicts that vibrant tradition than this sprawling museum right on Halifax's waterfront. See chapter 4.

o **Louisbourg** (Nova Scotia): This early-18th-century fort and village was part of an elaborate French effort to establish a foothold in the New World. It failed, and the village ultimately fell into ruin. In the 1960s, the Canadian government reconstructed much of it, and now it's one of the best historic sites in the Maritimes. See "Cape Breton Island" in chapter 4.

- **Village Historique Acadien** (New Brunswick): This huge complex near Caraquet depicts life as it was lived in an Acadian settlement of New Brunswick between 1770 and 1890. You'll learn all about the exodus and settlement of the Acadians from costumed guides, who also demonstrate skills ranging from letterpress printing to blacksmithing. See chapter 5.
- **Kings Landing Historical Settlement** (New Brunswick): This is a living history village devoted to those who settled the St. John River near Fredericton. There is always something happening that reflects life in the 19th century. Interpreters bring Loyalist (pro-British) farmers, tradesmen, and homemakers into the present so that you can meet them. See "Fredericton" in chapter 5.
- **Province House National Historic Site** (Prince Edward Island): Canadian history took shape in Charlottetown in 1864, when the idea of joining Britain's North American colonies into an independent confederation was first discussed seriously. Learn about what transpired at this Charlottetown edifice, which has been restored to appear as it did when history was made. See chapter 6.

THE most PICTURESQUE VILLAGES

- **Lunenburg** (Nova Scotia): Settled by German, Swiss, and French colonists, this tidy town is superbly situated on a hill flanked by two harbors, and it boasts some of the most unique and quietly extravagant architecture in the Maritimes. Bring your walking shoes for the hills. See "South Shore" in chapter 4.
- **Bouctouche** (New Brunswick): Despite just 2,500 year-round residents, this community abounds in visitor experiences. Le Pays de la Sagouine and local eateries are pure Acadian. Nearby beaches, the amazing boardwalks over impressive dunes, and an arboretum growing more than 10,000 types of trees are the best of ecotourism. This is one of the prettiest little communities anywhere. See "Moncton" in chapter 5.
- **Victoria** (Prince Edward Island): This tiny village west of Charlottetown is surrounded by fields of grain and potatoes, and hasn't changed all that much in the past, oh, 100 years or so. Try to time your visit to take in an evening show at the town's wonderfully old-fashioned playhouse. See "Prince County" in chapter 6.

THE best INNS

- **Rossmount Inn** (St. Andrews, New Brunswick): This three-story manor house is on a large estate between the forest and sea, which includes Chamcook Mountain, the highest point in Passamaquoddy Bay, and a great source for the foraged ingredients that make their menu stand above others. The licensed veranda and pool deck, fine market-fresh cuisine, walking trails, and garden make the steps from the parking area worthwhile. See p. 160.
- **The Great George** (Charlottetown, Prince Edward Island): This connected series of restored town houses is historic, central, welcoming, and quite comfortable. Continental breakfast is served in the open-concept lobby, where you can watch

the comings and goings without getting in the way. Rooms range from spacious doubles to huge family-size suites, and most of them have either a fireplace, a whirlpool bath, or both. See p. 230.

o **Inn at Bay Fortune** (Bay Fortune, Prince Edward Island): This exceptionally attractive shingled compound was once owned by actress Colleen Dewhurst (best known for portraying Marilla in TV's *Anne of Green Gables* miniseries). Current innkeeper David Wilmer pulled out all the stops during renovations. But the real draw here is the dining room, which is noted for the farm-fresh ingredients grown in the extensive gardens on the property. See p. 241.

THE best BED & BREAKFASTS

o **Shipwright Inn** (Charlottetown, Prince Edward Island): This right-in-town, nine-room B&B is within easy walking distance of all the city's attractions yet has a settled and pastoral feel. It's informed by a Victorian sensibility without being over-the-top about it. The owners have managed to include modern conveniences such as DVD players, decks, and Jacuzzis without spoiling the Victorian ambience. See p. 231.

o **Harbour's Edge B&B** (Yarmouth, Nova Scotia): The backyard is enough to encourage a stay. Located at the very head of Yarmouth Harbour, it's a perfect place to watch the tides, fishing boats, and shore birds. With just four guest rooms this is a personal service inn where you will feel right at home. There is fascinating history here. See p. 65.

THE MARITIME PROVINCES IN DEPTH

Canada's easternmost provinces can best be described as an eclectic mix of culture, history, nature, and geographic masterpieces, surrounded by mile after nautical mile of deep, gray-blue sea. You're never far from salt water when traveling the three provinces known as the Maritimes: Nova Scotia, New Brunswick, and Prince Edward Island; highways carry you alongside it, or to and from it, and most major cities cozy up to it.

This has been a fisherman's paradise since native Canadian times; abundant fish that thrive in icy waters rimming the region provided sustenance and income, and continue to do so today. The Bay of Fundy, Gulf of St. Lawrence, Atlantic Ocean, and the mighty rivers that flow into them influenced the pattern of settlement and provide the elements that hold such appeal for visitors today. The rich salmon fishing rivers of New Brunswick, the whales of the Bay of Fundy, the glorious beaches of Prince Edward Island, and the rugged scenic vistas of Cape Breton all translate into the foundation of a great vacation.

From the beginning, the Maritimes have been a challenging place to carve out a living. The abundance of natural bounty is offset by short summer growing seasons and long, storm-tossed winters. For travelers, those challenges become true benefits. Cooled by sea breezes, summers are appealing for those who suffer from the heat and humidity prevalent in other regions. Colder waters ensure an abundant year-round supply of delicious seafood—yes, they harvest in winter, often through the ice. Top-notch chefs and cooks are drawn to this region, where the emphasis has long been on local ingredients and natural bounty; wineries and distillers are a growth industry, and people eagerly seek out new culinary experiences. Winter snows bring enthusiasts for snowmobiling, pond hockey, cross-country skiing, skating, and more, in pristine white landscapes. Spring and fall are especially appealing for nature lovers and photographers lured by migrating sea birds, whales, and seals, as well as wildflowers and colorful forests; golfers looking for deals will find much to like in these seasons.

The oft-touted friendliness of Maritimers reflects a high value placed on lifestyle, people, and community. Indeed, you have to appreciate those who dug in and made the place their own. English, Scottish, Irish, and French colonists, as well as other nationalities, created unique communities that have retained their culture to this day. Some have grown into cities rich with nightlife, dining, museums, and shopping in historic markets and modern malls. Others remain small and continue to live life based around activities like kitchen parties and community dinners or picnics.

Today the ocean is a major tourist draw. If ever a place were built for eco-tourism and the quiet contemplation of nature, it's Eastern Canada. Wildlife-watching and deep-sea fishing are right up there with museum-hopping, toe-tapping music, and theater as top draws. Rappelling and zip-lining, as well as culinary and artistic learning experiences, speak to the breadth of what draws people here.

Tiring of megacities and life in the fast lane? Keening for a pie of locally harvested berries, a kayak in quiet waters, a private stretch of beach, or a spot of spontaneous fiddle music at the local pub? Well, then, this is the best place in North America. Kick off those shoes. They'll probably get wet anyway.

THE MARITIMES TODAY

NOVA SCOTIA   Canada's second-smallest province is almost entirely surrounded by salt water, giving its capital, Halifax, one of the best natural harbors in North America. As a result, the city became a financial and economic powerhouse back in the days of privateers and has never looked back. Modern Halifax, the region's largest city, is a transportation hub and center of industry and commerce. Culture and education, which came with European settlement, continue to impact city life today with colleges and universities fostering a youthful, edgy element to entertainment, restaurants, and outdoor activities.

Beyond city limits, a number of distinctive regions are blessed with beaches, spectacular cliffs, ocean vistas, forests, and farmlands to entrance photographers or nature lovers, as well as amazing history and culture to be savored. Music touches the soul on Cape Breton Island with its rich Scottish heritage and one of Canada's most spectacular national parks. The South Shore region, where German, Loyalist, and Acadian influence remains strong, embraces both the Atlantic Ocean and the Bay of Fundy. The isthmus between the Minas Basin and Northumberland Strait is world renowned for its rich fossil grounds, evidence of prehistoric times, as well as linking Nova Scotia with New Brunswick.

NEW BRUNSWICK   For many years, New Brunswick was sometimes referred to as a drive-through province that separated Nova Scotia, Prince Edward Island, and even Newfoundland from the rest of Canada and the United States. Smart tourists knew better and have been passing the message along. These days, New Brunswick—with its beautiful Bay of Fundy, St. John River Valley, Acadian Peninsula, quaint villages, and Appalachian Mountains—is a destination of choice. Its cities are unique. Fredericton is a genteel place where history and culture can be tasted and sampled like fine wine or perfectly aged cheese. The provincial capital offers exciting opportunities to expand your knowledge, your creativity, and your appreciation for art and nature. Saint John also reflects its past. As a seaport, it has always been a place to come ashore and enjoy great pubs, food, and entertainment. Today, it is also a cruise ship destination, and has wonderful nature parks and walking trails. Moncton capitalizes on its moniker, "Hub of the Maritimes," by offering great shopping, concerts, and consumer shows.

Culturally, New Brunswick is Canada's true bilingual province. With its population split between Anglophones and Francophones (a third of the province's residents speak French), and its heritage both proudly Acadian and proudly British, this province is a model for blending cultures. Head for the Tintamarre in Caraquet, a mid-August festival celebrating the Acadian National Holiday, and you will feel as warm a welcome as at a typical Loyalist Thanksgiving dinner—in fact, New Brunswick is sometimes called the Loyalist Province, since so many United Empire Loyalists (Brits still loyal to the crown) fleeing the United States after the American Revolution settled here.

PRINCE EDWARD ISLAND This island leaves the razzle-dazzle to cities on the mainland, choosing instead to soothe visitors' souls by offering places for quiet relaxation. An island of rolling hills, red soil, potato farms, and prolific wildflowers—plus healthy doses of fishing boats, golf, Acadian culture, and children's literature (you'll see what I mean)—PEI is the sort of place best explored via touring by car, RV, motorcycle, or bicycle (the ambitious can walk or cycle from tip to tip on quiet trails). The province's harborside capital city of Charlottetown is genuinely attractive, historic, and diverse; this was the place where the deal consolidating Canada into one nation ("Confederation") was born, and it's still a little gem of a town.

The island has, somewhat remarkably, managed to retain the bucolic flavor of a century ago, and pockets of sprawl are still few and far apart. You can see signs of growth in the suburbs outside Charlottetown, and small developments here and there, but basically, the population of the province remains that of a large town in "upper Canada" (Ontario). Much of the province is devoted to farming, fishing, arts and culture, and tourism; a rural lifestyle prevails. Residents and visitors like it that way.

LOOKING BACK AT THE MARITIME PROVINCES

Here's a brief look at some history and trends that have shaped Eastern Canada.

Indigenous Peoples

Maritime Archaic Indians, primarily a hunting-and-fishing culture, populated parts of Atlantic Canada beginning perhaps 7,500 years ago. These early natives relied chiefly on the sea for their food but eventually disappeared . . . why, nobody knows. Could it have been the long winters?

When Europeans discovered the region we now know as the Maritimes (Nova Scotia, New Brunswick, and Prince Edward Island) there were three Aboriginal groups: the Mi'kmaq, Maleseet, and Passamaquoddy, who have lived here for at least 500 generations. Part of the Algonquin linguistic family, these peoples lived a nomadic life of fishing, trapping, and hunting, changing camp locations several times each year to take advantage of seasonal fish runs, wildlife movements, and the like.

Today, more than 30,000 Mi'kmaq and Maliseet inhabit the region, adding to the cultural mix that is the Maritimes.

European Fishermen & British Loyalists

There are many theories about which Europeans were first to set foot in the Maritimes, but it is generally accepted that English explorer John Cabot visited in 1497. The Portuguese set up a small settlement in 1520, but left in 1523; apparently they didn't get along with the Mi'kmaq.

The French made the first significant attempts at establishing a new colony, though they were driven out time and again by the locals. They established a fur trade monopoly through the Acadia Company and were determined to establish permanent settlement in the New World. In 1604, a party led by Samuel de Champlain built a fort on St. Croix Island in Passamaquoddy Bay near St. Stephen, New Brunswick, but the site was unsuitable with few trees, no firewood or water, and harsh weather. Even worse, the native peoples were not interested in trade, just war. The French abandoned the settlement in the spring of 1605. The island is now a historic site.

Largely due to the aggressively—shall we say—protectionist actions of its native peoples, the region's first permanent settlement didn't come until 1605, when the group sailed across the Bay of Fundy and arrived in the Annapolis Valley at Port Royal—right across the river from present-day Annapolis Royal. Champlain called the lovely Annapolis Basin "one of the finest harbors that I have seen on all these coasts," and the strategic importance of that well-protected harbor was later proven during struggles for control of the region, when a series of forts was constructed on the low hills overlooking the water.

The settlement's impacts are still felt today. It was here that North American's first apple trees, grains, and dandelions were planted. As well, the Order of Good Cheer, the first social club, was established here.

Unaware of the Revolutionary troubles brewing to the south, the eastern provinces were settling organically. Farmers and fishermen slowly began filtering in from Europe and the colonies to the south. The Louisbourg fortress was built. The mid-1750s saw an explosion of settlement along the South Shore, including the towns of Chester (by Brits), Mahone Bay (by Anglican devotees), and Lunenburg (by German, Swiss, and French fisherfolk and boatbuilders, who laid it out in a grid with Germanic-Swiss precision, despite its hilly terrain). And, of course, there was Halifax, whose well-shaped natural harbor attracted Europeans in 1749 when Colonel Edward Cornwallis established a military outpost here.

But the separate peace would not last long. The signing of the Treaty of Paris in 1783, which recognized the American right of separation from Mother England, was like a bombshell. This single piece of paper would have profound effects on the subsequent composition and history of the Maritimes.

For those in America whose sympathies (or livelihoods) lay with the British, it created an untenable situation: They were men without a country. But England still held Eastern Canada. The solution was obvious.

A huge wave of fearful British Loyalist settlers and their families began fleeing New England and New York City by horse and foot, washing up at little harbors like Shelburne, Nova Scotia (which became a wooden boat-building stronghold—bigger, for a time, than both Montréal and Halifax). Before the arrival of the Loyalists, only about 5,000 peopled lived in the territory that would become New Brunswick, including indigenous peoples, uprooted Acadians, and first-generation settlers from Ireland, Great Britain, and New England. French settlers also ran for the eastern provinces. The Rustico region on the northern shore of PEI became one of the first in Canada to be permanently populated by the Acadians following the treaty's signing.

Would England be able to handle the strain of these new immigrants? How would it govern them? Would they eventually have ideas of their own independence? It was all up in the air, and things felt tenuous.

An Industrial Age

Tensions grew with the Maritimes' sudden spike in population, but somehow the British retained their hold on Canada for nearly another century, though that too would eventually crumble. The eastern provinces' place in Canadian history was forever cemented in 1864 when Charlottetown hosted the conference that would eventually lead to the creation of Canada as a separate nation—an event that is still remembered and celebrated on PEI today. The deeper significance was clear, too: This was no longer some backwoods fishing hole. The Maritime Provinces could be an engine of capitalism and growth for the new nation.

And so it was. The second half of the 19th century was a time of incredible growth and excitement for the Maritimes. No longer were they isolated fishing posts; now railroads, steamships, and the machination of certain production processes brought the fish to New York and Boston faster and fresher than ever. Boats could be built or fixed here, then sent anywhere in the world.

Demographics swung wildly as a consequence. Sydney, a working-class town, became northern Nova Scotia's industrial hub for decades, a legitimate rival to Halifax.

Yet this northern heyday would be sadly short-lived, lasting only three generations or so. As the highway and the jet airplane took over as means of transportation on the continent, the mill towns, factories, and airstrips began to wane.

And then the Great Depression hit.

Modern Times: Tourism & Natural Resources

In the wake of the Great Depression and the larger changes happening in the world—new transport methods; wars; a growing taste for production, consumption, and fashion—the Maritimes were forced to scramble. Fortunately, the treasure that the land and sea provided was recognized and a tourism industry was born. Rather than cutting down all the trees, forests were preserved, and national and provincial parks were developed. Golf courses, roads, inns, and expansive resort hotels began appearing at a furious pace. The spectacular Cabot Trail winding around Cape Breton Island was paved in 1939, ushering in decades of wide-eyed tourists. Salmon fishing drew the rich and famous to New Brunswick's great rivers.

During the years since, the Maritimes have gradually moved ahead with the times. Natural resources—specifically timber, paper, lobsters, and fish—remain the mainstays of the regional economy, just as they have for generations. The region's many protected natural harbors have also created important ports for oil and similar products imported from around the world to North America. New light industries and technology ventures have made inroads in the urban areas. And visitors continue coming for the unique charms of the eastern provinces; tourism income is still necessarily an important piece of the puzzle.

There is another subtle change occurring. Second homes and cottages in the Maritimes are lately more valuable than they have ever been, and an uptick in new development (during the boom times, at least) by outsiders worries many longtime residents. Meanwhile, the provinces' most remote parts have not really felt any economic kick from the past half-century of growth. For these locals, the Maritimes remain an enduringly difficult place to eke out a living—yet they continue doing so, just as their parents and grandparents did, choosing lifestyle and community over the comforts and the faster pace of life in more populated areas of the country.

ARCHITECTURE

History is reflected in the buildings, particularly in towns like Yarmouth, where glorious sea captains' homes reflect a prosperous era of seafaring; or Summerside, Prince Edward Island, where skilled craftsmen put out of work at the end of the era of building sailing vessels turned their skills to building homes for those who made their fortunes farming silver fox for their fur—now known as silver fox homes. The list of towns with unique architectural districts includes St. Andrews, N.B., and Nova Scotia's Lunenburg, Wolfville, and more. Cities like Halifax, Saint John, Fredericton, and Charlottetown all have well-cared-for architectural districts, particularly in the waterfront areas. Visitor information centers will provide you with maps of walking tours, and most have guided tours in the summer.

Those with an interest in architecture should factor visits to national historic sites and regional museums into their planning. Restorers and re-creators present the past with meticulous attention to detail.

THE MARITIMES IN POP CULTURE

Here's a "starter kit" of films, music, and literature that can prepare you for a rewarding visit to the Atlantic Provinces.

Books

Anne of Green Gables by L. M. Montgomery is a children's book for all time and a lovely evocation of life on Prince Edward Island. Originally published in 1908, Montgomery's fictional, ever-sunny Anne is the island's most famous export, hands down; this cycle of novels about an adopted red-haired girl remains enormously popular worldwide, thanks to both Montgomery's delineation of island characters and Anne's irrepressible optimism. It's less well known that there is an entire series of *Anne* books; *Gables,* the original in the series, only takes Anne's life through age 16. In future installments, Montgomery gave her a job as a school principal and took readers through Anne's marriage and motherhood. Montgomery was prolific beyond the *Anne* cycle as well, writing a series of spinoff novels about the lives of other townspeople in the fictional town of Avonlea; *Chronicles of Avonlea* (1912) and *Further Chronicles of Avonlea* (1920) are probably the best known. Montgomery also authored a number of other books and short stories set on the island not involving Anne at all, although none of these has achieved anywhere near the lasting fame of the *Anne* stories; these works include *Jane of Lantern Hill* (1937), *Mistress Pat* (1935), and *Along the Shore,* a 1989 collected volume. If you can locate it, the Oxford University Press edition of *Anne of Green Gables* is annotated with plenty of biographical material, excerpts from the author's girlhood journals, colloquial explanations of cookery, directions to locations featured in the book, and the like—it's a better choice for adult travelers. The Children's Classics edition is a simple hardcover version, great for kids.

No book with adult themes set in Atlantic Canada is more famous than *The Shipping News* by E. Annie Proulx (1993). Proulx won both a Pulitzer Prize and a National Book Award for her second novel, the tale of a crushed down-and-out New Yorker who moves to Newfoundland and takes up a job penning articles for a shipping newspaper in the land of his forebears—a position that puts him at an intersection with some of the more fascinating characters on (or just passing through) the Rock.

The protagonist must also battle the demons left him by his former wife. Yet he somehow begins to rebuild a life of dignity, hope, and purpose. Although often criticized for its overblown style, there's no denying this novel captures that peculiar blend of isolation, perkiness, and quirkiness that makes up a Newfie.

Author Howard Norman's novel, **The Museum Guard** (1999), is set in a fictional Halifax art museum, where a downbeat guard's female companion becomes obsessed with a Dutch painting. The stories of the guard's upbringing, his lady's obsession, and their dreary lives tell much about the often claustrophobic and hard-bitten lives of Maritimers. Norman turned to nonfiction for **My Famous Evening** (2004), recounting both his own personal travels and correspondences in Nova Scotia as well as some fantastic, seemingly unreal stories of real Nova Scotians and some folk tales from the province; definitely worth picking up if you will be in Nova Scotia.

The first Canadian book to sell more than a million copies, **Beautiful Joe,** the story of an abused dog, was written by Nova Scotia native Margaret Marshall Saunders in 1894. She wrote under the name Marshall Saunders to disguise the fact that she was a woman. Winner of a competition by the American Humane Society, it was translated into more than 14 different languages.

Another early publication, **Sailing Alone Around the World** by Joshua Slocum, was first serialized in *The Century* magazine in 1899, then turned into a book which, along with his adventures, gained him widespread fame. Born in Nova Scotia, Slocum was the first man to sail single-handedly around the world. His book was a must-read for adventurous boys and men, and it can still be found in bookshops.

Films

Many films have been made in the Maritimes (sharp-eyed film buffs may recognize parts of Nova Scotia during their travels), but precious few have been made *about* them. Among recent Academy Award winners made here are *Titanic, Bowling for Columbine,* and *The Shipping News.* Other films include *K-19* and *The Widowmaker.* Keep your eye out for movie stars in Halifax and surrounding areas.

Television series such as Tom Selleck's *Jess Stone, Trailer Park Boys, That's So Weird, Haven, This Hour has 22 Minutes, Black Harbour,* children's favorite *Theodore Tugboat,* and many, many more come out of Nova Scotia.

Children of a Lesser God with William Hurt and *Jericho Mansions* with James Caan were filmed in New Brunswick, the province that claims actors and filmmakers Mary Pickford, Walter Pidgeon, Donald Sutherland, Louis B. Mayer, Brett Somers, and Anna Silk as its own.

Music

It is often said that music ties together all of the Atlantic provinces. Nowhere is that more evident than at the East Coast Music Awards. This annual gathering demonstrates the diversity of both established and upcoming talent, be it traditional Celtic or Acadian, pop, blues, jazz, opera, classical—the list just goes on. Homegrown music in the Maritimes leans towards Celtic-inflected folk, or pop music greatly influenced by that sound, but certainly isn't limited to it.

Music from the region was entertaining the world as early as the 1930s when Hank Snow of Nova Scotia burst on the scene. His first massive hit, "I'm Movin' On" was followed by "The Golden Rocket," "I Don't Hurt Anymore," "I've Been Everywhere," And "Hello Love." The country singer charted more than 70 singles. One of Elvis

Presley's heroes, he's a member of the Country Music Hall of Fame and was a Grand Ole Opry staple for years. Today you can visit the Hank Snow Home Town Museum in Liverpool, Nova Scotia.

Another local country icon is Stompin' Tom Conners. Born in New Brunswick, he grew up on Prince Edward Island; his boot-stompin' style resulted in 20 albums, books, and loyal fans across the nation. The great Stan Rogers and his Maritime-influenced folk music are feted at an annual Stan Rogers Festival, also known as StanFest, in Canso, Nova Scotia, which brings songwriters and 50 or more performers from around the world together with music fans. His songs, "Northwest Passage" and "Barrett's Privateers," are often heard on television and extremely likely to be belted out in pubs and bars anywhere, when Maritimers gather and the beer flows free.

On the more classical side, one of the greatest contralto voices ever in Canadian music, Portia White of Truro, became an international sensation in the 1940s, helping to open the door to other black performers. In 1966, "The Men of the Deeps," coal miners from Cape Breton, formed and continue touring to this day. This world-renowned male choral ensemble was the first Canadian musical group to tour the People's Republic of China, and has toured most major cities in North America. Dressed in miners' coveralls and hard hats, these champions of miners around the world make an impressive statement when they enter a concert hall in total darkness, with their helmet lamps providing the only light. With country and folk tunes like "Flying On Your Own" and "Working Man" topping the charts internationally, Rita MacNeil's fame in Canada, the United Kingdom, and Australia led to her receiving the Order of Canada. MacNeil took her Cape Breton style to the world, but it was John Allan Cameron who showcased Nova Scotia's Celtic heritage to the mainstream. This ordained Catholic priest-turned-folk singer became known as "The Godfather of Celtic Music," who took Cape Breton music out of the kitchen and into the world. As did fiddler Natalie MacMaster who thrills audiences in Europe and North America, performing with such greats as Luciano Pavarotti, Paul Simon, and Faith Hill, and appearing on U.S. talk shows (the *Tonight Show, Late Night,* and *Good Morning America*). The Rankins of Cape Breton epitomize much about the Maritime music scene. From a family of 12 who entertained the neighbors at local *ceilidhs* these siblings have gone on to perform traditional jigs, reels, and Celtic folk songs with signature harmonies across Canada. With too many awards to list, they are a favorite element of the local music scene and one of the easiest to see in person, as one or a bunch of them always seems to be on tour. Nova Scotia native **Sarah McLachlan** has made it big around the globe, thanks to haunting pop classics: *Fumbling Towards Ecstasy* features the single, "Possession;" *Surfacing* features "Sweet Surrender" and "Building a Mystery;" and the live record, *Mirrorball,* includes the gem, "I Will Remember You."

Arguably the best-known Maritime star, Anne Murray, was the first Canadian female solo singer to reach #1 on U.S. charts with her signature song, "Snowbird." The Nova Scotia crooner has sold over 54 million albums and won so many awards and accolades that they had to have a special museum, the Anne Murray Centre, built in Springhill to house them all. In 2011, *Billboard* magazine ranked her number 10 on their list of the 50 biggest AC (adult contemporary) artists of all time.

Music is part of life in the Maritimes with festivals, concerts, and stage performances touching on every genre from blues to classical, Celtic to jazz. Search it out where ever you happen to be.

EATING & DRINKING

For generations, Eastern Canada has been known as the go-to place for great seafood; be it clams boiled up on the beach, deep-fried fish from a shack on the wharf, lobster from a "supper," chowder at a festival, or a top-level chef's culinary masterpiece. As self-sufficient communities, Maritime towns have always placed great value on locally produced foods. The Culinary Institute of Canada in Charlottetown boasts gold medal wins from Olympic and World competitions, as do many chefs from the region. The high level of culinary training that is available here has impacted all aspects of culinary tourism. Local offerings vary tremendously:

BERRIES Blueberries, cranberries, raspberries, and strawberries top a long list of local fruits that burst with flavor. Fresh berry pie or shortcake appear on most menus during their season, and farmers markets are treasure-troves for berry lovers. Natural blueberry and cranberry juices, as well as jams and jellies, are some of the region's best artisan products.

FIDDLEHEADS & GOOSE TONGUE GREENS Spring greens are popular in New Brunswick and indicative of fresh wild harvests that include such goodies as chanterelle mushrooms. Watch for them on seasonal menus at chef-operated restaurants and at farmers markets. See chapter 5.

FISH & CHIPS Fish-and-chips shops certainly aren't unique to Eastern Canada, but they do the chippie proud. Check around the Halifax area (see chapter 4), or the shoreline just to the south.

LOBSTER Wherever you see wooden lobster traps piled high on a wharf, a fresh lobster meal can't be far away. Among the most productive lobster fisheries are those around Shediac, New Brunswick, and along Nova Scotia's entire Atlantic coast (see chapters 4 and 5). Sunny days are ideal for cracking open a crustacean while sitting at a wharf-side picnic table, preferably with a locally brewed beer close at hand.

North central Prince Edward Island is famous for its church-sponsored lobster suppers. The typical supper might include a lobster or two, steamed mussels, and strawberry shortcake. See chapter 6.

MUSSELS & OYSTERS Some say you can't find better mussels or oysters anywhere in the world than those harvested in the shallow waters of Prince Edward Island. It's hard to argue with that sentiment; restaurants from New York to Tokyo covet (and pay big bucks for) these prized PEI shellfish. In fact, PEI produces 90% or so of the world's blue mussels. You can get them relatively cheap at local seafood outlets; sometimes you can even buy a bag off the docks or at the processors.

RAPPIE PIE Foodies in search of obscure-eats rapture might indeed feel they've died and gone to heaven when they reach the southwestern shore of Nova Scotia (see chapter 4). This area, a French enclave known as the Evangeline Trail, is one of the best places in Canada to sample tried-and-true Acadian cooking. (The other great areas can be found around New Brunswick's Acadian Peninsula). Rappie pie, a staple of the Acadian family restaurant, has several variations, such as a rich, potato-stock-and-onion casserole topped with a pile of pork rinds (yup), and baked. Your body fat percentage *will* change as a result of eating one of these.

SCALLOPS The waters off Digby Neck (on the southwestern shore of Nova Scotia; see chapter 4) produce some of the choicest, most succulent scallops in the world. They're ubiquitous on the menus of restaurants along the western shore of

Nova Scotia, and show up in lots of fine kitchens around the rest of the region, too. A light sauté in butter brings out their rich flavor best.

SMOKED FISH Here and there, particularly along the Atlantic shore of Nova Scotia and New Brunswick's Bay of Fundy, you'll come across the odd fish-smoking shack. That's not really surprising, given the huge supply of smoke-able fish just off-shore. The most organized and commercialized operation is the J. Willy Krauch & Sons operation in the village of Tangier, Nova Scotia (see chapter 4). Krauch & Sons' "hot-smoked" herring is a classic turn on the form.

WHISKY Deep in the highlands of Cape Breton, there's a distillery making lovely "Scotch" (which can't be called Scotch, this not being Scotland). So, single-malt whisky then. It's still fantastic, crafted from the pure local water. See chapter 4.

WINES, SPIRITS & MORE Each of the three provinces boasts a number of good artisan wineries and distilleries that have a legion of awards to their credit. Brochures detailing winery tours help you plan your own tastings in Nova Scotia and New Brunswick. Prince Edward Island boasts a first-class winery and two distillers in their eastern region. Tours will take you off the beaten path and to some of the most scenic areas in the region. Get details from local Visitor Information Centres.

WHEN TO GO

Weather

All the Atlantic Provinces lie within the **North Temperate Zone,** which means that they have weather much like New England in the United States. **Spring** is damp, cool, and short, though it can get warm and occasionally muggy as it eases into summer.

Summer's compact high season runs from mid-June to mid-September. That's when the great majority of travelers take to the road, enjoying the bright, clear days and warm temperatures. The average high is in the upper 70s°F (around 25°C) although in recent years, temperatures have been rising a few degrees. Nights can become cool, even approaching light frost, by mid-September. These cool nights are what make summers so appealing—less daytime humidity and a good night's sleep make summer in the Maritimes a joy.

Be aware that there is no "typical" summer weather in Atlantic Canada. The only thing typical is change, and you're likely to experience balmy, sunny days as well as howling rainstorms—quite possibly on the same day. Travelers who come here prepared for an occasional downpour, both psychologically and equipment-wise, tend to be happier than those who expect all blue skies. That's because the weather in all three provinces is to a large degree affected by the ocean. This means frequent fogs, especially on the Fundy Coast of New Brunswick and the Atlantic Coast of Nova Scotia. The ocean also offers an unobstructed corridor for high winds, should a storm be making its way up the Eastern Seaboard.

Note that the ocean does provide some benefits: Prince Edward Island's summer tends to linger into fall, thanks to the warm, moderating influence of the Gulf of St. Lawrence, and you'll rarely experience a sultry hot, humid day in the Maritimes because of the natural air-conditioning action of the sea breezes.

Fall is a time of bright leaf colors but also rapidly cooling temperatures, especially at night, and much shorter daylight hours. Bring winter sweaters and a heavy coat. It is possible for the tail end of tropical storms or hurricanes to make their way up the Eastern Seaboard. If a storm is forecast, stay put. Your accommodations will be your best source of advice on riding out the storm. **Best advice:** Cozy up with a good book and enjoy the experience—it can be awesome.

Few travelers, with the exception of winter sports enthusiasts, tackle the Maritimes in the dead of **winter,** as frequent blustery storms sweep in. If you're one of those hardy souls who might, be aware that snow or ice storms are a very real possibility at any time during winter, and they can blow in suddenly; if you're driving, make sure your car is equipped with good snow tires and special antifreeze windshield wash (you can get it from any gas station). And drive cautiously: Outside the major urban areas, most of this region's high-speed arteries are two-lane roads without medians. Watch for drivers coming your way.

Always be aware that the weather can be vastly different throughout the three provinces, especially in winter. Check the weather report for where you are going, as well as where you are at the moment. And remember that folks here live by the saying, "Stay where you're at," should bad weather make travel unsafe. It is perfectly acceptable to be "storm stayed" rather than take risks.

Halifax Average Monthly Temperatures

		JAN	FEB	MAR	APR	MAY	JUNE	JULY	AUG	SEPT	OCT	NOV	DEC
HIGH	(°F)	29	29	36	47	57	67	73	73	65	54	44	34
	(°C)	–2	–2	2	8	14	19	22	23	18	12	7	1
LOW	(°F)	14	14	22	32	41	50	57	57	50	40	32	20
	(°C)	–10	–10	–6	0	5	10	14	14	10	4	0	–7

Holidays

The national holidays in Canada are celebrated from the Atlantic to the Pacific to the Arctic oceans; for the traveler, this means all government offices and banks will be closed at these times. (Shops generally close on national holidays.) **National holidays** here include New Year's Day, Good Friday, Easter Monday, Victoria Day (the third Mon in May), Canada Day (July 1; this is a biggie—expect fireworks), Labour Day (first Mon in Sept), Thanksgiving (mid-Oct), Remembrance Day (Nov 11), Christmas Day (Dec 25), and Boxing Day (Dec 26).

Locally observed **provincial holidays** include: Islander Day (third Mon in Feb on Prince Edward Island), a civic holiday (Aug 2) in Nova Scotia, and New Brunswick Day (the first Mon in Aug). Acadians celebrate their national holiday, Tintamarre, on August 15, usually with celebrations for up to 2 weeks prior to the grand day.

For an exhaustive list of events beyond those listed here, check http://events. frommers.com, where you'll find a searchable, up-to-the-minute roster of what's happening in cities all over the world.

THE LAY OF THE LAND

The human history of Eastern Canada is usually thought of as beginning in or around the 17th century with the arrival of European colonists. But the clock actually turns back much farther than that—beginning thousands of years ago, when Native American tribes fished Atlantic shores and hunted these hills. Even they were here for only a sliver of the long period of time required to create this place. Situations like this call for the word *eons.* The rocks upon which you climb, sun yourself, and picnic are old—staggeringly old. Before arriving, then, it's a good idea to acquaint yourself with the natural history of the place. Armed with a little respect and appreciation for the landscape before you, you just might treat it more reverently while you're here—and help ensure that it remains for future generations to behold for many years.

Rocky Road: Geology of the Landscape

The beginnings of Eastern Canada are perhaps a half-billion years old. You read right: That's *billion*, with a B. At that time, deep wells of liquid rock known as magma were moving upward, exploding in underground volcanoes, then hardening—still underground, mind you—into granite-like rocks. Later, natural forces such as wind and water wore away and exposed the upper layers of these rocks. Their punishment was only beginning, however; soon enough (geologically speaking, that is), what is now eastern North America and most of Europe began to shove up against each other, slowly but inexorably. This "collision" (which was more like an *extremely* slow-motion car wreck) heated, squeezed, transformed, and thrust up the rocks that now form the backbone of the coastline. Ice ages came and went, but the rocks remained; the successive waves of great glaciation and retreat scratched up the rocks, and the thick tongues of pressing ice cut deep notches out of them. Huge boulders were swept up and deposited by the ice in odd places. When the glaciers finally retreated for the last time, tens of thousands of years ago, the water melting from the huge ice sheet covering North America swelled the level of the Atlantic high enough to submerge formerly free-flowing river valleys and give the coastline and places like Cape Breton their distinctively rocky, knuckled faces. (At Prince Edward Island, the boulders left behind tons of silt and sand; that's what the island is, basically: a big sandbox.)

Once the bones of this landscape were established, next came the flesh: plants and animals. After each ice age, conifers such as spruce and fir trees—alongside countless grasses and weeds—began to reform, then decompose and form soils. It was tough work: Most of Eastern Canada is a rocky, acidic place. Yet they persevered (as plants tend to do), and soon spruces, firs, and hemlocks formed an impenetrable thicket covering much of the coastal bedrock. Again, PEI was the exception: Mostly grasses, weeds, flowers, and pine trees sprouted up in the red mud and sand dumped here by the glaciers—because such an environment is inhospitable to almost everything else.

As the trees and flowers and fruits became reestablished, animals wandered back here, too—some now extinct (like the mastodon) but some still thriving today in the fields, hills, and woods of the region.

Eastern Canada's unique position—it is near the warm Gulf Stream—also bequeathed it plenty of marine (and economic) life: The current passes over the high, shallow undersea plateau known as Georges Bank, bringing an astonishing variety of microorganisms, and the marine life that follows, right to these provinces' doorsteps. Migrating whales make for a wonderful spectacle each year; seabirds travel similar passages, lighting upon the rocks and lakes of the region. And the waters teem—though not as they once did: Two of the three species of striped bass in the Bay of Fundy have disappeared from overfishing—along with fish, lobsters, crabs, dolphins, and a great deal more.

Then there are the coast's tidal pools, that precarious zone where land and rock meet ocean; a closer look at these pools reveals an ever-changing world of seaweed, snails, barnacles, darting water bugs, clams, shellfish, mud-burrowing worms, and other creatures. Interestingly, the type of life you find changes in well-marked "bands" as you get closer to water; rocks that are always submerged contain one mixture of seaweed, shellfish, and marine organisms, while rocks that are exposed and then re-submerged each day by the tides have a different mix. It's fascinating to note how each particular organism has found its niche. Move it up or down a foot and it would perish.

What follows is only the barest sketch of some of the nature you'll find in Eastern Canada. For a real look at it, go see it yourself. Whether you explore the provinces on foot, by bicycle, by kayak, by charter boat, or some other way, you're almost certain to see something that you've never seen before. If you're attentive, you'll come away with a deeper respect for things natural.

The Flora & Fauna

TREES & SHRUBS

BALSAM FIR   The best-smelling tree in the provinces must be the mighty balsam fir, whose tips are sometimes harvested to fabricate aromatic Christmas-tree wreaths and are farmed for Christmas trees. They're found in pockets of New Brunswick and Nova Scotia. It's sometimes hard to tell a fir from a spruce or hemlock, though the balsam's flat, paddle-like needles (white underneath) are unique—only a hemlock's are similar. Pull one off the twig to be sure; a fir's needle comes off clean, a hemlock's ragged. Still not sure you've got a fir tree on your hands? The long, glossy, almost purplish cones are absolutely distinctive. You can find tree farms around Lunenburg, Nova Scotia, and other areas in the Maritimes.

LOWBUSH BLUEBERRY   Canada is the world's largest producer of wild blueberries, officially known as lowbush blueberries, cultivating nearly C$70 million worth annually. All three provinces support significant blueberry production. With shrubby, tea-like leaves and thick twigs, the plants lie low on exposed rocks on sunny hillsides, or sometimes crop up in shady woods; most of the year, the berries are inconspicuous and trail harmlessly underfoot. Come late summer, however, they're suddenly very popular—for bears as well as people. The wild berries ripen slowly in the sun (look behind and beneath leaves for the best bunches) and make for great eating off the bush, pancake baking, or jam making. Roadside booths pop up, often beside the glorious fields that seem to be covered with a reddish green blanket as the berries ripen, and later when frosts pretty up the landscape.

RED & SUGAR MAPLE   These two maple trees look vaguely alike when turning color in fall, but they're actually quite different, from the shapes of their leaves to the habitats they prefer. **Red maples** have skinny, gray trunks and like a swampy or wet area; often, several of the slim trunks grow together into a clump, and in fall the red maples' pointy leaves turn a brilliant scarlet color almost at once. **Sugar maples,** on the other hand, are stout-trunked trees with lovely, substantial leaves (marked with distinctive U-shaped notches), which autumn slowly changes to red and flame-orange. Sugar maples grow in or at the edges of mixed forests, often in combination with birch trees, oak trees, beech trees, and hemlocks. Their sap, of course, is collected and boiled down to make delicious maple syrup—big business in Eastern Canada.

RED & WHITE PINE   These pines grow in sandy soils and like some (or a lot of) sunlight. The **eastern white pine** is the familiar "King's pine" once prevalent throughout the northeast portions of North America; you can recognize it by its very long, strong needles that are always arranged five to a clump, like a hand's fingers. Its trunk was prized for the masts of ships of war in the 16th to 19th centuries. Countless huge pines were floated down Canadian rivers by logger men. Sadly, old-growth white pines are virtually nonexistent today in many regions, but you can still find the tree throughout Eastern Canada. The less common **red pine** is distinguished by pairs of needles and a pitchy trunk. It grows on PEI (where it loves the sandy soil), and also in parts of New Brunswick and Nova Scotia.

EYES ON THE road

Wildlife can be very dangerous for traffic on the highways of this region. Moose, deer, bears, and smaller mammals are so prevalent that busy highways, like the Trans-Canada, are fenced in some areas to keep the animals from the road. Drivers should always be diligent about watching the road ahead, particularly in spring and fall, at dawn and dusk. The more remote or wooded the area, the more careful you need to be. Remember, a collision with a moose is often fatal for driver and passengers.

LAND MAMMALS

BEAVER   Often considered symbolic of Canada, beavers almost became extinct in the early 1900s due to a brisk world trade in beaver pelts and the rapid development of wetlands. Today the beaver's lodge-building, stick-chewing, and hibernating habits are well known once again; you'll find them in streams, lakes, and ponds, often in wet areas beside the road. Beavers seem to think that man invented culverts as an aid to dam building.

BLACK BEAR   Black bears still occur in Eastern Canada, though in small numbers (still, you may want to keep a cover on that campfire food). The bears are mostly—emphasis on *mostly*—plant eaters and docile; they're the smallest of the North American bears and don't want trouble. Though they'll eat just about anything, these bears prefer easily reached foods on the woodland floor, such as berries, mushrooms, nuts . . . and campers' leftovers. (Suspend leftovers in a "bear bag" away from your tent if you're camping in bear territory.) Black bears fatten up in fall for a long winter hibernation that averages 6 months.

MOOSE   Nothing says Canada like a moose, and the huge, skinny-legged, vegetarian moose is occasionally seen in the deep woods of Eastern Canada; in Nova Scotia, they're listed as a provincially endangered species, but New Brunswick holds a lottery dispensing hunting permits based on quotas determined annually. Moose are sometimes seen beside the road in New Brunswick and Nova Scotia. (But there are *no* moose—or even deer—on PEI.) The animal prefers deep woods, lakes, ponds, and uninhabited areas, and you can't miss it: The rack of antlers on the male, broad lineman-like shoulders, spindly but quick legs, and sheer bulk (it's as big as a truck) ensure you won't mistake it for anything else.

WHALES, DOLPHINS, PORPOISES & SEALS

DOLPHIN   Two very similar-looking species of dolphin—the **Atlantic white-sided dolphin** and the **white-beaked dolphin**—come to the Atlantic coast of the eastern provinces. Cute and athletic, these dolphins also occasionally turn up on beaches, for the same reason as pilot whales: Large groups are occasionally stranded by the tides, resulting in major rescue efforts, since they will die if unable to get back to sea in time.

FINBACK WHALE   A visitor to Eastern Canada's waters twice a year when migrating between polar and equatorial waters, the finback is the second largest of the world's whales. Finbacks are fast movers who spout up to 4m (13 ft.) above the surface and can be viewed from a mile away; even so, you will need a whale-watching excursion boat to see them. They often travel in pairs or groups of a half-dozen, leading to exciting sightings.

Shipping and added fishing are having an impact on world populations; thus finbacks, a type of baleen whale, are protected under Canada's Species at Risk Act.

HARBOR PORPOISE Quiet in behavior and habit, the porpoise is small and grey—their undersides are white. Just 1.5 to 2m (5–6 ft.) long, they can easily be seen from shore, particularly from Grand Manaan Island. Identified by their triangular dorsal fin and blunt snouts, they are sometimes referred to as a "puffing pig" because of the snuffling sounds made when they breathe. Year-round residents, porpoises are considered "threatened" in Canada.

HARBOR SEAL With beautiful, big round eyes, cat-like whiskers, and a look compared to a cocker spaniel, these seals often seem as curious about humans as we are about them. Common in all seasons in the Atlantic provinces, they are best seen by using a charter-boat service, as you'll often find them basking in the sun on rocks offshore. They are often spotted around the coast in harbors and in a few places their "haul-out" sites can be viewed from shore—the Irving Nature Park in Saint John and Charlottetown Harbour, for example.

HUMPBACK WHALE The gentle, gigantic humpback isn't often seen from shore in Eastern Canada, except in the Digby, Nova Scotia, area. Whale-watch tours often find humpbacks, and if you see them, you'll never forget the sight: They are huge and jet-black, blow tremendous amounts of water when surfacing, and perform amazingly playful acrobatics above water. The males also sing haunting songs, sometimes for as long as 2 days at a time. Because of their tendency to come close to shore to feed, they were highly vulnerable to whale hunters—estimates are that more than 100,000 were killed by whalers throughout the modern whaling era. The world's population has shrunk to perhaps 10,000 whales, making them an endangered species with a moratorium on whaling.

MINKE WHALE The smallest of the whales, the minke swims off the coast of Canada, usually moving in groups of two or three whales—but much larger groups collect in feeding areas and during certain seasons. They usually live at the surface. Sometimes curious, they may approach and congregate around boats, making this a whale you're quite likely to see while on a whale-watch tour. The minke is dark gray on top, the throat has grooves, and each black flipper fin is marked with a conspicuous white band.

PILOT WHALE These smallish whales swim up to 35kmph (22 mph), making successive leaps as they travel, much like dolphins. Since they often travel in groups which can reach in the hundreds, sightings are exciting, if rare. Summer residents of the Gulf of St. Lawrence and Atlantic Ocean off Nova Scotia, they are sometimes spotted by whale-watching boats, particularly along the northeast coast of Cape Breton. Not a lot is known about these whales. Even though there are occasional mass strandings, populations remain healthy.

INVERTEBRATES

AMERICAN LOBSTER Everyone knows the lobster by sight and taste; what few know is that it was once considered ugly, tasteless, and unfit to eat. There was a time not so long ago when children or workers who had lobster in their lunch pail were known to be poor. Today, the situation is quite different: This is one of Eastern Canada's major exports and a must-have for gourmands visiting the Maritimes. Lobsters are related to crabs, shrimp, and even spiders and insects (sorry to spoil your appetite); they feed by slowly scouring the ocean bottom in shallow, dark waters, locating food by smell (they see very poorly). The hard shell, which is periodically shed in order to grow larger, is the lobster's skeleton. A greenish-black or rarely blue color when alive, it turns bright red only after the lobster is cooked.

BIRDS

BALD EAGLE   Yes, they're here in Atlantic Canada—year-round—and they breed here. Sightings are common, especially near coastal areas such as Cape Breton Island in Nova Scotia, or on Prince Edward Island in the spring. (Their endangered status means you shouldn't get too close, but if you keep your eyes peeled, watching the tops of trees and cliffs, you might just be lucky.) The bald eagle's black body, white head, and yellow bill make it almost impossible to confuse with any other bird. It was nearly wiped out in the 1970s, mainly due to environmental poisons such as DDT-based pesticides. However, the bird is making a comeback.

DUCK   Between one and two dozen species of ducks and ducklike geese, brant, and teal seasonally visit the lakes, ponds, and tidal coves of Eastern Canada every year, including—though hardly limited to—the **red-breasted merganser** and the **common eider.** Mergansers, characterized by very white sides and very red bills (in males) or reddish crests (in females), occur year-round but are more common in winter months. So is the eider, which inhabits offshore islands and coastal waters rather than provincial freshwater lakes; in winter, these islands form huge rafts of birds. Males are marked with a sharp black-and-white pattern.

GREAT BLUE HERON   Everyone knows a great blue at once, by its prehistoric flapping wings, comb of feathers, and spindly legs. These magnificent hunters wade through tidal rivers, fishing with lightning strikes beneath the surface, from May through around October. The smaller, stealthier green heron and yellow-crowned night heron are rarely seen.

LOON   Two species of loon visit the region's lakes and tidal inlets, fishing for dinner. The **red-throated loon,** grayish with a red neck, is a spring passer-through and very rare in summer or winter. The **common loon** is, indeed, much more common— it can be distinguished by a black band around the neck, as well as black-and-white stripes and dots—and can be found in Canada year-round, though it's most easily spotted in late spring and late fall. Its habit of swimming low in the water helps to distinguish the loon from other water birds. It summers on lakes and winters on open patches of ocean inlets, giving a distinctively mournful, almost laughing call. Both loons have been decimated by environmental changes such as oil spills, acid rain, and airborne mercury.

PLOVER   Plovers inhabit and breed in certain muddy tidal flats, and their habitat is precarious; a single human step can crush an entire generation of eggs. Four species of plover visit Eastern Canada in a few spots, and they're here only for a relatively short time. The **lesser golden-plover** flocks in considerable numbers in September while passing through, and the **greater golden-plover** occasionally lands in Newfoundland during migration. The **semipalmated plover,** with its quite different brownish body and white breast, has a similar life cycle and is also usually only seen in spring, passing through. The bird most associated with the Maritimes is the Piping Plover, a species at risk, which is zealously protected during breeding season. If you see an area of beach barricaded off, don't venture forward; they build their nests amid the pebbles and sand. These lovely little birds have enough challenges raising their broods with storms and predators, so let's not add human encroachment.

SEAGULL   No bird is as closely associated with the sea as the seagull. A number of different gulls are found here, some year-round, a few seasonally, and a few more pop up only occasionally. Most common is the grayish **herring gull,** which is also the gull least afraid of humans. It's prevalent every month of the year. The **great black-backed gull** is also fairly common, and is nearly all white (except for that black back and wings). This aggressive bird will even eat the eggs of another gull but in general avoids humans. There's a huge colony on Lake George outside Yarmouth, Nova Scotia. You might also see **glaucous, ring-billed,** and even **laughing** and **Bonaparte's gulls** (rarely, and mostly in summer), not to mention the related **black-legged kittiwake.**

SONGBIRD   There are literally dozens of species of songbirds that roost in Acadia's open fields, forests, and dead snags—even in the rafters and bird boxes of houses. They are not so common in remote rocky places as in suburbia (greater Halifax, for instance) or in the farmlands of the provinces. One thing is for certain: Songbirds love human company, so look for them near the settled areas. The region hosts a dozen or so distinct types of chirpy little **warblers,** each with unique and often liquid songs; a half-dozen **thrushes** occurring in significant numbers; winter **wrens, swallows, sparrows, vireos, finches, creepers,** and **thrashers;** the whimsical **black-capped chickadee;** and occasionally lovely **bluebirds, cardinals,** and **tanagers,** among many other species.

STORM PETREL   The tiny storm petrel is a fascinating creature. These plucky little birds fly astonishing distances in winter, eating insects on the wing, only to return to the coast each spring like clockwork, usually in May. They spend an amazing 4 months incubating, hatching, and tending to their single, white eggs in nests eked out of rocks. **Wilson's storm petrels** sometimes follow behind offshore boats; the much less common **Leach's storm petrel** restricts its visits and nests solely to far-offshore rocks and islands and is also mostly nocturnal, which reduces the chances of seeing it further. Both breed in summer, then head south for winter.

RESPONSIBLE TRAVEL

I love Eastern Canada, and I'd never want to see what is special about the Maritimes disappear just because people visited it too much, or in the wrong way—loved it to death, as it were. There are ways to help ensure this won't happen. Here's a primer on some current environmental issues in the region, plus some tips on traveling as "lightly" as possible.

Fisheries

Fisheries have been *the* hot-button issue in Eastern Canada since forever. This region depends upon fishing and shellfish harvesting more than any other industry for both its economic lifeblood and its identity. Yet the native fishing stocks are imperiled, thanks to centuries of rampant overfishing; the national and provincial governments have enacted a series of emergency rules preventing fishing of certain fish. These restrictions make old-timers a bit tetchy, but they're probably a necessary poison if the fish are going to rebound and provide a living for future generations.

What can you do? Signing up for a fly-fishing or deep-sea fishing expedition isn't any different from joining a fishing crew, so don't feel guilty if you do. Just act responsibly. Don't fish for more than you need to eat. Catch and release (it is the law in some cases) if you're not planning to eat all of the fish you catch. Do not throw any trash overboard. And don't use any illegal fishing methods to coax out a bigger catch. (If you see your tour operator doing so, don't patronize them again. And you might think about writing a letter to the provincial authorities after you get home.)

Aquaculture has, to a degree, replaced harvesting of wild stocks. Mussels are a hugely successful farming venture on Prince Edward Island, as are Atlantic salmon in the Bay of Fundy. Scallops, oysters, halibut, and trout are among the other seafoods grown on fish farms.

Indigenous Culture

In Canada, they certainly don't refer to native peoples as "Indians," and they don't even call them "native Canadians;" they're referred to as members of the First Nation. There are First Nation reserves in all three Maritime Provinces.

However, reservations in Canada are not the same as those in the United States. There are few casinos here, no public religious ceremonies. There are some shops in places like Lennox Island on Prince Edward Island that carry native-made products. Individuals of the First Nations are also developing some attractions and programs that respectfully present their lifestyles, relationships with the land and sea, and traditions. The native peoples of Eastern Canada are proud of their heritage and valuable contributions to society. If you pass through or past a marked reserve, do so respectfully. Don't snap photos of signs, people, houses, or shops—it's just not cool.

You can view indigenous art at many art galleries in Eastern Canada (at the Confederation Centre Art Gallery, p. 228, in Charlottetown or the Beaverbrook Art Gallery in Fredericton to give just a couple of examples), and numerous museums throughout the region display artifacts from native settlements.

Staying Green

Yes, it's pretty hard to claim you're being "green" while you're staying in a resort hotel that pumps water into 300 rooms and also sprinkles it onto a golf course—or whose owners cleared off 20 acres of forest and marshlands to build it. But you can minimize your impact as a traveler in Eastern Canada. Here are just a few ways:

o **Stay in an accredited "green" hotel.** The **Hotel Association of Canada (HAC),** Canada's official hotel association, maintains a member-run "green" rating system called Green Key that assesses member hotels' practices, then assigns them a rating of two to five keys. This system doesn't differentiate a whole lot among properties—the majority of hotels and motels are rated at three keys, or "medium" greenness—but it might help you separate the most-green from the least-green ones. Visit the organization's website (www.greenkeyglobal.com) for more information.

o **Play golf on an eco-friendly course.** Hundreds of courses in North America have been certified by the Audubon Society as wildlife sanctuaries, including about 80 in Canada. Of these, unfortunately, only two are located in Eastern Canada, though both are visually stunning and historic: **Bell Bay** in Baddeck, Nova Scotia (p. 45) on Cape Breton and the **Algonquin Golf Course** in St. Andrews, New Brunswick (p. 149). Check course listings for those following an environmental program.

o **Take public transit.** Every major city in this book—from Halifax to Saint John to Fredericton to Charlottetown—operates some form of metropolitan bus system.

o **Ride a bike.** The parks of Eastern Canada are unusually tailor-made for great bicycle riding. What's better than getting in shape and burning calories while contributing exactly zero toxic emissions to the atmosphere? It's pretty hard to beat that for green travel. The following destinations provide superb cycling holidays:

stretches of the **Cabot Trail** (p. 117) on Cape Breton Island (but watch carefully for touring cars); the outstandingly scenic **Fundy Trail Parkway** in New Brunswick (p. 171), which has a dedicated bike lane; and the **Confederation Trail** (p. 207), which stretches the entire length of Prince Edward Island—the best parts are in northeastern PEI, around the area of Mount Stewart.

○ **Eat at restaurants that source locally.** The use of hyper-local or regional produce, meats, and fish—this is Atlantic Canada, after all—contributes to the local economy and cuts down on pollution by cutting out the freighters, trucks, planes, trains, delivery vans, and refrigeration units required to ship and preserve foods over very long distance. Luckily, numerous good restaurants in Eastern Canada now use this philosophy: **Lot 30** in Charlottetown (p. 233) is one great example. Read the restaurant listings closely to find more examples.

○ **Stay on the trail.** Trails have boundaries for a reason: you're safer inside the trail (cliffs and handholds can crumble away in an instant), and sudden erosion is bad for a mountainside, because it creates a cascade effect: Each subsequent rain will wash more and more topsoil, forest duff, and nutrients off the hill, preventing future plant life from gaining a toehold (and the animals who depend on it). Stay on-trail.

Respecting the Birds & the Bees

Canada officially began offering "green" holidays in 1885 with the creation of Banff National Park, over 125 years ago. The first national park in the country began a commitment to preservation and respect for the bounty of nature. Both national and provincial parks, and community initiatives, are at work to protect what is recognized as one of Eastern Canada's greatest assets—the environment. You can get up close and personal with anything from a bull moose to a black bear, a sperm whale to a harbor seal. Sometimes outfitters even bring you right up beside the objects of your desire. You can also come across wildlife in rural areas, on roadsides, or when boating.

That might look cool in your video or scrapbook, but it isn't necessarily best for the animal, whale, or landscape in question. **Remember:** These are wild animals, still unaccustomed to proximity with people. So don't try to get too close or harass them.

Here are a few tips and resources for more respectful travel:

○ **Don't collect.** Resist the urge to collect things from the sea or forest. Pulling sea creatures out of the ocean and yanking up flowers for your hotel room (or your kids' aquarium back home) is both gauche and prohibited; sometimes the penalties can be very steep, approaching those for a federal crime.

○ **Save the whales.** Whale-watching is enduringly popular throughout the Maritime Provinces, but operators are lightly regulated; if you think your captain is heading too close in to the animals, complain (nicely but firmly). To learn more about the whales you'll be glimpsing, and how to respect them, visit the online resources of the **Whale and Dolphin Conservation Society** (www.wdcs.org).

○ **Use a respectful outfitter.** You can find more eco-friendly travel tips, statistics, and touring companies and associations—listed by destination under "Travel Choice"— at the International Ecotourism Society (TIES) website, www.ecotourism.org. **Conservation International** (www.conservation.org) is another useful resource. This organization presents annual awards to tour operators that have made significant contributions toward sustainable tourism. Take a look at the latest award winners to see if any of them operate in Eastern Canada. While international organizations are critical to motivating and policing the eco-tourism cause, it is also important to check with Canadian sites such as Trails Canada

GENERAL RESOURCES FOR green travel

In addition to the resources for Eastern Canada listed above, the following websites provide valuable wide-ranging information on sustainable travel. For a list of even more sustainable resources, as well as tips and explanations on how to travel greener, visit www.frommers.com/planning.

- **Responsible Travel** (www.responsibletravel.com) is a great source of sustainable travel ideas; the site is run by a spokesperson for ethical tourism in the travel industry.

- In Canada, **www.greenliving online.com** offers extensive content on how to travel sustainably, including a travel and transport section and provincial information.

- **Greenhotels** (www.greenhotels.com) recommends green-rated member hotels around the world that fulfill the company's stringent environmental requirements. **Environmentally Friendly Hotels** (www.environmentallyfriendly hotels.com) offers more green

accommodations ratings. The **Hotel Association of Canada** (www.hacgreenhotels.com) has a Green Key Eco-Rating Program, which audits the environmental performance of Canadian hotels, motels, and resorts.

- Visit **www.eatwellguide.org** for tips on eating sustainably in the U.S. and Canada.

- For information on animal-friendly issues throughout Canada, visit www.wwf.ca; the world, visit **Tread Lightly** (www.tread lightly.org). For information about the whales you'll be glimpsing (and how to respect them) off the Atlantic coast, visit the Bay of Fundy (www.bayoffundy.com or www.novascotia.com).

- **Volunteer International** (www.volunteerinternational.org) has a list of questions to help you determine the intentions and the nature of a volunteer program. For general info on volunteer travel, visit www.volunteerabroad.org and www.idealist.org.

(www.trailcanada.com) or http://canadian365.com/html/137.html to know what is happening in regions you plan to visit. Responsible outfitters and tour operators always work to preserve and protect the environment that is their source of income, and usually their passion. Each provincial department of tourism will supply a list of responsible operators and information such as this from Fisheries department personnel: http://new-brunswick.net/new-brunswick/whales/ethics.html. See provincial chapters for other contact information.

- **Get educated.** Finally, for more information on traveling lightly in general, check the websites of involved groups such as **Tread Lightly** (www.treadlightly.org) and the **World Wildlife Federation** (www.wwf.panda.org) to search for species such as the North Atlantic Right Whale.

TOURS

Learning Vacations

This type of vacation is one of the hottest tickets in the Maritimes. Check out visitor guides for truly unique things to do as well as organizations such as writers groups or arts organizations; environmental groups or museums; national and provincial parks—the opportunities are amazing. Programs range from half-day to a week on-site. These are just a few examples:

The **Gaelic College of Celtic Arts and Crafts,** St. Ann's, NS (www.gaelic college.edu; ✆ **902/295-3411**), offers programs for children and adults that specialize in local culture—such as Highland bagpiping, dancing, drumming, and Cape Breton fiddling—on its campus near Baddeck. The college also sometimes sponsors Road Scholar associated programs and trips, such as half-day fall walking trips on Cape Breton Island.

At **Kings Landing,** near Fredericton, NB (www.kingslanding.nb.ca; ✆ **506/363-4999**), children dress up in period costume and learn about how the early Loyalist settlers lived. The programs range from a few hours to a week, from early June through mid-October. Admission is charged to all visitors. Adult programs are also offered. This is all part of **edVentures** Fredericton, an umbrella program for a huge variety of disciplines ranging from running groups to jewelry and metalwork, from meditation to spirit dolls. Check it out at (www.edventures.ca/en/workshops; ✆ **888/850-1333**).

Sunbury Shores Arts & Nature Centre, St. Andrews, NB (www.sunburyshores. org; ✆ **506/529-3386**), offers day- and weeklong trips and classes on various topics: plant dyes, printmaking, mosaic work, raku pottery, and watercolor and oil painting. Some summer classes and programs are specially geared toward children and teenagers. The center is located on the water in St. Andrews; lodging can be arranged locally, as well.

At **Village Historique Acadien,** near Caraquet, NB (www.villagehistorique acadien.com; ✆ **877/721-2200** or 506/726-2600), the lives and arts of early Acadian settlers are the focus of programs held at a re-created historic village. The continuous program of events includes various skits, theatrical performances, storytelling sessions, and popular reenactments of typical events in the Acadian settlers' lives (such as the arrival of the mail, or the birth of a child). The historic village is open from early June through mid-September.

If you prefer to eat your way to satisfaction, Holland College and the Culinary Institute of Canada **Boot Camps** in Charlottetown, PEI (www.hollandcollege.com/boot camps; ✆ **902/566-9305**) have great opportunities for learning culinary skills. The college also offers camps on photography and even bird-watching and animation.

Adventure Travel

Adventure travel is now a growth industry in Eastern Canada, and specialized adventure tour outfitters can be helpful if you're arriving by air—it's simply too much trouble for most folks to fly with bikes, canoes, kayaks, and so forth. Here's a sampling of well-regarded outfitters operating in Canada's Maritime Provinces.

○ **Backroads,** Berkeley, CA (www.backroads.com; ✆ **800/462-2848** or 510/527-1555): One of North America's largest adventure travel companies offers, for example, walking and biking trips through southeast Nova Scotia, among other programs in the eastern provinces. Pick according to your budget and inclination: You can stay at luxury inns or opt for more rustic camping trips.

○ **Coastal Adventures,** Tangier, NS (www.coastaladventures.com; ✆ **877/404-2774** or 902/772-2774): Sea kayak expert Scott Cunningham and his staff lead great trips ranging from 2-day paddles to weeklong adventures throughout the Maritimes. Things like a Mushroom Foray or Fall Foliage Tours often get added to their offerings. Scott's a marine biologist and avid paddler who's been doing this for nearly 30 years; this is probably the top local outfit in Eastern Canada for a paddle. His wife, Gayle Wilson, assists with everything—including the kayaking. Coastal also runs a local B&B, which is known as Paddler's Retreat. Located in a rustic 1860s fisherman's home, it retains the character of the past.

- **Freewheeling Adventures,** Hubbards, NS (www.freewheeling.ca; C **800/672-0775** or 902/857-3600): This popular outfitter based near Halifax offers excellent guided biking, kayaking, and hiking tours throughout Nova Scotia, as well as on Prince Edward Island and two challenging, exceptionally scenic areas of Newfoundland. It's operated by Cathy Guest, a former competitive cycler, who has been doing this since 1987. Freewheeling also has a reputation for traveling lightly. It's top rate.

Guided Tours

You can alternately choose to take an escorted tour of Eastern Canada, a structured group tour with a leader. The price of this kind of tour usually includes everything from airfare to hotels, meals, tours, admission costs, and local transportation.

Despite the fact that these tours require big deposits—and predetermine all your hotels, restaurants, and itineraries—some travelers enjoy the structure they offer. Basically, you sit back and enjoy the trip without having to worry about planning (or local transportation). Be aware that such tours usually bring groups to a large number of famous sights in a short time, without lingering much. They're especially convenient for people with limited mobility, provide great introductions to the Maritimes, and can be a great way to make new friends. (On the downside, you get little opportunity for spontaneous interactions with locals; the tours tend to leave little room for individual sightseeing; and you won't see "off the beaten track" spots.)

The best way to find tours is to check with a travel agent. These two firms offer especially good escorted tours of Eastern Canada.

- **Maxxim Vacations,** St. John's, NF (www.maxximvacations.com; C **800/567-6666** or 709/754-6666): A big travel package outfit based in Newfoundland? Yes. The province's largest travel provider has a top-rate reputation and offers a huge range of trips throughout the four Atlantic Provinces, just as you'd expect, including plenty of both guided and unguided excursions. From a "PEI Golf Getaway" to a "Romantic New Brunswick" (thankfully unescorted) tour, Scott and Judy Sparkes' family-owned company offers it all, professionally and well. And the prices of your tours helpfully come with airfare from your home city already factored into the equation. Call and ask for their extensive and colorful brochure.

- **Collette Vacations,** Pawtucket, RI (www.collettevacations.com; C **800/340-5158**): Collette offers a number of excellent tours of Eastern Canada (about 10 days each, on average) that range from fly/drive packages to the escorted everything's-done-for-you variety throughout the Maritimes. Sample tour names include "Canada's Atlantic Coast Featuring the Cabot Trail" (touching three provinces), and "Hidden Treasures of the Maritimes" (which *does* bring in some lesser-known sights). Additional side trips are even possible on Collette tours for an extra fee, but note that your airfare isn't included in the quoted base package prices. In addition to the Rhode Island HQ, this company maintains satellite offices in suburban Toronto, Vancouver, and London—helpful if you happen to live in one of those three cities.

SUGGESTED ITINERARIES IN THE MARITIME PROVINCES

The eastern provinces of Canada are big, yet intimate. You can be a long way between major destinations only to find yourself suddenly overwhelmed with wonder when you happen upon a small wooden church, fish stand, a rock outcropping—and you end up staying longer there than you intended. It happens time and again.

So here are two pieces of advice. First, leave a bit of flexibility in your itinerary, because these provinces are full of unexpected surprises. You'd hate to leave Lunenburg without jumping onto a whale-watching boat, or right on the eve of the fisherman's festival, right? Second, allow time for the long drives. Except when on Prince Edward Island, you'll log a few hours on the road to complete these tours. The provinces are big, and fast multilane highways just don't cut it when a touring holiday is the objective. After all, you are in the Maritimes to savor and enjoy, not to whiz by the best of the region.

The range of possible itineraries in Eastern Canada is practically endless (you could do a kayaking itinerary, or a French-towns itinerary, for example), so I've laid out a few general tours that take in favorite places. Don't hesitate to venture off and seek out whatever tickles your fancy. Although distances may seem long, you are never far from the next treasure. Just use your map and common sense. Even a month is not enough to see all of the Maritime provinces, but these four itineraries touching on some of the "greatest hits" of each province should get you started.

LIGHTS OUT: THE BEST OF NOVA SCOTIA IN 1 WEEK

This tour takes in lighthouses, quaint villages, a surprisingly vibrant city, and dramatic headlands plunging to the ocean. Begin in Digby, landing point for ferries from Saint John, New Brunswick.

Days 1 & 2: The Southernmost Coast

Downtown Digby offers a great place to enjoy scallops—you may see the fishing fleet tied up across the water—as you can't get seafood any fresher than here. Do take time to check out the wharf's tiny cafe, which dishes up awesome scallops.

From Digby, turn south on Route 101 to Yarmouth. Hop over to Route 1 at St. Bernard for a scenic coastal drive past several little-known (thus almost always empty) beaches, and a charming French-speaking region. Take a short side trip down Route 304 to Cape Forchu and its awesome lighthouse just before entering **Yarmouth.** This compact port city offers a few diversions, such as a **Firefighters' Museum** (p. 64).

Drive east along Route 103 about 40km (25 miles) to the villages Pubnico (there are several–all in a row) to experience a real Acadian community and savor their cuisine with the locals at funky little eateries See p. 66. After another 60km (37 miles) along Route 103, exit the main highway to reach **Shelburne ★**. This compact little town has a fine **historic complex** with water views, a cooper, boatbuilders, a few small museums, and a favorite fish-and-chips stand aptly named **Mr. Fish.** See p. 67.

Continue another 120km (75 miles) east along Route 103 to the exit for Route 324; exit and continue about 10km (6¼ miles) east to . . .

Days 3 & 4: Mahone Bay ★★ and Lunenburg ★★

These cute twin harbor towns, separated by just a 15-minute drive, are easily worth 2 nights to explore together. You can explore remote peninsulas—preferably by bike—hit the links, visit a great museum, or book a kayak tour. Some wonderful bed-and-breakfasts are tucked into these towns, too. I like to time my visit to coincide with one of the summertime fisherman's, arts, or music festivals. See p. 70 for Lunenburg details and p. 76 for Mahone Bay.

While here, also be sure to follow Route 3 about 10km (6¼ miles) northeast of Mahone Bay to **Chester ★★** (p. 79). This little port town has a scenic, first-rate golf course or two, a little summer theater company, a clutch of restaurants, and a ferry service to nearby **Tancook Island.** (Get a schedule so you don't miss the last boat back.) It's worth a couple hours, for sure.

From Lunenburg, Mahone Bay, or Chester, head northeast along Route 3 or Route 103 about 24km (15 miles) to the turnoff for Route 333.

Days 5–7: The Halifax Region

Down Route 333 about 24km (15 miles) lies **Peggy's Cove ★★★**. This famously picturesque village features a lighthouse, glacial carved rocks born as molten lava and polished by crashing surf, a somber memorial to a plane crash, and more cute souvenirs than you can shake a stick at. Sure, you can take a tour bus from Halifax, but why not just visit it yourself on the drive up? It's worth an hour or two; bring cameras. See p. 82.

From Peggy's Cove, continue on Route 333 to **Halifax ★★★**. This is Nova Scotia's crown jewel, a place where live bands play nightly, buskers sing in the streets, and there's plenty of grog and museum-going to be had. It's not huge as cities go, but the lodging and dining alone make it worth several nights. Be sure to explore the Historic Properties linked by waterside boardwalks to the **Maritime Museum of the Atlantic** (p. 88), especially for the Titanic artifacts, and

Pier 21 (p. 89), for a look at the immigrant experience in Eastern Canada. Or just wander up and down **Spring Garden Road** and back and forth along **Barrington Street,** hunting for brewpubs, record shops, and old buildings. You *will* eat well.

Bored with the bright lights? Head for a remote beach down a nearby peninsula, such as **Crystal Crescent Beach;** there are plenty, but you'll need a map to find the way. And roads are a bit rough on the suspension.

HIGH TIMES, HIGH TIDES: THE BEST OF NEW BRUNSWICK IN 1 WEEK

New Brunswick is spread out; to see a piece of it quickly and compactly, this tour takes in the highlights of the southernmost New Brunswick coast, from the province's largest city to its biggest tidal drops. Begin at St. Andrews, the first significant destination beyond the Maine state line (assuming you've driven north from Maine. If you've flown into Saint John, see it first or last and tinker with the order below a bit.)

Days 1 & 2: St. Andrews ★★

This compact seaside town is the perfect stopping point after driving miles and miles of empty downeast Maine roads. It's worth at least a night for shopping and walking, another day and a night if you're intent on taking a whale-watching trip or other excursion from the harbor—or playing the **Algonquin Hotel's golf course** (p. 149), one of the top courses in Eastern Canada.

A day trip to the nearby islands, such as **Deer Island** or **Campobello** (p. 150), is always nice in summer.

From St. Andrews, continue about 19km (12 miles) northeast (do not backtrack) along Route 127 to Route 1, the main road. Then continue 80km (50 miles) along Route 1 to . . .

Days 3 & 4: Saint John ★

Saint John (spelled out, please) isn't the capital of New Brunswick, but it is the province's chief economic engine. The central square downtown is lovely, and good for hanging out in; you can also wander downtown's grid of streets, choosing from gourmet and mid-priced restaurants, or pubs with ale and live music, or indulge in nature along the city's many walking trails. See p. 163.

The **city market,** also downtown, is a must-visit if you like fresh produce and good food.

From Saint John, continue about 90km (56 miles) northeast along Route 1 to Route 114; turn south along Route 114 and continue 42km (26 miles) to its end, which puts you in . . .

Days 5 & 6: Fundy National Park ★★

One of the most surprising things you can do in New Brunswick is hightail it to **Fundy National Park** overlooking Chignecto Bay, where the world's highest tides are formed by the narrowing "V" of the **Bay of Fundy.** Ask for a map of scenic lookouts, trails, and programs as you enter the park. Alma, as you leave the park, has accommodations, restaurants, and such. Side trips to Cape Enrage and the weirdly shaped **Hopewell Rocks** are a must to understand the tides and what is so unique here. This area is worth a day or two with the family—you'll have to stay in rustic accommodations, however, as there are no true resorts around here—who can enjoy some time on the bike or a hike. See p. 183.

From the park, continue north along Route 114 80km (50 miles) to . . .

Day 7: Moncton

This city at the crossroads of the Maritimes is showing new signs of life. Stay the night and use the city as a base for a day trip, or else press on to the big park an hour away. See p. 189.

Head 80km (50 miles) north, following routes 115 and 11, passing the big **Dune of Bouctouche** en route to **Kouchibouguac National Park ★★** (p. 194), where you can canoe, bike, or kayak, and the flat land makes for easy walking (or picnicking on the beach). Return to Bouctouche or Moncton at night, or just camp overnight in the park.

From Moncton, you're just 80km (50 miles) from the bridge to Prince Edward Island (see next itinerary), or a few hours from further coastal exploring, or a 170km (106-mile) trip to Fredericton.

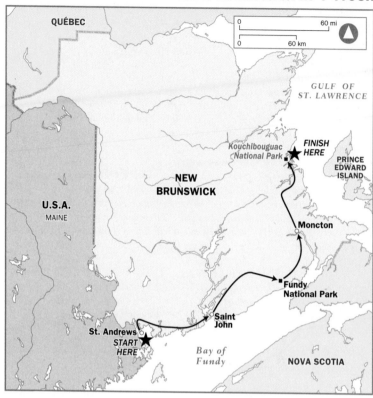

QUÉBEC

0   60 mi
0   60 km

GULF OF
ST. LAWRENCE

Kouchibouguac
National Park

**FINISH
HERE**

PRINCE
EDWARD
ISLAND

**NEW
BRUNSWICK**

U.S.A.
MAINE

Moncton

**Fundy
National Park**

**Saint
John**

St. Andrews
*START
HERE*

*Bay of
Fundy*

NOVA SCOTIA

REACHING THE BEACH: PRINCE EDWARD ISLAND FOR FAMILIES

This tour takes in a trifecta of the island's essential sights, giving each its due: Charlottetown, Anne's Land, and the lovely beaches of Prince Edward Island National Park. Kids will love all three places, and adults will feel a sense of tranquillity they may not have known in years.

Days 1 & 2: Victoria ★★ and Charlottetown ★★

From Confederation Bridge in Borden-Carleton, follow Route 1 east. Just past Crapaud, take a side trip to **Victoria** for a cute stop en route to the province's "big city." An hour or two and a cup of tea ought to do it, unless you're in the mood for some theater. See p. 244.

Take the Trans-Canada Highway 32km (20 miles) farther east to **Charlottetown.** The island's capital city has excellent restaurants, ins, B&Bs, a lot of history, and a plain friendly feel. Stay the night, or for . ral nights. Family activities here include the **Confederation Centre of the Arts** (p. 228), which offers an often-changing program of plays and performances (including an annual run of *Anne of Green Gables—The Musical*).

There are also excellent historic sites, shopping, and a surfeit of parks, plus a waterside boardwalk for walking. See p. 224.

From Charlottetown, follow signs west along Route 2 to Route 13, then turn north and follow Route 13 to . . .

Day 3: Anne's Land ★

The village of **New Glasgow** makes a good stop while heading to the island's north shore. There's a championship golf course, nice views from the country roads looping over hillsides, and the **Prince Edward Island Preserve** factory (p. 217), complete with a store and a good cafe. Everyone enjoys sampling the jams. Give this stop an hour or two to partake of some good food or if you just need a break from driving the slow island roads.

Continue north along Route 13 to **Cavendish** ★ (p. 210), the island's most tourist-friendly and developed area. The fictional redheaded Anne of Green Gables seems to be everywhere here, and some of the attractions related to her and the Anne books' authoress really are worth seeing—especially for young girls and their mothers. Not interested in all that? There are plenty of other touristy attractions for kids in and around the village, including amusement parks like the **Sandspit**.

Where to stay? Numerous "bungalow courts" (small cottage compounds) dot the area, some with cooking facilities, good for cooking up local lobster or mussels, and little playgrounds, though my first choice might be to pitch a tent in the national park (see next entry). This area is definitely worth a day or two with children.

From Cavendish, turn east on Route 6 and travel to Prince Edward Island National Park.

Days 4–6: Prince Edward Island National Seashore ★★★ & Souris ★

Some of the best beaches in Eastern Canada line the northern shores of Prince Edward Island. You'll surely want to spend a few days here with the family walking the beach, snapping photos of glorious sunsets and purple lupines against the red sand, camping among the dunes, hunting down obscure fish-and-chips shops, and just generally kicking back.

You'll find a wide range of accommodations in these parts, from Victorian resorts, to B&Bs, to well-maintained campgrounds (some with camping cabins), both within **Prince Edward Island National Park** and just outside it. Any family traveling in the Maritimes should camp together for at least a night; the quiet and fresh air should do you a world of good. The placid surroundings and warm waters here invite relaxation. While staying in and around the park, remember to take some scenic drives as well or explore the fishing and kayaking in North Rustico.

From the park, continue east on Route 6 to Route 2, turning east and continuing about 60 scenic kilometers (37 miles) through the towns of **Mount Stewart, Morell,** and **St. Peters** (the home of the Greenwich portion of PEI National Park and worth a stop).

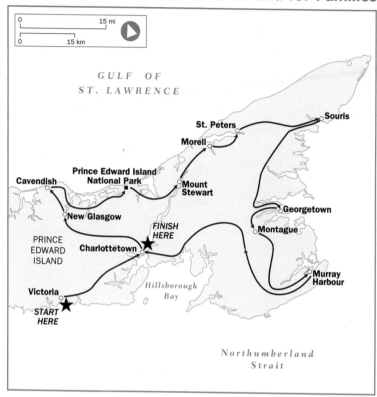

Finally you come to **Souris** (p. 240). Some outstanding inns, scenery, and beaches lie near the postage-stamp town. If you're an outdoors sort of family, rent yourselves a bike or three and go exploring. Visit the singing sands beach at Basin Head. Stay in a campground or in your pick of two of the island's most luxurious inns in the area.

On your way back to Charlottetown, nick the southeastern corner of PEI: Drop in on **Georgetown, Montague,** or **Murray Harbour,** each of which is worth a drive through (or even an overnight).

Locals are unfailingly nice throughout this island, an added bonus.

Return 80km (50 miles) along routes 2, 4, and 5 to . . .

Day 7: Charlottetown ★★, Once More

Charlottetown is worth a repeat visit while making a circuit of PEI. You probably didn't see everything on your first time through, anyway. Why not spend another night? Hit the **Confederation Court Mall** and wander the streets, snapping photos of the kids and looking for souvenirs for friends.

CAPE BRETON ISLAND: NATURAL ENCOUNTERS & CELTIC ENCHANTMENT

Crossing the causeway to Cape Breton puts you on the path toward one of the world's most beautiful drives. The Cabot Trail hugs the mountainous coast of the rugged northern highlands, a fitting crown for this land where Mother Nature did some of her best work, and Scottish and Acadian cultures create some of the best music you will ever hear. Consider taking this tour in the fall, when the trees are so magnificent they have their very own Celtic Colours International Festival, paying homage with music and feasting.

Day 1: Port Hastings to Margaree Harbour ★★

After crossing Canso Strait, take Route 19, also known as the **Ceilidh Trail,** into a region some say is more Celtic than Scotland itself. You may find bagpipes and fiddles, unique to Cape Breton music, Gaelic lore, the Mabou Highlands, beautiful beaches, scenery, and fishing villages, all of which will surely keep you at least 1 night. This is the land of the **Red Shoe Pub** (think Rankin family), the **Glenora Distillery** (a must-stop for a tour and tipple), and the **Inverness Miners Museum** (members.tripod.com/~Dongael/museum.htm, ℂ **902/258-3822**), all packed into 107km (66 miles). See p. 119 and 121.

Continue north until the Ceilidh Trail meets up with the Cabot Trail in Margaree Harbour. Choose the clockwise route towards Chéticamp and . . .

Days 2 & 3: Cape Breton Highlands National Park ★★★

At Chéticamp, decide what experiences to enjoy in this magnificent park and book accommodations accordingly. In addition to a scenic drive recognized as one of the world's best, the park offers superb hiking trails and programs. Pleasant Bay is just 44km (27 miles) from Chéticamp. While in Pleasant Bay, make a stop at the **Whale Interpretation Centre** or to take photographs. Whale-watching tours depart from here, as well as from many other communities along this northern island's coast. Until this point, you have been traveling along the Gulf of St. Lawrence side of Cape Breton. Now the road turns east toward the Atlantic Ocean. Ingonish marks the exit from the park, but not the scenery, beaches, golf, or natural attractions. Stop to enjoy the majestic view of Cape Smokey rising out of the sea, and Keltic Lodge. See p. 139.

Continue following the Cabot Trail to Baddeck. Note that the Cabot Trail (CT) joins the Trans-Canada Highway (Rte. 105) to go to Baddeck.

Day 4: Baddeck ★

More Scottish immersion is yours in St. Ann's at the **Great Hall of the Clans.** Once you have savored the tale of the great migration to Cape Breton, head for the **Alexander Graham Bell National Historic Site** and an overnight in the charming town of Baddeck. See p. 130.

Retrace your steps up Route 105, to Route 125, then Route 4 to . . .

Days 5 & 6: Glace Bay & Fortress Louisbourg ★★★

If you prefer a less direct route to visit North Sydney or Sydney (ferry terminals for Newfoundland), check your map. Otherwise, Glace Bay with its **Miners'**

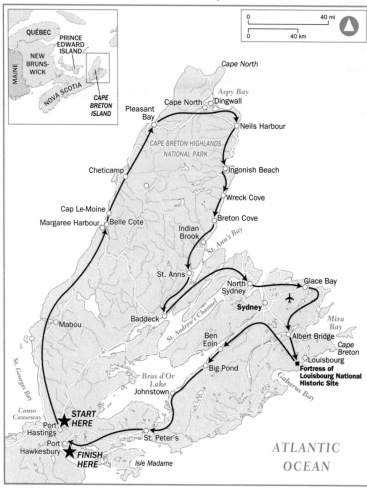

Museum and **Marconi National Historic Site** is the next stop. If you have lots of time, pick up Route 255 for a meandering coastal drive to Louisbourg, or the more direct Route 22 (about 65km/40 miles) for more time at **Fortress of Louisbourg National Historic Site,** a living history experience which can easily take up a day or more. See p. 137.

A 200km (124-mile) drive will take you back to Canso straight from Louisbourg. Take Route 22 to Route 4, which will take you back to the causeway over the Straight of Canso.

Day 7: Bras d'Or Lake ★

The final leg of your Cape Breton Tour runs beside Bras d'Or Lake, a playground for magnificent eagles and sailors. Stop at **Rita's Tea Room** in Big Pond for

Here's a great tip if you're planning to be in the Maritimes awhile and visit its national parks and national historic sites: You can now buy a **Parks Canada Discovery Pass** ★★★ for C$68 per adult or C$136 per family, plus tax. This pass gains you access to national parks, national marine conservation areas, and national historic sites across Canada for 1 full year. Passes for National Historic Sites only are available for approximately 25% less.

Buy the pass right at the entrance of the first national park or historic site you visit. For more info, see the "Parks Canada National Passes" section of the Parks Canada website at .pc.gc.ca.

home-style goodies and the skinny on Rita MacNeil, one of the Maritime's most beloved songstresses. St. Peter's Canal, with its 140-year-old tidal lock system, is a pleasant place to stretch your legs. See p. 133.

NOVA SCOTIA

With 7,400km (4,598 miles) of coastline, it's no wonder Nova Scotia is dubbed Canada's ocean playground. It is blessed with rolling hills, flowing rivers, stunning headlands, and beautiful beaches, all within manageable distances.

Halifax, with quality hotels, dining, entertainment, and shopping, is a good jumping-off point for exploring places like Cape Breton, where you're sure to see the Gaelic greeting, *Ciad Mile Failte*. Translated to "one hundred thousand welcomes," it reflects Nova Scotia's glad-to-see-you appeal.

Sightseeing This province is best appreciated by driving it. **Cape Breton's Highlands** are ranked among the country's top scenic drives; the **Bay of Fundy** is one of the top natural wonders in the world. With accommodations ranging from full resorts to campsites beside the sea, plotting a trip to feed your passions is easy. It's the leaving when your time is up that is difficult.

Eating and Drinking World-class chefs, particularly in bustling **Halifax,** are heavily committed to a "Taste of Nova Scotia" program. Traditional fare—Acadian or Scottish menus, takeout by the wharf, lobster boils at the beach—from down-home style cooks ensures delicious, fulfilling experiences. Freshly harvested seafood is the province's showcase, but drink is an often overlooked prime offering: award-winning wineries, microbreweries, distillers, and the production of North America's first single malt whisky prove it shouldn't be.

History With habitation dating back to 1605, there is much to see and savor. This is not a place of dusty artifacts behind glass. Interactive museums and historic sites reveal past conflicts and challenges through interpreters at **Annapolis Royal, Fortress Louisbourg,** and the **Halifax Citadel.** Daily life of founding cultures can be experienced at **Ross Family Farm, Acadian** and **Highland Villages,** or onboard a fishing vessel in **Lunenburg.** Natural history goes back millions of years to the time of mastodons and dinosaurs.

Nature Whether visiting with whales, riding the ocean surf, or watching sea birds fishing for dinner, the ocean that surrounds Nova Scotia is both a natural habitat and playground. What better way to savor the mountains of the highlands than to bike in their midst, to camp in a dark sky preserve, or to capture a soaring eagle or delicate orchid in your camera lens? The options to explore here are endless: Lace up your hiking boots to hunt fossils or ride the waves of the highest tides in the world.

EXPLORING NOVA SCOTIA

Visitors to Nova Scotia should spend a little time poring over a map and the province's visitor guide before leaving home. It's a good idea to narrow down your options, because numerous loops, circuits, and side trips are possible here—and the permutations only multiply once you factor in various ferry links to New Brunswick, Prince Edward Island, and Newfoundland. You don't want to spread yourself *too* thin. So figuring out where to go—and how to get there—is the hardest work you'll need to do in a place that is quite easy to travel around once you've arrived there.

The only travelers who complain about Nova Scotia are those who tried to see it all in a week. That sort of approach could leave you strung out and tired. Instead, prioritize your interests and decide accordingly.

Looking for picture-perfect scenes of coastal villages? Focus mostly on the South Shore, specifically the holy trinity of Chester, Lunenburg, and Mahone Bay. Drawn to hiking amid dramatic, rocky coastal vistas? Allow plenty of time for Cape Breton Island. Looking for more pastoral ocean scenery? Head for the Fundy Coast. Want to spend a quiet day canoeing? Build your trip around Kejimkujik National Park. Dying for some gourmet dining and urban buzz? Factor in a couple days in Halifax.

Above all, schedule time for simply doing not much of anything. Strolling or biking along quiet lanes; picnicking on a beach; and watching the tides from docks, boat decks, and hotel porches are the best ways to let Nova Scotia's charms sink in at their own unhurried pace.

Essentials

VISITOR INFORMATION Every traveler to Nova Scotia should get a copy of the massive (almost 400-page) official tourism guide. It's comprehensive, colorful, well-organized, and free, listing most hotels, campgrounds, and attractions within the province, plus brief descriptions and current prices. (Restaurants are given only limited coverage, however; investigate those using this book and your own nose for eats.)

The tome, called the *Nova Scotia Doers' & Dreamers' Guide*, becomes available each year around March. Contact the province by Internet (www.novascotia.com), phone (© **800/565-0000** or 902/424-5000), or mail (Nova Scotia Department of Tourism, Culture, and Heritage, P.O. Box 456, Halifax, NS B3J 2R5).You can wait until you arrive in the province to obtain the visitor's guide, of course. But then you won't be able to do much advance planning.

The provincial government administers about a dozen official **Visitor Information Centres** (known as "VICs") throughout the province, as well as in Portland and Bar Harbor, Maine. These mostly seasonal centers are amply stocked with brochures and tended by knowledgeable staffers. In addition, virtually every town of any note has a local tourist information center filled with racks of brochures covering the entire province, staffed with local people who know the area. You won't ever be short of information. Also be sure to request the province's excellent free road map, which will begin to give you a sense of how few roads there actually are here. (What the map *doesn't* convey is that driving places takes time here.)

In general, the local and provincial visitor information centers are run with cordiality and brisk efficiency. I have yet to come across a single one that wasn't remarkably helpful, although the press of crowds can sometimes require a few minutes' wait to get individual attention at the more popular stops, such as Amherst (outside Halifax) or Port Hastings (entering Cape Breton Island).

For general questions about travel in the province, call **Nova Scotia's informa-tion hot line** at © **800/565-0000** (North America) or 902/424-5000 (outside North America).

GETTING THERE

BY CAR & FERRY   Most travelers reach Nova Scotia overland by car from New Brunswick. Plan on at least a 4-hour drive from the U.S. border at Calais, Maine, to Amherst (at the New Brunswick–Nova Scotia border). Incorporating a ferry into your itinerary can reduce time behind the wheel if you catch the ferry across the Bay of Fundy, which works as long as that is where you are going.

To shorten the long drive around the Bay of Fundy, the 3-hour ferry (operated by Bay Ferries), known as the *Princess of Acadia*, links **Saint John, New Brunswick,** with **Digby, Nova Scotia.** Remarkably, this ferry sails daily year-round, with two sailings per day during peak travel periods. In 2011, the peak season one-way fare (June–Oct) was C$41 for adults, C$26 for children age 6 to 13, C$5 per child under age 6, and C$31 for students and seniors. Your car costs an additional C$82 (more for motor homes, trucks, vans, and buses), plus a C$20 fuel surcharge. Fares are a bit cheaper outside the peak travel months. If you walk on and return within 30 days, there are discounts available on the round-trip. Complete up-to-the-minute sched-ules and fares for the *Princess of Acadia* can be found at www.nfl-bay.com or by calling © **877/762-7245.**

For those traveling farther afield, ferries also connect Prince Edward Island to Caribou, Nova Scotia (see chapter 6 for more detailed information), and Newfound-land to North Sydney, Nova Scotia.

Also note that you can view the latest **updated highway conditions** around the province of Nova Scotia by logging onto the province's transportation website at http://511.gov.ns.ca/map. This map shows both road construction projects and unusual weather conditions affecting traffic flow.

BY PLANE   Halifax is the air hub of the Atlantic Provinces. **Air Canada** (www.aircanada.com; © **888/247-2262**) provides daily direct service from New York and Boston using its commuter partner, **Jazz** (www.flyjazz.ca), which also flies directly to Sydney, Charlottetown, Saint John, and St. John's, as well as several more remote destinations in Eastern Canada. But other contenders are jumping into the fray, as well: **Continental** (www.continental.com; © **800/231-0856**) flies direct from Newark to Halifax several times daily in summer, for one.

Several airlines fly into Halifax from points within Canada, including Air Canada and **WestJet** (www.westjet.com; © **888/937-8538**), connecting to several points in Ontario, as well as all other provinces. Regional carriers such as Jazz connect with cities throughout the region (see above). Porter Airlines (www.flyporter.com; © **888/619-8622**) connects with Ontario, Quebec, Newfoundland, and several U.S. cities.

BY TRAIN   **VIA Rail** (www.viarail.ca; © **888/842-7245**) offers train service 6 days a week on the *Ocean* run between Halifax and Montréal; the entire trip takes between 18 and 21 hours depending on direction, with a basic summertime fare of about C$200 each way, not counting sleeping accommodations. VIA Rail connects with AMTRAK in Montréal and trains to Vancouver in Toronto. Seasonal discounts, special fares, and such make it very worthwhile to start shopping early, and to be flexible about the day of the week you travel.

Nova Scotia

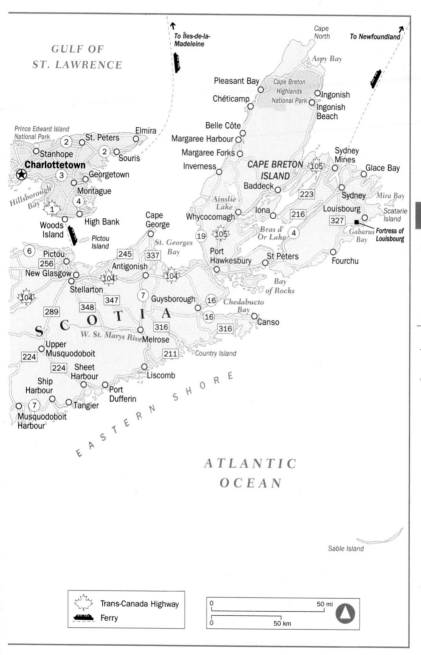

GULF OF
ST. LAWRENCE

To Îles-de-la-Madeleine

Cape North

To Newfoundland

Aspy Bay

Pleasant Bay

Cape Breton Highlands National Park

Chéticamp

Ingonish

Ingonish Beach

Prince Edward Island National Park

Elmira

Belle Côte

Margaree Harbour

St. Peters

2

Stanhope

Souris

2

Margaree Forks

Sydney Mines

Charlottetown

3

Georgetown

Inverness

CAPE BRETON ISLAND

105

Glace Bay

Montague

4

Baddeck

223

Sydney

Mira Bay

Hillsborough Bay

1

Ainslie Lake

Iona

216

Louisbourg

Scatarie Island

High Bank

Cape George

Whycocomagh

Woods Island

6

Pictou

Pictou Island

St. Georges Bay

19

105

Bras d' Or Lake

4

327

Gabarus Bay

Fortress of Louisbourg

St Peters

256

245

337

Port Hawkesbury

Fourchu

New Glasgow

Antigonish

104

Bay of Rocks

Stellarton

104

104

16

Chedabucto Bay

104

347

7

Guysborough

Canso

289

348

S C O T I A

16

316

316

W. St. Marys River

Melrose

224

Upper Musquodoboit

211

Country Island

224

Sheet Harbour

Liscomb

Ship Harbour

Port Dufferin

7

Tangier

Musquodoboit Harbour

E A S T E R N   S H O R E

ATLANTIC OCEAN

Sable Island

Trans-Canada Highway

Ferry

0   50 mi

0   50 km

Sleeping berths and private cabins are available at extra cost—the cheapest bed, in a double-bunked cabin, is about twice the cost of the no-bed fare—and VIA has created an even higher class of service (summer-only) known as the Sleeper Touring class aboard the *Ocean*. This class offers all-inclusive meals, sleeping accommodations, exclusive access to lounges and a panoramic car, and continuing presentations from an onboard educator about Maritime Province culture and history.

The *Ocean* runs daily (except Tues) each direction year-round, with standard overnight sleeper-cabin service; the Easterly option is available from mid-June through mid-October. Check the VIA Rail website for updates on routes, schedules, and online booking.

THE GREAT OUTDOORS

Nova Scotia's terrific official travel guide (the aforementioned *Doers' & Dreamers' Guide*) contains a very helpful "Outdoors" section in the back that's full of detailed listings of camping outfitters, bike shops, whale-watching tour operators, and the like. More specific information on the province's adventure outfitters can also be obtained from the trade association for providers, the **Nova Scotia Adventure Tourism Association,** 1099 Marginal Rd., Ste. 201, Halifax, NS B3H 4P7 (© **800/948-4267** or 902/423-4480).

BIKING The low hills and gentle, mostly empty roads of mainland Nova Scotia make for wonderful cycling. Cape Breton Island is the most challenging of the province's destinations; the south coast and Bay of Fundy regions yield wonderful ocean views while making fewer cardiovascular demands on the cyclist. A number of bike outfitters can aid in your trip planning. **Freewheeling Adventures** (www.freewheeling.ca; © **800/672-0775** or 902/857-3600) is highly recommended for its guided bike tours throughout Nova Scotia (as well as Prince Edward Island). Want to go it alone? Walter Sienko's guide, *Nova Scotia & the Maritimes by Bike: 21 Tours Geared for Discovery* (1995) is very helpful in planning a local bike excursion—though you don't need to follow all his recommended routes (they mostly stick to busier main roads). Order it from an online bookseller.

Also, for a good Internet introduction to cycling in Nova Scotia and beyond, point your Web browser to the website of **Atlantic Canada Cycling** (www.atlantic canadacycling.com) and click on "Tour Planning" for brief introductions to the regions of Nova Scotia and their respective characteristics (including strength of local winds). The site also offers group bicycle tours and events, and sells books and maps.

BIRD-WATCHING More than 400 species of birds have been spotted in Nova Scotia, ranging from odd and exotic birds blown off course in storms, to majestic **bald eagles.** Nova Scotia gained the distinction of having the highest concentration of breeding bald eagles in northeastern North America in 1975; by the mid-'80s, numbers were robust enough to supply eaglets to the northeastern United States to rebuild their population. The highest concentration is seen around Bras d'Or Lakes in the summer. In late January, eagle-watchers flock to Sheffield Mills in the Annapolis Valley on the Bay of Fundy. The populations there are estimated to be approaching 1,000 birds. Many whale-watching tours also offer specialized seabird-spotting tours, including trips to **puffin colonies.**

CAMPING With backcountry options rather limited, Nova Scotia's forte is drive-in camping. The 20 or so provincial parks offer some 1,500 campsites among them, and campgrounds are uniformly clean, friendly, well managed, and reasonably priced. For a brochure and map listing all provincial campsites, contact the **Nova Scotia Department of Natural Resources/Parks and Recreation Division** (© 902/ 662-3030). The division's website is located at **www.gov.ns.ca/natr/parks** and is well organized. Also try **www.novascotiaparks.ca**. As usual, the province's *Doers' & Dreamers' Guide* contains the fullest campground listings available in print. It is wise to make advance reservations at provincial or national parks during the summer.

Also check with the Campground Owners Association of Nova Scotia: Its website at **www.campingnovascotia.com** lists a number of privately held campgrounds. The free and helpful *Campers Guide,* available at visitor information centers, lists this information, as well.

CANOEING Nova Scotia offers an abundance of accessible canoeing on inland lakes and ponds. The premier destination is **Kejimkujik National Park** in the southern interior, which has plenty of backcountry sites accessible by canoe. You can even trace traditional trading routes of the Mi'kmaq—check in with park staff for details. A number of other fine canoe trips allow paddlers and portagers to venture off for hours or days. General information on paddling routes, classes, events, and local clubs is available from the organization **Canoe Kayak Nova Scotia,** 5516 Spring Garden Rd., 4th floor, Halifax, NS B3J 1G6 (© **902/425-5454,** ext. 316). The group's website can be found at **www.ckns.ca**.

FISHING Saltwater fishing tours are easily arranged on charter boats berthed at many of the province's harbors. Inquire locally at visitor information centers or consult the "Boat Tours & Charters" section of the *Doers' & Dreamers' Guide.* No fishing license is required for *most* saltwater species for those on charters. For questions, current fishing regulations, or lists of licensed fishing guides, check out the Nova Scotia **Department of Fisheries and Aquaculture** website at **www.gov.ns.ca/fish**.

Committed freshwater anglers come to Nova Scotia in pursuit of the tragically dwindling Atlantic salmon, which requires a license separate from that for other freshwater fish. **Salmon licenses** must be obtained from a provincial office, campground, or licensed outfitter. Other freshwater species popular with anglers are brown trout, shad, smallmouth bass, rainbow trout, and speckled trout. Again, for up-to-date information contact the Department of Fisheries and Aquaculture (see above).

GOLF Nova Scotia lays claim to more than 50 golf courses. Among the most memorable are the government-owned **Highlands Links** (www.highlandslinksgolf. com; © **800/441-1118** or 902/285-2600) course in Ingonish Beach, which features a dramatic oceanside setting, and **Bell Bay Golf Club** (www.bellbaygolfclub.com; © **800/565-3077** or 902/295-1333) near Baddeck—which is also wonderfully scenic and has appeared in *Golf Digest*. Highland Links costs C$91 plus tax for 18 holes in peak season; Bell Bay, C$79 for 18 holes in peak season. Both cost less during spring and fall, and Sunday or twilight rates are sometimes also available.

While the big names are fun, I prefer playing some of the less famous courses around the province. (And, yes that is a hint about my proficiency as a golfer.) The **Bluenose Golf Club** (© **902/634-4260**) has been operating on a beautiful tract of land known as Kaulbach Head overlooking Lunenburg's harbor since 1933. (It's visible in the distance from almost any point in the old town.) The short, 4,823m (5,275-yard) tract plays harder than it looks because of numerous slopes and side-hill lies. Views of the ocean and town are stupendous on both the starting and finishing holes; peak-season greens fees are just C$28 for 9 holes, C$45 for 18 holes (carts cost extra); and the clubhouse grill serves up mighty fine burgers and beers on tap. Rent at least a pull-cart to deal with the hills.

Two more nicely scenic tracts open to the public in Nova Scotia are the **Chester Golf Club** (www.chestergolfclub.ca; © **902/275-4543**), with amazing ocean views and fine course maintenance (C\$35 for 9 holes, C\$59 for 18 holes); and hilly, beautiful **Osprey Ridge** (www.ospreyridge.ns.ca; © **902/543-6666**) near Shelburne, designed by the noted course architect Graham Cooke and opened in 1999, which costs C\$35 weekdays and C\$30 to C\$55 on weekends.

New courses are always being constructed, too. For one-stop shoppers, **Golf Nova Scotia** (www.golfnovascotia.com; © **866/404-3224**), run by the tourism office, represents about 30 well-regarded properties around the province and can arrange customized golfing packages at its member courses. A handy directory of Nova Scotia's golf courses (with phone numbers) is published as a separate brochure and in the "Outdoors" section of the *Doers' & Dreamers' Guide* as well.

HIKING & WALKING   Serious hikers make tracks for **Cape Breton Highlands National Park,** which is home to the most dramatic terrain in the province. But other options abound—trails are found throughout Nova Scotia, although in some cases they're a matter of local knowledge. (Ask at the visitor information centers.) Published hiking guides are widely available at local bookstores. Especially helpful are the back-pocket-size guides published by **Nimbus Publishing;** call for a catalog (www.nimbus.ns.ca; © **800/646-2879** or 902/454-7404).

SAILING   Any area with so much convoluted coastline is clearly inviting to sailors and gunkholers. Tours and charters are available almost everywhere there's a decent-size harbor. The province's premier sailing experience for the non-sailor is an excursion aboard the *Bluenose II,* which is virtually an icon for Atlantic Canada and calls at Halifax, Lunenburg, and other ports. (See the "Lunenburg" section, later in this chapter.) Bras d'Or Lakes are very popular with sailing fans. A much more extensive listing of boat tour operators can be found in the "Outdoor Tours: Boat Tours & Charters" section of the *Doers' & Dreamers' Guide.* Skilled sailors will want to check in with the Nova Scotia Yachting Association. They have a race schedule, events, and sailing and cruising school information at www.nsya.ns.ca.

SEA KAYAKING   Nova Scotia's 7,600km (4,722 miles) of coastline is increasingly attracting the attention of kayakers worldwide. Sea kayak excursions are especially rewarding when seals, puffins, or porpoises come alongside. Kayakers traveling on their own should be especially cautious on the Bay of Fundy side; the massive tides create strong currents that overmatch even the fittest of paddlers. More than a dozen kayak outfitters do business in Nova Scotia, offering everything from 1-hour introductory paddles to intensive weeklong trips; once again, consult the directory in the *Doers' & Dreamers' Guide.*

Among the most respected outfitters is **Coastal Adventures,** P.O. Box 77, 84 Mason's Point Rd., Tangier, NS B0J 3H0 (www.coastaladventures.com; © **877/404-2774** or 902/772-2774). The company is run by veteran kayaker and doctorate-in-biology Dr. Scott Cunningham, who leads trips throughout the Maritimes and Newfoundland. For kayaking on the eastern side of Cape Breton, check with **North River Kayak,** R.R. #4, Baddeck, NS B0E 1B0 (www.northriverkayak.com; © **888/865-2925** or 902/929-2628). Owner Angelo Spinazzola is a native Cape Bretoner and a professional musician with several CDs to his credit; he's been running this award-winning outfit for more than a decade.

WHALE-WATCHING   When on the Nova Scotia coast, you're never far from a whale-watching operation. Around two dozen such tour outfits offer trips in search of finback, humpback, pilot, and minke whales, among others. The richest waters for whale-watching are on the Fundy Coast and Cape Breton. Fundy Bay is where the endangered right whale is often seen feeding in summer; thus, Digby Neck (the thin strand of land extending southwest from the town of Digby) has the highest concentration of whale-watching excursions in the province, but you'll find them in many other coves and harbors, as well. Pods of pilot whales on the Atlantic coast are a sight to behold. Ask staff at local visitor information centers to direct you to the whales, or check the provincial tourism guide, which contains a very good listing of whale-watchers.

CHIGNECTO BAY, MINAS BASIN & COBEQUID BAY

If you're only truly content when getting off the beaten track, a jaunt along the Minas Basin and Cobequid Bay might be one of the highlights of your trip to Nova Scotia. With the exception of Truro, this region is rural, quiet, and full of hidden surprises. You can turn down a dirt road, shut off your car's engine, and not hear much other than the wind and some birds. You can trek along spectacular hiking trails or picnic alone on a long stretch of remote and misty coast, literally watching the tides roll in—and you may well be alone. Tourists haven't wised up to this region yet.

There's a rich history here, though it tends to be hidden and subtle rather than preening and obvious. Don't look for the quaint seaside villages or the surf-washed rocky coast for which Nova Scotia is famous, either; that will have to wait until you get to Yarmouth and the South Shore. The natural drama here is pegged to the region's profound remoteness and the powerful but silent tides, among the highest in the world.

Wolfville ★

The trim Victorian village of Wolfville (pop. 3,800) has a distinctively New England feel to it, both in its handsome architecture and its compact layout—a small commercial downtown just 6 blocks long is surrounded by shady neighborhoods of

---

   A Scenic Drive

If you're headed from the Truro area southwestward along the Fundy Coast toward Digby, **Route 215** offers a wonderful **coastal detour ★** from Maitland to Windsor. This winding, fast, and rather narrow road (which is not recommended for bicyclists) passes through a number of quiet hamlets, some with handsome early buildings. But the chief appeal comes in the sudden vistas of lush green farmland (often accompanied by the redolent smells of cow

byproduct) and broad views of Minas Basin beyond. At the town of Walton, there's a handsome lighthouse on a rocky bluff with a nearby picnic area just off the main route (it's well marked). This detour runs about 90km (56 miles) from South Maitland to Brooklyn. Few services for tourists are offered along this route, other than a handful of restaurants, B&Bs, and campgrounds. Look for general stores and farm stands if you need a snack.

elegant homes. And it's not hard to trace that sensibility back to its source: The area was largely populated in the wake of the American Revolution by transplanted New Englanders, following the expulsion of the original Acadian settlers by the British.

The town's mainstay these days is handsome **Acadia University,** which has nearly as many full-time students as there are residents of Wolfville. The university's presence gives the small town an edgier, more youthful air. Don't miss the university's **Art Gallery** ★ (http://gallery.acadiau.ca; ✆ 902/585-1373), which showcases both contemporary and historical Nova Scotian art; it's located at 10 Highland Ave. (at the corner of Main St.) and is open Tuesday through Sunday from noon to 4pm, year-round. Admission is free.

EXPLORING WOLFVILLE

Strolling through the village is a good way to spend a half-day; the towering elms and maples that shade the extravagant Victorian architecture make for an ideal walk. Begin at the **Wolfville Tourist Bureau** (✆ 877/999-7117 or 902/542-7000) at 11 Willow Ave. (in Willow Park) on the northern edge of the downtown area; it's open daily from mid-April through October. Also be sure to check out the local tourism website at **www.wolfville.ca/visitors.** For a good printable map of Wolfville's downtown area, go to **www.downtownwolfville.com** and click on "Maps & Guides."

My memories of Wolfville include beautiful rhododendrons. Twelve were planted in the first **Peace Park,** representing the ten provinces and two territories. The nearby train station at 21 Elm Ave. is now a National Historic Site, and home to the **Wolfville Memorial Library** (www.valleylibrary.ca; ✆ 902/542-5760).

At **Blomidon Provincial Park** (parks.gov.ns.ca; ✆ 902/584-2332), 24km (15 miles) north of Route 101 (exit 11), some 14km (8.7 miles) of trail take walkers through forest and along the coast. Among the most dramatic trails is the 6km (3.7-mile) **Jodrey Trail** ★, which follows towering cliffs that offer broad views over the Minas Basin. It's open from mid-May through early October.

For a more demanding adventure, head north of Wolfville about 25 minutes on Route 358 and park off the side of the road near the beginning of the **Cape Split Trail** ★. This 16km (10-mile) trail offers some of the more breathtaking vistas in Nova Scotia, specifically cresting oceanside cliffs that approach 122m (400 ft.) in height. Allow most of a day to truly enjoy an in-and-back excursion on this hook of land that extends far into the Bay of Fundy.

EXPLORING GRAND-PRÉ

A side trip to neighboring Grand-Pré will happily fill a day and enhance your appreciation of the area and its Acadian heritage. Horticulturalists in particular should allow time to savor the area. The **Grand Pré Winery,** with its **LeCaveau Restaurant** ★★★ at 11611 Hwy. 1, Grand-Pré (www.grandprewines.ns.ca; ✆ 902/542-1753), specializes in lively celebration of food and drink. Just down the road, at 11827 Hwy. 1, Grand-Pré, the **Tangled Garden** (www.tangledgarden.ns.ca; ✆ 902/542-9811) transforms herbs and fruit into jewel-like jellies and vinegars. Their jars and bottles glisten in the sun, and taste as good as they look. Visit the gardens, labyrinth, gallery, and shop.

Grand-Pré National Historic Site ★   Hardworking Acadians vastly altered the local landscape, in large part by constructing a series of dikes outfitted with ingenious log valves, which allowed farmers to convert the saltwater marshes to productive farmland. At Grand-Pré, a short drive east of Wolfville just off Route 1, you can learn about these dikes, along with the history of the Acadians who populated the Minas

Basin from 1680 until their expulsion in 1755. More a memorial park than a history exhibit, Grand-Pré ("great meadow") features superbly tended grounds excellent for picnics or contemplative strolls. Among the handful of buildings on the grounds is a graceful stone church, built in 1922 on the presumed site of the original Acadian church. Evangeline Bellefontaine, the revered (albeit fictional) heroine of Longfellow's epic poem *Evangeline,* was said to have been born here; look for the tragic heroine's iconic statue in the garden, created in 1920 by Canadian sculptor Philippe Hérbert.

2241 Grand-Pré Rd. (P.O. Box 150), Grand-Pré B0P 1M0. www.grand-pre.com. ✆ **902/542-4040.** Admission C$7.80 adults, C$6.55 seniors, C$3.90 children age 6–16, C$20 families. Mid-May to mid-Oct daily 9am–6pm. Closed mid-Oct to mid-May.

WHERE TO STAY

Gingerbread House Inn ★   Ornate and brightly painted, thanks to a former owner who added all manner of swirly accouterments, the Gingerbread House Inn was originally a carriage house. Most guest rooms are an updated, modern interpretation of the gingerbread style and quite comfortable, though the two units in the back are darker and smaller than the rest. Each room has an exterior entrance, adding to the privacy, and each is unique: The airy Gaspereau suite has a modern-city loft feel, with luxe touches such as a sleek propane fireplace, big-screen television, and big eight-person hot tub beneath a mural of a lake. But the Country and Sunrise suites are much more, well, gingerbread, with their exposed unvarnished wood, throw rugs, rocking chairs and the like. Even some of the simpler rooms sport hot tubs. Breakfasts are elaborate.

8 Robie Tufts Dr. (P.O. Box 819), Wolfville, NS B4P 1X1. www.gingerbreadhouse.ca. ✆ **888/542-1458** or 902/542-1458. Fax 902/542-4718. 7 units. May–Oct C$120–C$129 double; C$175–C$205 suite; Nov–Apr C$95–C$115 double; C$140–C$199 suite. Rates include full breakfast. Ask about golf packages. AE, MC, V. No children permitted in suites. **Amenities:** Dining room. No Internet service for guests. *In room:* A/C, TV, DVD, fireplace, Jacuzzi (some), no phone.

Harwood House Bed & Breakfast ★   This former doctor's residence is downtown, beside Acadia University—in fact, when it was built in 1923 on a sloping lawn adjacent to the campus, it was built for then university provost Frank "Pa" Wheelock. Later home to a popular local family doctor, it was converted to an inn in 1999. The Juckers are warm and helpful, extending kindnesses far beyond those normally required of inn hosts; they even speak French and Swiss. Three queen-size-bedded rooms here are simple but airy, with white and floral linens and prints—the Glooscap unit is perhaps the best of the lot, overlooking the campus (though its private bathroom sits across the hall).

33 Highland Ave., Wolfville, NS B4P 1Y9. www.harwoodhouse.com. ✆ **877/897-0156** or 902/542-5707. 3 units, 1 with separate bathroom. C$120–C$175 double; off-season discounts available. Packages available. Rates include full breakfast. MC, V. *In room:* TV (2 units), no phone, Wi-Fi (free).

Tattingstone Inn ★★   This handsome Italianate-Georgian mansion is a registered heritage property dating from 1874. Decorated with a deft touch that mixes informal country antiques with regal Empire pieces, the carriage house rooms are a little smaller than in the main house, but still pleasant—and they showcase fine examples of modern Canadian art. Ask about the blue-and-cream "Toad Hall" room in the carriage house if you want privacy: There's a living room downstairs while the upstairs sports a queen-size bed and two-person Jacuzzi. The Tattingstone's spacious, semi-formal dining room is refined; diners eat off white tablecloths beneath stern

Doric columns. The heated outdoor pool is a bonus, as is the enclosed sun porch, which nicely captures the lambent early evening light.

620 Main St. (P.O. Box 98), Wolfville, NS B4P 1E8. www.tattingstone.ns.ca. ☎ **800/565-7696** or 902/542-7696. 9 units. July–Oct C$128–C$178 double; Nov–June C$98–C$165 double. Rates include full breakfast. AE, MC, V. **Amenities:** Restaurant; Internet; outdoor pool; steam room; tennis court. *In room:* A/C, TV/VCR, hair dryer, Wi-Fi (free), Jacuzzi (some), fireplace (some), no phone.

Victoria's Historic Inn ★★ Victoria's Historic Inn was constructed by apple mogul William Chase in 1893, and remains architecturally elaborate today. The sturdy Queen Anne–style building features bold pediments and pavilions adorned with balusters and ornate Stick-style trim. Inside, it feels like you've wandered into a Victorian parlor. There's dense mahogany and cherry woodwork throughout, along with some exceptionally intricate ceilings. Several of the inn's suites have fireplaces and Jacuzzis. The deluxe two-room Chase Suite (the most expensive unit), for instance, features a large sitting room with a gas fireplace, double Jacuzzi, queen-size bed, and an oak mantle. Less expensive third-floor rooms are smaller and somewhat less historical in flavor.

600 Main St., Wolfville, NS B4P 1E8. www.victoriashistoricinn.com. ☎ **800/556-5744** or 902/542-5744. Fax 902/542-7794. 16 units. Apr–Oct C$118–C$245 double and suite; Nov–Mar C$108–C$175 double and suite. Rates include full breakfast. AE, MC, V. *In room:* A/C, TV/VCR, Jacuzzi (some), Wi-Fi (free).

WHERE TO STAY & EAT

Blomidon Inn ★★ Two generations of the Laceby family operate this restored late 1800s sea captain's mansion, which offers 33 units ranging from modest rooms to apartments and suites fit for any executive. The only downside of this three-story inn is the lack of an elevator. That aside, it's one of my favorite places in the area. The ambience of an English manor house is enhanced by the extensive Victorian style gardens and a great shop, Blomidon Inn House of Gifts, where you can sometimes find garden goodies to tickle your fancy. Dining is amazing here, with the Chef Sean Laceby drawing on his five-acre vegetable garden and a fine array of ingredients ranging from lobster to caribou. Offerings in the two dining rooms and on the seasonal terrace are only bettered by a fine wine list and wonderful Victoria ambience. Great for when you want to do it up posh. Afternoon tea and continental breakfast available.

195 Main St., Wolfville, NS B4P 1C3. www.blomidon.ns.ca. ☎ **800/565-2291** or 902/542-2291. 29 rooms C$109–C$169; 3 suites C$159–C$199; cottage C$249–C$269. AE, MC, V. **Amenities**: Restaurant. *In room:* A/C, Internet (free).

WHERE TO EAT

If you're looking for something more elegant than these casual spots, many of the inns around Wolfville open their dining rooms at night and serve fancy food to the public, though prices will match.

Al's Homestyle Café ⬧ DELI This lowbrow, family-operated diner/deli is located in the nearby hamlet of Canning, about 10 miles northwest of Wolfville along Route 358. It has been a local favorite for years. Al Waddell no longer owns the place, but his popular recipes for sausages live on—choose from flavors like Polish, German, hot Italian, and honey garlic. They also pack the sausages to go. A sausage on a bun plus a cup of soup will run you less than C$5.

9819 Main St., Canning. ☎ **902/582-7270.** Most selections less than C$10. V. Mon–Sat 8am–6pm; Sun 8am–5pm.

Chignecto Bay, Minas Basin & Cobequid Bay

NOVA SCOTIA

The Coffee Merchant & Library Pub ★ ⛏ COFFEE SHOP Get your java and coffeehouse-culture fix at what's likely the hippest place in a pretty straight (not to say square) town. Besides an array of coffee drinks and an impressive array of organic teas, the shop also has a selection of pastries and sweets. After 9pm, the place transforms into a wine bar/pub upstairs, and musicians sometimes show up to gig. Great place to meet locals.

472 Main St., Wolfville. ℭ **902/542-4315.** Entrees $13–$24. MC, V. Daily 7am–midnight.

ANNAPOLIS ROYAL ★★

Annapolis Royal is arguably Nova Scotia's most historic town—it bills itself, with some justification, as "Canada's birthplace"—and it remains a treat to visit. Because the region was largely overlooked by later economic growth (the bulk of the trade and fishing moved to the Atlantic side of the peninsula), it requires very little in the way of imagination to see Annapolis Royal as it once was. (The current year-round population is less than 500.) The original settlement was rebuilt on the presumed site of explorer Samuel de Champlain's famous 1604 visit; the old Fort Anne still overlooks the upper reaches of the basin, much as it did when abandoned in 1854; and the village maintains much of its original historic charm, with narrow streets and historic buildings fronting a now-placid waterfront.

Annapolis Royal is also considered by many historians to be the birthplace of the continent's historic preservation movement. Town residents have been unusually activist about preserving the character of their town, and as a testament to their dedication, some 150 buildings and homes in town are now officially designated heritage sites (and presumably can't be altered much by future owners). For anyone curious about Canada's early history, Annapolis Royal is one of Nova Scotia's absolute don't-miss destinations.

Essentials

GETTING THERE Annapolis is located at exit 22 off Route 101. It is 200km (124 miles) from Halifax, and 129km (80 miles) from Yarmouth.

VISITOR INFORMATION The Annapolis Royal and Area Visitor Information Centre (ℭ **902/532-5454**) is 1km (⅔ mile) north of the town center at 236 Prince Albert Rd. (follow Prince Albert Rd. and look for the Annapolis Royal Tidal Generating Station). It's usually open daily 8am to 8pm, May 15 to October 15, and 10am to 6pm in spring and fall. Also check the town's official tourism site at www.annapolis royal.com for more local details.

Exploring the Town

Start at the tourist bureau, which is located at the **Annapolis Royal Tidal Power Generation Station** (ℭ **902/532-5454**), where the extreme fall in the tides has been harnessed since 1984 to produce electricity for the area in a generating station. It's the *only* such tidal generator in North America, and the world's largest straight-flow turbine—trust me, this will suddenly become important when the price of oil skyrockets. If you're so inclined, you can learn about the generator at the free exhibit center upstairs from the visitor information center, open roughly from mid-May until mid-October.

Even if you don't have time to visit the power station, do pick up a copy of the free walking-tour brochure at the tourism office. An annotated map provides architectural and historic context for a stroll downtown and around the waterfront. It's pretty amazing to stop and think, as you stroll down lower St. George Street, that you're walking down the oldest street in Canada.

Children and adults alike adore the **Upper Clements Parks** ★ (www.upper clementsparks.com; ℂ **888/248-4567** or 902/532-7557) on Route 1, about 5 minutes south of Annapolis Royal. It's an old-fashioned amusement park (you arrive after driving through an old orchard), full of low-key attractions that will delight younger kids. Highlights include the flume ride (originally built for Expo '86 in Vancouver), a wooden roller coaster that twists and winds through trees left standing during the coaster's construction, and a mini train. It's open daily in season from 11am to 7pm; admission to the grounds is C$10 plus tax, free for children 2 and under. The rate includes admission to the adjacent wild animal park. Single rides cost C$4, while bracelets permitting unlimited access to rides run from about C$22 to C$30 per day. AAA and CAA members receive a hefty 25% discount.

In the evening, there's often entertainment in downtown Annapolis Royal at **King's Theatre,** 209 St. George St. (www.kingstheatre.ca; ℂ **902/532-5466** or 532-7704). Shows range from movies to musical performances to variety shows to touring plays—and there are plenty of offerings for kids, too. Stop by or call to find out what's happening during your stay.

Fort Anne National Historic Site ★   What you'll likely remember about a visit here are the impressive grassy earthworks that cover some 14 hectares (35 acres) of high ground overlooking the confluence of the Annapolis River and Allains Creek. The French built the first fort here around 1643. Since then, dozens of buildings and fortifications have occupied this site. You can visit the 1708 gunpowder magazine (the oldest building among all the Canadian National Historic Sites), then look through a museum located in the 1797 British field officers' quarters. The model of this site as it appeared in 1710 is especially intriguing. If you find all the history a bit tedious, ask a guide for a croquet set and practice your technique on the green lawns. A good strategy for visiting is to come during the day to tour the museum and get a feel for the lay of the land. Then return later for the evening sunset, long after the bus tours have departed, to walk the **Perimeter Trail** ★, an easy 530m-long (⅓ mile) path that traces along the top of the star-shaped fort and features good river and valley vistas.

Entrance on St. George St. ℂ **902/532-2397,** 532-2321 off-season. Admission C$3.90 adults, C$3.40 seniors, C$1.90 children, C$9.80 families. May 15–Oct 15 9am–5:30pm; off season by appointment only (grounds open year-round).

Historic Gardens ★   You don't need to be a flower nut to enjoy an hour or two at these exceptional gardens, open to the public since 1981. The 4-hectare (10-acre) grounds are uncommonly beautiful, with a mix of formal and informal gardens dating from varied epochs. Set on a gentle hill, the plantings overlook a beautiful salt marsh (now diked and farmed), and they include a geometric Victorian garden, a knot garden, a rock garden, and a colorful perennial border garden. Rose fanciers should allow plenty of time—some 2,000 rosebushes (of 230 cultivars) track the history of the flower's cultivation from earliest days through the Victorian era to the present day. A garden cafe offers an enticing spot for lunch.

441 St. George St. www.historicgardens.com. ℂ **902/532-7018.** Admission C$10 adults, C$8.50 seniors and students, C$25 families. July–Aug daily 8am–dusk; May–June and Sept–Oct daily 9am–5pm. Closed Nov–Apr.

North Hills Museum   On the road to Port Royal, the North Hills Museum occupies a tidy shingled home, built in 1764, that's filled with a top-rate collection of English porcelain, glass, ceramics, and furniture. It's mostly thanks to local banker Robert Patterson, who accumulated the collection, then donated it to the province in the 1970s. The compact museum is of interest primarily to serious antiques collectors and history buffs; casual visitors might be just a bit frustrated by such opulently furnished rooms at arm's length, glimpsed at from roped-off doorways.

5065 Granville Rd., Granville Ferry. ⓒ **902/532-2168.** Admission C$3 adults, C$2 seniors and children age 6–17, C$7 families. June to mid-Oct Mon–Sat 9:30am–5:30pm, Sun 1–5:30pm. Closed mid-Oct to May.

Port-Royal National Historic Site ★   Canada's first permanent settlement, Port Royal was located on an attractive point with sweeping views of the Annapolis Basin. After spending the dreadful winter of 1604 on an island in the St. Croix River (along the current Maine–New Brunswick border), the survivors moved to this better-protected location. Settlers lived here for 8 years in a high style that approached decadence given such bleak surroundings, even forming the Order of Good Cheer, a feast designed to keep spirits up during the long, cold winters. Many of the handsome, compact, French-style farmhouse buildings originally here were designed by Samuel de Champlain to re-create the comfort they might have enjoyed at home.

Although the original settlement was abandoned and eventually destroyed, this 1939 reproduction is convincing in all the details. You'll find a handful of costumed interpreters engaged in traditional handicrafts like woodworking. Have the interpreters show you some of the techniques and tools (such as "rat-tailing" and "mortise and tenon") used in construction. They're also happy to fill you in on life in the colony during those difficult early years when the French first forged an uneasy alliance with local natives (demonstrations include ancient Mi'kmaw healing remedies). Allow 1 or 2 hours to wander and explore.

10km (6¼ miles) south of Rte. 1, Granville Ferry (turn left shortly after passing the tidal generating station). ⓒ **902/532-2898.** Admission C$3.90 adults, C$3.40 seniors, C$1.90 children, C$9.80 families. May 15–Oct 15 daily 9am–5:30pm. Closed Oct 16–May 14.

Outdoor Pursuits

A short drive from Annapolis Royal and Port Royal are the **Delaps Cove Wilderness Trails,** which provide access to the rugged Fundy coastline. The tricky part is finding the trail head, as signs tend to vanish. Directions and a brochure are usually available from the visitor information center. Otherwise, head to Delaps Cove from Granville Ferry; veer left on the dirt road that cuts steeply downhill at a rightward bend shortly before the cove. (If you get to Tidal Cove Campground and Cabins, you've gone too far.) Follow this dirt road to the end, where you'll find parking and trail maps.

Two trails lead from an overgrown farm road to the rocky coastline. Take the **Bohaker Trail ★** (2km/1.2 miles) first, then decide whether you want to continue on to **Charlies Trail ★** (1.9km/1.2 miles). Both trails are linked by the Shore Road Trail (2.7km/1.7 miles one-way). The return walk will take 3 to 4 hours. The Bohaker is a lovely loop through woodlands to a short coastline trail. The highlight is a cobblestone cove piled with driftwood, into which a small waterfall tumbles. This is a good place for a picnic. The trails are well marked—once you find them, that is.

Where to Stay

With its rich history, this region has a proliferation of mansions, heritage homes which have found a new life as inns, and bed-and-breakfast accommodations. This is your chance to experience the homes of movers and shakers, the sea captains and entrepreneurs of yesteryear—unless you choose to camp.

The closest campground to Annapolis Royal is on a handsome 9-hectare (22-acre) waterfront property, on Route 1 just across the bay from the famed tidal generating station. This facility, the privately owned **Dunromin Campsite ★** (www.dunromin campsite.com; © **902/532-2808**), has full hookups for trailers and RVs, and attractive tenting sites along the water's edge, plus high-speed Internet access, an on-site cafe, and a few cabins. Tent and RV sites cost C$27 to C$40, while the cabins are available for C$65 to C$110 per night. The campsite is open from May through mid-October.

For more modern, motel-like accommodations near town, try the **Annapolis Royal Inn** (www.portroyalinn.com/annapolis; © **888/857-8889** or 902/532-2323), south of town on Route 1 near Highway 101, exit 22. Doubles are C$120 to C$148 in high season, lower in off seasons.

Garrison House Inn ★ The historic Garrison House sits across the road from Fort Anne in the town center; it has been taking in guests since 1854, when it first opened to accommodate officers at the fort. Rooms are nicely appointed with antiques. Room nos. 1 and 2 are attractive with wide pine floors, braided rugs, and wing-back chairs, and face the street; room no. 7 is tucked in back, well away from the hubbub, and has two skylights and a big demilune window to let in light. The inn's very good restaurant (see below) includes a screened-in veranda with food and drink service.

350 St. George St., Annapolis Royal, NS B0S 1A0. www.garrisonhouse.ca. © **866/532-5750** or 902/532-5750. Fax 902/532-5501. 7 units. C$99–C$149 July–Aug, C$79-139 mid-Apr to June and Sept to closing double. AE, MC, V. Street parking. Open mid-Apr to Nov; call in advance for weekends rest of year. **Amenities:** Restaurant; bar. *In room:* A/C, TV, Jacuzzi (1 unit), no phone, Wi-Fi (free).

Hillsdale House Inn ★ This clapboard Italianate home's (built in 1849) first floor features a Georgian-style sitting room with furniture that's nice to look at and comfortable to sit on. The guest rooms are handsome, furnished with antique writing desks, claw-foot tubs, and poster beds. Only top-floor rooms have air-conditioning, although all units possess flatscreen televisions and CD-playing clock radios. This is a place on the rise.

519 St. George St. (P.O. Box 148), Annapolis Royal, NS B0S 1A0. www.hillsdalehouse.ns.ca. © **877/839-2821** or 902/532-2345. 13 units. July–Sept C$125–C$160; reduced rates in spring and fall; closed late Nov to mid-Apr. Rates include full breakfast. MC, V. *In room:* A/C (some units), TV/ DVD, Wi-Fi (free).

King George Inn ★ ☺ The handsome King George was built as a sea captain's mansion in 1868, and served a stint as a rectory before becoming an inn. It's still fittingly busy and cluttered for its era; guest rooms are furnished entirely in antiques, mostly country Victorian pieces. Most of the rooms have queen-size beds—ask if you want a king or two doubles—and the two family suites have separate bedrooms with a shared bathroom. The best room in the house might be no. 7, the Duchess of Kent suite, with its Jacuzzi and small private deck overlooking the garden. There is a second Jacuzzi room in the Queen Victoria suite, which also has a king-size bed and bay window. The inn features a pump organ and a 19th-century grand piano, and helpfully provides bikes for guests.

548 Upper St. George St., Annapolis Royal, NS B0S 1A0. www.kinggeorgeinn.20m.com. © **888/799-5464.** 8 units. C$75–C$150 double. MC, V. Closed Jan–Apr. **Amenities:** Bikes. *In room:* A/C, hair dryer, no phone, Wi-Fi (free).

Queen Anne Inn ★★ You can't miss this Second Empire mansion, built in 1865. Like the Hillsdale House across the street, the Queen Anne (built for the sister of the Hillsdale's owner) benefited from a preservation-minded owner, who restored Victorian detailing to its former luster. There's a zebra-striped dining-room floor (alternating planks of oak and maple) and a grand central staircase. Elegant guest rooms are furnished appropriately, although some have been updated to include Jacuzzis. Featherbeds and handmade soaps are other nice touches. A dining room is open to the public for dinner 5 nights a week; breakfast is a three-course affair. The two-story carriage house, split into two bi-level suite units, is good for families, while the park-like grounds, with towering elms, are shady and inviting.

494 Upper St. George St., Annapolis Royal, NS B0S 1A0. www.queenanneinn.ns.ca. © **877/536-0403** or 902/532-7850. Fax 902/532-2078. 12 units. June–Oct C$189–C$209 two-story suite; June–Sept C$109–C$179 rooms; reduced rates early May. Rates include full breakfast. MC, V. Closed Nov–Apr. **Amenities:** Dining room. *In room:* TV, Jacuzzi (some), no phone, Wi-Fi (free).

Where to Eat

The Garrison House ★★ ECLECTIC The Garrison House Inn's restaurant is arguably the most intimate, attractive, and innovative of Annapolis Royal's eating choices. Three cozy dining rooms in the inn each have a different feel: some with colonial colors, some with contemporary styling, most with black Windsor chairs and piscine art. (Check out the room with the green floors and the humpback whale.) Chef-owner Patrick Redgrave's menu ranges all over the world without ever losing its Canadian footing. Start with Thai shrimp soup, mushroom risotto, or mussels steamed in wine and finished with habanero cream. Main dishes might include Digby scallops, a Vietnamese coconut milk curry, strip loin of beef, salmon poached in bourbon and glazed with maple, "mumbo-jumbo" jambalaya—or the catch of the day.

350 St. George St. (inside the Garrison House Inn). © **866/532-5750** or 902/532-5750. Reservations recommended in summer. Main courses C$15–C$30. AE, MC, V. May–Oct daily 5:30–8:30pm; Nov–Apr open by arrangement.

Ye Olde Town Pub PUB FARE For a more relaxed bite than other places around town, head by this genial local pub located centrally in town and housed in an 1884 brick building that was once a bank (hence the bars on the windows). It's said to be the smallest pub in Nova Scotia—in the entire history of the province. But they've got a big heart. There's beer, of course, but also a kitchen that serves vittles all day, a kids' menu, and even Wi-Fi Internet access for those who just can't hoist a pint without updating their Twitter accounts about it at the same time.

9 Church St. © **902/532-2244.** MC, V. Daily 11am–11pm.

KEJIMKUJIK NATIONAL PARK ★★

About 45km (28 miles) southeast of Annapolis Royal is a popular national park that's a world apart from coastal Nova Scotia. Kejimkujik National Park, founded in 1968, is located in the heart of south-central Nova Scotia, and it is to lakes and bogs what the South Coast is to fishing villages and fog. Bear and moose are the full-time residents here; park visitors are the transients. The park, which was largely scooped and shaped during the last glacial epoch, is about 20% water, which makes it especially popular with canoeists. A few trails also weave through the park, but hiking is limited; the longest hike in the park can be done in 2 hours. Bird-watchers are also drawn to the park in search of the 205 species that have been seen both here and at the Kejimkujik Seaside Adjunct, a 22-sq.-km (8½-sq.-mile) coastal holding west of Liverpool. Among the more commonly seen species are pileated woodpeckers and loons, and at night you can listen for the raspy call of the barred owl. Kejimkujik was designated as Nova Scotia's first Dark Sky Preserve in 2010 by the Royal Astronomical Society of Canada, resulting in new programs relating to the ecological and cultural importance of night skies. Cultural heritage is also being preserved through presentations such as a guided walk to view petroglyphs which portray the observations of Mi'kmaq people in the 18th and 19th centuries.

Essentials

GETTING THERE   Kejimkujik National Park is approximately midway on Kejimkujik Scenic Drive (Rte. 8), which extends 115km (71 miles) between Annapolis Royal and Liverpool. The village of Maitland Bridge (pop. 130) is near the park's entrance. Plan on about a 2½-hour drive from Halifax. Kejimkujik Seaside park is located off Route 103 at Port Joli south west of Liverpool.

VISITOR INFORMATION   The park's **visitor center** (✆ **902/682-2772**) is open daily and features slide programs and exhibits about the park's natural history. It sometimes closes on late-fall weekends.

FEES   The park opens daily at 8:30am year-round, closing at 8pm in peak season (mid-June through Labour Day) and at 4:30pm the rest of the year. Entrance fees are C$5.80 for adults, C$4.90 for seniors, C$2.90 for children ages 6 to 16, and C$15 for families. Seasonal passes can cut the cost of a longer stay; they cost C$30 for adults, C$25 for seniors, C$15 for children ages 6 to 16, and C$74 for families. The campground kiosk stays open an hour later in peak season, until 9pm, to receive campers. Entry to the Seaside Adjunct is slightly less, with the family seasonal pass costing C$49.

Exploring the Park

The park's nearly 298 sq. km (150 sq. miles) of forest, lakes, and bogs are peaceful and quiet. Part of what makes the park so appealing is its lack of access by car: One short park road off of Route 8 gets you partway into the park—but from there, you're forced to continue either on foot or by canoe. Over 80% of the park is only accessible by foot or canoe.

A stop at the **visitor center** is worthwhile, both for its exhibits on the region's natural history, and a stroll on one of three short trails, including the Beech Grove loop (2km/1.2 miles), which takes you around a glacial hill called a drumlin. The park has an audio-taped walking tour available for borrowing, too; ask for it at the information center.

Canoeing is your best means of traversing the park, if you're into that. Bring your own craft or rent one at **Jakes Landing** (✆ **902/682-5253**), 3km (2 miles) along the park access road. (You can also rent paddleboats, kayaks, rowboats, and cycles at the facility.) Route maps are provided at the visitor center, and rangers also lead short, guided canoe trips for novices. Multiday trips from backcountry campsite to campsite are a good way to get to know the park intimately, or cobble together an excursion from one lake to another (which might involve portaging your canoe over dry land between bodies of water; bring a friend).

The park also has 15 **walking trails,** ranging from short and easy strolls to, well, longer easy strolls. In other words, there's no elevation gain here to speak of. The 5km (3½-mile) **Hemlocks and Hardwoods Trail** loops through stately groves of 300-year-old hemlocks; the 3km (2-mile) one-way **Merrymakedge Beach Trail** skirts a lakeshore to end at a beach. A free map that describes the trails is available at the visitor center. Several of the trails are multi-use so bikers and hikers should be aware of each other.

Mountain bikers can explore the old **Fire Tower Road,** a round-trip of about 19km (12 miles); the road becomes increasingly rugged until it ends at a fire tower near an old-growth forest of birch and maple. There are four other trails in the park where bikes are allowed, as well, including the 16km (10-mile) **New Grafton Distance loop.** The other three trails are somewhat shorter, and are shared with hikers.

Camping

Backcountry camping ★★★ is this park's chief draw for locals. The more than 40 backcountry sites here are in such demand that they actually cost as much as the drive-in campsites. Overnighting on a distant lakeshore is the best way to get to know the park, so even if you're planning to car-camp, it's worth the extra time and expense of renting a canoe and paddling off for a night to one of these campsites just for the experience.

The canoe-in and hike-in sites are assigned individually, which means you needn't worry about noisy neighbors playing loud music on their car stereo. Backcountry rangers keep the sites in top shape, and each is stocked with firewood for the night (the wood is included in the campsite fee). Most sites can handle a maximum of six campers. Naturally, the best sites are snapped up on weekends by urbanites from Halifax; midweek, you've got a much better shot. You can also reserve backcountry sites (C$25 per site) up to 60 days in advance; call the **visitor center (𝒞 902/682-2772)** to do so, though your deposit is nonrefundable even if you have to cancel.

The park's drive-in campground at **Jeremy's Bay ★** offers about 360 sites, a few quite close to the water's edge, and this campground is amazingly open year-round. Campground rates are C$18 to C$30 per night. Note that during the off season, November to April, there are no toilets or showers—just pits. Starting early each April, reservations at the drive-in campground may be made for an additional fee by calling 𝒞 **877/RESERVE** [737-3783] or online at **www.pccamping.ca.**

DIGBY TO YARMOUTH ★

The 113km (70-mile) shoreline from Digby to Yarmouth has been described as down-home Canada at its best. I'm going to assume that you are smart enough to choose the meandering coastal Route 1, rather than Route 101 (faster but ho-hum). Here you'll find Acadian enclaves, fishing villages, miles of sandy beaches with perhaps but a single walker and dog each, and spruce-topped basalt cliffs.

The unassuming port town of **Digby** is located on the water at Digby Gap—where the Annapolis River forces an egress through the North Mountain coastal range. Set at the south end of the broad watery expanse of the Annapolis Basin, Digby is home to the world's largest inshore scallop fleet. These boats drag the ocean bottom nearby and bring back the succulent Digby scallops famous throughout Canada. The town itself is an active community where life centers around the fishing boats, convivial neighborhoods of wood-frame houses, and no-frills seafood eating places. (It also serves as Nova Scotia's gateway for those arriving from Saint John, New Brunswick, via ferry. The ferry terminal is on Rte. 303, just west of Digby.)

Aside from the Digby Pines Golf Resort and Spa, which warrants its own trip (see below), the town is worth checking out.

Digby Neck ★

Look at a map of Nova Scotia and you'll see the thin strand of **Digby Neck** extending southwest from Annapolis Basin. This scenic peninsula is a nature lovers' paradise lying between the Bay of Fundy and St. Mary's Bay. You can catch a boat to watch whales, or kick back and relax secure in the knowledge that rush hour will never hit this long, bony finger of high ridges, spongy bogs, dense forest, and ocean views; you could also tug out your camera or paints and easel. Maybe you're like me and just get a kick out of following a road to its end. The last two knuckles of this narrow peninsula are islands, both of which are connected via quick, 10-minute ferries across straits swept by currents as strong as 9 knots.

Neither the neck nor the islands have a lot of services for tourists beyond a mix of basic accommodations (a lodge, B&Bs, and so on) and a few general stores. It's well worth the drive if you're a connoisseur of end-of-the-world remoteness. The town of **Sandy Cove** on the mainland is picture-perfect, with its three prominent church steeples rising from the forest and a town so narrow it has wharfs on both sides of the peninsula. There really is a sandy beach in this cove. Both Tiverton on Long Island and Westport on Brier Island are unadorned fishing villages where life is basic. You get the distinct feeling that things haven't changed much in the past few decades— and that is a good thing.

ESSENTIALS

GETTING THERE Digby is Nova Scotia's gateway for those arriving from **Saint John,** New Brunswick, via ferry. The ferry terminal is on Route 303, west of Digby. If you're indeed arriving by ferry and want to visit the town before pushing on, look sharp for signs directing you downtown from the bypass, lest you end up on Route 101 and headed out of town by mistake. Coming from the rest of Nova Scotia, take exit 26 off Route 101 to reach Digby.

Surprisingly, you can even get to Digby without a car. **Acadian Bus Lines** (**www. acadianbus.com**) runs a daily service from Halifax. The trip takes about 4½ hours and costs about C$50 one-way.

From Digby, Route 217 runs about 72km (45 miles) south to **Brier Island.** Two **ferries** bridge the islands, and they run 24 hours a day, year-round. The first boat leaves **East Ferry** (about a 45-min. drive from Digby) on the mainland for **Tiverton,** Long Island, every half-hour; the second ferry departs Long Island for **Brier Island** on the hour. (The ferries are timed so that you can drive directly from one ferry to the next, if you don't dally too much on the road between.) The fare is C$5 for each ferry (C$10 total), and you pay each full fare on the outbound leg.

VISITOR INFORMATION The province maintains a visitor information center (✆ 902/245-2201) in Digby on Route 303 (on your right shortly after you disembark from the Saint John ferry), at 237 Shore Rd. It's open from early May through October.

On Long Island, you can pick up local information inside the **Islands Museum** (✆ 902/839-2034) in Tiverton. The museum opens from June through late September and is free to enter.

If you're in the area in early August, don't miss Digby Scallop Days, a salty local celebration of the shellfish that gives the town its fame. Expect scallop-shucking contests (aw, shucks!), raffles, food, busking, and general merriment. A fancy event? No. A slice of real Nova Scotia life? Yes. Another don't-miss event for motorcycle enthusiasts: the **Wharf Rat Rally** (www.facebook.com/wharfratrally), held on Labour Day weekend, is the largest rally in Atlantic Canada, bringing thousands to town for the long weekend.

EXPLORING DIGBY NECK

BICYCLING   Brier Island is a great destination for mountain bikers. Just 6×2km wide (4×1½ miles), it's the right scale for spending a slow afternoon poking around the dirt roads that lead to two of the island's red-and-white lighthouses. Brier Island maps are available for free at island stores and lodges. If you park your car on the Long Island side and take your bike over on the ferry, you'll save money; there's no charge for bikes or pedestrians.

You can rent a bike cheaply at the local youth hostel, the **Digby Backpackers Inn** (© 902/245-4573) at 168 Queen St. (see "Where to Stay & Eat," below).

HIKING   On **Long Island,** two short but rewarding woodland hikes bring you to open vistas of St. Mary's Bay and the Bay of Fundy. The trail head for the first, the 800m (half-mile) hike to **Balancing Rock ★★**, is about 4km (2½ miles) south of the **Tiverton** ferry on Route 217; look for a well-marked parking area on the left. The trail crosses through swamp, bog, and forest and is straight and flat—until the last 91m (300 ft.), when it plummets nearly straight down a sheer bluff to the ocean's edge via some 169 steps. At the base, a series of boardwalks leads you over the surging ocean to get a dead-on view of the tall column of basalt balancing improbably atop another column.

For the second short hike, return to the parking lot and drive 5km (3 miles) south to the **picnic area** on the right. From the parking lot atop the hill, a hike of about 1km (a half-mile) descends gradually through a forest of moss, ferns, and roots to the Fundy shore. Note that the coastline here looks almost lunar, its dark rock marbled with thin streaks of quartz. You're likely to have this coast all to yourself, since few travelers ever venture here.

Farther along, **Brier Island** is also laced with **hiking trails** offering fantastic opportunities for seaside exploration. Pick up one of the maps offered free around the island. One good place to take a walk is at the **Grand Passage Lighthouse** (turn right after disembarking the ferry and continue until you can't go any farther). Park near the light and walk through the stunted pines to the open meadows on the western shore, where you can pick up a **coastal trail**.

WHALE-WATCHING ★   Here in the Bay of Fundy, ocean currents mingle and the vigorous tides cause upwelling, which brings a rich assortment of plankton up to the surface from the briny depths. That means a free, all-you-can-eat buffet for whales, which feed on these minuscule creatures. So your chances of seeing whales are good in these parts. As the fishing industry has declined, the number of fishermen offering whale-watching tours has boomed. Most of these are down-home operations on converted lobster boats—don't expect gleaming ships with comfy seats and full-service cafeterias like you might find in bigger cities or along the New England coast.

The decline of local fish stocks means that the boats need to head farther out into the bay to find whales than used to be, but you'll still almost always see fin, minke, or humpback whales. (Right, sperm, blue, and pilot whales, along with the seldom-seen orca, have also occasionally been spotted over the years.) Plan on spending around C$50 to C$60 per adult for a 3- to 4-hour cruise; less per child.

There are plenty of choices, depending only on which port you want to sail out of. Local resident Penny Graham operates **Mariner Cruises** (www.novascotiawhale watching.com; ✆ **800/239-2189** or 902/839-2346) in **Westport** on Brier Island, using the *Chad and Sisters Two,* which is equipped with a heated cabin. Both whale- and bird-watching tours are offered.

Pirate's Cove Whale & Seabird Cruises (www.piratescove.ca; ✆ **888/480-0004** or 902/839-2242), located in **Tiverton,** has been operating offshore cruises since 1990; several tours are offered daily aboard the *Fundy Cruiser* and *Fundy Voyager.*

Petite Passage Whale Watch (www.ppww.ca; ✆ **902/834-2226**) sails the *Passage Provider 04,* which has a partially covered deck, out of **East Ferry.** It runs two to three cruises daily from June through October for C$55 per person or C$28 per child age 2 to 12.

For a saltier adventure, **Ocean Explorations** (www.oceanexplorations.ca; ✆ **877/654-2341** or 902/839-2417) offers tours on rigid-hulled inflatable Zodiacs—they call it ocean rafting. The largest boat holds up to a dozen passengers and moves with tremendous speed and dampness through the fast currents and frequent chop around the islands and the open bay; guests are provided with survival suits for warmth and safety. The 2- to 3-hour trips cost C$60 per adult, less for children, seniors, students, and group members.

WHERE TO STAY & EAT

In addition to the choices listed below, there are two hostels in the area. The **Digby Backpackers Inn** ★ (www.digbyhostel.com; ✆ **902/245-4573**), at 168 Queen St., is newish and quite good. Run by an international couple, it offers dorm beds for C$25 a night and double rooms for C$60; all bathrooms are shared, but breakfast is included with the rate. The **Brier Island Hostel** (www.brierislandhostel.com; ✆ **902/839-2273**), on Brier Island, offers beds for C$20 adults, C$10 children 6 and under.

Brier Island Lodge ★ 🎒 Built to jump-start local eco-tourism, the Brier Island Lodge is a basic but great find, thanks to eye-popping views. You'll find a rustic-modern motif, with log-cabin construction and soaring glass windows overlooking the Grand Passage 40m (131 ft.) below; most rooms overlook the ocean and a lighthouse. Inside, they feature all the usual motel amenities, plus a few unexpected touches (double Jacuzzis in the pricier rooms). A well-regarded dining room serves up traditional favorites, and local fishermen congregate in an airy lounge in the evening to play cards and watch a satellite TV. Hiking trails connect directly from the lodge to the Fundy shore. Breakfasts feature fresh eggs from hens at the adjacent farm. But don't plan on sleeping in; as the lodge notes, "When the sun comes up, our roosters will be happy to let you know."

Brier Island (P.O. Box 33), Westport, NS B0V 1H0. www.brierisland.com. ✆ **800/662-8355** or 902/839-2300. Fax 902/839-2006. 40 units. C$89–C$149 double. MC, V. **Amenities:** Dining room; lounge; bike rental; exercise room. *In room:* A/C, TV, Internet (some rooms, free), Jacuzzi (4 rooms).

Digby Pines Golf Resort & Spa ★★ ☺ Red-roofed Digby Pines, situated on 121 hectares (299 acres), has marvelous views of the Annapolis Basin. The imposing stucco-and-stone resort, surrounded by pines, is a throwback to an era when mon-eyed families headed to fashionable resorts for the entire summer. Built in 1929 in

Norman château style, the inn is owned by the province of Nova Scotia—which does a good job emphasizing comfort over mere historical re-creation. The gracious lobby features old-world touches, and guest rooms vary in both size and views (ask for a waterview room; there's no extra charge). Thirty or so cottages have one to three bedrooms each, most of them featuring fireplaces, air-conditioning, and minirefrigerators. Amenities are a reason for coming: An Aveda spa offers a full menu of treatments and services, an 18-hole Stanley Thompson–designed golf course threads its way through pines and over a babbling brook, and the kids' program is exemplary. The resort's Annapolis Room is open for three meals daily, serving Nova Scotian cuisine with a French flair. Reserve and dress up.

Shore Rd. (P.O. Box 70), Digby, NS B0V 1A0. www.digbypines.ca. ⓒ **800/667-4637** or 902/245-2511. Fax 902/245-6133. 79 rooms, 6 suites, 31 cottages. C$159–C$442 double. Packages available. AE, DC, DISC, MC, V. Closed mid-Oct to mid-May. **Amenities:** Restaurant; bar; babysitting; bike rentals; children's center; concierge; golf course; health club; heated outdoor pool; sauna; spa; 2 tennis courts; Wi-Fi (free). *In room:* A/C (cottages only), TV, fridge (cottages only), hair dryer.

The Acadian Coast

The Acadian Coast (called the "French Shore" by English-speaking locals) runs roughly from Salmon River to St. Bernard. This hardscrabble coast, where the fields were once littered with glacial rocks and boulders, was one of the few areas where Acadians were allowed to resettle after their 1755 expulsion from English Canada.

Today, you'll find abundant evidence of the robust Acadian culture, from the ubiquitous Stella Maris (the Acadian tricolor flag, with its prominent star—you'll get what I mean as soon as you get here) to the towering Catholic church, around which each town seems to cluster. This region is more populous and developed than much of the rest of the Nova Scotia coast, and thus lacks somewhat the wild aesthetic that travelers often seek. It has also failed to put its best foot forward touristically; there's little to no PR seeping out of this stretch of coast, and few accommodations or fine-dining experiences to be found. On the other hand, of course, that's what makes it so charming: it is what it is, and won't change just to make a buck.

ESSENTIALS

GETTING THERE   The Acadian Coast is traversed by Route 1. Speedy Route 101 runs parallel, but some distance inland; take any exit from 28 to 32 and follow Route 1 to your heart's content.

VISITOR INFORMATION   It's best to collect information in the major towns bracketing either end of this stretch; that means heading to either the **Yarmouth Visitor Centre** (p. 63) at 228 Main St. or Digby's **information center** (p. 58) on Route 303.

EXPLORING THE ACADIAN COAST

A drive along this seaside route offers a pleasant detour, in both pace and culture. You can drive its whole length, or pick up segments by exiting from Route 101 and heading shoreward. The distance is only just over 100km (62 miles), so take your time and savor the sights.

What follows is a selected sampling of attractions along the coast, from north to south.

○ **St. Mary's Church** ★★★, Church Point. Many towns here are proud of their impressive churches, but none is quite so amazing as St. Mary's. You can't miss it; it's adjacent to the campus of Université Sainte-Anne, the sole French-speaking university in Nova Scotia. The imposing, gray-shingled church has the feel of a European cathedral made of stone—yet St. Mary's, built between 1903 and 1905, is made entirely of wood. It's said to be the tallest and biggest wooden building on the entire continent. How this tiny village afforded it is beyond me. Outside, the church is impressive enough—a steeple rises some 56m (184 ft.) above the grounds, with some 40 tons of rock helping to provide stability in the wind. Inside, though, it's even more extraordinary—entire tree trunks serve as columns (they're covered in plaster to lend a more traditional appearance), for instance, and there are plenty of windows and arches to give architectural weight to the place. A small museum in the rear offers glimpses of church history. Admission is by donation; leave one.

- **Rapure Acadienne Ltd.** (© 902/769-2172), Church Point. Rappie pie is an Acadian whole-meal pie, typically made with beef or chicken. The main ingredient is grated potatoes, from which the moisture has been extracted and replaced with chicken broth. The full and formal name is "pâté a la rapure," but look for signs for "rapure" or "rappie pie" along Route 1 on the Acadian Coast. Locals argue over which kitchen does it best, but as far as I'm concerned, one place is just good as the next—except this one, an unassuming shop on Route 1 just south of Church Point. You can pick up a freshly baked beef or chicken rappie pie here for about C$5. (It costs about a dollar more for a clam pie.) Commandeer an outdoor picnic table to enjoy your meal, or take it to the shady campus of Université Sainte-Anne, a few minutes' drive north. The shop is open daily year-round, usually from around 8am.

- **Rendez-vous de la Baie Cultural and Interpretive Centre** (© 902/769-2345), Church Point. Located on the Université Sainte-Anne campus, this center houses an artist-run gallery, souvenir boutique, theater, and an Internet cafe. The Interpretive Centre (admission C$5) is a great place to learn about Acadian culture. Enjoy music, check your e-mail, and check out the region at the Visitor Information Centre.

- **La Vieille Maison ★** (© 902/645-2389), Meteghan. One of the oldest Acadian houses on the French Shore is now a small historical museum displaying artifacts of Acadian life in the 19th century. Look for the scrap of original French wallpaper uncovered during restoration of the summer bedroom. Open daily in summer. Admission is free.

- **Smuggler's Cove,** Meteghan. This small provincial picnic area a few minutes south of town has a set of steps running steeply down to a cobblestone cove. From here, you'll have a view of a tidal cave across the way. Rum runners were said to have used this cave—about 5m (16 ft.) high and 18m (59 ft.) deep—as a hide-out during the Prohibition era. Admission is free.

- **Mavillette Beach ★★**, Mavillette. This beautiful crescent beach has nearly all the ingredients for a pleasant summer afternoon—lots of sand, grassy dunes, changing stalls, a nearby snack bar with ice cream, and views across the water to scenic Cape Mary. All that's lacking are picnic tables and an ocean warm enough to actually swim in; it's seriously frigid here, though some hardy souls do give it a try. The beach, managed as a provincial park, is 1km (⅔ mile) off Route 1, and the turnoff is well marked. It's open mid-May through mid-October. Admission is free.

- **Port Maitland Beach ★★**, Port Maitland. Another provincial park beach—and a very long one at that—Port Maitland Beach is near the breakwater and town wharf. It isn't as scenic or pristine as Mavillette Beach; it's closer to Yarmouth and attracts larger crowds, principally families. But I really enjoy it anyway, because you can walk for miles in solitude here. They have picnic tables, too. Signs direct you to the beach from the village center.

WHERE TO STAY

Accommodations are pretty thin on the ground here; most are small, unpretentious B&Bs offering varying degrees of comfort. They are quite affordable, however; you could pay as little as C$50 for a night in a double room. It all depends on what you want. Push to the Annapolis Valley if you want a fancy inn, or to Yarmouth for a family motel or chain hotel if you'll be heading for the South Shore next. Traipse inland to **Kejimkujik National Park** (p. 55) if you're longing to camp in the woods.

If you're determined to stay in the land of Evangeline, no sweat. There's a good B&B, **A la Maison D'Amitie** ★ (www.houseoffriendship.ca; ℭ **902/645-2601**), on a cliff top down a dirt road in Mavillette, with two oceanfront suites for C$175 in peak season and a much more expansive, ground-floor suite with vanity sinks and a Jacuzzi for C$350 per night. (Rates are a bit lower off season.) The home boasts an impressive 152m (500 ft.) of ocean frontage in addition to its views, and should be very welcoming—the name is French for "House of Friendship." You might also try **L'Auberge au Havre du Capitaine** (www.havreducapitaine.itgo.com; ℭ **902/769-2001**) on Route 1 in Meteghan River, a regular motel with 18 rooms at rates ranging from about C$75 to C$119 per night; a few even have air-jetted Jacuzzi tubs. As a bonus, there's a local Acadian-cuisine restaurant on the premises.

Yarmouth & the Acadian Shore

It is a mixed bag of people who have inhabited Yarmouth. Mi'kmaq called the area "Keespongwitk" meaning "lands end." France's Samuel de Champlain named a fishing village here Cape Fourchu in 1604 and Acadians exiled from Grand-Pré returned to settle here. United Empire Loyalists, settlers loyal to Britain who fled the United States, arrived in the late 1700s. Ideally located at the base of Nova Scotia, Yarmouth quickly became a thriving shipbuilding center and sea port at one point boasting more tonnage per capita than any other port in the world. One of the first screw propellers was built here. Seafaring history was made in 1932 when Molly Kool was issued master's papers, making her the first female ship captain in the world.

Visitors will see the legacy of this seafaring heritage when they visit Yarmouth today. There are some 400 sea captains' homes in the region, a testament to the historic legacy of this seaport. Built between 1850 and 1900 with riches gained at sea, the architectural styles of the homes reflect the ports of call and grandeur experienced by these men of the sea. Ask the folks in the Visitors Information Centre (see following) for information on the Sea Captains Homes and Mercantile Heritage Walk and go exploring, or you can just drive around and gape. Take time to explore this rocky sea coast, the heart of the world's largest lobster fishing grounds.

Yarmouth today is a great base for exploring the Acadian Shore. The loss of the ferry to Maine gave the citizens new impetus to develop their cultural attractions, festivals, and events, including their 250th anniversary in 2011. Today, visitors come to stay, instead of just driving through to the ferry terminal.

ESSENTIALS

GETTING THERE Yarmouth is at the convergence of two of the province's principal highways, routes 101 and 103. It's approximately 300km (186 miles) from Halifax.

VISITOR INFORMATION The **Yarmouth Visitor Centre** (ℭ **902/742-5033**) is at 228 Main St., in a modern, shingled building you simply can't miss. Both provincial and municipal tourist offices are located here, open mid-May through September, daily from about 9am to 7pm.

EXPLORING THE AREA

The tourist bureau and the local historical society publish a very informative walking-tour brochure covering downtown Yarmouth. It's well worth requesting at the Yarmouth Visitor Centre (see above). The guide offers general tips on what to look for in local architectural styles (how do you tell the difference between Georgian and Classic Revival?), as well as brief histories of significant buildings. The entire tour is 4km (2½ miles) long.

The most scenic side trip—an ideal excursion by bike or car—is to **Cape Forchu** and the **Yarmouth Light** ★ (www.capeforchulight.com). Head west on Main Street (Rte. 1) for 2km (1¼ miles) from the visitor center, then turn left at the horse statue. The road winds out to the cape, past seawalls and working lobster wharves, meadows, and old homes.

When the road finally ends, you'll have arrived at the red-and-white-striped concrete lighthouse that marks this harbor's entrance. (The lighthouse dates from the early 1960s, when it replaced a much older octagonal lighthouse that succumbed to wind and time.) There's a tiny photographic exhibit on the cape's history in the visitor center in the keeper's house. They also serve lunch, tea, boxed picnic lunches, and lobster dinners on Saturday nights. The food is down-home delicious and the setting gob-smacking gorgeous.

Leave enough time to ramble around the dramatic rock-and-grass bluffs—part of Leif Ericson Picnic Park—that surround the lighthouse. Don't miss the short trail out to the point below the light. Bright red picnic tables and benches are scattered about; buy or bring lunch or dinner if the weather is right.

Art Gallery of Nova Scotia (Western Branch) ★★ ☺ A satellite of the famous art gallery in Halifax, this AGNS is housed in the former Royal Bank building at the heart of Yarmouth's downtown. Its changing exhibits draw from the mother-ship's permanent collections, and might include a rumination on the history of flight; a curated showing of folk art from the Maritimes; or a collection of tall-ship paintings. The museum fills a much-needed gap in Yarmouth's cultural scene, and staff members even offer various summer art classes and workshops. You should definitely duck in here whenever you're in town and at a loss for things to do.

341 Main St. www.artgalleryofnovascotia.ca/en/AGNS_Yarmouth. ✆ **902/749-2248.** Admission by donation. Thurs–Sun noon–5pm.

Firefighters' Museum of Nova Scotia ☺ This two-story museum will appeal mostly to confirmed fire buffs, historians, and impressionable young children. The museum is home to a varied collection of early firefighting equipment, with hand-drawn pumpers the centerpiece of the collection. Kids love the 1933 vintage Chev Bickle Pumper because they can don helmets and take the wheel for some pretend-I'm-a-fireman time. Also showcased here are uniforms, badges, and pennants. Also look for the collection of photos of notable Nova Scotia fires.

451 Main St. ✆ **902/742-5525.** Admission C$3 adults, C$2.50 seniors, C$1.50 children, C$6 families. Open year-round, please call for specific times.

WHERE TO STAY

Fifteen kilometers (9⅓ miles) west of town on Route 1 is the **Lake Breeze Campground** (✆ **902/649-2332**), a privately run spot with the appealingly low-key character of a small municipal campground. It has 50 campsites for C$20 to C$28, some right on the shores of tiny **Lake Darling** (you can rent a boat inexpensively), as well as five small cottages (for C$65–C$104 per night); everything is well tended by the owners. The campground is open from around mid-May until mid-October. You can also rent boats here.

Yarmouth is home to a number of mom-and-pop and chain motels. Some of the better choices in town are the **Best Western Mermaid Motel,** 545 Main St. (© **800/528-1234** or 902/742-7821), with rates of around C$115 to C$180 double; **Comfort Inn,** 96 Starrs Rd. (© **800/228-5150** or 902/742-1119), at around C$85 to C$195 double; and the business-hotel-like **Rodd Grand Hotel,** 417 Main St. (© **800/565-7633** or 902/742-2446), more expensive at rates ranging from C$100 to C$225 double per night.

Guest-Lovitt House ★★　This small B&B owned by two locals is one of the town's best lodgings. Four rooms await the traveler, each with four-poster king-size or queen-size beds draped in white covers, lacy drapes, and lightly floral wallpapers or pastel schemes to accent. Antique furnishings in each room include touches such as fireplaces, writing desks, wingback chairs, loveseats, and even—in the case of the Dr. Webster Room—a little private balcony. An outdoor hot tub provides faux-California experiences, a good breakfast is included, and there's a gazebo for sitting. Two of the rooms can be combined into a suite (at a discount) when need be.

12 Parade St., Yarmouth, NS B5A 3A4. www.guestlovitt.ca. © **866/742-0372** or 902/742-0372. 4 units. C$119–C$159 double. Rates include full breakfast. AE, MC, V. **Amenities:** Jacuzzi. *In room:* TV/DVD, hair dryer, Wi-Fi (free).

Harbour's Edge B&B ★ 🏠　This attractive early Victorian home (built 1864) sits on a quiet hectare (2½ acres) and 76m (250 ft.) of harbor frontage, where the scenery changes twice per day with the tides. This was the very first parcel of land in Yarmouth to be owned by a European, but before that, local native peoples had camped and fished here for ages. Today you can lounge on the lawn watching herons, hawks, and kingfishers. The inn opened in 1997 after 3 years of restoration. Rooms are lightly furnished to highlight their architectural integrity; all four sport high ceilings and handsome spruce floors. The attractive Audrey Kenney Room is biggest, but the Clara Caie has better views of the harbor (though the private bathroom and its claw-foot tub are down the hall). The Georgie Allen has a private hallway and clear harbor view, as well. You'll feel safe here. One of the two innkeepers is a Mountie (a Canadian federal police officer). Head toward Cape Forchu and watch for the inn shortly after turning at the horse statue.

12 Vancouver St., Yarmouth, NS B5A 2N8. www.harboursedge.ns.ca. © **902/742-2387.** 4 units. C$135–C$150 double. Rates include full breakfast. MC, V. *In room:* Hair dryer, no phone, Wi-Fi (free).

Lakelawn B&B Motel　The clean, well-kept Lakelawn Motel offering basic motel rooms has been a downtown Yarmouth mainstay since the 1950s, when the main Victorian house (where the office is located) was moved back from the road to make room for the motel wings. The house has four B&B-style guest rooms upstairs, each furnished simply with antiques, if you're looking for something more traditional. Breakfast here, however, costs extra.

641 Main St., Yarmouth, NS B5A 1K2. www.lakelawnmotel.com. © **877/664-0664** or 902/742-3588. 34 units. C$59–C$99 double. AE, DC, DISC, MC, V. Open year round. **Amenities:** Restaurant. *In room:* TV, no phone (some units), Wi-Fi (free).

The MacKinnon-Cann Inn ★　The staff will ask you what decade you want to visit—the owners have highlighted 70 years of interior design (from the 1900s to the 1960s) in their rooms. What fun. The 1950s room inspired by Luci and Desi Arnez's

When you leave Yarmouth, travel east on Route 103 if you're making time, Route 3 if you're taking time. Pubnico, about 40km (25 miles) down the highway on Route 3, is the oldest Acadian Village in the world. Before the Acadians, it was known as Pobomcoup, Mi'kmaq for "a place where holes have been made through the ice to fish." Today there are several villages: West, Middle West, and Lower West on one side of the bay of the same name and East, Middle East, and Lower East on the other, and Pubnico itself at the top. There is a restored Acadian Village here, as well as a coastal wildlife habitat and a 19th-century lighthouse. But really, the best reason for the side trip is to experience the food and the people. For a real Acadian experience, be sure to visit Middle West Pubnico, where two eateries will give you a taste of *Acadie* (the French name for Acadia). At the

Red Cap Restaurant and Motel (www. redcapmotel-rest.com; ✆ **902/762-2112**) they say the true accomplishment of all the villagers is their ability to pleasantly meld the old with the new. You can experience that in the restaurant, where you'll rub shoulders with locals and where traditional foods like rappie pie share menu space with more modern choices. The motel is basic and reasonable at C$85 to C$130 a night, with the usual amenities. I have great fondness for it because we once rode out a hurricane in the end unit. Down facing the wharf (where one of the biggest fishing fleets in Atlantic Canada ties up), **Dennis Point Cafe** (www.dennis pointcafe.com; ✆ **902/762-2112**) is a great diner usually loaded with fishermen. Seafood here falls into the really, really good category, especially the hot lobster roll.

bedroom in the television series *I Love Lucy* features rabbit ears on the television and twin beds "because, after all, no one slept together in 50s television." The '40s room, inspired by films such as *Mommy Dearest,* is white on white, minimal and elegant. The inn owes its life to a former developer and hotelier, now the innkeepers, who specialize in restorations. It has many wellness options available, including yoga classes, lifestyle consultation, nutritional counseling, retreats, guided trips, and workshops presented through the Anne Willett Tedford Health and Wellness Centre located on the property. Dining at "Kabir's at the Inn" features traditional, authentic Indian cuisine prepared by chef Kabir Raj Rana from the Himalayan region of Northern India. A three-course meal runs about C$30.

27 Willow St., Yarmouth, B5A 1V2. www.mackinnoncaninn.com. ✆ **866/698-3142** or 902/742-9900. Fax 902/742-0326. 7 rooms. C$128–C$155 Oct 16–June 15; C$138–C$185 June 16–Oct 15. AE, MC, V. *In Room:* A/C, TV, Internet (free), whirlpool bath (4 rooms).

WHERE TO EAT

Quick-N-Tasty ☺ SEAFOOD   The name about says it all. This country-cooking joint has long been a hit with locals. The restaurant is adorned with the sort of paneling that was *au courant* in the 1970s, and meals are likewise old-fashioned and generous. The emphasis here is on seafood; you can order fish either fried or broiled, but go for the hot open-faced lobster club sandwich—it's gaining international foodie acclaim. The seafood casserole and the blueberry desserts are also notable.

Rte. 1, Dayton (from downtown Yarmouth, follow Rte. 3 west to Rte. 1). ✆ **902/742-6606.** Sandwiches C$3–C$12; main courses C$7–C$18. AE, DC, MC, V. Daily 11am–8pm. Closed mid-Dec to Feb. Just east of Yarmouth on the north side of Rte. 1.

Rudder's Seafood Restaurant & Brewpub ★ BREWPUB Yarmouth's first (and Nova Scotia's fourth) brewpub opened in 1997 on the waterfront. It occupies an old warehouse dating from the mid-1800s, where you can see the wear and tear of the decades on the battered floor and in the stout beams and rafters. The place has been nicely spruced up, though, and the menu features creative pub fare plus Acadian and Cajun specialties (like rappie pie and jambalaya), as well as lobster suppers and planked salmon. The steaks are quite good, as is the beer. In summer, there's outdoor seating on a deck with a view of the harbor across the parking lot.

96 Water St. ⓒ **902/742-7311.** Sandwiches C$9–C$11; entrees C$20–C$26. AE, DC, MC, V. Mid-Apr to mid-Oct daily 11am–11pm (shorter hours in spring and fall). Closed mid-Oct to mid-Apr.

Stanley Lobster Co., Ltd. ★★ 🍴 SEAFOOD You'll find fresh local goodness here: fresh steamed lobsters, corn on the cob, and homemade strawberry dessert. The owners (Ernie and Brian Williams) will even take you through the pound if you like, and tell you some fascinating stuff about lobsters and the industry. They'll also let you select your own lobster. They have a lovely, outdoor pavilion on the beach (walled in with windows in case the weather is foul), but no liquor license, so BYOB. The current market price for lobster varies from day to day, but the last time I was here it was C$25. Regardless, it's a huge hit with locals and visitors alike.

1066 Overton Road (Rte. 304), Yarmouth Bar, NS www.stanleylobster.com/lobsterretail.htm. ⓒ **902/742-8291**. Lobster costs fluctuate according to market prices but will be in the vicinity of C$25 and up, depending on the size of the lobster. MC, V. Open early June to late Sept (when the lobster runs out) noon-7pm Tues–Sat, 2–7pm Sun, or by appointment at other times.

SOUTH SHORE ★★

The Atlantic coast between Yarmouth and Halifax is that quaint, maritime Nova Scotia you see on calendars. Lighthouses and weathered, shingled buildings perch at the rocky edge of the sea, as if tenuously trespassing on the ocean's good graces. Rustic and beautiful, this coastline involves some 300-plus kilometers (186-plus miles) of slow, twisting road along the water's edge. If your heart is set on fully exploring this fabled landscape, then be sure to leave enough time for the many nooks and crannies. Towns such as Lunenburg, Mahone Bay, and Peggy's Cove are well worth the time.

It's sensible to allow more time here for one more reason: fog. When the cool ocean waters mix with the warm summer air over land, the results are predictably soupy. The fog certainly adds atmosphere. But it can, at times, slow driving to a crawl.

Shelburne

Shelburne is a historic town with unimpeachable pedigree. Settled in 1783 by United Empire Loyalists fleeing New England after the Revolution and the Treaty of Paris, the town swelled until by 1784 it was believed to have had a population of 10,000—larger than the Montréal, Halifax, or Québec of the time. With the recent declines in both boat building and fishing, however, the town has edged back into that dim economic twilight familiar to other seaside villages (it now has a population of about 2,000), and the waterfront began to deteriorate in spite of valiant preservation efforts.

Then Hollywood came calling. In 1992, *Mary Silliman's War* was filmed here. The producers found the waterfront to be a reasonable facsimile of 1776 Fairfield, Connecticut. The film crew spruced up the town a bit, and buried power lines along the waterfront.

Two years later, director Roland Joffe arrived to film *Scarlet Letter*, starring Demi Moore, Gary Oldman, and Robert Duvall. Those film crews buried more power lines, built 15 "historic" structures near the waterfront (most demolished after filming), dumped tons of rubble to create dirt lanes (since removed), and generally made the place look like 17th-century Boston. When the crew departed, it left behind three new buildings and an impressive shingled steeple you can see from anywhere in town. Among these "new old" buildings is the waterfront cooperage across from the Cooper's Inn. The original structure, clad in asphalt shingles, was generally considered an eyesore and was torn down, replaced by the faux-17th-century building. Today, coopers painstakingly make and sell traditional handcrafted wooden barrels in what amounts to a souvenir of a notable Hollywood film.

ESSENTIALS
GETTING THERE   Shelburne is about 223km (139 miles) southwest of Halifax on Route 3. It's a short hop from Route 103 via either exit 25 (southbound) or exit 26 (northbound).

VISITOR INFORMATION   The local **visitor information center** (© 902/875-4547) is in a tidy waterfront building at the corner of King and Dock streets. It's open daily mid-May to October.

EXPLORING HISTORIC SHELBURNE
The central historic district runs along the waterfront, where you can see legitimately old buildings, Hollywood facsimiles (see above), and spectacular views of the harbor from small, grassy parks. There's a lot more in the district, too: gift shops, a B&B, a husband-and-wife team of coopers making barrels in an open shop (technically, it's not open to the public, but ask nicely for a look), a kayaking and outdoor adventure center, and the **Sea Dog Saloon** (© 902/875-2862) at the very end of the road at 1 Dock St. It's sometimes open as late as 2am. A block inland from the water is Shelburne's more commercial stretch, where you can find services that include banks, shops, and snacks.

The town has developed a 3.5km (2.2-mile) section of an abandoned rail line as a trail, which links with a section that runs from the Roseway River to the Islands Provincial Park. A Bicycle Routes brochure contains four scenic routes. Pick one up at the visitor information center.

Shelburne Historic Complex ★ ☺   The historic complex is an association of three local museums located within steps of each other. The most engaging is the **Dory Shop Museum,** right on the waterfront. On the first floor you can admire examples of the simple, elegant boatbuilding craft (said to be invented in Shelburne) and view videos about the late Sidney Mahaney, a master builder who worked in this shop from the time he was 17 until he was 95. Then head upstairs, where all the banging is going on. While you're there, ask about the difference between a Shelburne dory and a Lunenburg dory.

The **Shelburne County Museum** features a potpourri of locally significant artifacts from the town's Loyalist past. Most intriguing is the 1740 fire pumper; it was made in London and imported here in 1783. Behind the museum is the austerely handsome **Ross-Thomson House,** built in 1784 through 1785. The first floor contains a general store as it might have looked in 1784, with bolts of cloth and cast-iron teakettles. Upstairs is a militia room with displays of antique and reproduction weaponry. You could easily spend a half-day here, particularly if you're bringing children who are captivated by the craftspeople.

Dock St. (P.O. Box 39), Shelburne, NS B0T 1W0. ☏ **902/875-3219.** Admission to all 3 museums C$8 adults, free for children 16 and under; individual museums C$3 adults, free for children 16 and under; all museums free on Sun mornings. June to mid-Oct daily 9:30am–5:30pm (Dory Shop, June–Sept).

WHERE TO STAY

Just across the harbor from Shelburne, the **Islands Provincial Park,** 183 Barracks Rd., Hwy. 3 ★ (☏ **888/544-3434** or 902/875-4304) offers 70 quiet campsites on 500 waterside acres from May through September. Some sites are right on the harbor, with a front-row seat and great views of the historic village; ask about those sites' availability first. There are no hookups for RVs here, another reason to consider it as a quiet overnight getaway. Campsites here cost C$25 apiece.

The Cooper's Inn ★★ ⚐   Facing the harbor in the Dock Street historic area, the impeccably historic Cooper's Inn was built by Loyalist merchant George Gracie in 1785. Subsequent additions and updates have been historically sympathetic. The downstairs sitting rooms set the mood nicely, with worn wood floors, muted wall colors (mustard and khaki green), and classical music in the background. A tranquil courtyard has a pond and bell fountain. Rooms are decorated in a comfortably historic-country style. A third-floor suite features wonderful detailing, two sleeping alcoves, and harbor views—worth the extra cost. The George Gracie Room has a four-poster bed and water view, the small Roderick Morrison Room a wonderful claw-foot tub perfect for a late-evening soak, and the Harbour Suite a harbor-view tub and massage chair. Owners Paul and Pat DeWar often leave treats and passes to the town's historic complex in rooms.

36 Dock St., Shelburne, NS B0T 1W0. www.thecoopersinn.com. ☏ **800/688-2011** or 902/875-4656. 8 units. C$100–C$185 double and suite. Rates include full breakfast. AE, MC, V. **Amenities:** 2 dining rooms; Wi-Fi (free). *In room:* TV/VCR, hair dryer, kitchenette (1 unit).

White Point Beach Resort ★★★ ☺   This is one of my favorite places to stay. Sitting right beside the ocean, its white sand beach is perfect for strolling, swimming, surfing, or storm watching—depending on the weather. If it's cold, just hit the indoor saltwater pool, with an ocean view. This is the resort that has it all when it comes to outdoor recreation, with two lakes, nature trails, a boathouse with canoes, kayaks and paddle boats, bicycles, and golf. Indoor recreation options equal those outdoors, and it is the indoors that holds my heart. The rustic ambience is immediately felt in the oceanview lounge off the lobby. A roaring fine in the huge fireplace, a refreshment from the bar, who needs more? That cozy rustic feel carries over to the cabins, each with a fireplace or woodstove—and actual wood-burning units. Snuggle up on a cold night and toast marshmallows. The dining is first-rate here, as are special culinary activities and events. White Point's laid-back atmosphere is immediately made obvious by the official greeters—bunnies, which kids love to feed with food from the front desk. Note: At the time of this writing, White Point Beach Lodge has just experienced a fire in its main lodge. They have announced that they will be rebuilding as quickly as possible. With the support of community, employees, and loyal guests, it will happen; but just what will be open when should be checked when you call for reservations.

Rte. 3, White Point B0T 1G0. www.whitepoint.com. ☏ **800/565-5068** or 902/354-2711. 164 rooms (in lodges or cottages), C$105–C$185; cottages C$140–C$325 depending on season and number of bedrooms. Specials and packages are worth exploring. AE, DC, DISC, MC, V. **Amenities:** Restaurant; babysitting; golf; pools; tennis courts. *In room:* TV/DVD, bar fridge, Wi-Fi (free).

Lane's Privateer Inn ★★ 🎒 There always seems to be something happening at this family-owned and operated inn in the heart of downtown Liverpool. They specialize in neat things to do: writing workshops, wine tastings, Fishermans' Breakfasts, harvest festivals, and Privateer Games; it's also a great location to explore the region's history of pirates and privateers. They have a great bookstore cum coffee shop, gourmet shop, and Captain Barss Pub and restaurant, specializing in local cuisine.

27 Bristol Ave., P.O. Box 509, Liverpool, B0T 1K0. www.lanesprivateerinn.com. 📞 **800/794-3332** or 902/354-3456. 27 rooms. C$70–C$105 winter rates; C$99–C$135 summer rates. AE, MC, V. **Amenities:** Restaurant. *In room:* A/C, TV, Wi-Fi (free).

WHERE TO EAT

In addition to the two choices listed below (one fancy, one very downscale), **Lothar's Café** (📞 **902/875-3697**) at 149 Water St., is also a good option when in town. Chef Lothar (yes, really) serves a sort of Swiss-Austrian-Germanic cuisine and, of course, fried fish, this being Nova Scotia. It's closed Tuesdays and Wednesdays.

Charlotte Lane Café ★★ CAFE Situated on a tiny lane between the village's waterfront and its main commercial street, it's a bit hard to find, but worth it once you do. The kitchen's eclectic lunch and dinner items range from straightforward pasta dishes to Thai-spiced tofu and noodles, racks of lamb with a port wine-orange sauce, seared scallops, and a filet mignon-lobster combination. You can go heavy or light, since the salads and starters like eggplant picatta are good as well. There's a wine list, too, plus the likes of brown sugar-and-buttermilk apple pie, sticky toffee pudding, sorbets, and baked cheesecakes for dessert.

13 Charlotte Lane (btw. Water and Dock sts.). 📞 **902/875-3314.** Lunch items C$11; dinner items and larger entrees C$16–C$32. MC, V. Tues–Sat 11:30am–2:30pm and 5–8pm. Reservations required.

Mr. Fish ★ 🐟 SEAFOOD You can't miss this little fried-fish stand on the side of busy Route 3, near a shopping center; what the place lacks in location, it more than makes up for in character and good simple seafood. Matronly line cooks fry messes of haddock, scallops, and shrimp, perfectly jacketed in light crusts, and the local clientele streams in for takeout. As if that weren't good enough, they then dole out great fries and crunchy coleslaw on the side—and a smile. You eat outside on the picnic tables (but watch for bees); if it's raining, you'll have to eat in your car.

104 King St. (Rte. 3, north of town center). 📞 **902/875-3474.** Meals C$3–C$13. V. Mon–Sat 11am–7pm (Fri and holidays until 9pm); Sun noon–7pm.

Lunenburg ★★★

Lunenburg is just plain lovable, compressing everything you came to see in Nova Scotia into one tidy package: ocean tides, fishing boats, terrain, architecture, museums, and fish. It's one of Nova Scotia's most historic *and* most appealing villages, a fact recognized in 1995 when UNESCO declared the old downtown a World Heritage Site.

The town was first settled in 1753, primarily by German, Swiss, and French colonists. It was laid out on the "model town" plan then in vogue. (Savannah, Georgia, and Philadelphia, Pennsylvania, are also laid out using similar plans.) The plan consists of seven north-south streets, intersected by nine east-west streets. Lunenburg is located on a harbor and flanked by steep hills—yet the town's planners decided not to bend the rules for geography. As a result, some of the town's streets go straight uphill, and can be exhausting to walk.

Still, it's worth trying. About three-quarters of the buildings in the compact downtown date from the 18th and 19th centuries; many of them are possessed of a distinctive style and are painted in bright pastel colors. Looming over all is the architecturally unique, red-and-white painted **Lunenburg Academy** with its exaggerated mansard roof, pointy towers, and extravagant use of ornamental brackets. The school sets a tone for the town the same way the Citadel fort does for Halifax. (The Academy's first two floors are still used as a public school—the top floor was deemed a fire hazard years ago—so the building is open to the public only on special occasions.)

What makes Lunenburg so appealing is its vibrancy. Yes, it's historic, but this is no village stuck in the 19th century. There's life, including a subtle countercultural tang that dates from the 1960s. Look and you'll see evidence of the tie-dye-and-organic crowd in the scattering of natural food shops and funky boutiques. A growing number of art galleries, crafts shops, and souvenir vendors are moving in, making for rewarding browsing.

ESSENTIALS

GETTING THERE Lunenburg is about 100km (62 miles) southwest of Halifax on Route 3.

VISITOR INFORMATION The **Lunenburg Visitor Information Centre** (© 888/615-8305 or 902/634-8100) is located at the top of Blockhouse Hill Road. It's open daily from May through October, usually from 9am to 8pm. It's not in an obvious location, but the brown "?" signs—and helpful locals—point you there. The staff are especially good at helping you find a place to spend the night if you've arrived without reservations. You can also call up local information on the Web at **www. lunenburgns.com**.

EXPLORING LUNENBURG

Leave plenty of time to explore Lunenburg by foot. An excellent walking-tour brochure is available at the tourist office on Blockhouse Hill Road, though supplies are limited. If that's gone, contact the **Lunenburg Board of Trade** (© 902/634-3170) for an excellent local and regional map.

St. John's Anglican Church ★★★ at the corner of Duke and Cumberland streets has got to be one of the most impressive architectural sights in all of Eastern Canada—even though it's a reconstruction. The original structure was built in 1754, of oak timbers shipped from Boston in simple New England meetinghouse style. Between 1840 and 1880, the church went through a number of additions and was overlaid with ornamentation and shingles to create an amazing example of the "carpenter Gothic" style—any local residents were baptized and attended services in this church throughout their adult lives. All this changed on Halloween night of 2001: A fire nearly razed the place, gutting its precious interior and much of the ornate exterior. In 2005 the church reopened after a painstaking 3-year restoration project using new materials but the old design. It's a must-see, and free to enter.

While exploring the steep streets of the town, note the architectural influence of its European settlers—especially the Germans. Some local folks made their fortunes from the sea, but serious money was also made by local carpenters who specialized in the ornamental brackets that elaborately adorn dozens of homes here. Many homes feature a distinctive architectural element known as the "Lunenburg bump"—a five-sided dormer-and-bay-window combo installed directly over an extended front door. (Other homes feature the simpler, more common Scottish dormer.) Also look for double or triple roofs on some projecting dormers, which serve absolutely no function other than to give the homes bearing them the vague appearance of a wedding cake.

Guided **walking tours** ★ are hosted daily in season by Eric Croft (www.lunenburgwalkingtours.com; ✆ **902/634-3848**), a knowledgeable native who brings his huge stock of local lore to the table when discussing local architecture and some rather murky legends surrounding the town's history. The tours traditionally depart three times daily (the last, by candlelight) from Bluenose Drive, across from the parking lot for the Atlantic Fisheries Museum. The cost is about C$15 for adults, C$10 for children.

Several boat tours operate from the waterfront, most tied up near the Fisheries Museum. **Lunenburg Whale Watching Tours** (www.novascotiawhalewatching.com; ✆ **902/527-7175**) sails in pursuit of several species of whales, along with seals and seabirds, on 3-hour excursions. There are four departures daily from May through October, with reservations recommended (and all bookings must be confirmed 24 hr. in advance with a phone call). Cost is C$48 per adult, C$30 for children age 5 to 14, and C$18 for children 5 and under (though infants are free). Alternately, if you have less time, **Star Charters** (www.novascotiasailing.com; ✆ **877/386-3535** or 902/634-3535) takes visitors on shorter, mellow 90-minute tours of Lunenburg's inner harbor five times daily from June through October. These tours cost C$24 for adults, C$15 for students, C$11 for children, and C$52 for a full family. (Rates are C$3 higher for sunset cruises, which depart around 7pm.)

Fisheries Museum of the Atlantic ★ ☺   The sprawling Fisheries Museum is professionally designed and curated, and deserves credit for taking a topic some consider dull—fishing—and actually making it relatively fun to learn about. The museum keeps pace with the times. You'll find aquarium exhibits on the first floor, including a touch-tank for kids and answers to questions like "Do fish sleep?" Look for the massive 7-kilogram (15-lb.) lobster, estimated to be more than 30 years old. Detailed dioramas depict the whys and hows of fishing from dories, colonial schooners, and other historic vessels. There's a newer exhibit called "Sea Monsters," and a third-floor section on "Rum Runners." You'll learn a whole bunch about the *Bluenose*, a replica of which ties up in Lunenburg when it's not touring elsewhere (see "The Dauntless *Bluenose*" box, below). Outside, you can tour several other vessels—a trawler and a salt-bank schooner among them—and visit a working boat shop and a scallop-shucking house. Allow at least 2 hours to probe this engaging museum, which is appropriately right on the waterfront, but take note: A friend and I once spent 2 days and weren't ready to leave.

On the waterfront. 68 Bluenose Dr. http://museum.gov.ns.ca/fma. ✆ **866/579-4909** or 902/634-4794. Mid-May to mid-Oct admission C$10 adults, C$7 seniors, C$3 children age 6–17, C$22 families; rest of the year C$4 per person (children free). May–Oct daily 9:30am–5:30pm (July–Aug to 7pm Tues–Sat); Nov–Apr Mon–Fri 9:30am–4pm.

SHORT ROAD TRIPS FROM LUNENBURG

Blue Rocks ★★ is a tiny, picturesque harbor a short drive from Lunenburg. It's every bit as scenic as Peggy's Cove, but without any of the tour buses. Head out of town on Pelham Street (which turns into Blue Rocks Rd.) and just keep driving east, watching for signs indicating either THE POINT or THE LANE, and steer in that direction. The winding roadway gets narrower as the homes get more and more humble. Eventually, you'll reach the tip of the point, where it's just fishing shacks, bright boats, rocks, and views of spruce- and heath-covered islands offshore. I love it out here. The rocks are said to glow in a blue hue in certain light, hence the name; bring a camera

THE DAUNTLESS bluenose

Take a Canadian dime out of your pocket and have a close look. That graceful schooner on one side? That's the *Bluenose*, Canada's most recognized and most storied ship. You'll also see it gracing license plates from Nova Scotia.

The *Bluenose* was built in Lunenburg in 1921 as a fishing schooner. But it wasn't just any schooner. It was an exceptionally fast schooner.

U.S. and Canadian fishing fleets had raced informally for years. Starting in 1920, the *Halifax Herald* sponsored the International Fisherman's Trophy, which was captured that first year by Americans sailing out of Massachusetts. Peeved, the Nova Scotians set about taking it back. And did they ever! The *Bluenose* retained the trophy for 18 years running, despite the best efforts of Americans to recapture it. The race was shelved as World War II loomed; in the years after the war, fishing schooners were displaced by long-haul, steel-hulled fishing ships, and the schooners sailed into the footnotes of history. The *Bluenose* was sold in 1942 to labor as a freighter in the West Indies. Four years later, it foundered and sank off Haiti.

What made the *Bluenose* so unbeatable? Several theories exist. Some said it was because of last-minute hull design changes. Some said it was frost "setting" the timbers as the ship was being built. Still others claim it was blessed with an unusually talented captain and crew.

The replica *Bluenose II* was built in 1963 from the same plans as the original, in the same shipyard, and even by some of the same workers. It has been owned by the province since 1971, and sails throughout Canada and beyond as Nova Scotia's seafaring ambassador. The *Bluenose*'s location varies from year to year, and it schedules visits to ports in Canada and the United States. In midsummer, it typically alternates between Lunenburg and Halifax, during which time visitors can sign up for 2-hour harbor sailings (C$40 adults, C$25 children age 3–12). Find each summer's sailing schedule online at http://museum.gov.ns.ca/blue nose. To hear about the ship's schedule, call the **Bluenose II Preservation Trust** (© **866/579-4909,** ext. 221 or 902/634-4794, ext. 221). The Bluenose underwent restoration in 2011, scheduled to be completed by the summer of 2012.

and see if you can capture some of it. There's a small bike shop along the road to the neighborhood, the **Lunenburg Bike Barn** (www.bikelunenburg.com; © **902/634-3426**) at 579 Blue Rocks Rd., run by the same family for what seems like ages. The Barn's helpful owners will rent you a bike for exploring the surroundings, dispense helpful info, even fix or otherwise service your bike in a pinch.

If you continue onward instead of turning toward "the point," you'll soon come to the enclave of **Stonehurst,** another cluster of homes gathered around a rocky harbor. The road forks along the way; the narrow, winding route to South Stonehurst is somewhat more scenic. This whole area is just ideal for exploring by bicycle, with twisting lanes, great vistas, and limited traffic.

Heading eastward along the other side of Lunenburg Harbor, you'll end up eventually at the **Ovens Natural Park** ★ (www.ovenspark.com; © **902/766-4621**) in Riverport, a privately owned campground and day-use park that sits on 1.6km (1 mile) of dramatic coastline. You can follow the seaside trail to view the "ovens" (sea caves, actually) for which the park was named. The park also features **Ol' Gold Miner Diner** that serves up traditional homemade meals, and a great view. Entrance fees are C$8 adults, C$5 seniors and children age 5 to 11, and campsites cost C$25 to C$55 per night—the most expensive sites are on the water, with the best views—and there are discounts for weekly stays. Nine camping cabins of various sizes are C$50 to C$180 nightly, C$350 to C$1,250 weekly. The park is open from May 15 to October 15.

WHERE TO STAY

Lunenburg is chock-full of good inns and B&Bs, but the situation seems to be in constant flux in recent years: most of the prominent properties in town always either seem to be for sale, or to have just recently been sold. As a result, ownership and rates can change on the fly. Call ahead to be sure.

The town's most diverse set of lodgings is that run by the folks at the pub-like the **Grand Banker Seafood Bar & Grill** (© 800/360-1181 or 902/634-3300) at 82 Montague St. The restaurant's owner rents out a total of 17 rooms and suites around the old town, including in the affiliated Brigantine Inn and the former Morash House. Rates depend on amenities and time of year, but usually range from around C$70 to C$185; check directly with the inn and restaurant for current prices, availability, and to make bookings.

For budget travelers, a great little **municipal campground** ★ is located next to (and managed by) the visitor center (© 888/615-8305 or 902/634-8100) on Blockhouse Hill. It has wonderful views and hookups for RVs. Be aware that the 55 sites are packed in tightly, but the location is well situated for exploring the town. Ask about pitching your tent on the less crowded far side of the information center, up on the grassy hill next to the fort's earthworks. The cost to camp is C$24 to C$33; it's open from mid-May through mid-October.

If that campground's full, **Little Lake Family Campground** (© 902/634-4308), 3km (2 miles) outside town in the village of **Centre** (head out Rte. 3), has 85 sites, most with electrical hookups and about half with water and sewer lines. Sites here cost about the same as those at the town's campground.

Alicion Bed & Breakfast ★★ 📖   Owners Lorne and Janet Johanson run this small B&B, formerly the Senator Bed & Breakfast, out of a large, shipshape house in a serene residential neighborhood within walking distance of Lunenburg's Old Town. It gets raves from Frommer's readers. Surprisingly for the house's size, there are four nature-themed guest rooms, all with en-suite bathrooms; two have jetted "hydrotherapy" tubs. Cheers to the Johansons, who have gone "green" with the property, adding organic fabrics and foods to what is already excellent lodging.

66 McDonald St. (P.O. Box 1215), Lunenburg, NS B0J 2C0. www.alicionbb.com. © **877/634-9358** or 902/634-9358. 4 units. C$99–C$155 double. Open year-round, rates reduced mid-Oct to mid-May. Rates include full breakfast. MC, V. **Amenities:** Bikes. Jacuzzi (2 units). *In room:* TV/DVD, hair dryer, Wi-Fi (free).

Boscawen Inn ★   This imposing 1888 mansion occupies a prime hillside site just a block from the heart of Lunenburg; it was built by local Senator H. A. N. Kaulbach, an influential figure in local history. Today it's considered one of the town's finest examples of the Queen Anne Revival style of architecture. The interior decor is Victorian, although not aggressively so. It's almost worth staying just to get access to the main-floor deck and its harbor views. The biggest (and costliest) room has a four-poster bed, Jacuzzi tub, turret sitting nook, and (the kicker) a harbor view. Three spacious suites are located in the nearby 1905 MacLachlan House—it's the building with the little octagonal tower and the only place where pets are allowed (C$25 fee). Note: Guests on the third floor need to navigate some pretty steep steps to get to their rooms (book a different floor if you have mobility concerns).

150 Cumberland St. (P.O. Box 489), Lunenburg, NS B0J 2C0. www.boscawen.ca. Ⓒ **800/354-5009.** 22 units. C$89–C$225 double; C$155–C$225 suite. Rates include continental breakfast. Pets in MacLachlan House only (C$25 fee). AE, DISC, MC, V. **Amenities:** Complimentary breakfast buffet; Jacuzzi (1 unit). *In room:* TV, hair dryer, Internet (free).

1880 Kaulbach House Historic Inn ★★   Owned by a pair of Brits, the 1880 Kaulbach House offers a perfect example of sympathetically restored architectural heritage combined with contemporary comfort. The house is decorated elaborately, as befits its architecture. Rooms are furnished in simple Victorian style, rendered somewhat less oppressive by welcoming, un-Victorian color schemes (one room is even ruby red). The biggest and best room (the Bluenose Suite) is on the top floor; it features two sitting areas and a great view; the former servants' quarters, on street level, are smaller. The included three-course breakfast is worth coming for. Just 2 blocks from the waterfront, this Registered Heritage home overlooks the ocean.

75 Pelham St. (P.O. Box 1348), Lunenburg, NS B0J 2C0. www.kaulbachhouse.com. Ⓒ **800/568-8818** or 902/634-8818. 6 units. C$99–C$169 double. Off-season discounts available. Rates include full breakfast. AE, MC, V. *In room:* A/C, TV/DVD, hair dryer, no phone, Wi-Fi (free).

Lennox Inn Bed & Breakfast ★   In 1991, this handsome but simple house in a quiet residential area was slated for demolition, but Robert Cram didn't want to see it go. He purchased and restored it to its original 1791 appearance, painting it deep red and furnishing with antiques and period reproductions. Things are more rustic than opulent (the wood-floored rooms are pretty spare), but the Lennox should be first on your Lunenburg list if you're into period atmosphere and historic homes. The inn claims, quite plausibly, to be the oldest unchanged inn in all of Canada (it was once a tavern back in the day). Spacious second-floor rooms have original plaster (in three of four), original fireplaces (no longer working), period prints, skinny four-poster beds, and French wingback chairs. The owner doesn't believe in TV, but added Wi-Fi access. An organic country breakfast is served in the former drinking room; do note the ingenious old bar.

69 Fox St. (P.O. Box 254), Lunenburg, NS B0J 2C0. www.lennoxinn.com. Ⓒ **888/379-7605** or 902/521-0214. 4 units, 2 with shared bathroom. C$95–C$120 double. Rates include full breakfast. MC, V. Open year-round; by reservation only mid-Oct to Apr. *In room:* No phone, Wi-Fi (free).

Lunenburg Arms Hotel & Spa ★★   In a town where nearly all the lodgings consist of former seamen's homes, this hotel converted from a gutted tavern-boardinghouse stands out as a modern and welcome alternative. It's what passes for a boutique hotel in these parts, offering an updated look, rooms that are wheelchair-accessible, and an elevator, amenities not often found in small-town Nova Scotia. Room furnishings wouldn't look out of place in a New York hotel. Yet there are thoughtfully homey touches such as a stuffed teddy bear (or two) in each room. (Pets are welcomed with open paws.) Bathrooms tend to be fairly small. No two rooms are laid out exactly alike, so examine a couple to get the configuration you want: some have Jacuzzis, some feature knockout harbor views. There are also two bi-level loft suites with beds upstairs. There is also an on-site spa that includes a soaker tub, hot tub, aromatherapy-and-steam showers. A little bit of modern-day pampering can be had with their full-service Spa at Ninety4.

94 Pelham St., Lunenburg, NS B0J 2C0. www.lunenburgarms.com. Ⓒ **800/679-4950** or 902/640-4040. Fax 902/640-4041. 26 units. Peak season C$129–C$199 double, C$199–C$269 suite; off-peak C$89–C$169 double and suite. AE, MC, V. **Amenities:** Dining room; conference room; spa. *In room:* A/C, TV, hair dryer, Wi-Fi (free).

4

NOVA SCOTIA | South Shore

WHERE TO EAT

As with Lunenburg's inns, many prominent restaurants in town always seem to be up for sale at any given moment. Check ahead to ensure your chosen eatery is open.

The Knot ★ 🍴 PUB FARE   Good beers on tap and a convivial English atmosphere make this pub a great place to take a break from more upscale eateries in town. Located smack in the center of a tiny commercial district, it serves surprisingly tasty pub fare—think juicy burgers, fried fish, local sausage, and a warming mussel soup—plus a selection of bitters and ales, including one specially brewed in Halifax by the folks at Propeller Brewery for the Knot. The crowd here is an agreeable, never-too-fancy mixture of fishermen, local families, and tourists, and bar staff are all too happy to help you decide what's good that day. Sign of the times: The bar now has a Facebook page.

4 Dufferin St. www.theknotpub.ca. ⓒ **902/634-3334.** Meals C$6–C$15. AE, MC, V. Daily 10am–midnight; kitchen closes 9pm in summer, 8:30pm in winter.

Old Fish Factory Restaurant ★ SEAFOOD   We always time visits to Lunenburg to include this restaurant in a former fish processing plant. Sharing space with the fishing museum (see "Exploring Lunenburg," above) heightens the experience. I love feeling steeped in the history of the fisheries; you can hear the creaking of the preserved vessels tied up dockside if you're early enough to nab a table on the patio or a window seat. The specialty is seafood and local fare like Lunenburg sausage and sauerkraut, salt fish cod cakes, or lobster (served at least four different ways). Of course, the menu also includes modern presentations such as baked halibut sided with strawberry salsa, along with basic steak and chicken. The large, popular restaurant sometimes seems to swallow whole bus tours, so reservations are recommended. Or you can grab a cold one at the Ice House bar and wait (the food is great here, too). Check out the entertainment: they often host *ceilidhs* and open mics.

68 Bluenose Dr. (at the Fisheries Museum). www.oldfishfactory.com. ⓒ **800/533-9336** or 902/634-3333. Reservations recommended. Lunch C$9–C$18; dinner C$17–C$29. AE, DC, DISC, MC, V. Daily 11am–9pm. Closed late Oct to early May.

Tin Fish ★ CANADIAN   The house restaurant of the Lunenburg Arms (see "Where to Stay," above) mostly features straight-ahead Canadian food, but done classier than the fried grub that predominates elsewhere around town. Start with scallops on the half-shell in béchamel sauce, crab cakes, mussels, or a tomato tart, then move on to entrees like local haddock peppered and fried in a *panko* crust, planked salmon, barbecued striploin, breast of duck, or a maple-curry pasta. Even the vegetarian entree, a grilled phyllo wrap filled with goat cheese, slivered almonds, and grilled veggies, is good. Eat inside by the fireplace, at the bar, or out on the stylish terrace opening onto a quiet street.

94 Pelham St. ⓒ **800/679-4950** or 902/640-4040. Reservations accepted. Lunch C$10–C$15; dinner C$18–C$29. AE, MC, V. Mon–Sat 7am–11pm; Sun 8am–2:30pm.

Mahone Bay ★★

The village of Mahone Bay, settled in 1754 by European Protestants, is picture-perfect Nova Scotia at its best. It's tidy and trim, with an eclectic Main Street that snakes along the lovely eponymous bay and is lined with inviting shops, markets, and eateries. Locals are friendly and knowledgeable. The winds attract plenty of sailboats to the bay. And the town's **three churches,** grouped closely together, are among the most famous in the province—expect *churcharazzi* politely clicking away. This is a town that's remarkably well cared for by its 900 or so full-time residents, a growing number of whom live here and commute to Halifax (about an hour away). Architecture buffs will find a range of styles to keep them ogling, too.

One of the best **visitor information centers** (www.mahonebay.com; ℂ **888/624-6151** or 902/624-6151) in Nova Scotia is located at 165 Edgewater St., near the three church steeples. It's open daily in summer from around 9am until 7:30pm, only until 5:30pm in the shoulder seasons.

Each year in early August, Mahone Bay pays homage to pirates with a fun-filled regatta in the Bay. In September, they celebrate scarecrows and then, come November, they put the focus on Father Christmas. It's all an excuse to dress up the town with various fun themes and activities for spectators and participants to enjoy.

There's also an annual summer series of **classical music and vocal performances** filling the three churches; the shows cost C$20 each, free for kids 12 and under. Call ℂ **902/634-4280** for information or to pre-order tickets.

EXPLORING THE TOWN

The free **Mahone Bay Settlers Museum,** 578 Main St. (ℂ **902/624-6263**), provides a historic context for your explorations. From June through September, it's open Monday to Saturday 10am to 5pm and Sundays 1 to 5pm. After Labour Day, they sometimes open on request; call if you want to have a look. A good selection of historic decorative arts is on display here. Before leaving, be sure to request a copy of "Three Walking Tours of Mahone Bay," a handy brochure that outlines easy historic walks around the compact downtown.

Thanks to the looping waterside routes nearby, this is a popular destination for bikers. And the deep, protected harbor offers superb sea kayaking. If you'd like to give kayaking a go, contact **East Coast Outfitters** (ℂ **877/852-2567** or 902/852-2567), based in the Peggy's Cove area near Halifax. They offer half-day introductory classes and a 5-day coastal tour of the area. Among the more popular adventures is the daylong introductory tour, in which paddlers explore the complex shoreline and learn about kayaking in the process. The price is about C$135 per person, C$35 extra for an optional lobster lunch. Rentals are also available, starting at about C$50 per half-day for a single kayak. (You can also rent for just an hour or two, but what fun is that?)

Ross Farm Living Agriculture Museum ★★ (www.rossfarm.museum.gov. ns.ca; ℂ **877/689-2210** or 902/689-2210) at 4568 Rte. 12, off Route 103, is one of those terrific living experience museums that draws you in to life as lived in the 1800s. Ride a horse-drawn sleigh, smell cookies or stew cooking over a wood fire, build a barrel, pet a lamb. The oxen are big, lumbering, and beautiful. Costumed interpreters help you learn about heritage animal breeds and many things related to running a farm or a family home. This is one of my favorite stops winter or summer. I love the slowdown to quieter times, walking the interpretative trails, and visiting both the people and the animals. Allow half a day to truly enjoy country life.

SHOPPING

Mahone Bay serves as a magnet for all manner of creative types, and Main Street has now become a mini-shopping mecca for those who enjoy buying handmade goods. Shops here are typically open from late spring until Christmas, when Halifax residents often travel down here for some offbeat holiday shopping. Among the more interesting options are these:

Amos Pewter   Watch pewter come fresh out of the molds at this spacious workshop and gallery located in an 1888 building. You can get anything from tie tacks and earrings to candle holders and vases here; the Christmas tree ornament is a popular souvenir. 589 Main St. © **800/565-3369** or 902/624-9547.

Jo-Ann's Deli Market & Bake Shop ★   Gourmet and farm-fresh basic fare are sold at this wonderful food shop, where a bag of carrots serves as a counterweight on the screen door. It's the best place for miles around to stock up on local and organic produce; fresh sandwiches; and knockout cookies, sweets, and Cape Breton–influenced oat cakes—the chocolate-covered ones blend chocolate, sugar, salt, and oats to perfect effect. If you're in the mood for a picnic, this is your destination. The homemade jams, sold to benefit a local museum, are well priced, and the coffee drinks from the bar are all exceptionally good, as well. Each fall, an amazing array of carved pumpkins greets the weary traveler. 9 Edgewater St. © **902/624-6305.**

Suttles & Seawinds   Vibrant and distinctive clothing designed and made in Nova Scotia is sold at this stylish boutique. (There are other branches stretching from Halifax to Toronto, but this is the original.) The adjacent shop is crammed with quilts and resplendent bolts of fabric. 466 Main St. © **902/624-8375.**

WHERE TO STAY

You'll find a clutch of bed-and-breakfast choices along Mahone Bay's Main Street, and also on the roads leading to surrounding coves; consult the **Chamber of Commerce** website (www.mahonebay.com) for a fairly complete listing.

Right in the center of town, the lovely **Mahone Bay Bed & Breakfast** at 558 Main St. (© **866/239-6252** or 902/624-6388) is a Victorian option with four rooms at rates from C$95 to C$135 per night. This restored, bright yellow house was built in the 1860s by one of the town's many former shipbuilders; expect plenty of wicker, a widow's walk, and some rather arresting curvature on the front detail of the home. A sitting room upstairs (known as the Mahone Bay Bump) contains cards, games, books, and a TV with DVD player.

There's also **Fisherman's Daughter Bed & Breakfast,** 97 Edgewater St. (© **902/624-0483**), with its maritime theme and four rooms costing C$100 to C$125 per night each. The rooms are predictably decked out with a little floral frippery (and claw-foot tubs), but they also have excellent views of the town and bay and cable televisions.

Amber Rose Inn ★★   There are three good size-units in this family-owned Main Street inn carved out of a blue heritage home built in 1875. Rooms are sparely furnished (in a good way), rose-themed, and floral-printed; they're accented by plentiful flowers and gardens outside. The side entrance has a lovely little porch with bird feeders, great for reading a magazine and taking in the coastal light. There's a patio with chairs, and more chairs in the backyard. Morning breakfasts are included and run to strudels, pancakes, quiche, waffles, and eggs Benedict. This former country general store also houses an art gallery.

319 W. Main St. (P.O. Box 687), Mahone Bay, NS B0J 2E0. www.amberroseinn.com. © **902/624-1060.** Fax 902/624-0363. 3 units. C$95–C$135 suite. Rates include full breakfast. AE, MC, V. Closed Jan–Apr. *In room:* A/C, TV, fridge, hair dryer, Wi-Fi (free).

WHERE TO EAT

Mahone Bay's little main street has more than its share of places in which you can nosh, though most of them are priced in *tourodollars*—which is to say, higher than they probably should be.

Maybe that's why the seasonally open **Gazebo Cafe** ★ at 567 Main St. (© **902/624-6484**) still remains my favorite casual eating spot in the town. Affable and affordable, the place dishes up filling, healthy sandwiches and thick bowls of seafood chowder. They also do juices, smoothies, and top-notch coffee. Fresh desserts are delivered several times weekly. This place is becoming the de facto arts headquarters of the town, so check the bulletin board for news about local art shows and musical performances, some of which even occasionally take place right at the cafe. If you're coming in fall, call ahead; every year's schedule is different. They might be closing up shop, or they might be serving lunch straight through until Christmas.

Innlet Café ★★ SEAFOOD/GRILL The Kralicks, the Bavarian owners of the Innlet, are carrying on the place's long tradition as Mahone Bay residents' upscale night out on the town. Everything here is good, particularly their specialties: stir fries, "boils," and stews. Check out the full menu, including dessert and tea. (The Kralicks couldn't resist sticking apple strudel on the dessert menu; try it.) The best seats in the house are on the stone patio, with its fine view of the harbor and the famous three steeples. If you end up sitting inside, though, that's okay: The airiness of the interior make it just as inviting. The atmosphere here is informal and relaxed, never stuffy. There's a wine list and cocktails.

249 Edgewater St. www.innletcafe.com. ⓒ **902/624-6363.** Reservations recommended for dinner. Most main course items C$12–C$21. MC, V. Daily 11:30am–9pm. Closed Jan to mid-Mar.

Chester ★★

Chester is a short drive off Route 103 and has the feel of a moneyed summer colony somewhere on the New England coast back in the roaring '20s. In any case, the town was first settled in 1759 by immigrants from New England and Great Britain, and today it has a population of about 1,600. The village is noted for its regal homes and quiet streets, along with the numerous islands offshore. The atmosphere here is uncrowded, untrammeled, lazy, and slow—the way life used to be in summer resorts throughout the world. Change may be on the horizon: Canadian actors and authors have apparently discovered the place and are snapping up waterfront homes in town and on the islands as private retreats, giving a bit of cultural edge to the lazy feel of the spot. There's not really a public beach here, but the views and boat rides are more than enough to compensate.

The **Chester Visitor Information Centre** (www.chesterareans.com; ⓒ **902/275-4616**) is inside the old train station on 20 Smith Rd., Route 3, on the south side of town. It's open daily from 10am to 5pm.

EXPLORING THE AREA

Like so many other towns in Nova Scotia, Chester is best seen from your car. But unlike other towns, where the center of gravity seems to be in the commercial district, here the focus is on the graceful, shady residential areas that radiate out from the tiny main street.

In your rambles, plan to head down Queen Street to the waterfront, then veer around on South Street, admiring the views out toward the mouth of the harbor. Continue on South Street past the yacht club, past the statue of the veteran (in a kilt), past the sundial in the small square. Then you'll come to a beautiful view of Back Harbour. At the foot of the small park is a curious municipal saltwater pool, filled at high tide. On warmer days, you'll find what appears to be half the town, out splashing and shrieking in the bracing water.

Some creative shops are finding a receptive audience in and around Chester, and there's good browsing for new goods and antiques, both downtown and in the outlying areas. A good stop is the **Village Emporium** at 11 Pleasant St. (📞 **902/275-4773**), an eclectic clustering of folk-arty lavender soaps, simple pottery, knit purses, and the like; it's in the same building as the Kiwi Café (see "Where to Eat," below).

For an even slower pace, plan an excursion out to the **Tancook Islands ★**, a pair of lost-in-time islands with 200 year-round (as opposed to year-old) residents. Historically, cabbage put the islands on the map. German farmers were so good at growing them and making sauerkraut that it became quite famous. You will still find Tancook Sauerkraut in stores throughout the region. The islands, accessible via a short ferry ride, are good for walking the lanes and trails. Read up on the beaches, which reveal fossils, gurgling rocks and bubble-like formations in the waves. There's a small cafe or two, but little else to cater to travelers. Several ferry trips are scheduled daily between 6am and around 6pm. The ferry ties up each night on one of the islands, however, so don't count on making a late trip back to the mainland. (But there's also an inn on Big Tancook, if you're inclined to stay over.) Ferry tickets are C$5 roundtrip, free for children under 12. You might also want to check out the story of Oak Island. One of many small islands in Mahone Bay, it periodically attracts treasure hunters and has history to titillate any lover of such mysteries. The Oak Island Money Pit is the site of one of the world's longest running hunts for lost treasure. Privately owned, the island is connected to the mainland by a causeway, but advanced permission is required for any visitation. The Friends of Oak Island Society (www.friends ofoakisland.com) organizes tours on occasion. In the evening, the intimate **Chester Playhouse ★★**, 22 Pleasant St. (www.chesterplayhouse.ca; 📞 **800/363-7529** or 902/275-3933), hosts plays, concerts, a summer theater festival, and other high-quality events from March through December; it's a town institution, and absolutely a mustvisit if you're a theater or folk music buff. Theater festival tickets are usually around C$25 per person for adults, cheaper for children; musical performance ticket prices vary. Call or check the Playhouse's website for a schedule or to purchase tickets.

The local **library** at 63 Regent St. is a great place to check out local history, too. It was a gift from a New Yorker in memorial of her sister, Zoé Vallé Lightfoot (related to Josiah Bartlett, who signed the U.S. Declaration of Independence).

WHERE TO STAY

Graves Island Provincial Park ★★ ☺   This 50-hectare (124-acre) estate-like park is one of the province's more elegant-looking campgrounds, as befits moneyed Chester. The park has expanded to 84 sites, many of them dotting a high grassy bluff with outstanding views out to the spruce-clad islands of Mahone Bay; camping is available from mid-May through early October. There's also a boat launch, swimming area, and playground for the kids.

Rte. 3 (3km/1¾ miles north of the village on East River). 📞 **902/275-4425.** 84 sites. C$23 per site. MC, V.

Mecklenburgh Inn ★★   This appealing, brightly painted inn, built around 1900, is located on a low hill in one of Chester's residential neighborhoods. Rather than being prepossessing, the building has a fun, lived-in feel (motto: "The door is always open"), dominated by two broad porches on the first and second floors which invariably are populated with guests relaxing in Adirondack chairs and watching the town wander by below. (They wander here because they have to: The town post office is next door.) This place has been ticking along with a casual bonhomie since the late 1980s. Rooms are modern Victorian; generally quite bright, with pine flooring, whose beauty has been newly restored. Other touches include amenities such as French truffles, Frette linens, bathrobes, and pillow-topped mattresses. Yet it's still a relative bargain for the price, considering how nice the touches are.

78 Queen St., Chester, NS B0J 1J0. www.mecklenburghinn.ca. ✆ **866/838-4638** or 902/275-4638. 4 units. C$95–C$155 double. Rates include full breakfast. AE, V. Closed Jan–Apr. In room: Hair dryer, no phone, Wi-Fi (free).

WHERE TO EAT

In addition to the eateries listed below, there's the **Rope Loft,** at 36 Water St. (✆ **902/275-3430**), one of the town's chief gathering spots for locals. The kitchen serves the expected pastas, pizza, fried clams, Digby scallops, lobster, and other seafood by the water; ask for a deck chair, if you can get one. The restaurant serves brunch on weekends. They have a kids' menu, too. It's open seasonally.

If it's baked goods you want, **Julien's Pastry Shop** (✆ **902/275-2324**) at 43 Queen St. does them extremely well, as does the Kiwi Café (see below).

Kiwi Café ★★ 🍴 CAFE   A little enclave of New Zealand culture on the nautical coast of Nova Scotia? Yes, indeed. Kiwi, a thank-goodness-it's-still-fun place reigns in what can be an occasionally starchy town. Proprietress Lynda Flynn—yes, she's really from New Zealand, and received training in the culinary arts in Auckland—serves up eggs and bagels (try the lobster scramble) for breakfast, plus an assortment of sandwiches, wraps, panini, fresh soups, Nova Scotian fish cakes with mango salsa, and gourmet salads for lunch. Wash it down with wine, Nova Scotia beer, or a good blended Halifax-roasted-coffee drink. On the go? No problem: Grab a "Dinner in a Box" (Flynn also runs a catering business) or some New Zealand honey from the little provisions shop on the premises. And don't forget a piece of hummingbird cake. A great little find, full of good cheer.

19 Pleasant St. www.kiwicafechester.com. ✆ **902/275-1492.** Main courses C$6–C$18. V. Daily 8am–4:30pm.

La Vista ★★ CONTINENTAL/SEAFOOD   This dining room inside the Oak Island Resort spa and convention center (just north of Chester, down a side peninsula) offers an upscale alternative to traveling diners in the Chester area. And the views out those windows—well, just be there at sunset on a clear day. Mains include sesame-crusted salmon over basmati rice, cedar-planked salmon with maple butter, pan-roasted halibut with pepper and lemon grass, roasted tenderloin with a Stilton crust, shrimp-and-lobster pasta, or whatever else has been invented for the season. The signature, decadent "Cordon Oak Island," stuffs a chicken with apple-wood smoked cheddar and Black Forest ham, but then tops it with (what else?) maple cream.

36 Treasure Dr. (inside the Oak Island Resort), Western Shore. ✆ **800/565-5075** or 902/627-2600. Main courses C$18–C$23. MC, V. Daily 7am–2pm and 5–9pm. Take Hwy. 103 to exit 9, continue 2km (1¼ miles) to Rte 3, turn onto Rte 3, continue 5km (3 miles) to resort.

Hubbards

Nova Scotia's last great dance hall has been luring folks to Hubbards for more than 65 years. From late April to Halloween, the Shore Club (see below) tunes up the music every Saturday for one great party. They serve up the best in classic and contemporary rock, blues, R&B, reggae, zydeco, swing and big band, so check the line-up on their website. Popular bands like the Persuaders, Late Nite Lover, Matt Minglewood, the Mellotones, Shameless, Sam Moon, Hal Bruce, the Hopping Penguins, and many more have kept the Shore Club hopping. But dancing is only part of the fun. The Shore Club's unique Lobster Suppers (see below) have been going even

About 42km (26 miles) southwest of Halifax is the fishing village of **Peggy's Cove** ★★ (pop. 120), which offers postcard-perfect tableaus: an octagonal lighthouse (surely one of the most photographed in the world), tiny fishing shacks, and graceful fishing boats bobbing in the postage stamp–size harbor. The bonsai-like perfection hasn't gone unnoticed by the big tour operators, however, so it's a rare summer day when you're not sharing the experience with a few hundred of your close, personal bus-tour friends. The village is home to a handful of B&Bs and a gallery, but scenic values draw the day-trippers with cameras. While there, make sure to check out the touching **Swissair Flight 111 Memorial** ★ among the rocks just before the turnoff to the cove; this site memorializes the passengers of that flight, which crashed into the Atlantic just off the coast. Pay attention to the wildflowers growing beside the walkways—some elusive plants grow here. Want to stay awhile? A good lodging choice in the area is **Peggy's Cove B&B** (www.peggyscovebb.com; ℂ **877/725-8732** or 902/823-2265), close to the lighthouse with five rooms costing C$99 to C$145 per night; breakfast is included. Units all have phones, Wi-Fi access, and DVD players. If it's full, **Code's Oceanside Inn** (www3.ns.sympatico.ca/oceanside.inn/; ℂ **888/823-2765** or 902/823-2765), about 2 miles away in West Dover, has two rooms and a suite for C$105 to C$195 per night. (The name isn't some mystic or cryptic puzzle. The owners are a couple whose last name is Code.)

longer, more than 75 years. Afterward, book into the **Dauphinee Inn** nestled on the shores of Hubbards Cove, just down the road.

WHERE TO STAY, PLAY & EAT

Dauphinee Inn ★★   This waterside inn boasts a magnificent view of their cove on St. Margaret's Bay, which can be enjoyed from decks or balconies outside, rooms, or from the waterside deck and panoramic dining room downstairs. Furnished with period antiques, all rooms have private bathrooms, comfy beds, and most have a magnificent view of the Cove. For a perfect evening, reserve a table on the deck and watch the sunset as you enjoy a meal. They offer a full menu, as well as several combinations of Hot Rock cooking, where you cook your own meal on a slab of granite, right at the table. The taste and smell are memory makers, and it's fun to do.

167 Shore Club Rd., Hubbards. www.dauphineeinn.com. ℂ **800/567-1790** or 902/857-1790. 6 rooms. C$99–C$195. Restaurant open mid-June to late Sept, 4pm–9pm. Sat–Sun brunch 10am–2pm. AE, DISC, MC, V. **Amenities:** Continental Breakfast included. *In room:* TV, Wi-Fi (free).

Shore Club Lobster Suppers ★★★ 🍴 LOBSTER SUPPER   It's simple here: As you enter, pass the crew cooking lobster and mussels, cross the "Red Carpet" and settle in for a feast that is an otherwise typical lobster supper. Lobster boiled fresh, unlimited cultivated mussels, all-you-can-eat salad bar, homemade rolls, and dessert (they have steak, chicken, and vegetarian options, as well). These folks specialize in hospitality and they are good at it. Be sure to get the details for the dance hall.

250 Shore Club Rd., Hubbards. www.lobstersupper.com. ℂ **800/567-1790** or 902/857-9555. Reservations highly recommended. Lobster C$29–C$40; alternates C$25–C$30; kids C$7.50. AE, MC, V. Open weekends last 3 weeks of May. Wed–Sun, June to early Oct 4–8pm.

HALIFAX ★★

Harborside Halifax is the biggest city in the Maritime Provinces by far, yet it doesn't *feel* big at all. It actually feels like a collection of loosely connected neighborhoods, which is, in fact, what it is; you often forget this is one of the central economic engines of Eastern Canada. Established in 1749, the city was named for George Montagu Dunk, second earl of Halifax. (Residents agree it was a huge stroke of luck that the city avoided being named Dunk, Nova Scotia.) The city plodded along as a colonial backwater for the better part of a century, overshadowed by nearby towns building more boats (Shelburne and Lunenburg, to name two); one historian even wrote of Halifax as "a rather degenerate little seaport town."

But the city's natural advantages—that well-protected harbor, its location near major fishing grounds and shipping lanes—eventually caused Halifax to overtake its rivals and emerge as an industrial port and military base for the ages. (Relatively speaking, of course.) And then, at long last, so came the tourists and scholars and urban escapees from Toronto: In recent decades, this city has grown aggressively (it annexed several adjacent suburbs in 1969) and carved out a niche for itself as the commercial and financial hub of the Maritimes.

Today, it's also the cultural cutting edge of Eastern Canada. Pop singer Sarah MacLachlan grew up here, and it's also the hometown of professional hockey's "next Gretzky," young Sidney Crosby of the Pittsburgh Penguins. So long as you're not allergic to beer, good food, ocean breezes, and good music, I think it's fair to say you'll never be at a loss for something to do during your time here.

Essentials

GETTING THERE   Coming from New Brunswick and the west, the most direct route to Halifax by car is via Route 102 from Truro; allow 2 or 2½ hours to drive here once you cross the invisible provincial border at Amherst. There is a bus service, the **Acadian Lines** (www.acadianbus.com; ✆ **902/454-9321**) which connects to the rest of the world.

Many travelers arrive in Halifax by air. Halifax's **Stanfield International Airport** (www.hiaa.com; ✆ **902/873-2091**; airport code YHZ) in Elmsdale is 34km (21 miles) north of the city center; to get to Halifax, take Route 102 south. Airlines serving Halifax currently include Air Canada (and its commuter airline Jazz), WestJet, American, Air Transat, Condor, Continental, Corsairfly, Delta, Porter Airlines, US Airways, United, and Icelandair (see "Fast Facts: The Maritimes," p. 258). Nova Scotia's variable weather means it's always a good idea to call your airlines before heading out to the airport to make sure your flight will depart on time, especially in winter.

For transportation to and from the airport, you can either take a cab (a flat fare of C$53–C$56 by law); rent a car (plenty of big-name chain options in the terminal); or take the **Airporter** (www.airporter.biz; ✆ **902/873-2091**) shuttle bus, which makes frequent runs from the airport to major downtown hotels daily from 6:30am to 11:15pm. The rate is C$20 per person one-way. There are also a surprising number of **long-haul shuttles ★** from the airport directly to Cape Breton, Yarmouth, Moncton, Antigonish, and Prince Edward Island. Some shuttle services require advance reservations, because they only run once per day and the vans may be full up on any given day. Check the airport's website (www.flyhalifax.com), or call the airport (✆ **902/873-4422**) for an updated list of these shuttle services.

There's also a province-run **Visitor Information Centre** (VIC) located in the domestic arrivals area of the main terminal of the airport (☎ **902/873-1223**), open year-round from 9am until 9pm.

You can even arrive by train. **VIA Rail** (www.viarail.ca; ☎ **888/842-7245**) offers overnight train service 6 days a week between Halifax and Montréal. The entire trip takes between 18 and 21 hours, depending on direction. Stops include Moncton and Campbellton (with bus connections to Québec City). Halifax's train station, at 1161 Hollis St. (adjoining the Westin Hotel), is within walking distance of downtown attractions. Cruise ships tie up adjacent to the train station, if you happen to want to arrive in style.

VISITOR INFORMATION   There's a ton of tourist info here. The government-run **visitor information center** (VIC) (☎ **902/424-4248**) on the waterfront at 1655 Lower Water St. (Sackville Landing on the boardwalk) is open daily, year-round until 9pm in summer, until 6pm in winter. There's another provincial VIC at Halifax's airport (☎ **902/873-1223**), also open year-round. Each is staffed with friendly staff who will point you in the right direction or help you make room reservations. For online information about the city, visit **www.halifaxinfo.com** or **www.halifax.ca/ visitors**.

GETTING AROUND   Parking in Halifax can be problematic. Long-term metered spaces are in high demand downtown, and many of the parking lots and garages fill up fast. If you're headed downtown for a brief visit, you can usually find a 2-hour meter. But if you're looking to spend the day in town, I'd suggest venturing out early and snagging a spot in an affordable parking lot or garage, or taking a taxi from your hotel. There's some parking near Sackville Landing, or try along Lower Water Street past Bishops Landing, where you can sometimes park all day for around C$9. A little gem in the world of parking can be found by the Historic Properties, at 1815 Upper Water (under the Law Courts); the entrance is hard to find, so go slow and look for the IMP Parking sign on the water side of the street.

Metro Transit operates buses throughout the city. Route and timetable information is available at the information centers or by phone (www.halifax.ca/metrotransit; ☎ **902/490-4000**). Bus fare is C$2.25 for adults and students; C$1.50 for seniors and children. Transfers are free.

EVENTS   The annual Royal Nova Scotia International Tattoo (www.nstattoo.ca; ☎ **800/563-1114** or 902/420-1114) features military and marching bands totaling some 2,000-plus military and civilian performers. The rousing event takes place over the course of a week in early July and is held indoors at the Halifax Metro Center. Tickets are C$34 to C$70 per adult, depending on the position of your seating, less for seniors and children.

The annual **Halifax Jazz Festival** (www.halifaxjazzfestival.ca; ☎ **902/492-2225**) has performances ranging from global and avant-garde to local and traditional music each July. Venues include nightclubs and outdoor stages, and prices vary considerably; consult the website for the latest details and specifics of performance and price.

In early August, expect to see a profusion of street performers ranging from folk singers and fire-eaters to clowns and jugglers. They descend on Halifax each summer for the 10-day **Halifax International Busker Festival** (www.buskers.ca). Performances take place along the waterfront walkway all day long and are often quite remarkable. The festival is free, though donations are requested—you can donate *and*

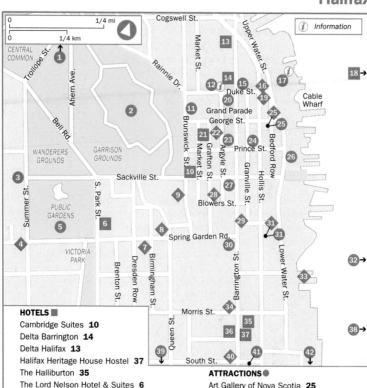

HOTELS ■

Cambridge Suites **10**
Delta Barrington **14**
Delta Halifax **13**
Halifax Heritage House Hostel **37**
The Halliburton **35**
The Lord Nelson Hotel & Suites **6**
The Prince George Hotel **21**
Super 8 Dartmouth **18**
Waverly Inn **36**
The Westin Nova Scotian **41**

RESTAURANTS ◆

The Bicycle Thief **33**
Cheapside Café **25**
Cheelin **31**
Chives Canadian Bistro **29**
daMaurizio **31**
Five Fishermen Restaurant & Grill **22**
Hart & Thistle Gastropub & Brewery **19**
Henry House **40**
Il Mercato **8**
Morris East **34**
Ryan Duffy's Steak and Seafood **7**
Saege Bistro **4**
Satisfaction Feast **28**
Sweet Basil Bistro **16**
Steve-O-Reno's **9**

ATTRACTIONS ●

Art Gallery of Nova Scotia **25**
Barrington Place **15**
The Brewery **31**
Fairview Lawn Cemetery **1**
Halifax Citadel National Historic Site **2**
Halifax Historic Properties **17**
Halifax Public Gardens **5**
Maritime Museum of the Atlantic **26**
McNab's Island **32**
Metro Centre **11**
Neptune Theatre **27**
Nova Scotia Centre for Craft
  and Design **38**
Nova Scotia Museum of
Natural History **3**
Old Burying Ground **30**
Old City Hall **20**
Pier 21 and Seaport Market **42**
Point Pleasant Park **39**
Province House **24**
St. Paul's Anglican Church **23**
Scotia Square **12**

get complete info by buying a comprehensive festival guide for just C$2 on the water-front before and during the festival. Any hotel reception desk in town worth its salt should also be able to give you updated info on what's happening where.

The **Atlantic Film Festival ★★★** (www.atlanticfilm.com; ☎ 902/420-3546) offers screenings of more than 150 films at theaters around Halifax over a 10-day period in mid-September. The focus is largely on Canadian filmmaking, with an emphasis on independent productions and shorts, and the quality level is high. The 2010 lineup included *Incendies* (Oscar nominee), *In a Better World* (Oscar Winner), *Carlos,* and *Barney's Version* (both Golden Globe winners). Panel discussions with industry players are also part of the festival, meaning you get a chance to see mid-level directors and stars up close and personal. Film screenings are C$12, with special packages offered. If you are a film buff, check their website for *alFresco filmFesto,* an outdoor summer film series on the Halifax waterfront and *ViewFinders: International Film Festival for Youth.*

In early August, a great new outdoor event showcases more than 200 different beers and ciders from the U.S. and Canada, including a bunch from Maine. I'm talking about the **Halifax Seaport Beerfest ★** (www.seaportbeerfest.com; ☎ 902/453-5343). It takes place at the Seaport Harbourwalk, at Terminal and Marginal streets, in two 3-hour sessions. If you're crazy for microbrews, and always wondered what a Muskoka Cream Ale or a Galt Knife Old Style tastes like, this is your chance. There's also food and live music, of course. Tickets cost C$40 to C$45 per person, and they get you a program plus a 4-ounce glass with which you can sample all the wonderful beers surrounding you. Bring a picture ID.

Finally, the annual mid-October **Nocturne** (☎ 902/233-0003) is a fun, free art museum-and-gallery walk that kicks off at 6pm and concludes around midnight, highlighting what's fresh on the local art scene. Free shuttle buses ease the load on your feet, too. Only drawback? It only lasts 1 night.

Exploring Halifax

These days, Halifax sprawls out for miles in every direction but east—that is the Atlantic Ocean. Downtown Halifax is fairly compact, thus easily reconnoitered if you don't mind steep hills and some traffic. The major landmark is the **Citadel**—that stone fortress looming over downtown from a grassy height. (From the ramparts, you can look into the windows of the 10th floor of downtown skyscrapers.) The Citadel is only 9 blocks uphill from the **waterfront**—9 *steep* blocks. The waterfront area crams a huge number of activities, experiences, restaurants, and shopping into about 9 city blocks. You can get a sampling in a day, but plan for longer if you want to go on tours, try sailing, visit the theater, or really explore the museums and eateries.

Another lively neighborhood worth seeking out runs along **Spring Garden Road** between the Public Gardens and the library (at Grafton St.). Here you'll find intriguing boutiques, bars, and restaurants along 6 blocks, set amid a bohemian street scene. If you have strong legs, start on the waterfront and walk uphill and over the Citadel, descend to the lovely **Public Gardens** (see later), then return via Spring Garden Road.

You will need wheels to get to the **Hydrostone Market ★★** (5515–5547 Young St.), a neighborhood often referred to as a "European experience." The district rose from the ashes of the catastrophic Halifax Explosion (1917) and was designed after an English garden suburb. On one block, the Market houses amazing eateries; the pastries and such from **Julien's Bakery** are amazing. An olive oil tasting bar is sheer fun, as are the boutiques and galleries.

THE WATERFRONT

Halifax's rehabilitated waterfront extends from the Casino Nova Scotia (near Purdy Wharf) south to Pier 21. To the north, naval dockyards and Canadian Forces Base Halifax are restricted but often provide a view of naval vessels from the Canadian fleet. On sunny summer afternoons, this good stretch of waterfront bustles with tourists enjoying the harbor, business folks sneaking ice-cream cones, or skateboarders trying to make (or stay out of) trouble.

To fortify yourself for what lies ahead, stop in at **Garrison Brewing** at 1149 Marginal Rd. (www.garrisonbrewing.com; ☎ **902/453-5343**) for a tour and sampling. It's at the south end of the waterfront boardwalk near Pier 21 and the cruise ship docks. **Seaport Farmers Market** at 1209 Marginal Rd./Pier 20 (www.halifaxfarmers market.com; ☎ **902/429-6256**) is tempting, but don't load up with goodies until you return. As you walk north, you have a terrific view of Georges Island, a small drumlin in the middle of Halifax harbor which has been the scene of constant military activity and harbor defense for 200 years. You can glimpse the top of fortifications from here, but most of it is hidden. In 2012, Parks Canada is scheduled to open the site to visitors.

You'll soon come across **Bishops Landing,** an upscale development of condos, and natty little shops will tempt you to linger. Among them, **Bishop's Cellar** (www.bishops cellar.com; ☎ **902/490-2675**) is a stellar little wine shop which stays open until midnight Friday and Saturday. **Sugah! Confectionery & Ice Cream Emporium** (www. sugah.ca; ☎ **902/421-6079**), just a few steps further on the boardwalk, is worth a stop. Their Brew Bar (no, not a place to drink) is made from roasted barley, black malt, and dark chocolate handcrafted into a decadent bar inspired by Garrison Brewing. **Rum Runners Rum Cake Factory** (www.rumrunners.ca; ☎ **902/421-6079**), where they bake the rum, or whisky, right into a delicious cake, is right next door.

Continue a short distance along the boardwalk, keeping the water on your right. **Sackville Landing** is studded with other small diversions, intriguing shops, takeout food emporia, artisans, and monuments. Think of it as an alfresco scavenger hunt.

If you're interested in fish or history, make your next stop the waterfront's crown jewel, the **Maritime Museum of the Atlantic** (see below). Pass North America's oldest operating **naval clock,** which was built in 1767 and chimed at the Halifax Naval Dockyard from 1772 all the way up until 1993.

Then check out the **ferry terminal,** which gets hectic during rush hour with commuters coming and going to Dartmouth across the harbor—but, outside rush hour, is a cheap and relaxing way to get a quick, sweeping city and harbor view. The passenger-only **ferry ★** runs every 15 minutes, with a fare of C$2.25 per adult each way, C$1.50 for seniors and children age 5 to 15. You need to have cash: change machines are nearby and remember to ask for transfers for a bus or to return. It only takes 15 minutes to get to Dartmouth, and 15 minutes to get back.

The waterfront's shopping core is located in and around the 3-block **Historic Properties.** These buildings of wood and stone are Canada's oldest surviving warehouses, and were once the heart of the city's shipping industry. Today, their historic architecture provides ballast for the somewhat precious boutiques and restaurants they now house instead. Especially appealing is the granite-and-ironstone **Privateers' Warehouse,** which dates from 1813.

If you're feeling like a pub crawl might be in order, the Historic Properties area is a good place to wander around during the early evening. There's a contagious energy that spills out of the handful of public houses here as workers get off work and tipple pints: You'll find a bustling camaraderie and live music.

Maritime Museum of the Atlantic ★★★ ☺ All visitors to Nova Scotia with even a passing interest in history owe themselves a stop at this standout museum, situated on a prime piece of waterfront. Exhibits are involving and well executed, and you'll be surprised how fast 2 hours can fly. Visitors are greeted by a cool 3m (10-ft.) lighthouse lens from 1906, then proceed through a series of shipbuilding and seagoing displays. Visit the deckhouse of a coastal steamer (ca. 1940) and learn the colorful history of Samuel Cunard, the Nova Scotia native (born in 1787) who founded the Cunard Steam Ship Co. to carry royal mail—but established a travel dynasty instead. Another highlight is the shocking exhibit on the tragic Halifax explosion of 1917, when two warships collided in the harbor not far from this museum, detonating tons of TNT; more than 1,700 people died, and windows were shattered 97km (60 miles) away. Naval convoy exhibits reveal just how close World War II came to North America.

But perhaps the most poignant exhibit is a single deck chair from the *Titanic*—a reminder that 150 victims of that disaster are buried here in Halifax, where rescue efforts were centered. Also memorable are an "Age of Steam" exhibit; Queen Victoria's barge; an interesting "Shipwreck Treasures of Nova Scotia" section with its stories and artifacts from more than a dozen local shipwrecks; and re-creations of a ship's chandlery, sail loft, and carpenter's shop. A fascinating place for adults and teens, especially on a rainy day.

1675 Lower Water St. www.maritime.museum.gov.ns.ca. © **902/424-7490.** May–Oct admission C$8.75 adults, C$7.75 seniors, C$4.75 children 6–17, C$23 family; Nov–Apr, admission discounted about 50%. May–Oct daily 9:30am–5:30pm (to 8pm Tues); Nov–Apr closed Mon and only 1–5pm Sun.

ON THE WATER

A number of boat tours depart from the Halifax waterfront. You can browse the offerings on **Cable Wharf,** near the foot of George Street, where many tour boats are based. On-the-water adventures range from 1-hour harbor tours (about C$18) to half-day deep-sea fishing trips (about C$55). **Murphy's on the Water** (© **902/420-1015**) runs the most extensive tour operation, with several boats and a choice of tours ranging from tall ship or cocktail sailing cruises to whale-watching and fishing trips to C$15 runs out to historic McNab's Island, which is located near the mouth of the harbor (see below). If you have little ones, *Theodore Too,* a replica of the tugboat from the Theodore cartoon series, will be a hit. It will cost you C$65 to take the family for a harbor tour.

The **Harbour Hopper** (© **902/490-8687**) amphibious craft, now also owned by Murphy's, crosses both land and sea during a harbor tour that takes about an hour. It costs C$26 for adults, C$24 for seniors, C$15 for children ages 6 to 15, and C$9 for children 5 and under. Families of four can travel for C$71 (the rates haven't changed in several years). The ticket office is located on the north side of the Maritime Museum.

CSS Acadia Now designated a National Historic Site, this unusually handsome 1913 steam-powered vessel is part of the Maritime Museum (their "largest artifact"). The *Acadia* was used by the Canadian government to chart the ocean bottom for 56 years until its retirement in 1969. Much of the ship is now open for self-guided tours, including the captain's quarters, upper decks, wheelhouse, and oak-paneled chart room. If you want to see more of the ship, ask about guided half-hour tours (they take place four times daily), which offer access to the engine room and more. Allow a half-hour to an hour to take it in.

1675 Lower Water St. (on the water, in front of Maritime Museum). ℂ **902/424-7490.** Admission C$2 per person or free with Maritime Museum ticket, which costs C$8.75 adults, C$7.75 seniors, C$4.75 children 6–17, C$23 family. 10am–5pm daily summer only; call in spring or fall.

HMCS Sackville   This blue-and-white corvette (a speedy warship smaller than a destroyer) is tied up along a wood-planked wharf behind a small visitor center. There's a short multimedia presentation to provide some background. The ship is outfitted just as it was in 1944, maintained as a memorial to the Canadians who served in World War II. Bedford Basin, at the western end of the harbor, served as the staging point for great convoys of ships that brought supplies and relief to war-torn Europe during that war. The thousands of seafarers who passed through this port are honored by nearby monuments. Plan to spend about an hour.

Sackville Landing (summer), HMC dockyard (winter). ℂ **902/429-2132,** off season 427-2837. Admission C$4 adults, C$2 seniors and students, C$9 family. June–Oct daily 10am–5pm; off-season hours vary.

Pier 21 ★ ☺   Between 1928 and 1971, more than one million immigrants arrived in Canada at Pier 21, Canada's version of America's Ellis Island. In 1999, the pier was restored and reopened, filled with engaging interpretive exhibits that vividly evoke the confusion and anxiety of the immigration experience. The pier is divided roughly into three sections: the boarding of the ship amid the cacophony of many languages, the crossing of the Atlantic (a half-hour multimedia show recaptures the voyage in a ship-like theater), and the dispersal of recent arrivals throughout Canada via passenger train. For those seeking more in-depth information (they say one in five Canadians today can trace a link back to Pier 21), there's also a reference library and computer resources. My family passenger records from 1951 popped up in just a few minutes. Pier 21 became the first National Museum outside of Ottawa in 2011, mandated to tell the story of immigration throughout Canada. Plan to spend at least an hour here, more if you're into immigration history.

1055 Marginal Rd. (on the waterfront behind the Westin Hotel). www.pier21.ca. ℂ **902/425-7770.** C$8.50 adults, C$7.50 seniors, C$5 children 6–16, C$21 family. May–Nov daily 9:30am–5:30pm; Dec–Mar Tues–Sat 10am–5pm; Apr Mon–Sat 10am–5pm.

THE CITADEL & DOWNTOWN

Downtown Halifax cascades 9 blocks down a hill between the imposing stone Citadel and the city's waterfront. There's no fast-and-ready tour route; don't hesitate to follow your own whims, ducking down quiet side streets and into bars or striding along the main roads as you wish. A good spot to regain your bearings periodically is the **Grand Parade,** where military recruits once practiced their drills. It's a lovely piece of urban landscape—a broad terrace carved into a hill, presided over on either end by **St. Paul's** (see below) and Halifax's **City Hall**, a sandstone structure built between 1887 and 1890 and exuberantly adorned with all the usual Victorian architectural trifles: prominent clock tower, dormers, pediments, arched windows, pilasters, Corinthian columns. (Alas, there's not much to see inside.)

If the weather is nice, the Grand Parade is a prime spot to bring an alfresco lunch and enjoy some people-watching.

Art Gallery of Nova Scotia   Located in a pair of sandstone buildings between the waterfront and the Grand Parade, Halifax's Art Gallery is arguably the premier gallery in the Maritimes, with a nice focus on local and regional art. Yet you'll also find a selection of other works by Canadian, British, and European artists, too, and well-chosen exhibits of folk and Inuit art. In 1998, the gallery expanded to include the Provincial Building next door, where the entire tiny house of Nova Scotian folk artist Maud Lewis was reassembled and put on display. The museum can be comfortably perused in 60 to 90 minutes. Overwhelmed? Sign up for the once-a-day tours. Also consider a lunch break in the attractive Cheapside Café (see "Where to Eat," later).

1723 Hollis St. (at Cheapside). © **902/424-5280.** Admission C$12 adults, C$10 seniors, C$7 students, C$5 children age 6–17, C$30 families. Daily 10am–5pm (Thurs to 9pm). Tours daily at 2:30pm (2nd tour 7pm Thurs only).

Halifax Citadel National Historic Site ★★ ☺ The Citadel is the perfect introduction to Halifax: It provides a good geographic first look at the city, and anchors it in history, as well. Even if a big stone fort weren't here, it would still be worth the uphill trek just for the astounding views—the panoramic sweep across downtown, the city's harbor, and the Atlantic Ocean make for some great sightseeing. The ascent quickly makes it obvious why this spot was chosen for Halifax's most formidable defense: There's simply no sneaking up on the place. Four forts have occupied this hilltop since 1749, but today the Citadel has been restored to look much as it did in 1856, when the final fort was built out of concern over American expansionist ideas. Yet the fort has never been attacked, a testament to its effectiveness as a deterrent.

Sturdy granite fortress walls topped by grassy embankments form a star. In a sprawling gravel and cobblestone courtyard, convincingly costumed interpreters in kilts and bearskin hats march in unison, playing bagpipes, and firing a cannon at noon. The former barracks and other chambers are home to exhibits about life at the fort. If you have questions, just stop a soldier, bagpiper, or washerwoman and ask. Don't expect to be alone—this National Historic Site is one of the most heavily visited in all of Canada, and it's not hard to see why. On the plus side, you won't need more than an hour to see everything here unless you want to linger and snap lots of pics of tartan-clad 78th Highlanders pageantry.

Citadel Hill. © **902/426-5080.** Admission June to mid-Sept C$12 adults, C$10 seniors, C$5.80 children 6–16, C$29 families; May and mid-Sept to Oct C$7.80 adults, C$6.55 seniors, C$3.90 children 6–16, C$20 families; free rest of the year. Parking C$4. July–Aug daily 9am–6pm; May–June and Sept–Oct daily 9am–5pm. Nov–Apr, visitor center closed but grounds open. No guides or tours in fall or winter.

Nova Scotia Centre for Craft and Design ★ 📇 Nova Scotia's provincial government runs this center near the Seaport Market and Pier 21, at the south end of the waterfront. The idea: to encourage and develop crafts- and design-based industries across the province. The Mary E. Black Gallery features constantly changing exhibits of the best that Nova Scotia craftspeople are producing in silver, pewter, ceramic pottery, precious jewelry, fabric, needlepoint—even whalebone. Depending on your interest, you could spend up to an hour here. There is also a small shop nearby, selling student work.

1061 Marginal Rd., Ste. 140. www.craft-design.ns.ca. © **902/492-2522.** Free admission. Tues–Fri 9am–5pm; Sat–Sun 11am–4pm.

Nova Scotia Museum of Natural History ★ ☺ Situated on the far side of the Citadel from downtown, this modern, midsize museum offers a good introduction to the flora and fauna of Nova Scotia. Galleries include geology, botany, mammals, and birds, plus exhibits of archaeology and Mi'kmaq culture. There's a cool butterfly house, filled with the winged wonders from July to September. Also noteworthy are an extensive collection of lifelike ceramic fungus and a colony of honeybees that freely come and go from their indoor acrylic hive through a tube connected to the outdoors. Allow an hour or more if your kids are really excited by this sort of science.

1747 Summer St. www.nature.museum.gov.ns.ca. (© **902/424-7353.** Admission C$5.75 adults, C$5.25 seniors, C$3.75 children 6–17, C$12–C$17 families. June to mid-Oct Mon–Sat 9:30am–5:30pm (Wed until 8pm); Sun noon–5:30pm; mid-Oct to May, closed Mon.

Province House ★ Canada's oldest seat of government, the three-story stone Province House has been home to the tiny Nova Scotian legislature since 1819. This exceptional Georgian building is a superb example of the rigorously symmetrical Palladian style. And like a jewel box, its dour stone exterior hides gems of ornamental detailing and artwork inside, especially the fine plasterwork, which is rare in a Canadian building from this era.

A free, well-written booklet is available when you enter; it provides helpful background about the building's history and architecture. (Sample legend that may or may not be true: It's said the headless falcons in several rooms were decapitated by an agitated, free-swinging legislator with a cane who mistook them for eagles during a period of feverish anti-American sentiment in the 1840s.) If the legislature is in session (it's not always), you can obtain a visitor's pass and sit up in the gallery, watching the business of the province unfold. They also offer tours, which you book by calling the information number below. History buffs should allow an hour for this visit.

1726 Hollis St. (near Prince St.). www.gov.ns.ca/legislature. (© **902/424-4661.** Free admission. July–Aug Mon–Fri 9am–5pm, Sat–Sun and holidays 10am–4pm; Sept–June Mon–Fri 9am–4pm.

St. Paul's Anglican Church ★★ Forming one end of the Grand Parade, this classically handsome white Georgian building was the first Anglican cathedral established outside of England, and as such is Canada's oldest Protestant place of worship. It was once the figurehead for all church doings in Eastern Canada—all the way to Ontario. That makes it pretty significant. (Part of the 1749 church was fabricated in Boston and erected in Halifax with the help of a royal endowment from King George II.) Later, history continued happening here: A piece of flying debris from the great explosion of 1917 (see Maritime Museum of the Atlantic, p. 88) is lodged in the wall over the doors to the nave. Just a quick visit is enough to get a sense of the place, especially the fine stained-glass windows; take one of the summertime guided tours if you want to see more. But the exterior alone is amazing.

1749 Argyle St. (on the Grand Parade near Barrington St.). www.stpaulshalifax.org. (© **902/429-2240.** Mon–Fri 9am–4:30pm; Sun services 8, 9:15, and 11am. Free guided tours June–Sept Mon–Sat; call for scheduling.

GARDENS & OPEN SPACE

Fairview Lawn Cemetery ★ When the *Titanic* went down on April 15, 1912, nearly 2,000 people died. Ship captains from Halifax were recruited to help retrieve the corpses. (You can learn about this grim mission at the Maritime Museum, described on p. 88.) Some 121 victims, mostly ship crewmembers, were buried at this quiet cemetery located a short drive north of downtown Halifax. Some of the simple graves have names, but many others only bear numbers. Plaques and signs highlight some poignant stories from the tragedy. It's definitely worth an hour or more for *Titanic* fans; others might just spend a few minutes here. (Without a car, though, skip it entirely—too far.) A brochure with driving directions to this and two other *Titanic* cemeteries in the city can be obtained either at the Maritime Museum or the city's visitor information centers. The 100th anniversary of the *Titanic* sinking will be marked here in 2012.

Chisholm Ave., off Connaught Ave. (about 4km/2½ miles northwest of the Citadel). © **902/490-4883.** Daylight hours year-round.

McNab's Island ★ This island wilderness is located within city limits near the mouth of the busy harbor, yet it's a world apart from downtown Halifax. Once part of the city's military defenses and later the site of a popular amusement park, McNab's hasn't had any permanent residents since 1985. Today it is a provincial park where you'll find miles of wooded roads and trails to explore, some 200 species of birds, and great views of the city skyline and Point Pleasant. Some camping is permitted. The fort at the island's southern tip dates from 1888—it was manned during both world wars, when all ships visiting Halifax harbor were required to signal the fort. (Those that failed to comply were warned with a shot across the bow.) Vital supply convoys of World War II, assembled in Bedford Basin and Halifax Harbour, were subject to attack by enemy submarines as soon as they passed the Island. Bring a picnic (and a ferry schedule) and plan to spend 2 hours or so.

In Halifax Harbor. www.mcnabsisland.com. © **800/326-4563** or 902/465-4563 (ferry service). Admission to island free; ferry from Eastern Passage C$15 round-trip adult, C$10 round-trip seniors and children 5–17.

Old Burying Ground Fully restored in 1991 as an outdoor museum and park, this was the first burial ground in Halifax, and between 1749 and 1844, some 12,000 people were interred here. (Only 1 in 10 graves is marked with a headstone, however.) You'll find examples of 18th- and 19th-century gravestone art—especially winged heads and winged skulls. (No rubbings are allowed, however.) Also exceptional is the Welsford-Parker Monument from 1855, which honors Nova Scotians who fought in the Crimean War. An ornate statue near the grounds' entrance features a lion with a Medusa-like mane. Go at dusk, when the grounds are imbued with a quiet grace, a few hours before sunset. The light slants through the trees and city traffic seems far, far away. Cemetery buffs could spend an hour or more; others can easily drop by for 10 minutes en route to downtown attractions or eateries.

Corner of Spring Garden and Barrington. © **902/429-2240.** Free admission. Daily mid-May to mid-Oct 9am–5pm; guides until late Aug. Closed rest of year.

Point Pleasant Park ★★ ☺ Point Pleasant is one of Canada's finer urban parks, and there's no better place for a walk along the water on a balmy day. This 75-hectare (186-acre) park occupies a wooded peninsula today, but for years it actually served as one of the linchpins in the city's military defense. Look carefully and you'll find the ruins of early forts, plus a nicely preserved Martello tower built to protect British sea batteries from French landward attack. (Halifax still has a 999-year lease from Great Britain for this park, for which it pays 1 shilling—about US10¢—per year.) You'll also find a lovely gravel carriage road around the point, a small swimming beach, miles of walking trails, and groves of graceful fir trees. The park is located about 2km (1¼ miles) south of the Public Gardens. Take note, though, that no bikes are allowed in here on weekends or holidays; you'll need to use pedi-power.

Point Pleasant Dr. (south end of Halifax; head south on S. Park St. near Public Gardens and continue on Young). www.pointpleasantpark.ca. Free admission. Daily 6am–midnight.

Halifax Public Gardens ★★ The Public Gardens took seed in 1753, when they were founded as a private venture. The tract was acquired by the Nova Scotia Horticultural Society in 1836, and these gardens assumed their present look around 1875 during the peak of the Victorian era. As such, the garden is one of Canada's Victorian masterpieces, rarer and more evocative than any mansard-roofed mansion. You'll find here wonderful examples of 19th-century trends in outdoor landscaping, from the "naturally" winding walks and ornate fountains to the duck ponds and Victorian band shell. (Stop by the shell at 2pm any summer Sun to catch a free concert.) There are plenty of leafy trees, lush lawns, cranky ducks who have lost their fear of humans, and little ponds. You'll also usually find everyone from octogenarians to kids feeding pigeons there, and smartly uniformed guards slowly walk the grounds. Spring Garden Rd. and S. Park St. www.halifaxpublicgardens.ca. Free admission. May–Nov 11 8am–dusk.

BOAT TOURS

Murphy's on the Water (www.mtcw.ca; ✆ 902/420-1015) runs daily boats from Cable Wharf in downtown Halifax in summer for C$15 and up round-trip; a range of harbor, whale-watching, nature, and sightseeing tours are offered by Captain Gerard Murphy and his family. Or, to see McNab's Island, drive instead to Eastern Passage (south of Dartmouth), park free at Government Wharf, and take the McNab's Island Ferry (www.mcnabsisland.com; ✆ 902/465-4563). For the brief trip, Captain Mike Tilley (known locally as "Red Beard") charges C$15 for adults, C$10 for seniors and children, and there's no extra charge for bikes or dogs. Captain Tilley will also charter you around the harbor for C$100 per hour.

SHOPPING

Halifax has a pleasing mix of shops, from mainstream retailers to offbeat boutiques. There's no central retail district to speak of; shops are scattered throughout downtown. Two indoor malls are located near the Grand Parade—**Scotia Square Mall** and **Barrington Place Shops,** flanking Barrington Street near the intersection of Duke Street. Another downtown mall, the 85-shop **Park Lane Shopping Centre,** is on Spring Garden Road about 1 block from the Public Gardens.

For souvenir shopping, head to the Historic Properties buildings on the waterfront; one of the star attractions is **Nova Scotian Crystal** at 5080 George St. (novascotian crystal.com; ✆ 902/492-3044), where mouth-blown, hand-cut crystal is made in full view. For idle browsing, try the shops on and around Spring Garden Road between Brunswick and South Park streets. Queen Street is the destination for vintage and local clothing. For big-box stores and specialty shops like Lee Valley Tools, head for Bayers Lake Business Park at the junction of routes 102 and 103.

Art Gallery of Nova Scotia Shop The museum's gift shops feature limited but choice selections of local crafts, ranging from creative postcards to birdhouses and tabletop sculptures. There's also work by Mi'kmaq artisans. 1723 Hollis St. ✆ 902/424-4303.

Atlantic News ★★ 📗 A huge selection of magazines for just about any passion and a wide range of newspapers can be found here (they will print your very own copy of today's paper from many places around the world). They claim to have over 5,000 magazines and 350 newspapers to choose from. Corner of Morris and Queen sts. www. atlanticnews.ns.ca. ✆ 902/429-5468.

John W. Doull, Bookseller ★★ A virtual rabbit warren of books (old, new, and ancient) in piles, boxes, and on shelves is like the treasure at the end of the rainbow for lovers of the written word. 1684 Barrington St. www.doullbooks.com. © **902/429-1652.**

Drala Books & Gifts This shop specializes in Japanese imports: crystal balls, incense, calligraphy and ikebama materials, paper screens, chopsticks, teas, teapots, books on design and philosophy, pillows, meditation cushions, local greeting cards—and some mystical/offbeat stuff too. Instructors sometimes teach meditation, tea ceremony, and the like. 1567 Grafton St. www.drala.ca. © **877/422-2504** or 902/422-2504.

Newfoundland Grocery Store A wee touch of "The Rock" for those interested in sampling the culture of Canada's easternmost province. Products range from bake-apple jam to salt pigs tails and salted corned beef—the real stuff stored in pails on the floor. Purity candy, cookies, syrups, crackers, and of course, candy, is made right in Newfoundland. 6061 Willow St. © **902/423-6209.**

Pete's Frootique A haven for foodies. Picnic fare, snacks for your hotel room, or specialty items for gifts. I always stock up with treats for home in the Best of Britain section. They have several locations—the best in Bedford. 1515 Dresden Row off Spring Garden Rd., © **902/425-5700,** and 1595 Bedford Hwy. in Bedford. www.petesfrootique.com. © **902/835-4997.**

Urban Cottage This consignment store in the middle of downtown has an eclectic and sizable selection of furniture, housewares, and collectibles, nicely displayed and generally reasonably priced. 1819 Granville St. © **902/423-3010.**

Where to Stay

EXPENSIVE

Cambridge Suites Hotel Halifax ★ ☺ The attractive, modern Cambridge Suites is nicely located near the foot of Citadel Hill, well positioned for exploring the city. It's perfect for families—about 40 of the units are two-room suites, bigger spaces featuring kitchenettes with microwaves and extra phones. Expect above-average service and a comfortable, inoffensive decor. They also offer the usual business-hotel amenities such as a fitness center and a business center. **Dofsky's Urban Grill** on the first floor is open for all three meals. Look for pasta, blackened haddock, burgers, jerk chicken, and the like. Four-legged travelers get VIP treatment here.

1583 Brunswick St., Halifax, NS B3J 3P5. www.cambridgesuiteshalifax.com. © **800/565-1263** or 902/420-0555. Fax 902/420-9379. 200 units. C$139–C$299 suite. Children 17 and under stay free in parent's room. AE, DC, DISC, MC, V. Indoor parking C$16. **Amenities:** Restaurant; roof-top health club. *In room:* A/C, TV/VCR, fridge, hair dryer, kitchenette, Wi-Fi (free).

Delta Barrington ★ Convenience and location are reasons to consider the Delta Barrington. It's just 1 block from the waterfront and the Grand Parade, and connected to the Metro Centre and much of the rest of downtown by a covered walkway. While it's a large, modern hotel, the design and furnishings are more oriented to comfort than flash. Guest rooms are decorated in a contemporary country decor. King rooms are spacious, furnished with sofas and easy chairs. Some rooms face the pedestrian plaza and have been soundproofed to block out the noise from below; the downside is that these windows don't open as they do in most other rooms. Thus the quietest rooms face the courtyard, but lack a view.

1875 Barrington St., Halifax, NS B3J 3L6. www.deltabarrington.com. © **877/814-7706,** 888/890-3222, or 902/429-7410. Fax 902/420-6524. 200 units. C$134–C$294 double. AE, DC, DISC, MC, V. Valet parking C$20. Small pets allowed. **Amenities:** Restaurant (breakfast only); babysitting;

children's programs; concierge; Jacuzzi; indoor pool; room service; sauna. *In room:* A/C, TV, hair dryer, Internet (C$9.95 day), minibar.

Delta Halifax ★

The Delta Halifax (formerly the Hotel Halifax, which was formerly Chateau Halifax) is a slick, modern downtown hotel that offers premium services. It's located just a block off the waterfront with great walking and eateries nearby. In inclement weather you can connect via a pedway to the casino, shops, and the waterfront. During the week, guests are largely business travelers. Ask for a room in the "resort wing" near the pool, which feels farther away from the chatter of downtown and the press of business. Some rooms have balconies and many have harbor views. Ask when you book. The **Harbour City Bar & Grill** offers good local Maritime-inflected cuisine, while **Sam Slick's Lounge** next door features Friday night piano and a surprisingly varied bar menu.

1990 Barrington St., Halifax, NS B3J 1P2. www.deltahalifax.com. ✆ **800/268-1133** or 902/425-6700. Fax 902/425-6214. 296 units. C$134–C$284 double. AE, MC, V. Valet parking C$23, self-parking C$20. **Amenities:** Restaurant; bar; concierge; health club; Jacuzzi; indoor pool; room service; sauna. *In room:* A/C, TV, hair dryer, Internet (C$9.95 day), minibar.

The Halliburton ★★

A well-appointed, well-run, country inn in the heart of downtown. Named after former resident Sir Brenton Halliburton (Nova Scotia's first chief justice), the inn is spread out among three town house–style buildings connected via gardens and sun decks in the rear (though not internally). The main building, constructed in 1809, was converted into an inn in 1995; it was somehow modernized without the loss of its considerable charm. Guest rooms are subtly furnished with fine antiques, yet few are so rare that you'd fret about damaging them. Things are rich and masculine in tone, and light on frilly stuff. Among the best: room no. 113, small but with a lovely working fireplace and unique skylighted bathroom. Room nos. 102 and 109 are suites with wet bars and fireplaces; there's also a studio apartment. Popular with business travelers, it also has romantic appeal. The intimate first-floor dining room, **Stories ★**, serves dinner nightly.

5184 Morris St., Halifax, NS B3J 1B3. www.halliburton.ns.ca. ✆ **888/512-3344** or 902/420-0658. Fax 902/423-2324. 29 units. C$145–C$350 double; off-season discounts available. Rates include continental breakfast and free parking (limited; first-come, first-serve). AE, MC, V. **Amenities:** Restaurant; babysitting; room service. *In room:* A/C, TV, hair dryer, Internet (free), MP3 docking station.

The Lord Nelson Hotel & Suites ★

Built in 1928, this was the city's preeminent lodging for years. It sank in esteem, ending up as a flophouse, but not for long. In 1998, new owners restored it to former glory reminiscent of the golden-age of classic hotels through both architecture and Georgian reproduction furnishings. It certainly has location going for it: it's across from the lovely Public Gardens and abuts lively Spring Garden Road. Business-class Flagship Rooms feature desks, ergonomic office chairs, robes, free local calls, and morning newspapers. The hotel charges a premium for rooms facing the street or gardens. You can tipple a pint off the lobby at the **Victory Arms,** a cozy and convincing English-style pub serving British fare like bangers and mash, and fish and chips, but also rotating more inventive dishes.

1515 South Park St., Halifax, NS B3J 2L2. www.lordnelsonhotel.com. ✆ **800/565-2020** or 902/423-6331. Fax 902/423-7148. 260 units. C$159–C$259 double and suites. AE, DC, DISC, MC, V. Valet parking C$25, self-parking C$20. Pets allowed with C$100 deposit. **Amenities:** Restaurant; bar; babysitting; concierge; health club; limited room service; sauna. *In room:* A/C, TV, hair dryer, Wi-Fi (free).

The Prince George Hotel ★   This large, contemporary, downtown hotel features understated styling, polished wainscoting, carpeting, and the discreet use of marble. Expect modern and comfortably appointed rooms, most with balconies. Nicely situated near the Citadel, theater, and restaurants, it's perfect for events at the Halifax Metro Centre and the business core. It's also connected by the city's indoor pedestrian walkway to shopping and other parts of the city. The hotel's **Gio restaurant ★** features contemporary bistro styling, with a trendy menu to match. If you're in town on a Sunday, an attractive and popular Sunday brunch is served at the hotel's **Terrace restaurant** for C$35 per person (reservations required).

1725 Market St., Halifax, NS B3J 3N9. www.princegeorgehotel.com. © 800/565-1567 or 902/425-1986. Fax 902/429-6048. 203 units. C$169–C$299 double. AE, DC, DISC, MC, V. Valet parking C$25, self-parking C$20. **Amenities:** Restaurant; babysitting; concierge; health club; pool; room service; sauna. *In room:* A/C, TV, hair dryer, Internet (free), minibar.

The Westin Nova Scotian ★★★ ☺   Feeling like an oasis in the middle of the city with its peaceful setting, the Westin is one of those grand hotels associated with the railroad era. In fact, VIA Rail travelers walk straight into the lobby from the station. It's just steps to the seaport (where cruise ships tie up), the Seaport Farmers Market, Garrison Brewing, Pier 21 Museum, and the entry point for the waterside boardwalk, which takes you all the way to the Historic Properties. This is a very family-friendly place: A Westin Kids Club provides neat activities such as train station tours. They've also mapped out jogging/walking routes from the hotel and can supply a kids' running stroller or fix you up with the local running club. Diana Princess of Wales hosted her only official royal dinner on her Eastern Canadian tour in their ballroom. Ask about Harbour View rooms; they allow you to watch the ships come and go.

1181 Hollis St., Halifax, NS B3H 2P6. westin.ns.ca. © **877/9WESTIN** [877/993-7846] or 902/421-1000. 310 units. C$139–C$299 double; C$395 suites. Luxury suites also available. Valet parking C$23, self-parking C$18, complimentary shuttle service in downtown area. AE, MC, V. **Amenities:** Restaurant; health club; Internet (free in lobby and lounge); pool; spa; tennis courts. *In room:* A/C, TV, hair dryer, minibar, Wi-Fi or Internet (C$9.95 per 2-hr. period).

MODERATE

Super 8 Dartmouth   Yes, it's a chain property, but if you have kids and a car, this all-suite hotel right across the harbor from Halifax is just a short walk to the Dartmouth waterfront and commuter ferries. It is definitely one of the better options for travelers on a beer budget. Housed in a modern concrete building, it features rooms that are large and tidy. Many of the 84 units have separate sitting areas, kitchenettes, and balconies. Don't expect anything super-fancy; rooms are basic, simple, and clean, but some have wonderful views of the harbor, sometimes for no extra cost—ask about getting a prime view when you book. Reach the hotel by crossing the Angus MacDonald bridge from Halifax's waterfront and quickly exiting onto Windmill Road (east), which becomes Alderney; go left at Queen Street, then left again on King.

65 King St., Dartmouth, NS B2Y 4C2. www.super8dartmouth.com. © **877/518-7666** or 902/463-9520. 84 units. C$109–C$400 suite. AE, DC, MC, V. Parking C$6 underground/outdoor. **Amenities:** Restaurant; health club; Internet. *In room:* A/C, TV, fridge (some), hair dryer, kitchenette (some), Wi-Fi (free).

Waverley Inn ★   The Waverley is adorned in high Victorian style, as befits its 1866 provenance. Flamboyant playwright Oscar Wilde was a guest here in 1882; perhaps he had a hand in the decorating? There's walnut trim, red upholstered furniture, and portraits of sourpuss Victorians at every turn. Headboards in the guest rooms are especially elaborate—some look like props from Gothic horror movies. Among the rooms, no. 130 has a unique Chinese wedding bed and a Jacuzzi, one of about 10 with private Jacuzzis. Some rooms have canopy beds.

1266 Barrington St., Halifax, NS B3J 1Y5. www.waverleyinn.com. © **800/565-9346** or 902/423-9346. Fax 902/425-0167. 34 units. Mid-May to Oct C$129–C$229 double; Nov to mid-May C$109–C$179 double. DC, MC, V. **Amenities:** Breakfast; snacks; afternoon tea; Jacuzzi (some units); parking. In room: A/C, TV, hair dryer (some units), no phone (some units), Wi-Fi (free).

INEXPENSIVE

The 75-bed Hostelling International–Maritimes **Halifax Heritage House Hostel** (www.hihostels.ca; © **902/422-3863**) is located at 1253 Barrington St., within walking distance to train and bus stations, many downtown attractions, and a number of convivial bars. You'll usually share rooms with other travelers (several private and family rooms are available, though); there are lockers in each room, shared bathrooms for all, and a shared, fully equipped kitchen. Bring coins for the Internet terminals and the coin-op laundry. Rates are C$35 and up per person in dormitories, C$68 and up for a double bed in a private room.

A short distance from downtown, but convenient to bus lines, are the dorm rooms at **Dalhousie University** (www.conferenceservices.dal.ca; © **888/271-9222** or 902/494-8840), furnished with plain single beds and each rented to the traveling public when school isn't in session (mid-May to mid-Aug). Many rooms even have private bathrooms and kitchenettes (you have to rent dishes for a small fee), making them an especially good deal for families on the road. Rooms are C$40 single, C$60 double. Varied-size apartments cost somewhat more. Check with the university about current pricing and options. Remember, summer demand is high, so book as far in advance as possible. Also note that a 2-night minimum stay is required for some units.

Where to Eat

Coffee emporia have cropped up throughout Halifax over the last decade, just as they have everywhere. Many also stock sandwiches, pastries, and light snacks in addition to the java. A few of the best downtown options are **Caffé Ristretto** (© **902/425-3087**) at 1475 Lower Water St. (Bishop Landing), notable mostly for its nice harborside location; **Cabin Coffee** (© **902/422-8130**) at 1554 Hollis St., with its bohemian feel and good espresso and cappuccino; and the dependable Canadian chains that seem to appear every few blocks, **Second Cup** and **Tim Hortons.** Down at the seaport, the **Java Factory** (© **902/431-9500**) at 1113 Marginal Rd. serves mean sandwiches and samosas, along with free Wi-Fi.

When you get away from the waterfront downtown area, Halifax is home to universities and large regional hospitals. It created a need for numerous quick-fix eateries and a proliferation of fast-food outlets in neighborhoods beyond downtown. Spring Garden Road and tiny side streets happily mix upscale fare with more basic grub. Good snacks, pastries, coffees, teas, and light meals can be found at **Annie's Place** (© **902/420-0098**), 1592 Queen St. (available 7am–3pm). Outstanding all-day breakfast and bargain lunch specials include a changing menu of offerings, such as a slab of grilled meatloaf on focaccia.

The **Brewery** ★★ complex, on the uphill side of Lower Water Street just above the docks, is an interesting one-stop shopping and dining expe ·nce. Originally the site of the Alexander Keith brewery—North America's oldest· .ie space here was eventually redesigned and renovated to enclose courtyards from the weather, link the various structures of the abandoned brewery, and create a kind of interior market of shops and restaurants. It's working. The complex houses the city's finest Italian restaurant (see daMaurizio, below), as well as a range of other drinking, dining, and shopping options. Make time for the Alexander **Keith's Brewery Tour** (www.keiths. ca; ✆ **902/455-1474**), where you can savor the samples at tours' end along with the history. Tours cost C$16 for adults, C$14 for students/seniors, and C$8 for children, lasting about an hour. You must phone for tour times. While navigating the labyrinthine courtyards can be a bit confusing, it's great fun to see what is around the next corner.

The Saturday morning **farmer's market ★★** held within the Brewery's walls is a weekly highlight for Haligonians, rain or shine. It's Canada's oldest such market—and possibly its most interesting. The market runs from 7am until just 1pm, and you'll need to go early for the best selection. The market became so overcrowded that the vendors split and a second market opened just blocks away. **Seaport Farmers' Market** at Pier 20 on Marginal Road opens 7am to 4pm Saturday, 8am to 4pm Sunday, 8am to 4pm Tuesday to Thursday, and 8am to 6pm Friday. Closed Monday. It has some growing pains, but is still a great place to go for lunch if you don't mind balancing it on your knee; tables and chairs are sadly lacking.

EXPENSIVE

Haligonians and their visitors love fine dining enough to support a number of excellent (if pricey) and trendy spots. Critics love **Onyx** (www.onyxdining.com; ✆ **902/428-5680**) at 5680 Spring Garden Rd. It's the sort of place with wine flights and specialty mojitos, a menu of Asian-influenced selections combined with a dab of French flair; supposedly rock stars eat and drink here when they're passing through town.

Several of Halifax's hotels also have very good fine-dining restaurants tucked within them, notably the Prince George Hotel's **Gio ★** (www.giohalifax.com; ✆ **902/425-1987**) at 1725 Market St., which has won raves and culinary awards.

The Bicycle Thief ★★★ 🍴 NORTHERN ITALIAN   Nova Scotian culinary wizards Maurizio and Stephanie Bertossi struck again when they transformed elegant Bish World Cuisine into the Bicycle Thief, with a more relaxed, come-as-you-are feel. They live up to their claim of offering North American food with an Italian soul. The experience begins with the menu: Invariably diners read aloud, rolling the Italian ingredients and dishes from the tongue like musical notes. Not as magic as enjoying dishes like Shellfish Zuppa (half-lobster, clams, mussels, scallops, jumbo shrimp, king crab, garlic tomato Marinara) or local rabbit (braised long and slow with a great Valpolicella, garlic and fresh herbs, alongside seared polenta). This is perfect fare for a summer's eve on the waterside patio, cooled by Atlantic breezes. It's popular to the point where it is often crowded and noisy—reservations are a must, as is time, since its popularity sometimes means service is less than prompt; make an evening of it.

1475 Lower Water St. (in Bishop's Landing, entrance at end of Bishop St.). ✆ **902/425-7993.** Reservations highly recommended. Main courses C$20–C$29. AE, DC, MC, V. Mon–Sat 5:30–10pm.

Chives Canadian Bistro ★★★ REGIONAL BISTRO   The menu constantly changes at Chives because it relies so heavily on what is fresh, in season, and local on any given day. That element of celebrating the harvest, as well as the Canadian landscape (through the use of water, wood, rock, and sand in the decor), make for an unpretentious atmosphere in what is best described as casual fine dining. The dedication to sourcing first Nova Scotian, then Maritime ingredients, rouses a great sense of Canadiana. I also enjoy the fact that the wine is stored in a vault, left from the days when the building was a bank, and the "Moving Menu," which broadcasts the live action of the kitchen on the street to passers-by in an attempt to show the many faces behind the food. It's vibrant and cool.

1537 Barrington St. www.chives.ca. © **902/420-9626.** Daily for dinner 5–9:30pm. Reservations suggested. C$31–C$50. AE, MC, V. Breakfast and lunch available in their Ciboulette Café next door, Mon–Fri 7:30am–5pm.

daMaurizio ★★★ ITALIAN Owner/Chef Andrew King maintains the high standards of the founder for whom the restaurant is named. The atmosphere and anticipation are in keeping with a menu often described as amazing and innovative, if pricey. First-timers would do well choosing the prix-fixe menu, which allows you to choose one each of three courses for C$40. The menu is a bit mind-boggling in its grandeur, making the prix-fixe a grand introduction to complementary dishes. A knowledgeable waiter steered us towards selections we shared and sampled. Antipasti selections of truly tender calamari, flash-fried with tomato and chilies and a delicious foie gras, set the tone for the experiment in flavor that followed as we savored a memorable feast. Our evening ended with a selection of European cheeses, served with a sweet raisin compote and an apple walnut and cinnamon bread, served with specialty coffee.

1479 Lower Water St. (in the Brewery). © **902/423-0859.** Reservations highly recommended. Main courses C$29–C$35; pasta dishes C$10–C$16. AE, DC, MC, V. Mon–Sat 5–10pm.

Five Fishermen Restaurant & Grill ★★★ SEAFOOD Ask where to find seafood in Halifax and invariably the response will be Five Fishermen. They have 35 years' experience dishing up fine seafood and have been voted Best Seafood Restaurant in Halifax five years in a row. The big decision is what to choose: Select your own Steak and Seafood Combo, a prix-fixe menu, try the evening mussel and salad bar, or make your selections from the menu, which counters varied seafood offerings with such inspired goodies as grilled bison tenderloins, roast vegetable Napoleon, and a truffle-and-sage marinated chicken breast. You may prefer the downstairs Grill, slightly more casual, which offers a hearty weekend brunch, oyster happy hours, and its own menu. If you have any mobility problems, opt for the Grill rather than the stairs up to the restaurant. No matter whether you sit upstairs or downstairs while waiting for your meal, take a moment to read about the Five Fishermen History & Hauntings to get in touch with the rich history of the place. The 1817 building has a fascinating story. Anna Leonowens opened an art school here. Name not familiar? She wrote a book about her earlier life called *Anna and the King of Siam*, inspiring Broadway and film versions of *The King and I*. They also have a resident ghost. But go for the food.

1740 Argyle St. www.fivefishermen.com. © **902/422-4421.** Dinner (reservations recommended) C$40–C$50; Grill C$30–C$45, reservations not usually needed. AE, MC, V. Daily 5pm–10pm. Grill daily 11am–10pm.

MODERATE

Hart & Thistle Gastropub & Brewery ★★ GASTROPUB This British-style pub, specializing in high-quality food a step above basic pub grub, is a popular meeting spot. Enjoy one of the largest waterside patios in Halifax (it seats 200), from which you can watch sailing vessels, ferries, and seagoing traffic. Indoors, a fireplace takes care of chilly weather. It isn't all about the ambience: chefs work with the brewmaster to keep taste buds hopping as they marry food (often bordering on gourmet) with the local passion: beer. The brewery produces a variety of well-crafted, balanced brews including a very bitter Hop Mess Monster—a tasting challenge for locals—and a variety of local micro-brews. Hand-thrown pizza, a club sandwich best described as "kickin'," and a variety of pastas, seafood, and "real" meat dishes are consistently good eating. Check the schedule for live music in the pub.

1869 Upper Water St. www.hartandthistle.com. © **902/407-4278.** Main dishes C$11–C$30. AE, MC, V. Daily 11am–11pm.

Ryan Duffy's STEAKHOUSE   The house specialty here is steak, for which the place is justly famous. The beef, local AA tenderloin and Alberta AA short loin in-house, dry-aged cuts, are tender worth talking about! Steaks are grilled over natural wood charcoal to order (no broiling here; Hallelujah), and can be dressed up with garlic, cilantro butter, or other extras as you wish. The more expensive cuts, such as the strip loin (weighed and cut tableside; priced by the ounce) are so juicy you might not need a knife. They'll even cook it "blue rare" if you want it that way. If you don't feel like steak, though, there's a lot less to get excited about on the menu here.

1650 Bedford Row. www.ryanduffys.ca. © **902/421-1116.** Reservations recommended. Main courses C$11–C$35 at lunch, C$25–C$48 at dinner. AE, DC, MC, V. Mon–Fri 6:30am–11pm; Sat–Sun 7am–11pm, close at 10pm during winter.

Saege Bistro ★★ FUSION   Geir Simensen's Saege Bistro is a member of the family-owned catering team that handles Cheapside Café (see below). Think of it as "Scandinavia meets Canada" (with a sprinkling from the rest of the world). Lunches run to Norwegian fish cakes, corn-crusted crab cakes, schnitzel, Asian stir-fries, lobster ravioli with pesto cream, and mussels steamed in Calvados; dinners to bouillabaisse, seared Digby scallops, pork chops, cumin rack of lamb, and salmon with coconut and peach chutney—not to mention plenty of interesting pizzas and pastas. Dessert could be a lemon flan, a gianduja torte, a pistachio mousse with mango sorbet, or a chili-and-chocolate *pot de crème*—yum. Saege also does a nice affordable Sunday **brunch** ★ with items like real muesli, huevos rancheros, and brioche French toast filled with apple chutney.

5883 Spring Garden Rd. www.saege.ca. © **902/429-1882.** Reservations recommended. Main courses C$9–C$21 at lunch, C$15–C$26 at dinner. AE, DC, MC, V. Tues–Fri 11:30am–10pm; Sat 9:30am–10pm; Sun 9:30am–9pm.

INEXPENSIVE

Cheapside Café ★★ 🍴 ☺ CAFE   Yes, it's cheap, but that's not the point; the name actually comes from an open market that once occupied this street, named after a similar market in London. This cheerful and lively cafe is a fantastic find. Menus vary daily. A card of soups and sandwiches might feature choices like jerked pork tenderloin on rye with an apple-blackberry compote, open-faced shrimp with dill mayonnaise, phyllo with chevre and mushrooms, or grilled red pepper and portobello. Other daily fare: haddock fish cakes, simple pastas, Caesar salads, and crepes. Desserts really go over the top: Linzer tortes, raspberry mousse tarts, Florentines, cheesecake slices, and the eponymous Cheapside Café torte with its combination of milk and dark chocolates and pavé of sweet crunchy hazelnut.

1723 Hollis St. (inside the Art Gallery of Nova Scotia). © **902/425-4494.** Sandwiches and entrees C$9–C$12. MC, V. Tues–Sat 10am–5pm (Thurs to 8pm); Sun 11am–2:30pm.

Cheelin ★ CHINESE Possibly Halifax's best Chinese restaurant, Cheelin achieves a seemingly improbable balance between authentic Asian cuisine and a funkier, Haligonian vibe. The Szechuan- and Beijing-influenced kitchen serves normally hard-to-find dishes like *mapo* tofu (spicy tofu, cubed and stir-fried, often mixed with ground pork or beef) and *yu xiang* pork (pork with Szechuan sauce). The brightly painted, pastel interior, and hip young staff and crowd—plus a few interesting dishes like scallops with mango sauce—tell you that you're in Halifax. Despite surprisingly low prices, this is definitely not a hole-in-the-wall eatery. Go for the spicy Hunan haddock, the excellent vegetable spring rolls, the tofu bao, spicy calamari, orange beef, shredded pork with bitter melon, or maybe a daily special such as peppery shrimp with sautéed bok choy and squash. They also do takeout and delivery to the downtown area—good to know when you're hungry in your hotel.

1496 Lower Water St. (inside the Brewery). www.cheelinrestaurant.com. ✆ **902/422-2252.** Most items C$10–C$16. AE, MC, V. Mon–Sat 11:30am–2:30pm; Tues–Sun 5:30–10pm.

Henry House ★ BREWPUB Eastern Canada's first brewpub is housed in an austere building on the far western reaches of Barrington Street, down near the youth hostel. The starkly handsome 1834 stone building has a medium-fancy dining room upstairs with red tablecloths and captains' chairs, plus a pub downstairs that's more informal (and louder). You order off the same menu at either spot, and the food's mostly what you'd expect at a brewpub, though better-tasting. Entrees could include beer-battered fish, salmon, steak sandwiches, a smoked-salmon club sandwich, burgers, beef-and-beer stew, or a chicken-and-leek pie. The half-dozen locally brewed beers are fresh and good, as is the black-and-tan and amber-and-tan.

1222 Barrington St. www.henryhouse.ca. ✆ **902/423-5660.** Main courses C$8–C$15. AE, DC, MC, V. Mon–Sat 11:30am–12:30am; Sun noon–11pm.

Il Mercato ★★ ITALIAN Another leg in the daMaurizio empire, this fun bistro features Tuscan sponged walls and a terra-cotta tiled floor, setting an appropriate mood amid the clamor of Spring Garden. Come early or expect to wait. You'll find a great selection at prices that approach bargain level. Start by selecting antipasti from the deli counter (you point; waitstaff bring them to your table). Focaccias are superb and come with salad, while the ravioli filled with roast chicken and wild mushrooms is sublime. There are plenty of pastas and thin-crust pizzas on the menu, too, while non-Italian entrees include a grilled rack of lamb with Dijon, veal scallopine, a seafood medley cooked up with peppers, and a strip steak topped with Gorgonzola. The desserts, Italian coffees, aperitifs, and cocktails are similarly tasty. Try a toffee crunch, a chocolate tart, a sambuca, a Campari, or an espresso if you like—but save room for the fantastic homemade gelati, too.

5650 Spring Garden Rd. www.il-mercato.ca. ✆ **902/422-2866.** Reservations not accepted. Main courses and pastas C$10–C$20. AE, DC, MC, V. Mon–Wed 11am–10pm; Thurs–Sat 11am–11pm.

Morris East ★★ ITALIAN This is an excellent thin-crust pizza joint (though it's fancier than "joint" suggests) that uses a wood-fired oven bought from Naples, which burns premium orchard apple wood from the Annapolis Valley. Sometimes you can smell the place before you can see it.

5212 Morris St. www.morriseast.com. ✆ **902/444-7663.** Entrees $16–$25. MC, V. Tues–Thurs 11:30am–2:30pm and 5pm–9pm; Fri–Sat 11:30am–2:30pm and 5pm–10pm; Sun 5–9pm.

Satisfaction Feast ★ VEGETARIAN   Halifax's longest-running vegetarian restaurant (it opened in 1981) has been voted one of the top 10 veggie restaurants in Canada by the national *Globe and Mail*. Its offerings run to curries, samosas, quesadillas, veggie burgers, wraps and sandwiches, and other cow-friendly entrees. There's also "neatloaf" for those who like their food with cute names. The vegan fruit crisp is the dessert to hold out for. They also now serve breakfast and Sunday brunch, which include free-range eggs, if you vegetarians out there are keeping track. Anyway, consider a picnic atop nearby Citadel Hill: They're happy to bundle up something as takeout for you.

3559 Robie St. www.satisfaction-feast.com. © **902/422-3540.** Main courses C$6–C$14. AE, DC, MC, V. Tues–Thurs 11am–8pm; Fri 11am–9pm; Sat–Sun 10am–8pm.

Steve-O-Reno's ★ 🍴 CAFE   Tucked on a quaint side street off Spring Garden Road, this coffee shop is a popular lunch stop for the locals. You'll have your choice of potent coffee and other beverages (such as chai tea latte), along with inventive fruit smoothies, a small selection of sandwiches and salads, and a pleasantly relaxed atmosphere. They do everything well and inexpensively, and the hip young staff is friendly and cheerful as can be. There's a drive-through location of Steve-O's on Robie Street, open similar hours and also within the Seaport Farmers Market.

1536 Brunswick St. www.steveorenos.com. © **902/429-3034.** Meals C$4–C$7. No credit cards. Mon–Sat 7:30am–6pm; Sun 8am–6:30pm.

Halifax by Night

For starters, stop by the visitor center or the front desk of your hotel and ask for a copy of *Where Halifax* (www.wherehalifax.com), an excellent and comprehensive monthly guide to the city's entertainment and events. Among the city's premier venues for shows is the downtown **Halifax Metro Centre,** 1800 Argyle St. (www. halifaxmetrocentre.com; © **902/421-8000**), which hosts sporting events (wrestling, pro hockey) as well as concerts by a variety of big-name artists. Note that tickets are sold by the Ticket Atlantic Box Office (© **902/451-1221**).

PERFORMING ARTS

Shakespeare by the Sea ★ (www.shakespearebythesea.ca; © **902/422-0295**) stages a whole line of bardlike and non-bardlike productions July through Labour Day at several alfresco venues around the city. Most are held at Point Pleasant Park, where the ruins of old forts and buildings are used as the stage settings for delightful performances, with the audience sprawled on the grass, many enjoying picnic dinners with their *Taming of the Shrew*. Shows are technically free, though the players suggest a donation of C$15. The occasional more elaborate productions at other locations (past shows have included *King Lear* at the Citadel and *Titus Andronicus* at the park's Martello tower) have limited seating, with ticket prices that might range up to C$30. Check the website for new shows, tickets, and schedules.

The **Neptune Theatre,** 1593 Argyle St. (www.neptunetheatre.com; © **800/565-7345** or 902/429-7070), benefited from a big, multimillion-dollar renovation and now also runs an intimate 200-seat studio theater. Top-notch dramatic productions are offered throughout the year. (The main season runs Sept–May, with a summer season filling in the gap with eclectic performances.) Main-stage tickets range generally from around C$15 to C$45.

For a more informal night out, there's the **Grafton Street Dinner Theater,** 1741 Grafton St. (www.graftonstdinnertheatre.com; © **902/425-1961**), which typically offers light musicals and mysteries with a three-course dinner. Tickets cost C$42 per adult, C$23 for children 12 and under.

THE CLUB & BAR SCENE

Halifax's young and restless tend to congregate in pubs, nightclubs, and on street corners along two streets that converge at the public library: Grafton Street and Spring Garden Road. If you're thirsty, wander the neighborhoods around here and you're liable to find a *Cheers*-type spot to drink elbow-to-elbow with the locals.

One of the coolest places to hang out is **Economy Shoe Shop** (www.economyshoe shop.ca; © **902/423-8845**), at 1663 Argyle St., not a shop but rather a cafe-bar where many of Halifax's prettiest people wind up sooner or later. Helpfully, they serve food from 11am all the way until 2am from an eclectic mix of menus, and the wine list is impressive. In the evening (and late afternoons on Sat), you'll also find lively Maritime music and good beer at the **Lower Deck Pub** (© **902/425-1501**), one of the more popular restaurants in the Historic Properties complex on the waterfront. There's music nightly, and on Saturday afternoons (out on the patio in summer).

Local rock bars include the **Marquee Club** at 2037 Gottingen St. (© **902/429-3020**). And the **Maxwell's Plum** at 1600 Grafton St. (© **902/423-5090**) is an English pub where peanut shells litter the floor and patrons quaff from a list of dozens of 150 import and Canadian draft and bottled beers. The nightly happy-hour and pitcher specials can considerably cut your cost.

Also check out *The Coast* (www.thecoast.ca), a free newspaper widely available around Halifax, for good listings of upcoming performances.

THE EASTERN SHORE

Heading from Halifax to Cape Breton Island (or vice versa), you need to choose between two routes. If you're burning to get to your destination, take **Route 102** to Route 104 (the Trans-Canada Highway, the one with the maple leaf). If you're in no particular hurry and are more content venturing down narrow lanes, destination unknown, allow a couple of days to wind along the Eastern Shore, mostly along **Route 7.** (**Note:** Official tourism materials refer to this stretch as the Marine Drive instead of the Eastern Shore, for whatever reason.) Along the way, you'll be rewarded with glimpses of a rugged coastline that's wilder and more remote than the coast south of Halifax. Communities here tend to be farther apart, less genteel, and stocked with far fewer services—or tourists. With its rugged terrain and remote locales, this region is a good bet for those drawn to the outdoors and seeking coastal solitude.

Be forewarned that the Eastern Shore isn't breathtakingly scenic along the main road. You'll drive mostly through cutover woodlands and scrappy towns. To get the most out of this section of the coast, become committed to making periodic detours. Drive down dead-end roads ending in coastal peninsulas, where you might come upon wild roses blooming madly in the fog, or point your car inland to the enormous interior forest, where you can still find moose—and an overarching quiet.

Essentials

GETTING THERE   Routes 107 and 7 run along or near the coast from Dartmouth to Stillwater (near Sherbrooke). Other local routes—including numbers 211, 316, 16, and 344—continue onward along the coast to the causeway to Cape Breton. An excursion along the entire coastal route—from Dartmouth to Cape Breton Island with a detour to Canso—is about 400km (250 miles) in length. Driving time would vary wildly, depending on your capacity for making detours.

VISITOR INFORMATION Several tourist information centers are staffed along the route. You'll find the best stocked and most helpful centers in **Sheet Harbour** inside the **MacPhee House Museum** (next to the waterfall; ✆ **902/885-2595**); in **Sherbrooke Village,** in the little yellow building at the entrance to the historic complex that also serves as the museum's info center (✆ **902/522-2400**); and in **Canso** at 1297 Union St., on the waterfront (✆ **902/366-2170**). All are open daily in summer.

A Driving Tour of the Eastern Shore

This section assumes you'll drive northeastward from Halifax toward Cape Breton Between Halifax and Sheet Harbour, the route plays hide-and-seek with the coast, touching coastal views periodically and then veering inland again. The most scenic areas are around wild, open-vista **Ship Harbour** and **Spry Harbour,** noted for its attractive older homes and the islands looming offshore. But before you get there, a side trip to Lawrencetown Beach is in order (p. 106).

At the **Fisherman's Life Museum** (✆ **902/889-2053**) on Route 7 in Jeddore Oyster Pond, you'll get a glimpse of life on the Eastern Shore a century ago. The humble white-shingle-and-green-trim cottage was built by James Myers in the 1850s; early in the 20th century it became the property of his youngest son, Ervin, who raised a dozen daughters here—a popular stop for local boys, evidently—and the home and grounds have been restored to look as they might have around 1900 or 1920. It's replete with hooked rugs and a reproduction pump organ, among other period touches. A walk through the house and barn and down to the fishing dock won't take much more than 20 minutes or so. Open June to mid-October, daily 9am to 5pm. Admission is C$3.50 adults, C$2.50 seniors and children age 6 to 17, C$7.75 families.

At the town of Lake Charlotte, you can opt for a side road that weaves along the coast (look for signs for Clam Harbour). The road alternately follows wooded coves and passes through inland forests; about midway you'll see signs for a turn to **Clam Harbour Beach Park** ★, one of the best beaches on this coast. A long, broad crescent beach attracts sunbathers and swimmers from Halifax and beyond; it also helps that there's a boardwalk, clean sand, and toilets and changing rooms, plus lifeguards supervising the action on summer weekends. Look for the picnicking area set amid a spruce grove on a bluff overlooking the beach. There's a funky **sand castle competition** here once a year (which draws big crowds), so you know the sand is plentiful and good. There's no admission charge; gates close around 8pm. Continue on up the coast from the park and you'll reemerge on Route 7 in Ship Harbour.

Between Ship and Spry Harbours is the town of Tangier, home to the great tour outfit **Coastal Adventures** (✆ **877/404-2774** or 902/772-2774) at 84 Mason's Point Rd., which specializes in kayak tours. It's run by Scott Cunningham, who literally wrote the book on Nova Scotia kayaking (he's the author of the definitive guide to paddling this coast). This well-run operation is situated on a beautiful island-dotted part of the coast, but it specializes in multiday trips throughout Atlantic Canada. You can write (P.O. Box 77, Tangier, NS B0J 3H0) or call for a brochure well in advance of your trip, or check the company's website at **www.coastaladventures.com**.

There's also a terrific little fish-smoking business just outside Tangier, **J. Willie Krauch & Sons** ★ (✆ **800/758-4412** or 902/772-2188). The Krauch family (pronounced *craw,* not *crotch,* thank goodness) sells wood-smoked Atlantic salmon, mackerel, and eel in an unpretentious little store. They'll give you a tour of the premises, if you like, where you can check out the old-style smoking process in action. Take some to go for a picnic. It's open until around 6pm daily.

Continuing northeast, **Sheet Harbour** is a pleasant little town of 800 or so souls, with a campground open May through September, a couple small grocery stores, two motels, and a **visitor information center** (✆ 902/885-2595), behind which is a short nature trail and boardwalk that descends along low, rocky cascades. Inland from Sheet Harbour on Route 374 you can find the **Liscomb Game Sanctuary,** a popular destination for the sort of hearty explorers who come equipped with their own maps, compasses, canoes, and fishing rods. (There are no services to speak of here for casual travelers.) Then, east of Sheet Harbour, you pass through the wee village of **Ecum Secum,** which has nothing to attract the tourist—but is unusually gratifying to say out loud to friends after the journey.

Adjacent to the well-marked Liscombe Lodge (see below) and just over the main bridge is the **Liscomb River Trail** system. Trails follow the river both north and south of Route 7. The main hiking trail follows the river upstream for 5km (3 miles), crosses it on a suspension bridge, and then returns on the other side. The Mayflower Point Trail follows the river southward toward the coast, then loops back inland.

Continuing on Route 211 beyond historic Sherbrooke Village (see description below), you'll drive through a wonderful landscape of lakes, ocean inlets, and upland bogs, and soon come to the scenic **Country Harbour Ferry** (✆ 902/387-2200). The 12-car cable ferry crosses the broad river every half-hour, year-round, weather and river conditions permitting. The fare is C$5.25 per car, which includes driver and passengers. If the ferry isn't running, you'll have to turn right around and head back, so it's wise to check at the Canso or Sherbrooke visitor centers before detouring this way.

Farther along (you'll be on Rte. 316 after the ferry), you'll come to **Tor Bay Provincial Park.** It's 4km (2½ miles) off the main road but well worth the detour on a sunny day. The park features three sandy crescent beaches backed by grassy dunes and small ponds that are slowly being taken over by bog and spruce forest. The short boardwalk loop is especially worth a walk.

Way out on the eastern tip of Nova Scotia's mainland is the end-of-the-world town of **Canso** (pop. 900), a rough-edged fishing town and oil port, wind-swept and foggy. The main attraction here is the ruined fort at the **Grassy Island National Historic Site** (✆ 902/295-2069; also known as the Canso Islands National Historic Site). A park-run boat takes you out to the island, which once housed a bustling community of fishermen and traders from New England, where a small interpretive center on the waterfront (open daily 10am–6pm June to mid-Sept) features artifacts recovered from the island and boat schedules. A trail also links several historic sites within the island, which feels a bit melancholy. Admission to the island and park are by voluntary donation; pay what you wish—I recommend a few dollars per person.

If you're coming to Canso in summer, also watch out for the annual music festival held the first week of July to honor late Canadian folk musician Stan Rogers, who perished in an airline fire in Cincinnati in 1983 at the age of just 33. The **Stan Rogers Folk Festival** (www.stanfest.com; ✆ 888/554-7826), also known in these parts as StanFest, focuses on the craft of songwriting. But big names do sometimes play here. Day passes start at C$35 per adult.

Route 16 between the intersection of Route 316 and Guysborough is an especially **scenic drive.** This road runs high and low along brawny hills, giving soaring views of

surf's up AT LAWRENCETOWN BEACH

Word that the surf is up spreads like a fever among those who get their kicks from riding the waves and spectators who get their thrills watching from shore. Lawrencetown Beach, a provincial park supervised by the Nova Scotia Lifeguard Service, is renowned as a prime destination for local and international surfers. A south-facing stretch of sand unfurls for nearly 1.5km (.9 miles) along the Atlantic Ocean. It's positioned perfectly to experience exceptionally high surf conditions resulting from tropical storms and hurricanes. Beach conditions are recorded daily by lifeguard staff and can be accessed by calling the Beach Line at ℰ **902/429-0635.** You don't have to be a pro to enjoy the beach, which is also popular with body boarders. There are folks on hand to give lessons and rent surf boards, boogie boards and wet suits. Board rental costs about C$20 a day, lessons C$30 (group) to C$100 (private). Swimmers need to be cautious of undertows so are advised to stay in the areas with life guards. Hikers and mountain bikers love the great trail system near the beach. Nature enthusiasts will find the area home to lots of watchable wildlife, especially seabirds, and enjoy outings such as guided flora and fauna walks.

Happy Dudes Surf Emporium (www.happydudes.ca; ℰ **902/827-4962**) located at 4891 Hwy. 207 in Three Fathom Harbour, just 3km (1.9 miles) east of Lawrencetown Beach, is open 9am to dusk daily. They sell or rent everything you need for surfing but you don't have to go there. When the surf is up, look for their rental van on the head bank overlooking the beach.

One Life Surf School (www.onelife surf.com; ℰ **902/880-7873**) offers surf lessons for all ages and abilities; it is women-run and women-owned, but they also teach guys. Private, semi-private, and group lessons, and surf yoga classes are announced on their website. The business does not have a physical address.

Kannon Beach Wind and Surf (www.kannonbeach.com; ℰ **902/471-0025**) has just about everything you'll need for surfing and windsurfing in their shop at 4144 Lawrencetown Rd. in East Lawrencetown. It overlooks popular surf spots and one of the more popular windsurf and kite spots (Stoney Beach). Open Monday to Friday 9am to 6pm; Saturday 9am to 5pm; Sunday depends on the waves.

Chedabucto Bay and grassy hills across the way. Also pleasant, although not quite as distinguished, is Route 344 from Guysborough to the Canso causeway. That road twists, turns, and drops through woodlands with some nice views of the strait. It might make you wish you were the owner of a large and powerful motorcycle.

Sherbrooke Village ★★ ☺   About half of the town of Sherbrooke comprises Sherbrooke Village, a historic section surrounded by low fences, water, and fields. You'll have to pay admission to wander around, but the price is well worth it: This is the largest restored village in all of Nova Scotia, and is unique in several respects. For one, almost all the buildings here are on their original sites (only two have been moved). That's very rare in museums like this. Second, many of the homes are still occupied by local residents—and other private homes are interspersed with the ones open to visitors. So it's not just a historic exhibit. About two dozen buildings have been restored and opened to the public, from a convincing general store to an operating blacksmith shop and post office. Look also for the former temperance hall, courthouse, print shop, boatbuilding shop, drugstore, and schoolhouse. All are capably staffed by genial interpreters in costume, who can tell you what life was like around here from the 1860s forward. Be sure to ask about the source of the town's early prosperity; you might be surprised. You could easily spend up to a half-day here, depending on your (or your kids') interest level.

Rte. 7, Sherbrooke. http://museum.gov.ns.ca/sv. ℰ **888/743-7845** or 902/522-2400. Admission C$11 adults, C$8.75 seniors, C$4.75 children age 6 to 17, C$30 families. June to mid-Oct daily 9:30am–5pm.

Where to Stay & Eat

Other than a handful of motels and B&Bs, few accommodations are available on the Eastern Shore beyond these three inns/resorts.

Liscombe Lodge Resort ★★ ☺ This modern complex, owned and operated by the province, consists of a central lodge plus smaller cottages and outbuildings. It's situated on a remote part of the coast, adjacent to hiking trails and a popular boating area at the mouth of the Liscomb River. The lodge bills itself as a nature lover's resort, and indeed it offers access to both forest and sea. But it's not exactly wilderness here; the well-tended lawns, modern architecture, shuffleboard, marina, and outdoor chessboard testify to the middle-to-upper income summer-camp feel of the place. What makes it great for vacationing families are the tons of kid-friendly offerings (table tennis, horseshoe pitches, and so forth). Outdoor types will enjoy the guided kayak trips, hikes, and bird-watches. Rooms here are modern and motel-like; the cottages and chalets have multiple bedrooms: again, good for families. The dining room is open to the public and serves resort fare (steaks, fish).

Rte. 7, Liscomb Mills, NS B0J 2A0. www.liscombelodge.ca. ℰ **800/665-6343** or 902/779-2307. Fax 902/779-2700. 54 units. C$140–C$350 double. Packages and meal plans available. AE, DC, DISC, MC, V. Closed mid-Oct to mid-May. Pets allowed in chalets. **Amenities:** Restaurant; free bikes; fitness center; indoor pool; sauna; whirlpool; tennis courts. In room: TV, fridge (some units), hair dryer, no phone, Wi-Fi (free).

SeaWind Landing Country Inn ★★ Located on a secluded peninsula, just steps from the shore of the Atlantic Ocean, the location puts guests in touch with the flora and fauna and migrating birds. Some of the guest rooms are located in the handsome, 130-year-old home, which has been tastefully modernized and updated. The rest are in a more recent outbuilding, whose rooms feature a whitewashed brightness, terrific peninsula and ocean views, and double Jacuzzis. The innkeepers are very knowledgeable about local art—much of the work on display in the inn was created locally—and they have compiled a literate, helpful guide to the region for guests. The 8-hectare (20-acre) property also has three private sand beaches, and coastal boat tours and picnic lunches can be arranged for an extra charge. The inn also serves dinner as part of some of its packages, featuring local products and wines.

159 Wharf Rd., Charlos Cove, NS B0H 1T0. www.seawindlanding.com. ℰ **800/563-4667** or 902/525-2108. 10 units. C$99–C$169 double. Packages available. AE, MC, V. Closed mid-Oct to mid-May. **Amenities:** Dining room; Jacuzzi (most units). In room: Hair dryer, no phone, Wi-Fi (free).

AMHERST TO ANTIGONISH

The northernmost shore of Nova Scotia—dubbed the **Sunrise Trail** by visitor information centers and provincial tourism publications—is chock-full of rolling hills, water views, and pastoral landscapes. Driving along Route 6, you pass through farmlands along the western reaches from **Amherst** to **Pugwash** and beyond; around **Tatamagouche** (locally: "Ta-Ta"), the landscape sometimes mirrors the one found on the other side of the straits on Prince Edward Island: softly rolling fields of grain, punctuated by well-tended farmhouses and barns, and rust-red soil appearing wherever the vegetation has been scraped off. Cows might dominate one field; massive bull's-eyes of rolled hay the next. This Amherst-to-Pictou drive is especially scenic very early or late on a clear day, when the low sun highlights the green of the local fields and forests. After **Pictou,** back on the Trans-Canada Highway, you'll see more forest and hills as you make your way toward Cape Breton Island.

Amherst

Amherst is known chiefly by travelers for the busy, bustling information center staffed by provincial tourism officials just off the Trans-Canada Highway (see "Visitor Information," below). Yet it's also a lovely small town, perched on a low hill at the edge of the sweeping **Amherst Marsh,** which demarcates the border between Nova Scotia and New Brunswick. It's worth slowing and taking a detour through town just to appreciate the historic streetscapes here. You might even be surprised enough to linger an hour or two.

ESSENTIALS

GETTING THERE Amherst is the first Nova Scotia town you encounter when heading east on the Trans-Canada Highway from New Brunswick; it's the terminus for Nova Scotia Route 6 (from the north) and Route 2 (from the south). It's only about 40 minutes east of Moncton, and **VIA Rail**'s (www.viarail.ca; ✆ **888/842-7245**) six-times-weekly *Ocean* train service between Montréal and Halifax stops here. Note that there is a C$4 **toll** if you head east from Amherst on the Trans-Canada toward Halifax.

VISITOR INFORMATION The huge Nova Scotia Visitor Information Centre (✆ **902/667-8429**) is on Amherst's western edge, just off exit 1 of the Trans-Canada Highway. In addition to the usual vast library of brochures and pamphlets, there are videos, helpful staff, extraordinary views across the usually windy marsh, and often a bagpiper providing the appropriate mood out in front. It's open year-round, and staffed during daylight hours. (A wing of the center with washrooms, vending machines, brochures and maps, and pay phones is open 24 hr. a day in summer.)

Just east of the provincial visitor center is the **local visitor information center,** housed in a handsome old rail car. It's got more detailed information on activities in the area and usually opens daily from late May through early September. There's also a detailed (though slow-to-load) street map online at the town website, **www.amherstns.com**.

EXPLORING AMHERST

Downtown **Amherst** is compact (just a few blocks, really), though attractive in a brick-and-sandstone way. A half-dozen or so buildings are rough gems of classical architecture, nicely offset by the trees—including a few elms that continue to soldier on despite Dutch elm disease. Notice the elaborately pedimented 1888 **courthouse** at the corner of Victoria and Church; a short stroll north is the sandstone Amherst First Baptist Church, with its pair of prominent turrets. Farther north are the stoutly proportioned Doric columns announcing the 1935 Dominion Public Building.

Heading east on Route 6 from the center, you'll glimpse homes dating from the past 150 years or so, displaying an eclectic range of architectural styles and materials.

Those seeking more information on Amherst's history can visit the **Cumberland County Museum,** 150 Church St. (© **902/667-2561**), located in the 1836 home of R. B. Dickey, one of the Fathers of Canadian Confederation. This museum is especially strong in documenting details of local industry and labor—it's big on rugs, fabrics, and knitting. There are also tons of local census records, oral histories, and other ephemera. The museum is open Tuesday through Friday from 9am to 5pm and Saturdays from noon to 5pm. Admission costs C$3 per adult or C$5 per family.

While this isn't really a town to linger in before heading into such a lovely province, you might want to check out the authentic **Old Germany Restaurant ★** (© **902/667-2868**) at 80 Church St. The owner cooks traditional German cuisine and fantastic desserts. It's in a strange location that looks like it once housed a fast-food joint, but never mind: The meat and beer here are very good, plus there's a kids' menu. Owner Holger Renner, as you might have guessed, is originally from Germany. The restaurant is open for lunch and dinner 5 days a week (closed Mon–Tues).

Pugwash & Tatamagouche

If you're in the planning phase of your trip, note that it takes roughly 2 hours to drive from Amherst to **New Glasgow,** whether you take the Trans-Canada Highway (which dips southward through Truro) or Route 6 along the northern shore. If speed is your chief objective, take the Trans-Canada; there's nothing to slow you and the driving is typically steady and fast. But you'll also notice your eyes glazing over and find yourself twirling the radio dials and singing to yourself for entertainment. And you'll pay that C$4 **toll** I mentioned in "Getting There," above.

Route 6 ★ has far more visual interest, and you'll still move speedily among sprawling farms, fields of wheat and corn, blue ocean inlets, and green coastal marshes. Look sharp and you can even spot the wide **Northumberland Strait** dotted with sails, with Prince Edward Island right over there across the way. The landscape changes frequently enough to prevent it from ever growing repetitious. As I mentioned, both routes require about the same amount of time—assuming you don't stop. But, when traveling on Route 6, you probably will be encouraged to stop and walk on beaches, order up french fries with vinegar, or shop at one of the crafts stores in the middle of nowhere. If you take Route 6, you'll also pass through **Pugwash** and **Tatamagouche,** described below.

ESSENTIALS

GETTING THERE   Both towns are located on Route 6; you can't miss them from either direction.

VISITOR INFORMATION   The Tatamagouche Visitor Information Center (© **902/657-3285**) is in a lovely yellow house which doubles as the Fraser Cultural Centre at 362 Main St.

EXPLORING THE REGION

This region is home to a number of picnic parks, as well as local and provincial beaches. Signs along Route 6 point the way; most require a detour of a few miles. Pack a picnic and make an afternoon of it.

Pugwash, which comes from the Mi'kmaq word *pagweak,* meaning deep waters, has a slightly industrial feel, with a factory, mine, and midsize cargo port on the Pugwash River. That white stuff you see piled across the water, or being loaded onto ships is salt—yes, Pugwash has a salt mine. Pugwash sits on top of a salt deposit some 450m (492 yards) thick, and Windsor Salt brings it up from underground. **Seagull**

WHERE thinkers MEET

Pugwash gives the impression of being a sleepy little town, but remarkably, this is the site where some of the world's great thinkers came together and had a huge impact on world politics and world peace. When World War II ended, Bertrand Russell, Albert Einstein, and several scientists published the Russell-Einstein Manifesto, calling for nuclear disarmament. They wanted to debate these issues in a location free from scrutiny from any government. Finding funding with "no strings attached" was a problem until Cyrus Eaton, an American industrialist, stepped forward and agreed to fund the entire project with one condition: They must hold the conference in Pugwash. In his honor, attendees named it the Pugwash Conferences on Science and World Affairs. The first Peace Conference was held in 1957 at what is now known as the "Thinkers' Lodge." The

Pugwash Movement grew and is now held in cities throughout the world. Important conferences are still held periodically at the Lodge.

Mr. Eaton received the Lenin Peace Prize in 1960. In 1995, the Pugwash Conferences on Science and World Affairs won the Nobel Peace Prize.

In 2011, a restoration project for Thinker's Lodge was announced, inspiring the president and secretary-general of the Pugwash Conferences to say, "We are pleased that Thinkers' Lodge is envisioned to be a living, working monument to those who dared at the height of the Cold War to envision a world without nuclear weapons and war. Thinkers' Lodge is a symbol not only for the 'Pugwash movement' that was born there, but to all those who seek to promote dialogue across political divides on key issues that threaten humanity."

Pewter (© 888/955-5551 or 902/243-3850) is well known throughout the province and is made in a factory on the east side of town; look for the retail store (which also stocks antiques) on the other side of town, just west of the Pugwash River bridge on Route 6. It's open 7 days a week in the summer.

Between Pugwash and Tatamagouche you'll drive through the scenic village of **Wallace** (town motto: "A Friendly Place") as the road winds along the water and takes in fine views of the forested shores on the far side of Wallace Bay. Or should it be Wallaces? Last time through, I counted about eight villages with "Wallace" in their name. They're all tiny. East of the "main" Wallace, watch for the remains of ancient Acadian dikes in the marshes—they were built to reclaim the land here for farming (and signs point the dikes out).

Tatamagouche is a pleasant fishing village with a cameo on TV (the CBC miniseries *The Week the Women Went* was based here) and a surprisingly large annual **Oktoberfest** of German beer and dancing, held at the local recreation center. For details on the festival, visit the event's website at **www.nsoktoberfest.ca**. The town is also home to the **Fraser Cultural Centre,** 362 Main St. (© 902/657-3285), a former hospital and rest home which strives to preserve the region's cultural heritage through ongoing exhibits and arts and crafts-related activities. It's open daily from June through September, and admission is free.

You can even go craft shopping here with several shops in town. **Sara Bonnyman Pottery** (© 902/657-3215) has a studio and shop just outside town on Route 246, where you'll find rustic country-style plates, mugs, and more in a speckled pattern embellished with blueberries, sunflowers, and other pleasing country motifs.

WHERE TO STAY

Train Station Inn 🏨 This is one of the most unique lodgings in the province—or in Canada, for that matter, and it's great fun. You won't find Jacuzzis, but you will get a souvenir-worthy digital photo for all time. Located down a side street in Tatamagouche's former railyard, the Train Station (a lovely, century-old brick building) contains just one unit. The Station Master's Suite, the entire second floor of the station, comes with three double-bedded rooms, a TV room, small Victorian parlor, kitchenette, and balcony. It's a good deal if you have six or seven to sleep.

The rest of the units sit in the railyard, in Canadian National cabooses and boxcars. Honest. The rail cars have been refurbished as very simple rooms and vary in comfort and character. Some are decorated in Edwardian parlor motifs with beadboard paneling and striped wallpaper; others come outfitted with hardwood floors, gas woodstoves, kitchenettes, king-size beds, and little sitting areas with plastic patio chairs. All bookings include a continental breakfast served in a men's waiting room lined with lanterns and railway memorabilia. (It doubles as a cafe.) The reception area and gift shop is located in the ladies' waiting room; pick up an engineer's cap if you like. Amazingly, there is even a dining car here, serving lunches and dinners of salmon, steak, lobster, and the like from mid-May through mid-October. Expect train buffs to be your fellow guests and diners, rather than a hip, young crowd.

21 Station Rd., Tatamagouche, NS B0K 1V0. www.trainstation.ca. ⓒ **888/724-5233** or 902/657-3222. 9 units. Caboose and boxcar rooms C$120–C$180 double; station suite C$320. Rates include continental breakfast. AE, DC, MC, V. Closed Nov–Mar. Pets allowed with advance notice. **Amenities:** Restaurant; shared guest kitchenette Wi-Fi (free hot spots on the property). *In room* (caboose only): A/C, TV, kitchenette (2 units), fridge, Wi-Fi.

Pictou

Pictou was established as part of a development scheme hatched by speculators from Philadelphia in 1760. Under the terms of their land grant, they needed to place some 250 settlers at the harbor. That was a problem: Few Philadelphians wanted to live there. So the company sent a ship called the *Hector* to Scotland in 1773 to drum up a few hundred desperately impoverished souls who might be amenable to starting their lives over again in North America.

They were. The ship returned with some 200 passengers, mostly Gaelic-speaking Highlanders. The stormy voyage was brutal, and the passengers nearly starved, but they made it—disembarking in high style, wearing tartans and victoriously playing bagpipes. Now, really: Isn't that the way a town *should* be settled?

The town is still genuinely Scottish enough that you might find *haggis* (a dish containing sheep heart, liver, and lung) slipped into a meal if you're not paying attention. One time you're sure to see that squeamish treat is during the annual anniversary of the settlers' arrival, celebrated in mid-August each year at Pictou's 3-day **Hector Festival** (ⓒ **800/353-5338** or 902/485-8848). Members of the clans wear kilts and dine out in high style in memory of their ancestors; the rest of us listen to storytellers, enjoy Highland Dance, take in the re-enacted landing (bagpipes and all), and dance to talented *ceilidh* fiddlers. Ticket prices vary per event, from free to C$30.

ESSENTIALS

GETTING THERE Pictou is located on Route 106, which is just north of exit 22 off Route 104 (the south branch of the Trans-Canada Hwy.) or on Route 6 if you are coming in from Amherst via the Sunrise Trail. The **Prince Edward Island ferry** is several kilometers north of town at the coast near Caribou. (See chapter 7 for details on this ferry.)

VISITOR INFORMATION The provincial Visitor Information Centre (© **902/485-6213**) is located just off the big rotary, just west of downtown (at the junction of Rte. 6 and Rte. 106). A bit surprisingly, this info center is open daily from May all the way through to mid-December. Considering its size, Pictou also maintains an amazingly well-organized, designed, and researched Web page at www.townofpictou.ca. Kudos for that; check it out.

EXPLORING PICTOU

Pictou is a historic harborside town, with lots of interesting buildings. It's debatable whether it's worth an overnight visit, though: There's not a whole lot to do, and the town isn't terribly outward-looking in terms of welcoming visitors. Still, it does have architecture. There are so many sandstone edifices adorned with five-sided dormers here that you might feel at times like you've wandered into an Edinburgh side street by mistake. Water Street is especially pleasing to the eye, with a few boutiques, casual restaurants, and pubs filling the storefronts.

The harbor is well protected and suitable for novices who want to explore by sea kayak or canoe. Also look in on the **Hector Heritage Quay Visitor's Marina** (© **902/485-6960**) on the waterfront at 37 Caladh Ave., with its twice-weekly live music in summer and a variety of other events. It's open from May through October.

Look for the headquarters and factory outlet of **Grohmann Knives** at 116 Water St. (© **888/756-4837** or 902/485-4224), too. Located in a 1950s-mod building with a large knife piercing one corner, you'll find a good selection of quality knives (each with a lifetime guarantee) at marked-down prices. It's open daily; free half-hour factory tours are offered on weekdays between 9am and 3:30pm—but only if you can get four people together to take one.

Hector Heritage Quay Learn about the brutal hardships endured on the 1773 voyage of the singularly unseaworthy *Hector*, the boat that brought Scottish settlers to the region, at this modern small museum on the waterfront in downtown Pictou. You'll pass several intriguing exhibits en route to the museum's centerpiece: a full-size replica of the 33m (108-ft.) *Hector* at water's edge. Stop by the blacksmith and carpentry shops to get a picture of life in the colonies in the early days, too.

33 Caladh Ave. www.shiphector.com. © **902/485-4371.** Admission C$6 adults, C$5 seniors and students. Mid-May to mid-Oct Mon–Sat 9am–5pm, Sun 10am–5pm; longer hours July–Aug.

WHERE TO STAY

Pictou is a convenient stop for those planning to catch the PEI ferry the next day. Generally speaking, the terminal is about 15 minutes' drive from any of these accommodations, however you should get in line about half-an-hour before sailing time, earlier if it's a summer or holiday weekend.

Auberge Walker Inn ★ This handsome downtown B&B located in a brick town house–style building dating from 1865 overlooks one of Pictou's more active intersections. The innkeepers have done a good job of making the place comfortable while still retaining its historic sensibilities. Some rooms (such as no. 10, on the third floor) have nice harbor views. A first-floor suite has a small kitchen, Jacuzzi, and dark bedroom in back. All rooms have private bathrooms, but the conversions have come at some sacrifice—upstairs rooms have showers only, and some are very, very small. On the upside: The inn is perfectly situated to enjoy Pictou's restaurants and attractions.

78 Coleraine St. (P.O. Box 629), Pictou, NS B0K 1H0. www.walkerinn.com. ⓒ **800/370-5553** or 902/485-1433. Fax 902/485-1222. 11 units. May to Sept C$79–C$99 double; C$149 suite. Off-season rates lower. Rates include continental breakfast. AE, MC, V. Parking on street, at rear of building, and in lot 1 block away. **Amenities:** Conference room. *In room:* Kitchenette (1 unit), no phone, Wi-Fi (free) in most rooms.

Braeside Inn

This three-story hotel on a hill at the edge of downtown was built in 1938 as an inn, and it has been one of the town's more enduring places of lodging. Guest rooms are carpeted and comfortable, though smallish. The dining room has hardwood floors, views down a lawn to the harbor, and a varied menu. Reservations for dining are suggested.

126 Front St., Pictou, NS B0K 1H0. www.braesideinn.com. ⓒ **800/613-7701** or 902/485-5046. Fax 902/485-1701. 18 units. C$65–C$175 double. Rates include continental breakfast. AE, MC, V. At the end of Water St., turn right on Coleraine St. and left on Front St. **Amenities:** Dining room; Jacuzzi (some units). *In room:* A/C, TV/VCR, fridge (some units), hair dryer, Wi-Fi (free).

Consulate Inn ★

No surprise: This 1810 historic home of sandstone and ivy really was originally a consulate. Three guest rooms upstairs in the main inn building share a handsome sitting area; seven larger, more modern rooms are located next door in a wing; and there's yet another room off-property. The decor has a country feel (simple white walls, understated furniture, floral-print bedspreads, lots of wood paneling and beams). Innkeepers Debbie and Garry Jardine work to impart a romantic mood. Newer rooms located in a walk-in basement are smaller, but feature nice touches such as Jacuzzis and mood lighting; three more suites also have Jacuzzis. The Thistle Room has its own private patio with harbor view and awning, a big plus. The whole thing is well situated for exploring Pictou.

115 Water St., Pictou, NS B0K 1H0. www.consulateinn.com. ⓒ **800/424-8283** or 902/485-4554. Fax 902/485-1532. 11 units. June–Sept C$75–C$159 double. Rates include full breakfast. Ask about off-season rates Oct–May. AE, DC, MC, V. **Amenities:** Jacuzzi (some units). *In room:* A/C, TV/VCR, fridge (some units), Wi-Fi (free).

Pictou Lodge Resort ★★

The original lodge and log outbuildings here have gone through a number of ownership changes—including the Canadian National Railway—since entrepreneurs built the compound on a grassy bluff overlooking a nice beach early in the 20th century. It's now owned privately and has been upgraded and improved with new three-bedroom Oceanview Villas and executive "chalets." (They're modern-looking and full of windows to let in the view.) The splendid ocean views, of course, never go out of style, nor do the outdoor playgrounds, lawn games, nature trails, and canoes. The lodge is located about a 10-minute drive from downtown Pictou, yet has a very remote feel. The log rooms, most of which have kitchenettes, have a lot more character (but also look a bit dowdy); newer rooms have the blandness of modern motel rooms anywhere. Lunch and dinner are served in an Adirondack-style lodge that was hammered together with classic beams; there's both a lounge with windows opening onto the stunning view, and a restaurant with a fireplace (see "Where to Eat," below).

172 Lodge Rd. (P.O. Box 1539), Pictou, NS B0K 1H0. www.pictoulodge.com. ⓒ **800/495-6343** or 902/485-4322. Fax 902/485-4945. 49 units. C$139–C$229 double; C$165–C$449 chalets and cottages (for up to 6 people). Packages available. AE, DC, DISC, MC, V. Closed mid-Oct to mid-May. Follow Shore Rd. from downtown toward PEI ferry; watch for signs. **Amenities:** Restaurant; outdoor pool; room service. *In room:* A/C, TV (some units), fridge (some units), Jacuzzi (some units), Wi-Fi (free).

WHERE TO EAT

The **Pictou Lodge Resort ★★** (see above) features several distinct dining areas, one with ocean views and one with fireplaces, plus special jazz nights (on Tues) and full brunches (on Sun). It's definitely the preferred pick in town.

If you want something more casual, a wide choice of cafes, pubs, chip shops, and tearooms line **Water Street** and its continuation to the east (Front St.). Several more choices can be found by walking a block to the water and Caladh Avenue. The downtown area is so compact here that you can just go from place to place, checking the menus until you find something you like.

Piper's Landing CONTINENTAL   This contemporary, attractive dining room on a stretch of residential road just outside Pictou remains a local favorite and your best bet in the area for a sophisticated meal. The interior is sparely decorated and understated. Likewise, the menu looks simple—European-influenced entrees of grilled beef tenderloin, pork schnitzel, and big seafood platters—but there's some flair in the preparation. There's a small wine list, as well.

Rte. 376, Lyons Brook (5km/3 miles west of downtown Pictou). © **902/485-1200.** Reservations recommended. Main courses C$20–C$30. AE, MC, V. Mon–Sat 5–8pm. From the Pictou Rotary take Rte. 376 toward Lyons Brook; it's 3km (1¾ miles) on your left.

Antigonish

Antigonish can trace its European roots back to the 1650s (the French came first; the Irish, Black Loyalists, and Scottish Highlanders later), and today the town of 4,000-plus residents is still the local market town, with a bustling main street and St. Francis Xavier University, which was founded in 1853. For rural Nova Scotia, the town has a relatively busy commercial center; be prepared for some traffic midsummer. This is a good spot to stock up on groceries or grab a bite for lunch. There are several cafes on Main Street and a shop or two worth browsing.

For a mild outdoor adventure, drive about 8 to 9km (5 or 6 miles) northeast of town on Route 337 (past the hospital) and look for the **Fairmont Ridge Trail ★**. Here you'll find a half-dozen gentle hiking loops, ranging from 3 to 11km (2–7 miles) in length, that take you through hayfields and past babbling brooks into ravines and forests of old-growth trees. There are many junctions and intersections on the trail, but trail maps are posted. Eagles and even bears have reportedly been sighted in these woods; check with the tourist office (see "Visitor Information" below) about current conditions on the trail if you're serious about hiking it.

The Name Game

The origins of the name Antigonish—correctly pronounced, it sounds more like "ahn-tee-gun-ish" than "anti-goan-ish," "anti-matter," "anti-aircraft fire"—has created a little contention among linguists with the time on their hands to research the matter. In the original native tongue, it meant either "five-forked rivers of fish" or "the place where branches get torn off by bears gathering beech nuts to eat." There's no real consensus. But that's all right; I like both versions just fine.

ESSENTIALS

GETTING THERE   Antigonish is on Route 104 (Trans-Canada Hwy.) 53km (33 miles) west of the Canso Causeway (the connection to Cape Breton Island).

VISITOR INFORMATION   The **Tourist Office** (© **902/863-4921**) is located at the **Antigonish Mall Complex** (exit 33 north off the Trans-Canada Hwy., Rte. 104 to Church St.). It's open daily from 10am to 8pm, May to October.

SPECIAL EVENTS   The Highland Games ★ have been staged in mid-July annually since 1861. What started as a community diversion has become an international event—these are now the oldest continuously played Highland games in North America, a place to experience everything Scottish from piping to dancing to the feat of dexterity known as "tossing the caber" (the caber being a heavy log or pole that's tossed for accuracy, not distance). Contact the folks at the local **Antigonish Highland Society** (www.antigonishhighlandgames.ca; © **902/863-4275**) for each summer's dates and details. Rooms are scarce during the 3-day games (Fri–Sun), so if you plan to attend, be sure to book well ahead. You can buy daily and event tickets (C$10–C$30 per adult, free to C$5 per child age 6–16).

The **Festival Antigonish** ★ (© **800/563-7529** or 902/867-3333) is a different event, a summer-long program of theater and live performances held on the campus of St. Francis Xavier University. It usually begins in late June or early July and runs through Labour Day. Shows might range from productions written by local playwrights to Agatha Christie tales, *Rumpelstiltskin*, or a Woody Guthrie tribute act. Tickets for children's and "Stage 2" productions are C$10 or less; tickets for the mainstage, grown-up performances range from about C$15 to C$30. Or you can pre-order one of several all-inclusive passes for about C$90. The organization's website is at **www.festivalantigonish.com**.

WHERE TO STAY

Antigonish is located just off the Trans-Canada Highway, the last town of any size before you reach Cape Breton Island. As such, it's home to a number of chain motels, both downtown and on the "strip" leading into town. If nightfall is coming, and you're bound for Cape Breton, I'd suggest overnighting here and pushing off the next morning. That's because Port Hastings and Port Hawkesbury—the first towns you encounter on Cape Breton—are also full of chain motels. Antigonish is a better choice, with better restaurants.

Budget travelers can also book a no-frills dorm room or apartment at **St. Francis Xavier University** (© **902/867-2855** or 877/STAY-AT-X [782-9289]) from mid-May through mid-August. The dorm rooms are mostly simple and share hallway washrooms, but they include all the basics: linens, pillows, towels, and soap. Apartments have private bathrooms and kitchens—but no utensils; bring your own. Dorm room rates here range from about C$40 to C$125 for two, including tax, while the dorm apartments (four single bedrooms, two bathrooms, and a living room) cost from C$115 to C$145 per night. Meals are available in the Morrison Dining Hall for a small charge. The best thing about staying here is that you get the use of some campus facilities—and walk-to-it proximity to the summer theater festival. If you're looking for a room and it's after business hours, head to the Security Office in the basement of MacKinnon Hall and ask nicely.

At the west edge of town on the Trans-Canada Highway (3055 Rte. 104), you'll find the plain **Chateau Motel** (www.antigonishchateauinns.com; ☏ **877/339-8544** or 902/863-4871) with about 16 double rooms (queen-size and king-size beds) and simple cottages (double beds, but full kitchens). There's also a laundromat on the premises. Rates are C$70 to C$99 per night.

Maritime Inn Antigonish   The basic, modern Maritime Inn Antigonish has benefited from renovations. Rooms are comfortable and clean, if unexceptional. The best thing about the place? Its location on Antigonish's Main Street, where you can easily walk to the city's best restaurant cafe and take care of your basic shopping needs without getting back in the car. The cheapest rooms are drive-up, motel style, while the more expensive suites include two bedrooms (one with a queen-size bed, one with a king), plus a sitting room with sofa and several televisions. A restaurant on the premises also serves three meals daily.

158 Main St., Antigonish, NS B2G 2B7. www.maritimeinns.com/antigonish. ☏ **888/662-7484** or 902/863-4001. Fax 902/863-2672. 32 units. C$119–C$189 double. AE, DC, DISC, MC, V. **Amenities:** Restaurant. *In room:* A/C, TV, Wi-Fi (free).

WHERE TO EAT

Lobster Treat ☺ SEAFOOD   Housed in a red-shingled former schoolhouse (note the hanging lamps, which are original) west of town on the Trans-Canada Highway, Lobster Treat has been doing seafood for a few decades and is something of an institution around here. Foodies have even made the trip from the United States to check it out. It's not fancy, featuring family-restaurant decor like potted plants and mauve carpeting. But the seafood is fresh. The menu ranges from a traditional Nova Scotia boiled lobster dinner to surf-and-turf combos and seafood concoctions. You can get haddock just about anywhere in the Maritimes, but it's particularly good here. Complete meals for kids are available for about C$5, and the place also serves pasta, chicken, and steaks in case you don't want lobster. But everyone does.

241 Post Rd. (Rte. 104). ☏ **902/863-5465.** Main courses C$10–C$30 at dinner; most dishes under C$20. AE, DC, MC, V. Daily 11am–10pm. Closed late Dec to mid-Apr.

CAPE BRETON ISLAND ★★★

Isolated and craggy Cape Breton Island—Nova Scotia's northernmost landmass—should be tops on a list of don't-miss destinations for travelers to Nova Scotia, especially those who like outdoor adventures or great views. The island's chief draw is **Cape Breton Highlands National Park,** a knockout park up at the top of the island's western lobe. Celtic music and the lure of Scottish heritage, the historic fort at **Louisbourg,** and scenic **Bras d'Or Lake,** an inland saltwater lake that nearly cleaves the island in two, are just a few of the reasons for visiting.

Above all, there are the drives: It's hard to find a road on this island that's *not* a scenic route. Some of the vistas are wild and dramatic, some green and pastoral, but all of them will have you clicking your camera furiously.

When traveling on this island, be aware of the cultural context. Just as southern Nova Scotia was largely settled by Loyalists fleeing the United States after England lost the War of Independence, Cape Breton was principally settled by Highlander Scots whose families came out on the wrong side of rebellions against the crown overseas. You can still hear their heritage here, both in the accents of people in the villages (listen carefully, you might even hear the Gaelic language) and in the great

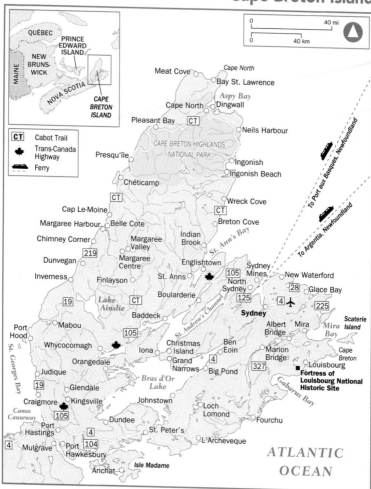

popularity of Scottish-style folk music throughout the island. For a primer on things Celtic, check out www.celticheart.ca—some say this place is more Celtic that Scotland.

You'll often hear references to the **Cabot Trail ★★★** while on the island. This is the official designation for the 300km (186-mile) roadway circling around the northwest corner of the island and the national park. It's named for John Cabot, whom many believe first set foot on North American soil near Cape North. (However, many scholars disagree; it's not a fact, and Cabot may have made landfall on Newfoundland first. Or even somewhere else.)

The one "challenge" with this island is that it's perceived as being remote, so tourism hasn't really developed with the times. Accommodations tend towards B&Bs in small towns and a number of rural resorts, with most hotels and motels in larger communities. Some travelers base themselves in **Baddeck,** which is centrally located and has a small concentration of lodgings and restaurants. You can reach both the national park and the historic settlement of Louisbourg from Baddeck, but I would recommend doing your planning ahead to map your route, then book appropriate lodgings (see the suggested itineraries in chapter 3) along the way. I'd much prefer staying in a small local village such as **Mabou,** or in the Margaree Valley, or scoping out a cottage rental somewhere. If you only have a few days, focus on the Cape Breton Highlands, Fortress Louisbourg, or western Celtic region and enjoy it rather than logging lots of miles but not really experiencing any place properly.

Oh, and one more thing: If you've got golf clubs and some game, bring 'em. The golfing is wonderfully scenic here—but it's tough. Cape Breton is a place to follow your passions: photography, sport fishing, nature gazing, painting, music, history, or whale-watching.

For your convenience, this section is divided into two parts: one on the bulk of Cape Breton Island, and then one on Cape Breton Highlands National Park itself. (For specific information on just the park, jump ahead to the next section on p. 139.) Geographically, though, the park is likely second on your itinerary: Most travelers enter the island, scoop up info, then make a beeline for lovely uplands areas in Mabou or the Margaree Valley for the night. Then they head straight for the **Cabot Trail,** the winding, spectacular coastal road which takes you right into the national park.

Essentials

GETTING THERE Cape Breton is connected to the mainland via the Canso Causeway, a man-made stone causeway built in 1955 with 10 million tons of rock. (You can see the mountain which was sacrificed for the cause as you approach the island on the Trans-Canada Hwy.) The causeway, which is 61m (200 ft.) high and 1km (¾-mile) long, is 262km (163 miles) from the New Brunswick border at Amherst and 272km (169 miles) from Halifax—a little less than 3 hours' drive from either point if you take the fastest route possible and don't stop.

But you're just getting started: Once you cross the causeway onto the island, it takes another 2 to 3 hours to reach the best parts, such as the national park. Baddeck, Mabou, the Margaree Valley, and Louisbourg are a little closer—they can all be reached in 1 to 2 hours' driving, maximum, but you may want to take longer to savor the sights.

VISITOR INFORMATION A number of tiny local tourist information centers dot Cape Breton Island, but you're best off grabbing a pile of info at the bustling **Port Hastings Info Centre** (© 902/625-4201), which is on your right just after you cross the causeway onto the island. It's open daily from around 8am until about 8:30pm most of the year, closed only from January through April.

SPECIAL EVENTS Celtic Colours ★★★ (www.celtic-colours.com; © 877/285-2321 or 902/562-6700) is a big, island-wide annual music shindig timed to approximate the peak of the lovely highland foliage in early October. Few tourists know about it, and the concentration of local Celtic musicians getting together for good times and music beneath lovely foliage is simply breathtaking, if you're into this sort of thing. Some 350 artists put on 45 or more shows throughout the island, so you can take in many artists in many communities. It usually begins in the second week of October and lasts more than 10 days: a foot-stompin', pennywhistlin', fiddle-playin' 10 days. The musical performances, by such international stars as the Chieftains and Barra MacNeils—or, even better, the up-and-coming stars of tomorrow—are the obvious highlight, though they can cost as much as C$60 per person for a real head-line act. More typical *ceilidh* nights (see below) cost about C$20, and popular local performers sell out months in advance; check the website or call well ahead if you've got your heart set on a particular act. Otherwise, just buy a ticket to anything. You can't go wrong. Stages and venues are scattered all over Cape Breton Island.

Mabou & Vicinity ★★

The little village of Mabou sits on a deep, protected inlet along the island's western shore. This former coal-mining town has made itself over as a lobster-fishing town, though you don't come here for crustaceans; the seafood is shipped out to Halifax and beyond. Instead, the lovely scenery and culture are what you come for. Attractive drives and bike rides are easy to find in the area; almost any road you choose is an opportunity to break out the camera. The town itself consists of a short main street, a clump of homes, a gas station, a few eateries and services, plus (if you can find it) a scenic little beach.

But there's a hidden bonus to the area, giving it an importance disproportionate to its size: Local residents are strongly oriented toward **music,** even more so than is usual on already-musical Cape Breton Isle. The local kids, nearly all of Scottish descent, grow up playing instruments, singing, and dancing; amazingly, this tiny town has produced not only several international hit Celtic music acts, but also the former premier of Nova Scotia (Rodney MacDonald), a former step dancer and fiddler who was elected in 2006 at the age of just 34 and served as premier for 3 years.

Evening entertainment in Mabou revolves around fiddle playing, square dancing, and the traditional gathering of musicians and storytellers known as a *ceilidh* (*kay-lee*) ★★★. These planned and impromptu musical events take place in pubs, civic buildings, outdoors, people's homes . . . anywhere. To find out what's going on, stop by the village **grocery store,** the **Mull** pub right across the street, or the **Red Shoe** pub (see "Where to Eat," below) and scope out their bulletin boards and calendars. You might also check with the **Strathspey Place Theatre** (www.strathspeyplace. com; ℂ **902/945-5300**) at 11156 Rte. 19. It offers occasional Celtic music events too, usually for C$15 to C$20 per person.

In a handsome valley between Mabou and Inverness is the distinctive post-and-beam **Glenora Distillery** ★ (ℂ **800/839-0491** or 902/258-2662). This modern distillery—North America's only single-malt whisky ("scotch") producer—began producing spirits from the pure local stream in 1990, and selling it in 2000. Your tour guide will tell you that the Cape Breton water is what makes all the difference, and is in fact the reason the owner chose to put the factory here—seemingly in the middle of nowhere. They use Kentucky bourbon casks to age the whisky, because the distill-ers here believe those impart a mellower taste to their spirits than the traditional sherry casks. Production runs take place each fall; tours of the facility are offered May through October. Tours cost C$7 and last about a half-hour (offered daily 9am–5pm), culminating in welcome free samples; they also conveniently end near the gift shop, where you can buy local music CDs, gift glasses, even bottles of the whisky itself (for at least C$80 a pop). The owner can't call the product scotch, by the way, since it isn't made in Scotland, hence "Canadian single malt whisky."

The distillery complex also includes an adjoining **restaurant** (open seasonally) and a nine-room **hotel** with rooms and chalets on a hillside overlooking the valley (see below); traditional music is often scheduled for weekends or evenings in the contemporary pub.

WHERE TO STAY

Glenora Inn & Distillery ★★ When was the last time you spent the night sleeping next to a distiller of single-malt whisky (see above)? Well, this is your chance. Glenora offers nine modern hotel rooms over a courtyard next to a pub, beside the distillery. They're contemporary yet rustic, with easy access to said pub and a restaurant (which often feature live performers from the area). There are also a half-dozen attractive log chalets, of one to three bedrooms each, with woody interiors on the hills overlooking the distillery. These are perfect for either lovebirds or families. Each chalet has a Jacuzzi, satellite TV, and wonderful view of the mist-covered valley below. It all has the feel of being tucked in a remote vale in the Scottish Highlands.

Rte. 19, Glenville, NS B0E 1X0. www.glenoradistillery.com. ⓒ **800/839-0491.** 15 units. C$125–C$180 double; C$175–C$299 chalet. AE, MC, V. Closed Oct 31 to mid-May. **Amenities:** Restaurant; bar; Jacuzzi (some units). *In room:* TV, Wi-Fi (free).

Haus Treuburg Country Inn and Cottages ★ Located a few miles from Mabou in the undistinguished oceanside fishing village of Port Hood, Haus Treuburg is a handsome Queen Anne–style home dating from 1914. The three guest rooms in the main building (one is a suite) are nicely furnished in a spare style, with down duvets and lots of wood. As nice as they are, the cottages behind the house are a better deal. Each comes with a private deck, ocean view, and gas barbecue. Four-course dinners at the inn cost about C$40 (expect German-Italian cuisine, including apple strudel), and a full "Sunday morning breakfast" is available to guests (for an extra charge) every morning of the week.

175 Main St. (P.O. Box 92), Port Hood, NS B0E 2W0. www.haustreuburg.com. ⓒ **877/787-2116.** 902/787-2116. Fax 902/787-3216. 6 units. C$100–C$120 double; C$140–C$195 cottage. AE, DC, MC, V. **Amenities:** 2 dining rooms; babysitting. *In room:* TV/VCR, Wi-Fi (free).

Mabou River Inn ★★ 🏠 Located not far from the river and adjacent to the Mother of Sorrows Pioneer Shrine (dedicated to the settlers of the Mabou area), this former boarding school was converted twice, first into a winning youth hostel and then into this homey little inn just off the main road. Hosts Donna and David Cameron keep things running smoothly and dispense great advice; nature lovers will appreciate the opportunity to hike, kayak, fish, and mountain-bike on the scenic Ceilidh Trail using the inn's rental equipment, while night owls can stroll a few minutes across the bridge to check out the local traditional music offerings that fill Mabou in summer. Note that while all of the main inn rooms come with their own private bathrooms, you have to put on your slippers and cross the hall to get to three of them. Four now have king-size beds. Three two-bedroom apartment suites are good for families. The kitchen and dining room for guests are useful: At night the staff cooks up good pizzas and serves beer and wine with them, or you can pick up lobster at the wharf and they will help cook them. They bake all of their own bread, making for a delicious breakfast.

19 Southwest Ridge Rd. (P.O. Box 255), Mabou, NS B0E 1X0. www.mabouriverinn.com. ⓒ **888/627-9744** or 902/945-2356. Fax 902/945-2605. 10 units. C$105–C$135 double; C$145–C$165 suite. AE, MC, V. **Amenities:** Complimentary continental breakfast; restaurant; bike and sea kayak rentals. *In room:* TV, kitchenette (some units), no phone (some units), Wi-Fi (free).

WHERE TO EAT

The Mull Café & Deli CAFE   Owned by the same folks who own the Duncreigan Inn in town, the Mull is a simple country deli that serves simple food. You can get something basic like seafood chowder, fish and chips, a burger, or one of the deli-style sandwiches. There's also a dinner-type menu, with entrees like grilled salmon, chicken potpie, thick-cut pork chops, and good pasta selections. Translation: This is more than just bar grub. Don't expect to be bowled over by fancy food; do expect a filling meal and good company.

Rte. 19 (just north of the village), Mabou. (C) **902/945-2244.** Reservations accepted for parties of 6 or more. Sandwiches C$6–C$9; main courses C$8–C$22. AE, MC, V. Daily 11am–8pm (7pm in winter).

The Red Shoe Pub ★★ 🏛 CANADIAN   I like this place a lot. You can't find a more local pub than "the Shoe" (as it's known here), owned by the famous Rankin family of musicians and open from June through mid-October. Time was when this was a gloriously hazy dive of fiddle music, cigarette smoke, sassy waitresses, and heavy pub fare. Not now: The province is smoke-free, and the menu has been completely revamped—you can get a pulled-pork sandwich, some beautifully caloric Nova Scotia *poutine* (french fries covered in cheese curds and gravy), a bowl of seafood chowder with cheddar biscuits, steak frites, or char-broiled salmon. There are requisite ales on tap and in bottles, of course. The real highlight, though, is the daily scheduled musical performances in the pub—the next Celtic music star might be playing for a small donation or cover charge on the night you swing by. Be aware that this place is small, so it can get a bit crowded and claustrophobic; it helps to know a local, though the influx of summer tourists keeps the mix interesting. A small but welcome kids' menu, and surprisingly yummy desserts, are two more reasons to stop by. Don't miss it if you're in town.

11573 Rte. 19, Mabou. (C) **902/945-2996.** Entrees C$11–C$19. MC, V. Mid-June to Oct Mon–Wed 11:30am–11pm; Thurs–Sat 11:30am–2am; Sun noon–11pm.

Margaree Valley ★

Continuing up the western coast brings us to Margaree Harbour, south of Chéticamp. It is here that the Margaree River enters the Gulf of St. Lawrence, and this is also where you pick up the Cabot Trail. The experts tell us that the trail should be driven clockwise, for the best views and such, so I do suggest you treat the Margaree Valley as a side trip to be traveled both ways (thus bringing you back to enter the Cape Breton Highlands at Chéticamp) or tack it on to the end of your Cabot Trail odyssey.

The **Margaree Valley** consists of the area from the village called Margaree Valley (near the headwaters of the Margaree River) to Margaree Harbor, downriver on Cape Breton's west coast. Some seven small Margaree-themed communities are clustered along this valley floor, a world apart from the rugged drama of the surf-battered coast—it's more reminiscent of Vermont than Maine. The **Cabot Trail ★★★** gently rises and falls here on the shoulders of rounded hills flanking the valley, offering views of farmed floodplains and glimpses of a shining river. The whole area is best explored by slow and aimless driving, or by bike or canoe if you've brought one along with you. And, in autumn, the foliage here is often among Eastern Canada's very best.

The **Margaree River** is a bona fide celebrity in fishing circles—widely regarded as one of the most productive Atlantic salmon rivers in North America, and the salmon have continued to return to spawn here in recent years, which is unfortunately *not* always the case on many waterways of Atlantic Canada. The river has been closed to all types of fishing except fly-fishing since the 1880s, and in 1991 it was designated a Canadian Heritage River.

Learn about the river's heritage at the **Margaree Salmon Museum ★** (www.margareens.com; ℂ **902/248-2848**) in North East Margaree. The handsome museum building features a brief video about the life cycle of the salmon, and its exhibits include fishermen photos, antique rods (including an impressive 16-footer), examples of seized poaching equipment—plus hundreds of skillfully hand-tied salmon flies. (You've got to be a buff to appreciate those.) If you want to fish, museum docents can help you find a guide to bring you out on the river; late spring and early fall are usually the times of year when the fish are biting. The museum is open daily mid-June through mid-October, 9am to 5pm. Admission is C$2 per adult, C$1 per child.

Also make a point of dropping by **Cape Breton Clay ★★** (www.capebretonclay.com; ℂ **902/235-2467**), northeast of the salmon museum. Margaree Valley native Bell Fraser's work is truly unique. Fish, crab, lobster, starfish, ear of corn, and other motifs are worked into her platters and bowls in ways that will surprise and delight even pottery haters. Bell's colorful hand-painted lobster and starfish platters bring a whole new interpretation to the serving plate, while her fish-handled serving bowl is reminiscent of the local river's leaping, silvery trout. The shop is open daily from June through mid-October, 10am to 5pm, it's definitely worth a stop; individual pieces might run from C$40 to C$400. Don't miss "the Koop" next door, either, a place where real—and Bell's ceramic—chickens comingle.

WHERE TO STAY

The Normaway Inn ★   Down a drive lined with Scotch pines, the Normaway, built in 1928 and run by the same family since the 1940s, was once the sort of place anglers dressed in tweed. It's no longer a luxury getaway; families and honeymooners come to the 500-acre (202-hectare) compound for fresh air, quiet, and local music. Ten rooms are situated in the main lodge, which is rugged in a loveable stonework-and-exposed beam way. There are also 17 cottages a short walk from the lodge—none have kitchens or air-conditioning. The original four Normaway cottages have hardwood floors and spare interiors; built in the '40s, they're smaller and rougher around the edges. Newer cottages have touches like whirlpool tubs, and all but two have wood-stoves. The newest additions are three expensive suites in the MacPherson House, about 400m (a quarter-mile) from the lodge. The lodge's dining room is known for its salmon and lamb; subscribe to a meal plan if you want your breakfast and dinner cooked daily. Guests really seem to enjoy the entertainment here, ranging from films to live music, storytelling, and fiddling. (A weekly dance is held in the inn's red barn, attracting hundreds of locals and guests.) All in all, Normaway offers a great local experience—so long as you can cope with the simplicity and occasional mosquito.

691 Egypt Rd., P.O. Box 121, Margaree Valley, NS B0E 2C0. www.thenormawayinn.com. ℂ **800/565-9463** or 902/248-2987. Fax 902/248-2600. 30 units. C$139–C$179 double; C$179–C$259 suite; C$139–C$199 cottage. 2-night minimum stay (some dates) July–Aug. MAP meal plans and packages available. DC, MC, V. Closed late Oct to May. Pets allowed in cottages only. Paved landing strip. **Amenities:** Dining room; free bikes; tennis court. *In room:* No phone, Wi-Fi (free).

Chéticamp ★

The Acadian town of **Chéticamp** is the western gateway to Cape Breton Highlands National Park, and the center of French-speaking culture on Cape Breton. The change is rather obvious as you drive northward from Margaree Harbour—the family names suddenly go from MacDonald to Doucet, and the cuisine turns on its head all at once. The town is an assortment of restaurants, boutiques, and tourist establishments spread along a Main Street closely hugging the harbor. A winding **boardwalk** ★ follows harbor's edge through much of town, and this is a great spot to stretch your legs from the drive and have a look at the local geography. Chéticamp Island sits just across the water; the mighty coastal hills of the national park are visible just up the coast.

Chéticamp is famous worldwide for its hooked rugs, a craft perfected here by the early Acadian settlers. Those curious about the craft should allow time for a stop at **Les Trois Pignons,** which houses the **Elizabeth LeFort Gallery** and the **Hooked Rug Museum** ★ (www.lestroispignons.com; © **902-224-2642**). It is located on Main Street in the north end of town and displays some 300 fine tapestries, many created by Elizabeth LeFort, who was Canada's premier rug-hooking artist for many decades until she passed away in 2005—check out her tableau of U.S. presidents from 1959, which required 1.7 *million* loops to be hooked. You can also view tools used for the craft. The museum and gallery are usually open from mid-May to mid-October, daily 9am to 5pm (until 7pm in July and Aug). Admission is C$5 per adult, C$4 for seniors, C$3.50 students, C$12 for families, and free for children 5 and under.

In the 1930s, artisans formed the **Co-opérative Artisanale de Chéticamp,** located at 5067 Main St. (www.cheticamphookedrugs.com; © **902/224-2170**). A selection of hooked rugs—from tiny ones on up—are sold here, along with other trinkets and souvenirs. There's often a weaver or other craftsperson at work in the shop. A small local museum downstairs (admission is free) chronicles the life and times of the early Acadian settlers and their descendants. It's closed from mid-October to May.

Several boat tour operators are based in Chéticamp Harbor. **Love Boat Seaside Whale Cruises** (www.loveboatwhalecruises.ca; © **800/959-4253** or 902/224-2400) sets out in search of whales, seals, and scenery, and has hydrophones on board for listening to any whales you may encounter. (No, Captain Stubing will not be your captain.) The tours take 2½ to 3 hours.

The most pleasing drive or bike ride in the area is out to Chéticamp Island, connected to the main highway by a road and bridge. Look for the turnoff just south of town; the road is just north of the gift shop.

WHERE TO STAY

A handful of motels service the thousands of travelers who pass through each summer. **Laurie's Motor Inn,** on Main Street (www.lauries.com; © **800/959-4253** or 902/224-2400), has more than 50 motel rooms and newer suites in a string of buildings situated right in town; rates run from C$109 to C$249 per night (mostly toward the lower end of that range). The inn also manages some nice rental homes and apartments around town for longer stays; inquire if you're interested in something bigger or need cooking facilities. Open April through October.

Parkview Motel   This basic, comfortable motel's biggest advantage is its location—within *walking distance* of the national park's visitor center, and away from the bustle of Chéticamp's downtown. Don't expect anything fancy; rooms have cable TV and somewhat upgraded bathrooms, and that's about it. There's a dining room and lounge in a building across the street, where a half-dozen newer rooms are also located—these units have a number of amenities (coffeemakers, refrigerators, microwave ovens) unavailable in the main building's 11 motel units, plus better, actually quite scenic, views of the Chéticamp River and the island's mountains.

Cabot Trail (P.O. Box 117), Chéticamp, NS B0E 1H0. www.parkviewresort.com. ✆ **877/224-3232** or 902/224-3232. Fax 902/224-2596. 17 units. C$79–C$109 double. AE, MC, V. Closed mid-Sept to Apr. Hotel is 3 miles north of downtown Chéticamp on Cabot Trail. **Amenities:** Dining room; bar. *In room:* A/C (some units), TV, fridge (some units), Wi-Fi (free).

Pilot Whale Chalets ★   These spare, modern cottages each have at least two bedrooms and full housekeeping facilities, including microwaves, gas barbecues for firing up steaks, coffeemakers, decks, and woodstoves; some even have Jacuzzis and fireplaces, as well. They're plain but attractive, and their best feature is the great view northward toward the coastal mountains. The lodge has also added some basement apartment suites to several of the cottages, which does impinge upon the privacy of both cottage dwellers and suite dwellers. For more space and comfort, ask about the three-bedroom cottage with king-size beds, two bathrooms with whirlpools, Wi-Fi, and a private laundry—it sleeps up to six people. A small beach sits adjacent to the hotel.

Rte. 19, 15775 Cabot Trail, Chéticamp, NS B0E 1H0. www.pilotwhalechalets.com. ✆ **902/224-1040.** Fax 902/224-1540. 15 units. C$95–C$125 double; C$159–C$249 cabin. AE, MC, V. **Amenities:** Jacuzzi (some units). *In room:* TV/VCR/DVD, Internet (free), kitchenette (some units).

WHERE TO EAT

La Boulangerie Aucoin (✆ **902/224-3220**) has been a staple of Chéticamp daily life since the 1950s. Located just off the Cabot Trail between the town and the national park (look for signs), the place is full of fresh-baked goods; ask what's just out of the oven when you get to the counter. Among the potential options: croissants, scones, fresh bread, and (yum) berry pies. This is a great place to fuel up on snacks before setting off into the park.

Restaurant Acadien ACADIAN   This local restaurant is attached to a crafts shop on the south side of town (the Co-opérative Artisanale; see above) and has the feel of a cafeteria. Servers wear costumes inspired by traditional Acadian dress, and the menu draws heavily on tried-and-true Acadian cuisine, just as you'd expect it to. Look for *fricot* (a sort of chicken-and-potato soup), stewed potatoes, and the meat pies for which this region is renowned. They also do lobster, fried fish, turkey dinners, and other more traditionally Anglo fare. Also on the menu: baked beans, bottled beer, blood pudding (for the brave of heart), and butterscotch and blueberry pies (among others).

15067 Main St. ✆ **902/224-3207.** Reservations recommended. Breakfast items C$3.50–C$5; lunch and dinner entrees C$4–C$17. AE, MC, V. Daily 7am–9pm. Closed Nov to mid-May.

Pleasant Bay ★

At the north end of the Cabot Trail's exhilarating run along the island's western cliffs, the road turns inland to the village of **Pleasant Bay.** You need to sneak off the Trail (down Harbour Rd., naturally) to find a surprise: a simple, attractive little harbor protected by a man-made jetty, complete with bobbing brightly painted fishing boats. It's just a short walk off the main road and sits at the base of rounded, forested mountains that plunge down to the sea. You know what to do: Break out that camera and impress friends with your foray into the "real" Nova Scotia off the main roads.

The **Whale Interpretive Centre** (✆ **902/224-1411**), built on a rise overlooking the harbor, features exhibits to help explain why the waters offshore are so rich with marine life—not to mention *life-size* models of some of the local whales. It's open daily, June through mid-October 9am to 5pm; admission is C$5 for adults, C$4 for children and seniors, and C$16 for families.

Whale-watching tours are offered three to five times daily from June through October from the harbor by Capt. Mark Timmons of **Capt. Mark's Whale and Seal Cruise** (www.whaleandsealcruise.com; © **888/754-5112** or 902/224-1316). Timmons's 2½-hour cruises on his 13m (42-ft.) cabin cruise *Double Hookup* provide unrivaled glimpses at the rugged coast both north and south, and often a close-up look at whales (almost always pilot whales, frequently finbacks and minkes, occasionally humpbacks). The boat has a hydrophone on board, so you can hear the plaintive whale calls underwater. Trips are C$28 per adult, C$25 students and seniors, C$12 children age 6 to 15, and reservations are encouraged. The same outfit also offers Zodiac sea tours in 6m (21-ft.) inflatable boats, though you'll spend more—and get considerably wetter—if you take one: The cost is C$39 per adult, C$19 for kids age 8 to 15. Discounts on first or last sailings.

If you bear right at the "Y" and continue northward, the road wraps around the coastal hills and turns to gravel after 5km (3 miles). Keep going another 3 to 5km (2 or 3 miles). Here you'll come to a spectacular **coastal hiking trail ★★**, which runs to **Pollett's Cove,** about 10km (6 miles) up the coast. A dozen families once lived here; all that remain now are two cemeteries. The cove and the trail are on private land, but hiking and other quiet recreation are allowed.

Cape North ★★

Cape North is a recommended detour for adventurous travelers hoping to get off that heavily trafficked Cabot Trail. Outdoor types say Cape North is much like the Cabot Trail used to be 20 or 30 years ago—before the glossy travel magazines showed up and started trumpeting its glories, leading to a huge influx of tourists. So if you're really here to see wild nature, this is worth the extra driving and backtracking.

The cape is reached via a signed turnoff at the northern tip of the Cabot Trail, after you descend into the Aspy Valley. You'll soon come to **Cabot Landing Provincial Park,** where local lore claims that John Cabot first made landfall in North America in 1497. (We're still not sure, though.) Debate the issue among yourselves near the statue of Cabot, or take a long walk on the lovely 3km (2-mile) ocher-sand beach fronting the bay. The views of the remote coastline are both noteworthy and camera worthy.

The road then winds onward to the north; at a prominent fork, you can veer right to **Bay St. Lawrence,** if you wish, and find the tiny harbor and several summertime whale-watching outfits.

Family-owned **Oshan Whale Watch**'s (www.oshan.ca; © **877/383-2883** or 902/383-2883) thrice-daily tours on Captain Cyril Fraser's 13m (42-ft.) lobster boat cost C$30 per adult, C$20 senior and student, and C$12 per child from July through October. These folks can also take you deep-sea fishing (and clean your fish for cooking afterward). They're even on Twitter. (Sample entry: "On our 4:30pm whale watching tour we sighted 80 pilot whales . . .") **Captain Cox's Whale Watch** (www. whalewatching-novascotia.com; © **888/346-5556** or 902/383-2981) costs more but also offers a different experience: Its whale-watching cruises are aboard an 8m (24-ft.) inflatable Zodiac craft, fully safety-certified, from mid-June through September. These tours cost C$45 adults (discounts for seniors) and C$25 per child, but require a four-person minimum; don't show up expecting a tour unless you are four or more. Instead, call ahead to check on the status of tours.

From Bay St. Lawrence, go left at the fork in the road and continue along the stunning cliffside road to **Meat Cove.** The last 5km (3 miles) are along a dirt road that runs high along the shoulders of coastal mountains, then drops into shady ravines to cross brooks and rivers. The road ends at a rough-hewn settlement that's been home to hardy fishermen—seemingly all named McClellan—for generations.

There's a private campground here, **Meat Cove Camping ★★** (© **902/383-2379**), with some of the most dramatic ocean and cliff views of any campground in Nova Scotia. It's open from June through October; the two dozen campsites are unserviced, but there are hot showers, bathrooms, and firewood for sale. The sites cost C$25 per night. Several cabins on the same site cost C$60 a night, with the same knockout views and grills (bring your own blanket). Also ask the staff about hiking trails in the nearby hills above the campground (there's a day-use fee for non-campers). The campground is located at 2479 Meat Cove Rd., almost at the very end of the road.

WHERE TO STAY

Four Mile Beach Inn ★ 🖎 This rambling, interesting inn, which opened in the late 1990s, is one of the most interesting hotels on Cape Breton. Located in an old inn and former general store dating from 1898, it's run by innkeepers doing a superb job keeping pace with the ravages of time and weather, making it feel as comfortable as possible. Sometimes described as funky or eccentric, it's funky in a good way—if you can handle a few quirks. (Two rooms share a bathroom, while another has its bathroom across the hall, for instance; and you won't find flatscreen TVs or phones anywhere here.) The old general store has been spruced up and stocked with not-for-sale items; it's sort of like a little museum. An included breakfast is filling and tasty. The innkeepers also dispense great advice about local outings: walk, pedal, or paddle; a dirt road through the backyard leads right to the bay. Too tired for that? Hang out in the parlors chatting and playing cards, or just listening to the music that sometimes wafts through the place. Good value for the money.

R.R. No. 1 (P.O. Box 3), Aspy Bay, Cape North, NS B0C 1G0. www.fourmilebeachinn.com. © **888/602-3737** or 902/383-2282. 8 units. C$79–C$139 double. Rates include full breakfast. Packages available. AE, MC, V. Closed Nov–May. **Amenities:** Canoe, kayak, and bike rentals. *In room:* Kitchenette (some units), Wi-Fi (free).

Markland Cottage Resort ★ The Markland is sited on 28 hectares (69 acres) at a point where a meandering river meets a long sand beach fronting spectacular Aspy Bay. It's hard to imagine a more idyllic spot, especially in the morning when the sun illuminates mountains to the north. The property features two kinds of accommodations, both furnished in a simple, uncluttered style. Eleven one- and two-bedroom log cabins have kitchens, sitting areas, and porches—most with good views of the bay—and lots of pretty unvarnished wood, though some visitors complain these are getting a bit dated. Then there are a dozen more rooms, carved out of four other shared cottages. The Markland also hosts occasional performances and events at the **Octagon Arts Centre ★**, a lovely little performance space of wood beams and a high ceiling; the Celtic Colours series touches down here each October.

802 Dingwall Rd., P.O. Box 62, Dingwall, NS B0C 1G0. www.themarkland.com. © **855/872-6084** or 902/383-2246. Fax 902/383-2246. 23 units. C$99–C$200 double and cottage. Packages available. Children 16 and under stay free in parent's room. AE, DC, DISC, MC, V. Closed Oct 30–Apr 30. "Well-behaved pets" allowed. **Amenities:** Babysitting; bike rentals; canoes; outdoor pool. *In room:* A/C (some units), Wi-Fi in main lounge and some cottages (free).

WHERE TO EAT

For inexpensive eats, check out **Angie's Family Restaurant** (© **902/383-2531**) in Cape North, serving a menu of pizzas and dependable local shellfish. There's also a local **cafe** in Bay St. Lawrence; a tiny **pizzeria** and **takeout fish** in Dingwall; and the seasonal **chowder house**—with a great view of the coast—in Meat Cove.

White Point & Neil's Harbour ★

From South Harbor (near Dingwall) you can drive on the speedy Cabot Trail inland to Ingonish, or stick to the coast along an alternate route that arcs past White Point, continues onward to **Neil's Harbour,** then links back up with the Cabot Trail.

If the weather's clear and dry, this **coastal road** ★★ is a far better choice. Bear left at **South Harbour** onto White Point Road. Initially, the road climbs upward amid jagged cliffs with sweeping views of Aspy Bay; at **White Point** ★, you can veer a mile-and-a-half out to the tip of the land for even *more* dramatic views.

The road then changes names (to New Haven Rd.) and tracks inland before emerging at **Neil's Harbour** ★, a postcard-worthy fishing village of a few hundred souls. On a rocky knob located on the far side of the bay is a square red-and-white lighthouse (now an ice-cream parlor). From Neil's Harbour, it's just a 2-minute drive back to the Cabot Trail.

Ingonish ★

The Ingonish area includes a gaggle of similarly named towns—Ingonish Centre, Ingonish Ferry, South Ingonish Harbour—which collectively add up to a population of perhaps 1,300 or so (on a good day). Like Chéticamp on the peninsula's east side, Ingonish serves as a gateway to the national park and is home to a park visitor information center and a handful of motels and restaurants. There's really no critical mass of services in any one of the villages, though—instead, they're spread along a lengthy stretch of the trail. So you never quite feel you've arrived in town. You pass a liquor store, some shops, a bank, a post office, a handful of cottages. And that's it—suddenly you're there, in the wild park.

Highlights in the area include a sandy beach (near Keltic Lodge) good for some chilly splashing around, and a number of shorter hiking trails. (See "Cape Breton Highlands National Park," later in this chapter.)

For golfers, the wind-swept **Highlands Links course** ★★★ (www.highlands linksgolf.com; ✆ **800/441-1118** or 902/285-2600)—adjacent to the Keltic Lodge (see "Where to Stay," below) but under completely separate management—is considered one of the best in Nova Scotia, if not all of Atlantic Canada. It's a 6,035m (6,600-yard), links-style course with stupendous views and some stupendously difficult holes. Peak-season rounds cost about C$90 per adult (C$27–C$45 for children); spring and fall rates are about C$20 lower, and twilight rates are also available. Ask about packages whenever booking a hotel room, and be sure to reserve your tee time in advance—it's popular.

South of Ingonish, the **Cabot Trail** ★★★ climbs and descends the hairy 305m (1,000-ft.) promontory of Cape Smokey, which explodes into panoramic views from the top. At the highest point, there's a free **provincial park**—really little more than a picnic area and a trail head—where you can cool your engines and admire the views. A 10km (6-mile) hiking trail studded with unforgettable viewpoints leads to the tip of the cape along the high bluffs.

WHERE TO STAY

A number of serviceable cottage courts and motels are located in the area. (If you're booking by phone, be sure to find out *which* Ingonish you're staying in; the town names in this area all sound the same, which could create confusion.)

In addition to the choices below, **Glenghorm Beach Resort** in Ingonish (www. glenghormbeachresort.com; © **800/565-5660** or 902/285-2049) has about 75 units on a spacious 8-hectare (20-acre) property that fronts a sandy beach. Calling it a resort is a little bit of a stretch. Some rooms feature painted cinderblock walls and decor that's plain and a bit dated, though others feel a bit fresher and nicer. The expensive two-bedroom deluxe suite on the second floor is quite nice, though, featuring Jacuzzi tubs, kitchen units, and fireplaces. (Other suites are in a building out back, and aren't as nice.) Options include motel rooms and efficiencies, along with cottages and some elaborate suites. Prices are C$110 to C$120 for the motel rooms, C$139 to C$189 for the cottages, and C$299 to C$399 for one- and two-bedroom suites.

Castle Rock Country Inn   The squat, two-story Castle Rock Country Inn sits boldly on a high hill overlooking Ingonish harbor, with a pristine view of the hillside flanking Cape Smokey. The exterior is whitewashed, shingled, and solidly basic, and rooms are surprisingly basic too—furnished the way you might expect rooms in a midrange business or chain hotel to be, with queen-size beds, armoires, and writing tables. Rooms facing north have outstanding ocean views, though they cost extra. The **dining room ★** and patio have even more stunning water views; the kitchen serves a menu of updated traditional cuisine.

39339 Cabot Trail, Ingonish Ferry, NS B0C 1L0. www.ingonish.com/castlerock. © **888/884-7625** or 902/285-2700. Fax 902/285-2525. 17 units. C$129–C$173 double. Rates include continental breakfast. Packages and off-season discounts available. AE, MC, V. **Amenities:** Restaurant; bar. *In room:* TV, hair dryer, no phone, Wi-Fi (free).

Keltic Lodge Resort & Spa ★★ ☺   The Keltic Lodge is reached after a dramatic drive through a grove of white birch trees and across an isthmus topping big cliffs. The Tudor-looking resort is impressive at first glance, and the views just extraordinary. Yet most rooms here remain plainly furnished; you might expect more for the price. Some units are located in the more modern Inn at Keltic building a few hundred yards away. It has better views though a more sterile character. (Also, one reader wrote to lament the soundproofing in this annex, recommending an upstairs room to avoid hearing footfalls.) The cute log-cabinesque cottages are better, set among the birches—half with two bedrooms, half with four—but you'll share space with other travelers. If you rent one bedroom of a cottage, for instance, you'll share your living room with one to three other sets of guests; that may or may not be the sort of "resort" experience you wanted. Escape to the amazing Highland Links golf course (see above), a newish spa (with full treatments, yoga classes, and a hair salon), or the nice heated outdoor swimming pool (with one of the best pool views you can find anywhere in the province). Amenities like these somewhat compensate for the in-room inexperience. The resort is especially nice to young kids, too—free meals, bedtime snacks, and various programs and recreational offerings. Food in the **Purple Thistle ★★** dining room is among the best on the island; the menu might run to prime rib or salmon filet. Another restaurant, the **Atlantic,** serves lighter fare.

383 Keltic Inn Rd., Middle Head Peninsula, Ingonish Beach, NS B0C 1L0. www.kelticlodge.ca. © **800/565-0444** or 902/285-2880. Fax 902/285-2859. 105 units. C$155–C$395 double and cottage. Rates include breakfast and dinner. Packages available. AE, DC, DISC, MC, V. Closed mid-Oct to late May. **Amenities:** 2 restaurants; lounge; children's programs; golf course; outdoor pool; spa; tennis courts. *In room:* A/C (2 units), TV, fridge (some units), hair dryer, no phone, Wi-Fi (free).

St. Ann's

Traveling clockwise around the Cabot Trail, you'll face a choice when you come to the juncture of Route 312. One option is to take the side road to the **Englishtown ferry** and cross over St. Ann's Harbor in slow but dramatic fashion. The crossing of the fjordlike bay is scenic, and it only takes about 2 minutes (if there's no line—this is the province's busy "small" ferry). The ferry runs around the clock, for C$5 per car.

Your second option for making the Cabot Trail circuit is not to cross via ferry but rather to stay on the Trail, heading down along the western shore of St. Ann's Harbor.

One good launching point for exploring the waters is **North River,** where local guide/musician Angelo Spinazzola offers tours through his **North River Kayak Tours** (www.northriverkayak.com; ✆ **888/865-2925** or 902/929-2628) company from mid-May through mid-October. The full-day tour (C$109 per person) includes a steamed-mussel lunch on the shore; 3-hour tours cost C$64; and there's also a more expensive "romance tour" offered, where couples camp overnight on a remote beach—the owner cooks dinner, sets up a tent, and then departs for the night. Most every trip, claims Spinazzola, involves sightings of a bald eagle or two. Kayaks can also be rented (or even purchased) from the outfit.

In the village of St. Ann's, be sure to drop by the **Gaelic College of Celtic Arts and Crafts** (www.gaeliccollege.edu; ✆ **902/295-3411**), 51779 Cabot Trail Rd., located about a kilometer (⅔ mile) off the Trans-Canada Highway at exit 11. The school was informally founded in 1938, when a group of area citizens began offering instruction in Gaelic language in a one-room log cabin. Today, both campus and curriculum have expanded significantly, with classes offered in bagpiping, fiddle, Highland dance, weaving, spinning, and Scottish history, among other things.

The expansive, 142-hectare (350-acre) campus is home to the seasonally open **Great Hall of the Clans ★**, a museum where visitors can get a quick lesson in Scottish culture via interactive displays. Exhibits provide answers to burning questions like "What's the deal with the plaid?" and "What do Scotsmen really wear under a kilt?" Pretty impressive. Even better, one of poet Robert Burns's walking sticks is on display here, and you can buy one of the intriguing clan histories if you've got Scots blood running through your veins. The museum is very heavy on Gaelic music history, too. The Hall is open daily in July and August, 9am to 5pm, Monday to Friday only in June and September. Admission is C$7 per adult, C$5.50 for students, and C$20 for families. A crafts shop offers Gaelic souvenirs such as bolts of tartan plaid and CDs of traditional music. Live music performances happen from time to time; call or ask at the crafts shop for a schedule.

If you're driving from Ingonish south to St. Ann's during summer, be sure to drop by the Giant MacAskill Museum as well (see "One Giant Detour," below).

WHERE TO STAY

Luckenbooth Bed & Breakfast   Built in 1999, this modern, log-accented B&B has three guest rooms on 305m (a thousand feet) of wooded shore frontage. Guests get the run of several common areas, including a living room with a cozy fireplace and a basement-level TV room decorated in the clan tartans of genial owners Frances and Wayne McClure. Rooms each have modern furnishings. Try to book into no. 3 upstairs, with its hardwood floors, views of the bay, and a sitting area outside the door.

📷 ONE GIANT DETOUR

If you happen to pass through English-town—it's about 64km (40 miles) south of Ingonish, on the way down to the middle "lobe" of Cape Breton Island—you can find one of Canada's most fascinating and Ripley-esque museums. I'm talking about the seasonal **Giant MacAskill Museum** (www.macaskill.com; ⓒ **902/929-2875**) on Route 312. This museum honors the memory of local Scottish transplant Angus MacAskill, who lived here from 1825 to 1863 and gave new meaning to the term "living large." Angus, you see, was *huge*.

Supposedly MacAskill's father was of normal height, and Angus was a regular-size baby, too. But when he hit adolescence, something went haywire: The boy shot up to 7 feet tall before he was even 20. At 7 feet 9 inches tall and 425 pounds, MacAskill is believed to have been perhaps the tallest natural giant who ever lived. According to the

Guinness Book of World Records, he was the strongest man in recorded history. MacAskill's feats of strength—tipping over his fishing boat to drain water from it; lifting 1-ton anchors off a dock easily—are still legend, and he later made a successful go of it as owner of English-town's local general store. Angus was well-liked (he would have to have been), but caught a fatal infection during a trip to Halifax to purchase supplies and died a week later, not yet 40. He is buried nearby.

Children might enjoy sitting on MacAskill's massive chair (if they can reach it, that is) and trying on his sweater; the actual-size replica of the coffin MacAskill was buried in is simply astounding. The museum is open daily mid-May to mid-September from 9am to 6pm. Admission is C$4 for adults, C$2.50 for seniors and youth, and C50¢ for kids 11 and under.

(The other two units are in the basement, and feature cork floors.) There's a trail going down to the water for your daily walk, but the inn has a no-shoes-inside policy (slippers are furnished to guests) and a number of other rules—be prepared. Candle-light breakfast gets raves.

50671 Cabot Trail (R.R. 4), St. Ann's, NS B0E 1B0. www.bbcanada.com/3624.html. ⓒ **877/654-2357** or 902/929-2722. Fax 902/929-2503. 3 units. C$120–C$140 double. Rates include full breakfast. AE, MC, V. *In room:* TV, Wi-Fi (free).

Baddeck

Although **Baddeck** (pronounced *Bah*-deck) is some distance from the national park, it's often considered the de facto "capital" of the Cabot Trail. This is partly because Baddeck is centrally positioned on the island, and partly because the main drag happens to offer more hotels, B&Bs, and restaurants than any other town on the loop. (That's how thinly populated it is up here.) There are also a clutch of practical services here you can't easily find on the Trail: grocery stores, laundromats, gas stations, and the like.

Baddeck does have one claim to fame: For years, it was the summertime home of telephone inventor Alexander Graham Bell, now memorialized at a national historic site (see below). It's also a compact, easy town to explore by foot and is scenically located on the shores of big Bras d'Or (say bra-*door*) Lake. If you're on a tight schedule and plan to drive the Cabot Trail in just a day (figure on 6–8 hr.), this might be the best place to bed down afterward, if only because it's on the way to Sydney and/or Louisbourg.

If, however, your intention is to spend a few days exploring the hiking trails, bold headlands, and remote coves of the Trail and the national park (which I certainly recommend), find an inn farther north; this town's single street can get packed with tourists and tour buses.

The friendly **Baddeck Welcome Center** (© **902/295-1911**) is located just south of the village at the intersection of routes 105 and 205. It's open daily from June through mid-October.

EXPLORING THE TOWN

Baddeck, skinny and centered around a single main street (called Chebucto St. rather than Main St.), is just off the lake. You can ask for a free walking-tour brochure at the welcome center, although a complete tour of all the architectural highlights probably won't take long.

Government Wharf (head down Jones St. from the Yellow Cello restaurant) is where you go for summer boat tours, the best way to experience Bras d'Or Lake up close. **Loch Bhreagh Boat Tours** (© **902/295-2016**), for one, offers thrice-daily sightseeing tours on a 13m (42-ft.) cruiser motorboat. They pass Alexander Graham Bell's palatial former estate and other attractions at this end of the lake. (Moonlight tours are available by arrangement, if you've got a big enough group together.)

About 180m (197 yards) offshore is **Kidston Island ★**, owned by the town of Baddeck. It has a wonderful sand beach with lifeguards and an old lighthouse to explore. The local Lion's Club offers frequent pontoon boat shuttles across St. Patrick's Channel, warm and clear weather permitting; the crossing is free, but donations are encouraged.

Alexander Graham Bell National Historic Site ★★ ☺   Each summer for much of his life, Alexander Graham Bell—of Scottish descent, but his family emigrated to Canada when he was young—fled the heat and humidity of Washington, D.C., for this hillside retreat perched above Bras d'Or Lake. The mansion, still owned and occupied by the Bell family, is visible across the harbor from various points around town. Today it's part homage, part science center. The modern exhibit center highlights Bell's amazing mind; you'll find exhibits on his invention of the telephone at age 29, of course, but also information about other projects: ingenious kites, hydrofoils, and airplanes, for instance. Bell also invented the metal detector—who knew? Science buffs will love the place, and most visitors are surprised to learn Bell actually died in this home. (He's buried on the mountaintop.) Then there's an extensive "discovery" section, where kids are encouraged to apply their intuition and creativity to science problems. All in all, it's a very well-thought-out attraction—and attractive, too.

559 Chebucto St., Baddeck. © **902/295-2069.** Admission C$7.80 adults, C$6.55 seniors, C$3.90 youth age 6–16, C$20 families. June daily 9am–6pm; July to mid-Oct daily 8:30am–6pm; May and mid- to late Oct daily 9am–5pm. Late Oct to Apr by appointment only.

WHERE TO STAY

There are lots of choices in and around Baddeck, but none really jumps out head-and-shoulders above the rest. If the places below are booked, you could just as easily try **Auberge Gisele's Inn,** 387 Shore Rd. (www.giseles.com; © **800/304-0466** or 902/295-2849), a nicely modern 75-room hotel that's open May to late October and popular with bus tours; regular rooms cost C$115 to C$150, upgraded rooms and suites run from C$140 up as high as C$300 (with fireplace and Jacuzzi). There's also the cost-effective **Cabot Trail Motel** (www.cabottrailmotel.com; ✆ **902/295-2580**) on Route 105 about a mile west of Baddeck, with 38 motel units and four chalets overlooking the lake, a nice little heated outdoor pool, and private saltwater beach. Its rates run from C$65 to C$125 per night.

Green Highlander Lodge   The Green Highlander is located atop the Yellow Cello, a popular eatery on Baddeck's main drag. The three rooms here are decorated in a sort of gentleman's fishing camp motif, quite simple but pleasing. Rooms are named after Atlantic salmon flies; Blue Charm has a private sitting room and blue-quilted twin beds, while all three have private decks with views looking out toward Kidston Island. Ask about moonlight paddle trips, kayak rentals, and the private beach located 2km (a mile) away. The inn also manages a cottage nearby, hewn in unvarnished wood paneling with a kitchenette and propane grill for alfresco cookery on the deck.

525 Chebucto St. (P.O. Box 128), Baddeck, NS B0E 1B0. www.greenhighlanderlodge.com. ✆ **866/470-5333** or 902/295-2303. Fax 902/295-1592. 3 units. C$90–C$120 double. AE, MC, V. Closed Nov–Apr. Pets welcome. **Amenities:** Restaurant; pool; kayak rentals. *In room:* A/C, TV, hair dryer, Wi-Fi (free).

Inverary Resort   This sprawling property, located on 5 lakeside hectares (12 acres) within walking distance of town, is an option for families with active kids—but it's not a luxe "resort." Activities run the gamut from fishing and paddleboats to bonfires on the beach; sports fans will enjoy the volleyball, tennis, and shuffleboard courts. Guest rooms and facilities are spread around well-maintained grounds, mostly in buildings painted dark brown with white trim and green roofs. Rooms vary in size and style, but most are good enough—even the snug motel-style units in the two-bedroom cottages (a few have kitchens). Rooms are gradually being upgraded. The boathouse is a popular gathering place (events take place there). The resort operates two dining rooms: a cafe overlooking the marina serves informal fare, including various pastas, plus a more formal dining room serves classier food on a sun porch.

368 Shore Rd. (P.O. Box 190), Baddeck, NS B0E 1B0. www.inveraryresort.com. ✆ **800/565-5660** or 902/295-3500. Fax 902/295-3527. 190 units. C$99–C$189 double; C$159–C$390 suite. Packages available. MAP plans available. AE, DC, MC, V. Closed Dec 20–Jan 10. **Amenities:** 2 restaurants; pub; bikes; Jacuzzi; indoor pool; room service; sauna; spa; 3 tennis courts; watersports equipment. *In room:* A/C, TV, kitchenette (some units), Wi-Fi (free).

Telegraph House ★   Rooms in this 1861 hotel on Baddeck's main street are divided between the original building, an annex of motel units on a hill behind it, and a set of cabins. This is actually where Alexander Graham Bell stayed when he first visited Baddeck. (Oddly enough, rooms here *don't* have phones; what would Bell think?) The bigger motel rooms in back have small decks with glimpses of the lake; some of the newest rooms in the main lodge now have lovely polished wood floors and whirlpool baths; you can even stay in Bell's room, a Victorian space of flowery wallpaper print. The cottages are quite small, yet they're as brightly furnished as a child's playroom, and come with air-conditioning and whirlpool tubs. The dining room serves breakfast plus straightforward lunches and dinners of meat, fish, fowl, and huge desserts. Fiddle and piano music sometimes fill the inn, and guests can linger on the front or side porches.

479 Chebucto St. (P.O. Box 8), Baddeck, NS B0E 1B0. www.baddeck.com/telegraph. ✆ **888/263-9840** or 902/295-1100. Fax 902/295-1136. 41 units. C$80–C$130 double; C$100–C$275 cabins. AE, MC, V. **Amenities:** Restaurant. *In room:* A/C (some units), TV (some units), Jacuzzi (some units), no phone, Wi-Fi (free).

WHERE TO EAT

In addition to the listings below, many of Baddeck's hotels and inns have their own dining rooms. **Auberge Gisele's** dining room (see above) features Continental cuisine, for instance, though bus tours often feed here. At the Inverary Resort (see above), the aptly named **Lakeside Cafe** is a popular spot with a view of the marina and a moderately priced menu; the resort's main dining room features more creative (and more expensive) fare. And **Silver Dart Lodge** on Shore Road (✆ **902/295-2340**) has the informal **McCurdy's.**

Baddeck Lobster Suppers 🍴 SEAFOOD   This no-frills restaurant has the charm of a Legion Hall and charges an arm and a leg, but tourist crowds chow down here every summer nonetheless. You might want to, too. The lobster dinner—everyone orders it—is only available from 4 to 9pm, and includes a smallish steamed lobster, all-you-can-eat mussels, chowder, biscuits, dessert, and soda. Beer and wine cost extra and can push the bill for a family into the "expensive" range. Not in the mood for lobster? There's also cedar-planked salmon and a grilled steak. A kids' menu is also available, and you can order smaller meals—lobster rolls, a bowl of chowder, even pizza or a hot dog—during the lunch hour only.

Ross St. ✆ **902/295-3307.** Reservations accepted for groups of 10 or more. Lobster dinner C$34. MC, V. Daily 4–9pm. Closed Nov–May.

Yellow Cello Café PUB FARE   Despite its arty name, this eatery located inside the Green Highlander Lodge (see "Where to Stay," above) is a pubby, family-restaurant sort of place, not a gourmet luncheny. (It began as a takeout pizza joint.) If you don't set your culinary expectations too high, it's a decent spot to grab a bite. Angle for a seat outdoors under the awning facing the street: There are two decks, each featuring the work of Maritime painter David Stephens. The menu will be familiar to those who watch a lot of sports on TV; it consists mostly of pizza, pasta, nachos, chili, and sandwiches. They also serve basic, hearty breakfasts in the morning.

525 Chebucto St. ✆ **902/295-2303.** Reservations suggested during peak season. Main courses C$8–C$15. AE, MC, V. May–Oct daily 8am–10pm.

Bras d'Or Lake

With so much beauty on Cape Breton Island, Bras d'Or Lake hardly gets noticed by travelers. That's amazing; almost anywhere else in the world, Bras d'Or—a vast inland sea that's so big it nearly cleaves the island in two—would be a major tourist attraction ringed by motels, boat tour operators, water parks, and chain restaurants. But today, along the twisting shoreline of this 112km (70-mile) saltwater lake, you find—well, next to nothing. Yes, roads circumnavigate the whole lake, but there are few services for tourists because there are few tourists.

Bras d'Or is a difficult lake to characterize, since it changes dramatically from one area to the next—wild and rugged in some parts, pastoral and tamed in others. Wherever you go on the lake, though, keep an eye peeled for the regal silhouettes of **bald eagles** ★★★ soaring high above the water (or for a telltale spot of bright white in the trees, indicating a perching eagle). Dozens of eagle pairs nest along the lake's shores or nearby, making this one of the best places in Canada for observing eagles in their natural habitat.

EXPLORING BRAS D'OR LAKE

What's a good strategy for touring the lake? For starters, I would caution against trying to drive around it in 1 day—or even 2 days. There's no equivalent to the Cabot Trail

Bras d'Or Lake is huge and scenic—in fact, that's the problem. It's simply *too* big (and too hard to see from most roads) to be worth the trouble of circumnavigating. I don't know anyone who's ever done it. So what's a traveler to do? Take the lake piece by piece, that's what. Here are some picks for the three best short sections of Bras d'Or to tour by car when you're pressed for time (get a map to check them out):

○ Drive the stretch of quiet shoreline that begins in **Iona** and hugs the St. Andrews Channel on **Route 223;** if you're headed to **Sydney,** go this way as far as **Barrachois.** It's about a 40km (25-mile), 45-minute ride—longer if you stop awhile at the good **Highland Village Museum** (p. 135).

○ Another nice section is the hump of land that rises and falls

between **Dundeed** and **St. Peter's,** which runs attractively over hill and dale. There are two or three different ways you can go; each takes about a half-hour.

○ A third segment is the stretch of **Route 4** that heads northeast from **St. Peter's** to **East Bay,** running along the eastern arm of the lake as it narrows to a point. You'll get the very best views of the lake from this route, and the best sense of its surprisingly vast size. You'll also pass little coves, a famous tearoom (see "Where to Eat," below), and even a native Canadian reserve (at **Chapel Island**). This is a longer haul—about 64km (40 miles)—but the road is mostly straight and quick, and it'll very likely take you less than an hour to traverse.

tracing the lake's outline. The circumnavigating road serves up breathtaking views from time to time, but much of the route frankly is on the dull side, running some distance from the lake's shore and offering little more than views of scratchy woods.

It's far better to pick one or two small sections of the lake and focus on those; fortunately, we have already done the grunt work of sorting out the best routes for you. (See "Three for the Road: Lakeside Drives," below.)

On the southeastern shore is the historic little town of **St. Peter's** ★, where the lake comes within 800m (900 yards) of breaking through to the Atlantic Ocean and splitting Cape Breton into two half-islands. There's evidence this neck of land was settled as early as the 16th century by Portuguese. Later the French used it strategically for shipping out timber—it was known as Port Toulouse at that time. Still later, the British built a fort and the town grew by leaps when Loyalists began fleeing America.

Nature couldn't quite manage to split the mass up here, but humans did it when they built **St. Peter's Canal** in 1854. This canal still operates, and you might see some pretty impressive pleasure craft making their way up-canal to the lake. The pathway along the canal makes for a good walk, too.

The village of **Marble Mountain** ★, on the lake's southwestern shore, is hard to find but offers an intriguing glimpse into island history. (If you intend to come here, get a *good* local map of the island first, then take the back roads from **Dundee, West Bay,** or **Orangedale.**) Believe it or not, this town was briefly a little metropolis. In 1868, a beautiful seam of marble was discovered here, and by the early 20th century, full-scale mining operations were digging it out and sending it to builders and craftsmen around the world as fast as they could. At its peak, the quarry employed 750 miners, and the town was home to a thousand or more souls.

Now the marble has played out, though, and the village has reverted to form: a sleepy backwater. You can glimpse the scar of the former mine (which offers great views over the lake) by car or on foot from town (ask a local for directions), and there's a **beach** right in town with scenic swimming. The beach looks like it features pure white sand from a distance, but it doesn't: It's made up of marble chips washed down from the old quarry.

If you're hungry, pop into the **Cape Breton Smokehouse** ★ (www.capebreton restaurant.com; ⓒ **902/756-3332**), a family eatery that smokes its own salmon and also serves beef, chicken, and even buffalo steaks. It's about 8km (5 miles) north of the village, on the main road (7004 Marble Mountain Rd., in Malagawatch).

Also worth a quick detour is **Isle Madame** ★—which is the largest in an archipelago; a group of small islands—just south of the lake off Route 104 and Route 4 as you return west from St. Peter's to the island's "entrance" at Port Hawkesbury. Shortly after Columbus discovered North America, French, English, and Basque fishermen used these islands as a base for fishing, whaling, and walrus expeditions. Over the years, people settled, fished, and survived both the wars between French and English and being exploited by business monopolies. A few turned to smuggling, giving the island a bit of a romantic history, but cod was the mainstay. Today, this region is almost entirely French-speaking (though they speak English too, of course). Drop by a local bakery or restaurant for a croissant or other local treat.

Highland Village Museum ★ ☺   Highland Village is located outside Iona, on a grassy hillside with sweeping views over the lake. When you finally turn your back on the great panorama, you'll find a good living history museum. This 16-hectare (40-acre) village features a set of buildings reflecting the region's Gaelic heritage, some of them actual historic structures relocated here from elsewhere on the island and some of them quite impressive replicas. Inside, they contain rug-hooking tools, furniture, old Celtic music scores, info on the Gaelic language, and many more artifacts. Poke through the (ca. 1790) Black House, a stone-and-sod hut of the sort an immigrant would have lived in prior to departing Scotland, or the schoolhouse and general store, which date from the 1920s. Staffers dressed in historical costumes are happy to answer your (or your kids') questions about island life in the early days. It's worth spending at least an hour, more if you've got a group of kids keenly interested in history.

4119 Hwy. 223, Iona, NS B2C 1A3. http://museum.gov.ns.ca/hv. ⓒ **866/442-3542** or 902/725-2272. Admission C$9 adults, C$7 seniors, C$4 children 6–17, C$22 families. June to mid-Oct daily 9:30am–5:30pm. Closed mid-Oct to May.

WHERE TO STAY

Highland Heights Inn ★ 🐟   Highland Heights is a well-managed motel, with clean, well-maintained rooms. The views set it apart from other motels; every room has a view of the lake bordering on the spectacular. Second-floor rooms cost a little more, but they're worth the splurge because they all have balconies from which you can watch the lake in all its shifting moods. (These rooms are also a bit larger and brighter.) All the motel's units have fans and windows that open and phones—not always found in rural Nova Scotian lodgings. The motel's dining room is cheerful and sunny in a '70s sort of way (apropos, since the inn was built in 1972), with lake views from some tables. It's open daily and features home cooking, including excellent chowder.

Hwy. 223, Iona, NS B2C 1A3. www.highlandheightsinn.ca. © **800/660-8122** or 902/725-2360. Fax 902/725-2800. 32 units. C$80–C$130 double. Ask about multinight packages. AE, DISC, MC, V. Closed mid-Oct to mid-May. **Amenities:** Dining room. *In room:* TV, hair dryer, Internet (free).

WHERE TO EAT

Rita's Tea Room ★ ![icon] CAFE   Singer/songwriter Rita MacNeil grew up in Big Pond, and she never forgot her roots during her rise to fame. She always told audiences to stop by for a cup of tea if they were in the neighborhood. Problem was, they did. So Rita opened a tearoom for her fans, housing it in a converted 1939 schoolhouse. Today it contains a thriving gift shop (offering the music of Rita but also others), plus a comfortable dining room where you can buy baked goods, sandwiches, and soups—with tea, of course. Rita herself periodically shows up for meet-and-greets with her fans here, about a half-dozen times each summer. The teas and sweets are great.

8077 Hwy. 4, Big Pond (about 40km/25 miles southwest of Sydney). © **902/828-2667.** Snacks, soups, and sandwiches C$7–C$15; afternoon tea sets C$10–C$15. V. Late June to mid-Oct daily 10am–6pm. Closed mid-Oct to late June.

4 Sydney

The province's third-largest city (pop. 30,000) was northern Nova Scotia's industrial hub for decades, and three out of four Cape Breton Islanders still live in or around Sydney. Recent economic trends have not been kind to the area, however, and the once-thriving steel mills and coal mines are quiet now. So this gritty port city has thus been striving to reinvent itself as a tourist destination, though with limited success—partly because Cape Breton's natural wonders offer such tough competition for your tourist dollar. Although its commercial downtown is a bit bland, some of Sydney's residential areas might appeal to architecture and history buffs. Three early buildings are open to the public in summer, all within easy walking distance of one another. Spend a few hours visiting the trifecta if you're a fan of old buildings.

The **Cossit House Museum,** 75 Charlotte St. (© **902/539-7973**), is Sydney's oldest standing house, built in 1787 and now carefully restored and furnished with a fine collection of 18th-century antiques. It's open from June through mid-October, Monday through Saturday 10am to 5pm and Sunday 1pm to 5pm. Admission costs C$2 for adults, C$1 for seniors and children age 6 to 17.

The **Jost Heritage House,** 54 Charlotte St. (© **902/539-0366**), was built in 1787 and had a number of incarnations in the intervening years, including service as a store. Open June through August Monday through Saturday from 9am to 5pm; hours are shorter during the fall. Highlights of the home include an early apothecary. Admission costs C$2 per person.

The handsome **St. Patrick's Church,** 87 Esplanade (© **902/539-1572**), locally known as "St. Pat's," is the island's oldest Roman Catholic church and dates to 1830. It's suitably impressive, made of rugged stone. From June through Labour Day, a **museum** in the church opens daily from 9am to 5pm.

PUFFIN STUFF

Looking for something you can't see anywhere else (almost)? Thirty minutes west of Sydney (just off the Trans-Canada Hwy., en route to St. Ann's or Baddeck) is the home port of **Bird Island Boat Tours** ★ (www.birdisland.net; © **800/661-6680**). On a 2¾-hour narrated cruise, you'll head out to the Bird Islands, home to a colony of around 300 nesting puffins. You'll get within 18m (60 feet) of the colorful endangered birds (which nest in grassy burrows above rocky cliffs); you may also see razorbills, seals, guillemots, and the occasional eagle. Two or three tours are offered daily from mid-May through late September, though the timing varies by day; cost of the tours is C$35 for adults, C$15 for children 7 to 12, and reservations are suggested.

The same outfit also maintains a campground and some rental cottages in the area. To find directions to the landing, check the website.

AN UNDERGROUND TOUR

Northeast of Sydney is the town of **Glace Bay,** a former coal-mining center. The mines have slipped into an economic twilight, but the province made lemonade from lemons by creating the surprisingly intriguing **Cape Breton Miners' Museum ★★** at 17 Museum St. (www.minersmuseum.com; ✆ 902/849-4522). The museum provides some background on the geology of the area, and offers insight into the region's sometimes-rough labor history. But the highlight of the trip is the 20-minute descent into the mine itself (for an extra charge), with damp walls and cool, constant temperatures. Retired miners lead the tours, because they can tell you what it was like to work here better than anyone else. One reader reported two teenage sons were all groans and eye rolls when she announced this destination—but came away in awe of the place afterward. Plan to spend at least an hour here.

Admission is C$6 adults, C$5 children for the museum, and then an additional C$6 adults or C$5 children if you want to take the mine tour. The museum is open daily from June through October, 10am to 6pm (Tues until 7pm Jul–Aug), but weekdays only the rest of the year from 9am to 4pm. There is also a restaurant on premises.

Louisbourg ★★

Louisbourg, on Cape Breton's remote and wind-swept easternmost coast, was once one of Canada's most impressive French settlements. Despite its brief prosperity and durable construction, the colony basically disappeared after the British forced the French out (for the second and final time) in 1760. Through the miracle of archaeology and historic reconstruction, much of the imposing settlement has now been re-created, and today this is among Canada's most ambitious national historic parks.

However, a visit does require a little effort. Being 35km (22 miles) east of Sydney means this attraction isn't on the way to anyplace else, and it's an inconvenient detour from the national park. So it's easy to justify skipping it. But if you're interested in local history, make the trip. For the right kind of traveler, the hours spent wandering the wondrous rebuilt town and then walking among ruins and along the coastal trail could be one of the highlights of a trip to Eastern Canada. If the opportunity to partake in one of their re-enactments or festivals presents itself, don't pass it up.

EXPLORING THE VILLAGE

The hamlet of Louisbourg—which you pass through en route to the historic park—is low-key. A short **boardwalk** with interpretive signs runs along the town's tiny waterfront. (You'll get a glimpse of the historic site across the water.) Nearby is a cool faux-Elizabethan theater, the **Louisbourg Playhouse ★** (www.louisbourgplayhouse.com; ✆ 902/733-2996), at 11 Aberdeen St. The 17th-century-style playhouse was originally built near the old town by Disney for the movie *Squanto*. After production wrapped, Disney donated it to the village, which dismantled it and moved it to a side street near the harbor. Live theater and Cape Breton music are staged here throughout the summer.

One fun summer event here is the **Race Through Time,** a mid-August 13km (8-mile) road race that takes runners right into the heart of Old Europe—er, Louisbourg. Nothing like the sight of the old gallows to get the blood pumping.

As you come into town on Route 22, you'll pass the **Sydney and Louisbourg Railway Museum** (© 902/733-2720), which shares the gabled railway depot with the local **visitor information center** (same phone). The museum commemorates the former railway, which shipped coal from the mines to Louisbourg harbor between 1895 and 1968. You can visit some of the old rolling stock (including an 1881 passenger car) and view the roundhouse. It's open daily from June through September; in July and August, from 9am to 6pm, and in spring and fall Monday to Friday, 10am to 5pm. Admission is free. There's a gift shop here, as well.

Since you're already here, you might detour a few additional miles out of your way to **Lighthouse Point ★**, the site of Canada's very first lighthouse. (The lighthouse you see there today is a replacement version, however.) The rocky coastline at this spot is quite dramatic and undeveloped, and open—no trees. It's a great spot for a little hike, a picnic, and some photographs. Look for Havenside Road (the lighthouse access road), which diverges from the main paved road near the visitor information center in the center of town. You might pass lobstermen at work on the way.

Fortress of Louisbourg National Historic Site ★★★ ☺ Though it feels like the end of the world today, the village of Louisbourg has had three lives. The first was early in the 18th century, when the French colonized the area aggressively and built a stone fortress—imposing but not impregnable, because the British captured it in 1745. The fort was returned to the French following negotiations in Europe. War soon broke out again, however, and the British recaptured it in 1758 (and blew it up for good measure). That appeared to be the end, but the Canadian government decided to re-create about a quarter of the stone-walled town in the 1960s, based on over 750,000 documents about what had been there. The park is built to show life as it might have been in 1744, as an important French military capital and seaport that had not yet been captured; you arrive at the site after walking through an interpretive center and taking a short bus ride. (Keeping cars at a distance definitely enhances the historical feeling.) After walking through an impressive gatehouse—complete with costumed guard on the lookout for English spies—you can wander narrow lanes and poke through the faux-historic buildings, some of which contain informative exhibits, others furnished with convincingly worn reproductions. Chicken, geese, and other barnyard animals peck and cluck away, and vendors hawk freshly baked bread from wood-fired ovens. It really does feel like old Europe. To get the most out of the experience, explore their activities or programs: there's Louisbourg After Dark Dinner Theatre, "Tragic Tales: The Haunted at Louisbourg" rendezvous, or the Feast of St. Louis re-creation of an 18th-century celebration. Ask for the free tour, and don't hesitate to question the costumed guides; come in June or October, and your cost is 60% less to compensate for the weather. Allow a full day for the experience.

Louisbourg, NS. © **902/733-3552** or 733-3546. Mid-June to mid-Oct: Admission C$18 adult, C$15 seniors, C$8.80 children, C$44 families; daily 9:30am–5pm. Mid-Oct to mid-June: Admission C$7.30 adult, C$6.05 seniors, C$3.65 children, C$18 families; daily 9:30am–4pm. Some programs and services by pre-arrangement only mid-Oct to mid-June.

WHERE TO STAY

Cranberry Cove Inn ★★ You can't miss this attractive in-town inn en route to the fortress: it's the three-story Victorian farmhouse painted cranberry red. Inside, it's decorated in a light Victorian motif. Upstairs rooms are carpeted and furnished on themes. Anne's Hideaway is the smallest, but has a nice old tub and butterfly collection; Isle Royale is done up in Cape Breton tartan patterns. The quirky Field and Stream room comes with a twig headboard, mounted deer head, and stuffed pheasant. Note that, due to the three-story open staircase, this inn really isn't suitable for those with toddlers. It is very suitable for anyone who likes to borrow a book from their library and relax on the veranda.

12 Wolfe St., Louisbourg, NS B1C 2J2. www.cranberrycoveinn.com. © **800/929-0222** or 902/733-2171. 7 units. C$105–C$160 double. Rates include full breakfast. MC, V. Closed Nov–Apr. *In room:* TV, fireplace (some units) Jacuzzi (some units), Wi-Fi (free).

Louisbourg Harbour Inn Bed & Breakfast ★★ This yellow clapboard inn is just a block off Louisbourg's main street and overlooks the fishing wharves, harbor, and fortress. The lovely pine floors within are nicely restored, and guest rooms are tidy, attractive and well thought out. (Six of the eight units face the ocean, five have Jacuzzis.) The best rooms are probably on the third floor, up the stairs; room no. 6 is bright and cheerful, while room no. 7 is spacious and boasts a handsome wooden bed and a pair of rockers overlooking the fish pier. Room nos. 1 and 3 have private balconies, as well.

9 Lower Warren St., Louisbourg, NS B1C 1G6. www.louisbourgharbourinn.com. © **888/888-8466** or 902/733-3222. 8 units. C$115–C$180 double. Rates include breakfast. MC, V. Closed mid-Oct to mid-June. **Amenities:** Jacuzzi (some units). *In room:* TV, fridge (some units), no phone, Wi-Fi (free).

WHERE TO EAT

Louisbourg has a handful of informal, family-style restaurants. For more casual eating out, hit the **Grubstake** at 7499 Main St. (© **902/733-2308**), open mid-June to early October from noon to about 9pm. The place was founded in 1972, and ever since it has embraced the philosophy that food should be fresh and honest. Expect straightforward steaks, pastas, pork, burgers, and an array of seafood (the house specialty).

There's also the **Lobster Kettle,** locally and touristically popular, at 41 Commercial St. (© **902/733-2723**). It's just what you'd expect: an emphasis on lobsters, chowder, and broiled fish, everything done well enough.

CAPE BRETON HIGHLANDS NATIONAL PARK ★★★

Cape Breton Highlands National Park is one of the two crown-jewel national parks in Atlantic Canada (Gros Morne in Newfoundland is the other). Covering nearly 1,000 sq. km (370 sq. miles) and stretching across a rugged peninsula from the Atlantic to the Gulf of St. Lawrence, this park is famous for its starkly beautiful terrain. It also features one of the most dramatic coastal drives in North America. One of the great pleasures of this park is that it holds something for everyone, from tourists who prefer to sightsee from the comfort of their cars to those who prefer backcountry hiking in the company of bear and moose.

The mountains of Cape Breton are probably unlike those you're familiar with elsewhere. The heart of the park is fundamentally a huge plateau; in the vast interior, you'll find a flat, melancholy landscape of wind-stunted evergreens, bogs, and barrens. This is called the "taiga," a name that refers to the zone between tundra and the northernmost forest. In this largely untracked area you might find 150-year-old trees that are still only knee-high.

It's the park's edges that really capture your attention, though. On the western side of the peninsula, the tableland has eroded right into the sea, creating a dramatic landscape of ravines and ragged, rust-colored cliffs pounded by the ocean. The **Cabot Trail ★★★**, a paved road built in 1939, winds dramatically along the flanks of these mountains, offering extraordinary vistas and camera shots at every turn. On the park's eastern flank—the Atlantic side—the terrain's a bit less spectacular, but those lush green hills still offer a backdrop that's exceptionally beautiful.

Note that this section of the book focuses only on the park proper, which offers *no* lodging or services other than campgrounds. You can find limited lodging and restaurants in the handful of villages that ring the park, however. See the previous section, which begins on p. 116, for detailed information about local inns and hotels in the various towns (such as Chéticamp and Ingonish) near the park's boundaries.

Essentials

GETTING THERE   Access to the park is via the **Cabot Trail,** which is very well marked by provincial signage. The entire loop is about 305km (190 miles), though the section that passes through the national park—from the entrance at Chéticamp to the one at Ingonish—is only about 105km (65 miles). You'll drive slowly to take in the vistas. Although the loop can be done in either direction, I would encourage you to drive it in a clockwise direction; the visitor center in Chéticamp offers a far more detailed introduction to the park.

VISITOR INFORMATION   Two **visitor information centers** are located at either end of the park, in **Chéticamp** and **Ingonish.** Both are open daily from mid-May through mid-October, 8am to 8pm in summer (Jul–Aug) and 9am to 5pm during the shoulder seasons. The Chéticamp center has much more extensive information about the park, including a slide presentation, natural history exhibits, a cool large-scale relief map, and a very good bookstore specializing in the natural and cultural history. The park's main phone number is ✆ **902/224-2306.**

FEES   Entrance permits are required from mid-May through mid-October and can be purchased either at information centers or at tollhouses at the two main park entrances. Permits are required for any activity along the route, even stopping to admire the view. Daily fees are C$7.80 adults, C$6.80 seniors, C$3.90 children age 6 to 16, and C$20 families. If you'll stay in the vicinity of this park for a week or more, buy an **annual pass,** which saves you money; the yearly pass is about C$98 for families, about C$39 per adult. Or buy an all-Canada National Pass (see "The Great Outdoors," p. 44).

Exploring the Park
SCENIC DRIVES
Cape Breton Highlands National Park basically only offers one drive, but it's a doozy: With few exceptions, it's jaw-droppingly scenic along nearly the entire route. The most breathtaking stretch is probably the 40km (25-mile) section from **Chéticamp to Pleasant Bay** ★★★ along the island's northwestern coast. Budget lots of extra time for driving this part, because you'll want to spend plenty of time at the pullouts gawking at the views, reading signs, and snapping digital photos. Other drivers will poke along, too. If you have time, there's even a nice little detour at the northern apex of the loop to **Meat Cove;** see "Cape North," earlier in this chapter, for details.

If it's a foggy day, though, you might want to save yourself the entrance fee and time. Some folks say that without the views, there's little reason to drive the loop, and advise waiting for a day when the fog has lifted. Personally, I find a foggy landscape ethereal and enchanting (as long as it doesn't get too thick to be safe). Fog usually hangs low, near the water or over the bogs, so I slow down and savor the unique views.

Cape Breton Highlands National Park

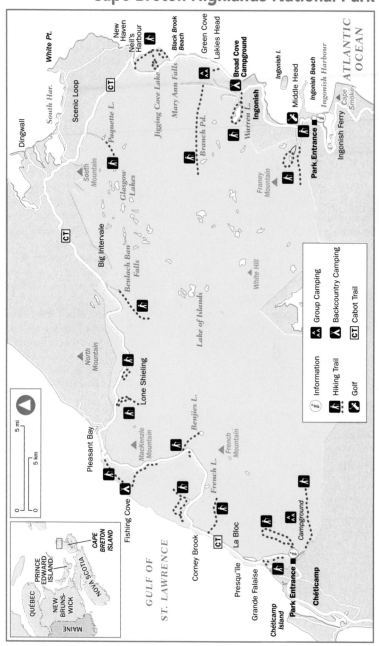

If you don't appreciate it, or are nervous about driving in fog, explore villages near your hotel in the atmospheric mist instead.

HIKING

The park offers no fewer than 25 distinct hiking tracks departing from the Cabot Trail. Many excursions are quite short and have the feel of a casual stroll rather than a vigorous tramp, but those determined to get a workout will find suitable trails, too. All the trails are listed, with brief descriptions, on the reverse side of the map you get when you pay your park entry fee at the gates.

The **Skyline Trail ★★★** offers oodles of altitude and views, without the climbing. You ascend a tableland from Chéticamp by car, then follow a 9km (6-mile) loop out along dramatic bluffs and through wind-stunted spruces and firs. A spur trail descends to a high, exposed point overlooking the surf; it's capped by blueberry bushes. Moose are often spotted along this trail, though it's a very popular trek for visitors and thus often crowded.

Farther along the Cabot Trail, **Lone Shieling ★** is an easy 800m (.5-mile) loop through lush hardwood forest in a valley that's home to 350-year-old sugar maples. The re-created hut of a Scottish crofter (shepherd) is another cool feature of this trail. Another short trail, **Bog ★**, is my favorite at just .5km (.35-mile). I've spent hours lying on the boardwalk, photographing delicate orchids and pitcher plants.

If you're looking to leave the crowds behind, the **Glasgow Lakes Lookoff ★** is a relatively gentle 9km (6-mile) round-trip hike that takes you through barrens and scrubby forest to a rocky bald overlook with distant views of the ocean and some highland lakes. This trail is alternately swampy and rocky, so wear rugged footwear.

On the eastern shore, try the 4km (2.5-mile) **hike to Middle Head ★★**, which starts beyond the Keltic Lodge resort. This dramatic, rocky peninsula thrusts well out into the Atlantic. The trail is wide and relatively flat, and you'll cross open meadows with wonderful views both to the north and south. The tip of the peninsula is grassy and open, a good spot from which to watch for passing whales—or see waves crashing in after a storm. Allow about 2 hours for a relaxed walk out to the point and back.

BIKING

The full 290km (180-mile) **Cabot Trail loop ★★★** is the ironman tour for bike trekkers, both arduous and rewarding. The route twists up ravines and plummets back down toward the coast. One breathtaking vista after another unfolds, and the plunging, brake-smoking descent from Mt. MacKenzie to Pleasant Bay is one serious cyclists aren't likely to forget in a lifetime. Campgrounds and motels are well spaced out here, too, making a 3- or 4-day excursion easy. Disadvantages? The road is almost uniformly narrow and free of shoulders, so you'll be battling constantly with errant drivers for the side of the road. That can be a bit harrowing. If you're not inclined to pedal the entire loop, pick and choose. Especially scenic stretches for bikers in good shape include the sections from **Chéticamp to Pleasant Bay ★★** and back, and the climb and descent from **Lone Shieling eastward to the Aspy Valley ★★**.

Note that mountain bikes are allowed on just a few trails within the park—check with the visitor center when you arrive for details about any new restrictions. The longest backcountry trail is the 13km (8-mile) route into the **Lake of Islands ★**, which doesn't appear on all the maps. Ask about it at one of the park's visitor centers.

Camping

The best way to experience the park is to stay awhile: to live close to nature by camping. The park has five drive-in campgrounds. The largest are at **Chéticamp** (on the west side) and **Broad Cove** (on the east), both of which have the commendable policy of never turning a camper away; even if all regular sites are full, they'll still find a place for you to pitch a tent or park your RV. All these campgrounds are well run and well maintained, though Chéticamp and Broad Cove have the most facilities, including three-way hookups for RVs. Rates run from around C$18 to C$38 per night, depending on the level of services you require, time of year, and the campground you've selected. Remember that you're also required to buy park entry (or have a park pass in hand) when camping at Cape Breton, and that you can only make advance reservations at Chéticamp and Broad Cove, where sites are set aside for advance bookings, made by calling © **877/737-3783** or using the website **www. pccamping.ca**. At all the other campgrounds, it's first-come, first-served. Winter camping is allowed in some park campsites, as well, for a flat fee of C$15.

The park also has a stunning **backcountry campsite at Fishing Cove ★★**, set on a pristine, scenic cove. It's an 8km (5-mile) hike into the site from your car, and there's no potable drinking water once you arrive; pack enough in. (No campfires are allowed there, either.) Once there, however, you can watch for pilot whales at sunset from the cliffs to your heart's content. The site costs C$9.80 per night; make arrangements at one of the visitor information centers.

NEW BRUNSWICK

U nspoiled and beautiful, New Brunswick is waiting to reveal new and unexpected adventures to you. There is much to explore: two distinctly different coastal areas, interior wilderness, mighty rivers, peaceful farmlands, refined cities, peaceful towns, neat villages, and encounters with nature that are truly special; prepare for a vacation of discovery.

5

Sightseeing Tremendous diversity sets the tone: Cliffs and islands sculpted by wind and sea dominate the **Bay of Fundy,** beaches and dunes line the eastern shore, and river valleys dot the interior. Renowned scenic drives tie them all together. Little equals the views you get from a boat tour, the top of Mount Carleton, the side of a cliff as you rappel down, or a lighthouse at lands' end. If you crave the arts, heritage, and urban life, you'll find three distinct cities to explore: **Fredericton, Saint John,** and **Moncton** each have something unique to offer.

Eating & Drinking Since food aficionados don't always think of New Brunswick as a culinary destination, be prepared to be surprised. Fine dining is usually focused on local ingredients; happily, many takeouts and small eateries have the same dedication. Seafood is the headliner, thanks to coastal waters that yield salmon, lobster, oysters, clams, and more. Traditional regional dishes—such as ploye, poutine, fricote, and wild fiddleheads—enhance the culinary adventure.

Nature The province's most recognizable natural wonder, the **Bay of Fundy,** Canada's only finalist (one of two in North America) in the recent New 7 Wonders of Nature worldwide campaign, is home to the highest tides in the world, and is a rich feeding ground for marine mammals. Three impressive river systems (the **St. John, Miramichi,** and **Restigouche**) and the Appalachian mountain range ensure a proliferation of wildlife: whales, moose, huge flocks of migrating birds, rare peregrine falcons and exotic orchids, plus forests as far as the eye can see.

History The original inhabitants—the Mi'kmaq, Malecite, and Passamaquoddy Nations—were followed by Acadian, English, Scottish, and Irish settlers. Many of these cultures are celebrated today through festivals, concerts, heritage sites, museums, and attractions. Communities reflect their distinct heritage: **Caraquet** is pure Acadian, **St. Andrews** is English Loyalist; **Edmunston** celebrates Madawaska, **Miramichi** its Irish. Visitors can experience history at **King's Landing** and **Acadian Village** historic sites, learn heritage crafts or trades, master traditional cooking, or learn about history and nature through educational adventures.

EXPLORING NEW BRUNSWICK

Here's a bit of advice: It's beneficial to come to New Brunswick with a strategy already in hand, one that takes into account geography and driving times. Key attractions are spread out, but the distances between then can turn into great road trips through beautiful countryside with a bit of planning and map reading. There are multilane highways traversing the province, which are great when you need to cover the distance quickly, but they miss what is one of the jewels in New Brunswick's crown: its beautiful scenery.

If you're drawn to rugged beauty, plan to focus mostly on the **Fundy Coast** with its stupendous dropping tides, rocky cliffs, and boreal landscape. This part of the coastline actually feels a lot more remote and northerly than the more densely settled (and tamer) northeastern coast.

Those who want to sip a pint to the strains of traditional music, shop at a great farmer's market, or visit a museum or gourmet restaurant should swing through **Saint John** instead. A lovely country drive will take you to Fredericton, rich in Loyalist (read British) history, a riverfront and parks to stroll, great eateries, and pure gentle relaxation. Those interested in Acadian history or sandy beaches, on the other hand, can keep moving and drive to the **Gulf of St. Lawrence,** which brings Acadian heritage, seafood, and a laid-back feel to the table.

Think you are simply interested in hurrying *through* the province to get to Prince Edward Island or Nova Scotia? Well, you've paged to the wrong chapter of this book. Take at least a day to detour through Fundy National Park to see **Cape Enrage** and **Hopewell Rocks**—two of Eastern Canada's most dramatic attractions. If nothing else, you'll be able to tell your friends that New Brunswick should never again be written off on any tour of Eastern Canada.

Essentials

VISITOR INFORMATION New Brunswick publishes several free annual directories and guides that are helpful in planning a trip to the province, including the comprehensive *New Brunswick Official Touring Guide* vacation planner listing attractions, accommodations, campgrounds, and adventure packages, as well as the official New Brunswick travel map. Contact the **New Brunswick Department of Tourism and Parks,** P.O. Box 12345, Campbellton, NB E3N 3T6 (www.tourismnewbrunswick.ca; ✆ 800/561-0123).

The province staffs six official visitor information centers; more than 50 cities, towns, and villages also have their own municipal information centers. A complete listing of phone numbers for these centers can be found in the *Experience New Brunswick* guide, or look for "?" direction signs on the highway. Phone numbers and addresses for the appropriate visitor information centers are provided in each section of this chapter.

GETTING THERE

BY CAR AND FERRY The Trans-Canada Highway bisects the province, entering from Québec at St. Jacques. It follows the St. John River Valley before veering through Moncton and exiting into Nova Scotia at the hamlet of Aulac. The entire distance is about 530km (329 miles).

Entering from the USA The fastest route from New York City or New England to New Brunswick is the Maine Turnpike (a toll road). Take the turnpike north to Bangor, Maine, then slice east on Route 9 to connect to Route 1. Continue to Calais, Maine, which is just across the river from **St. Stephen,** New Brunswick.

A more scenic variation is to drive across a bridge onto **Campobello Island** from Lubec, Maine (see the "Passamaquoddy Bay" section below), then take a ferry to Deer Island, drive the length of the island, and board a second ferry to the mainland.

Those headed to **Fredericton** or **Moncton** can speed their trips somewhat by following the Maine Turnpike to its conclusion, then continuing north on I-95 all the way to Houlton, Maine, and beyond; you'll connect with the Trans-Canada after crossing the border.

Bay Ferries (www.nfl-bay.com; ℭ **888/249-7245**) operates the ferry known as the *Princess of Acadia* that links **Saint John** with Digby, Nova Scotia. The ferry sails year-round, with one to two crossings daily (travel time: 3 hours) each way. The peak-season (June–Oct) one-way fares are C$41 for adults, C$31 for seniors and students, C$26 for children ages 6 to 13, C$5 per child 5 and under, and C$82 and up per vehicle, plus a C$20 fuel surcharge; fares are cheaper during the rest of the year. Also, 15% discounts are available on round-trips completed within 30 days, so be sure to buy a round-trip ticket if you'll return the same way you came. Reservations are advised.

BY AIR The province's main airports are at Fredericton (the provincial capital), Saint John, and Moncton, all of which are chiefly served by **Air Canada** (www.air canada.com; ℭ **888/247-2262**) and the major car-rental companies. **United** (www. united.com; ℭ **877/932-4259**) also flies nonstop from Newark, New Jersey's Liberty International Airport to Moncton, while **WestJet** (www.westjet.com; ℭ **888/937-8538**) links Moncton with Toronto. **Porter Airlines** (www.flyporter.com; ℭ **888/619-8622** or 416/619-8622) offers flights from Moncton to several Canadian and U.S. cities, usually connecting through Ottawa or Toronto City Airport.

BY TRAIN Canada's government-operated cross-country railroad, **VIA Rail** (www. viarail.ca; ℭ **888/842-7245**), offers train service through the province to and from Montréal 6 days a week (no departures on Tues) year-round. The train stops in **Campbellton, Miramichi,** and **Moncton.** Check the VIA Rail website for more details on routes, schedules, stopping times in New Brunswick, and online booking. Also see p. 253 in chapter 7 for more details on pricing of seats on the overnight train.

BY CRUISE SHIP Yes, indeed, you read that correctly. Popular **Carnival Cruise Lines** (www.carnival.com; ℭ **888/CARNIVAL [888/227-6482]**) is just one of the major cruise lines to dock in New Brunswick, with a series of summertime cruises. Optional shore excursions during the day and night at port in Saint John (for an extra charge) have included a bike tour of local covered bridges; visits to a dairy farm; kayak trips around the bay; and a visit to a local brewery. Other big cruise lines also stop in this port—see the Saint John tourism website **www.cruisesaintjohn.com** for fuller listings and links to cruise-booking sites.

THE GREAT OUTDOORS

The province has put together a well-conceived campaign to encourage visitors of all budgets to explore its outdoor attractions and activities. The provincial travel guide outlines dozens of multiday and day adventures ranging from a C$10 guided hike at Fundy National Park to fancy biking packages that include overnight inn accommodations and gourmet dinners. For more information on these programs, call the tourism department at ℭ **800/561-0123** or check the official website www.TourismNew Brunswick.ca.

Readers who really want to see the wild should think about visiting the outdoor center at **Cape Enrage** (see the "Fundy National Park" section later in this chapter),

QUÉBEC

New Richmond
Tide Head
Dalhousie
Campbellton
132
Chaleur Bay
Miscou I.
Lamèque I.
Matapedia
Caraquet
Shippagan
L. Témiscouata
Kedgwick
11
Bathurst
Sainte-Quentin
17
MOUNT CARLETON PROV. PARK
Nepisiguit
GULF OF
Edmundston
Ste.-Anne-de-Madawaska
2
11
ST. LAWRENCE
St.-Léonard
8
Neguac
Grand Falls
Square L.
Chatham
Newcastle
KOUCHIBOUGUAC N.P.
Alberton
Caribou
Presque Isle
Perth-Andover
St. Louis de Kent
P.E.I.
161
1
2
SW Miramichi
Doaktown
Summerton
MAINE
Hartland
Salmon R.
Bouctouche
126
11
Shediac
Houlton
8
Chipman
Moncton
Pt. Elgin
Woodstock
Grand L.
Sackville
Fredericton
Petitcodiac
Amherst
95
Grand L.
Oromocto
Washademoak L.
Sussex
1
Alma
114
Oxford
Spednic L.
McAdam
4
Norton
FUNDY N.P.
NOVA SCOTIA
7
Long Reach
6
West Grand L.
St. Stephen
St. George
Grand Bay
Quispamsis
Saint John
Chignecto Bay
Kentville
St. Andrews
1
Passamaquoddy Bay
Fundy
Middleton
101
Windsor
Bangor
9
Eastport
Campobello I.
Grand Manan I.
Bay of
Digby
0   50 mi
0   50 km

Trans-Canada Highway
Ferry

where one can canoe, rappel, rock-climb, zip-line and/or kayak—all in the same dramatic coastal setting.

BACKPACKING   Among the best destinations for a backcountry hike in this province are **Mount Carleton Provincial Park** (p. 201) and **Fundy National Park** (p. 183), both of which maintain backcountry campsites for visitors. The two landscapes are quite different to hike through—see the appropriate sections for more information on each park, then take your pick.

BICYCLING   The islands and peninsulas of **Passamaquoddy Bay** lend themselves nicely to cruising in the slow lane—especially **Campobello Island** (p. 150), which also has good dirt roads for mountain biking. **Grand Manan** (p. 160) holds lots of appeal for cyclists, too, even if the main road (Rte. 776) has some rather narrow shoulders and some pretty quick local drivers. Some of the best coastal biking is around **Fundy National Park**—especially the back roads to Cape Enrage—and the **Fundy Trail Parkway,** an 11km (7-mile) multiuse trail that hugs the coast of Fundy Bay. Along the Acadian Coast, **Kouchibouguac National Park** has limited but unusually nice biking trails through mixed terrain (and rentals are available right in the park). A lovely network of trails run beside the St. John River in Fredericton, taking you from the historic downtown to country, and even across the river on a former railway bridge that now caters to pedestrians and bicyclists. Several trails (South Riverfront, Salamanca, and Old Train Bridge) join up to create a 5.4km (3.6 miles) multiuse trail. A few blocks north, the North Riverfront Trail adds another 5.6km (3.5miles).

A handy guide is *Biking to Blissville,* by Kent Thompson. It covers 35 rides in the Maritimes and costs C$15, plus tax and shipping. Look in local bookshops, check online, or contact the publisher directly: Goose Lane Editions, 500 Beaverbrook Ct., Ste. 500, Fredericton, NB E3B 5X4 (www.gooselane.com; ☎ **888/926-8377** or 506/450-4251).

Mountain bikers would be well advised to check out St. Andrews and Sugar Loaf Provincial Park near Campbellton (p. 200).

BIRD-WATCHING   Grand Manan is the province's most notable destination for birders, right on the Atlantic flyway. (The great John James Audubon lodged here while studying and drawing bird life more than 150 years ago.) Over the course of a typical year, as many as 275 species can be observed on the island; September is often the best month for sightings. Boat tours from Grand Manan can also take you farther out to **Machias Seal Island,** with its colonies of puffins, Arctic terns, and razorbills. It's fun to swap information with other birders, too; during the ferry ride, look for excitable folks with binoculars and floppy hats dashing from one side of the boat to the other and back.

Campobello Island's mixed terrain attracts a good mixture of birds, including the sharp-shinned hawk, common eider, and black guillemot. Ask for a checklist and map at the visitor center. The lower St. John River is a birder's paradise and the folks here have produced a free guide, "The Birding Route," that details exactly how to get to the best viewing areas. It's online at www.discoverthepassage.com. Download it or pick up a paper copy at any Visitor Information Centre. Shorebird enthusiasts also flock to **Shepody Bay National Wildlife Area,** which maintains preserves in the mudflats between **Alma** (near the entrance to Fundy National Park) and Hopewell Cape. There's good birding in the marshes around **Sackville,** near the Nova Scotia border.

CANOEING   New Brunswick has some 3,500km (2,175 miles) of inland waterways, plus countless lakes and protected bays. Canoeists can find everything from glass-smooth waters to daunting rapids; several guides and tour operators can help you plan your trip if you visit www.tourismnewbrunswick.ca (select canoeing from the Activities). In Kouchibouguac National Park, for example, a **Voyageur Canoe Adventure** (☎ **506/876-2443**) goes out weekday mornings at 8:30am for just C$30 per person for a morning with grey seals, Common Terns (the largest single-species colony in Canada is here), and learning about the Mi'kmaq way of life. More experienced canoeists looking for a longer expedition should head for the **St. Croix River** along the U.S. border, where you can embark on multiday paddle trips and get lost in the woods—so to speak. If you want some background on paddling in the province, check out www.canoekayaknb.org.

FISHING   The Miramichi River has long attracted anglers lured by its wily Atlantic salmon. Some experts consider it to be among the best salmon rivers on the planet. There are strict laws regarding river fishing of the salmon: The fish must be caught using flies, not hooks, and nonresidents must hire a licensed guide. (There's an exemption from this rule during Fish New Brunswick Days in early June, when you don't need to use a guide but still need a license; check ahead with your lodging if you are interested.) For other freshwater species, including bass, as well as open-ocean saltwater angling, the rules are less restrictive. Get up to date on the rules and regulations by requesting two brochures: "Sport Fishing Summary" and "Atlantic Salmon Angling," available from the **Fish and Wildlife Branch** of the Department of Natural Resources ✆ **506/453-2440** or P.O. Box 6000, Fredericton, NB E3B 5H1. The Department's information can also be found online at www.gnb.ca/natural resources.

GOLF With more than 36 courses to choose from (visit www.golfnb.com for a list), golf can be enjoyed to its fullest. In St. Andrews, the **Algonquin Hotel**'s redesigned golf course is a beauty—more than 100 years old, it was retouched by Donald Ross's plans in the 1920s, then rethought and expanded in the late 1990s—easily ranking among Eastern Canada's top 10. The course features newer inland holes (the front 9), in addition to the original seaside holes that become increasingly spectacular as you approach the point of land separating New Brunswick from Maine. All 18 of them are challenging, so bring your "A" game. Service and upkeep are impeccable, and there's both a snack bar on premises and a roving club car with sandwiches and drinks. Greens fees are C$59 to C$99 for 18 holes (carts extra; discount at twilight time). Lessons are offered, and there's a short-game practice area with a huge putting green in addition to the usual driving range. Call ✆ **506/529-8823** or go to www. fairmontgolf.com/algonquin for tee times and other details. In Fredericton, lovely **Kingswood** (www.kingswoodpark.com/golf.php; ✆ **800/423-5969** or 506/443-3333)—located inside a family entertainment park—was ranked among the top 12 in North America in 2006 by *Golf Range Magazine*, and one of the "Best Places to Play" by *Golf Digest*. It features 27 holes, a par-3 course, and a double-ended driving range. A round of 18 holes costs C$59 to C$89, with twilight discounts.

HIKING The province's highest point is on top of **Mount Carleton Provincial Park** (✆ **506/235-0793**), in the center of a vast area of woodlands far from all major population centers. Several demanding hikes in the park yield glorious views. The park is open daily from mid-May to mid-October and costs C$8 to enter; you get there either by following Route 17 from **Campbellton** or taking various local roads (routes 105, 108, and then 385, to be specific) from the border crossing at Limestone, Maine. This should take less than 3 hours from either Campbellton or Caribou, Maine. There's also superb hiking at **Fundy National Park,** with a mix of coastal and woodland hikes on well-marked trails. The multiuse, 11km (7-mile) **Fundy Trail Parkway ★★** has terrific views of the coast and is wheelchair-accessible. **Grand Manan ★** is also a good destination for independent-minded hikers who enjoy the challenge of *finding* the trail as much as they enjoy hiking itself.

An excellent resource is *A Hiking Guide to New Brunswick* by Marianne Eiselt, published by Goose Lane Editions. It's C$17 and is available in bookstores around the province, online, and directly from publisher Goose Lane Editions (www.goose lane.com; ✆ **888/926-8377**).

SEA KAYAKING The huge tides that make kayaking so fascinating along the **Bay of Fundy** also make it exceptionally dangerous—even the strongest kayakers are no match for these fierce ebb tides if they're in the wrong place. Fortunately, a number of skilled sea-kayaking guides work the province.

Among the most extraordinary places to explore in New Brunswick is **Hopewell Rocks.** At high tide, there are plenty of sea caves and narrow channels to explore. **Baymount Outdoor Adventure** (www.baymountadventures.com; ✆ **877/601-2660** or 506/734-2660), run by the Faulkners in Hillsborough, offers 90-minute sea kayak tours of Hopewell Rocks from June through early September for C$59 adults, C$49 children, or C$199 per family.

Other good kayak outfitters along the coast include **FreshAir Adventure** (www. freshairadventure.com; ✆ **800/545-0020** or 506/887-2249) in Alma (near Fundy National Park) and Bruce Smith's **Seascape Kayak Tours** (www.seascapekayak tours.com; ✆ **866/747-1884** or 506/747-1884) down in Deer Island (with an amazingly international staff).

SWIMMING   Parts of New Brunswick offer surprisingly good ocean swimming. The best beaches are mostly along the "Acadian Coast," especially near the town of **Shediac** and within **Kouchibouguac National Park.** If you're coming to this province with plans to swim, bear in mind that the water is much warmer (and the terrain more forgiving) along the Gulf of St. Lawrence than it is in the frigid, rocky Bay of Fundy.In fact, random testing has shown temperatures can reach 25°C (77°F), validating claims that these waters are warmer than any other salt water north of Virginia.

WHALE-WATCHING   The **Bay of Fundy** is rich with plankton, and therefore rich with whales. Some 12 types of whales can be spotted in the bay, including finback, minke, humpback, the infrequent orca, and the endangered right whale. Whale-watching expeditions sail throughout the summer from various wharves and ports, including Campobello Island, Deer Island, Grand Manan, St. Andrews, and St. George. Any visitor information center can point you in the right direction; the province's travel guide also lists lots of tours, which typically cost around C$40 to C$60 for 2 to 4 hours of whale-watching.

PASSAMAQUODDY BAY

The **Passamaquoddy Bay** region is often the point of entry for those arriving overland from the United States. The deeply indented bay is wracked by massive tides that produce currents powerful enough to stymie even the sturdiest fishing boats. It's a place of deep fogs, spruce-clad islands, bald eagles, and little development. Fortunately for you, it's also home to grand summer colonies, spectacular islands, and a peninsula that boast five-star inns, a rambling turn-of-the-20th-century resort, great camping, charming B&Bs and economical digs for tight budgets.

Campobello Island ★★

Campobello is a compact island (about 16km/10 miles long and 5km/3 miles wide) at the mouth of Passamaquoddy Bay. Connected by a graceful modern bridge to Lubec, Maine, it's easier to get to from the United States than from Canada. (To get here from the Canadian mainland requires two ferries, one of which operates only during the summer.) This is a great quick trip into Canada if you're already in Downeast Maine; from Bar Harbor it's about a 2½-hour drive—into another world that feels a century or more older.

 Don't Forget Your Passport

Remember that passports will be required, as you are crossing international borders if choosing the Lubec route.

Campobello has been home to both humble fishermen and wealthy families over the years, yet both have coexisted quite amicably. (Locals approved when the summer folks wanted to build a golf course, for example—because it gave them a nice place to graze their sheep.) Today, the island is a mix of elegant summer mansions and simpler local homes.

Campobello offers excellent shoreline **walks** ★ at **Roosevelt Campobello International Park** (see below) and **Herring Cove Provincial Park** (✆ **506/752-7010**), which opens from late May until mid-October and in other marked locations. The landscapes are extraordinarily diverse. On some trails you'll enjoy a Currier & Ives tableau of white houses and church spires across the channel in Lubec and Eastport; 10 minutes later you'll be walking along a wild, rocky coast pummeled by surging waves. Herring Cove's thousand or so acres include a mile-long beach that's perfect for a slow stroll in the fog, camping (see "Where to Stay & Eat" below), and a good golf course with a pro shop. Watch for bald eagles and osprey, too. Look for whales, porpoises, and seals from observation decks at Ragged Point or Liberty Point.

ESSENTIALS

GETTING THERE   Campobello Island is accessible year-round from the United States. From Route 1 in Whiting, Maine, take Route 189 to Lubec, then cross the free **FDR International Bridge** from the mainland onto Campobello.

In summer only, there's a second fun option, although it will cost you. From **St. George** on the Canadian mainland, drive down Route 172 to the dock at **L'Etete.** Board the **provincial ferry** that runs year-round (operates on the half-hour 7am–5pm, hourly until 10pm) to **Deer Island**'s northern tip. Then drive the length of that island to Cummings Cove—it's only about 24km (15 miles or 20 min. drive)—and board the small ferry to Campobello. This second ferry is operated by **East Coast Ferries** (www.eastcoastferries.nb.ca; ✆ **877/747-2159** or 506/747-2159) from late June through September, running once per hour from 8:30am to 6:30pm. The ride takes about a half-hour. The fare is C$16 for a car and driver, plus C$3 for each additional passenger and a small fuel surcharge (currently C$2). You can later retrace your steps for another C$16, or just drive on across the border into Maine. Remember: These ferry times are in local Atlantic time, 1 hour ahead of Eastern Standard Time.

VISITOR INFORMATION   The Campobello Welcome Center, 44 Rte. 774, Welshpool, NB E5E 1A3 (✆ **506/752-7043**), is on the right side just after you cross the bridge from Lubec. It's usually open from mid-May until early September, 9am to 7pm, then from 10am until 6pm through mid-October.

ROOSEVELT CAMPOBELLO INTERNATIONAL PARK ★★

This free park south of Welshpool, on Route 774 (www.fdr.net; ✆ **506/752-2922**), is truly international, run by a commission with representatives from both the U.S. and Canada. It offers scenic coastlines, 16km (10 miles) of walking trails on 1,134 hectares (2,800 acres)—and tons of history, thanks to Franklin Delano Roosevelt's still-looming presence here. Like any number of affluent Americans, FDR's family made annual treks to this prosperous summer colony to experience cool air and presumed near-magical powers of restoration. ("The extensive forests of balsamic firs seem to affect the atmosphere of this region, causing a quiet of the nervous system and inviting sleep," reported one 1890 real-estate brochure.) You'll learn a lot about Roosevelt and his early life at the visitor center, where you can watch a short film and take a self-guided tour of his family's elaborate mansion, still covered in cranberry-colored shingles. For a "cottage" this big, it's surprisingly comfortable and intimate.

The park's visitor center closes late October until mid-May, but the extensive grounds and parklands remain open year-round sunrise to sunset; maps and walk suggestions are available at the visitor center. From mid-May to September, the center is open daily from 10am to 6pm; the last tour leaves 15 minutes before closing. This is easily worth half a day or more.

WHERE TO STAY & EAT

There's camping at Herring Cove Provincial Park (© **506/752-7010**). Nightly fees at the 88 sites range from C$22 (for a simple site) to C$35 (for a rustic shelter to somewhat protect you from the elements) with discounts for seniors.

Owen House, A Country Inn & Gallery This three-story clapboard captain's house dates from 1835 and sits on four tree-filled hectares (10 acres) at the edge of the bay. First-floor common rooms are decorated in a Victorian manner, with Persian and braided carpets and mahogany furniture; watch the water from a nautical-feeling sunroom that has big windows. The guest rooms are a mixed bag, furnished with a mixture of antique and modern furniture. Some units are bright and filled with salty air (room no. 1 is biggest and most expensive, with waterfront views on two sides and attractive antiques such as a cane chair and an iron-frame bed). Others are simpler, dark, or tucked beneath stairs. Some rooms have private bathrooms; others share. Ask when you call.

11 Welshpool St., Welshpool, Campobello Island, NB E5E 1G3. www.owenhouse.ca. © **506/752-2977.** 9 units, 4 with shared bathroom. C$104–C$210 double. Rates include full breakfast. MC, V. Closed Nov–Apr. No children under 6 in Aug. *In room:* No phone, Wi-Fi (free).

St. Stephen

St. Stephen is the Canadian gateway for many travelers arriving from the United States. It's directly across the tidal St. Croix River from Calais, Maine. The two towns share a symbiotic relationship—it's a local call across the international border from one town to the other, fire engines from one country sometimes respond to fires in the other, and during an annual summer parade, bands and floats have marched right through Customs. Downtown St. Stephen is a handy pit stop—and the smell of chocolate (as you'll read below) entices you into a longer stay.

A second border crossing located just outside the town of Calais and St. Stephen avoids passing through either town. If you are in a hurry, this crossing is a better choice, steering you directly onto a multilane highway heading east toward Saint John. However, it lacks the charm of the border towns, restaurants, or interesting things to see.

ESSENTIALS

VISITOR INFORMATION The Provincial Visitor Information Centre (© **506/466-7390**) is open daily from 9am to 8pm in summer (mid-June to Labour Day), 9am to 6pm during the shoulder seasons (mid-May to early Oct). It's in the old train station at Milltown Boulevard and King Street, about a mile from Canadian Customs—turn right after crossing the border (follow signs toward St. Andrews and Saint John), watching for the information center at the stoplight where the road turns left.

EXPLORING ST. STEPHEN

St. Stephen has labeled itself Canada's Chocolate Town, having earned the moniker as the home of Ganong Bros. Ltd., Canada's oldest candy company. As you'd expect, there is lots of chocolate around town, and plenty of reasons to indulge. If you feel the need to work off the sweet stuff, there is a lovely Riverfront Walking Trail easily found between downtown buildings and the river, or from the Visitor Information Centre. I've even watched eagles over the river while enjoying a picnic. Just out of town, the **Ganong Nature Park** (www.ganongnaturepark.org) has even more walking trails, a spectacular coastline, and a large intertidal area. It is located at 350 Todd's Point Rd. in Charlotte County, about 10km (6 miles) out of town. You might want to

Road Trip to St. Andrews

When leaving St. Stephen on Route 1, take exit 25 onto Route 127 to St. Andrews. This lovely rural road soon takes you to **Saint Croix Island International Historic Site** in Bayside (about 24km (15 miles) from St. Stephen) overlooking the site of the first European colony in North America. In 1604 and 1605, 79 men spent the winter here creating the first "capital of l'Acadie," beginning a process of adapting to the environment and interacting with aboriginal people that led to an enduring French presence in what we now call Canada. The site went on to be the first use of archaeological techniques in North America to determine an international boundary. During the war of 1812, officers from the United States and Britain met on what was a neutral island. Enjoy the view as you take a few moments to read up on survival and history. Once you have enjoyed this site, which is the only international historic site in the United States Park Service, just keep going to St. Andrews.

get directions from the Visitor Centre. The lumber industry and wood trades that were responsible for those handsome brick and stone buildings along main street have mostly dried up. The town now depends on its paper mill, the large Ganong chocolate factory, and tourists for its economic mainstays. There's not much in the way of stylish shopping or restaurants, but this is a good place to stock up on groceries and such if you are camping or cottaging.

You can learn more about the region's history at the **Charlotte County Museum** (*©* **506/466-3295**), in a handsome mansard-roofed home at 443 Milltown Blvd. quite close to the tourist office (see above). Besides information about the chocolate factory—who knew Ganong invented both the chocolate bar and the heart-shaped candy box?—you can learn about the city's formerly impressive cotton mill (which was the second largest in Canada in its heyday) and soap factory. It's open June through August only, daily from 9:30am until 4:30pm.

The Chocolate Museum ★ ☺ St. Stephen's claim to fame is that it's the home of the chocolate bar. In 1910, someone first thought to wrap chocolate pieces in foil and sell them. Chocolate is still big around here—a huge part of the local psyche and economy. The Ganong brothers began selling chocolate from a general store in 1873, and from there an empire was built, employing up to 700 workers by the 1930s. They were first to package chocolates in heart-shaped boxes for Valentine's Day, and still make 30% of Canadian Valentine chocolates. The modern plant on the outskirts of town isn't open to the public, but this museum is in one of the company's original factories. Exhibits explain 19th-century chocolate boxes; there are interactive multimedia displays about the candymaking; kids can play games like "Guess the Center." (I always get them wrong.) One highlight is watching expert hand-dippers make chocolates the old-fashioned way—samples follow. Need more? Ganong's Chocolatier, an old-fashioned candy shop, is located in the storefront adjacent to the museum—pick up discounted bags of factory seconds. A "Heritage Chocolate Walk" combines a factory tour with a walk through downtown's historic areas. Plan to spend an hour or more.

73 Milltown Blvd. www.chocolatemuseum.ca. *©* **506/466-7848.** Admission C$7 adults, C$6 students and seniors, free children 4 and under, C$22 families. Downtown tour plus museum C$13 adult, C$10 seniors, C$5 children 5 and under, C$40 families. July–Aug Mon–Sat 9:30am–6:30pm, Sun 11am–3pm; June and Sept Mon–Sat 10am–4pm; Oct–Nov Mon–Fri 10am–4pm.

5

NEW BRUNSWICK

Passamaquoddy Bay

St. Andrews ★★

St. Andrews—or St. Andrews-by-the-Sea as it's sometimes called—traces its roots back to the United Empire Loyalists. After the American Revolution, New Englanders who supported the British needed a new life. They moved first to seaside Castine, Maine, which they thought was safely on British soil. But it wasn't; the St. Croix River was later determined to be the true border between Canada and the United States. Forced to uproot once more, these Loyalists dismantled their homes, loaded the pieces aboard ships, and rebuilt them on the welcoming peninsula of St. Andrews (not so far away from Castine, by water). Some of these remarkably resilient saltbox houses *still* stand in the town today.

The community emerged as a fashionable summer resort in the 19th century, when many of Canada's affluent built homes and gathered here annually. The Tudor-style Algonquin Hotel was built in 1889 on a small rise overlooking the town and quickly became the area's social hub and defining landmark.

St. Andrews is beautifully situated at the tip of a long, wedge-shaped peninsula. Thanks to its location off the beaten track, the community hasn't been spoiled by modern development. Walking the wide, shady streets—especially around the Algonquin—takes one back to a simpler time, as do century-old homes in the town. A number of appealing boutiques, shops, and interesting eateries are spread along Water Street on the town's shoreline, and it's easy to grab a whale-watching or boat tour at the wharf. I definitely recommend this town if you're seeking an easy touristic dip into New Brunswick. Don't miss the weekly farmer's market, held Thursday mornings in summer on the waterfront.

ESSENTIALS

GETTING THERE   St. Andrews is located at the apex of Route 127, which dips southward from Route 1 between St. Stephen and St. George. It's an easy drive north from **St. Stephen** or south from **Saint John** (but more scenic coming from Saint John); the turnoff is well marked from both directions.

In case you don't have wheels, **Acadian Bus Lines** (www.acadianbus.com; ✆ 800/567-5151) runs a bus between St. Andrews and Saint John several days a week; the trip takes less than 90 minutes, and the adult one-way fare is C$29, C$49 round-trip. Even better, the bus line offers discounts to children, students, and seniors.

VISITOR INFORMATION   St. Andrews' seasonal **Welcome Centre** (www.townofstandrews.ca; ✆ 800/563-7397 or 506/529-3556) is located at 24 Reed Ave., on your left as you enter the village. Look for the handsome 1914 home overarched by broad-crowned trees (which is also home to the local Chamber of Commerce). The center opens daily from mid-May through mid-October; the rest of the year,

---

 Single Track Alert

If you are a mountain biking fan, ask about opportunities here. **Ripple Fitness** (www.ripplefitness.ca; ✆ 506/466-8388) organizes tours and rentals. There is an Off-Kilter Mountain Bike event in October, which takes riders from sea floor to mountaintop, plus an unprecedented chance to don a kilt and challenge the trails with like-minded mountain biking enthusiasts.

St. Andrews

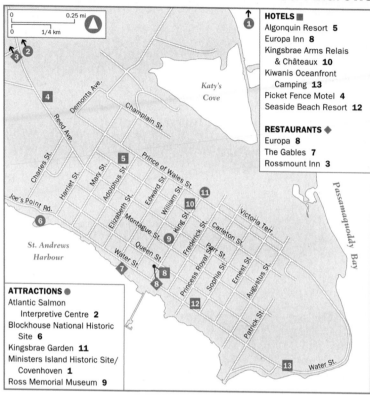

HOTELS ■
Algonquin Resort **5**
Europa Inn **8**
Kingsbrae Arms Relais
& Châteaux **10**
Kiwanis Oceanfront
Camping **13**
Picket Fence Motel **4**
Seaside Beach Resort **12**

RESTAURANTS ◆
Europa **8**
The Gables **7**
Rossmount Inn **3**

ATTRACTIONS ●
Atlantic Salmon
Interpretive Centre **2**
Blockhouse National Historic
Site **6**
Kingsbrae Garden **11**
Ministers Island Historic Site/
Covenhoven **1**
Ross Memorial Museum **9**

contact the **Chamber of Commerce** (www.standrewsbythesea.ca; *©* **506/529-3555**) at the same address.

EXPLORING ST. ANDREWS

The local chamber of commerce produces brochures, a town map and directory, and the St. Andrews-by-the-Sea historic guide, all free. Also look for *A Guide to Historic St. Andrews,* produced by the St. Andrews Civic Trust. Many of the private dwellings in St. Andrews feature plaques with information on their origins—look for them especially on the sides of the town's saltbox-style homes. The village's compact and handsome downtown flanks **Water Street,** the long commercial street paralleling the bay. You'll find understated commercial architecture here, much of it from the turn of the 20th century, in a variety of styles. Allow an hour or so for browsing through the boutiques and art galleries. There's also a mix of restaurants and inns.

Two blocks inland on King Street, get a dose of local history at the **Ross Memorial Museum ★**, 188 Montague St. (*©* **506/529-5124**). This brick Georgian mansion was built in 1824; in 1945, it was left to the town by American reverend Henry Phipps Ross and his wife Sarah Juliette Ross, who summered in St. Andrews for 40 years before dying within days of each other. The house was full of their eclectic and intriguing collection of period furniture, carpets, and paintings—and it has remained that way. The museum is open June through early October, Monday through Saturday from 10am to 4:30pm. Admission is by donation—leave a few dollars. Just uphill from the museum, at the head of King Street, is the growing **Kingsbrae Garden** (see below).

Toward the western end of Water Street, you'll come to Joe's Point Road at the foot of Harriet Street. The stout wooden **blockhouse** that sits just off the water behind low, grass-covered earthworks was built by townspeople during the War of 1812, when the colonials anticipated a U.S. attack (which never came). This structure is almost all that remains of the scattered fortifications created around town during that war—well, there are cannons here, too—but it's in pretty good shape, and has good bay views. The fortification is administered to visitors as the **Blockhouse National Historic Site** (✆ **506/529-4270**). It's open June through August; entry is only a paltry C90¢ per person. Across the street from the blockhouse sit peaceful lawns and gardens, established in 1967 to mark the centenary of Canadian Confederation. The compact **Centennial Park** has nice views of the bay and is a pleasant spot for a picnic.

At the other end of Water Street, headed east from downtown, is the open space of **Indian Point** and a local campground. Now the views of the bay become even more panoramic, and they're especially dramatic on foggy days or at sunrise. The water is swimmable, but quite frigid. Better to beachcomb: You might turn up worn, rounded pieces of flint and coral on the shoreline. It's not native, but imported—early traders loaded up their holds with flint from England and coral from the Caribbean to serve as ballast during the long crossings. When they arrived, they simply dumped the rocks overboard, and today they still churn up from the deep.

For a more protected swimming spot, wander down **Acadia Drive,** which runs downhill behind the Algonquin Hotel. You'll come to popular **Katy's Cove** (✆ **506/529-3433**), where floating docks form a sort of natural saltwater swimming pool along a lovely inlet. You'll find a snack bar, playground, and sense of ease. There's a small fee to swim and use the playground, but it's worth it.

Atlantic Salmon Interpretive Centre   The splashy visitor center of the Atlantic Salmon Federation educates the general public about the surprisingly intriguing Atlantic salmon. Located in a bright, airy post-and-beam building, the center allows visitors to get oriented through exhibits and by viewing salmon through underwater windows or strolling outdoor walkways along Chamcook Stream. Plan to spend an hour here.

24 Chamcook Rd. (6.4km/4 miles from St. Andrews, via Rte. 127). www.salarstream.ca. ✆ **506/529-1384.** Admission C$6 adults, C$4 students, C$3 children. Daily 9am–5pm. Closed Sept to mid-May.

Kingsbrae Garden ☺   This 11-hectare (27-acre) horticultural garden, opened in 1998 on the grounds of several former estates, was named one of the "Top Five North American Gardens Worth Traveling For" at the International Garden Tourism Conference in 2011. Its designers incorporated existing hedges and trees as they developed theme gardens where every turn reveals stunning new vistas. Almost 2,000 varieties of trees (including old-growth forest), are among the 50,000 plants. Notable features include a day lily collection, extensive rose garden, cedar maze, fully functional Dutch windmill, animals, duck ponds, and a children's garden with an elaborate Victorian-mansion playhouse. The Garden Cafe has a patio and excellent views over the lawns to the bay below. There's a gift shop, art gallery, and plant center on the premises. Special things happen here. Every summer morning, they release ladybugs, delighting the young at heart; croquet and bocce ball are ready for anyone to play; annual sculpture competitions bring art to the garden. Anyone who has a hard time walking the 11 hectares (27 acres) can book a personal, motorized golf cart tour. Those with a horticultural bent should plan to spend a few hours here, strolling and enjoying.

220 King St. www.kingsbraegarden.com. © **866/566-8687** or 506/529-3335. Admission C$15–C$17 adults, C$10–C$13 students and seniors, C$32–C$42 families, free for children 5 and under. Gardens open mid-May to mid-Oct daily 9am–6pm; cafe, mid-May to mid-Oct daily 10am–5pm. Closed mid-Oct to mid-May.

Ministers Island Historic Site/Covenhoven ★★ 🎁

Twelve hours before visiting Ministers Island, we checked the access: The tide was in, the road disappearing into the surf. The trip to Ministers Island is part of the adventure, as it requires driving across the ocean floor revealed by low tide. You meet your tour guide on the mainland, then drive your car in a convoy to the island estate, the amazing 1890s sandstone mansion, Covenhoden. Fifty rooms (17 bedrooms), some, like the grand drawing room, as big as modern homes, wait to be explored. This, the summer home of Sir William Van Horne, the visionary president of Canadian Pacific Railway, is now a protected Provincial Historic Site which reveals his ingenuity, and the wealth he had to indulge his passions. Stroll to the circular stone bathhouse and tidal swimming pool, or the innovative windmill, gigantic livestock barn and creamery. When Van Horne was stuck working in Montréal, he shipped dairy products from the creamery and vegetables from the greenhouse to himself daily—by rail, of course. (He extended the rail line here.) You'll learn all this, and much more, on the available tours.

At the end of Bar Rd. off Rte. 127 (northeast of St. Andrews), Chamcook. www.ministersisland.net. © **506/529-5081.** Tours C$15 adults, C$10 seniors and students, C$45 families, free for children 6 and under. Tours mid-May to mid-Oct; closed mid-Oct to mid-May.

BOAT TOURS

The docks of St. Andrews are an excellent spot from which to launch an exploration of Passamaquoddy Bay, which is very much alive, biologically speaking. That means you'll very likely see a combination of whales, porpoises, seals, and bald eagles, no matter what tour you select. All 2- to 3-hour tours generally run the same price: C$55 to C$60 per adult, less for children. Reservations are strongly advised. Your selection really comes down to the type of vessel and experience you prefer.

Quoddy Link Marine (www.quoddylinkmarine.com; © **877/688-2600** or 506/ 529-2600) offers seasonal (late June to late Oct) whale-watch tours, one to three times daily on a 17m (56-foot) power catamaran, and the tour includes seafood snacks and use of binoculars; the tours take 2½ to 3 hours. Two-hour tours in search of wildlife aboard 7m (24-ft.) rigid-hull Zodiacs are offered by **Fundy Tide Runners** (www.fundytiderunners.com; © **506/529-4481**). Flotation suits (provided) are a must as the boats cruise through the West Isles archipelago to the whale feeding grounds. This outfitter opens May through October, offering 2-hour cruises.

For a more traditional experience, though, sign up for a trip aboard the 22m (72-foot) square-rigged cutter the *Jolly Breeze of St. Andrews* ★ with **Tall Ship Whale- Watching** (www.jollybreeze.com; © **866/529-8116** or 506/529-8116). The outfit offers three 3½-hour sails a day from mid-June through mid-October. Complimentary breakfast or soup is included. A flat-fee deal for families of four (or more) is also offered. Watch for whales, seals, dolphins, and eagles—all have been sighted from the sailboat's deck.

Bruce Smith's **excellent Seascape Kayak Tours** ★ (www.seascapekayaktours. com; © **866/747-1884** or 506/747-1884) outfit on nearby Deer Island (see "Getting

There," in the Campobello Island section, earlier) offers a different sort of up-close and personal view of the bay's natural wonders. Seascape's talented international staff leads kayak trips lasting from 2 hours (C$55 per adult) to a full day (C$150) through the islands and bays of the Campobello/Deer Isle/St. Andrews area; you might see whales, seals, porpoises, and/or eagles, snacks are provided, and no prior kayaking experience is required to sign up for a tour.

WHERE TO STAY

Those traveling on a budget instead of seeking the luxury digs below might head for the low-slung **Picket Fence Motel,** 102 Reed Ave. (www.picketfencenb.com; 🌮 **506/529-8985**). This trim and tidy property offers 17 cost-effective rooms, all with air-conditioning, close to the handsome Algonquin golf course (see "Golf," earlier) and within walking distance of St. Andrews' village center. The queen- and double-bedded rooms cost C$65 to C$95 double. It's a good deal.

Or, for something slightly more upscale that won't break your bank, contact the **Europa Inn** (www.europainn.com; 🌮 **506/529-3818**), an outgrowth of the successful Europa restaurant (see "Where to Eat," below) in the heart of town at 48 King St. The inn's owners rent out a series of rooms, suites, and an apartment collectively rated a very respectable 3½ out of 4 stars by Canada's government hotel-rating agency, Canada Select. Nightly rates run from C$89 (for a simple room, off season) to C$175 (for a suite in high season). Helpfully, the suites and apartment all have kitchenettes or full kitchens.

Algonquin Resort ★★ The Algonquin's pedigree dates from 1889, when it opened its doors to wealthy vacationers seeking respite from the city heat. The original structure was destroyed by fire in 1914, but surviving annexes were rebuilt in Tudor style; in 1993 an architecturally similar addition was built across the road, linked by a gatehouse-inspired bridge. This red-tile-roofed resort commands attention through its sheer size and bearing—and kilt-wearing, bagpipe-playing staff. Several blocks from the water's edge, the inn is perched on a hill and affords panoramic bay views from a second-floor roof garden and many of the guest rooms. Updated rooms are comfortable and tasteful. In addition to its outstanding seaside golf course (see "Golf," earlier), there's now a spa at the hotel with a full card of treatments ranging from facials and nail services to body wraps and massage. The resort's **dining room** ★, open May through October, is one of the better spots in town to eat—it's often bustling with summer folks, and the kitchen produces surprisingly creative meals. Informal dining options include the **Library Lounge & Bistro** (off the main lobby) and a downstairs lounge. Farther afield, the food at the **Clubhouse Grill** on the resort's golf course is worth the drive. Note that this hotel markets itself aggressively to tour and conference operators; when they're here, the place feels a little bit like an in-joke to which you're not privy. *Note:* Management of the Algonquin changed at the end of 2011, resulting in a possible change of contact information, rates, and some amenities; be sure to ask when you call.

184 Adolphus St., St. Andrews, NB E5B 1T7. 🌮 **506/529-8823.** Fax 506/529-7162. 234 units. C$99–C$459 double; C$299–C$1,169 suite. Rates include continental breakfast. AE, DC, MC, V. Free valet parking. Small cats and dogs C$25 per night. **Amenities:** 2 restaurants; 2 bars; babysitting; bike rentals; children's programs; concierge; golf course; health club; Jacuzzi; outdoor heated pool; sauna; spa; 2 tennis courts; Internet (paid) some rooms. *In room:* TV, hair dryer, minibar.

Kingsbrae Arms Relais & Châteaux ★★★ Part of the Relais & Châteaux network, this Kingsbrae Arms is a luxe five-star inn with an upscale European feel.

Occupying an 1897 manor house built by jade merchants, the inn sits next to Kingsbrae Garden (see above); some guest rooms have wonderful views of the gardens, others a panoramic sweep of the bay. Guests are pampered by a guest-services suite stocked with complimentary snacks and refreshments. Some rooms also have Jacuzzis and steam showers. Two suites in the carriage house are especially suited for those with pets or young children. For an extra charge, guests can eat **five-course meals ★★** around a single table in the private dining room during summer—the chef brings a Mediterranean influence, while using the local bounty of land and sea.

219 King St., St. Andrews, NB E5B 1Y1. www.kingsbrae.com. ✆ **506/529-1897.** 8 units. C$395–C$995. Packages and meal plans available. 2-night minimum; July–Aug 3-night minimum. 5% room service charge additional. AE, MC, V. Open Mother's Day to Canadian Thanksgiving. Pets allowed with advance permission. **Amenities:** Babysitting; pool. *In room:* A/C, TV, CD player, hair dryer, Wi-Fi (free).

Kiwanis Oceanfront Camping ★

Overlooking Passamaquoddy Bay, this little campground is a lovely walk from downtown St. Andrews and just steps from the intertidal beach. A morning coffee at a picnic table, watching fishing boats, kayakers, or excursions heading out for whale-watching is just about a perfect way to start the day. Caravans often stop here for a few days, so you can meet folks from far and wide. Clean and air-conditioned by sea breezes, this campground should rank up with the Algonquin Resort for most valued asset in this town. All buildings are wheelchair accessible.

550 Water Street, St. Andrews E5B 2R6. www.kiwanisoceanfrontcamping.com. ✆ **877/393-7070** or 506/529-3439. RV with full hookups (oceanfront) C$42 night; tents (unserviced) C$31. AE, MC, V. **Amenities:** Washrooms; laundry; playground.

Seaside Beach Resort ★ ☺

Two dozen cabins, cottages, and apartment units of various shapes and sizes cluster closely together by the waterfront in a simple but central complex, right beside a boardwalk, all just a 5- or 10-minute stroll from downtown. All units are equipped with surprisingly up-to-date kitchens or kitchenettes, and there's a beachy feel enhanced by the naturally weathered shingling on many of the buildings and the cottages' exposed-pine interiors. Views range from direct shots to the ocean to the honestly advertised "no view of any sort" in one unit. The newest cottage, Spruce, is the biggest and best (and priciest); it has a deck with a grill and a view, skylights, a dishwasher, and lovely woodwork. This property is a great pick when you want something more affordable; just bring groceries, everything else you need to prepare and enjoy your own meals is there. Open year-round; leashed dogs welcome.

339 Water St., St. Andrews, NB E5B 2R2. www.seaside.nb.ca. ✆ **800/506-8677** or 506/529-3846. 24 units. Mid-June to Aug C$130–C$220 cottage; Apr to mid-June and Sept to mid-Nov C$90–C$150 cottage; mid-Nov to Mar C$70–C$150. 3-night minimum (some units). AE, MC, V. **Amenities:** Wi-Fi (free). *In room:* TV, fridge, kitchenette, no phone.

WHERE TO EAT

Locals swear by the **Gables,** 143 Water St. (✆ **506/529-3440**), a waterside spot where you can relax and nosh on some seafood, lobster, or burgers. It isn't fancy, but it's friendly. Coming or leaving town, on Route 1 between the turnoffs for St. Andrews and St. George, the **Ozzie's Lunch** (that's Hwy. 1 in Bethel; ✆ **506/755-2758**) parking lot tells a story. Cars and trucks from "away" are surpassed by locals at this takeout that feels like it's in the middle of nowhere. Highway crews, law enforcers on a break, fishermen; all happily rub shoulders with tourists as they line up to place their order at the takeout window. Ozzie's claims to have "the best seafood in North

America," at least according to their sign. The demand seems to back that up. It's cash only, and don't pass on dessert. Homemade donuts for a *loonie* (C$1) or pies top the list. If you have a cooler along, follow the little gravel road to **Oven Head Salmon Smokers** (101 Oven Head Rd., Bethel; www.ovenheadsmokers.com; © 877/955-2507 or 506/755-2507). They cold smoke using maple chips. Yum.

Europa ★★ 🏛 CONTINENTAL   In an intriguing building that once housed a movie theater and dance hall, Bavarian husband-and-wife transplants Markus and Simone Ritter whip up French-, Swiss-, and Austrian-accented cuisine for a 35-seat room. Starters could run to lobster bisque, smoked salmon with *rösti* and capers, or seared scallops in Mornay sauce baked with cheese (a house specialty). Main courses usually include several versions of schnitzel with different fillings, toppings, and sauces; steak Béarnaise; duck a l'Orange; haddock in lemon butter or champagne sauce; and tiger shrimp with mango chutney. Finish with a chocolate mousse, almond parfait, or homemade ice cream or sorbet. The wine list is surprisingly strong. All in all, a lovely slice of Europe—just as the name promises.

48 King St. © **506/529-3818.** Reservations recommended. Main courses C$18–C$27. MC, V. Mid-May to Sept daily 5–9pm; Oct Tues–Sat 5–9pm; Nov to mid-Feb Thurs–Sat 5–9pm. Closed mid-Feb to mid-May.

Rossmount Inn ★★★ CONTEMPORARY CANADIAN   When the waiter placed a side dish of goose tongue greens in front of me, I knew I was in diner's heaven. These edible marsh greens (actually a seaside plantain) are only found in the wild in the spring. Chef Chris Aerni focuses on local ingredients and seasonal hand-picked wild foods, such as fiddleheads, cattails, and chanterelles. Foraged ingredients are as likely to grace the menu as the daily catch of local fishermen, or organics from their own garden—the menu changes daily. The burgeoning reputation of this 60-seat inn, located in a stately manor house on a 35-hectare (87-acre) estate, means that you have to call ahead to reserve a table. To extend your experience, book a stay in their guest rooms priced from C$80 to C$145 (they have feather beds!), perfect when you want to finish off your evening in their old English–style lounge bar, where single malt whiskies are a specialty.

4599 Rte. 127, St. Andrews. www.rossmountinn.com. © **506/529-3351.** Reservations required. Main courses C$15–C$28. AE, MC, V. Mid-Apr to Oct daily 6–9:30pm. Closed Mon–Wed in Nov–Dec and Apr. Closed Jan to mid-Apr.

GRAND MANAN ISLAND ★

Grand Manan is the main island of an archipelago at the mouth of the Bay of Fundy. Geologically rugged, profoundly peaceful, and indisputably remote, the handsome island of 2,700 year-round residents is just a 90-minute ferry ride from the port of Blacks Harbour, southeast of St. George. This is a much-prized destination for adventurous travelers, often a highlight of their vacation. Nature lovers, whale-watchers, and those who seek solitude will relish the rough-hewn charm of this land surrounded by the sea.

Grand Manan is a special favorite of serious birders. When hiking the island's trails, don't be surprised if you come across knots of quiet people peering intently through binoculars—these are the birders on a quest to see all 300 or so species of birds that either nest here or stop by during their long migrations. This is *the* place to pad your "life list" if you're accumulating one, with birds ranging from bald eagles to puffins (you'll need to pay for a boat tour to catch a glimpse of the latter). You're practically guaranteed to see something you've never seen before. John James Audubon came here to paint; Pulitzer Prize winning author Willa Cather kept a cottage here. This unique island continues to attract artists, photographers, and others who seek out special places.

Essentials

GETTING THERE   Grand Manan is reached from Blacks Harbour on the Canadian mainland via frequent ferry service. **Coastal Transport car ferries** (www. coastaltransport.ca; © **506/642-0520**), each capable of hauling 60 cars, depart from the mainland and the island every 2 hours between 7:30am and 5:30pm during July and August, four times daily the rest of the year. The ferry does not sail on Christmas or New Year's Day. The round-trip fare is C$11 per adult, C$5.40 per child age 5 to 12, and C$33 per car. Boarding the ferry on the mainland is free; you buy tickets when you leave the island.

Caution: This island is exceptionally popular in summer. A new ferry, Grand Manan Adventure, introduced in August 2011, has a larger carrying capacity but you still get in line early, or you might not get a spot on the boat. Departures from Blacks Harbour are on a first-come, first-served basis. One time-tested strategy is to bring a picnic lunch, arrive an hour or two early, put your car in the line, then head for the grassy waterfront park adjacent to the wharf and eat alfresco. It's a nicely attractive spot; there's even an island to explore during low tide while you wait. Reserve your return trip at least a day ahead to avoid getting stranded overnight (unless that's what you want); again, get in line early to secure a spot in Blacks Harbour. You can only reserve for crossings leaving Grand Manan, as there are no ticket agents in Blacks Harbour; there it is only first-come, first-served.

VISITOR INFORMATION   The island's Visitor Information Centre (www.grand manannb.com; © **888/525-1655** or 506/662-3442), is located at the island's museum (see "Exploring the Island," below) in the village of Grand Harbour at 1141 Rte. 776, one of three villages on the island's eastern shore; the center is open weekdays and Sunday afternoons through the summer, until it closes down in mid-September until the following June. If you come when it's closed, ask at island stores or inns for a free island map published by the Grand Manan Tourism Association (www.grandmanannb. com), which also has a listing of key island phone numbers.

Exploring the Island

Start exploring before you even land. As you come abreast of the island aboard the ferry, head for the starboard (right) side : You'll soon see the **Seven Days' Work** in the rocky cliffs of Whale's Cove, a spot where seven layers of hardened lava and sill (intrusive igneous rock) have come together to create a sort of geological Dagwood sandwich.

Get an even better understanding of the local landscape at the **Grand Manan Museum** (© **506/662-3424**) in Grand Harbour. The museum's geology exhibit teaches you what to look for as you roam around the island. Serious birders might enjoy the collections donated by island birder Allan Moses, which feature 200-plus stuffed and mounted birds behind glass. The museum also houses an impressive lighthouse lens from the Gannet Rock Lighthouse, plus a collection of items that have washed up from shipwrecks. The museum is open fro June to September, Monday through Friday 9am to 5:30pm; it's also open Saturda (same hours) in July and August. Admission is C$4 for adults, C$2 for seniors and students, and free for children 12 and under.

The relatively flat and compact island is perfect for cycling; the only stretches to avoid are some fast, less scenic segments of Route 776. Any of the side roads offer superb biking, and the paved cross-island road to **Dark Harbour** is especially nice; when you get there, you'll find a scenic little harbor with a few cabins, dories, and salmon pens. Eat your Wheaties before coming: This route is wild and hilly for a stretch, but then offers a memorably scenic coast down to the ocean on the island's western side as your reward.

Bike rentals are available at **Adventure High** ★ (www.adventurehigh.com; *©* **800/732-5492** or 506/662-3563) at 83 Rte. 776 in **North Head,** not far from the ferry. If you're fit enough, consider leaving your car at Blacks Harbour and taking only a bike onto the boat, then returning on the last ferry; you'll save money and burn calories. The outfitter also offers sea kayak tours around the island, for those who prefer to get a rarely-seen, whale's-eye view of the impressive cliffs. Bikes rent for C$22 per day, C$16 for a half-day. Kayak tours run from C$45 for a 2-hour sunset tour to C$110 for a full day's excursion. The same folks can even rent you a cabin—or add a lobster dinner on the beach to your kayak trip, for an extra charge.

While Grand Manan is about as quiet as it gets, you can find even more silence and solitude (and cross one more island off your "life list") by driving to **White Head Island,** population 190 on a good day. To get there, drive to Ingalls Head (follow Ingalls Head Rd. from Grand Harbour) and catch a free ferry to the island. You walk along the shore to a lighthouse guarding the passage between Battle Beach and Sandy Cove. The ferry holds nine cars and sails year-round, several times per day during the summer.

HIKING

Numerous hiking trails lace Grand Manan, particularly around the coast, with several overland routes crossing the island. The degree of difficulty varies, from easy strolls along boardwalks to more challenging terrain for experienced hikers. Don't hesitate to ask at your inn or the tourist information center about trail access, or good places to walk. The Grand Manan Tourism Association publishes a trail guide, *Heritage Trails and Footpaths of Grand Manan,* which can be purchased on the island for C$6 or by mail order. Also check out www.grandmanannb.ca or visit Grand Manan Hikers on Facebook.

The most accessible clusters of trails on Grand Manan are at the island's northern and southern tips. Head north up Whistle Road to Whistle Beach, and you'll find both the **Northwestern Coastal Trail** ★ and the **Seven Days' Work Trail** ★, both of which follow the rocky shoreline. Near the low lighthouse and towering radio antennae at Southwest Head (follow Rte. 776 all the way to its end), trails radiate out along cliffs topped with scrappy trees. The views are remarkable (when the fog's not in, that is). Just be sure to watch your step. As you travel Route 776, watch for signs to trails painted on the road surface.

WHALE-WATCHING & BOAT TOURS

A fine way to experience island ecology is to mosey offshore. Several outfitters offer complete nature tours, providing a nice sampling of the world above and beneath the sea. On an excursion you might see minke, finback, or humpback whales, along with exotic birds including puffins and phalaropes. **Sea Watch Tours** (www.seawatchtours. com; *©* **877/662-8552** or 506/662-8552), run by Peter and Kenda Wilcox, operates a series of excursions from late June through September, with whale sightings guaranteed or your money back, aboard a 13m (43-ft.) vessel with canopy. Rates run C$63 to C$90 for adults and C$43 to C$45 per child 12 or younger.

Where to Stay

The **Anchorage Provincial Park** ★ (© 506/662-7022) has about 100 campsites scattered about forest and field, available mid-May through mid-September. There's a small beach and a hiking trail on the property, and it's well situated for exploring the southern part of the island. It's very popular midsummer; call before you board the ferry to ask about campsite availability. Sites are C$24 to C$35, some with hookups for RVs, others better suited for a simple tent—including some involving crude shelters to help you fend off the weather.

Inn at Whale Cove Cottages ★★ This family-run compound is set in a grassy meadow overlooking the aforementioned cove. The original building is a farmhouse dating to 1816, furnished with antique Shaker furniture. There are three comfortable guest rooms, two with a water view. The living room features good reading material and a fireplace. Five cottages are scattered about the property, varying in size from one to four bedrooms; most rent only by the week. (One was built by author Willa Cather.) The John's Flat and Cove View units are the most modern, sporting extra bedrooms and dining rooms, decks, televisions, laundry service, and (in one case) a Jacuzzi. The four hectares (10 acres) of grounds, especially the pathway to the beach, are lovely. Innkeeper Laura Buckley received culinary training in Toronto and the **dining room** ★ demonstrates a deft touch with Continental cuisine. Dinners are served nightly from mid-June through mid-October, weekends only in May and early June.

26 Whale Cove Cottage Rd., North Head Grand Manan, NB E5G 2B5. www.whalecovecottages.ca. © **506/662-3181.** 9 units. C$125–C$135 double; C$850–C$1,000 per week cottage. Rates include full breakfast. MC, V. All but 1 unit closed Nov–Apr. Dogs allowed in all but 1 unit, C$5 per day. **Amenities:** Dining room; Jacuzzi (1 unit). *In room:* TV (2 units), kitchenette (3 units), Wi-Fi (free).

Where to Eat

Options for dining out aren't exactly extravagant on Grand Manan, but the Inn at Whale Cove Cottages (see "Where to Stay," above) serves great meals incorporating fresh local ingredients. **Shorecrest Lodge** (www.shorecrestlodge.com; © 506/662-3216) in North Head, another local inn, has a country-style dining room with fireplace and hardwood floors, and serves a menu of seafood, chicken, and beef daily during the summer months. You must make a reservation before 4pm. You'll also encounter a few other family restaurants and grocers along the main road.

The seasonal, summer-only **North Head Bakery** ★ (© 506/662-8862) on Route 776 is superb. The artisanal bakery has been using traditional methods and whole grains since 1990. Breads made here daily include a crusty, seven-grain loaf and a delightful egg-and-butter bread—nor should the chocolate-chip cookies be overlooked. The bakery is on the main road, on the left as you're heading south from the ferry.

If you're here on Saturday morning between late June and early September, check out the weekly **farmer's market** in North Head.

SAINT JOHN ★

Wrapped around a commercial harbor, Saint John meanders uphill from the water's edge. Hills are part of life here in the province's largest city and help define a

Note that Saint John is always spelled out, never abbreviated as "St. John," nor do you ever tack on an s. St. John's is another city, hundreds of miles northeast in Newfoundland.

character that is rich in parks and natural attractions: **Rockwood Park** boasts 13 lakes, a campground, and golf course; **Harbour Passage**, a series of interconnected waterfront park and heritage sites, links past and present; the **Reversing Falls** provides adventure for thrill seekers. In fact, Saint John is at the center of **Stonehammer,** North America's first global geopark: a UNESCO site that has exceptional geological heritage.

Down at the harbor, cruise ships almost equal cargo vessels, bringing a festive air downtown. Ironically, this waterfront area is known locally as "Uptown Saint John." Shopping, dining, artisans, entertainment, and history all come together at or near **Market Square.** Something is happening here every day during the summer.

An eclectic mix of old and new is found throughout the city. Impressive mansions tucked into the side streets reflect the timber barons and shipping magnates of the past. Yet the modern city is full of life: Streets often bustle with skateboarders, merchants, carousers, out-for-the-weekenders, and local old-timers casing the public market for bargains. Here the St. John River empties into the Bay of Fundy (except when the tide is coming in) on the Fundy Coastal Drive, 90 minutes from the U.S. border, and linked by ferry to Nova Scotia. For all of its history and access to nature, Saint John is an industrial center and active transportation hub—which can sometimes leave the air with pungent reminders of its existence.

GETTING THERE   Saint John is located on Route 1. It's 106km (66 miles) from the U.S. border at St. Stephen and 427km (265 miles) around the bend from Halifax. Reach downtown by taking exit 122 or 123 off Route 1.

A year-round **ferry service** connects Saint John with Digby, Nova Scotia. For more details, see "Exploring New Brunswick" at the beginning of this chapter. Saint John's **airport,** coded YSJ (www.saintjohnairport.com; ℂ 506/638-5555), has regular flights to and from Montréal, Toronto, and Halifax on **Air Canada** (www.air canada.com; ℂ 888/237-2262). There are auto-rental kiosks in the terminal, and a taxi ride into the city costs about C$30.

VISITOR INFORMATION   Saint John (www.tourismsaintjohn.com) is fully stocked with four visitor information centers (VICs). All except City Hall open Victoria Day Weekend (mid-May) and close at Thanksgiving (early Oct). City Hall is open year-round. Hours are daily 9am to 7pm in July and August; daily 9am to 6pm the rest of the year. Arriving from the west, look for the contemporary triangular building near the Route 1 offramp: This is the **Route 1 West visitor information center** (ℂ 506/658-2940). You'll find a trove of information and brochures here.

There's also a seasonal VIC (open mid-May to early Oct), the **Reversing Falls information center** (ℂ 506/658-2937). It's located inside the observation building overlooking those popular falls (see "Outdoor Pursuits," below) on Route 100, which is also labeled on maps as Bridge Road. Get there from Route 1 by taking exit 119 or 119B.

If you're already downtown, or you're visiting town outside the peak seasons, look for the **City Hall Tourist Information Centre** (ℂ 886/463-8639 or 506/658-2855) in the Shoppes of City Hall on the pedestrian walkway connecting Brunswick Square and Market Square. It's open Monday through Saturday, 9am to 5pm, year-round.

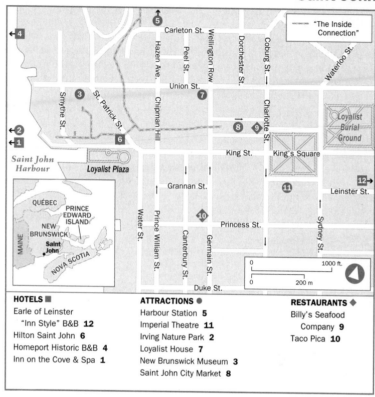

There is a seasonal downtown location at Barbour's General Store, 10 Market Square (**© 506/658-2940**).

Exploring Saint John

If the weather's good, begin by wandering around the **waterfront.** Tourism Saint John has published a historical walking-tour brochure that offers plenty of history and architectural trivia, including a rundown of the oddly fascinating gargoyles and sculpted heads that adorn downtown's 19th-century buildings. If you have time for only one walk, architecture buffs should go on **"Prince William's Walk,"** an hour-long, self-guided tour of the city's impressive commercial buildings. (Personally, though, I like to wing it and just wander.) You can obtain tour brochures at the **Market Square information center** (see "Visitor Information," above).

Wherever you ramble, be sure to drop by the **Saint John City Market** (detailed below) and to work the **Old Burial Ground ★** (across from King's Square) into your itinerary; it's a good place to rest for a spell. The ancient cemetery dates from 1784, but it was renovated quite recently—note the beaver pond. When the famous Irving family refurbished the cemetery in 1995, they installed this monument, comparing their employees (a good number of the local residents) to hard-working beavers.

If you have a car, you'll also want to visit at least two of the city's tremendous **nature preserves ★★**, described below in the section "Outdoor Pursuits." I can't tell you how surprising it is to find so much lovely, varied green space in the midst of a city.

If the weather's disagreeable (it could be), head indoors. Saint John has helpfully linked up quite a number of uptown malls, hotels, and attractions with each other through an elaborate network of underground passageways and overhead pedestrian walkways. The whole thing has been dubbed the **Inside Connection ★** and the system makes the city approachable even in heavy rains or snow.

Loyalist House ★   A mandatory destination for antiques buffs or Anglophiles, this stately white Georgian mansion was built in 1817 for the Merritts, a family of wealthy Loyalists who fled from New York. Inside you'll find an extraordinary collection of furniture; most pieces were original to the house and have never left. Especially notable are the extensive holdings of Duncan Phyfe Sheraton furniture and a rare piano-organ combination. The house also features its original brass knocker, doors steamed and bent to fit into the curved sweep of the stairway, and intricate carvings on the wooden chair rails. It even managed to avoid being burnt to the ground during a great fire that razed much of the city in 1877. Tours last 30 to 45 minutes.

120 Union St. ✆ **506/652-3590.** C$5 adults, C$2 children, C$7 families. July to mid-Sept daily 10am–5pm (last admission 4:45pm); mid-May to June Mon–Fri 10am–5pm; Sept–Apr by appointment only.

New Brunswick Museum ★★ ☺   If anything in the city should be classified as a crown jewel, it should be this gem located in Uptown Saint John—the imposing-looking building is a must-stop for anyone seriously curious about this province's natural or cultural history. Collections are displayed on three open floors, an exhaustive mixture of traditional artifacts and quirky objects. First stop: the Tidal Tower, a 29-foot tube showing the comings and goings of the Bay of Fundy tides in the adjacent harbor. Take note of the water level, then go exploring. Exhibits include Delilah, a North American Right Whale, whose skeleton and a life-size model hang from the ceiling; the *Marco Polo*, once the fastest sailing ship in the world; the complete interior of Sullivan's Bar (where longshoremen used to slake their thirst a few blocks away); and even a sporty white Bricklin car from a failed stab at auto manufacturing in the province during the mid-'70s. Be sure to check the What's Happening calendar; activities for all ages (especially kids), as well as new exhibitions, are constantly changing. Allow at least 4 hours to enjoy the eclectic, uncommonly well-displayed exhibits here. Before you leave, make sure to return to the Tidal Tower to see the change in water level since you arrived. You will be amazed.

1 Market Sq. www.nbm-mnb.ca. ✆ **506/643-2300.** Admission C$8 adults, C$6 seniors, C$4.50 students and children 4–18, C$17 families. Mon–Fri 9am–5pm (Thurs until 9pm); Sat 10am–5pm; Sun noon–5pm. Closed Mon Nov to mid-May.

Saint John City Market ★★   Hungry travelers, venture here at your peril. This spacious, bustling marketplace is crammed with vendors hawking meat, fresh seafood, cheeses, flowers, baked goods, and bountiful fresh produce. (You can even sample *dulse*, a snack of dried seaweed from the Bay of Fundy.) The market, built in 1876, has been a constant draw for city residents ever since. Note the construction of the roof—local lore claims it resembles the hull of an inverted ship because it was made by boatbuilders. Also look for small, enduring traces of tradition: Handsome iron gates at either end have been in place since 1880, and a loud bell is rung daily by the Deputy Market Clerk to signal the opening and closing. A number of vendors offer meals to go, and there's bright seating in an enclosed terrace on the south side. It's definitely worth an hour or two, and perfectly positioned for an eating break. Just don't make the mistake of coming on a Sunday or a Canadian holiday: It'll be closed.

47 Charlotte St. (facing King's Square). ℂ **506/658-2820.** Mon–Fri 7:30am–6pm; Sat 7:30am–5pm. Closed Sun and holidays.

Outdoor Pursuits

Just after construction workers found a 500-million-year-old rock formation called the Hinge in 2010, the United Nations named **Stonehammer Geopark** North America's first UNESCO-recognized geopark. Saint John lies in the heart of the swath of land along the Bay of Fundy that is recognized for natural attributes, geoscientific significance, and beauty. Many of the outdoor activities enjoyed here are part of the Stonehammer landscape. There are big natural attractions in town, some of them simple adventures of drive-walk-and-look; others a little more intense.

Reversing Falls Jet Boat Rides (www.jetboatrides.com; ℂ **888/634-8987** or 506/634-8987) offers trips through the Reversing Falls or out through the harbor in two configurations: a sightseeing tour and a "thrill ride." The always-breezy, sometimes-damp Thrill Rides don't take long (about 20 min.), but climbing, jumping, and crossing the rapids is sheer exhilarating fun. They only go for the 2 hours at low tide, so call for a reservation to get times, and ask about height and age restrictions. The hour-long Sightseeing Tour takes in the reversing falls, whirlpools, local lore and history from native and European settlers, and the port. Figure C$38 per adult, C$27 per child, or C$115 for a family; all tickets include the use of raincoats and mandatory life jackets. Reservations are recommended during peak season. The tours depart from a narrow cove at **Fallsview Park** (see "Reversing Falls," below).

Irving Nature Park ★★ ☺   Oil giant founder J. D. Irving donated and maintains one little gem of a park within the Saint John city limits. Located at the west end of the city, across the St. John River, the Nature Park consists of 243 dramatic hectares (600 acres) on a coastal peninsula. As many as 240 species of birds have been spotted, while trails and marsh boardwalks provide access to a lovely forest and wild, salty seascapes. The observation tower on the "Squirrel Trail" gives a fine vantage of the park and mud flats, where migrating sandpipers devour shrimp before flying 4 days nonstop to Surinam. Throngs of seals visit the park, usually in mid-June and mid-October, often so thick on the rocks that they have been beautifully described as "a great gray noisy carpet." This park can get very busy—it sees 125,000 visitors a year—so avoid summer Sundays, which are busiest. Call ahead to ask about the excellent program of tours and events (moonlight snowshoeing, meteor shower watches, day camps for children); even if there's nothing in particular going on, you might still stick around an hour or two—or more. There are even barbecue pits, in case you want to grill while you green.

Sand Cove Rd. www.jdirving.com. ℂ **506/653-7367.** Take exit 119A off Rte. 1, then follow Bleury St. to Sand Cove Rd. and continue to the end. Free admission and tours. Daily dawn–dusk; information booth staffed daily May–Oct.

Reversing Falls 🖐   Just west of downtown, Reversing Falls is located within an impressive rocky gorge, a natural phenomenon which has been turned into a tourism site. The falls here reverse because of huge local tides battling against the St. John River's flow; rapids, small waterfalls, and big, slurping whirlpools flow one way up through the gorge during the incoming tide, then reverse during the opposite tide. It's somewhat dramatic, and offers thrills to the thrill-seeker through jet-boat rides (see above) and zip-lining (see following), but it is in a busy part of the city and next to a paper mill. This isn't a wild natural place like the Irving Nature Park (see above). It is best enjoyed for what it is. There are several ways to observe the falls. You can scramble down wooden steps to a park at river's edge, or climb atop a rooftop viewing platform, both for free. You can cross the river to **Fallsview Park** (go left on Douglas Ave., then left again on Fallsview Ave.) and get a water-level view. The adventurous can take a Zip Line Tour with **Saint John Adventures** (www.saintjohnadventures. ca; ℭ **877/634-9477** or 506/634-9477), which offers an amazing view of the falls from six towers (five zip lines). Allow about 90 minutes and C$70 for adults; students and seniors get a discount. Or, you can dine at the **Falls Restaurant** (ℭ **506/635-1999**), open year-round, where the view gets rave reviews. It's a casual eatery with basic good food and service. Get there early for the best views.

Rte. 100. ℭ **506/658-2937.** Free admission to viewing platform. Early June to mid-Oct daylight hours, but best at low or high tide. Call for tidal schedule.

Rockwood Park ★★ ☺   Extensive footpaths attract walkers and joggers to these 890 hectares (2,200 acres) of lovely urban preserve, which take in lakes, forests, and rocky hills. There's swimming at sandy beaches, horseback riding and wagon rides, golf at a pretty 18-hole municipal golf course (ℭ **506/634-0090;** greens fees C$25–C$37), picnic areas, a campground, minigolf, and the small Cherry Creek Zoo with several dozen species of exotic animals, including six species of monkeys on the endangered species list. In short, there's something for everyone in the family. Boat rentals include canoes and kayaks. There's even an eco-friendly aquatic driving range; golfers practice by hitting floating balls into a lake. The park, located just 5 minutes' drive north of downtown, gets especially popular on weekends. The park and gardens are operated by the Saint John Horticultural Association.

Lake Dr. S. ℭ **506/658-2883.** Free admission to park; Cherry Creek Zoo C$7–C$9 adults, C$4.50–C$6 children; various fees for equipment rental and golf. Interpretation Centre late May to early Sept daily 8am–dusk.

Where to Stay

Budget travelers should head for Manawagonish Road, where many of the city's lower-priced motels congregate. *A bonus:* Unlike most other motel strips, this one's actually reasonably attractive as it winds along a high ridge of residential homes west of town, providing views out to the Bay of Fundy. It's about a 10-minute ride back to town. Nightly rates at many of the mom-and-pop motels on the strip are unbelievably low, sometimes as low as the C$60 range even during peak summer season. The chain property **Econo Lodge Inn & Suites,** 1441 Manawagonish Rd. (ℭ **800/55-ECONO** [553-2666] or 506/635-8700), is somewhat more expensive but a bit more comfortable, and the rooms have those sweeping views.

In-town camping is available summers at **Rockwood Park Campgrounds** (ℭ **506/652-4050**), where 201 sites are spread across a rocky area and a few overlook the harbor, downtown, the main highway, and a railyard (campers in those sites may experience nighttime noise). Large RVs requiring hookups (electricity and water only) are directed to an area resembling a parking lot. Other sites vary widely in privacy and scenery. Rates start at around C$23 for a tent site and around C$33 for hookups. Follow signs to the park from either exit 122 or exit 125 off Route 1.

EXPENSIVE

Hilton Saint John ★★
This 12-story waterfront hotel has all the amenities and the dependability you'd expect from an upscale chain hotel. Executive rooms offer more amenities and space than traditional guest rooms—as they should. Perks here include electronic safes and such. This hotel boasts one of the best locations in the city, overlooking the harbor yet just steps from the rest of Uptown by street or the indoor walkway. Windows in guest rooms open, allowing sea breezes in. Hilton Saint John is connected to the city's convention center, so attracts large groups and lots of associated events; ask if anything is scheduled if you don't want to be overwhelmed. Their lounge offers light meals until midnight. The main dining room serves more refined food in an understated harborside setting nightly.

1 Market Sq., Saint John, NB E2L 4Z6. www.hiltonsaintjohn.com. ℭ **800/561-8282** in Canada, 800/445-8667 in the U.S., or 506/693-8484. Fax 509/657-6610. 197 units. C$119–C$219 double. AE, DC, DISC, MC, V. Self-parking C$17 per night. Pets allowed. **Amenities:** Restaurant; lounge; concierge; fitness room; indoor pool; 24-hr. room service. In room: A/C, TV, hair dryer, minibar, Wi-Fi (free in executive rooms, otherwise paid).

Homeport Historic Bed & Breakfast ★★ ☺
This architecturally impressive home, built by a prominent shipbuilding family, sits high atop a rocky ridge north of Route 1, overlooking downtown and the harbor. Built around 1858—that's before Canada was even Canada yet—it's one of southern New Brunswick's best options for an overnight if you're a fan of old houses. The Veranda Room is spacious, with fine harbor views, walls decorated with steel engravings, floors of hand-cut pine, and locally made antique furniture. The Harbour Master Suite has a four-poster bed and small sitting room good for those traveling with a child or two. All units have individually controlled heat—a rarity in small inns. Breakfasts are served family-style around a long antique table in the dining room.

80 Douglas Ave. (take exit 121 or 123 to Main St.), Saint John, NB E2K 1E4. www.homeport.nb.ca. ℭ **888/678-7678** or 506/672-7255. 10 units. C$109–C$175 double and suite. Rates include full breakfast. AE, MC, V. Free parking. In room: A/C, TV, fridge (1 unit), kitchenette (1 unit), Wi-Fi (free, although coverage might not be the best in some rooms—ask for a good spot).

Inn on the Cove & Spa ★★
This is a lovely inn in a pretty setting, overlooking the ocean, about a 15-minute drive from downtown Saint John. The house, built in 1910, was once a classic late Victorian; subsequent changes to the architecture created bright, spacious rooms that take full advantage of the terrific views. Some rooms offer decks. All guests can enjoy the wonderful view while bathing in the privacy of their room; two-person Jacuzzi or Air Tubs sit in front of a full picture window overlooking the Bay of Fundy. Meals are excellent, and there's a highly rated day spa offering mud wraps and facials for an extra charge. The wonderful Irving Nature Park (see "Outdoor Pursuits," above) is next door, so guests can hike right from the inn to dramatic Sheldon's Point.

1371 Sand Cove Rd., Saint John, NB E2M 4X7. www.innonthecove.com. ℭ **877/257-8080** or 506/672-7799. 7 units. Late June to mid-Oct C$165–C$225 double; spring and fall C$135–C$195 double; winter C$99–C$135 double. Rates include breakfast. MC, V. Pets allowed in 2 garden rooms with access to the yard. Children 12 and up welcome. **Amenities:** Restaurant; spa. In room: A/C, TV/DVD, hair dryer, Internet and Wi-Fi (free).

MODERATE

Earle of Leinster "Inn Style" Bed & Breakfast ⚑
This handsome Victorian row house in a working-class neighborhood not far from King's Square is welcoming and

casual rather than fancy. It feels like a small European hotel and its uptown location is a bonus. There's a kitchen for guests, plus a pool table and TV in the basement. The Fitzgerald and Lord Edward rooms in the main house are the most historic, with high ceilings and regal furniture; most of the rest are out in the carriage house and feel motel-like, though a second-floor loft is quite spacious and some units resemble minisuites with their microwave ovens. Bathrooms, while private, are on the small side.

96 Leinster St., Saint John, NB E2L 1J3. www.earleofleinster.com. ℂ **506/652-3275.** 7 units. C$89–C$115 double. Rates include full breakfast. AE, DC, MC, V. *In room:* TV/VCR, fridge, microwave, Wi-Fi (free).

Where to Eat

For lunch, don't overlook Saint John's **city market** (see above)—grab a light meal and some fresh juice to go, then eat it either in the alley atrium or right on King's Square.

Billy's Seafood Company ★★ ☺ SEAFOOD   It's not fancy but it's not a dive; it's just right. Billy Grant's seafood eatery off King's Square gets big points for its friendly staff, fresh-off-the-boat seafood (they sell it to City Market customers during the day), better pricing than the tourist-oriented seafood restaurants on the water-front, and great attitude toward kids. They really know how to cook fish here without *over*cooking it. Specialties of the house include cedar-planked salmon, Billy's bouil-labaisse, and delicious lighter entrees: lobster rolls, oysters-and-chips, and a chicken breast club sandwich. They also serve steak, pasta, and even a rack of lamb if you're somehow not in the mood for fish.

49–51 Charlotte St. (at City Market). www.billysseafood.com. ℂ **888/933-3474** or 506/672-3474. Reservations suggested. Entrees C$8–C$29. AE, DC, MC, V. Mon–Thurs 11am–10pm; Fri–Sat 11am–11pm. Closed Sun.

Lily's Café ★ 🍴 ECLECTIC CANADIAN   There is a feeling of going off for a relaxing visit to the cottage at this cafe on Lily's Lake in Rockwood Park. During the summer, soaking up the sun on the lakeside deck is almost as nice as the cozy ambi-ence of a massive stone fireplace in winter. The chef offers a few traditional favorites, like Guinness beef stew and turkey dinners, then goes wild with an eclectic mix on the rest of the menu, from entrees like maple curry chicken or lobster crepe to a col-lection of pizzas, pub grub, and munchies. Paninis tickled our taste buds on the lunch menu, as did a collection of salads. One of the joys of Lily's is its status as a nonprofit organization that returns profits to the community. There are a number of activities year-round, thanks to the presence of Rockwood Park, including pond hockey, bike rentals, and even a soapbox derby.

The Lily Lake Pavilion, 55 Lake Dr. S. www.lilylake.ca/lilyscafe.html. ℂ **506/693-5033.** Dinner C$10–C$20; lunch C$7–C$14; weekend brunch C$7–C$10. AE, MC, V. Mon–Fri 11am–9pm; Sat 9am–9pm; Sun 9am–8pm.

Taco Pica ★ 🍴 LATIN AMERICAN   Here's something refreshingly different: a restaurant that's cooperatively owned by the chefs, servers, and managers, and some of their friends. (Its full name is "Taco Pica Worker Cooperative Restaurant.") It's bright, festive, and just a short stroll off King Street. The restaurant developed a devoted local following, thanks to a menu that's a notch above the usual staid local adaptations of Latin American and Mexican fare. Reliable dishes prepared here by the Guatemalan staff include *pepian* (a spicy beef stew with chayote); garlic shrimp; and shrimp tacos with potatoes, peppers, and cheese. Vegetarian items are available, as are a good variety of fresh juices and libations—fruit margaritas definitely put out the fire in a hot dish. ***Insiders' tip:*** There's sometimes a live guitarist at night, and the place even occasionally turns into an impromptu Latin-flavored dance club on weekend nights (after the dinner service, of course).

96 Germain St. ☎ **506/633-8492.** Reservations recommended on weekends. Main courses C$8–C$17. AE, MC, V. Mon–Sat 10am–10pm. Closed Sun and holidays.

Saint John After Dark

The best theater entertainment in town can be found at the **Imperial Theatre ★** (☎ **506/674-4100,** or 800/323-7469 from Maine and the Maritimes) on King's Square—not just because of the acts, but because of what the Toronto *Globe and Mail* called the "most beautifully restored theatre in Canada." It opened in 1913 and hosted such luminaries as Edgar Bergen, Al Jolson, and Walter Pidgeon (the latter a Saint John native). Driven out of business by movie houses, it served for a time as a Pentecostal church and was threatened with demolition. That's when concerned citizens stepped in. The Imperial reopened in 1994, and has since hosted a wide range of performances from Broadway road shows to local theater productions and music concerts. See the theater's website at www.imperialtheatre.nb.ca for performance schedules.

If you're looking to catch a big-time recording act passing through town, head for **Harbour Station** (www.harbourstation.nb.ca; ☎ **506/657-1234,** or 800/267-2800 from Maine or the Maritimes) at 99 Station St. The acts here run the gamut—during your stay in town, you might coincide with anyone from Mötley Crüe, WWE wrestling, and Brad Paisley (we'll pass) to pre-season hockey and Willie Nelson (we're in).

The rest of Saint John's nightlife revolves around the city's seemingly unending selection of **pubs,** most featuring live music and concentrated in the downtown district. Among the best is **O'Leary's on Princess,** a fun Irish pub at 46 Princess St. (☎ **506/634-7135**), where music on weekends and an open mic on Wednesdays are tradition. The rest are all more or less the same experience, and fit the bill if you want beer, music, iffy food, and noisy conviviality. For something a little different, try **Happinez Wine Bar** (☎ **506/634-7340**) at 42 Princess St.—a perfect spot for an intimate interlude for couples or friends.

A Road Trip to the Fundy Trail Parkway

Fundy Trail Parkway ★★ ☺ Less than an hour's drive from downtown Saint John, the amazing Fundy Trail Parkway is almost unknown outside New Brunswick. Get to know it. An ambitious multiuse trail that will eventually extend for 48km (30 miles) and link up with the Trans-Canada Trail, the parkway so far counts about 16km (10 miles) of hiking and biking trails—paralleled by about 11km (7 miles) of paved road for autos—all planned to show off the spectacular local bays and cliffs. The trail is wide and easy to hike or bike, with wheelchair-accessible pullouts that have spectacular coastal views; side trails lead to various beaches, some of which can only be reached at low tide. Admission is the same for cars or bikes. You can also catch a free shuttle (with paid admission) that stops at each of nine parking lots, and there are even water stations and picnic tables spaced out along the way. The interpretive center has interesting displays, but don't linger: The real thing is much better. Two-hour guided tours are offered (weekdays only) for C$4 per person in summer, while a half-day foliage tour is C$40 for adults and C$20 per child; you can rent bikes for C$40 per day.

If you want to stay overnight on the trail, you can. The **Hearst Lodge,** built by the newspaper magnate, is a rustic cabin about a 1-hour (3km/2-mile) hike off the trail.

Saint John is located at the mouth of the river known as the Rhine of Canada, which dissects the province north to the French-speaking Republic of Madawaska, a region near the Québec border with a unique heritage, customs, and dialect. The St. John River Heritage Corridor has four regions: Lower River Passage, Capital, River Valley, and Madawaska. Each has an official visitors' guide that will enhance any road trip to this region. If you enjoy exploring roads less traveled, without completely entering the wilderness, consider exploring this great river and the communities that surround it. Consider one often overlooked area, north of Fredericton. The road to Edmundston takes you past several worthwhile stops: Hartland, home of the world's longest covered bridge; Florenceville-Bristol, French Fry Capital of the World with a natty potato museum; Grand Falls, with its gorge and waterfall, where you can ride the zip line for a bird's-eye view, hike and climb to the "Wells in the Rocks," or take a lazy ride on a pontoon boat. Edmundston itself has a fine botanical garden. This region surrounded by the Appalachian Mountains is the heart of Madawaska. For other activities in the Heritage Corridor, read on.

Open June through September for C$99 per person double occupancy, breakfast and dinner included.

Serious hikers can pick up the Fundy Footpath, a challenging 41km (25-mile) wilderness trail; it crosses one of the last remaining coastal wilderness areas between Florida and Labrador. Plan for 4 days, with primitive campsites and challenging terrain. No permit is required; however, you must register and obtain maps at the Interpretive Centre in Big Salmon River (C$20, C$23 if mailed to you). You can hike in the off season but will have an additional 10km (6 miles) to get to the gate.

Rte. 111 (at St. Martins) 229 Main St. www.fundytrailparkway.com. © **866/386-3987** or 506/833-2019. Day pass C$5 adult, C$4.50 senior, C$3.50 child 12 and under, C$20 family. AE, MC, V. Mid-May to mid-Oct trail gates daily 6am–8pm, interpretive center from 8am. Take Rte. 111 east; entrance is 10km (6¼ miles) east of St. Martins (watch for signs). Leashed dogs allowed.

FREDERICTON

It is all too easy to overlook New Brunswick's riverside capital city. The Trans-Canada skirts around it, and it isn't located in either of the province's magnificent coastal regions. But it does have its own unique charm. Nestled along the shores of the mighty St. John River, Fredericton likes to refer to itself as Atlantic Canada's riverfront capital. With a population of just 50,000 (not including its 'burbs), the city's handsome buildings, broad streets, and wide sidewalks make the place feel more like a big village than a small city. If your passions include history—especially the history of British settlements in North America—Fredericton's well worth the detour.

Lower Fredericton, along the river, is considered the downtown area, and is the most pleasing for visitors with its mix of heritage and modern buildings, restaurants, and nightlife. The main artery—where you'll find the bulk of the attractions and restaurants—is **Queen Street,** which parallels the river. The **Green,** a pathway that follows the river, protects the river's edge from development and provides a great place for walkers and bicyclists. In the summer, several hotels have lovely patios

Fredericton

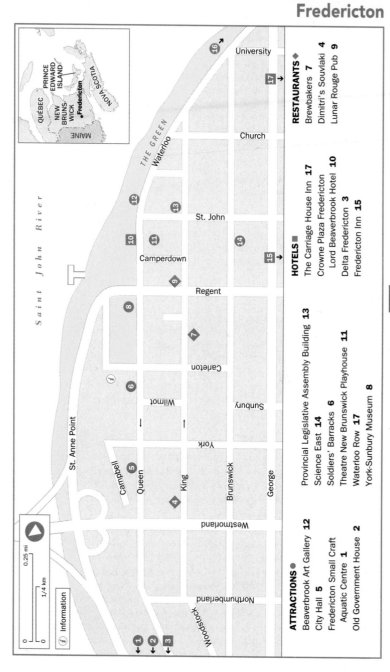

University

THE GREEN
Waterloo

Church

Saint John River

St. John

Camperdown

Regent

St. Anne Point

Carleton

Wilmot

Sunbury

York

Campbell
Queen

King

Brunswick

George

Westmorland

Northumberland

Woodstock

0   0.25 mi
0   1/4 km
ⓘ Information

ATTRACTIONS ●
Beaverbrook Art Gallery **12**
City Hall **5**
Fredericton Small Craft
  Aquatic Centre **1**
Old Government House **2**

Provincial Legislative Assembly Building **13**
Science East **14**
Soldiers' Barracks **6**
Theatre New Brunswick Playhouse **11**
Waterloo Row **17**
York-Sunbury Museum **8**

HOTELS ■
The Carriage House Inn **17**
Crowne Plaza Fredericton
  Lord Beaverbrook Hotel **10**
Delta Fredericton **3**
Fredericton Inn **15**

RESTAURANTS ◆
Brewbakers **7**
Dimitri's Souvlaki **4**
Lunar Rouge Pub **9**

QUÉBEC
NEW BRUNSWICK
MAINE
PRINCE EDWARD ISLAND
NOVA SCOTIA
●Fredericton

5

NEW BRUNSWICK | Fredericton

173

Surprisingly, Fredericton has been named one of the most wired cities in all of North America; it's easier to find a free (and legal) hotspot with a laptop than it is in New York City or San Francisco. That's thanks to the 2003 installation of a citywide Wi-Fi network. Known by the odd name of **Fred-e-Zone** (www.fredezone.ca), the city's network offers numerous access points—not only downtown, but at the local airport, in shopping malls, even in parks and sports arenas. Fredericton was the first city in Canada to offer such a service, and while coverage isn't guaranteed on *every* street corner, it is available in most of the downtown. And it's *free*.

overlooking the river, a nice break when exploring historic areas, art galleries, and the magic of downtown.

Up the hill from downtown, away from the river, a charming area ruled over by the Georgian-style University, parks, and residential areas serves as a buffer zone between the quiet, genteel downtown and the hustle and bustle at the top of the hills, near the main highways, where shopping malls, motels, small industry, and services are found.

5 Essentials

GETTING THERE Located beside the Trans-Canada Highway, Route 2, linking the Maritimes to the rest of Canada, Fredericton is 265km (165 miles) from Edmundston, to the northwest, near the Québec border. From Saint John to the south, it's only about 112km (70 miles) via Route 7. From the U.S.-Canadian border at Houlton, Maine, it's about the same distance: Take Route 95 to Woodstock, New Brunswick, then turn onto the Trans-Canada Highway and follow it east for an hour. Look for signs directing you downtown. (From the west, follow Woodstock Road, which tracks along the river. From Saint John, look for Route 7 to Regent Street, and then turn right down the hill.)

Fredericton International Airport (www.frederictonairport.ca; © **506/460-0920**), coded YFC, is located 10 minutes southeast of downtown on Route 102 and is served by cab and rental-car companies. For flight information, contact **Air Canada** (www.aircanada.com; © **888/247-2262**), which is basically the only carrier here. The airline connects Fredericton daily with Montréal, Ottawa, Halifax, and Toronto with nonstop direct flights.

VISITOR INFORMATION Always careful to cater to visitors, Fredericton maintains several central visitor information centers. There's one in **City Hall** at 397 Queen St. (© **506/460-2129**), open May through October; one in an Irving Big Stop gas station, near the airport; and a third at **King's Landing** (© **506/460-2191**), at 5804 Rte. 102. Another is just west of town in River Valley, open mid-May through early October. No matter which one you visit, ask for a Visitor Parking Pass, which allows visitors from outside the province to park free at city lots and meters in town for several days without penalty. Fredericton's tourism office is open year-round at 11 Carleton St. You can also request travel information in advance by visiting the city's website at www.tourismfredericton.ca or by calling © **888/888-4768** or 506/460-2129.

Exploring Fredericton

The free *Fredericton Visitor Guide,* available at the information centers and many hotels around town, includes a well-written and informative **walking tour** of the downtown area, as well as several driving tours. It's worth tracking down before exploring the city and surroundings.

City Hall, at 397 Queen St., is an elaborate Victorian building with a prominent brick tower and a 2.5m (8-ft.) clock dial. The second-floor City Council Chamber occupies what used to be Fredericton's opera house until the 1940s. Tapestries adorning the **visitor's gallery** tell the town's history. Learn about these tapestries—and the rest of the building—during free tours, offered twice daily from mid-May through mid-October (both in English and French). Contact the tourism office (𝄐 506/460-2129) to arrange a tour.

For visitors, the **Historic Garrison District** is a must. This National Historic Site sits behind a wrought iron-and-stone fence and covers a 2-block area between Queen Street and the river. There are all kinds of activities and things to see here—all free. Check out a visitor center or www.HistoricGarrisonDistrict.ca to see what is happening, or just drop by.

Officers' Square, on Queen Street between Carleton and Regent streets, is a handsome city park now, but in 1785 it was the center of the city's military activity; it was chiefly used for drills, first as part of the British garrison and then, until 1914, by the Canadian Army. Today, a changing of the guard ceremony and daily outdoor theater happen during the summer, as well as a variety of festivals and events throughout the year. (In winter, the square becomes a magical outdoor skating rink.). That handsome colonnaded stone building facing the parade grounds is the former officers' quarters, now the **York-Sunbury Museum** (see below).

In the center of the square, there's a prominent statue of a robed Lord Beaverbrook. It's a name you hear a lot in Fredericton—a street, a museum, and a hotel also bear his name—though it wasn't actually his name; he was born Max Aitken in Newcastle, New Brunswick. Aitken amassed a fortune, primarily in publishing, during his life and was made a lord in Britain in 1917, using the name of a stream near Newcastle where he had fished as a boy. Aitken later donated an art collection and a modern building to house it in (the Beaverbrook Art Gallery), along with a modern playhouse, now home to the **Theatre New Brunswick,** built the same year Beaverbrook died (1964).

Two blocks upriver from Officers' Square are the Soldiers' Barracks, housed in a similarly grand stone building. Check your watch against a sundial high on the end of the barracks, a replica of the original timepiece. A small exhibit explains the life of enlisted men during the 18th century.

Fredericton is well noted for its distinctive architecture, especially its neighborhoods of fine Victorian and Queen Anne residences. Particularly attractive is **Waterloo Row ★**, a group of privately owned historic homes just south of the downtown area. Follow the river bank south (near the University of New Brunswick).

One entertaining and enlightening way to learn about the city's history is to sign up for a walking tour with the **Calithumpians Theatre Company ★**. Costumed guides offer free tours in July and August, pointing out highlights with anecdotes and dramatic tales. Recommended is the nighttime "Haunted Hike" tour, done by lantern light, which runs 6 nights each week (no Sunday tours). The tour takes about 2 hours and costs C$13 for adults, C$8 for children; meet at the Coach House at the corner of Church and Queen streets (behind Gallery 78). Call the theater company at 𝄐 **506/457-1975** for more information.

If you're in town on a Saturday, do not miss the **Boyce Farmers' Market** ★ (www.frederictonfarmersmarket.ca; ℂ **506/451-1815**) at 665 George St. (corner of Regent St.)—it's adjacent to **Science East** (see below). This award-winning market, which runs from about 6am until about 1pm, has existed here in one form or another since the late 18th century (although the current building was constructed in the 1950s, and later expanded). Something approaching 250 indoor and outdoor vendors—butchers, bakers, even some candlestick makers—still hawk everything from fresh produce to crafts, croissants, and artisanal smoked meats, just as they always have done. *Harrowsmith* magazine once selected this market as one of the top farmer's markets in Canada. It's well worth an hour of your Saturday morning.

Also, don't miss any event hosted by the local artists' co-op **Gallery Connexion** (www.galleryconnexion.ca; ℂ **506/454-1433**) at 440 York St. The collective presents talks, video artworks, exhibitions, musical performances, and other events. Check the website or call the gallery office, located (for now) at the Fredericton Playhouse.

Outdoor Pursuits

Fredericton's trail system for walkers and bikers includes 85km (52 miles) of trails. The centerpiece is undeniably the **Green** ★, a 5km (3-mile) path that follows the river from the Delta hotel (see "Where to Stay," below) to near the Princess Margaret Bridge. It's a lovely walk, and passes by most of the city's key sightseeing points: the **Old Government House** (see below), the downtown area, and open parklands near Waterloo Row.

Connecting with the Green a well-used pedestrian bridge crosses the St. John River using an abandoned railroad trestle just east of downtown. From this vantage point, you get great views of downtown and the surrounding river valley. If you continue, the **Nashwaak/Marysville Trail** ★ follows an abandoned rail bed along the attractive Nashwaak River; after about 4km (2.5 miles) you can cross the river at Bridge Street and loop back to the pedestrian rail bridge via the 5km (3-mile) **Gibson Trail.**

A number of other trails link up to this network, as well. A free trail guide is available at the information centers, or contact the **New Brunswick Trails Council** (ℂ **800/526-7070**), which builds and maintains bridges and trails throughout the system.

Bikes may be rented by the hour or the day until the snow flies at both the River Trails Bike Rentals & Tours at the **Lighthouse Adventure Centre** (www.lighthouseonthegreen.ca; ℂ **506/476-7368**), 615 Queen St., near **Regent St. Wharf** in the Fredericton Lighthouse, and at **Radical Edge,** 129 Westmorland St. (www.radicaledge.ca; ℂ **506/459-1449**). Figure C$25 per day or C$7.50 per hour for a rental.

An option for getting on the water is the **Small Craft Aquatic Centre** on Woodstock Road (behind the Victoria Health Centre and near the Old Government House; www.fredericton.ca/en/recleisure/smallcraftaquaticcentre.asp; ℂ **506/460-2260**). It's open daily from the middle of May to early October and rents rowing shells, canoes, and kayaks. Also ask about naturalist-guided tours of the river. There are many other opportunities to get on the river as well, including houseboat rentals, pontoon boat tours, and tubing. Ask at the Visitor Centre.

Finally, the **Kingswood** golf course (www.kingswoodpark.com/golf.php; ℂ **800/423-5969** or 506/443-3333) is among the province's finest. It consists of 27 holes, a par-3 course, and a driving range. Greens fees for 18 holes run from C$49 to C$89.

Attractions Downtown

Beaverbrook Art Gallery ★ 🖌 Even if you don't fancy yourself an art lover, you will get lost for hours gazing at the works here. This surprisingly impressive gallery, just steps from the Historic Garrison District, is home to an extensive collection of British paintings, including works by Reynolds, Gainsborough, Constable, and Turner. Antiques buffs gravitate to the rooms with period furnishings and early decorative arts, while others find themselves drawn to Dalí's massive *Santiago El Grande*. Exhibits of modern art are increasing. Other shows have touched on more conventional ground, such as 19th-century French realism and the cities of Canada drawn from the Seagram Collection. This gallery is especially strong when showing the art of First Nations (native Canadian) artists. Stop by, or check the website, to find out what's currently on display.

703 Queen St. www.beaverbrookartgallery.org. 🕐 **506/458-2028.** Admission C$8 adults, C$6 seniors, C$3 students, C$18 families; Thurs evenings after 5:30pm pay what you wish. Tues–Wed and Sat 9am–5:30pm; Thurs 9am–9pm; Sun noon to 5:30pm. Closed Mon Jan–May.

Old Government House ★ Government House, constructed in 1828, was built as the official residence of the lieutenant governor and governor of the province of locally quarried sandstone in a rigorously classical style. It features a Palladian symmetry and intricate plasterwork. Over time it has housed a school, a military hospital, and a detachment of Mounties. Spared from the wrecking ball, the home was restored and reopened in 1999, and is now once again the official residence of the lieutenant governor, who has an apartment and an office here. Bilingual tours begin in the interpretive center and last about 45 minutes. You hike sweeping staircases and view extraordinarily high-ceilinged reception rooms; there's an art gallery on the second floor, and the rooms are full of intriguing period pieces and fixtures. Ask the helpful guides anything.

51 Woodstock Rd. www.gnb.ca/lg/ogh. 🕐 **506/453-2505.** Free admission. Mid May to Aug tours Mon–Sat 10am–4pm and Sun noon–4pm; off season by appointment only.

Provincial Legislative Assembly Building ★ New Brunswick's official Assembly Building, built in 1880, boasts an exterior in Second Empire style, but the dressed-up interior is the star. The assembly chamber itself nearly takes your breath away, especially when viewed from the visitor gallery on the upper floors. If you're visiting when the legislature is not in session you can take pictures; if in session you can watch the elected officials in action. Half-hour-long tours are available; plan to spend at least an hour here if you really love old buildings.

706 Queen St. (across from the Beaverbrook Art Gallery). www.gnb.ca/legis. 🕐 **506/453-2506.** Free admission. June to mid-Aug daily 9am–5pm.

Science East ★★ ☺ Children usually enjoy a visit to this science center for two reasons. First, it's located in an old jail, a sturdy stone structure built in the 1840s (and used as a jail as late as 1996). Then there are great exhibits: more than 150 interactive displays. Kids can fool around with a huge kaleidoscope, use a periscope to people-watch, check out a solar-powered water fountain, make patterns with a laser beam, even create a miniature tornado—though, truth be told, the dungeon museum probably will impress them more than all that. It's an ideal place to visit with the kids on a chilly or rainy day, and there's a lot to do on nice days, too. A human gyroscope and climbing wall are part of an outdoor science playground, and there are science shows twice daily in summer. This is one of Canada's preeminent science museums, and if you have kids with a spark of curiosity, this place is easily worth up to 4 hours of your time.

668 Brunswick St. www.scienceeast.nb.ca. ⓒ **506/457-2340.** Admission C$8 adults, C$7 seniors, C$5 children 16 and under or students, C$22 families. June–Aug Mon–Sat 10am–5pm, Sun noon–4pm; rest of the year, Mon–Fri noon–5pm, Sat 10am–5pm, closed Sun.

York-Sunbury Museum ☺ This small museum lures visitors with the promise of a stuffed 42-pound frog, supposedly fattened on a diet of June bugs, cornmeal, buttermilk, and whiskey, known throughout the province as the Coleman Frog (for its supposed owner). Displays feature over 30,000 artifacts, including many from former aboriginal, Acadian, and Loyalist inhabitants of the area. And kids might like the claustrophobically re-created World War II trench on the second floor. The building, the former Officers' Quarters, built in 1853, faces the old Parade Square.

571 Queen St. near Regent St. www.yorksunburymuseum.com. ⓒ **506/455-6041.** Admission C$5 adults, C$2 students, C$10 families. July–Aug Mon–Sat 10am–5pm, Sun noon–5pm; Apr–June and Sept–Nov Tues–Sat 1–4pm. Closed Dec–Mar.

Attractions Outside of Town

Kings Landing Historical Settlement ★★ ☺ The huge (121-hectare/300-acre) site on the banks of the St. John River, about 32km (20 miles) from Fredericton, is a living museum that depicts the evolution of life in rural New Brunswick from the era of the Loyalists to the late Victorians. Rescued buildings and artifacts span from the 1820s to the 1920s: children play in the orchard, women stir pots in kitchens, men labor in fields or at trades, each home and trade restored to a different time period. Interpreters stay in character, performing tasks and depicting the lives of Scots, Irish, and English settlers. What's most impressive? It feels real. The transition from the Loyalist 1860s Joslin Farm to a 1900s carpenter shop to a 1830s cabin of an Irish immigrant works because the artifacts and the people have been so well chosen to reflect their era. To complete your experience, partake of the Bill of Fare served at the King's Head Inn (see below).

You could spend two full days if you want to really immerse yourself in the past, but realistically most people should plan for 4 to 8 hours. Watch for special events: the popular Pauper Auction, Duel & Trial, a literary festival, or Christmas Dinner. Begin your visit at the Information Centre with an introduction, grab your map, and head out to explore. There's a horse-drawn wagon, but walking is best for meeting people and truly seeing the settlement. It's all uphill coming back, so the ride is most appreciated then.

If vacation learning appeals, time your visit with the Heritage Workshops held in the summer: Topics include Herbs and Medicine, Open Hearth Baking, Quilting, Rug Hooking, and 19th Century Trades. Children (ages 9-15) have a chance to actually live in the past for week through the Visiting Cousins and Family Kin programs.

5804 Rte. 102, Prince William (exit 253 off the Trans-Canada Hwy., on Rte. 2 west). www.kingslanding.nb.ca. ⓒ **506/363-4999.** Admission C$16 adults, C$14 seniors, C$13 students 17 and over, C$11 children 6–16, C$38 families. June to mid-Oct daily 10am–5pm. Closed mid-Oct to May.

Shopping

Fredericton is home to a growing number of artists and artisans, as well as entrepreneurs who have launched a handful of offbeat shops. If you love collectible, rare, or used books, check out Queen and King Streets between Wilmont Alley and York Street, in the downtown core. It's worth setting aside an hour or two for browsing.

Aitkens Pewter   This well-known shop sells classically designed pewter dishes and mugs based on historical patterns, as well as modern adaptations and jewelry, at a downtown shop. Walk-through tours of the actual pewter work studio (in an industrial park, about 9km/6 miles southeast of the city center) are also allowed, twice per day, on weekdays. 408 Queen St. ✆ **800/567-4416** or 506/453-9474; studio 450-8188.

Cultures Boutique   This is one of a chain of YMCA-run shops that promote alternative trade to benefit craftspeople in the Third World. Look for goods from foreign lands as well as North American native cultures, mostly from community-based cooperatives. 383 Mazzucca Lane (off York St. btw. King and Queen). ✆ **506/462-3088.**

Gallery 78   In a handsome Queen Anne–style mansion with a pointy turret, you can find one of the province's oldest private art galleries. The sunny spaces upstairs and down showcase a range of regional art, much of it sold at affordable prices, from talented local painters, sculptors, printmakers, and photographers. It's closed Mondays. 796 Queen St. (near the Beaverbrook Art Gallery). ✆ **506/454-5192.**

The Barracks Fine Craft Shops   Artisans sell their ware in the historic district at the lower level of the Soldier's Barracks. They create, demonstrate, and sell their handmade, one-of-a-kind items from June to September. Corner of Carleton and Queen sts. ✆ **506/460-2837.**

The Kings Landing Gift Shop   A wide selection of handcrafted items, quilts, wooden ware, pottery, and jewelry—as well as homemade jams, jellies, and maple products—are carried here. History and how-to books are noteworthy. 5804 Rte. 102 in Prince William. ✆ **506/363-4999.** Open June to early Oct.

Where to Stay

In addition to the properties listed below, a clutch of motels and chain hotels are bunched up in a bustling mall zone on the hillside above town (along Regent and Prospect sts.), about 10 minutes' drive from downtown.

The dependable local entrant in this pack is the **Fredericton Inn,** 1315 Regent St. (✆ **800/561-8777** or 506/455-1430), situated in between two malls. It's a typical soothing-music-and-floral-carpeting sort of place that does a brisk business in the convention trade. But with its indoor pool, nice little whirlpool, and surprising fitness center, it's an adequate overnight stay for vacation travelers, as well—and the price is right. Peak season rates run from C$119 to C$139 for a double room, up to C$199 for an apartment or suite.

The Carriage House Inn ★ 🛏   Fredericton's premier B&B is a short stroll from the riverfront pathway, in a quiet residential neighborhood—and B&B travelers love it. A former mayor and local lumber baron built the imposing three-story Victorian home in 1875; inside, it's all dark wood trim, deep colors, floral-printed sofas, and a few steep stairs. Rooms—nine with a queen-size bed, one with a double and a single—are furnished with period art and antiques; some public areas have so many artifacts, you feel you're inside a museum instead of a hotel. Delicious, big breakfasts are included with the rate; they're served in the sunny ballroom at the rear of the mansion by bilingual hosts, who get raves far and wide for their hospitality. Not a luxury inn, but very restful if you're the sort who doesn't mind sleeping in historic old homes. It's open year-round.

230 University Ave., Fredericton, NB E3B 4H7. www.carriagehouse-inn.net. ✆ **800/267-6068** or 506/452-9924. Fax 506/452-2770. 10 units. C$99–C$129 double. Rates include full breakfast. AE, MC, V. **Amenities:** Restaurant. *In room:* A/C, TV, hair dryer, Wi-Fi (free).

Crowne Plaza Fredericton Lord Beaverbrook Hotel ★ ☺ This water-front hotel looks boxy and dour from the street. But inside, the mood lightens, thanks to interesting composite stone floors, Georgian pilasters, and happy chandeliers. The indoor pool and recreation area downstairs are positively whimsical, a sort of tiki-room grotto motif that kids love. Guest rooms are appointed with traditional repro-duction furniture in dark wood—freshened up since Crowne Plaza acquired the property—though the standard, lowest-priced rooms can be somewhat dim and most windows don't open (ask for a room with windows that do open if that's important to you). However, the suites here are spacious, and many have excellent river views. Some Jacuzzi suites have now been added, but this is still an old-fashioned hotel at its heart. There are several choices for dining: The Terrace Room is the main dining area, with a deck overlooking the river. The more intimate Governor's Room strives for fine-dining superiority with a modern take on French classics, a chef's tasting menu and a specialty reserved wine list. Finally, the Maverick lets you select your cut of beef, then grills it to your specs while a Caesar salad is made at your table.

659 Queen St., Fredericton, NB E3B 5A6. www.cpfredericton.com. ⓒ **877/579-7666** or 506/455-3371. Fax 506/455-1441. 168 units (12 deluxe suites). C$109–C$199 double; suites up to C$599. Packages available. AE, DC, MC, V. **Amenities:** 3 restaurants; babysitting; Jacuzzi; indoor pool; sauna. In room: A/C, TV, hair dryer, Wi-Fi (free).

Delta Fredericton ★★ This urban-resort hotel, built in 1992, occupies a prime location on the river about a 10-minute walk from downtown via the riverfront pathway. In summer, life revolves around an outdoor pool (with its own poolside bar) on a deck overlooking the river. On Sundays, the lobby is taken over by an over-the-top brunch buffet. Though obviously up to date, the Delta's interior is done with classical styling; some suites are positively huge, and some come with Jacuzzis and river balconies. The hotel's lounge is an active and popular nightspot, especially on weekends. **Bruno's** is a good alternative to the restaurants downtown. The chef usually cooks with whatever's fresh; look for seasonal and regional specialties (even fiddleheads in early summer), local vegetables and fruits in season, and good steaks. They claim to like unique requests and will cook to your specific needs; nice for those with dietary restrictions.

225 Woodstock Rd., Fredericton, NB E3B 2H8. www.deltafredericton.com. ⓒ **888/462-8800** or 506/457-7000. Fax 506/457-7000. 222 units. C$119–C$219 double; suites C$249–C$800. AE, DC, MC, V. Free parking. Pets accepted. **Amenities:** Restaurant; 2 bars; babysitting; bike and kayak rentals; fitness room; Jacuzzi; heated indoor pool and heated outdoor pool; sauna; spa. In room: A/C, TV, fridge (some units), hair dryer, minibar, Jacuzzi (some units), Wi-Fi and Internet (free).

Hartt Island River Valley RV Resort Tent and RV sites are clean and spa-cious, located on the banks of the St. John River, and conveniently located just minutes from downtown. There is access to the river for boating, as well as evening guided boat tours, tube rides, and canoes and kayaks for those who want to explore this unique chain of islands. There are also riverside biking and hiking trails that go into the city. Washrooms and other facilities are in need of an upgrade, but the water park's pool and slides are great for kids.

2475 Woodstock Rd, Rte. 105, Fredericton E3C 1P6. www.harttisland.com. ⓒ **866/462-9400** or 506/462-9400. C$29-C$45 May–Oct. **Amenities**: Pools; some watersports equipment rentals; minigolf; dairy bar or canteen; playground.

On the Pond Country Retreat & Spa ★ 🎒 Billing itself as a wilderness lodge, On the Pond is located just 15 minutes out of Fredericton. Nestled in a lovely woodland setting overlooking the St. John River, it is designed in the tradition of a fine country inn. Guests can take spa treatments and also enjoy the adjacent Mactaquac Provincial Park's natural beauty, beaches, nature trails, and marina. The lodge itself is lovely. Two downstairs common rooms—one with a wood fireplace, one lined with bookshelves, lure guests to hang out and mingle. Guest rooms upstairs feature queen-size beds and a woodland theme; they're a bit larger than your average hotel room, with nice extras. The spa is in the basement and offers massage, a hot tub, a sauna, an aesthetics room (manicures, pedicures, and facials), and a fitness center. There's also Wi-Fi access throughout.

Notably, the lodge sits on "The Arm"—an impoundment of the St. John River behind the nearby hydroelectric dam—in a marshy setting better for bird-watching than swimming. (Beach swimming is available across the road at the provincial park.) The Kings Landing Historical Settlement (see "Attractions Outside of Town," above) is nearby.

20 Scotch Settlement Rd. (Rte. 615), Mactaquac, NB E6L 1M2. www.onthepond.com. ✆ **800/984-2555** or 506/363-3420. 8 units. C$125–C$145 double. Packages available. MC, V. Drive west of Fredericton on Woodstock Rd.; cross Mactaquac Dam and continue to Esso station; turn right and look for sign on right. No children. **Amenities:** Jacuzzi; sauna; spa. *In room:* A/C, TV/VCR, hair dryer.

Where to Eat

You don't have to spend big bucks for good food in Fredericton, although you'll find a proliferation of tony eateries. Locals will tell you that the **Sunshine Diner** at 7 Brookmount, across from the Delta (✆ **506/458-8470**), or tiny the **Cabin Restaurant** at 723 Woodstock Rd. (✆ **506/459-0094**), serve great breakfast and lunch. You can't beat them for local home-style diner food in a casual setting.

Brewbakers ★★ MEDITERRANEAN   This is a fun pub, cafe, and restaurant on three levels in a cleverly adapted downtown building. It's a bustling and informal spot—a meeting spot of sorts—creatively cluttered with art and artifacts. Lunch hours and early evenings get very busy. The cafe section is quieter, as is a mezzanine dining room, while the third floor bustles with the open kitchen. Lunch features excellent sandwiches: smoked salmon, pulled pork, triple-cream Brie, and oven-roasted peppers with garlicky mayo are just samples. For dinner, pastas are the main attraction, as is haute cuisine (a maple-curry-chicken-cream pasta is just one offering). Other good nighttime choices: pizzas, pan-roasted scallops, strip loin, and herb-crusted tenderloin. The cocktail menu takes in some Asian- and martini-influenced libations.

546 King St. ✆ **506/459-0067.** Reservations recommended. Main courses C$10–C$19 at lunch, C$18–C$30 at dinner. AE, DC, MC, V. Mon–Thurs 11:30am–10pm; Fri 11:30am–11pm; Sat 4–11pm; Sun 4–10pm.

Dimitri's Souvlaki 🌶 GREEK   Dimitri's is hard to find and easy to walk past. But the generic, chain-restaurant interior belies decent cooking for budget-conscious diners. You'll get a big plate of food without spending a lot of money. Greek specialties include moussaka (with and without meat), souvlaki, and dolmades (rice-and-herb-stuffed grape leaves). Deluxe dinner plates are served with excellent potatoes—hearty wedges cooked crispy on the outside, yet hot and soft within.

349 King St. (in Piper's Lane area). ✆ **506/452-8882.** Main courses C$8–C$18. AE, DC, MC, V. Mon–Sat 11am–10pm.

King's Head Inn ★★ 🍴 TRADITIONAL CANADIAN   Great care is taken to ensure that everything you find here is appropriate to the 1850s, from the furnishings to costumed staff, fine food, and entertainment. Daily menu options include venison stew, skoodawabskoosis salad (a cold poached filet of fresh Atlantic salmon on a bed of garden greens with capers and slices of red onion, served with tarragon mayonnaise and a warm herb biscuit with butter), bang belly (made with fruits of the season served warm with whipped cream) and pies: buttermilk or maple-brandy-squash or Acadian sugar. Open daily during the season, they also do themed dinners around most holidays: Valentine's Day, Easter, Mother's Day, and so on. Reserve ahead, they sell out fast. You don't have to pay site admission if you just want a meal.

5804 Rte. 2, at King's Landing Historic Settlement, Prince William. www.kingslanding.nb.ca. ℂ **506/363-4999.** Main courses C$11–C$16; themed dinners C$25–C$35. AE, MC, V. June to early Oct 11:30am–5pm.

Fredericton After Dark

Being a university town insures a goodly number of nightclubs; you can find out what is currently happening where at www.clubzone.com/Fredericton. Downtown is often lively with university students and young professionals after hours. Your best bet is the **Lunar Rogue Pub ★★**, 625 King St. (ℂ **506/450-2065**), which features more than 100 single-malt whiskies, a dozen draft beers, and the requisite grub (mostly fried food and burgers) in a comfortable, pubby atmosphere. It was anointed "Greatest Whisky Bar in the World" by *Whisky* magazine, who should know what they're talking about. Its patio is popular in warm weather. The pub is open 9am to 1am weekdays, from 10am Saturdays and from 11am to 10pm Sundays.

   Dolan's Pub, 349 King St. (ℂ **506/454-7474**), is the place to go for live Maritime music, which is on tap most Thursdays through Saturdays. Also on tap is the city's largest selection of microbrews. It's open from lunchtime all the way until 2am.

Road Trip to Gagetown ★★

About 56km (35 miles) southeast of Fredericton is the village of **Gagetown,** a scenic driving detour en route to or from Saint John. (Don't confuse this with Canadian Forces Base Gagetown; it's up the road in Oromocto). Gagetown's been named one of the 10 prettiest villages in Canada, and has somehow remained largely unchanged through the years—still backed by farm fields on one side, and cozied up to by Gagetown Creek, a deep water anchorage off the St. John River, on another. The peaceful surroundings and simple country architecture have attracted craftspeople and artists, who have settled here and slowly made it over into a quiet arts colony—quaint and creative, but never annoyingly so. Look for low-key enterprises like art galleries, a decoy carver, bookstore, cider press, crafts cooperative, and several potters. **Creek View Restaurant** (www.thecreekviewrestaurant.com; ℂ **506/488-9806**) at 38 Tilley Rd. makes new use of a former 1900s automobile dealership. Memorabilia on the walls complements the country-style cuisine. We love this place: cornbread and molasses is C65¢, fiddleheads find their way into soup in season, and haddock is offered in a half-dozen ways. The menu will leave you laboring over what to choose.

   You can also **bird-watch** and explore; the region is noted for the avian life enjoying the local marshes, forests, and fields. (Nearly 150 species have been reliably identified rein and around Gagetown.) Where to do it? **Gagetown Island** is just offshore and easily accessible by kayak or canoe, which some local inns provide. The island features a glacial deposit that rises some 23m (75 ft.) high, plus the ruins of a stone house dating from the early 19th century. That's all nice, but birders go for the osprey-viewing platform. There are also two Ducks Unlimited marsh preserves with trails.

   While in town, drop by the **Queens County Museum** (www.queenscounty heritage.com; ℂ **506/488-2966**), birthplace of Sir Samuel Leonard Tilley, one of the fathers of Canadian Confederation. The 1786 home, located at 69 Front St., is open daily from mid-June to mid-September; admission costs C$3 per person, free for children 11 and under. You can also buy a pass (C$5–C$7, free for children) allowing access to several more historic homes including the Flower House and a simple courthouse.

If you want to stay the night, check with the simple bed-and-breakfast in town, the **Step Aside B&B** (© **506/488-1808**) at 58 Front St. Owners Elaine and Maurice Harquail maintain four rooms costing from C$70 to C$100 per night, and their inn's open year-round.

If Canadian military history is of interest, head up Route 102 to Oromocto, where the **CFB Gagetown Military Museum** (www.museumgagetown.ca/EngRNBR. htm; © **506/422-1304**) and the **Canadian Military Engineers Museum** (www. cmemuseum.ca; © **506/422-2000**) collect, preserve, and promote the country's military history. Both have free admission, lots of free parking, and are open year-round. Also of interest to military or World War II buffs, just 50km (31 miles) east of Fredericton on Route 10 in Minto, is the **New Brunswick Internment Camp Museum** (www.nbinternmentcampmuseum.ca; © **506/327-3573**) located on the site where prisoners of war (POWs) were detained. In its early days, the camp housed German and Austrian Jewish refugees, then later on German and Italian Merchant Marines, and even some Canadians who spoke out against the war effort.

FUNDY NATIONAL PARK ★★

The **Fundy Coast** (btw. Saint John and Alma) is for the most part wild, remote, and unpopulated. It's crisscrossed by few roads other than the Fundy Drive, making it difficult to explore deeply—unless you happen to have a boat with you, which I'm guessing you don't. The best access is at **Fundy National Park,** a gem of a destination that's hugely popular in summer with travelers of an outdoors bent. Families often settle in here for a week or so, filling their days with activities in and around the park such as hiking, sea kayaking, biking, and splashing around in a seaside pool.

One of the best aspects of a stay in Fundy Park is the activities and interpretation programs: outdoor theater presentations and concerts; guided paddles; bike hikes; forays to catch and count eels; fossil walks; even photo safaris. For kids there are bedtime stories and evenings gathered around the campfire, or looking for night birds, bats, and bugs. Pick up a schedule as you enter the park or check at the information center.

Nearby there are also some lovely drives, plus an innovative adventure center at **Cape Enrage.** You can even vary your adventuring according to the weather: if a muffling fog moves in and smothers the coastline (and it might), head inland for a hike to a waterfall through lush forest. If it's a day of brilliant sunshine, on the other hand, venture along the rocky shores by foot, bike, or boat, and bring a camera.

Essentials

GETTING THERE   Route 114 runs through the center of Fundy National Park. If you're coming from the west, follow the prominent national park signs just east of **Sussex.** If you're coming from Prince Edward Island or Nova Scotia, head southward on Route 114 from Moncton.

VISITOR INFORMATION   The park's main **Visitor Centre** (© **506/887-6000**) is located just inside the **Alma** (eastern) entrance to the park. The stone building is open daily during peak season from 8am to 10pm, and until 4:30pm the rest of the year. You can watch a video presentation, peruse a handful of exhibits on wildlife and tides, and shop at the nicely stocked nature bookstore. The smaller **Wolfe Lake Information Centre** (✆ **506/432-6026**) is at the park's western entrance; it's open until 6pm daily, from late June through late August.

The small town of **Alma** also maintains a seasonal information center at 8584 Main St. (✆ **506/887-6127**), open from late spring through September.

FEES   Park entry fees are charged from mid-May to mid-October. The fee is C$7.80 adults, C$6.80 seniors, C$3.90 children ages 6 to 16, and C$20 families. Seasonal and annual passes are also available.

Exploring Fundy National Park

Most national park activities are centered around the Alma (eastern) side of the park, where the park entrance has a cultivated and manicured air, as if part of a landed estate. Here you'll find stone walls, well-tended lawns, and attractive landscaping, along with a golf course, amphitheater, lawn bowling, and tennis.

Also in this area is a **heated saltwater pool,** set near the bay with a sweeping ocean view. There's a lifeguard on duty, and it's a popular destination for families. The pool is open from late June through early September. Entrance costs C$3.40 adults, C$2.90 seniors, C$1.65 children, and C$8.80 for families.

Canoes, rowboats, and kayaks can be rented at Bennett Lake for C$8 to C$12 an hour, and there are some guided events. Geocaching is a new activity at the park. Sea kayaking tours are a great way to get an up-close look at the marine environment here—but you want expert help when kayaking the world's highest tides. **FreshAir Adventure** (www.freshairadventure.com; ✆ **800/545-0020** or 506/887-2249) at 16 Fundy View Dr. in Alma offers tours that range from 2 hours to several days. The half-day tours explore marsh and coastline (C$52–C$64 per person, including snack); the full-day adventure includes a hot meal and 6 hours of exploring the wild shores (C$90–C$110 per person).

Birders are always pleased to learn that some 250-plus species have been sighted within park boundaries, and almost half of them breed here. Notably, the endangered peregrine falcon has been reintroduced to the bay's steep cliffs.

HIKING

The park maintains miles and miles of scenic trails for hikers and walkers, with good signage and stairs where necessary. These range from a 20-minute loop to a 4-hour trek, and pass through varied terrain. The trails are arranged such that several can be linked into a full 48km (30-mile) backpacker's loop, dubbed the **Fundy Circuit** (which typically requires 3–5 nights camping in the backcountry; pre-registration is required, so check in at the visitor center if you're serious about doing it).

Among the most accessible hikes is the **Caribou Plain Trail ★**, a 3km (2-mile) loop that provides a wonderful introduction to the local terrain. You hike along a beaver pond, across a raised peat bog via boardwalk, then through lovely temperate forest. Read the interpretive signs to learn about deadly "flarks" which lurk in bogs and can swallow a moose whole.

The **Third Vault Falls Trail ★★** is an 8km (5-mile), in-and-back hike that takes you to the park's highest waterfall (it's about 14m/46 ft. high). The trail is largely a flat stroll through leafy woodlands—until you begin a steady descent into a mossy gorge. You round a corner and there you are, suddenly facing the cataract. How cool is that?

All the park's trails are covered in the trail guide you'll you receive when you pay your entry fee at the gatehouse.

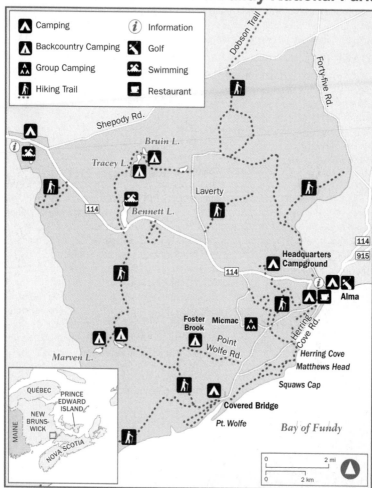

Legend:
- Camping
- Backcountry Camping
- Group Camping
- Hiking Trail
- Information
- Golf
- Swimming
- Restaurant

Dobson Trail

Forty-five Rd.

Shepody Rd.

Bruin L.

Tracey L.

Laverty

114

Bennett L.

Headquarters
Campground

114

114

915

Alma

Foster
Brook

Micmac

Point
Wolfe Rd.

Herring Cove Rd.

Marven L.

Herring Cove

Matthews Head

Squaws Cap

Covered Bridge

Pt. Wolfe

Bay of Fundy

QUÉBEC

PRINCE
EDWARD
ISLAND

NEW
BRUNS-
WICK

MAINE

NOVA SCOTIA

0   2 mi

0   2 km

BIKING

The roads east of Alma offer superb bicycling terrain, at least if you get off busy Route 114 and are in good shape. Especially appealing is **Route 915 ★** from Riverside-Albert to Alma; combined with a detour to Cape Enrage, it makes for lovely touring. Along this scenic road you'll pedal through rolling farmland and scattered settlements, past vistas of salt marshes (as well as the wonderfully named Ha Ha Cemetery). The hills here look low, but they get steep in spots and require a serious grind at times. Route 915 runs for about 27km (17 miles) in all; the detour to Cape Enrage adds about 13km (8 miles).

Also note that the park allows **mountain biking** on six trails: Goose River, Marven Lake, Black Hole, Bennett Brook (to the top of Point Wolfe valley), East Branch (must take right-hand side trail only, and return from river on same path), and Maple Grove. These first two trails are *steep*; be prepared.

Bike rentals have not been available in Alma in recent years, but check with the Alma visitor information center (see "Visitor Information," above) to see if the situation has changed. Otherwise, bikes can be rented in Saint John or Moncton.

CAMPING

The national park maintains three drive-in campgrounds and about 15 backcountry sites. The two main campgrounds are near the Alma entrance. **Headquarters Campground ★** is within walking distance of Alma, the saltwater pool, and numerous other attractions. Since it is near the bay, this campground tends to be cool and subject to fogs. **Chignecto North Campground ★** is higher on the hillside, sunnier, and warmer. You can hike down to Alma on an attractive hiking trail in 1 to 2 hours. Both campgrounds have hookups for RVs, flush toilets, and showers, and both can be reserved in advance online (www.pccamping.ca; 🕿 **877/737-3783**); sites cost C$16 to C$35 per night, depending on services offered. Rates drop in the shoulder seasons.

The **Point Wolfe** and **Wolfe Lake** campgrounds lack RV hookups and are slightly more primitive, but they are the preferred destinations for campers seeking a quieter camping experience. Rates at Point Wolfe, where showers and flush toilets are available, are about C$25 and it too can be reserved online via Canada's national parks campground website at www.pccamping.ca. Wolfe Lake lacks showers and has only pit toilets—thus a night there costs only about C$16. Call the park directly to reserve.

Backcountry sites are scattered throughout the park, with only one located directly on the coast (at the confluence of the coast and Goose River). Ask at the visitor centers for more information or to reserve a site (mandatory). Backcountry camping fees are about C$10 per person per night.

Before leaving the park, check the tide tables. Your visits to the next two sites are best made at low tide, or ideally, arrive at high tide and stay until it is totally out—or vice versa.

Road Trip to Cape Enrage ★★

Cape Enrage is a blustery and bold cape that juts out into Chignecto Bay. It's home to a wonderful adventure center that could be a model for centers worldwide. It costs C$15 for adults, C$4 seniors and students, C$2.75 children to enter the cape. There you'll find lots of places to explore and walk (including the sea bottom when the 15m/50-ft. tides are out), great views from platforms, a gift shop and an unexpectedly fine restaurant. The Cape Enrage Interpretive Centre is open from mid-May to mid-October, but the real draw here is its adventure center.

Tight Turns

The road in and out to Cape Enrage—which is actually a rocky island soaring up from marshes and tidal flats—is steep and narrow in places. RVs towing a car would be best advised to take the car in, or drop it in the upper parking area. The RV-designated area is tight for turning, and the road down steep.

Cape Enrage Adventures ★ traces its roots to 1993, when a group of high school students from Moncton decided to arrest the decay of the cape's historic lighthouse, which had been abandoned a few years earlier. They put together a plan to restore the light and keeper's quarters and establish an adventure center. And it worked. Today, with the help of experts in rock climbing, rappelling, and local

Mary's Point

On your way to Hopewell Rocks, take the loop road around Mary's Point. The coastal nature preserves are a stopover for migrating sea birds whose flight displays can be spectacular. At 255 Mary's Point Rd., the widow of Lars Larsen, one of Canada's premier wildlife artists, continues to operate **Studio on the Marsh** (www.studioonthemarsh.com; ☏ **506/882-2917**). Larsen's work and that of other fine artists is available at this lovely little gallery.

history, you can indulge in a day of adventure; appointments are needed for rappelling and rock climbing. Part of what makes the program so notable is its flexibility. You can pick and choose from day adventures, which are scheduled throughout the summer, as though from a menu. Prices vary; you might pay about C$78 per person for a 2-hour rock-climbing or rappelling workshop. In 2011, they introduced zip-lining at a cost of about C$43 for two runs. They have packages and group discounts.

Families looking to enjoy outdoor challenges together should inquire about **custom adventures.** For something like C$200 to C$300 per person, the center can draw up a 2- to 5-night adventure vacation that includes equipment, instruction, food, and lodging.

For more information about the program, contact **Cape Enrage Adventures** (www.capenrage.com; ☏ **888/280-7273** or 506/887-2273).

The restaurant here boasts a surprisingly upscale menu for a remote location—think lobster poutine, hand-rolled pasta, pheasant cannelloni, or Santa Fe steak. The view is fabulous and you may even see zip liners speeding across in front of you.

Road Trip to the Hopewell Rocks

There's no better place in Canada to witness the extraordinary power of ocean tides than at the **Hopewell Rocks ★★★** (www.thehopewellrocks.ca; ☏ **877/734-3429**), located about 40km (25 miles) northeast of Fundy National Park on Route 114. Think of it as a natural sculpture garden. At low tide (the best time to visit), these eroded columns as high as 15m (50 ft.) stand on the ocean floor like Brancusi or Easter Island statues, and you can walk right out among them and gawk. (They're sometimes called the "flowerpots," on account of the trees and plants that still flourish on the narrowing summits.) But don't linger: Most of those rocks will be under water in a few hours.

When you arrive, park at the visitor center and restaurant and wander down to the shore. (There's also a shuttle service that runs from the interpretive center to the rocks for C$2.) Signboards fill you in on the natural history of the rocks. If you've come at low tide, you can descend the steel staircase to the sea floor and admire these wondrous free-standing rock sculptures, chiseled by waves and tides. Even the **visitor center** is a pleasant place to spend some time. It not only has intriguing exhibits (look for the satellite photos of the area, and a time-lapse video of the tides) but the cafeteria-style restaurant has terrific views from its floor-to-ceiling windows and serves good, simple food. The park charges an entry fee of C$9 adults, C$7.75 students and seniors, C$6.75 children ages 5 to 18, and C$24 families. It's open daily mid-May to mid-June, 9am to 5pm, then 8am to 8pm from mid-June until mid-August (mid-Aug to late Aug to 6pm only), and from 9am to 5pm from September until it closes in mid-October. Note that the site can get crowded at peak times, which is understandable given its uniqueness and beauty, but might not jive with your ideal of peace and quiet. If your schedule allows it, come early in the day, when most travelers are still in bed, remembering to time your visit to low tide if possible. If you arrive at the top half of the tide, consider a sea kayak tour around the islands and caves. **Baymount Outdoor Adventures** (www.baymountadventures.com; ☏ 877/601-2660 or 506/734-2660) runs 90-minute kayak tours of Hopewell Rocks from June through early September for C$59 per adult, C$49 per child, or C$199 per family. A Walk on the Ocean Floor tour provides before- and after-the-tide photo-ops. Caving tours of nearby caverns are also offered by this family outfit; contact them for details.

Where to Stay

Broadleaf Guest Ranch ★ ☺   Two-bedroom cottages at this homey, family-operated ranch are a great choice for families or couples traveling together, particularly those with an interest in horses: The ranch offers rides of varying duration, cattle checks, even some basic spa packages. Cottages sport full kitchens, small sitting areas with gas stoves, and lovely sweeping views of the 607-hectare (1,500-acre) ranch and bay. You won't mistake these lodgings for a luxury experience: Bedrooms are furnished with bunk beds (a single over a double). Staying here is like sinking into a favorite chair: comforting. So is the home-cooking dished up in a large, cafeteria-style dining area. In addition to the cottages, there are bed-and-breakfast rooms in the main house, a lodge, a little nine-site campground (with hookups) in an apple orchard, and an annex known as "Broadleaf Too."

5526 Rte. 114, Hopewell Hill NB E4H 3N5. www.broadleafranch.com. ☏ **800/226-5405** or 506/882-2349. Fax 506/882-2075. 7 units. Main inn rooms C$60 double; chalets and apts C$150–C$200. Packages available. MC, V. **Amenities:** Restaurant; bike rentals; room service; spa; watersports equipment; Wi-Fi (free in office or restaurant). *In room:* TV/VCR (some units), kitchenette (some units), no phone.

Fundy Highlands Inn and Chalets ★ ☺   This property's 24 cottages are furnished with color televisions, beach towels, and kitchenette units. Some of the cottages even have built-in bunk beds, a good choice for travelers with young children. It's also notable for its grounds, rose beds, and good views of the bay and coastline from many of the cottages' windows. If the chalets are all fully booked up, the same owners run the adjacent **Fundy Park Motel,** with 20 basic rooms for C$74 to C$94 each; all of the motel rooms have kitchenettes, too, and second-floor rooms have a veranda. Just be aware that all rooms in the motel are furnished with bunk beds only.

8714 Rte. 114, Fundy National Park, NB E4H 4V3. www.fundyhighlandchalets.com. ☏ **888/883-8639** or 506/887-2930. 24 units. Cottages C$84–C$109. Packages available. MC, V. *In room:* TV, kitchenette, Wi-Fi (free).

Parkland Village Inn ✦   The Parkland, located right on the oceanfront beside the village wharf, opened the same day that the park did, back in 1948. It's an old-fashioned seaside hotel in the village of Alma, offering rooms and suites that have been renovated. Some rooms have fine views of the bay, others the mountains. It's handy to the park, beach, and village shops, and offers good value for families. A dining room, the **Tides,** specializes in seafood (prepared with flair by Chef Marc Casey) and has pretty views out over the water so that you can watch the small fishing fleet come and go. Enjoy delightful dining at window tables where hummingbirds provide entertainment. Breakfast is complimentary in the shoulder seasons.

8601 Main St. (Rte. 114), Alma, NB E4H 1N6. www.parklandvillageinn.com. ⓒ **866/668-4337** or 506/887-2313. Fax 506/887-2315. 10 rooms, 2 suites. C$95–C$140 double; C$125–C$145 suites. MC, V. Closed Nov–Mar. **Amenities:** Restaurant; parking. *In room:* TV, no phone, Wi-Fi (free).

Vista Ridge ★   Simple cabins are set amid birch and pines very near the park's eastern entrance, on a pretty little site overlooking a beach and the headlands of the park (hence the name). The owners have put in the elbow grease to update cottages, installing satellite televisions, electric fireplaces, and full kitchens in all of the units. These three-bedroom cottages are small and basically furnished, but they do have lots of exposed wood and those good kitchen appliances; bring food and cook it up on-site. Children of any age can ride a pony in the corral for C$10. There's an RV campground on-site, too—call the owners for more details if you're seeking a scenic place to park a big rig.

41 Foster Rd., Alma, NB E4H 4Y8. www.fundyparkchalets.com. ⓒ **877/887-2808** or 506/887-2808. Fax 506/887-2282. 29 cabins. C$99–C$150 cabin. Discounts in spring and fall. MC, V. Closed Dec–Apr. Pets accepted (C$10 per pet). *In room:* TV, electric fireplace, full kitchen, no phone.

Where to Eat

Amid the scattering of seafood takeout and lobster shops in and around the park, one good picnic pick is **Butland's** (www.fundylobster.com; ⓒ **506/887-2190**) at 8607 Main St. in Alma beside the town wharf. They sell locally caught crustaceans, scallops, and smoked salmon. You can cook the lobster yourself in your cabin, or have these guys do it; there are no tables here. The shack is open daily from mid-May through Labour Day, then weekends until New Year's.

There's also a bakery in Alma, **Kelly's Bake Shop,** at 8587 Main St. (ⓒ **506/887-2460**), open year-round. They serve big, locally famous sticky buns.

MONCTON

Moncton makes a claim that it's the crossroads of the Maritimes, and it hasn't been bashful about using this lucky geographic position (it *is* at the crossing of several major highways) to promote itself as a regional business hub. As a result, the majority of downtown's hotels and restaurants here cater to people in suits, rather than travelers, at least on the weekdays. But there is some life here; take a walk down Main Street at night or on a weekend, and you'll spot spiky hairdos, flannel, skateboards, and other youthful fashion accouterments.

For families, Moncton offers a decent way station if you're traveling with kids. A concentration of family-friendly attractions, including **Magnetic Hill** and **Crystal Palace** (see "Exploring Moncton," below), offer entertaining—if somewhat pricey—ways to fill an idle afternoon.

Essentials

GETTING THERE   Moncton is at the crossroads of several major routes through New Brunswick, including Route 2 (the Trans-Canada Hwy.) and Route 15.

Moncton's small **international airport** (www.gmia.ca) on Aviation Avenue in Dieppe, is about 11km (7 miles, or 10 min.) from downtown Moncton via Route 132; you basically head straight out Main Street (which becomes Champlain St.) to Dieppe and follow the airport signs. (From the airport, take Rue Champlain straight into town.) **Air Canada** (www.aircanada.com; ⓒ **888/247-2262**) has long served the city, and Canadian carrier **WestJet** (www.westjet.com; ⓒ **888/937-8538**) now also connects Moncton with Toronto and other points in Canada. From the U.S., **Continental** (www.continental.com; ☎ **800/231-0856**) flies to and from Newark daily. **Porter Airlines** (www.flyporter.com; ☎ **888/619-8622**) flies to and from Toronto, via Ottawa, Ontario daily. At last count, there were four international-chain car rental agencies at the airport.

The **VIA Rail** (www.viarail.com; ☎ **888/842-7245**) *Ocean* train from Montréal to Halifax stops in Moncton 6 days a week. Moncton's station is located off Main Street, behind Highfield Square.

VISITOR INFORMATION There's a downtown visitor information center located centrally in **Bore Park,** just off Main Street at 10 Bendview Court (☎ **506/853-3540**), open daily from mid-May through September. The city's tourism website is located at www.tourismmoncton.ca.

Exploring Moncton

Moncton's downtown is easily reconnoitered on foot—if you can find parking. (Look for lots a block just north and south of Main St.) **Downtown Moncton, Inc.,** publishes a nicely designed "Historic Walking Tour" brochure that touches upon some of the most significant buildings; ask for it at the visitor center. They have also developed some really good walking trails and have more than 2,000 acres of parkland for outdoor lovers. The most active stretch of Main Street is the section between City Hall and the train underpass: an accumulation of cafes, newsstands, hotels, and restaurants, plus a handful of shops. On Saturdays, check out the great farmers' market just one block off Main. There's also quite a mix of architectural styles here, the earliest examples of which testify to Moncton's former prosperity and prominence as a regional center of commerce. **Exploring by bike** is a good idea, especially if you go pedaling along **Riverfront Park** or through the 121 hectares (300 acres) of popular **Centennial Park.** The local bike club, Hub City Wheelers, sometimes schedules group bike rides, which nonmembers are welcome to join; it's a good way to meet local cyclists and find the most scenic routes. Ask about the rides at the visitor center. Centennial Park is also home to **Treego** (www. treegomoncton.com; ☎ **877/707-4646** or 506/388-4646) aerial adventure courses designed for use by all ages (C$30 adults, C$25 16 and under).

Crystal Palace ★ ☺ This indoor amusement park at can make a rainy, hot, or freezing day with the kids go by quickly. The spacious, enclosed park includes shooting arcades, numerous games (ranging from Skee-Ball to video games), a medium-size roller coaster, a carousel, swing ride, laser tag, bumper cars, miniature airplane and truck rides, miniature golf, batting cages, and even a virtual-reality ride. The park especially appeals to kids under 12, though teens will likely find a few video games to occupy them, too. Families never have to go outside if they book a room at the adjoining Ramada Plaza Crystal Palace Hotel (see "Where to Stay," below). A restaurant, four-screen cinema, laser center, miniature golf, climbing wall, and large bookstore are located within the same complex.

499 Paul St., Dieppe, next to Champlain Place Shopping Centre (Trans-Canada Hwy., exit 504-A W.). www.crystalpalace.ca. ☎ **506/859-4386** or 877/856-4386 (Eastern Canada only). Free admission. Rides are 1–4 tickets each (book of 25 C$24); unlimited ride bracelets C$24 adults, C$20 children shorter than 4 ft., C$75 families. Game tokens C$20 per 100. Late June to early Sept daily 10am–9pm; rest of year Mon–Thurs noon–8pm, Fri noon–9pm, Sat 10am–9pm, Sun 10am–8pm.

Magic Mountain Water Park ★ ☺ This water park, adjacent to famous/infamous Magnetic Hill (see below), features wave pools and eight slides, including the towering Kamikaze Slide, where daredevils can reach speeds of up to 60kmph (40 mph). (Yes, it's safe.) Kids can race their friends side-by-side down a slide on a tube or mat (sign me up) and play miniature golf at the site. Little kids might be more interested in the Splashpad, a more passive attraction that sprays water in four directions from a plastic whale, boat, and lighthouse onto shrieking kids.

2875 Mountain Rd. (Trans-Canada Hwy., exit 488), Moncton. www.magicmountain.ca. ⓒ **800/331-9283** or 506/857-9283. Admission C$26 adults full day, C$15–C$20 children under 4 ft. tall (children under age 3 free), C$85 families. Afternoon tickets (enter after 3pm) about 33% lower. July to late Aug daily 10am–7pm; mid-June to end of June and late Aug to early Sept daily 10am–6pm.

Magnetic Hill ☺ Located on Moncton's northwest outskirts, this natural phenomenon has been puzzling folks since the 1800s when, reportedly, wagons and barrels rolled uphill. With the coming of the automobile, cars that stopped at the bottom of a short stretch of downhill started to roll back uphill—or *appeared* to do so. In fact, it's an optical illusion. (The "hill" is on the side of a far larger hill tilted at a different angle, so that skews your perspective.) Starting in the 1930s, locals capitalized on the phenomenon by opening gift shops; by the 1950s, this hill boasted the biggest souvenir shop in the Maritimes. Today it's not so quaint; you enter a well-marked drive with magnet-themed road signs and streetlights, pay a toll at a gatehouse, and wind around a comically twisting road to wait your turn before being directed to the hill. You might find the "uphill roll" entertaining for a few meters while you wonder how it can be real. Attractions nearby include Wharf Village (souvenir shops and snack bars designed to look like a seaside village); a popular **zoo ★**; video arcades, driving ranges, and the like; and the Magic Mountain water park (see above). Despite—maybe because of—its utter cheesiness, this is a decent stop for families weary of beaches and hikes. If you don't mind forking over a few bucks to roll "up" a hill, that is.

Mountain Rd. (Trans-Canada Hwy., exit 488), Moncton. No phone. Admission Magnetic Hill C$5 per car, free if the gate is open and unstaffed; Magnetic Hill Zoo C$9.50 adults, C$8.50 seniors and children 12–18, C$6.50 children 4–11, C$22 families in summer, cheaper off season. June–Oct Mon–Fri 10am–6pm, weekends 9am–6pm; off season some attractions closed, call for info. Closed Nov to mid-May.

Where to Stay

In addition to the properties listed below, a welter of inexpensive and mid-priced chain hotels have set up shop near the complex of services around Magnetic Hill. They include the **Comfort Inn,** 2495 Mountain Rd. (ⓒ **800/228-5150** or 506/384-3175); **Country Inn & Suites,** 2475 Mountain Rd. (ⓒ **800/596-2375** or 506/852-7000); and **Holiday Inn Express,** also just off the exit at 2515 Mountain Rd. (ⓒ **866/570-7666** or 506/384-1050). Double rooms range from as little as C$65 up to as high as C$199, though they tend toward the lower end of that range. To get here from the Trans-Canada Highway, take exit 450.

Delta Beauséjour ★ Ideally located to enjoy the restaurants and shops of downtown, the Delta Beauséjour is accessed through towering wrought iron gates which, combined with very helpful doormen, make arrival feel special. The inviting decor inside and some of the friendliest staff you can imagine make this a top-choice hotel. Comfortable rooms are appointed in usual business-hotel style; a third-floor indoor pool offers year-round swimming, and a pleasant outdoor deck overlooks the distant marshes of the Petitcodiac River. Riverfront Park, behind the hotel, is a great place for a run or leisurely stroll. The hotel is a favorite among corporate travelers, but in summer and on weekends, leisure travelers largely get it to themselves. In addition to the elegant **Windjammer** restaurant (dinner only; see "Where to Eat," below), the hotel also has **Triiio** (a restaurant/lounge serving three meals a day) and a cafeteria space serving breakfast, lunch, and snacks all day.

750 Main St., Moncton, NB E1C 1E6. www.deltahotels.com. (📞 **888/351-7666** or 506/854-4344. Fax 506/858-0957. 310 units. C$129–C$199 double. Rates include continental breakfast. AE, DC, MC, V. **Amenities:** 3 restaurants; bar; babysitting; fitness center; indoor heated pool; 24-hr. room service. *In room:* A/C, TV, fax (some units), minibar, Internet (free).

Ramada Plaza Moncton ★ 🏨   This modern, three-story chain hotel adjoins the Crystal Palace amusement park (see above), a short walk from the region's largest mall. It's surrounded by asphalt and has little in the way of native charm. Most rooms are modern (a number are suites), unexceptional but well furnished with amenities like minifridges and minibars. But there's a surprise here: a handful of "fantasy suites" that go way over the top with themes like Deserted Island (you sleep in a thatched hut) and Rock 'n' Roll (you sleep in a bed that's a replica of a pink '59 Cadillac). This is corny, kitschy hostelry the way it used to be. Some rooms face the Tropics-themed indoor pool, but others face that vast parking lot. For entertainment without going outside, there's the adjacent amusement park, large Chapters book store, and movie theaters. Their restaurant, McGinnis Landing, serves basic pub grub and buffet brunches. It's a bit pricey, but does cater well to kids' appetites. Some of the package offerings include tickets to the amusement park.

499 Paul St., Dieppe, NB E1A 6S5. www.crystalpalacehotel.com. (📞 **800/561-7108** or 506/858-8584. Fax 506/858-5486. 115 units. C$90–C$275 double. Packages available. AE, DC, DISC, MC, V. **Amenities:** Restaurant; bar; babysitting; whirlpool; indoor pool; room service; sauna, fitness center. *In room:* A/C, TV, fridge, hair dryer, minibar, Wi-Fi (free).

Where to Eat

If you're visiting this area in summer, also check out the seasonal (mid-May to mid-Oct) restaurants that spring up along **Pointe-du-Chêne wharf ★**, a marina complex on the waterfront in **Shediac** about 24km (15 miles) east of the city via routes 11 and 15. You'll find everything from fish and chips to barbecue to ice cream here—even some adult beverages.

City Grill ★ CANADIAN   These folks boast about giving a city experience, using prints of city skylines and a black-and-white color scheme to help create the right ambience. The kitchen integrates old favorites (steaks, prime rib, and burgers are very much on the menu) with much healthier choices such as salads and sandwiches and food cooked over one of Eastern Canada's only working charcoal grills—hence the name. This wine bar has a unique late-night food menu, and don't overlook the stone-oven pizzas.

130 Westmoreland St. (📞 **506/857-8325.** Call-ahead seating in lieu of reservations. Lunches C$9–C$15; dinners C$17–C$28. AE, DC, DISC, MC, V. Mon–Thurs 11:30am–2pm and 5–10pm; Fri 11:30am–2pm and 5–11pm; Sat 5–11pm.

The Homestead Restaurant ★ CANADIAN   Cross the river to Riverview for this local favorite. Cross the bridge, turn left, and pretend you are going to Fundy. They are on the right before you leave town. Child- and senior-friendly. Their home cooking and folksy atmosphere get rave reviews, and prices are affordable. Servings are ample; in fact, they serve half portions if you request. Do check out dessert; people travel miles for their peanut butter pie.

358 Coverdale Rd., Riverview. (📞 **506/386-1907.** Lunch C$9–C$18; dinner C$10–C$25. AE, MC, V. Daily 6:45am–8pm.

The Windjammer ★★ SEAFOOD/CONTINENTAL   Tucked off the lobby of Moncton's top business hotel, the Windjammer is consistently rated one of the top

A road trip AROUND SOUTHEASTERN NEW BRUNSWICK

Although it's easy to think that the roads to the south and east of Moncton simply lead to Nova Scotia or Prince Edward Island, that ignores some beautiful country to be seen and some nice areas to visit. Take Route 106 (country) or 2 (multilane) south 28km (18 miles) from Moncton to Memramcook. The **Lefebvre National Historic Site** (www.pc.gc.ca/lhn-nhs/nb/lefebvre/index.aspx; ☎ 506/758-9808) and **Memramcook Museum** (☎ 506/758-0087) will interest history buffs, especially those keen on understanding the rebirth of l'Acadie after the great expulsion of 1755. Continue on 106 through Dorchester and into Sackville. You are in a fabulous area for bird-watching. A diversion on Route 935 to the village of **Johnson's Mills** might reveal tens of thousands of migrating sandpipers who stop here to feed during summer migration. The Johnson's Mills Shorebird Reserve Interpretive Centre (☎ 506/379-6347) is open in July and August. Back on Route 106 there is 55-acre wetland preserve to wander at the **Sackville Waterfowl Park on the Tantramar Marshes** (www.sackville.com/visit/attractions/waterfowl; ☎ 800/249-2020 or 506/364-4930). Boardwalks take you out over the wetlands where more than 150 species of birds and about 200 species of plants have been recorded, making it one of the most productive wetland sites in the region. Guided tours are available May to August, or take a self-guided tour with the information available at the Visitor Information Centre. Just 10 minutes down Route 2, you'll find the **Fortress Beausejour-Fort Cumberland National Historic Site** at 111 Fort Beausejour Rd. in Aulac (www.pc.gc.ca/lhn-nhs/nb/beausejour/index.aspx; ☎ 506/364-5080). Kids will love clambering over the grassy ramparts of the fort that played a pivotal role in the struggle for North America. Adults may be more interested in the site's museum or the spectacular view of the head of Fundy Bay. As the crow flies, you are about 60km (37 miles) from Moncton, so your day isn't spent driving, but rather exploring and enjoying.

From Aulac, Route 16 takes you about 25km (16 miles) to a traffic circle where you can either continue on Route 16 to **Cape Jourimain,** where there is another natural wildlife area and a spectacular view of Confederation Bridge to Prince Edward Island; or, take Route 15 to **Shediac.** The 80km (50-mile) stretch between Port Elgin and Shediac is home to four great beaches: Murray, Cap-Pele, l'Aboiteau, and Parlee. Parlee Beach and the town of Shediac bustle with holidayers in season, so they have all the services you could want.

100 restaurants in Canada. It is probably this city's best fine dining; years ago, the *Globe and Mail* described Chef Stefan Müller's culinary efforts as a "virtuoso performance." This has been proven accurate over and over again, as he and his team served VIPs ranging from the queen to visiting celebrities. Check out the 100 Mile Table offering first: Four courses are served using local seasonal ingredients. A sample menu might include Wolfhead cold smoked salmon dulse brioche toast, served with chopped eggs, capers and onions, or chilled New Brunswick potato and fiddlehead "vichyssoise" garnished with rooftop herb clippings (C$63 a person). Their regular menu items include Atlantic beef, bison, boar, lamb, and loads of regional seafood. If you love seafood, do check out their Regional Seafood Tasting, which includes local scallops, smoked sturgeon, salmon, halibut, mussels, and oysters—quite a catch and a good sampling of local harvests; meat lovers might savor their Trio of New Brabant

Boar. It's pricey for New Brunswick, but an excellent find in an unlikely place. Not staying at the hotel? Guests of the Windjammer get free valet parking.

750 Main St. (inside the Delta Beauséjour). © **506/877-7137.** Reservations recommended. Main courses C$28–C$90. AE, MC, V. Mon–Sat 5:30–10pm.

En Route to Kouchibouguac National Park

If you decide to head directly to Kouchibouguac from Moncton, you might want to consider a few hours in Bouctouche area—take Route 15 east out of Moncton, then turn north on Route 11 at its intersection with **Shediac.** The drive takes about an hour. The area has some interesting spots to visit: **Le Pays de la Sagouine** (51 Acadie Rd., Bouctouche; www.sagouine.com; © **800/561-9188**), where music, kitchen parties, comedy, food, storytelling, and dinner theater are all part of a day's activities; **Savonnerie Olivier Soapery** (821 Rte. 505 in Sainte-Anne-de-Kent; © **888/775-5550**), an econo-museum that serves up a learning experience about soap making which is full of color and fragrance (who knew skin care could be so much fun!); and the **Seawind Buffalo Farm** (136 St. Pierre Rd., in Sainte-Anne-de-Kent; www.seawindbuffalo.com; © **506/743-6200**) for a wagon ride out to see the herd, learn about bison, and perhaps indulge in a buffalo burger.

Bouctouche Dune ★★, on the coast road at 1932 Rte. 475, makes for a good stop along the way. This striking white-sand dune stretches an impressive 13km (8 miles) across **Bouctouche Bay;** it's home to the endangered piping plover, a unique butterfly species, and some rare plants. The sensitive dune area itself can be viewed from a wheelchair-accessible, 2km (mile-plus) boardwalk that snakes along its length. On a sunny day, the sandy beach is a lovely spot to while away a couple hours, or even take a dip in the (relatively) warm seawater. The visitor center is fairly straightforward in its explanations of the flora and fauna indigenous to the dune; kids will probably be amused. There are also regular programs here. Admission is free; the boardwalk is open year-round (in good weather) and the visitor center is open daily May through October, from 10am to 8pm (until 5pm in the off season). Contact the dune's visitor center (administered by the Irving Oil folks) at © **888/640-3300** or 506/743-2600.

If you're interested in spending the night in the area or grabbing a bite to eat, check out the **Dune View Inn ★** at 589 Rte. 475 (www.aubergevuedeladune.com; © **877/743-9893** or 506/743-9893). It's open year-round, where the owners (one a trained chef who previously cooked in Montréal) serve up French-inflected local seafood. The six units here feature TVs, telephones, and private bathrooms (five with whirlpool tubs). They're pretty and light, if somewhat cramped. A double with breakfast costs from C$90 to C$135. The inn can also arrange local golf and kayaking packages, or even a romance package, with advance notice.

KOUCHIBOUGUAC NATIONAL PARK ★★

Much is made of the fact that big **Kouchibouguac National Park** (local slang: "the Kooch") has all sorts of ecosystems worth studying, from sandy barrier islands to ancient peat bogs. But that's like saying Disney has nice lakes: It misses the point. In fact, this artfully designed park is a wonderful destination for cycling, hiking, and beachgoing, too—yes, it has beaches. If you're an outdoorsy type, plan to spend a few days here, doing nothing but exercising. The varied natural wonders (which *are* spectacular) will just be an added bonus—a big one.

The tongue-tangling name is a Mi'kmaq Indian word meaning "river of the long tides." It's pronounced "Koosh-uh-*boog*-oo-whack," or something like that. The place is great for **cyclists,** because the park is laced with well-groomed bike trails made of finely crushed cinders that traverse forest and field or meander alongside rivers and lagoons. In those areas where bikes aren't permitted (such as on boardwalks and beaches), there are usually bike racks handy for locking up while you keep going on foot. In fact, if you camp here and bring a bike, there's no need to even use a car.

The only group this park might disappoint is gung-ho hikers. There isn't any hard-core hiking or climbing, just gentle walking and strolling. The pathways are wide and flat. Most trails are short—on the order of a half-mile to a mile—and seem more like detours than destinations.

Although the park is ideal for **campers,** day-trippers also find it a worthwhile destination. Plan to stay until sunset. The trails tend to empty out in the afternoon, and the dunes, bogs, and boreal forest take on a rich, almost iridescent hue as the sun sinks over the spruce.

Be aware that this is a fair-weather destination only—if it's blustery or rainy, there's little to do save a damp stroll on the beach.

Essentials

GETTING THERE   Kouchibouguac National Park is located about 112km (70 miles) north of Moncton; figure less than 90 minutes' driving time. The exit for the park, off Route 11, is well marked.

VISITOR INFORMATION   The park is open daily from April through November, while a **Visitor Reception Centre** (✆ **506/876-2443**) opens daily from mid-May until mid-October. The visitor center is just off Route 134, a short drive past the park entrance. (It's open 8am–8pm from mid-June through Aug, 9am–5pm in the shoulder seasons.) There's a slide show here to introduce you to the park's attractions, plus some field guides.

FEES   A daily pass costs C$7.80 adults, C$6.80 seniors, C$3.90 children 6 to 16, and C$20 families. (Rates are discounted 50%–60% Apr–June and Oct–Nov.) Seasonal passes are also available, but are only worth the dough if you're planning to visit for more than 3 days. Though there are no formal checkpoints here, occasional roadblocks during the summer check for pass-holding compliance. Note that, for a small extra charge, you can also get a helpful map of the park at the information center.

Outdoor Pursuits

CAMPING   Kouchibouguac is at heart a camper's park, best enjoyed by those who plan to spend at least a night.

South Kouchibouguac ★, the main campground, is centrally located and very nicely laid out with 300-plus sites, most rather large and private. The 50 or so sites with electricity are nearer the river and somewhat more open, while the newest sites (nos. 1–35) lack grassy areas for pitching a tent—campers there must pitch their tents on gravel pads. Bring a thick sleeping pad or ask for another site. Sites here cost C$22 to C$33 per night, depending on time of year and the level of comfort you require. Reservations are accepted for about half of the sites; call ✆ **506/876-2443** starting in late April. The remaining sites are doled out first-come, first-served.

Other camping options within the park include the more remote, semiprimitive **Côte-à-Fabien,** across the river on Kouchibouguac Lagoon. It lacks showers and some sites require a short walk, but it's more appealing for tenters. The cost is C$16 per night. The park also maintains three backcountry sites. **Sipu** is on the Kouchibouguac River and is accessible by canoe or foot only, **Petit Large** by foot or bike, and **Pointe-à-Maxime** by canoe or kayak only (no fresh water available at this campground). These sites cost a flat C$9.80 per night, or C$69 annually.

BEACHES   The park features about 16km (10 miles) of sandy beaches, mostly along barrier islands of sandy dunes, delicate grasses and flowers, and nesting plovers and sandpipers. **Kellys ★** is the principal beach, one of the best-designed and best-executed recreation areas in Eastern Canada. At a forest's edge, a short walk from the main parking area, you can find showers, changing rooms, a snack bar, and some interpretive exhibits. From here, you walk about 480m (⅓-mile) across a winding boardwalk that's plenty fascinating as it crosses a salt marsh, lagoons, and some of the best-preserved dunes in the province.

The long, sandy beach here features water that's comfortably warm, with waves that are usually mellow—they lap rather than roar, unless a storm's passing offshore. Lifeguards oversee a roped-off section about 91m (300 ft.) long; elsewhere, though, you're on your own. For kids, there's supervised swimming on a sandy stretch of the quiet lagoon.

BOATING & BIKING   Ryans ★★ (✆ 506/876-8918)—a cluster of buildings between the campgrounds and Kellys Beach—is the recreational center where you can rent bikes, kayaks, paddleboats, and canoes. All rent relatively cheaply, even the double kayaks. Canoes can be rented for longer excursions. And since Ryans is located on a lagoon, you can explore around the dunes or upstream on the winding river.

With over 60km (37 miles) of bikeway, the park is a prime biking destination. The Major Kollock Creek Mountain Bike Trail, which starts near Petit-Large, is ideal for those who want to try mountain biking. This one-way bicycle trail is 6.3km (4 miles) and takes 45 to 90 minutes to ride.

The park sometimes offers a "Voyageur Canoe Marine Adventure" during summer, with a crew paddling a sizable canoe from the mainland out to offshore sandbars, and a naturalist-guide helps identify the wildlife. You'd probably see osprey, bald eagles, and, if you're lucky, seals. It's an inexpensive 3-hour excursion with a nice little wilderness payoff; inquire about these trips at the park's information center when you enter. You need to reserve, and pay the C$30 per-person fee by 2pm the previous day.

HIKING   The hiking and biking trails are as short and undemanding as they are appealing. The one hiking trail that requires slightly more fortitude is the **Kouchibouguac River Trail,** which runs for some 13km (8 miles) along the banks of the river.

The **Bog Trail ★** runs just 2km (1.25 miles) in each direction, but it opens the door to a wonderfully alien world: The 4,500-year-old bog here is a classic domed bog, made of peat created by decaying shrubs and other plants. At the bog's edge you'll find a wooden tower ascended by a spiral staircase that affords a panoramic view of the eerie habitat.

The boardwalk crosses to the thickest, middle part of the bog. Where the boardwalk stops, you can feel the bouncy surface of the bog—you're actually standing on a mat of thick vegetation that's floating on top of water. Look for the pitcher plant, a carnivorous little devil that lures flies into its bell-shaped leaves and then digests them with acid, allowing the plant to thrive in an otherwise hostile environment.

Callanders Beach and **Cedar Trail ★** are both located at the end of a short dirt road. There's an open field with picnic tables here, a small protected beach on the lagoon (with fine views of dunes across the way), and an 800m (about .5 mile or so) hiking trail along a boardwalk that passes through a cedar forest, past a salt marsh, and through a mixed forest. This is a good alternative for those who prefer to avoid the crowds (relatively speaking) at Kellys Beach.

THE ACADIAN PENINSULA

The **Acadian Peninsula** is the bulge on the northeast corner of New Brunswick, forming one of the arms of the **Baie des Chaleurs** (Québec's Gaspé Peninsula forms the other). It's a land of tidy houses, miles of shoreline (much of it beaches), harbors filled with commercial fishing boats, and residents proud of their Acadian heritage. You'll see the Stella Maris flag—the French tricolor with a single gold star in the field of blue—everywhere up here. You are in Acadian country, a warm, welcoming culture where time seems to slow down and relaxation is the norm.

After leaving Kouchibouguac, it's just a short drive to **Miramichi**, the gateway to the Acadian Peninsula. Miramichi and the river of the same name have long been known for sport fishing and hunting—numerous outfitters in the region still help anglers in their quest for the salmon. The town is developing its tourism offerings and can provide a delightful stopping point with river tours and music ranging from Country Music Opry to kitchen parties featuring local talent. There are several good chain hotels in town. From Miramichi, follow Route 11 around the coast of the peninsula or, if you want to get to Bathurst in a hurry, take Route 9. Presuming you enjoy scenery and want to explore, take Route 11.

VISITOR INFORMATION The **Caraquet Tourism Information** at 39 St-Pierre Blvd. W. (© **506/726-2676**), is a seasonal (mid-May to mid-Sept) office in the heart of downtown. The village of **Shippagan** dispenses its information from a wooden lighthouse near the Marine Centre at 200 Hotel de Ville Ave. (© **506/336-3993**); it's only open from mid-June through August.

GETTING THERE Route 11 is the main highway serving the Acadian Peninsula. Caraquet is about 260km (160 miles, or a 3½-hr. drive) north from Moncton, about 160km (100 miles, or 2+ hr.) north from the entrance to Kouchibouguac National Park, or 70km (43 miles) from Bathurst.

A Side Trip to Shippagan ★ & Miscou Island ★★

Both Shippagan and Miscou Island require detours off Route 11, but they're worth it if you're interested in glimpsing Acadian New Brunswick in the slow lane. As an added bonus, Miscou Island boasts some fine beaches and a historic lighthouse. I think this side trip is worth a half-day to a day. There are places to stay and eat; they are often smaller, more intimate, and obviously local, so keep your eyes peeled.

Shippagan ★ lies off routes 11 and 345. It's a quiet, leafy village that's also home to sizable crab and herring fleets. (Go down to the harbor and snap pictures of the various boats in their slips; it's better than buying a postcard.)

Shippagan is home to the surprisingly modern **New Brunswick Aquarium and Marine Centre** ★★, 100 Aquarium St. (© **506/336-3013**), near the harbor; it's a good destination if you're the least bit curious about local marine life. Here you'll learn about the 125 species of native fish hereabouts, many of which are on display. Kids are especially drawn to the **harbor seal tank** outside, where trainers prompt the sleek creatures to show off their acrobatic skills. Little ones will also love watching the twice-daily feedings, when the seals down pounds of herring. Admission is C$9 adults,

C$7 seniors and students, C$6 children age 6 to 18, and C$23 families. Open late May to late September 10am to 6pm daily; seal feedings are at 11am and 4pm.

Keep driving north on Route 113 across a low drawbridge onto **Laméque Island ★★**. If you're traveling through in mid-July, don't be surprised to hear fine baroque music wafting from the **Sainte-Cecile Church.** Since 1975, the island has hosted the **Laméque International Baroque Music Festival** (℃ **877/377-8003** or 506/344-5846). For about 10 days, talented musicians perform an ambitious series of concerts in an architecturally striking, acoustically wonderful church in a small village on the island's north coast. Tickets often sell out well in advance, and most are priced at C$20 to C$35 per adult. If you miss the festival, do drop into the Laméque Island Church and take a look at the paint job inside—it has to be seen to be believed. Hand-painted in dazzling turquoise, green, yellow, and orange, the inside is sometimes compared to a Ukrainian Easter egg.

The **Saint-Marie church ★★**, a gorgeous twin-towered white wooden structure, is also worth finding; it's located in the hamlet of **Saint-Raphael-sur-Mer,** about 16km (10 miles) from Shippagan—bear right onto Route 305 a few miles after crossing the drawbridge onto Laméque Island. From the church, continue north on 305 another couple of kilometers (a mile or two) to find **Cap-Bateau Arch ★★**, a remarkable natural stone formation that looks like it should be somewhere in the canyons of Utah.

Backtrack to Route 113 and keep traveling north. You'll soon cross onto **Miscou Island ★★**, which for decades was connected by a simple ferry. In the mid-1990s, an arched bridge was finally erected across the strait. Happily, this wee island still retains a sense of remoteness, especially north of the village of Miscou Centre when you start getting into boggy territory.

If you continue northward across the island until you run out of road (it won't take long), you'll come to New Brunswick's oldest lighthouse. The **Miscou Island Lighthouse ★** (℃ **506/336-1302**), built in 1856, marks the confluence of the Gulf of St. Lawrence and the Baie des Chaleurs. It's only open to the public in August and September, from dawn until dusk.

The dominant natural feature of Miscou might be its **bog ★**. The bog landscape here is as distinctive as that of the Canadian Rockies; it's flat and green, and stretches for miles in places. You'll see much of this bog habitat on northern Miscou Island, where some of the bogs have been harvested for their peat. There's a well-constructed **nature trail** on Route 113, just north of Miscou Centre; a boardwalk loops through the bog and around an open pond. Learn about the orchids and lilies that thrive in the vast and spongy mat of shrubs and roots, and watch for the pitcher plants. The loop takes about 20 minutes, and it's free. If you come in fall (late Sept to mid-Oct), you'll find these bogs suddenly aflame in coats of gorgeous crimson. It happens every year.

There's also a saltwater **beach** (℃ **506/336-1302**) on Miscou Island's northern end where you can swim, change, and shower.

Caraquet ★

The historic beach town of Caraquet—widely regarded as the spiritual capital of Acadian New Brunswick—is the town that keeps going and going. (Geographically speaking, anyway.) It's spread thinly along a single commercial boulevard that parallels the beach; this town once claimed the honorific "longest village in the world" when it ran to some 20km (13 miles) long.

A good place to start a tour is the **Carrefour de la Mer,** 51 Blvd. St-Pierre Est, a modern complex overlooking the man-made harbor. It has a spare, Scandinavian feel to it, and you'll find a seafood restaurant, a snack bar, a children's playground, and two short strolls that lead to picnic tables on jetties with fine harbor views. Carquet is well-known as the premier place to be for the **Tintamarre,** a festival celebrating the national Acadian holiday on August 15. Accommodations can be hard to come by during this time, so if you plan to visit the first 2 weeks of August, reserve ahead.

Village Historique Acadien ★★ If you only have time to see one Acadian Museum, this is the place to visit. Some 45 buildings—most transported from villages elsewhere on the peninsula—depict life as it was lived in Acadian settlements between 1770 and 1890. The buildings are set among hundreds of acres of woodlands, marshes, and fields. You'll learn all about the exodus and settlement of the Acadians from costumed guides, who also demonstrate skills ranging from letterpress printing to blacksmithing. And that's not all. Another area focuses on more recent eras; this section continues the saga, showing Acadian life from 1890 to 1939 with a special focus on industry. Plan on spending 4 to 8 hours on-site. Or alternatively, stay over-night. The attractive yellow **Chateau Albert Hotel** (**©** **877/721-2200** or 506/726-2600) is good for those who wish to experience a night in a fine hotel from the last century (C$69–C$125; ask about packages that include dinner theater and site admission). Rooms are snug and wonderfully peaceful due to the lack of phones and televisions (to fit the period), but there's a dining room, convivial bar area, and lost-in-time vibe. There are also several restaurants within the village. The simple, hearty 18th- and 19th-century traditional Acadian cooking in **La Table des Ancêtres** is a must for those who love food history, a chance to sample Fricot, Poutine, Fayots, and more. The hotel dining room is home to musical dinner theater, or, on other evenings, a select menu. Simpler, modern fare is available in several other eateries.

Rte. 11 (6 miles west of Caraquet). www.villagehistoriqueacadien.com. **©** **506/726-2600.** Summer admission C$16 adults, C$14 seniors, C$11–C$13 children 6 and over, C$38 families; late Sept rates discounted about 60%. Early June to mid-Sept daily 10am–6pm; mid-Sept to late Sept daily 10am–5pm. Closed late Sept to early June.

WHERE TO STAY

Hôtel Paulin ★★ A three-story red building with a green-shingled mansard roof, the Hotel Paulin was built in 1891, the first hotel in Caraquet. It's still the best in town; it has been operated by a member of the Paulin family for three generations. Overlooking the bay, the beautifully restored country inn has an old-world France feel, both for the decor and the hospitality. Rooms and suites are comfortably furnished with antiques. (Four luxury suites on the top floor are more stylish and contemporary.) The hotel's first floor houses a handsome, well-regarded **restaurant** ★★ featuring seafood and fusion with French influences. This hotel is especially known for experiences such as food-and-wine getaways.

143 Blvd. St-Pierre Ouest, Caraquet, NB E1W 1B6. www.hotelpaulin.com. **©** **866/727-9981** or 506/727-9981. Fax 506/727-4808. 16 units. Mid-June to mid-Sept C$195–C$315 double and suite; mid-Sept to mid-June C$179–C$235 double and suite. Minimum 2-night stay first 2 weeks of Aug. MC, V. **Amenities:** Restaurant; massage; spa. In room: A/C, TV, hair dryer, no phone, Internet (free).

WHERE TO EAT

Caraquet is a good place for seafood, naturally. The **Hôtel Paulin's restaurant** ★★ is the best in town for its charm, but there are several inexpensive-to-moderate spots along the main drag that also serve fresh seafood as well.

For a delicious and sophisticated picnic snack, head to **Les Blancs d'Arcadie** ★, 488 Blvd. St-Pierre Est (**©** **506/727-5952**), just east of town. The specialties here are artisanal cheeses made from the milk of local cows; they include variations made with smoke, salt, pesto, French herbs, sun-dried tomato, and barbecue flavoring.

Grande-Anse

Grande-Anse is a wide-spot-in-the-road village of low, modern homes near bluffs overlooking the bay, lorded over by the stone Saint Jude church. The best view of the village—and a pretty good spot for a picnic—is along the bluffs just below the church. (Look for the sign indicating QUAI 45m/147 ft. west of the church.) Here you'll find a small man-made harbor with a fleet of fishing boats, a small sandy beach, and some grassy bluffs where you can park overlooking the bay.

If you'd prefer picnic tables, head a few miles westward to **Pokeshaw Park,** open from mid-June through August. Just offshore is a large kettle-shaped island ringed with cliffs that rise from the waves, long ago separated from the cliffs on which you're now standing. An active cormorant rookery thrives among the trees. There's a small picnic shelter for use in inclement weather; the park's open daily from 9am to 9pm, and a small admission fee is charged.

For an ocean swimming experience, head to **Plage Grande-Anse,** located 2km (a mile) east of the town. This handsome beach has a snack bar near the parking area and is open from 10am to 9pm daily. There's a small entrance fee for adults.

Bathurst on to Campbellton

The beautiful Chaleur Bay draws eyes northward—that's Québec and the road to Gaspe across the water. You might want to pick up Route 134 into Bathurst. They have put some effort into developing their waterfront into a charming stop for refreshments or exploring. The boardwalks and observation tower, which rewards a climb with a great view, make for a nice break in driving. You'll also find a beach, golf, shopping, museums, and walking trails—if you overnight, you might want to take in the live local entertainment on the boardwalk every night. Bathurst is a VIA Rail stop, as is Campbellton up the line.

Chaleur Bay has been voted one of the most beautiful bays in the world, and at its top end Campbellton acts as a welcome point for travelers from Québec's Gaspe Peninsula. That puts it at the top of New Brunswick, a region famous worldwide for the superb salmon fishing in the Restigouche River. Today it's a center for canoeing, kayaking, fishing, backpacking, hunting, nature trails, and bird-watching. **Sugar Loaf Provincial Park** (www.nbparks.ca; ✆ **506/789-2366**) has a great ski hill for winter enthusiasts. In the summer they have the only lift-service mountain bike trail in Atlantic Canada and they offer a "Defy Gravity 101" program which, for just C$50 gives 2 hours of instruction with a guide, bike rental, and a full-day lift pass.

Campbellton is at the beginning (or end, depending on your direction of travel) of the Appalachian Range driving route, which cuts across the province to Perth-Andover. This region speaks to those who are enamored of wilderness, forests, and mountain ranges, huge skies and rock formations—409-million-year old fossils have been found near the Campbellton coast. Learning about forests and lumberjacks, cowboys and horses, native peoples and their ceremonies and crafts, even ghosts and history, are part of the journey to San Quentin and Mount Carleton.

MOUNT CARLETON PROVINCIAL PARK ★

In 1969, the province of New Brunswick carved out some of its choicest woodlands and set them aside as a wilderness park—a wise decision. Today, Mount Carleton Provincial Park consists of 2,800 hectares (7,000 acres) of lakes, streams, thick boreal forest, and gently rounded mountains, the tallest of which afford excellent views of the surrounding countryside. It is the highest point in the Maritimes and you can hike to the top. The park's home to moose, black bear, coyotes, bobcat, and more than 100 species of birds. It's so pristine that fishing isn't allowed. If you're anywhere in the area and crave a truly wild experience, it's well worth a visit—though you have to *want* to get there.

The International Appalachian Trail cuts through the park, allowing a long-distance backpacker to head northwest into Québec or southwest into Maine and on to Georgia.

Essentials

GETTING THERE The park's access road and entrance is on Route 180, about 40km (25 miles) east of Saint-Quentin, the nearest community for supplies; there are no convenient general stores anywhere near the park's gates, so stock up. The park is also accessible from Bathurst to the east, but that's a rugged, 112km (70-mile) drive on a road that's gravel in spots, has no services, and is buzzed regularly by logging trucks. Use the other route.

VISITOR INFORMATION It costs C$8 per car (cash only) to enter, and the park's gates are open daily from mid-May through mid-October (7am–10pm in summer and 8am–8pm in spring and fall). A small **interpretive center** (✆ **506/235-0793**), located at the entrance gate, offers background on the park's natural and cultural history. The park remains open, though unstaffed, the rest of the year.

Camping

Armstrong Brook ★★ is the principal destination for visiting campers coming to Mount Carleton. It has 88 sites split between a forest near Lake Nictau's shore and an open, grassy field; campers can also avail themselves of hot showers and a bathhouse for washing up. A path leads to lake's edge, where there's a spit of small, flat pebbles good for swimming and sunbathing. Camping fees are C$25 per site.

Four backcountry sites are located high on the slopes of Mount Carleton (preregistration required). These sites, which require a 4km (2½-mile) hike, offer views into a rugged valley and a great sense of remoteness. Water is available but should be treated (beavers live nearby). No fires are permitted, so bring a stove. The fee up here is C$5 per night. Two other remote campsites on the shores of Lake Nictau are accessible either by canoe or a moderate walk. Register in advance for these, as well; the fee is C$8 to C$9 per night.

Note that all water supplies and toilets are shut off after September 15 due to concerns about pipes freezing.

Hiking & Biking

The park has 11 hiking trails totaling nearly 64km (40 miles). The helpful park staff at the gatehouse will be happy to direct you to a hike that suits your experience and mood. (There's even one wheelchair-accessible trail.)

The park's premier hike, of course, is to the summit of **Mount Carleton ★★**, the province's highest point at 820m (2,690 ft.). Although that doesn't *sound* impressive, it's all relative: Views from the peak to the tablelands below seem endless. A craggy comb of rocks with a 360-degree view of the lower mountains and the sprawling lakes marks the summit. The trailhead is about a 25-minute drive from the gatehouse; allow about 4 hours for a round-trip hike of about 10km (6 miles).

Overlooking Nictau Lake is Mount **Sagamook Trail,** at an altitude of about 762m (2,500 ft.). This circular trail is a steep and demanding hike of about 8km (5 miles). At the summit you're rewarded with spectacular views of Nictau Lake. For the truly gung-ho, there's the ridge walk that connects Sagamook and Carleton via **Mount Head.** The views from high above are unforgettable; but you'll need to set up a shuttle system (with a friend and two cars) to do the entire ridge in 1 day.

If you have a **mountain bike,** bring it. The cross-country ski trails, consisting of three interconnected loops (almost 14km/8 miles.), are open to mountain biking in the summer. As well, the park's gravel roads here are perfect for exploring, and non-park vehicles are banned from several of these roads, which take you deep into the woods past clear lakes and rushing streams.

Finally, in winter the park becomes part of a regional **snowmobile** trail system and also offers an 8km (5-mile) **cross-country ski trail** through the woods.

Where to Stay & Eat

Auberge Evasion de Rêves ★ ☺ If the weather's bad, or you're just not into camping in the park with the kiddies, check out this property in nearby Saint-Quentin. Its name roughly translates as "Dream-Escape Inn," though that might be a bit generous. Inside, it's made up of simply furnished business-hotel-type rooms but with small flourishes of design on various themes (nature, golf, and so forth). The unpretentiousness is actually refreshing, and kids enjoy the indoor swimming pool. There's also a dining area, a lounge, and a nice high-ceilinged common area that feels like a lodge. There are a few single rooms here, and a few specially equipped for travelers with disabilities as well.

11 Canada St., Saint-Quentin, NB E8A 1J2. ✆ **866/443-7383** or 506/235-3551. 14 units. C$97–C$133 double. Rates include continental breakfast. MC, V. **Amenities:** Restaurant; bar; Jacuzzi; indoor pool. *In room:* A/C, TV, DVD (some units), fridge (some units), hair dryer, Internet (free).

PRINCE EDWARD ISLAND

So small it occasionally gets overlooked by map-makers, Prince Edward Island rises like a gem from the Gulf of St. Lawrence. For Canada's smallest province, it is rated highly for a surprising number of things. It's a top golfing destination, has the longest running dinner theater and musical production in Canada, and ice creams named the world's best. Part of the reason for such success is repeat visitors who appreciate the getting-away-from-it-all factor of this gentle island, where life is simpler, the pace less harried, and the roads less traveled.

Sightseeing   PEI's size is a bonus: Never far to anywhere, it's natural for unhurried sightseeing. Beautiful **Charlottetown**, the "birthplace of Canada," brings history to life. **Prince Edward Island National Park** and the north shore region boast miles of white-sand beaches and soaring dunes. A drive east reveals a beach where the sand sings, and a distillery makes legal "shine." Up west, past **Summerside,** discover a reef you can walk on and a lighthouse to sleep in.

Eating & Drinking   Evidence of the fishing and farming that stocks Island pantries is everywhere: fields of potatoes, mussel harvesting, and amazing ingredients at local farmers' markets. Add dedicated restaurateurs and blend with the influence of the **Culinary Institute of Canada,** and you have a recipe for unique food encounters ranging from lobster on the wharf (the world's best finger food) to fine dining at country inns. For real foodies: Culinary Bootcamps, an International Shellfish Festival, and organized Culinary Experiences.

Arts & Culture   Known world-wide as the birthplace of *Anne of Green Gables*, the story that brings Prince Edward Island to life, the province rightly celebrates author Lucy Maud Montgomery's contribution to world literature. Her success created an environment which fosters creativity: first-class music, handcrafts, art, photography, and live theater are showcased at venues like the **Confederation Centre of the Arts** and the **Dunes Studio Gallery,** *ceilidhs,* markets, and artisans shops.

Relaxation   PEI's slow, relaxed pace is immediately obvious. Arriving feels like coming to the home we dream of: warm, welcoming, safe, and for want of a better phrase, laid-back. Take relaxation how you wish—golf first-rate courses, cycle or walk tip to tip on **Confederation Trail,** laze on a beach serenaded by the surf, tour museums. It's a perfect place to let children experience nature and relaxed play, and for all ages to learn to kayak or cook. The peace and tranquillity that Montgomery treasured still inspires visitors to de-stress and appreciate what surrounds them.

EXPLORING PRINCE EDWARD ISLAND

PEI is, by far, Canada's smallest province—it's only about 280km (175 miles) long from tip to tip, which is amazing—and that keeps your transit down to a minimum. With one or two smart bases, you can easily explore the whole province in a week. However, traffic on island roads—slowed by farm tractors, shutterbugs, leisurely drivers, terrain, and odd twists and turns along the route—tends to be slower than you'd expect. So don't count on the sort of speedy travel common on a fast mainland four-lane. After all, one of the reasons people come here is to recharge and relax. Just kick back and enjoy the scenery; you'll get there soon enough.

In recent years, a number of PEI hotels and attractions have banded together to market a ton of different vacation packages that offer discounts ranging from moderate to generous. There are some good values hidden in there. Call the provincial tourism office at ✆ **800/463-4734** or 902/368-4444 to discuss or receive information about these island packages, or click Packages Guide at www.tourismpei.com/about-pei.

Essentials

VISITOR INFORMATION   Tourism PEI publishes a comprehensive **free Visitor's Guide** to island attractions and lodgings that's well worth picking up. It is available at all information centers on the island, or in advance by calling ✆ **800/463-4734** or 902/368-4444. The official PEI website is located at **www.tourismpei.com**.

PEI has a Visitor Information Centre at each entry point to the province. Charlottetown boasts two, one at the airport and another on the waterfront where cruise ships dock. People arriving via Confederation Bridge can exit directly to **Gateway Village** (✆ **902/437-8570**), as you come off the bridge. The Visitor's Centre is a worthwhile stop for gathering brochures and asking questions. There's also an exhibit about the building of the bridge. The Gateway features a number of retail shops, food, a liquor store, and a park to let the kids or dog burn off steam. Be sure to check out **Cavendish Figurines** (www.cavendishfigurines.com; ✆ **800/558-1908**), a fun place with some great photo-ops inside and out. The main activity here is the production of Anne of Green Gables figurines, the only craftsmanship of its type in North America, but they also have a great gift shop, tours, and a warm welcome with a sense of humor to keep you smiling. If you are a photography buff, take the side road back toward the bridge, through Borden-Carleton. A little park at the lighthouse offers a great perspective. The road ends where the former ferries linking the island to the mainland year-round used to dock.

Visitor Information Centres at Wood Islands and Souris (seasonal) welcome those arriving by ferry. There are also welcome centers in Cavendish, on the Summerside waterfront, in St. Peters, and West Prince.

WHEN TO GO   PEI's peak tourism season is brief, running 8 to 9 weeks from **July through August.** If you plan to visit in June or September (lovely times to come), expect some restaurants and attractions to be closed. My advice? Check the listings

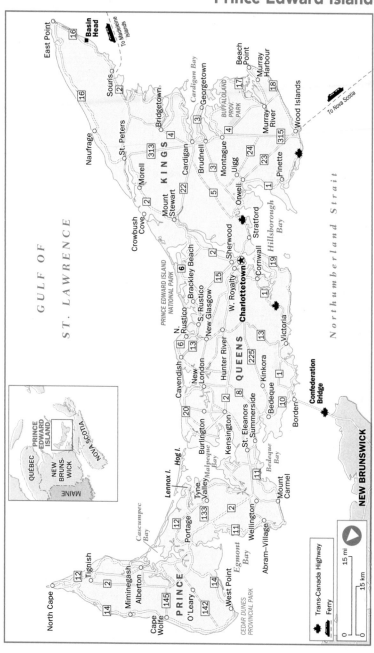

in this book carefully for restaurant, hotel, and attraction opening seasons, or contact a Visitor Information Centre. Definitely think about basing yourself in Charlottetown for a while if you'll be taking a number of day trips around the island. Determine whether you want a beach or rural-based vacation, or the convenience of being in town for restaurants and entertainment. After all, nothing is far away in Canada's smallest province.

Getting There

If you're coming by car, as the vast majority do, you'll either arrive by ferry (see below) or drive onto the island via the big **Confederation Bridge** (www.confederation bridge.com; ☎ 888/437-6565 or 902/437-7300), which opened with great fanfare in 1997. (On the island, you'll sometimes hear this bridge referred to as the "fixed link," a reference to the guarantee Canada made back in 1873 to provide a permanent link with the mainland. These people have long memories!) Whatever you call it, though, the dramatic 13km (8-mile) bridge is open 24 hours a day and takes 10 to 12 minutes to cross. If the winds are high, call ahead; it is occasionally shut down for bad weather. Unless you're high up in a van, truck, or RV, however, side views are mostly obstructed by the concrete barriers that form the guardrails along both sides. This is the longest bridge in the world that crosses ice-covered water (in the winter), so relax and enjoy the trip.

The round-trip bridge toll as of 2011 was C$43 for passenger cars (more for vehicles with more than two axles); the toll is collected when you leave the island, not when you enter it. (If you drive on in a rental car and fly off, you escape the toll altogether.) Credit cards are accepted at the bridge plaza. **Cyclists and backpackers** can cross the bridge, but not on the road. They must use the bridge's shuttle van, which charges C$4 per pedestrian or C$8 per cyclist.

SHUTTLES & BUSES   Even if you didn't bring wheels or rent any after arriving, you can get here via several long-distance shuttle, bus, or limo services. **PEI Express Shuttle** (www.peishuttle.com; ☎ 877/877-1771), one of them, runs one van daily each way between Halifax, Halifax's airport, and Charlottetown. The ride takes about 5 hours from downtown Halifax (about 4 hr. from the airport) and costs C$65 one-way for adults, C$60 for students and seniors, C$45 for children under age 12. (There's an additional C$5 surcharge if you're picked up at or dropped off from Halifax airport, and a C$5 fuel surcharge during certain high-gas-price times.) **Acadian Bus** (www. acadianbus.com; ☎ 800/567-5151) takes passengers from Moncton, New Brunswick, to Prince Edward Island daily. The trip takes about 3 hours and costs C$38 one-way (adult). There are connections to and from other major centers.

BY FERRY   For those arriving from Halifax, Cape Breton Island, or other points east, **Northumberland Ferries Limited** (☎ 877/882-8685 or 800/761-3806; www.nfl-bay.com) provides seasonal service between Caribou, Nova Scotia (just north of Pictou), and Woods Island, PEI. Ferries with a 220-car capacity run from May to mid-December. During peak season (June to mid-Oct), ferries depart each port approximately every 1½ to 2 hours throughout the day, with the last ferry departing as late as 8pm or 9:30pm in midsummer, depending on which direction you are traveling. The crossing takes about 75 minutes. Reservations are accepted, by booking online at www.nfl-bay.com, or call ☎ 866/775-8284. Early morning ferries tend to be less crowded. Fares are C$65 for a regular-size car (more for campers and RVs), plus C$16 per person (C$14 for seniors, free for kids 12 and under). There's a small fuel surcharge, as well, and major credit cards are honored.

Note that this round-trip fare is only collected when leaving the island. If you take the ferry onto the island and drive off, you pay the cheaper bridge toll only; drive on and take the ferry off, and you pay the higher ferry toll only.

A second ferry run from Souris, PEI, takes automobiles to Îles de la Madeleine, Québec, however you must return to PEI if traveling by car as there is no other link to the mainland that takes vehicles.

BY AIR The island's main airport, Charlottetown Airport (call sign YYG; www.fly pei.com), is located within the city of Charlottetown, just minutes from downtown. In summer, you can get here easily from either the U.S. or Canada. **Air Canada** (www.aircanada.com; *C* **888/247-2262**) commuter flights from Halifax take just a half-hour, and the airline also flies daily to Toronto and Montréal. Calgary-based **WestJet** (www.westjet.com; *C* **888/937-8538**) also connects Charlottetown with Toronto. **Delta** (www.delta.com; *C* **800/221-1212** or 800/325-1999) runs direct weekend summertime service from Boston's Logan and New York's JFK airports. **Sunwing** (www.sunwing.ca; *C* **800/761-1711**) provides seasonal service to Cuba and the Dominican Republic, two favorites of islanders during the winter.

A taxi ride into Charlottetown from the airport costs a flat fee of C$11 for the first passenger, plus C$3 each for additional passengers; two strangers can even share a single cab into town for a city-mandated fare of C$9 each. (Cabs also run to other parts of the island, for higher flat fares.) There are also limousine firms and several chain auto-rental outfits in the terminal.

THE GREAT OUTDOORS

Prince Edward Island doesn't have much wildness to speak of. It's all about cultivated landscapes that have long ago been tamed by farmers. That doesn't mean you can't find outdoor adventures, though. Here are some places to start.

BICYCLING There's no finer destination in Atlantic Canada for relaxed cycling than Prince Edward Island. The modest size of this island, the gentleness of the hills (the island's highest point is just 142m/466 ft. above sea level), and the loveliness of the landscapes all make for memorable biking trips. Although you won't find much rugged mountain biking here, you can find plenty of idyllic excursions, especially in the northern and eastern portions of the island. Don't get the idea that it is flat; with the exception of a couple of areas, the land is made up of gently rolling hills and vales. Just be sure to avoid the busy Trans-Canada Highway on the south coast, and main roads like Route 2. You'll find less traffic and superb backroads biking throughout the network of secondary routes.

There's also a very significant off-road bike trail here: the **Confederation Trail ★★★**, an impressive system of several hundred miles of pathway built along the former trackbed of an ill-fated provincial railway. The main trail runs from Tignish (on the island's far northwestern shore) to Elmira (up in the northeastern corner), while good branch trails stretch right into downtown Charlottetown and touch on a number of towns mentioned in this book, such as Souris, Montague, and Georgetown. One spur even reaches all the way to the Confederation Bridge (see above). The pathway is mostly covered in rolled stone dust, which makes for good traveling with either a mountain bike or hybrid. Services are slowly developing along this route, with more rental services and inns cropping up every year. Ask at tourist bureaus for updated information. Do remember the trail is also used by hikers and walkers (often with dogs), so be attentive.

The Prince Edward Island National Park has bike lanes along its coastal roads.

The experts at **MacQueen's Island Tours & Bike Shop,** 430 Queen St. in Charlottetown (www.macqueens.com; ℂ **800/969-2822** or 902/368-2453), organize a range of bicycle tour packages with all-inclusive prices covering bike rentals, accommodations, route cards, maps, luggage transfers, and emergency road repair service. They run shuttle vans out to the trail. A customized 5- to 7-night tour of a section of the island for two might run C$1,000 to C$1,360 per person, double occupancy; a custom group tour would be cheaper per person. Bikes can be rented at the shop for C$25 per day and C$125 per week (kids' bikes are cheaper, touring bikes a bit more expensive). And, of course, they do all repairs. Another pure cycle shop in Charlottetown doing rentals, repairs, bike tune-ups, and shuttle runs out to either end of the trail (no tours) is **Smooth Cycle,** at 330 University Ave. (ℂ **800/310-6550** from Eastern Canada or 902/566-5530). Rentals here including helmet, water bottle, and a lock cost C$17 per half-day, C$25 per day, or C$110 per week. Note that the shop is closed Sundays.

FISHING With 1,700km (1,100 miles) of coastline, inland rivers and streams, and more than 800 ponds, the island can be a fisherman's dream. If you're interested in deep-sea fishing, head to the north coast, where you'll find plenty of fishing captains and outfitters happy to take you out on the big waves in search of cod, mackerel, and others. The greatest concentrations of services are at the harbors of North Rustico and Covehead Bay; see the "Queens County" section, below, for more details on specific outfits. Rates are quite reasonable, generally about C$40 for adults, C$30 for children, for 3 hours or so, and most will clean and fillet fish to take home if you wish.

North Lake Harbour gives itself the moniker "Tuna Capital of the World" and is home to deep sea charter vessels who will take you out in search of the giant bluefins, who can top 1,000 pounds. Whale, seal, and bird sightings can sweeten the experience. **Tony's Tuna Fishing** (www.tonystunafishing.com; ℂ **902/357-2207**) will take you on a private tuna charter July through September for C$1,000 a day. They also offer scenic tours for C$125 an hour for the family. Or you can go lobster fishing for C$100 in May or June, but be warned they will probably put you to work.

Trout fishing attracts inland anglers, although, as always, the very best spots are a matter of local knowledge. A good place to start your inquiries is at **Going Fishing** in the Sherwood Shopping Centre at 161 St. Peters Rd. in Charlottetown (ℂ **902/367-3444**). The store specializes in fly-fishing equipment, but also stocks conventional rods and reels as well. **Ben's Lake** in Bellevue (www.benslake.com; ℂ **902/838-2706**) offers catch-and-release fly-fishing and fee fishing by the pound on their 18-acre (7.2 hectare) lake. A great place to try fishing or take the kids, they even have tackle for rent and a campground on-site. Information on required fishing licenses can be obtained from any visitor information center, or by contacting the province's **Department of Fisheries, Aquaculture & Rural Development,** P.O. Box 2000, Charlottetown, PEI C1A 7N8 (www.gov.pe.ca/eef/fishing; ℂ **902/368-6330**).

GOLF PEI's reputation for golf has soared in recent years, earning the province the title of 2011 Undiscovered Golf Destination of the Year from the International Association of Golf Travel Operators, thanks largely to the variety and convenience of 32 courses within a short driving distance—and the LPGA success of Charlottetown native Lorie Kane. (The island now possesses 10 of Canada's top 100 courses, according to the Toronto *Globe & Mail.* And *ScoreGolf* magazine says the Canadian Golf Academy in Stratford was voted the #1 teaching facility.) You can golf beside the ocean, within city limits, or in a pastoral setting—PEI has more golf courses per capita than anywhere else in Canada.

One of the best-regarded courses on the island is the **Links at Crowbush Cove ★** (𝄞 **800/235-8909** or 902/961-7306). Sand dunes and persistent winds off the gulf add to the challenge at this relatively young course, which is on the northeastern coast; greens fees run C$60 to C$110 per person. Another perennial favorite is the **Brudenell River Golf Course** (𝄞 **800/235-8909** or 902/652-3015), near Montague along the eastern shore at the Rodd Brudenell River Resort; in the late 1990s the course added a second 18-holer, designed by Michael Hurdzan, and a double-ended driving range. Greens fees are C$40 to C$85 per person.

Golf PEI (www.golfpei.ca; 𝄞 **866/465-3734**), a trade association, has a reservation system with great golf packages which takes the work out of planning a complete vacation. It publishes a booklet and website outlining the essentials of member island courses available from island information centers, the provincial tourist information office, or check the website at **www.golfpei.ca**; the organization's mailing address is 565 N. River Rd., Charlottetown, PEI C1E 1J7.

SEA KAYAKING   Little PEI packs in more than 1,200km (800 miles) of attractive coastline, most of it touched by relatively warm seawater, making for some excellent sea kayaking. Paddlers can vary the scene from broad tidal inlets ringed with marsh to rusty-red cliffs sculpted by the wind to dunes topped with swaying waves of marram grass. **Outside Expeditions** (www.getoutside.com; 𝄞 **800/207-3899** or 902/963-3366) in North Rustico hosts half- and full-day excursions and clinics daily at the national park and nearby (including one that takes in a drop-in to the PEI Preserve Co.). Rates vary, but you can usually figure on C$50 to C$100 per person. More ambitious paddlers can sign up for 1- to 7-day kayak trips departing throughout the summer. Excursions are also available from Brudenell River Provincial Park in eastern PEI, a more sheltered environment with calmer waters than the north shore. They'll also rent you a kayak if you want to plan your own itinerary.

SWIMMING   PEI's chief attraction is its beaches, which are generally excellent for swimming. You'll find them ringing the island, tucked in between dunes and crumbling cliffs. Generally speaking, the beaches along the Northumberland Strait, or south shore, have red sand and long shallows, while those along the Gulf of St. Lawrence are white sand, often backed by soaring dunes. These north shore beaches can be subject to rip tides, so stay in the shallows unless in an area with lifeguards. Thanks to the moderating influence of the Gulf of St. Lawrence, the water temperature is more humane here than elsewhere in Atlantic Canada. The most popular beaches (by far) are at **Prince Edward Island National Park** along the north shore, but you can easily find other local or provincial beaches with great swimming by asking anywhere locally. Good choices include **Cedar Dunes Provincial Park** (on the island's southwestern coast), **Red Point Provincial Park, Basin Head Beach** (on its northeastern shore), and **Panmure Island Provincial Park** on the southeastern coast. Basin Head, on the eastern shore, is known as the "singing sands" because the sand squeaks when you walk on it.

QUEENS COUNTY

Queens County occupies the center of PEI. It's home to the island's largest city **(Charlottetown),** which is also the provincial capital, and hosts the greatest concentration of traveler services by far.

Cavendish on the north shore is the most tourist-oriented place in the entire province. Its popularity began because of visitors seeking the home of Lucy Maud

Montgomery and her fictional character Anne of Green Gables, as well as the glorious beaches of this coastal area. Today, attractions such as amusement parks, shops, interactive attractions, golf courses, paintball, and water activities are particularly appealing to families. On the other hand, much of the rest of the county—besides Charlottetown, of course—is extremely pastoral and untrammeled. Villages are the hidden gems. **New Glasgow,** for instance, has three top eateries, a preserve maker, and a toy shop, all located along River Clyde, known for its proliferation of geese and ducks, and the eagles that soar overhead. The fishing community of **North Rustico** is a must: Wander the wharfs or the seaside boardwalk, go deep sea fishing, or trace Acadian roots dating back to 1790. Or, Stanley Bridge, where kids diving from the highway bridge entertain patrons of Carr's Oyster Bar, who specialize in shucking oysters from their own aquaculture operation.

Two areas of Queens County merit their own sections within this chapter: Charlottetown on the south shore, of course, and **Prince Edward Island National Park** on the north shore. Flip ahead to those sections if you're seeking detailed information on those destinations in a hurry.

Essentials

GETTING THERE   Three main routes travel east and west through the county. Route 1 in the south connects Charlottetown with the Confederation Bridge, and then Summerside. Route 2, the fastest way to travel east or west, runs through the center. Route 6, the main route along the county's northern reaches, involves a number of turns at stop signs at intersections. Keep a sharp eye on the road signs or you'll lose the trail.

VISITOR INFORMATION   The snazzy, well-stocked **Cavendish Visitor Information Centre** (© **902/963-7830**) is open daily from mid-June through mid-October. It's located just north of the intersection of routes 13 and 6.

Cavendish

There are three things that make Cavendish a prime tourist destination: the Prince Edward Island National Park with its legendary white-sand beaches, two top golf courses, and a huge dedication to fantasy. Cavendish is the home of the fictional redhead Anne of Green Gables, a somewhat heroic figure in Canadian literature (and, in fact, Anne is well known around the world). She's a plucky girl who perseveres through the sheer force of her optimism. Her fictional hometown features a bucolic mix of woodlands, fields, rolling hills, and sandy dunes, the ideal setting for the pastoral novels that made Anne so famous.

Fortunately for those who love and appreciate Anne and her creator, important sites, images, and concepts have been preserved and cared for, either by Parks Canada or, in some cases, descendants of the author who created Anne, Lucy Maud Montgomery. The enduring popularity of the novels attracts droves of tourists. It didn't take savvy entrepreneurs long to realize that the area could support attractions, amusement parks, and shopping arcades, plus a surfeit of motels and "cottage courts," which are a popular option for families or groups traveling together. The majority of what you want to find is conveniently located along the main road (Rte. 6). Most attractions are set back from the road, spread out well apart from each other and somewhat limited—you only need head east or west of town on Route 6 for a few miles to get back to the lovely vistas that made this region famous in the first place.

As for "downtown" Cavendish, there's no discernible village center, just an intersection of roads and a tourist information center; everything is sprawled out along the approach roads. If you're on PEI to stroll quaint lanes and villages, rather than because of an interest in Anne, you're probably much better off heading east to North Rustico or south to New Glasgow. If beaches, nature, walks in the woods, or quiet relaxation by the sea appeals, then turn north at any of the entrances to the national park. You can check in to the Interpretive Centre on the northwest corner of routes 6 and 13 to find out what is happening during your visit. If your kids do enjoy amusements, though—or you do know who Anne is—buckle in for a day or two. This village has the most kid appeal of any community on the island, but don't expect a high-tech Disney-like experience or exciting nightlife.

EVERYTHING ANNE

Visitors to Prince Edward Island owe it to themselves to at least think about picking up a copy of *Anne of Green Gables* at some point. If you don't read it, you might feel a bit left out of the fun—and unable to understand what the fuss is all about. The novel has inspired the longest running musical theater in Canada, a television miniseries, movies, and spin-off fiction and nonfiction books. In fact, Anne has become so omnipresent and popular that a licensing authority was created in the 1990s to control the crush of Anne-related products popping up everywhere.

In case you don't have time to read it, here's a little background. In 1908, island native Lucy Maud Montgomery published *Anne of Green Gables,* her very first book—and an instant success. The book is a fictional account of Anne Shirley, a precocious 11-year-old orphan who's mistakenly sent from Nova Scotia to the farm of dour islanders Matthew and Marilla Cuthbert, who had requested an orphan *boy* to help with their farm chores. Anne's vivid imagination and outsized vocabulary get her into a series of increasingly more hilarious pickles, from which she generally emerges beloved by everyone who encounters her. It's a bright, somewhat bittersweet story that touched a serious nerve and became such a hit worldwide that it spawned a number of sequels. (The book is still taught in many elementary schools in Japan. It's probably Anne's always plucky attitude in the face of crushing real-life circumstances that attracts her to the Japanese.) Whatever the reason, throngs of Japanese tourists congregate in Cavendish each year to relive Anne's fictional life for a few days.

The nucleus of tourism in Cavendish is the preservation of all things Anne, as people come from around the world to pay homage and seek some of the magic. Even with the increased commercialism, there is a certain sweetness to both Anne's story and the landscape in which she lived. Except for a dozen or so attractions along Route 6, this area still looks more or less the same as it did during the era when Montgomery wrote the original book.

If you're a traveler who has never heard of Anne until this moment, and you're more interested in locating fine foods and scenic bike tours than the house where Anne "grew up," head for nearby communities or the national park.

Anne of Green Gables Museum at Silver Bush ★   West of Cavendish, where Route 20 runs along the shore, Silver Bush, a farm that has been in the Campbell family since 1776, welcomes visitors from around the world to celebrate Lucy Maud Montgomery and the connections the author has to this white-shingled two-story home. She referred to it as "the wonder castle of my childhood." Her love for the Campbell Home, and the aunt and uncle who lived there, was so strong that she chose to marry in the homestead. In a letter to a cousin, she once revealed that "I love this old home more than any place on Earth." If you visit, don't be surprised if you see a bride, all decked out in traditional white, in the parlor beside the Lake of Shining Waters. Romantics from as far away as Japan come to the island to exchange their marital vows in the parlor just as Lucy Maud did in 1911. The Campbell Home is now known as the Anne of Green Gables Museum, with many significant treasures to be seen. Of special appeal are the carriage rides, which take passengers by the Lake of Shining Waters, down a country lane to a private white-sand beach—the very waters that inspired the author. The family prides itself on its flower gardens, the lovely countryside, the preserved furniture, linens, photos, and personal effects. Plan 2 hours to explore the museum, grounds, and gift shop; if you take the long carriage ride (a worthy experience), then plan 3.

Rte. 20, Park Corner (about 6 miles north of intersection with Rte. 6). www.annemuseum.com. ⓒ **800/665-2663** or 902/886-2884 (weekends only). Admission C$5 adults, C$1 children age 6–18. Carriage rides: Short (10 min.) C$4 adults, C$1.50 children, half-hour C$55 for up to 5 people, 1 hour C$90 for up to 5. May and Oct daily 11am–4pm; June and Sept daily 10am–4pm; July–Aug daily 9am–5pm.

Anne of Green Gables—The Musical A must-do for anyone who loves live musical theater, or the spirit of Anne of Green Gables, is this sprightly, professional musical rendition of Anne's story (complete with 19-piece orchestra). The high-energy, sometimes emotional production has been selling out the house for 47 years, making it Canada's longest-running musical. The play brings the early story of Anne to the stage for a 2-hour show from late June through late September, usually Wednesdays and Saturdays. Shows take place at 2pm and then again at 7:30pm. Definitely call ahead, as tickets go fast during the limited summer run. Every so often they take Anne on a tour, but there is nothing quite as special as seeing the show on its own turf, in the Land of Anne.

Confederation Centre of the Arts, 145 Richmond St., Charlottetown. www.charlottetownfestival. com. ⓒ **800/565-0278** or 902/566-1267. July–Aug. Tickets C$55–C$75 adult, C$39–C$53 child, C$50–C$68 student and senior.

Avonlea Village ★ ☺ If the idea of introducing your family to a day of old-fashioned fun appeals, then Avonlea Village is the place to be. The hosts here do their best to help you feel like you have traveled back in time, to that idyllic period before electronic entertainment. Don't expect glitz, glamour, or heart-stopping thrills from rides. Personally, I love to see children learning to play the spoons, shuffling into a sack for a sack race, or giggling until they roll over during the Farmer's Pig Race. Basically, this is a stroll-around attraction that portrays a village from Anne's time. Ride in a horse and wagon, visit the barns, eat ice cream, chocolates, or lunch in a box, all made on-site. Many of the buildings are of historic significance, moved there on big trucks, and even those that are new re-creations provide a good backdrop for the roving characters who do little skits, re-create musical kitchen parties, and reinforce the concept of stepping back to the good old days. Admission to the village is a bit pricey, but you can stay all day long. The price drops dramatically in September, but the village also has less going on.

8779 Rte. 6, Cavendish. www.avonlea.ca. ⓒ **902/963-3050.** Day-pass admission C$19 adults, C$17 seniors, C$15 children 3–18, C$65 families; Sept admission C$10 per person flat fee. Musical variety show, small extra charge. Mid-June to Aug daily 10am–5pm; early Sept 10am–4pm. Closed mid-Sept to mid-June.

Cavendish Cemetery ★ This historic cemetery, protected by a grove of trees, was founded in 1835 and is best known as the final resting spot for author Lucy Maud Montgomery. It's not hard to find her gravesite: Follow the pavement blocks from the arched entryway, which is across from the Anne Shirley Motel. She's buried beside her husband, the Rev. Ewen MacDonald (thus the stone reads "MacDonald," not Montgomery).

Intersection of routes 13 and 6, Cavendish. Free admission. Open daily dawn–dusk.

Green Gables Heritage Place at L.M. Montgomery's Cavendish National Historical Site ★★

If you have even an inkling of knowledge about Anne, the very best place to begin your Anne experience in Cavendish is at Green Gables. This is a historic site, not a theme park. Operated by Parks Canada, the emphasis is preservation of artifacts and the site itself, as well as interpretive programs. Lucy Maud Montgomery grew up nearby and used this farm as the chief inspiration for the Cuthbert farm in the books, and it has since been furnished according to descriptions in the books. She wandered the woodlands, naming special places such as Lover's Lane and the Haunted Wood. She loved the home and modeled the fictional Green Gables after it. The real-life settings preserved at this historic site fed the creativity that led to Montgomery becoming the first Canadian female author to be made a member of the Royal Society of Arts and Letters of London, England. For many, visiting Green Gables is a pilgrimage of sorts. They come not just to celebrate the fictional character, but the author and the idyllic way of life she presented. In 1936, the farm was purchased and became part of Prince Edward Island National Park, along with the site of the homestead. They have been caretakers ever since for the 200,000 people visit each year (6,000 of them from Japan). If you see buses in the parking lot, plan to explore the farm before the house, as the lines to enter the home will be lengthy. Allow 2 hours for a visit, more if the idea of seeking a special place for quiet introspection appeals.

8619 Rte. 6, Cavendish (just west of intersection with Rte. 13). www.pc.gc.ca/eng/lhn-nhs/pe/greengables/index.aspx. © **902/963-7874** or 566-7050 (off season) Admission mid-June to late Aug, C$7.80 adults, C$6.55 seniors, C$3.90 children, C$20 families; rates discounted 25% May to mid-June and late Aug to Oct; C$6.30 adults, C$5.40, seniors, C$3.15 youth, C$16 families/groups; winter C$3.90 adults, C$3.15 seniors, C$1.90 youth, C$9.80 family. May 1–Oct 31 daily 9am–5pm; Nov–Apr by appointment only.

Lucy Maud Montgomery Birthplace

A few miles south of the Silver Bush Anne of Green Gables Museum is this simple white home, where the author was born in 1874. Today the house is once again decorated in the Victorian style of Montgomery's era, and it includes mementos like the author's wedding dress and scrapbooks. Just like the (separately owned and operated) Silver Bush, this is historically authentic and worth an hour for Anne fans.

Intersection of routes 6 and 20, New London. © **902/886-2099** or 836-5502. Admission C$3 adults, C50¢ children 6–12. Mid-May to mid-Oct daily 9am–5pm. Closed mid-Oct to mid-May.

Site of Lucy Maud Montgomery's Cavendish Home at L.M. Montgomery's Cavendish National Historic Site ★★

The place where the girl behind the girl lived . . . sort of. Authoress Montgomery lived in a house on this site with her grandparents, Alexander and Lucy Macneill, from 1876 (when she was 21 months old) until 1911. She wrote *Anne of Green Gables* and her other books at the home, which unfortunately is no longer standing; visitors can roam the grounds and read interpretive signs and plaques about the property's literary history. A small bookshop features books by and about the author. Again, as with so many others around the area, this site is mainly of interest to Anne buffs, but it does also give a nice flavor of the surroundings in which she worked and from which she drew inspiration. Allow 1 hour.

Rte. 6. Cavendish (just east of Rte. 13 intersection). www.peisland.com/lmm. © **902/963-2969.** Admission C$4 adults, C$2 children, C$12 families. Mid-May to Oct daily 10am–5pm (July–Aug 9am–6pm).

WHERE TO STAY

Cottage courts, properties that offer a number of cottages in one location (sort of like a small village), are an integral part of the accommodations scene in and around Cavendish. Families particularly appreciate being able to put the kids to bed in their own room, giving adults time to relax. With kitchens, a place to let the kids run and play, and costs similar to one good hotel room, cottages are a great option for families. Cavendish can boast enough cottage choices to fit your budget; just remember you will pay more for the best amenities: pools, better quality furnishings, private locations, proximity to the beaches, access to the trolley. This area has a proliferation of options ranging from bare basics to luxurious. Your best move is to study the listings in the visitors' guide, check off what is important to you and your family, and book ahead.

If you've arrived without reservations, check the board at the **visitor information center** (see above), which lists vacancies. You might also find a great deal (people do) by asking local residents about rentals; checking local bulletin boards at laundromats and general stores; or browsing free local "shopper" newspapers. Certainly can't hurt. But it takes time and energy.

Cavendish Beach Cottages ★★ ☺ Location, location, location. This compound of closely spaced cottages is located on a grassy rise within PEI's lovely national park (where the beaches are), just past the entrance. The pine-paneled one-, two-, and three-bedroom units won't win any prizes for design, but do come with the basics you need. All feature direct ocean views; some have tubs while others have showers only, but generally speaking these are a great choice for couples and families—all the more so, since every cottage is no more than a 5-minute walk from the beach. There's easy access right onto Gulf Shore Drive, where you find some of PEI's best walking and biking trails.

1445 Gulf Shore Pkwy. W., Cavendish C0A 1N0 (mailing address P.O. Box 3088, Charlottetown, PEI C1A 7N9). www.cavendishbeachcottages.com. © **902/963-2025.** Fax 902/963-2025. 13 housekeeping units. Mid-June to Aug C$120–C$215 double; May to mid-June and Sept to early Oct C$95–C$140 double. MC, V. Closed early Oct to mid-May. **Amenities:** Laundromat. *In room:* A/C, TV, kitchenette w/microwave and dishwasher, no phone, Wi-Fi (free).

Shining Waters Luxury Cottages ★★★ ✦ Part of the Resort at Cavendish Corner, the six cottages of Shining Waters are the most luxurious of a large offering from the Wood family, who have been at the business of accommodating guests since 1942. The two-story cottages—with fireplaces, Jacuzzis, and loads of space for getting together—have only one fault: no bathroom upstairs. After a multimillion dollar upgrade, the resort combines the benefits of being located in the heart of old Cavendish, with a 200-seat restaurant, art gallery, and gift shop, and lots to do off-site and nearby. Perfect for a couple's golf weekend or family vacation.

7600 Cawnpore Lane (off Rte. 6), Cavendish, PEI C0A 1N0. www.resortatcavendishcorner.com. © **877/963-2251** or 902/963-2251. 39 cottages, 6 luxury. C$130–C$298 2–3 bedroom, C$825–C$1800 weekly; C$665-C$1230 off season. MC, V. Closed Oct–June. **Amenities:** Heated outdoor pools; playgrounds; exercise room. *In room:* TV, Internet (free), whirlpool tubs, large kitchen.

WHERE TO EAT

Cavendish offers limited opportunities for creative dining, though it's well stocked with places offering hamburgers, fried clams, and the like. For a fine dining experience, check out the **Pearl Café** ★★★ (© **902/963-2111**) on Route 6 between

Cavendish and North Rustico. Locals like the home cooking at **Chez Yvonne's** (© 902/963-2070) on Route 6 at the west end of town. Two of the restaurants listed below require an easy, 10- to 15-minute drive via country roads from Cavendish, but they're worth it. (Also see the "PEI's Seasonal Lobster Suppers" box, p. 218 below, for info on a uniquely PEI style of family dining.)

Café on the Clyde ★★ 🗡 ☺ CANADIAN   Part of the popular Prince Edward Island Preserve Co. (p. 217), a worthwhile stop for delicious homemade preserves. Foodies regularly stop in to this cheerful cafe. Breakfasts run to French toast, granola, toast with their own preserves, frittata, or a hearty country platter. Lunch choices include a rarity in this land often known as Spud Island: a decadent main dish made with local potatoes, the Preserve Company Potato Pie. Other traditional favorites include seafood chowder, fish cakes, and lobster quiche. Dinner could be sautéed pork tenderloin or pan-seared seafood. Finish with their popular Raspberry Cream Cheese Pie, homemade ice cream, or a delectable cake, pie, or cheesecake. You'll also find a kids' menu, afternoon tea, and jazz guitar (weekend nights). Just be prepared for the tour-bus crowd: Buses get their own parking lot, close to the door.

Intersection of routes 224 and 258 (4 miles south of Rte. 6, on Rte. 13), New Glasgow.© **902/964-4301.** Reservations recommended for dinner. Main courses C$5–C$10 at breakfast, C$12-18 at lunch, C$13–C$18 at dinner. AE, DC, MC, V. July–Aug daily 9am–9pm; June and Sept limited hours. Closed Oct–May.

Olde Glasgow Mill Restaurant ★ CANADIAN   This casual restaurant, originally built as a late-19th-century feed mill in New Glasgow, has been a restaurant since 1997 and is nicely shielded from the tourist throngs over in Cavendish. The place overlooks a river and features an eclectic assortment of dinner options. Appetizers like Moroccan fried dumpling set the tone for dinner, which serves up such choices as a rack of lamb encrusted in herbs, served with the traditional mint; lobster thermidor; inventive pastas, or bouillabaisse.

5592 Rte. 13, New Glasgow. www.oldeglasgowmill.ca. © **902/964-3313.** Reservations recommended. Dinner C$19–C$38. MC, V. June to early Oct daily 5–9:30 pm. Closed early Oct to May.

Rachel's Restaurant ★ ITALIAN   These folks boast about having the north shore's best pizza, along with seafood, traditional favorites, and Italian specialties. Don't expect authentic Italian; it is North Americanized, but generally very good with a few tempting twists, like Island Scallop Pie or Lobster and Scallop Cannelloni al Forno. The oceanview deck or one of three dining areas can make for a decent meal out in a community that offers few choices. Best options are lunch and dinner; breakfast is overpriced.

8554 Cavendish Rd. (Rte. 6) near Rte. 13. www.cavendishresort.com. © **902/963-3227.** C$9.95–C$14 lunch; C$15–C$25 evening; C$6.95–C$11 breakfast. Children's menu. MC, V. May–Sept daily 7:30am–8:30pm. Closed Oct–Apr.

North & South Rustico to Brackley Beach

A few miles east of Cavendish are the Rusticos, five in all: North Rustico, South Rustico, Rusticoville, Rustico Harbour, and Anglo Rustico. (Don't feel bad if you can't keep them straight.) It's a fun, relaxing place to head if you're seeking beaches, small harbors, and friendly locals.

The region was first "settled" by Acadians in 1790, and many present-day residents are descendants of those original settlers. (This was one of the first Canadian regions to be populated by Acadians following the Treaty of Paris, and is the oldest Acadian presence on PEI.) The Rusticos are attractive villages with far fewer tourist traps and auto traffic than Cavendish—which means they're much easier to explore by car or bike. Out of the hubbub, they're all still close enough to the national park *and* Anne's land, so they work well as a base. And the island's famous beaches are virtually at your doorstep.

North Rustico ★ clusters around a scenic harbor with views out toward Rustico Bay. Leave time for parking, walking around, perusing deep-sea fishing opportunities (see below), and peeking into shops. The village curves around Rustico Bay to end at North Rustico Harbour, a sand spit with fishing wharves, summer cottages, a fisheries museum, and a couple of informal restaurants. A wood-decked promenade follows the water's edge from town to harbor, a worthy destination for a quiet afternoon ramble or a picnic. Also, here is **Outside Expeditions** (www.getoutside.com; ✆ **800/207-3899** or 902/963-3366), one of PEI's best outfitters; they offer sea kayaking excursions around the harbor and into surrounding areas (see "Sea Kayaking," earlier in this chapter). If you crave a good read, watch for **Jem Books** (✆ **902/ 963-3802**) as you leave North Rustico on Route 6, one of the best-organized used book stores I've ever seen.

To find **South Rustico ★★**, continue east on Route 6 to **Route 243** and ascend the low hill overlooking the bay. Here you'll find a handsome cluster of buildings that were once home to some of the most prosperous Acadian settlers. Among the structures is the sandstone **Farmers' Bank of Rustico Museum ★** (✆ **902/963-3168**), beside the church. A bank that's historic? In this case, yes. The bank was established with the help of a visionary local cleric, the Reverend Georges-Antoine Belcourt, in 1864 to help local farmers get their operations into the black. The Father and parishioners actually built the bank themselves, timber by timber, stone by stone. It operated for some 30 years and helped inspire the credit union movement in North America before it was, ironically, forced to shut down by legislative banking reforms. Open for tours from June through September, Monday through Saturday, 9:30am to 5:30pm, and Sundays 1 to 5pm. (You can call during the off season and try to schedule a walk-through, as well, if you're in town.) Admission costs C$4 per adult, C$3 per senior, C$2 per student, and C$8 per family.

Right next door to the bank, there are two more structures worth checking out. **Doucet House ★**, a sturdy log building of Acadian construction dating from 1772, was the home of Jean Doucet, who arrived in these parts on a type of boat called a "shallop." It's believed that this might be the oldest extant home on the entire island. The house was moved from its waterside location in 1999 and completely restored— which it badly needed—and period furnishings have since been added to bring back that ages-old flavor. Its opening hours and admissions fees are the same as those for the Farmers' Bank; in fact, one ticket gets you into both.

Then there's the handsome **St. Augustine's Parish Church** (dating from 1838, with a cemetery beyond), also next door. If the church's door is open, enter and have a look around the graceful structure.

Brackley Beach ★ is the gateway to the eastern section of the main part of PEI's national park, and it has the fewest services of any town in these parts. It's just a quiet area, with no village center to speak of; it can be best appreciated by those who prefer their beach vacations only lightly touched by civilization or noise.

DEEP-SEA FISHING

PEI's north shore is home to the island's greatest concentration of deep-sea fishing boats. For something like C$40 per person (check on the latest rates, but it's never very costly), you'll get about 3 hours' worth of time out on the open seas to fish for mackerel, cod, flounder, and the like. Don't worry about a lack of experience: All the necessary equipment is supplied, crewmembers are usually helpful as coaches, and some boat hands will even gladly clean and fillet your catch before you debark so that you can cook it after you hop back onto dry land and drive back to your cottage.

In North Rustico, at any given time, at least a half-dozen captains offer fishing trips, including **Aiden's Deep Sea Fishing** (www.peifishing.com; 🕿 **866/510-3474** or 902/963-3522). There's also **Salty Seas Deep-Sea Fishing** (www.virtuo.com/salty; 🕿 **902/672-3246**), about a 20-minute drive east of North Rustico at Covehead Harbour (within the national park).

SHOPPING

Between Cavendish and Brackley Beach, you'll find a number of shops offering unique island crafts and products. Browsing is a good option on days when the weather doesn't lure you to the beach.

Cheeselady's Gouda 👜 A short detour off Route 6, but well worth it. Watch a brief video about the making of Gouda, then get down to the real business of tasting and buying some of the excellent cheeses produced here. If you don't feel like the usual aged Gouda, try the flavored varieties with peppercorns, garlic, or herbs. Sizes range from a wedge to a wheel. Rte. 223, Winsloe N., southeast of Oyster Bed Bridge. 🕿 **902/368-1506**.

The Dunes Studio Gallery and Café ★★★ 📷 This architecturally striking modern gallery on the road to the eastern section of PEI National Park is the best place to browse works by international, Canadian, and island artisans and craftspeople. It calls you to sit back and savor the flowers, gardens, and tranquillity. The owner/potter can often be seen at his potter's wheel, producing the distinctive, elegant items that the Dunes is known for. Housed on several open levels, the gallery features pottery, furniture, lamps, woodworking, sculptures, and paintings, along with more accessible crafts, soaps and jewelry. The gallery is also home to serene gardens and an appealing **cafe** ★★, covered below in "Where to Eat." Allow a couple of hours to explore all the levels of the Dunes. The gallery is open daily from May through October; the cafe, daily from June through September. Rte. 15, Brackley Beach. www.dunesgallery.com. 🕿 **902/672-2586** (gallery) or 672-1883 (cafe).

Gaudreau Fine Woodworking ★ Set beside Rustico Bay, this store sells woodworking made right on-premises by Jacques Gaudreau. Items for sale might range from big, deep salad bowls to plates, elegant sushi trays, or even wrist rests for computer keyboards (crafted from bird's-eye maple). As a bonus, you can browse a wide selection of pottery from regional potters while you're here. Open year-round; call for winter hours. Rte. 6, South Rustico. www.woodmagic.ca. 🕿 **902/963-2273.**

North Shore Island Traditions Past & Present Rug Shop ★ 👜 If you enjoy working with your hands, then this little gem of a shop, so tiny that three people constitute a crowd, is for you. That is because it is chock-full of unique supplies for those who papercraft: scrapbooking, card making, and paper embroidery. You'll find luxury yarns, traditional rug-hooking supplies, and handcrafted items, including greeting cards and hand-hooked rugs. Open year-round, Monday to Saturday 10am to 5:30pm in summer, Thursday to Saturday 11am to 4pm in winter. Rte 6 and Legion St., North Rustico. www.hookamat.com. 🕿 **902/963-2453.**

Prince Edward Island Preserve Co. ★★ PEI Preserve sells accessible luxury—a little piece of PEI to take home. The company makes a variety of preserves at a renovated butter factory in a lovely valley; abundant sampling is encouraged, and

If you have a must-do list for Prince Edward Island, the experience of an Island-style lobster supper should be on it. Lobster suppers have a long history here, beginning several decades ago as community suppers. The opening of lobster season was celebrated in community halls, church basements, or even outdoors. Not only did it mark the arrival of spring (the ice having departed from the harbors and fishing grounds), it also brought welcome income. As is the way with Islanders, they began using these events to raise funds for worthy projects or to support the church.

The logic behind the menu was simple. Local fishermen donated the lobster, farmers the potatoes and milk for chowder. Someone's cold cellar would provide cabbage and carrots for coleslaw. Strawberries were the first fruit of the season. Biscuits, bread, pies, and squares came from local housewives, along with their own pickles. Everyone pitched in.

Soon word spread. Townfolk wanted to go, as did savvy tourists. In 1963, Father Denis Gallant, pastor at St. Ann's Church in Hope River, started serving Lobster Dinners in the basement of the church to help pay off the mortgage. At the time, they charged C$1.50 for a full dinner. St. Ann's continues to operate Lobster Suppers and boasts they are the "original." As a nonprofit organization, they support charities close to the heart of the community, as well as the church.

St. Ann's Church Lobster Suppers (www.lobstersuppers.com; ✆ **902/621-0635**) is just off Route 224. It's open mid-June to late September, Monday through Saturday from 4 to 8:30pm. Cost is C$33 to C$47 lobster dinner; C$30 to C$40 for alternates: chicken, salmon, scallops, shrimp haddock, steak, or surf and turf. Credit cards are accepted and there is a children's menu.

The other star in my lobster supper showcase, New Glasgow Lobster Suppers, began in 1958 when the Junior Farmers Organization held a fundraiser. Twelve Junior Farmers turned it into a business in 1972, building ever bigger halls to accommodate the crowds. The Nicholson and MacRae families purchased

you can watch the preserve-making process through a glass window. Single jars of jam are frankly a little pricey, but fans tend to stock up on their favorites. Mine: black currant, raspberry and champagne jam, sour cherry marmalade, and whatever I can't resist after a taste. The flavor continues in their **Café on the Clyde,** open seasonally and serving everything from hearty breakfasts to surprisingly gourmet lunches and dinners (see "Where to Eat" in the Cavendish section, p. 214, for more details). Intersection of routes 224 and 258 (just off Rte. 13), New Glasgow. ✆ **902/964-4300.**

WHERE TO STAY

Barachois Inn ★★ 🎁   If walks down country lanes, quiet pastoral countryside touching the sea, and lazy days in the garden are your idea of an ideal vacation, then this inn is just the ticket. Topped by a fine mansard roof, this Victorian country home keeps company with a noteworthy cluster of historic buildings, including an impressive Acadian church, Farmers' Bank, and Doucet House. Barachois (pronounced bar-a-schwa) Inn was derelict when purchased by Judy and Gary MacDonald in 1982. Its restoration won them a Heritage Preservation Award and offers guests a luxurious stay among period antiques. Rooms range from spacious to under-the-eaves cozy. Adjacent MacDonald House offers executive suites with kitchenettes, fireplaces, balconies, and all shares and continue operating New Glasgow Lobster Suppers to this day. Meals include unlimited chowder, mussels, bread, desserts, and beverages. Both suppers are important to their communities, providing employment in a region where jobs have been scarce. Many, many students have put themselves through school on their supper earnings.

The food set out at those original gatherings set the tone for the more authentic of today's lobster suppers. Begin your feast with chowder, mussels, and salads. Be careful you don't fill up on the delicious homemade rolls. Lobster is served at its best, fresh cooked, with a touch of the sea to keep it honest (hot or cold, your choice). The size of lobster you order will determine the price. They crack it for you and provide the tools to help you get every morsel. Finish off your meal with home-style desserts. These suppers still have the feel of the community events—informal, with lots of people chattering and having a good time. If it's busy it can seem noisy

at first, but it's all part of the gathering experience. Credit cards accepted. Expect to pay up to C$40 each plus your liquor.

New Glasgow Lobster Suppers (www.peilobstersuppers.com; © **902/ 964-2870**) is on Route 258 (just off Rte. 13), open daily from June through mid-October, 4 to 8:30pm. Lobster supper ranges from C$30 to C$65 per person, depending on the size of the lobster. Less expensive alternatives: scallops, roast beef, ham, vegetarian, salmon, and chicken. There's a good kids' menu, and credit cards are accepted.

There are lots of lobster-eating opportunities here. **Fisherman's Wharf** (www. fishermanswharf.ca; © **877/289-1010** or 902/963-2669) in North Rustico is one. They keep their 60-foot salad bar well stocked, so if down-and-dirty eating is your goal, you will love it here. If you happen to be on a budget and want a taste of lobster, try a lobster roll. McDonald's in Charlottetown serves up an awesome lobster roll during the summer.

rooms for exercise, sauna, and meetings. Packages for history buffs, golfers, Anne fans, and romantics are available.

2193 Church Rd., Rte. 243 (Hunter River R.R. 3), Rustico, PEI C0A 1N0. www.barachoisinn.com. © **800/963-2194.** 8 units. C$125–C$399. Rates include full breakfast. Packages available. MC, V. Open year-round **Amenities:** Sauna. In room: A/C, cable TV, hair dryer, kitchenette, Wi-Fi (free).

Shaw's Hotel ★★ ☺ One of three grand old hotels located adjacent to PEI's National Park, Shaw's holds the distinction of being the oldest hotel in Canada continuously operated by the same family. Welcoming guests since 1860, an era of New Englanders making "excursions to PEI," it retains the classic charm of a Victorian seaside hotel, even with additions such as sun decks. Antiques-furnished rooms at this Canadian National Historic Site maintain the ambience of days past. Cottages (one to four bedrooms) range from rustic to modern. Luxury chalets have fireplaces. The charming dining room lives up to its stellar reputation for "French country" meals. It's perfect for outdoor lovers: who can resist walking down a country lane, over the dunes, to miles of white-sand beach? Summer children's programs, menus, and a playground make Shaw's a good choice for families, too. I think of Shaw's as a place where kids can run free, and adults are free to run, relax, and rejuvenate.

99 Apple Tree Rd. off Rte. 15, Brackley Beach, PEI C1E 1Z3. www.shawshotel.ca. ℂ **902/672-2022.** Fax 902/672-3000. 15 hotel units, 10 cottages, 9 luxury chalets. C$95–C$145 double; C$140–C$240 suite; C$190–C$5,000 cottage for 2–8 people. Reduced rates for extended stays. MAP plan about C$80 per night additional (double occupancy). Packages available. AE, MC, V. Closed Nov to late May. Cottages open year-round, hotel early June to late Sept. Well-mannered dogs allowed in cottages only. **Amenities:** Restaurant; bar; babysitting; canoe, kayak, and bike rentals; children's program. *In room:* TV (some units), fridge (some units), kitchenette (some units), no phone, Wi-Fi (free in rooms and cottages).

WHERE TO EAT

This is one of PEI's neat dining regions during the summer. For fine dining, in addition to the two selections listed below, consider sampling the fare from the resort dining rooms at **Shaw's Hotel** (see "Where to Stay," above) and at **Dalvay by the Sea ★★** (described in the "Prince Edward Island National Park" section of this chapter on p. 221).

As I've just said, there's certainly plenty to eat in this area, but there's also a great local restaurant in Margate, the **Shipwright's Café,** about 24km (15 miles) due west of North Rustico on Route 6. Its menu falls somewhere between the refined gourmet fare of the Dunes and the fried-up grub of a roadside takeout—and sometimes that middle ground is what you want to eat. See p. 248 in this chapter for details about the cafe.

The Dunes Café ★★ CAFE   Once the in-house cafe/coffeehouse of a gallery (see "Shopping," above), the Dunes now serves lunches and dinners equal to those almost anywhere in rural PEI. Foodies are taking notice. A great spot for a gourmet lunch or dinner of island fish chowder, crab cakes, grilled chorizo, seafood cioppino, lobster Pad Thai, or one of the salads; it's amazing how the chef balances fresh local ingredients with international spices and influences. They also serve good coffee here, of course, as well as tea and knockout house cocktails at night—drinks like the gingery A Dunes Life, or the island Rhubarb-A-Rita made with local "shine." The restaurant's kids' menu is considerate of the little ones, but limited.

Rte. 15, Brackley Beach. www.dunesgallery.com. ℂ **902/672-1883.** Lunch main courses C$7–C$15; dinner entrees C$17–C$34. MC, V. June–Sept daily 11:30am–10pm. Closed Nov–May.

Orwell ★★

In southeastern Queens County, the village of **Orwell** is a great little historic detour off busy Route 1, about 32km (20 miles) east of Charlottetown. (Rte. 1 is the fast main road travelers drive to get from C-town to Montague, the Murrays, Georgetown, or the Wood Islands ferry.) Both sites mentioned below are near each other on a side road; there are few landmarks other than simple signs directing you here, so keep a sharp eye out for the corner and the turnoff.

The **Orwell Corner Historic Village ★★** (www.orwellcorner.ca; ℂ **902/651-8515**) is one of the most aesthetically pleasing historic parks in the province. One of several sites on the island managed by the PEI Museum and Heritage Foundation, the village re-creates life as it might have been in a small island town of the 1890s. You can visit a general store, stop by a blacksmith shop, or wander through lush gardens and make a picnic in the shade of a tree. Events scheduled during summer include activities such as folk-music performances, lively Wednesday evening *ceilidhs* (Scottish concerts), working horse or artisan demonstrations, and Sunday afternoon themed family programs. The Tea Room packs picnics to enjoy on-site.

The village is open from 9:30am to 5:30pm daily in July and August; 9am to 5pm weekdays only in June; and 9am to 5pm Sunday to Thursday from September through early October, when it closes for the season. Admission is C$7.50 for adults, C$4.50 for children 6 to 18, and C$20 for families.

A few minutes' drive from the village is the handsome, white-shingled **homestead of Sir Andrew Macphail** ★★ (www.macphailhomestead.ca; ℂ **902/651-2789**). Macphail, a gifted polymath born in this tiny village in 1864, gained renown as a doctor, pathologist, professor, writer, editor, and agricultural tinkerer; you learn a lot about his exceptional mind and career by walking through the house, which includes a handful of exhibits and some period furniture. There's also a tiny restaurant which offers simple soup-and-sandwich type fare with some special presentations from time to time. But the real allure is a stroll across the green lawn and through the 40-plus hectares (more than a hundred acres) of farmlands laced by several **trails ★**. These walks are lush, pastoral, and quiet, filled with the summer sounds of crickets and songbirds—a great antidote to city life. Admission is free, though donations are happily accepted. The house is open daily from spring through fall, with shorter hours in the shoulder seasons. Also note that the gardens and grounds here remain open later into the fall, even after the home has closed.

PRINCE EDWARD ISLAND NATIONAL PARK ★★

Located along PEI's sandy north central coast, Prince Edward Island National Park is big and it's small all at once. In total, the park encompasses just 40 skinny kilometers (25 miles) of white-sand beaches and wind-sculpted dunes topped by marram grass, red-sandstone cliffs, salt marshes, and gentle inlets. Even what length it possesses is broached in several places by broad estuarine inlets that connect to harbors; as a result, you can't drive the entire park's length in one stretch, but rather must break away from the coastal road (and views) and backtrack inland.

You don't mind, though, because this is *the* reason many people come to the island. These bright sand, empty beaches, and lovely dunes define the park for a hefty percentage of PEI visitors. My advice? There's really little point in trying to tour the whole length of the park in 1 day. It's better to simply pick out one stretch of beach, stake a claim, and settle in and enjoy the gentle surroundings. Participate in the programs to enrich your knowledge of local nature and history.

There's more to this national park than just beaches and dunes. Within its boundaries you can also find considerable woods and meadows, full of wildlife—you might spot red foxes (who den in the dunes), muskrats, mink, eagles, or osprey. In the marshes and tidal flats, great blue heron stalk their aquatic prey near sunset. And, where beach and dune meet, watch for the piping plover, a tiny, endangered beach bird that scratches its shallow, hard-to-spot nest right out of the beach sand. Walking trails and interpretive programs enrich your stay. Be sure to consider a visit to Greenwich at the far eastern reaches of the Park, near St. Peters. With fewer visitors finding their way here, this part of the park is a great place for communing with nature, relaxing, and just enjoying a bit of solitude in one of PEI's special places. The interpretive center has very informative displays about the ecology and nature, and some educational programming. The national park also administers the Green Gables house and grounds, but they're a bit of a drive from the beaches and a world apart from them, aesthetically speaking; see "Cavendish," earlier in this chapter, for details on what tourism officials call "Anne's Land."

Essentials

GETTING THERE From downtown Charlottetown, Route 15 (which passes the airport, then continues north) is the most direct route to central sections of the national park. To reach the lovely eastern sections and Dalvay by the Sea, you can also drive east on Route 2, then turn north on Route 6 at Bedford. Alternately, to reach the Cavendish (western) area and the attractive Rusticos most quickly, take Route 2 west to Hunter River, then turn north on Route 13. The entire drive from city to beach is probably 30 or 40km (20 or 25 miles) at most, yet it can still take up to 45 minutes or more, depending on traffic conditions. Once you arrive at the park, if you want to drive its length and survey it more closely, enter at North Rustico and follow the Shore Road. Otherwise you'll be forced to use Route 6 to inch your way along to the Cavendish entrances. Keep your cool; the route wiggles, waggles, and sometimes swells with summer traffic.

VISITOR INFORMATION The **Cavendish Visitor Information Centre** (✆ **800/463-4734** or 902/963-7830), north of the intersection of routes 6 and 13, furnishes information on the park's destinations and activities. It opens daily from mid-May through early September.

At the far eastern end of the park, past St. Peters, the modern **Greenwich Interpretation Centre** (✆ **902/961-2514**) is open daily from 10am to 5pm, June through September. For other questions or during the off season, the park administration (located in Charlottetown) can be reached at ✆ **902/672-6350.**

FEES The park is open year-round. Between June and early September, however, visitors must stop at one of the two tollhouses and pay entry fees. From July through September, the fees are C$7.80 adults, C$6.80 seniors, C$3.90 children ages 6 to 16, and C$20 per family; all these rates are discounted by 50% in June. Ask about multiday or annual passes if you plan to visit for more than 3 days.

Beaches

PEI National Park is home to two kinds of sandy beaches: popular, sometimes crowded strands with changing rooms, lifeguards, snack bars, and other amenities; and all the rest. Where you go depends on your temperament. If it's not a day at the beach without the aroma of other people's coconut tanning oil, head for Brackley Beach, Dalvay Beach, or Cavendish Beach. (The latter is within walking distance, at least a kilometer through the fields of the Green Gables Historic Site and many amusements, thus making it good for families with kids; see "Cavendish," earlier in this chapter for details on said attractions.)

If you'd just as soon be left alone with the waves, sun, and sand, though, you need to head a bit farther afield—or just keep walking very far down the beaches from parking lots until you have left the crowds behind. I won't reveal the very best spots,

| Rip Currents |

If the surf is up, or waves are breaking, you would be best advised to swim at beaches with a lifeguard. Rip currents form when waves breaking near the shoreline rush back out to sea through breaks in sandbars just offshore. It is easy for even the strongest swimmer to get pulled out to sea, so check out conditions and take appropriate care of yourself and your children.

for fear they'll get crowded. But suffice it to say they're out there. Get thee a map of the national park, and study it closely. A hint: "Fewer facilities" almost always translates to "far fewer people."

Hiking & Biking

For the true enthusiast, hiking is rather low-key in PEI National Park, especially when compared with the trails in Atlantic Canada's other national parks, but you can still find a number of pleasant strolls here, with 14 trails to choose from. You won't find challenging grinds, or hard-to-navigate landscapes, but you will find what PEI is known for: gently rolling trails, scenic vistas, and very walkable trails. (Of course, there's also the beach, which is perfect for long, leisurely walks.)

The park maintains a total of 45km (28 miles) of trails, so there's plenty of room to roam. They have also added walking/bicycling lanes, separated from traffic by a grass verge, along paved roads throughout the park.

Among the most appealing is the **Homestead Trail ★**, which departs from the Cavendish campground. The trail offers both a 6.7km (4-mile) loop and an 8.8km (5.5-mile) loop and skirts wheat fields, woodlands, and estuaries, with frequent views of the distinctively lumpy dunes at the west end of the national park. Very unusually, mountain bikes are allowed on this trail, so it can become a relatively busy place on sunny days. If you are going into Green Gables (admission is charged in season), the two **short trails**—Balsam Hollow and Haunted Wood, each less than 2km (a mile)—are lovely but invariably crowded when buses are in the parking lot. **Cycling** the seaside roads in the park is sublime. Traffic is generally light, and it's easy to make frequent stops along the way to explore beaches, woodlands, or the marshy edges of inlets. The two **shoreline roads ★★** within the national park—between Dalvay and Rustico Island, and from Cavendish to North Rustico Harbour—are especially beautiful as sunset edges into twilight. As a bonus, there are snack bars located both at Brackley Beach and again at Covehead Bay. Both have bike lanes.

It's easy to rent bikes in **Charlottetown,** year-round. There are two good rental outfits: **MacQueen's** (www.macqueens.com; ✆ 800/969-2822 or 902/368-2453) at 430 Queen St. and **Smooth Cycle** (✆ 800/310-6550 or 902/566-5530) at 330 University Ave. Rentals at each run about C$25 per day. If you make a last-minute decision to cycle, don't sweat it: You can also find hybrid and mountain bike rentals, for roughly the same rates, at **Dalvay Beach Bike Rentals** (✆ 888/366-2955 or 902/672-2048). The facility is located at the venerable Dalvay by the Sea resort (see "Where to Stay & Eat," below). These folks even smartly offer a half-day package deal that includes a packed picnic lunch for two for about C$15 more.

Camping

Prince Edward Island National Park maintains excellent campgrounds, which open for the short season in mid-June, with hundreds of sites in total. This is one of the best ways to enjoy the island, and it's not very expensive: Campground fees start at about C$25 per night, with serviced sites costing no more than C$36 per night. Both of the following campsites are open mid-June to the second week of October.

The most popular (and first to fill) is **Cavendish,** located just off Route 6 west of Green Gables and in the park's western reaches. It has hundreds of sites, spread among piney forest and open, sandy bluffs; sites at the edge of the dunes overlooking the beach are the most popular, but most aren't especially private or scenic. A limited number of two-way hookups are available for RVs, and the campground also has free showers, kitchen shelters, and evening programs.

The **Stanhope** ★ campground lies just across the park road from lovely Stanhope Beach, on the eastern side of the park (you enter through Brackley Beach). The park road isn't heavily traveled, so you don't feel very removed from water's edge. Most sites are forested, and you're afforded more privacy than at Cavendish; all things considered, it's a better choice. Two-way hookups, free showers, and kitchen shelters are offered. There is also a group camping area in Brackley. Reserve a site at either by using the national park service's reservation website (www.pccamping.ca) or calling ☏ 877/737-3783 or 405/505-8302. Just remember: You can only reserve in advance between mid-April and early September, at which point the reservation system shuts down.

You can try to walk on to either campsite, of course, but I wouldn't recommend trying at the height of summer and expecting a spot—you might get shut out. In the shoulder seasons, things are much less hectic and you could show up last-minute.

Where to Stay & Eat

See also listings for "Cavendish" and "North & South Rustico to Brackley Beach," earlier in this chapter, for more choices in the vicinity of the park. Don't overlook Covehead Wharf, located on the Gulf Shore Highway between the Brackley and Stanhope park entrances. There is a deep-sea fishing and diving charter outfit here, as well as local fishing boats, not to mention lots of activity to enjoy if you indulge in takeout from Richards. You cannot get fresher lobster than that found here—32 steps from boat to pound. Buy it from the Fishmart to take with you (live or cooked) or better yet, order from **Richard's Eatery** (☏ 902/672-3030). The menu ranges from beef tenderloin sandwich (C$10) to steamed clams (C$10), mussels (C$8), or lobster (roll, club, or sandwich, C$11).

Dalvay by the Sea ★★   Many resorts claim to offer a quieter stay, reminiscent of a less harried era; but at this seaside resort hotel they really do enhance that experience. No phones, television, or radios will be found in the guest rooms. Windows, open to cooling sea breezes, replace the hum of air-conditioning. Withdrawal from hi-tech is tempered by complimentary wireless Internet. Doubling as the White Sands Hotel in the *Road to Avonlea* television series, Dalvay presents the best of days past. Guest rooms are elegantly appointed; period furniture has the solid feel of permanence present throughout the hotel. Large cottages providing everything but cooking facilities are in big demand. Nestled beside a small lake, Dalvay is just steps from the ocean, with pristine beaches and sand dunes stretching as far as the eye can see. The highly regarded kitchen turns out Continental dishes and superb desserts; their sticky date pudding with toffee sauce was featured in *Gourmet* magazine. Afternoon tea is delicious, but very pricey and a bit overrated.

Rte. 6, Grand Tracadie (P.O. Box 8, Little York), PEI C0A 1P0. www.dalvaybythesea.com. ☏ **888/366-2955** or 902/672-2048. Fax 902/672-2741 (summer only). 34 units. June to late Oct C$199–C$404 double, C$379–C$419 (some meals included), cottage; extra charges for all children age 4 and above and more than 2 adults. Rates include full breakfast and dinner. B&B rates and packages also available. National park entrance fees also charged. 2-night minimum in summer. AE, DC, MC, V. Closed late Sept to May. **Amenities:** 2 dining rooms; bike rentals; canoeing; croquet; horseshoes; lawn bowling; tennis court. *In room:* Fridge (cottages only), minibar (cottages only), no phone, Wi-Fi (free).

CHARLOTTETOWN ★★

It's not hard to figure out why PEI's earliest settlers situated the province's political and cultural capital where they did: It's on a point of land between two rivers and within a large, protected harbor. For ship captains plying the seas, this quiet harbor with ample

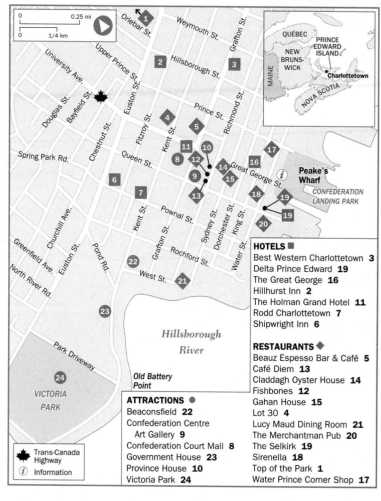

HOTELS ■
Best Western Charlottetown **3**
Delta Prince Edward **19**
The Great George **16**
Hillhurst Inn **2**
The Holman Grand Hotel **11**
Rodd Charlottetown **7**
Shipwright Inn **6**

RESTAURANTS ◆
Beauz Espesso Bar & Café **5**
Café Diem **13**
Claddagh Oyster House **14**
Fishbones **12**
Gahan House **15**
Lot 30 **4**
Lucy Maud Dining Room **21**
The Merchantman Pub **20**
The Selkirk **19**
Sirenella **18**
Top of the Park **1**
Water Prince Corner Shop **17**

ATTRACTIONS ●
Beaconsfield **22**
Confederation Centre
  Art Gallery **9**
Confederation Court Mall **8**
Government House **23**
Province House **10**
Victoria Park **24**

anchorage and wharf space was a welcome sight. Of course, travelers rarely arrive by water these days (unless a cruise ship is in port), but Charlottetown's harborside location and compactness still translate into a lovely setting. This remains one of Atlantic Canada's most graceful and relaxed cities, and one of my very favorites.

Named for Queen Charlotte (wife of the infamous King George III), metro Charlottetown and its suburbs are now home to about 60,000 people—nearly one out of every two islanders. To Canadians, the city is everlastingly famous for hosting the 1864 conference that 3 years later led to the creation of the independent Dominion of Canada. (In a historic twist of fate, PEI itself actually declined to join the new confederation it spawned for 9 years, until it relented in 1873 when promised a railroad and fixed link with the mainland.)

Today, the downtown has a brisk feel to it, with its mixture of modern and Victorian commercial buildings, government and cultural centers, buttoned-down bureaucrats, and folkies/artists hanging out around town. Outside the business core, you'll find leafy streets and large, elegant homes dating from different eras (the most dramatic were built in the late 19th c.). Charlottetown is blessed with a number of pocket parks (or squares), which provide a quiet respite amid the gentle clamor. If you are a fan of big box stores, check out those located at the northern entrance to the city. Grocery and department stores as well as malls, gas stations, and fast food outlets are located along routes 1 and 2, but not in the historic downtown. Charlottetown is centrally located and a good base for exploring the rest of the island; only the western tip is too far for day-tripping. You can be touring Green Gables, relaxing on a north-shore beach, or teeing off at Brudenell Provincial Park—all within 45 minutes of leaving Charlottetown. The capital has—by far—the island's best selection of inns and hotels, plus a fine assortment of restaurants. You can dine out every night for a week, and still be pleasantly surprised each time—no fried-fish capital, this. The establishment of the Culinary Institute of Canada ensures a high level of cuisine. Students here have brought home gold from the World Culinary Olympics—just a sampling of their many accolades.

The city itself can occupy a couple of days, especially if you like history or leisurely walks around old neighborhoods, waterfronts, or parks. Then of course there is the theater, a night at the races, pub tours, the sidewalk cafes on Victoria Row, and coffee shops. Be sure to take time to chat with the locals; they're a friendly bunch.

Essentials

GETTING THERE   Coming by car from the mainland and across the Confederation Bridge, Route 1 (the Trans-Canada Hwy.) makes more or less a straight shot east into downtown Charlottetown. From the Woods Island ferry, you also take Route 1 (the route begins at the ferry dock), except you go west.

Charlottetown Airport (www.flypei.com) is just north of the city center. In summer, you can get here easily from either the U.S. or Canada via several carriers. **Air Canada** (www.aircanada.com; $\textcircled{C}$ 888/247-2262) offers daily flights from Halifax, Toronto, and Montréal, and **WestJet** (www.westjet.com; $\textcircled{C}$ 888/937-8538) also connects Charlottetown with Toronto. **Delta Air Lines** provides seasonal service from New York (www.delta.com; $\textcircled{C}$ 800/221-1212).

If you're coming from Montréal by VIA Rail train, debark at Moncton and rent a car or take an **Acadian** (www.acadianbus.com; $\textcircled{C}$ 800/567-5151) bus to Charlottetown; the cost is C$36 per adult for the trip, which takes about 3 hours. Do check ahead: Bus and train schedules don't always work together, so you may have a long wait. If you're coming from Halifax, **PEI Express Shuttle** (www.peishuttle.com; $\textcircled{C}$ 877/877-1771) operates one daily van trip between Charlottetown and Halifax. The trip takes 4 to 5 hours and costs C$65 one-way for adults, C$60 for students and seniors, C$45 for children 11 and under.

VISITOR INFORMATION   The city's main Visitor Information Centre ($\textcircled{C}$ 902/368-7795) is in a historic brick railroad building, now known as Founders' Hall. It's at the very end of Prince Street, near the entrance to Confederation Landing Park. (Brown question-mark signs help direct you there.) This place is loaded with helpful staffers, an interactive computer kiosk, a cafe, free Internet, and an ample supply of brochures; there's also a vacancy service to let you know where rooms are currently available around town, and it's the jumping-off point for city-sponsored walking or motorized vehicle tours (for a charge). The center is open daily in July and August, weekdays only in the off season.

There's also a tourism office, **Tourism Charlottetown** (www.walkandsea charlottetown.com; ℂ **800/955-1864** or 902/629-1864), nearby at 91 Water St.

Exploring Charlottetown

Charlottetown is a compact city that's easy to walk around. Focus on three areas: the waterfront, the downtown area near Province House, Confederation Court Mall, and the parks and residential areas near Victoria Park. You're best off first heading to the **information center** (see above), by the waterfront, for a little orientation and then starting your first tour right from there. That's because parking is generally scarce downtown, but relatively abundant near the visitor center, both on the street and in free and paid lots. Be sure to ask for a map and free walking-tour brochures. If you have kids along, ask for the Eckhart club brochure and have them seek out the little bronze mice hiding at historic sites around the city. Eckhart is a character in a children's book and cartoons produced locally. The **waterfront** is anchored by **Peake's Wharf,** a collection of touristy boutiques and eateries that attract hordes in summer. The complex offers good people-watching, plus a kid-friendly "marine touch tank" (watch out for the lobster spines). **Free concerts,** featuring local tunesmiths and a folksy vibe, take place afternoons and evenings (weather permitting) most of the summer. Next to the wharf is **Confederation Landing Park** ★, an open, modern park with a boardwalk along water's edge; lush lawns; and benches nicely situated for lazing about awhile with the kids. There's also a big marina, where you can scope out the pleasure craft. Cruise ships tie up in this area, affording a wonderful look at their size and majesty.

From the wharf, stroll up **Great George Street** ★★★, one of the best-looking streets in Eastern Canada with its leafy trees, perfectly scaled Georgian row houses, and stately churches. Designated as a National Historic District, this street is noteworthy because you are tracing the steps of the Fathers of Confederation who, in 1864, walked from the wharf to meetings at Province House, which led to the formation of Canada. Costumed reenactors lead walking tours that bring history alive. At the top of Great George Street, stop into the **Province House,** then explore Victoria Row with its outdoor restaurants and entertainment. Visit **Confederation Centre Art Gallery** (see below), then explore downtown's shops and restaurants.

For a pleasant walk affording fine water views, head southwest on **Kent Street** (just north of the Confederation Mall). At 2 Kent St., you'll see **Beaconsfield** ★ (ℂ **902/368-6603**), a mansard-roofed mansion designed in 1877 by local architect William Harris for a prosperous shipbuilder. The architecture boasts an elegant mix of Georgian symmetry and Victorian exuberance, and rooms are furnished in high Victorian style. The home, operated by the Prince Edward Island Museum and Heritage Foundation, hosts lectures and events throughout the year. It's open daily in summer from 10am to 5pm. Call ahead for opening hours if you'll be visiting September to June; hours vary. Admission is C$4.50 adults, C$3.40 students, C$12 families, and free for children 12 and under.

From Beaconsfield, look for the boardwalk that follows the edge of the harbor for about a mile into **Victoria Park** ★★, a quiet place of ball fields, grassy picnic areas, and lovely paths through the woods. This walk along the water has unobstructed views of the harbor and the "gut" (also known as the channel btw. the cliffs) out to Northumberland Strait.

Along the way, look for the handsome **Government House** ★★ (www.govpe.ca/lg/governmenthouse.php3; ℂ **902/368-5480**), also known as Fanningbank. Built in 1834, this sturdy white-shingled residence with eight Doric columns is set back on a broad lawn. It's the official residence of the island's lieutenant governor, who serves

The Port-la-Joye/Fort Amherst National Historic Site is easily seen across the harbor from Charlottetown; it's on the eastern side of the gut that takes shipping from the harbor out to Northumberland Strait. A 20km (12-mile) drive from Charlottetown, west on Route 1 to Cornwall, then south on Route 19 (part of the Red Sands Shore Drive), this site provides a panoramic view of Charlottetown and the harbor, and a lovely place for a walk or to fly kites with the kids. While the Visitor Reception and Interpretive Services are only available 9am to 5pm daily in July and August, the grounds are open June to October. This is a great place to view the city at night—fireworks on Canada Day (July 1) are awesome! For a special experience, check the cruise ship schedules and view their passing—so close you feel you can almost touch them. This history of this place goes back to 1720 and involves French, Acadian, and English settlers.

as the queen of England's personal representative to the province. The home is only opened to the public in July and August, Monday to Friday, 10am to 4pm, when there are guided tours. (The grounds are also open to the public, but again only in summer.) The place probably looks familiar to you if you've been in Charlottetown for a few days: That famous photo of the Fathers of the Confederation you see around town was taken on the front portico. The cannon overlooking the water were placed there after an attack by Yankee Privateers, who took a kidnapped resident back to George Washington, perhaps anticipating a ransom for their coffers.

Confederation Centre Art Gallery ★ 🍴   One of the largest art galleries in Atlantic Canada, the center is housed in a boxy complex—a casualty of the "modern" architecture wave that swept the continent in the 1960s and 1970s. (Canadian writer Will Ferguson has referred to the building as "one of the greatest unprosecuted crimes of urban planning in Canadian history.") Inside, the gallery is spacious and well arranged on two levels, featuring displays from a 15,000-piece permanent collection as well as imaginatively curated changing exhibits. Admission is free. Shows might range from an exhibit on Canadian legal history to knit rugs from war-torn Afghanistan, from Uruguayan paintings to photographs of islands. The museum focuses partly on hanging the work of up-and-coming artists. Spend an hour or more here if you appreciate art.

145 Richmond St. www.confederationcentre.com. Ⓒ **902/628-6142.** Mid-May to late Aug daily 9am–5pm; rest of the year Wed–Sat 11am–5pm, Sun 1–5pm.

Province House National Historic Site ★   PEI's official legislative building, this imposing landmark of sandstone was built in 1847. When it served as a colonial legislature, the massive building rose up from dust and mud; but today it's ringed by handsome trees and an inviting lawn. A bustling downtown area lies just beyond it. The building occupies a special spot in Canada's history: This is where details of Confederation were hammered out in 1864. (During the 1980s, the building was restored to appear as it would have looked in that year.) Start with a film that documents the process of Confederation. Afterward, wander the halls and look in on the Legislative Assembly, where the island's legislators have been meeting since 1847. It's surprisingly tiny, but that's appropriate given that PEI's legislature has just 27 members—the smallest in Canada. Especially impressive is the second-floor Confederation Chamber, where a staffer is usually on hand to explain the place and answer that burning question: Why did PEI wait 9 years to join Canada? History buffs could spend an hour here.

Intersection of Richmond and Great George sts. ☏ **902/566-7626.** Free admission (donations requested). June–Sept daily 9am–5pm; rest of the year Mon–Fri 9am–5pm.

Shopping

Charlottetown has a number of shops and boutiques, but you have to seek them out. An artisan studio walking-tour map, available at Visitor Information Centres or brochure racks in many hotels, will help. Ask at the visitor information center if you have a special interest like quilting fabric or models, and they'll direct you where to go. The area has something for most needs, but with smaller, more intimate shops—for example, enthusiasts of boat, plane, and automobile models will love **Great Hobbies** across the bridge at 17 Glen Stewart Dr., Stratford (☏ **902/569-3262**). If you're looking for malls and big box stores, head up University Avenue to the outskirts of town.

Peake's Wharf on the waterfront contains a number of tourist-oriented shops. It's a good destination if you're in search of that souvenir mug or bumper sticker emblazoned with PRINCE EDWARD ISLAND or some such slogan. You'll also find casual dining and ice cream here.

The **Confederation Court Mall** (☏ 902/894-9505), downtown right across from the Province House at 134 Kent St., is bigger and better. Architecturally, the 90-store complex blends in nicely with its historic neighbors, although the city's newest hotel, the Holman Grand, physically part of the mall, is testing that. Inside, though, the place is less distinctive—nice, but the restaurants, escalators, and chain stores look like upscale malls anywhere. Come chiefly if you (or your kids) need a rainy-day shopping fix.

Anne of Green Gables Store Everything Anne, from dolls to commemorative plates. There's another branch in Avonlea Village. Check out the chocolate shop next door—they might be hand-dipping. 110 Queen St. ☏ **902/368-2663.**

The Bookman Located across from the mall, this small shop has the city's best selection of used books, with a strong inventory of PEI and Canadian titles. 177 Queen St. ☏ **902/892-8872.**

COWS Canada's best ice cream (according to *Reader's Digest*), plus tons of cow-themed T-shirts and other bovine whimsy. Ice-cream flavors here include Wowie Cowie Coffee Toffee Crunch and Cotton Candy Bunny Tails. Stop for a factory tour to see ice cream (yes, there are samples!) and award-winning cheeses being made (on Rte. 1 on the outskirts of town). They also have a shop downtown and other locations around the island. 397 Capital Dr. www.cowscreamery.ca ☏ **800/565-2697.**

Paderno Cookware Serious cooks seek out the elegant, stainless-steel Paderno brand cookware made right on island (with heat-conducting pads); these pots and pans are so dependable that they come with a 25-year warranty. Special sales take place in the area from time to time or look for them at Peake's Wharf in the summer. Confederation Court Mall (Grafton St.). www.paderno.com. ☏ **902/566-2252.**

Northern Watters Knitwear This knit shop sells a diverse line of unusually well-made sweaters handcrafted right here on PEI. They can also be purchased at shops in the other eastern provinces, and at the Rustico Bay Wool Sweater Shop in North Rustico. 150 Richmond St. www.nwknitwear.com. ☏ **800/565-9665** or 902/566-5850.

Where to Stay

If you're traveling on a tight budget, there are a number of moderately priced motels situated along the main access roads running into and out of town (namely, routes 1 and 2), and also out by the airport. These places are generally basic and clean but with few frills. They are easier on your pocketbook, so if cost is a prime consideration, they'll do—and they're all a short drive from the central attractions. Properties with double rooms for less than C$100 per night include **Canada's Best Value Inn & Suites Charlottetown** (20 Capital Dr., which is Rte. 1 as you enter the city from the west; ✆ 877/890-2481 or 902/892-2481), and the **Winfield Motel** (✆ 800/267-5525), where 16 of the 18 units don't crack the century mark. It's located right where routes 1 and 2 merge, north of the city near the university.

If you want a motel even closer to downtown—one within easy walking distance of everything, in fact—try the **Best Western Charlottetown ★** (✆ 800/937-8376 or 902/892-2461), in two buildings (one a brick mélange, one surprisingly attractive in a shingled-cottage way) across the street from each other at 238 Grafton St. (a couple blocks east of the Confederation Court Mall). Of course, you're paying more due to the very central location, pool, hot tub, and fitness center; rooms and suites range from around C$100 up to as much as C$235 per night in peak season; check all rate configurations carefully (AAA and CAA discounts are applied if you're a member). But parking is free, which saves you some dough. For affordable accommodations, check out the **University of Prince Edward Island** residences from May through August at 550 University Ave. Apartments at C$85, suites C$109 to C$133 are suitable for four to six people (www.upei.ca/rfcs; ✆ 877/734-7327 or 902/566-0442). Includes Internet and parking.

EXPENSIVE

Delta Prince Edward ★★ ☺ This 10-story hotel is ideally located on the waterfront just 5 minutes from downtown shopping, theater, restaurants, and historic olde Charlottetown. Step out to designated walking tours, which skim the water's edge, or tour the historic district. Located between two marinas, the hotel is ideally situated to watch cruise ships navigate the narrows into the harbor. Seventy percent of rooms have a water view; ask if you want one, the higher the better. Current renovations (scheduled to be completed in mid-2012) will open up even more water views and patio dining. Contemporary rooms vary in price and style; the very best "deluxe" have two-person Jacuzzis, and apartment-like "Home Suites" are good for extended stays. Kids enjoy the indoor wading pool and creative play area, while adults hang out in an adjacent heated pool, hot tub, or well-equipped fitness center. The venerable Selkirk restaurant (see below) is one of the city's top regional gourmet comfort food venues. The level of service and pleasant staff set this one ahead of other hotels.

18 Queen St., Charlottetown, PEI C1A 8B9. www.deltaprinceedward.com. ✆ **866/894-1203** or 902/566-2222. Fax 902/566-1745. 211 units. Peak season C$169–C$390 double, C$225–C$905 suite; call for off-season rates. Packages available. AE, DC, DISC, MC, V. Valet parking C$19, self-parking (indoor) C$15 per day. Pets allowed. **Amenities:** Restaurant; lounge; babysitting; concierge; fitness room; Jacuzzi; indoor pool; room service; sauna; spa; golf simulator. *In room:* A/C, TV, minibar, hair dryer, Jacuzzi (some units), Internet (free).

The Great George ★★★ The Great George, Charlottetown's historic boutique hotel is, without doubt, its classiest. A complex rather than a single inn, the property encompasses a collection of striking buildings on and around historic Great George Street, many of which were painstakingly restored. The Fathers of Confederation walked here to meetings that led to the formation of the nation. Today, the Great George goes a long way toward preserving the historic integrity of the downtown neighborhood. Accommodations range from traditional rooms through efficiency units to romantic and super luxurious suites. No two are alike, instilling a true sense of individuality. The pièce de résistance is found in the lobby. Comfortable groupings of seating welcome guests for complimentary breaks, continental breakfast prepared by their baker, and "Happy Hour," all of which foster a convivial atmosphere. The old-world charm continues in the gardens amid pampering by skilled staff. Although there is no restaurant in the Great George, there are several nearby. On a summer's eve, an outside table at a nearby Victoria Row eatery is sheer delight.

58 Great George St., Charlottetown, PEI C1A 4K3. www.thegreatgeorge.com. © **800/361-1118** or 902/892-0606. Fax 902/628-2079. 54 units. C$179–C$358 double; C$269–C$899 suite; C$224–C$358 efficiency units; C$2,000 week luxury condo. Rates include continental breakfast. Open year-round. Packages available. AE, DC, MC, V. Free parking. **Amenities:** Babysitting; concierge service; elevator; fitness room; limited room service. *In room:* A/C, TV (some units), hair dryer, kitchen (some units), Jacuzzi (some units), Internet, Wi-Fi (free).

The Holman Grand Hotel ★★ This contemporary boutique hotel is the newest accommodations in Charlottetown. The central downtown location features spectacular views of the city and harbor from most rooms. The posh 10th-floor penthouse with a wraparound terrace features a "Master King" bedroom, with fireplace and a hospitality suite. All rooms and suites are located around a 7-story atrium, making it one of the most modern establishments in the city. Spa-inspired bathrooms have walk-in showers (but not all have tubs). A lovely place for a winter stay, it's connected physically to a shopping mall, and via an underground walkway to Confederation Centre of the Arts.

123 Grafton St., Charlottetown, C1A 1K9. www.theholmangrand.com. © **877/455-4726** or 902/367-7777. 68 rooms, 12 suites. Standard room C$159–C$259, suites C$310–C$439, penthouse C$875. AE, DC, MC, V. Valet parking (no parking on-site). **Amenities:** Restaurant; pool; hot tub; fitness room. *In room:* A/C, TV, fridge, Wi-Fi (free).

Shipwright Inn ★★★ Even though located right in the city, the Shipwright has a settled, pastoral feel to it: a perfect combination, and very PEI. The sturdy Victorian home, built in the 1860s by a local shipbuilder, has been expertly renovated and refurbished. It's decorated in period furniture, without the over-the-top Victorian floral patterns that dampen many B&Bs. Rooms show off gorgeous wooden floors (some made from ship planking). The best units have something extra. The romantic Officer's Wardroom, a suite with an Asian feel, has a living room, private balcony, fireplace, headboard made from the inn's original doors, and a skylight-view Jacuzzi. The Crow's Nest features a king-size bed, claw-foot Jacuzzi (really), fireplaces, attractive unvarnished wood furniture, and a shared deck. Other units are each distinctive and handsome. The business center, with computer and fax, is a nice bonus; afternoon tea service is a good introduction to the island; and the innkeepers and staff are unfailingly helpful.

51 Fitzroy St., Charlottetown, PEI C1A 1R4. www.shipwrightinn.com. © **888/306-9966** or 902/368-1905. Fax 902/628-1905. 9 units. C$99–C$299 double. Rates include full breakfast. AE, DC, MC, V. Free parking. **Amenities:** Dining room. *In room:* A/C, TV/DVD, fridge (most units), hair dryer, Jacuzzi (some units), kitchenette (some units), minibar, Wi-Fi (free).

MODERATE

Hillhurst Inn ★ A fine mansion built in a fine neighborhood northeast of Province House around the turn of the 19th century, Hillhurst features a number of nice touches—including some extraordinarily detailed woodworking carved by early shipbuilders throughout the home. Rooms vary in size and style, but all have been upgraded. Only drawback? Many bathrooms are on the smallish side (some had to be shoehorned into former closets), and the furnishings are perhaps a bit less historical and creative than those at the comparatively priced Shipwright down the street.

181 Fitzroy St., Charlottetown, PEI C1A 1S3. www.hillhurst.com. (*) **877/994-8004** or 902/894-8004. Fax 902/892-7679. 9 units. May–Nov C$145–C$235 double; spring and fall off-season rates C$99–C$165. Rates include full breakfast. AE, DISC, MC, V. Free parking. **Amenities:** Internet (free). *In room:* A/C, TV, hair dryer, Jacuzzi (some units).

Rodd Charlottetown ★   Built in 1931 of handsome brick by CN Railways, this five-story business hotel—now part of the eastern provinces' Rodd Hotel mini-empire—is right next to a shady park, a short walk from most of downtown's attractions. It features Georgian flourishes inside and out, and has been updated and remodeled with a nod to its heritage. Rooms have been tastefully remodeled. There are several newer suites, and the rooftop patio is worth a look. A low-ceilinged indoor pool is open to guests on the ground floor. The hotel's **Chambers Restaurant** is open daily for dinner and features hotel favorites such as prime rib and salmon; there's also a lobby bar and during the summer the Feast Dinner Theatre.

Kent and Pownal sts. (P.O. Box 159), Charlottetown, PEI C1A 7K4. www.rodd-hotels.ca. (*) **800/565-7633** or 902/894-7371. Fax 902/368-2178. 115 units. C$109–C$250 double; C$185–C$350 suite. Packages available. AE, DC, DISC, MC, V. Free parking. Pets accepted (C$10 charge). **Amenities:** Restaurant; bar; babysitting; Jacuzzi; indoor pool; limited room service; sauna. *In room:* A/C, TV, hair dryer, Wi-Fi (free).

Where to Eat

For a quick pick-me-up while traversing the city, try **Beanz Espresso Bar & Café** at 38 University Ave. ((*) **902/892-8797**), just a block from Province House. The espresso drinks are good, and they also sell pastries, sandwiches, soups, and other light items. Casual dining at waterside is found at **Lobster on the Wharf** at 2 Prince St. (www.lobsteronthewharf.com; (*) **902/368-2888**). They have a great menu, are right on the water, and have their own lobster pound. Thinking of taking lobster home? This is the place to buy it.

On the east side of town, overlooking the Hillsborough River, **Top of the Park Restaurant** at 46 Kensington Rd. (www.redshores.ca; (*) **877/620-4222** or 902/620-4264) offers lunch buffets Wednesday through Friday and dinner buffets Fridays and race nights. As well as serving up excellent food, the staff here is extremely helpful to those with special food requirements such as gluten or ingredient allergies. A chef will walk you through the buffet, or prepare special desserts—a unique bit of pampering. The former grandstand at the Charlottetown Driving Park, this trendy restaurant boasts a panoramic race track view from every table. Watch the standard-bred horses go through the paces during training sessions or reserve a table for race night. Placing bets from your table adds to the harness racing experience at Red Shores, a gaming, racing, and dining facility.

Claddagh Oyster House ★ SEAFOOD   The Claddagh Room is a place for seafood—starting with the famous PEI oysters and mussels, which have become a focus of the place. A seafood chowder is good as a starter, as are the lobster spaghetti, lobster strudel, and lobster-crab cakes with a lemony rémoulade. Seafood entrees include seared scallops with ginger-pea puree, and PEI-farmed halibut; there are also grilled steaks, Moroccan-spiced rack of lamb, a beef tenderloin topped with crab and sided with whipped potato, and other landlubber entrees. Preparation and service are a notch above most other fish joints. There's a great, convivial vibe as locals pop in for the live Irish music and beer upstairs.

131 Sydney St. (*) **902/892-9661.** Reservations recommended. Main courses C$22–C$30; oysters C$2 each. AE, DISC, MC, V. Mon–Fri 11:30am–2pm; Sun–Thurs 5–10pm; Fri–Sat 5–10:30pm.

Lot 30 ★★★ CONTEMPORARY   Gordon Bailey has struck again! The enfant terrible (self-described as a "biker chef") and former Dayboat restaurant owner has opened his own place in downtown Charlottetown. Bailey reportedly uses no freezers in his restaurants, only fresh items from the market, and it shows. Start with one of his creative seafood appetizers, such as white wine and white-cheddar steamed mussels, a cioppino incorporating seared salmon, or house-cured pork. Entrees are more spread out between land and sea, running to such choices as butter-poached lobster with braised beef and fingerling potatoes or grilled duck breast with Yukon gnocchi. The rotating desserts are as fancy and well-prepared as you'd expect them to be. If you're a serious foodie, don't pass up a chance to dine here while on island.

151 Kent St. www.lot30restaurant.ca. © **902/629-3030.** Reservations recommended. Main courses C$25–C$55. MC, V. Tues–Sun 5–9pm. Closed Jan.

Lucy Maud Dining Room ★★ REGIONAL   The Lucy Maud is located in the respected Culinary Institute of Canada. The building is a bit institutional; the 80-seat dining room has the feel of a hotel restaurant. But touches like custom china offset the lack of personality, and there's a lovely view of the bay and Victoria Park from the big windows. Best of all, diners taste some excellent island cuisine, prepared and served by Institute chefs-in-training. Lunch and dinner menus change every semester. Dinner entrees could be anything from duck or venison (the kitchen is known for it) to chicken, steaks, and seafood prepared with local twists such as blueberry puree. There's always salmon, and sometimes a curry-inflected seafood chowder. A wine list is also available.

4 Sydney St. © **902/894-6868.** Reservations recommended. Main courses C$8–C$13 at lunch, C$15–C$28 at dinner. AE, MC, V. Oct–Apr Tues–Fri 11:30am–1:30pm; year-round Tues–Sat 6–8pm. Closed holiday weekends and Oct–May.

The Merchantman Pub ★★ 🍴 GASTROPUB   More upscale than a bar, less fancy than a sit-down dining room, the Merchantman broke new ground when it opened in the mid-'90s. It's as close a thing to a "gastropub" (pub serving gourmet food) as there is on this island; even the nachos are gourmet. The kitchen specializes in seafood, often cooked with Thai or Cajun spices, but they cook a little of everything. Start with lobster bruschetta (yes, please), bacon-dusted scallops, local mussels or oysters, crab cakes, or chowder. Move on to hearty sandwich (steak on a baguette), island fish cakes, or a burger from the pub menu and be plenty happy. But you can also order something considerably more substantial and refined—here's where the place separates itself widely from other drinking houses around town. Gourmet items include a pair of aged beef medallions served with a whiskey lemon butter sauce; lobster linguine; rack of lamb in a spiced onion and olive sauce; or barbecue-roasted salmon. Sweetish desserts, including a maple tart, complete the menu.

23 Queen St. www.merchantmanpub.com. © **902/892-9150.** Pub and gourmet items C$8–C$35. MC, V. Mon–Thurs 11:30am–10pm; Fri–Sat 11:30am–11pm.

The Selkirk ★★★ CANADIAN/FUSION   Charlottetown's most stylish restaurant is right in the lobby of the high-end Delta Prince Edward Hotel (see "Where to Stay," above) with a more informal character than many hotel dining rooms. The menu is more ambitious and creative than it has to be; lunch choices can begin with fish and chips and burgers, but include steak sandwiches, veggie Wellington, and pasta carbonara with scallops. Dinners might start with a grilled chicken brochette, local seafood chowder, wine-steamed island mussels, or a salad of local greens and goat cheese; main courses from Chef Javier Alarco could include a full lobster dinner, a cut of beef tenderloin, a filet of haddock, or some pan-seared scallops. Standard hotel-dining selections, but they're prepared right—and for a price that's not nearly as high as you'd expect. The lobby location gets noisy at times, though, so try for a table under the mezzanine.

18 Queen St. (in the Delta Prince Edward). © **902/566-2222.** Reservations recommended. Lunch entrees C$12–C$21; dinner entrees C$18–C$35. AE, DC, DISC, MC, V. Mon–Fri 7am–1:30pm and 5:30–9pm; Sat 7–11am and 5:30–9pm; Sun 7am–2pm and 5:30–9pm.

Sirenella ★ ☺ ITALIAN Restaurateur Italo Marzari was already running Italian eateries in two other Maritime Provinces when he decided to open Sirenella on PEI in 1992. Right across from the Delta Prince Edward, it has since become a popular spot. When all systems are functioning smoothly, it's a decent family option. Locals swear by dishes such as veal; grilled calamari; "mussels in love" (cooked in Pernod); ravioli stuffed with ricotta, spinach, and prosciutto; and the seafood pastas. They also serve lobster, garnished with the famous local shellfish. This restaurant is tucked on a quiet side street and is tiny enough to be considered romantic. There's a kids' menu for the little ones.

83 Water St. © **902/628-2271.** Reservations recommended. Main courses C$14–C$27 at dinner. AE, MC, V. Mon–Fri 11:30am–2pm and 5–10pm; Sat 5–10pm.

Water Prince Corner Shop ★★ 🏚 SEAFOOD Located a block from the waterfront, in the historic district, this hidden gem looks at first glance like a newsstand or convenience store. Inside, though, you'll find a convivial seafood joint, serving lobster dinners and rolls, seafood chowder and cooked mussels, as well as burgers, chicken fingers, and such to kids or the shellfish-allergic. They also ship lobsters by air. The exceptionally rare mounted blue lobster that is their claim to fame is fading, so ask waitstaff to point it out.

141 Water St. © **902/368-3212.** Reservations recommended. Lunch and dinner C$8.95–C$23. AE, DC, DISC, MC, V. May–June and Sept–Oct daily 9am–8pm; July–Aug daily 9am–10pm.

Charlottetown After Dark

One good resource for planning evening adventures is *The Buzz,* a free monthly newspaper that details ongoing and special events around the island with an emphasis on Charlottetown. It's widely available; look for it in visitor centers at area bars and restaurants. You can read an online version at **www.buzzon.com**.

Outdoor libations are on tap at **Victoria Row ★**, a section of Richmond Street beside the Confederation Centre that is blocked off to auto traffic each summer. Restaurants and pubs cluster here, serving meals and drinks on outdoor or street-side patios; things get fun and lively, and there's usually live music. Two locally favorite spots here are **Café Diem** (© **902/892-0494**) at 128 Richmond St. and **Fishbones** (© **902/628-6569**), an oyster bar and seafood grill with good live music at 136 Richmond St.

Olde Charlottetown is a great spot for those who enjoy pubs, be it for the food, the music, or the good times. **Gahan House Pub ★** (www.gahan.ca; © **902/626-2337**) at 126 Sydney St. is the only microbrewery on PEI. They serve a pubby menu (fish and chips are served in a bag). Sample the house-brewed ales and stout. They do tours of the brewery, twice a day (except Sun), in July and August.

For live Celtic-flavored music and lobster and roast-beef dinners, head for the **Olde Dublin Pub,** above the Claddagh Oyster House (see above) at 131 Sydney St. (© **902/892-6992**). **Churchill Arms,** a tiny eatery at 75 Queen St. (© **902/367-3450**) is known for British fare, especially traditional curries and fish and chips (which are reputed to be the best on the island and rank as my personal favorites). The menu includes such delights as Chip Butty and Deep Fried Mars Bars.

For high culture, always check first with the **Confederation Centre of the Arts** (www.charlottetownfestival.com; ✆ **800/565-0278** or 902/566-1267), where the stage bustles with dramatic and musical activity throughout the warm-weather months. The musical *Anne of Green Gables,* a perennial favorite, is performed here throughout the summer—but so are revivals and new shows. The **Guild ★** (www. theguildpei.com; ✆ **866/774-0717** or 902/368-4413), a black-box theater at 111 Queen St., showcases emerging and professional artists and is a hotbed of fund-raising events, giving it a unique community feel. Music, comedy, theater, dance: It's always affordable. Finally, the art-house **City Cinema ★**, at 64 King St. (✆ **902/368-3669**), has an excellent lineup of domestic and foreign films throughout the year; typically, there's a choice of two films each evening. Movie tickets cost C$8 per adult, C$5.50 for seniors and kids 14 and under.

KINGS COUNTY

After visits to Charlottetown and the island's north shore area, Kings County comes as a bit of a surprise. It's very tranquil and uncluttered. Best described as a little more rustic rural, the landscapes feature woodlots alternating with corn, grain, and potato fields and superb water views. Although locals play up this county's two largest commercial centers—**Souris** and **Montague**—it's good to keep in mind that each of these coastal hamlets has a population of less than 2,000. So don't arrive here expecting attractions to amuse and entertain you; you'll have to do that yourself.

One way to do so is to plot your course for a spirited tour. Kings County is home to the province's only award-winning winery and two distilleries. **Rossignol Estate Winery ★** on Route 4 (www.rossignolwinery.com; ✆ **902/962-4193**) in Little Sands is a great start. The vineyards offer a panoramic view of Northumberland Strait; the winery has an impressive array of table and fruit wines, as well as liqueurs and an art gallery. Try the Blackberry Mead—yum. **Myriad View Artisan Distillery** on Route 2 in Rollo Bay (www.straitshine.com; ✆ **902/687-1281**) is creating a glimpse into the days of Prohibition by producing "Strait Shine" collected straight from the still. It's something that doesn't happen anywhere else. The distillery also produces rum, gin, vodka, and Pastis. Up on the north shore, at Hermanville on Route 16, **Prince Edward Distillery** (www.princeedwarddistillery.com; ✆ **902/687-2586**) has won international gold medals for its potato vodka. Take a tour to learn more about the art of craft distilling. They also produce a wild blueberry vodka and gins. Remember drivers can't sample and drive; PEI has tough drinking and driving laws.

Fortunately, there is a lot more to do. This is prime cycling territory, while walking trails and walks on the empty beaches are other good tonics for life. Long drives in the country, with occasional stops for eats or to snap photos, are usually the order of the day. Luckily, the tourism industry has taken great steps to develop the **Points East Coastal Drive,** a 475km (298-mile) coastal route that hits most of the local highlights and points out many easily missed. You can pick up a free map and brochure, which details the route that circles the eastern end of the Island at any Visitor Information Centre. And they have provided good highway signs to various points of interest. One of my favorite things to do here is visit the lighthouses. Each has a unique story to tell, wonderful scenery, and its own magic. Top of the list are **Wood Island's Lighthouse** and **East Point Lighthouses,** located at Wood Island and East Point respectively, which have been developed with museums, shops, and places to partake of a bit of refreshment after you tour the lighthouse. Welcome after climbing to the top, where views are always fabulous.

Note that if you're heading to Kings County from Charlottetown, you may pass right through **Orwell** and its historic sites en route. It's a worthwhile stop. For more information on Orwell, see the village's listings earlier in this chapter in the "Queens County" section.

Essentials

GETTING THERE　Several of the Island's main roads, including Highways 1, 2, 3, and 4, connect Kings County with Charlottetown. So it's easy to get here; get out a map, plot a cool route, and point your car east. If you're coming from Nova Scotia, the **Woods Island** ferry docks up on the southern coast. See "Exploring Prince Edward Island," earlier in this chapter, for more information about the ferry.

VISITOR INFORMATION　There's a provincial Visitor Information Centre at 95 Main St. in Souris (which is also Rte. 2; ✆ **902/687-7030**), open daily from mid-June through mid-October. There's another VIC at the head of pretty St. Peters Bay, on Route 2 at the intersection of routes 313 and 16 (✆ **902/961-3540**); this info center, which borders the lovely Confederation Trail, opens daily June through October. Yet another is located where Route 1 meets Route 4, just after you roll off the ferry at Wood Islands.

Wood Islands to Murray Harbour & Murray River ★

Assuming you are starting your eastern tour from Charlottetown on Route 1, you'll soon find yourself tempted to leave the main road to explore treasures like the **Point Prim Lighthouse** (www.pointprimlighthouse.com; ✆ **902/659-2768**), the only round, brick lighthouse on the island, now a historic site (open daily mid-June to mid-Sept). Follow Route 1 to the ferry terminal, turning left just before the compound, to get to the **Wood Islands Lighthouse and Interpretive Museum** (www. woodislandslighthouse.com; ✆ **902/962-3110**) to get the lowdown on rum-running, phantom ships, ice boats, and much more. A great little park here provides a photo-op of ferries and the shoreline of Northumberland Strait.

Leaving Wood Islands, watch for Route 4 and turn east. This beautiful drive takes you 9km (5½ miles) on Route 4 to **Rossignol Estate Winery** (www.rossignolwinery. com; ✆ **902/962-4193**) in Little Sands. Sample an award-winning wine or two, or just relax in their vineyard by the sea. Bearing right on Route 18 watch for the signs to **Cape Bear Lighthouse ★**. Built in 1881 on a (crumbling) cliff, it was one of Marconi's wireless stations—and the one where an operator first heard the Titanic's desperate SOS calls. The lighthouse was later used to track German U-boats during World War II. A **small seasonal museum ★** (✆ **902/962-2469**) documents the station, which is no longer here, and it includes audio from Thomas Bartlett, the man who received the Titanic call. You can also climb about 40 steps to get a great view of the red-sand beaches and cliffs of the point. Admission costs C$3.50 for adults, C$2.50 for seniors, C$1.50 for children, and C$7.50 for families. Continue on to **Beach Point ★** beach, which is almost never crowded and is especially good for families with kids. When the tide is out, there's room to roam and tide pools aplenty. Route 18 will take you to the Murrays.

These two small and tidy villages offer little in the way of drama but lots of repose: the sounds of crickets, wind in the trees, and water; the soothing sights of red cliffs of sand, little boats returning to harbor, and seals.

As you drive, watch for the tight lines of buoys in the coastal waterways: The island's famous blue mussels are cultivated in the rivers here in mesh "socks" suspended underwater by ropes attached to those buoys, then shipped out to fine kitchens world-wide when they've grown to proper eating size.

EXPLORING THE MURRAYS

Murray River has several natural attractions beyond the views. One short **interpretive trail,** about half a kilometer (.35 mile) long, skirts the local golf course; another trail takes you through a grove of tall, ancient pine trees on the east side of McLure's Pond.

But the town is probably more famous for its local harbor seals, which are more common than cows in this part of PEI—if you know where on the river to look. The best way to view the sleek creatures is from the water. Visit the island's largest **seal colony ★★** by booking a trip with **Cruise Manada Marine Adventures ★** (www.cruisemanada.com; © **877/286-6532** or 902/566-5259) in Murray River. You'll travel in enclosed boats (rain or shine) and see seals, mussel farms, herons, and, with luck, bald eagles. The tours are offered three times daily Saturday through Thursday, two departures Friday, and a *ceilidh* in the evening. (From June through the end of Aug, one departure daily June and Sept at 1 pm; the cost is C$38 adults, C$19 children age 12 and under. Allow at least 2 hr. for the entire trip.)

Young children enjoy corny **Kings Castle Provincial Park** (© **902/962-7422**), an old-fashioned kiddy park of the sort that was popular in the 1950s and 1960s. This pleasant spot on the shores of the Murray River (with swimming at a small beach) features life-size depictions of storybook characters scattered about the fields and woodlands and an array of playground equipment. It's open daily from 9am to 9pm from June through mid-September; best of all, admission is free. The park is on Route 348, about 3km (2 miles) east of Murray River on the south bank of the river.

A short drive from Murray River, along the north bank of the river (take Rte. 17), is remote, empty **Poverty Point Beach.** Dunes back this long strand of eastward-facing beach. You park at the end of the road and walk along the beach watching for bird life. Swimming is problematic; the beach is pebbly at low tide, and currents can be troublesome. But it's certainly quiet: You might not see another soul, even in summer, on the entire strand.

A few miles north is **Panmure Island ★** and its **provincial park ★**, open from early June through the middle of September. This island is connected to the mainland via a sand-dune isthmus; the contrast between the white sands (on the ocean side) and the red beach of the inner cove is striking. It's a lovely spot, with swimming on the ocean side (lifeguards in summer); bathrooms and changing rooms; a viewing tower; and views northward to a striking little **lighthouse ★**. *Note:* If you see a lot of broken sea shells on the road, drive with care. Seagulls drop clams and such from high in the air, to break open dinner. They can puncture a tire. There's also a 9-hole golf course to occupy you in the **Murrays.** And if you're here at the end of July, don't miss the **Murray River Fisheries Festival ★**, a very local celebration involving dory-rowing competitions, log-rolling, a parade, and food and drink.

WHERE TO STAY

It's nice to be able to camp within sight of a white-sand beach, and you can do just that in **Panmure Island Provincial Park ★** (© **902/838-0668**). There are 43 sites here, some with hookups, some nicely sited in grassy fields with water views. Cost is from C$24 to C$30 per night. They accept credit cards. The campground, like the park, is open from early June through the middle of September.

Fox River Cottages ★ These modern two-bedroom cottages with kitchenettes are beautifully situated on 5 hectares (13 acres) down a winding dirt road at the edge of a field overlooking the islands of Murray Bay. The cottages are tidy units of exposed wood and high cathedral ceilings, furnished with televisions and DVD players, and all with views of the bay. They're near one another, yet also staggered to create a sense of personal privacy. Two units have woodstoves; all are heated with electric heat and have decks, Wi-Fi access, and gas barbecues for evening grilling. Relax on your cottage's screened porch, then wander down to the river and dabble around on a thousand-foot beach (swimming and good clam digging) or in one of the property's canoes (remember your life jacket). One unit has a private washer and dryer and its own dishwasher, but there's also laundry on premises that all guests can use for free.

239 Machon Point Rd. (off Rte. 18 on the north side of the river), Murray Harbour, PEI C0A 1V0. www.foxriver.ca. © **902/962-2881.** 3 units. Cottages (double occupancy) peak season C$120–C$140 nightly, C$500–C$925 weekly; spring and fall, C$80–C$95 nightly, C$500–C$600 weekly. MC, V. Closed Nov–May. **Amenities:** Canoes. *In room:* TV/DVD, kitchenette, no phone, Wi-Fi (free).

Montague

Montague may be the Kings County region's main commercial hub, but it's a hub in pretty low gear: compact and attractive, with a handsome business district on a pair of flanking hills sloping down to a bridge across the Montague River. Shipbuilding was the economic mainstay in the 19th century; today, though, dairy and farming are the main local endeavors. Montague has a lovely little waterfront on the river where you can enjoy refreshments overlooking the marina. A walking trail along the river will whip up an appetite, and there are several good eateries nearby.

EXPLORING THE OUTDOORS

East of Montague at Three Rivers, the **Roma National Historic Site** brings to life the story of a French merchant who, in 1732, established an international trading post. You'll find lively interpretive events, a heritage lunch with bread baked in Roma's outdoor oven, and lots to see and do. Southeast of Montague (en route to Murray River) is **Buffaloland Provincial Park** ★ (© **902/652-8950**), home to a small herd of buffalo. A gift from the province of Alberta, the magnificent animals number about two dozen. Walk down the fenced-in corridor and ascend the platform for the best view. Often they're hunkered down at the far end of the meadow, but be patient, they sometimes wander closer. The park is right off Route 4, about 6km (4 miles) outside town; watch for signs. Like so many PEI parks, it's free.

A bit north of Buffaloland on Route 4, between routes 216 and 317, is the **Harvey Moore Wildlife Management Area** ★, a delightful place for a stroll. A privately owned park named for the naturalist who created this sanctuary in 1949, its centerpiece is a 45-minute trail that loops around a pond and through varied ecosystems. Watch for waterfowl (with which Moore had an unusually close rapport) such as black ducks, blue-winged teal, ring-necked ducks, pintails, and plenty of Canada geese. Open during daylight hours June to mid-September. Once again, admission is free.

Brudenell River Provincial Park ★ is one of the province's best parks and a great spot to work up an athletic glow on a sunny afternoon. You'll find two well-regarded championship golf courses, an executive course, a full-blown resort (see "Where to Stay," below), tennis, lawn bowling, a playground, a campground, and nature trails. There are also interpretive programs for kids and adults. You can rent canoes, kayaks, and jet skis from private operators within the park. The park is open daily from mid-May through early October, and is free to enter. Head north of Montague on Route 4, then east on Route 3 to the park signs.

WHERE TO STAY

In addition to the park's own resort, described below, **Brudenell River Provincial Park** ★ (© **902/652-8966**) also maintains a large campground of 95 sites with various levels of services and amenities. Rates range from C$24 to C$33 per night. The park is open from mid-May through early October.

Rodd Brudenell River Resort ★★ ☺ This is an especially popular destination for golfers, with three types of lodgings. The hotel proper has 99 well-appointed guest rooms and suites, most with a balcony or terrace looking out onto either the river or one of the resort's showpiece **golf courses** ★★. The expensive, modern "gold cottages" each have two bedrooms, a Jacuzzi, a wet bar, cathedral ceilings, kitchens with dishwashers, fireplaces, decks, barbecue sets, and big-screen TVs; they can also be split in half, so you might share a cottage with another set of guests. In addition to the excellent golf courses, the resort has indoor and outdoor pools and a spa. The main dining room, on the first level of the property, is a huge place (high-backed chairs try to establish a sense of intimacy) but there's a bistro and pool bar here, as well.

Rte. 3 (P.O. Box 67), Cardigan, PEI C0A 1G0. www.rodd-hotels.ca. © **800/565-7633** or 902/652-2332. Fax 902/652-2886. 181 units. C$139–C$260 double; C$90–C$183 cabin; C$167–C$568 suite and cottage. Packages available. AE, DC, MC, V. Closed mid-Oct to mid-May. Pets allowed (C$10 per pet per night). **Amenities:** 2 restaurants; bar; babysitting; canoe, kayak, and bike rentals; children's center; 3 golf courses; golf school; fitness center; Jacuzzi; indoor and outdoor pools; sauna; spa; 2 tennis courts. *In room:* A/C, TV, fridge (some units), hair dryer, kitchenette (some units), minibar (some units), Wi-Fi (free).

WHERE TO EAT

Although it doesn't seem so when you drive into Montague, there are some terrific little eateries here during the summer. **Sir Isaac's and Mister Gabe's Restaurant** at 576 Main St. (© **902/836-2628**) is cozy and welcoming in cool weather. If it's warm, they have a great second-story patio overlooking the waterfront. Oh, and the food? Suffice it to say their Lord of Montague Burger won them a first place from the cattlemen's association—they should know good beef. The homemade fish cakes, beans, and bacon served the island way with tomato chow, makes a person think of grandma's kitchen. Across the river (you can use the bridge) a small outdoor cafe located under the Visitors Centre is a great place to check out the activity at the marina. A short drive away, at 7 West St. in Georgetown, **Clamdiggers Beach House Restaurant** (© **902/652-2466**) buys its seafood fresh and hand cuts it. In fact, food is prepared in the classical eastern PEI tradition. The spectacular waterfront location is enjoyed from their deck. Open year-round.

Windows on the Water Café ★★ SEAFOOD If you haven't yet dined on those internationally famous PEI mussels, this enjoyable seasonal cafe is the place to do it. The blue mussels are steamed in a *mirepoix* (French vegetable soup stock) adulterated with flavors of sesame, ginger, and garlic—a tasty take. Dinnertime main courses here could include sole stuffed with crab; fish burgers; or peppered steak served with sautéed vegetables. Lunches are lighter, but still great—chicken salads, house-made maritime fish cakes, and the like. For dessert, the bread pudding is highly recommended. If the weather's good, ask for a seat on the (covered) deck and enjoy a great view of the Montague River; if not, that's okay, because the open dining room is lively enough on its own.

106 Sackville St. (corner of Main St.), Montague. © **902/838-2080.** Reservations recommended. Main courses C$8–C$10 at lunch, C$15–C$35 at dinner. AE, DC, MC, V. June–Sept daily 11:30am–9:30pm. Closed Oct–May.

Souris & Northeast PEI ★★

Some 40km (25 miles) northeast of Montague—take Route 4 north out of town, merge with Route 2, and keep going east—is the little town of **Souris,** an active fishing town attractively set on a gentle hill overlooking its harbor. Yet things weren't always so great here. Souris (pronounced soo-*ree*) is actually French for "mice"—not too flattering, is it? And, in fact, the town owes its name to its frustrated early settlers, who were beset by waves of voracious field mice that repeatedly destroyed their food crops. Finally they named the place "Mouse-town" and concentrated on the fishing, which worked out rather better. But "Mouse-town" it remains today, though the mice are (mostly) gone. To learn more about Souris, visit the tiny **Matthew & McLean Museum** located in the Visitor Information Centre on Main Street.

In addition to its own little charms, this town is the launching base for ferry boats to the **Magdalen Islands** (actually part of Québec; see box on p. 242 for ferry details). It also makes a good central base for exploring northeastern PEI, a place that's remote, less populated, and more greenly forested than the rest of PEI, where farming prevails. Since a spur of the **Confederation Trail** ends in Souris, this is a good spot from which to launch a bike excursion of the area. You can ride to the main trunk trail, then turn northeast and continue to land's end at the East Point Lighthouse (see "Exploring the Area," below).

EXPLORING THE AREA

Several good beaches can be found ringing this wedge-shaped peninsula that points like an accusing finger toward Nova Scotia's Cape Breton Island. **Red Point Provincial Park** (✆ 902/357-3075) lies about 13km (8 miles) northeast of Souris, on Route 16. Open from June through mid-September, it offers a handsome beach and supervised swimming, along with a **campground** that's popular with families (see "Where to Stay," below).

Just a little farther along Route 16 there's another inviting beach at **Basin Head,** which features **"singing sands" ★** that allegedly sing (actually, they more like squeak) when you walk on them. The dunes are especially nice. Access is via the **Basin Head Fisheries Museum ★** (✆ 902/357-7233), a provincially operated museum that offers insight into the life of the inshore fisherman. Admission is C$4 adults, C$3.50 students, and C$12 families (free for children 12 and under). It's open daily 9am to 5pm, then closed from mid-September through May.

At the island's far eastern tip is the aptly named **East Point Lighthouse ★** (www. eastpointlighthouse.com; ✆ 902/357-2106). You can simply enjoy the dramatic setting overlooking the sometimes turbulent meeting of the tides or take a tour of the lighthouse from mid-June through early September. Ask for your East Point ribbon while you're here; if you also made it to the North Cape Lighthouse on PEI's western shore, you'll receive a Traveler's Award documenting you've traveled the island tip-to-tip. Admission to the octagonal lighthouse tower is C$3 adults, C$2 seniors and students, C$1 children, and C$8 families. There's also a craft shop on-site purveying jewelry, soap, sand paintings, local books and music, and other island goods.

WHERE TO STAY

There's camping at **Red Point Provincial Park** (✆ 902/357-3075). There are about 120 sites here, costing from C$24 to C$33, most of them built to handle the annual summer influx of RVs. They take reservations beginning in April and accept credit cards; there are kids' programs throughout July and August.

Inn at Bay Fortune ★★ This lovely brick-and-shingle compound on 18 hectares (45 acres), beside the bay in the hamlet of Bay Fortune, was built in 1910 as a summer home for playwright Elmer Harris and actress Colleen Dewhurst. It became the nucleus for a colony of artists, actors, and writers. Current innkeeper David Wilmer bought it in the 1980s, renovating to create a unique collection of rooms and suites. Overlooking Fortune Harbour and the sea beyond, it remains a perfect place to relax. Home to the television series *The Inn Chef*, the Inn is known for its cuisine and extensive gardens, which are showcased each evening in one of the island's best known restaurants (below). The **Inn Chef Experience Package** includes your room, a gourmet dinner, and full breakfast for C$260 to C$445 per couple.

758 Rte. 310 (turn south off Rte. 2 about 5 miles west of Souris), Bay Fortune, PEI C0A 2B0. www. innatbayfortune.com. ℂ **902/687-3745.** Fax 902/687-3540. 17 units. C$135–C$150 double; C$200-C$335; suite off-season discounts available. Rates include full breakfast. Packages available. DC, MC, V. Closed mid-Oct to mid-May. **Amenities:** Restaurant. *In room:* Internet (free), fireplace (most units), Jacuzzi (some units), no phone.

Inn at Spry Point ★★ 🏠 Folks who crave getting away from it all will love the location of this inn. Set on the tip of a peninsula with over 2,743m (9,000 ft.) of shore frontage, it is a little corner of paradise. Eleven of 15 rooms have private balconies, the rest garden terraces; all have king-size beds. The complex began as a United Nations–funded, self-sufficient community affiliated with the New Alchemy Institute: Think windmills, solar power, greenhouses, trout ponds, and such. But oil prices dropped, interest in conservation waned, and the experiment faded. Enter David Wilmer, owner of the Inn at Bay Fortune (see above), who purchased and converted the 32-hectare (80-acre) property. Appetites built by walking trails and beaches are appeased in their dining room. The chef creates a new breakfast menu each day. Lunch is served in-house, dinner at their sister property, the Inn at Bay Fortune, just 10 minutes away.

Spry Pt. Rd. (turn off from Rte. 310 about 6 miles south of Rte. 2), Little Pond, PEI C0A 2B0. www. innatsprypoint.com. ℂ **888/687-3745** or 902/583-2400. Fax 902/583-2176. 15 units. Off season C$159–C$249, peak season C$179-C$299 double. Rates include full breakfast. Packages available. DC, MC, V. Closed mid-Sept to late June. **Amenities:** Restaurant; Internet (free). *In room:* A/C.

WHERE TO EAT

Sometimes great food experiences are found in the most unlikely places. Such is the case in the region just south of Souris, where what is arguably PEI's most famous restaurant, the Inn at Bay Fortune (see below) seems to be miles from anywhere. Beautiful miles, but miles nonetheless. This northeastern tip seems to delight in surprises. Another is found at 2065 Rte. 2 in Fortune Bridge, where the sheltered **Harbour Café** (ℂ **902/687-1997**) is easily passed by—it's a gas station restaurant. The proprietors have ignored that fact to create a warm atmosphere with local dishes, a coming together of home-style and chef-created cuisine. We were blown away by our meal and the sheer good value for the dollar. Later we visited the **Evergreen Café,** right in Souris at 99 Maine St. (ℂ **902/743-3330**), a small coffee shop that would fit in any trendy city neighborhood.

Inn at Bay Fortune ★★★ CONTEMPORARY This became a culinary destination when its already stellar reputation was enhanced by the television program, *Inn Chef*. The TV cameras are gone, but dedication to great dining remains. Chef Serio focuses on local, first from their own gardens, then from local farmers and fishermen. This dedication to freshness was the norm here long before it became trendy. Those with a serious passion for a food experience dine in the kitchen, choosing 7, 10, or 12 courses served in a glass-enclosed **Chef's Table** ★★. A five-course

AN EXCURSION TO THE magdalen islands

The **Magdalen Islands (Les Îsles de la Madeleine),** a 5-hour ferry ride north of PEI, are a dozen low-lying islands linked to each other by sand spits. Around 13,000 people live here, in peaceful fishing villages and farming communities; the red-sand cliffs look like PEI, but the farmhouses, wharves, cows, boats, and accents are reminiscent of the Atlantic coast of France. (The Magdalens are actually part of Québec, even though they're closer to PEI.) The islands boast nearly 320km (200 miles) of uncrowded beaches, and urban Montréalers in search of leisure time love the place. The islands are also famous for their persistent winds, which seemingly never cease blowing.

Advance planning is necessary for a trip to the islands, since the summertime demand for accommodations far outstrips supply. A free island tourist guide is available by calling ☏ **877/624-4437** or 418/986-2245. On the web, head to **www.tourismeilesdelamadeleine.com**.

Ferry service from Souris to Cap-aux-Meules is provided by the **Coopérative de Transport Maritime** (www.ctma.ca; ☏ **888/986-3278** or 418/986-3278), also known as the CTMA. The long river crossing takes 5 hours one-way on a seven-deck ferry that can carry 95 cars and 400 passengers. The boats sail as many as 11 times weekly in summer; the schedule is reduced to as few as three weekly boats in the off season, so check a schedule online before arriving on PEI.

One-way rates during high season (mid-June to mid-Sept) are C$47 per adult, C$38 per senior, and C$24 per child age 5 to 12, plus C$87 for a normal-size automobile (more for vans and campers). *Tip:* Those rates plunge by about 40% outside of the 3 peak months.

Chef's Tasting Menu is offered nightly for C$70 to C$100. Or order from the menu, beginning with starters such as a charcuterie board of house-cured and smoked meats and fish. Offerings and prices change daily as ingredients come and go. Their award-winning wine list is well-chosen. Dine on the veranda, where open windows take advantage of the porch aspect of summer and present a great view overlooking Fortune River and the Northumberland Straight.

758 Rte. 310 (turn south off Rte. 2 about 8km/5 miles west of Souris), Bay Fortune, PEI C0A 2B0. ☏ **902/687-3745.** Reservations strongly recommended. Main courses typically C$25–C$35; tasting and chef's table menus C$70-C$100 per person. AE, MC, V. Daily 5–9pm. Closed mid-Oct to late May.

St. Peters Bay & Environs

The easternmost sector of Kings County attracts fewer tourists—the majority are speeding through en route to East Point with the goal of a tip-to-tip car crossing of the island or heading to the ferry to Îles de la Madeleine.

Yet it's worth slowing down to see this region—the pastoral landscapes are sublime, and the best vistas are found off the paved roads. It's also an area blessed with a number of appealing bike routes and what might be the island's top golf course. While it has few prominent natural landmarks, **St. Peters Bay ★**, a narrow and attractive inlet that twists eastward from the coast, is a worthy exception. This is also the real PEI: full-service filling stations that look like they could be straight out of the Midwestern U.S. in the 1950s; farmers cycling and fishing from bridges; wildflowers such as bold purple lupines far outnumbering cows, cars, and people.

Restless travelers with attention-deficit disorder might not enjoy this region as much, but for the rest of us, a bit of rambling around here isn't a bad way at all to spend a day.

To really learn about the area, visit the **Turret Bell** (© **902/961-1070**) at St. Peters Landing, a collection of shops next to the bridge at the head of the bay. This nifty little shop is a great spot to pick up a book or two, have a coffee or sign up for a historic walking tour or a Geo Treasure Hunt—an adventure that involves learning how to use a GPS to find hidden caches. Artisans run a pewter shop, **St. Peters Bay Craft and Giftware** (www.stpetersbay.com; © **902/961-3223**), nearby at 15465 Northside Rd. where you can even learn to pour your own piece of pewter, and up at 9984 Rte. 16, in Hermanville, **Prince Edward Distillery** (www.princeedwarddistillery.com; © **877/510-9669** or 902/687-2586) produces true potato vodka and other handcrafted spirits.

EXPLORING THE AREA

Follow Route 313 along the north shore of St. Peter's Bay to its tip and you'll come to the **Greenwich Dunes ★**, a stunning area of uniquely wind-carved migrating sand dunes capped with grasses. This region was slated for vacation-home development until 1997, when it was acquired (and thus saved) by Parks Canada, which added it as an extension to Prince Edward Island National Park. Thank goodness for that.

The cute little town of **Mount Stewart** (on Rte. 2, just over the county line in Queens County) is located near the confluence of several spurs of the **Confederation Trail,** the excellent island-wide recreation trail described earlier (see "The Great Outdoors," p. 207). The Mount Stewart area is home to some of the best-maintained eastern segments of this trail.

Drop in to the **Hillsborough River Eco-Centre** at 104 Main St. (www.hrec.mount stewartpei.ca; © **902/676-2050** or 676-2881) and ask about the best viewing area for eagles and other wildlife, as well as the history of the area. The village is located on the Hillsborough, designated a Canadian Heritage River. If you are in need of refreshments, check out **Kristie's Family Restaurant,** just down the street at 141 Maine (© **902/676-2732**). It's just a regular village eatery, clean with the usual fare, but I heartily recommend their Loose Meat Sandwich. Also take a look at the **Trailside Inn** across from the Eco-Centre (www.trailside.ca; © **888/704-6595**). They offer rooms and a cafe that serves lunch and some refreshments Thursday through Sunday in July and August and sometimes offer evening musical performances in a cozy atmosphere.

Greenwich Interpretation Centre ★ A spectacular parabolic dune system, white-sand beaches and an extensive trail system, complete with a floating boardwalk, make Greenwich a favorite spot to spend the day. Visits to this part of the Prince Edward Island National Park are best begun with a visit to their interpretive center (open seasonally). Using the state-of-the-art learning center, you can have fun while getting an appreciation for how natural forces and 10,000 years of human settlement shaped this place. A supervised (July and Aug) beach with facilities and observation tower are nearby. You are entering the National Park, which carries a summertime admission fee of C$7.80 per adult, C$6.80 per senior, and C$2.90 per child. All these rates are slashed by 50% during spring and fall.

Rte. 313, Greenwich (from St. Peters Bay, cross the bridge to the north side and drive a few miles west on Rte. 313), Prince Edward Island National Park. © **902/961-2514.** July–Aug daily 10am–6pm; June and Sept daily 10am–5pm. Closed Oct–May.

WHERE TO STAY & EAT

Rodd Crowbush Golf & Beach Resort ★★★ The Rodd's Kings County property is impressive, anchored by access to what's ranked as the island's best golf course and a nearby beach. The range of accommodations here include 25 rooms, 24 king-bedded suites (some with balconies on the bay and golf course), 32 colorful one- and two-bedroom cottages with luxe touches, and free Wi-Fi throughout. The hotel's dining room (serving three meals daily) is complemented by an adjacent lounge and the clubhouse grill at the golf course.

632 Rte. 350 (P.O. Box 350), Morell, PEI C0A 1S0. www.roddvacations.com. (C) **800/565-7633** or 902/961-5600. Fax 902/561-5601. 81 units. C$128–C$589 double. Packages available. MC, V. Closed late Oct to mid-May. **Amenities:** 2 restaurants; lounge; golf course; fitness center; Jacuzzi; indoor pool; spa; 2 tennis courts. *In room:* A/C, TV/DVD, hair dryer, Wi-Fi (free).

PRINCE COUNTY

Prince County encompasses the western end of PEI, and offers a mixture of lush agricultural landscapes, rugged coastline, and unpopulated sandy beaches. Generally speaking, this region is a working-farm, working-harbors kind of place. In other words: Real people live and work here.

Within this landscape, you can find pockets of charm, such as the village of **Victoria** on the south coast (at the county line) and in **Tyne Valley** near the north coast, which is vaguely reminiscent of a Cotswold hamlet. Two of the province's tourism icons, **West Point Lighthouse** and **North Cape** complex, are located "up west" and the province's second city, **Summerside** resides on the narrow isthmus between Malpeque and Bedeque Bays. These two bays are some of the best environments in the world for harvesting oysters.

In addition, the **Confederation Trail** (described in "The Great Outdoors," p. 207) offers quiet access to the rolling countryside throughout much of northwestern Prince County. As well, several provincial parks here rank among the best on the island.

Essentials

GETTING THERE   From Confederation Bridge, take Route 1A to connect with Route 2 west, the main highway connecting Prince County with the rest of the island. Route 2 goes right up the middle to North Cape and is the fast way to get to the western tip. A better route if you have time is to pick up the North Cape Coastal Drive in Summerside and follow it around the coast for a spectacular loop (about 350km/218 miles). Be prepared to linger—you might want a couple of days.

VISITOR INFORMATION   The best source of travel information for the county is **Gateway Village** ((C) **902/437-8570**) at the end of the Confederation Bridge, described in the introduction to this chapter (see "Essentials," p. 204). It's open daily, year-round. There is also a Visitor Information Centre on Summerside's waterfront.

Victoria ★★

The town of **Victoria**—located a short detour off Route 1, between the Confederation Bridge and Charlottetown—is a tiny, scenic village that has attracted a clutch of artists, boutique owners, and craftspeople. What there is of the village is perfect for strolling—parking is near the wharf and off the streets, keeping the narrow lanes free for foot traffic.

Wander these short, shady streets while admiring the architecture, much of which is in an elemental, farmhouse style or dotted with elaborate Victorian homes. The village, which was first settled in 1767, has escaped the creeping sprawl that has plagued so many otherwise attractive places. The entire village consists of a grand total of four square blocks, surrounded by potato fields and the Northumberland Strait. I'm pretty sure the village looked almost the same (except for the cars puttering through) a century or more ago.

EXPLORING VICTORIA

The **Victoria Seaport Lighthouse Museum** (no phone) is located inside the shingled, square **lighthouse** ★ near the town parking lot. (You can't miss it.) You'll find a rustic local history museum with an assortment of artifacts from the past century or so. It's open daily in summer; admission is by donation.

In the middle of town is the well-regarded **Victoria Playhouse** ★ (victoria playhouse.com; ☏ **902/658-2025**). Built in 1913 as a community hall, the building has a unique raked stage (it drops 17cm/7 inches over 6m/21 ft. to create the illusion of space), four beautiful stained-glass lamps, and a proscenium arch—pretty unusual for a community hall. It's hard to say which is more fun: the quality of the performances or the fun-night-out air of a professional play being staged in a small town with little else going on. Monday-night concerts offer up everything from traditional folk to Latin jazz. Most tickets are C$26 adults, C$24 seniors, and C$20 students, though a few performances are priced higher; matinees cost about C$20.

Among the dozen or so businesses in the village, the most intriguing is **Island Chocolates** (☏ **902/658-2320**), where delicious Belgian-style chocolates are made. The shop is open daily from mid-June through mid-September (they do workshops on chocolate making, for C$45 per person. You must book in advance).

With a little hunting, you can also find artisans, eateries, a small **provincial park** ★, an antiques shop, and a lobster outlet (great for a picnic in the park).

WHERE TO STAY & EAT

Café Maplethorpe   The restaurant has a focus on local and organic food that reflects the region. Priding themselves on cooking from scratch, they offer soups, salads, and sandwiches for lunch. A three-course fixed price (C$25) meal unleashes the chef's creativity in the evening, or they have just started offerings such as barbequed short ribs, vegetarian Madras curry, seafood pie, and spinach and feta stuffed chicken breast. One of the pluses about this inn's cafe is their commitment to accommodating dietary restrictions. Call ahead to discuss your needs and also ask about any specials. Pastry Chef Diane creates wonderful breads and desserts as part of an imaginative menu. Reasonably priced.

2123 Rte. 112, P.O. Box 4109, Bedeque C0B 1C0. historicmaplethorpe.com. ☏ **866/770-2909** or 902/887-2909. C$7–C$13 lunch; C$13–C$30 dinner. MC, V. Open to public 11am–3pm for lunch Tues–Fri, 5–9pm for dinner Fri–Sat, year-round.

Historic Maplethorpe B&B ★★   French and colonial antiques, a meticulous attention to comfort, and creating a genteel atmosphere reflects the heritage of this former merchant's home. Flowers fresh from the garden, and locally made toiletries are indicative of the owners' dedication to creating rooms you want to return to at the end of a day sightseeing. The owners arrived in 2002, fell in love with the house and worked to restore it to its 1860 grandeur. Happily for their clientele, they achieved their goals, brought culinary skills into the mix, and created an award-winning destination that really speaks of where it is. Part of their adventure has been to explore and capture the essence of Prince Edward Island. I often think that someone from away (as locals describe anyone not born here) has a deeper appreciation because they see the island through fresh, new perspective. Ask about having your own culinary adventure with the chef. Beach nearby. Breakfasts created by this pastry chef get rave reviews.

2123 Rte. 112, P.O. Box 4109, Bedeque C0B 1C0. www.historicmaplethorpe.com. ☏ **866/770-2909** or 902/887-2909. 3 rooms, 1 cottage. Rooms (double) are C$110–C$160 high season, C$90–

C$130 mid-Sept to mid-May; 2-bedroom cottage C$850 week available June to mid-Sept. MC, V. **Amenities:** Restaurant; breakfast; computer; crib available; complimentary laundry service. *In room:* TV/DVD, Wi-Fi (free).

Landmark Café ★ 🍴 CAFE Right across from the Victoria Playhouse (see "Exploring Victoria," above), this popular cafe occupies a small green building that was once this town's general store and post office. Today the food is squarely the main focus. The menu, while limited, is inviting, served in a funky, slightly bohemian setting that keeps the same summer people and locals coming back, year after year. Daily offerings usually include sandwiches and lobster rolls for lunch, and such things as steamed mussels, salads, lasagna, meat pie, and salmon for dinner. Yes, there's a wine list.

12 Main St. www.landmarkcafe.ca. © **902/658-2286.** Reservations recommended. Sandwiches around C$6; main courses C$11–C$16. MC, V. June–Sept daily 11am–3pm and 5pm–close.

Orient Hotel Bed & Breakfast ★ 🛏 The Orient has been a Victoria mainstay for years—a 1926 guide says the inn offered rooms for C$2.50 per night. (Of course, back then a trip to the bathroom required a walk to the carriage house.) Modernized, all rooms now have private bathrooms, and the hotel still retains much of its original charm and quirkiness. The century-old building with bright yellow shingles and maroon trim is at the edge of the village. Rooms are painted in warm pastel tones and furnished in flea-market antiques; most have good water views, and all have ceiling fans. The place has a friendly, low-key demeanor much like that of the village itself, and a television-and-games room for playing cribbage, crokinole (an old-fashioned Maritime game), and *ceilidhs* (Celtic folk dances). **Mrs. Proffit's Tea Room,** on the first floor, serves light lunches (sandwiches, lobster rolls, soup, salad) plus an afternoon tea featuring good scones.

34 Main St. (P.O. Box 55), Victoria, PEI C0A 2G0. www.theorienthotel.com. © **800/565-6743** or 902/658-2503. 8 units. C$95–C$160 double and suite. Rates include full breakfast. Packages available. MC, V. Off-street parking. Closed mid-Oct to mid-May. Not suitable for children under 12. **Amenities:** Tearoom; bicycle storage. *In room:* TV, Wi-Fi (free).

Summerside ★★

Prince Edward Island's second city has a fantastic waterfront boardwalk stretching 6.5km (4 miles) alongside Bedeque Bay, and overlooking Indian Head Lighthouse. There is much more to enjoy here than the **Baywalk,** but it is a biggie. Add to the mix the **College of Piping and Celtic Performing Arts,** which puts on stirring performances during the summer; Canada's longest running dinner theater known as the **Feast; Harbourfront Theatre,** home to *Anne & Gilbert: The Musical;* free live music along the waterfront; numerous museums; and harness racing. Summerside is known as the Gateway to the North Cape Coastal Drive and offers a variety of accommodations and eateries to warrant a stay of a couple of days. Harness racing and baseball are popular with spectators. History buffs will find lots of museums devoted to local topics like the silver fox.

EXPLORING SUMMERSIDE & AREA

The city waterfront is best explored by following Water Street from the east, right through the town. A number of eateries are located along the way, as is a continuous walking trail alongside the water. If you stay on this road long enough you will see signs for **Linkletter Provincial Park.** Follow it to Route 2. The majority of shopping is found on Granville Street, which also takes you to Route 2.

Slemon Park off Route 2 is a former military base, now home to businesses that take advantage of the airport. An interesting stop for plane or military buffs can be found at the entrance to the former Canadian Forces Base Summerside. **Air Force Heritage Park** is home to three historical aircraft along with interpretive displays. On Route 2, the **Acadian Museum** (23 Main Dr., Miscouche; www.peimuseum. com; ✆ **902/432-2880**) is a great introduction to the Acadian region that lies to the west. Learn about the 300-year Acadian presence here, stroll their Heritage Trail, or access their genealogy resources. It's open year round (9:30am–5pm daily July–Aug, 9:30am–5pm Mon–Fri and 1–4pm Sun Sept–June).

WHERE TO STAY & EAT

As you enter Summerside along Water Street, there are a number of mom-and-pop motels that are clean and moderately priced—good value for the dollar.

The Loyalist Country Inn ★★   This urban hotel is well located: overlooking the Summerside waterfront and adjacent Harbourfront Jubilee Theatre, and just a short walk to downtown. Clean, well placed, and reasonably priced, it is comfortable without being luxurious. The restaurant and lounge offer up good meals, if a little pricey. Ask about special-occasion buffet suppers, consistently better than most such offerings. Confederation Trail passes outside the door, for walkers and bicyclists.

195 Harbour Dr., Summerside. 84 rooms, 8 housekeeping units. www.lakeviewhotels.com. ✆ **877/355-3500** or 902/436-3333. C$99–C$199 double; C$129–C$299 suite. AE, MC, V. Parking. Open year-round. **Amenities:** Restaurant; lounge; exercise room; indoor pool; sauna; bike rental. In room: TV, sauna (some rooms), Wi-Fi (free).

Quality Inn & Suites—Garden of the Gulf ★★   This hotel has the advantage of being beside the Feast Dinner Theatre and across the street from the College of Piping and Celtic Performing Arts of Canada. The waterfront property offers free golf (9 holes), two swimming pools, and easy access to walking, biking, and hiking trails. One unique aspect is the wide corridor, with seating areas, used to access rooms. Almost an indoor streetscape, it adds a nice atmosphere to what are typical chain-hotel rooms, especially at night when fairy lights decorate plants and trees. Very comfortable beds at this very well-run family operated hotel.

618 Water St. E. (Rte. 11) Summerside, C1N 2V5. www.qualityinnpei.com. ✆ **800/265-5551** or 902/436-2295. 94 units. C$99–C$199 double. AE, MC, V. Parking. **Amenities:** Indoor and outdoor pool; complimentary golf; coffee shop; exercise room; picnic area. In-room: TV, free local calls, whirlpool bathtubs (some), Wi-Fi (free).

SUMMERSIDE AFTER DARK

For the summer months, Summerside is a hotbed of nighttime things to do. Along with a number of pubs and eateries that offer entertainment, the city boasts good stage performances. **Harbourfront Jubilee Theatre** (www.harbourfronttheatre. com; ✆ **800/708-6505** or 902/888-2500) at 124 Harbour Dr. on the waterfront is a 520-seat theater year-round productions—*Anne & Gilbert* is a summer mainstay. **Credit Union Place** hosts sporting events and whatever high-demand performers come to town (Elton John was here in 2011). For even more rousing entertainment, head for the **College of Piping and Celtic Performing Arts of Canada** (www. collegeofpiping.com; ✆ **877/224-7473** [BAG-PIPE] or 902-436-5377), located at 618 Water St., the only year-round institution of its kind in North America. Their summer stage production, *Highland Storm*, is an exhilarating presentation of highland dance, bagpipers, drummers, and step dancers. Daytime activities also captivate lovers of all things Celtic. The **Feast Dinner Theatre** (www.brotherstwo.ca; ✆ **902/436-9654**), at **Brothers Two Restaurant,** 618 Water St., began here in 1979 and has been running every summer since, making it Canada's longest-running

Head out in the morning, following Route 20 northeast of Summerside, until you get to the hamlet of Indian River. Watch for signs to St. Mary's Church, home to the **Indian River Festival** (©️ 866/856-3733 or 902/836-3733), a summer-long presentation of classical, jazz, world music, choral, and Maritime music. This rural church, known for its architecture and acoustics, attracts world-class musicians to play, and sometimes record. Take note of the location and performance schedule. You might be able to return for a performance. As you continue driving east on Route 20, note the body of water to the west. This is Malpeque Bay, where the famous Malpeque oysters were first found. Long considered a delicacy, they are now "farmed" in these same waters and make their way to eager diners around the world. Walk on the beach at Cabot Park, just off Route 20 or continue on Route 20 to Park Corner for the Anne of Green Gables Museum (p. 211). Book a carriage ride which takes you around the Lake of Shining Waters and to a beautiful beach. Continue on Route 20 to Route 6, turn right and you'll end up at the Shipwright's Café (below) to dine before taking in a concert at St. Mary's Church. You did make reservations, right? A late night refreshment at Brothers Two (p. 247) or the Loyalist Country Inn (p. 247) in Summerside will suitably close a great day.

dinner theater. Shows change each season but the entertainment value stays high. In 2011, they sold their 500,000th ticket. The musical comedy—with lots of singalong and hand clapping—makes for a fun night out.

The Shipwright's Café ★★ REGIONAL   This friendly and locally popular restaurant moved to the village of Margate in 2001. It's elegant yet informal, and you'd be comfortable here in neat jeans or sport clothes. Expect great service, a short but serviceable wine list, and salads with organic greens to begin your meal. Dishes here include lunchtime lamb wraps, chili tostadas, curried mussels, iced or broiled-with-cheese local oysters, and the "Margate Clipper" (a lobster sandwich on potato bread with greens). Dinners run more to fish cakes, herb-crusted Atlantic salmon with lime salsa, vegetable potpie, seafood paella with bread and aioli, and a chowder rich with plenty of those famous plump PEI mussels. It's a great local find—*if* you can find it.

11869 Rte. 6 (at junction of Rte. 233), Margate, PEI C0B 1M0. www.shipwrightspei.com. ©️ **902/836-3403.** Reservations recommended. Lunch items C$9–C$20; dinner entrees C$15–C$20 (more for lobster). MC, V. June–Sept daily 11:30am–3:30pm and 5–8:30pm. Closed Oct–May.

Tyne Valley ★

Although the village is tiny, there is much to admire in this area: verdant barley and potato fields surrounding gingerbread-like homes, plus azure inlets nosing in on the view from the long distance. (Those inlets are the arms of the bay, world-famous for its succulent oysters.) A former 19th-century shipbuilding center, Tyne Valley now attracts artisans and others in search of the slow lane; the gorgeous scenery is a bonus. A handful of good restaurants, inns, and shops cater to summer travelers.

EXPLORING TYNE VALLEY

Just north of the village on Route 12 is lovely **Green Park Provincial Park** ★★ (©️ **902/831-7912**), open from mid-June through early September. Once the site of an active shipyard, this 80-hectare (200-acre) park is now a lush riverside destination with emerald lawns and leafy trees. It still has the feel of a turn-of-the-20th-century estate—which, in fact, it was. In the heart of the park is the extravagant 1865 gingerbread mansion built by James Yeo, a merchant, shipbuilder, and landowner who in his time was the island's wealthiest and most powerful man.

The historic Yeo House and the **Green Park Shipbuilding Museum ★** (© 902/831-7947), open June through September, are now the park's centerpieces. Managed by the province's museum and heritage foundation, they together provide a good glimpse into the prosperous lives of shipbuilders during the golden age of PEI shipbuilding. The museum and house are open daily from mid-June through mid-September, 9am to 5pm. Admission is C$5 adults, C$3.50 students, C$14 families, and free for children 12 and under.

WHERE TO STAY

Green Park Provincial Park ★★ (© 902/831-7912), on Route 12 just outside Tyne Valley, may be the most gracious and lovely park on the entire island, and it offers camping on 58 grassy and wooded sites overlooking an arm of Malpeque Bay for about C$23 to C$30 per night. There are cabins, a coin-op laundry, a playground, and a camp store. The campground usually opens for a season of mid-June through early September; you can begin making reservations for the current season in April.

Caernarvon Cottages & Gardens ★ ☺ The sense of quiet and the views over Malpeque Bay are the lures at this attractive, well-maintained cottage complex a few minutes' drive from Tyne Valley. Four red-roofed pine cottages, built around 1990, are furnished simply but comfortably with two bedrooms, cathedral ceilings, a sleeping loft, an outdoor gas barbecue, a porch with a bay view, board games, and a well-kitted kitchen. It's a great place to get away with the kids; there's a playground out back, and croquet sets and kites available. One caveat: The owner keeps large, energetic dogs (pets are very welcome here). If you're allergic, or your kids are nervous around big dogs, be aware.

4697 Rte. 12 (about 11–13km/7–8 miles south of Tyne Valley), Bayside, PEI, C0B 1Y0. www.cottagelink.com/caernarvon. © **902/854-2765.** 4 cottages. C$135 night for 4 people; C$450–C$800 weekly cottage for 2 people. Inn rates include full breakfast. V. Cottages open mid-May to mid-Nov. Pets welcome. *In room:* TV/DVD (some units), hair dryer, fully equipped kitchen w/dishwasher, no phone, propane fireplace.

WHERE TO EAT

The Doctor's Inn ★★ CONTEMPORARY CANADIAN   The best food in this area is the nightly dinner service here, where four-course meals are built around what is fresh in the organic market garden. Meals are served around a large oval dining room table and prepared on the woodstove. Entrees vary according to what is fresh: scallops, Arctic char, veal, salmon; all served with bread warm from the oven, wine, and homemade dessert. Guests must make reservations at least 24 hours in advance to arrange your meal time and discuss your menu.

Rte. 167 (at junction with Rte. 12), Tyne Valley, PEI C0B 2C0. www.peisland.com/doctorsinn. © **902/831-3057.** C$45–C$60. MC, V.

Tignish & North Cape ★★★

The road west, Route 12, takes travelers through Alberton, the only town in the region; take a short side trip down Route 152 to the picturesque fishing village of Northport. Northport Pier is home to a good-size fishing fleet. A Great Blue Heron rookery means you are sure to find the great birds posing for photos in the shallows near the lighthouse. The **Sea Rescue Interpretive Centre** displays will give insight into life of fishermen from the past.

Locals like to tell you that the first European to visit the island came ashore at Kildare Capes in 1534 and recorded it as being "the fairest land 'tis possible to see!" Today **Jacques Cartier Provincial Park,** named for that French explorer, offers a beautiful beach with supervised swimming, nature walks, and children's games during the summer.

Continue on Route 12 to Tignish, home to one of the largest fleets of inshore fishing vessels in Atlantic Canada, and mile "0" of the Confederation Trail. The wharf at Tignish Run is a great place to take pictures and soak up atmosphere. Depending on the time of year you visit, watch for crates of lobster, or giant bluefin tuna being off-loaded. In Tignish proper, **St. Simon & St. Jude Catholic Church,** the largest in PEI, is home to one of only four Louis Mitchell Tracker pipe organs in the world. The convent next door has been turned into the **Tignish Heritage Inn and Gardens** (www.tignish.com/inn; ✆ 877/882-2491 or 902/882-2491). Consider checking in before moving on to North Cape, where Mother Nature will lure you to linger past sunset.

It's just a short drive to North Cape, past Sea Cow Pond. The skyline ahead will be dominated by huge sweeping blades outlined against the sky. You have arrived at the Energy Institute of Canada and the **North Cape Wind Farm.** This test facility has been a leader in developing wind energy and now has an interpretive display to tell you all about it. It's part of the North Cape complex (www.northcape.ca; ✆ 902/882-2991) that houses a restaurant, gift shop, aquarium, and historical information about shipwrecks, ghost ships, storms, and natural history. Black Marsh Nature Trail will take you back to nature.

North Cape is famous for the natural wonders found here. At low tide you can walk out to sea, atop the longest natural rock reef in North America: About 2.4km (1½ miles) long, it is the dividing point between the Gulf of St. Lawrence and Northumberland Strait. As the tide moves in, their waters merge over the reef. It's a great place for seal watching; seabirds and bank swallows soar and the tide pools are great for checking out sea life.

WHERE TO STAY & EAT

Tignish Heritage Inn & Gardens ★   This restored heritage property built in 1868 is filled with atmosphere. Formerly the parish convent for St. Simon and St. Jude Church, it now offers modern amenities such as use of a kitchen—should you wish to cook up your own lobster—with its guest rooms and honeymoon suite. Decorated with a sparse country-chic style, rooms manage to reflect the heritage, yet are very comfortable. The gardens are a big attraction, luring guests out for a morning or evening stroll. Located within the village of Tignish, near mile '0' of the Confederation Trail.

206 Maple St., Tignish, PEI C0B 2B0. www.tignishheritageinn.ca. (✆ **877/882-2491** or 902/882-2491, 17 units. C$70–C$140 double. AE, MC, V. Open year-round. **Amenities:** Breakfast included; gardens; laundry. In room: TV, Wi-Fi (free).

Wind & Reef Restaurant ★ 🍴 SEAFOOD   Sitting down to a good meal is a welcome respite after exploring the natural rock reef, coast, and walking trails, and you can continue to enjoy the beauty outdoors through the many windows overlooking the sea and reef the restaurant is named for. Seafood heads a full menu, and rightfully so. Local oyster are superbly fresh and they excel at pan-fried fish. If you are really hungry, the Lightkeeper's Platter is great for sampling several choice shellfish and fish, and enough to share. Part of the North Cape Nature and Technology Interpretive Centre at the western tip of the Island, this spot verifies the importance of location, location, location. We've never had an unsatisfactory meal here.

North end of Rte. 12, North Cape. www.northcape.ca. ✆ **905/882-2991.** Main courses $13-$30. AE, MC, V. July–Aug daily 9am–8pm; June and Sept daily 10am–6pm; May and Oct Sat-Sun 10am–6pm.

The southern shore, Route 14, back toward Summerside takes you to **Skinner's Pond,** home to spectacular dunes and legendary singer Stompin' Tom Connors. At **Miminegash,** you are also in Irish Moss country (after a storm you may see heavy horses out in the surf, raking up this valuable seaweed with large rakes they drag behind them). Learn all about it at the **Seaweed Pie Café** in the Irish Moss Interpretive Centre (✆ **902/882-4313**) on Route 14; the gals here make the tasty dessert the place was named for, a delicious seafood chowder and more homemade-style fare. If you like a little whimsy in life, take a detour on Route 151 to **Back Roads Folk Art** (www. birchgate.ca/kerras; ✆ **902/853-3644**) in Lauretta. They claim to have the world's largest egg beater. Resident artist Kerras Jeffery will make you smile, even laugh out loud, with his whimsical creations. Backtrack to Route 14. Your next stop is West Point, the home of the black-and-white striped lighthouse that so often represents Prince Edward Island in promotional material. **West Point Lighthouse Inn** (see listing below) is one of a kind; a preserved lighthouse, housing a museum and an inn. A short walk or drive past **Cedar Dunes Provincial Park** takes you to the West Point waterfront, where the West Point Lighthouse restaurant, **Sandals** (159 Cedar Dunes Park Rd.; ✆ **902/ 859-1674**), serves up a delightful meal to enjoy while you overlook the marina, working fishing village, the shore, and sea. Interpretive walking trails, boardwalk, and miles of beautiful beach make West Point a very worthwhile place to stop and explore.

After lingering for a day or two, continue to follow the North Cape Coastal Drive. It will take you to the town of O'Leary for an hour or so at the **PEI Potato Museum** located on Dewar Lane (www.peipotatomuseum.com; ✆ **800/565-3457** or 902/ 859-2039). Spuds are a big thing here and the museum claims to have the largest collection of potato-related artifacts in the world. There is also a natty quilt shop in town, the **Quilt Gallery and Fabric, Crafts and More,** at 534 Main St. (www. soswebhosting.com/quiltgallery; ✆ **800/889-2606** or 902/859-1888).

The final leg of the North Cape Coastal Drive is through the region known as Evangeline. Culturally rich, this community's artisans, festivals, and traditional foods celebrate their Acadian heritage. And just to prove they are creative, one of the chief attractions is a house made of bottles. The **Bottle Houses** (www.bottlehouses.com; ✆ **902/854-2987**) at 6891 Rte. 11 in Cap-Egmont are life-size buildings created from 25,000 recycled bottles. Described as symphonies of light and color, they have been featured by Ripley's Believe It Or Not!

WHERE TO STAY & EAT

West Point Lighthouse Inn ★★ 🛎 The inn boasts walkout seaside decks overlooking the beach and sea for all rooms except the Tower Room and the Keepers Quarters, which are actually located in the lighthouse tower museum. Here, the song of the ocean waves rippling onto shore will lull you to sleep. Spacious rooms have hardwood floors and new furniture but retain the homey ambience the inn is known for. The Lighthouse underwent a major upgrade and change in 2011, which relocated the restaurant and expanded rooms in the inn. A lovely walk past Cedar Dunes Provincial Park will take you to the Point Restaurant on the village wharf. Continental breakfast is served in the inn, and delivery of meals can be arranged. This is a destination that will tempt you to relax for a few days of R & R. A boardwalk over the dunes, a museum right in the lighthouse, glorious beaches, and walking trails await.

364 Cedar Dunes Park Rd., West Point. www.westpointlighthouse.com. ✆ **800/764-6854** or 902/ 859-3605. 13 rooms. C$137–C$160 double. Open late May to Sept. AE, DC, MC, V. **Amenities:** Continental breakfast included. *In room:* A/C, TV/DVD, Internet (free).

PLANNING YOUR TRIP TO THE MARITIME PROVINCES

The three eastern provinces of Canada (also known as the Maritimes) are safe and scenic yet stretched out, with limited travel options. And the tourist season here is short, with many seasonal operations in rural areas that only open for the 2 to 4 months of summer. As such, the region requires some care when planning if you want to be sure about getting maximum value for your travel expenditures, and find available accommodations that fit both your budget and your needs.

On the other hand, you won't need to worry at all about things that vex travelers to some destinations: violent crime, snakes, sharks, inoculations against disease, and the like. All in all, this is one of the easiest, most comfortable places to travel with a family or as a lone traveler. If you dislike long drives, then pick one area and concentrate on enjoying that rather than trying to squeeze three provinces into one short vacation.

Reading the planning information in the following chapter before you set out could save you money, time, and the headache of distance between attractions, accommodations, and so on. Also order each province's free visitor guide; they are chock-full of information. Plan realistically, allowing yourself time to enjoy the places you want to see and experience rather than trying to cram it all into a few days. A good map will help put the Maritimes into perspective and be an amazing help in planning. In these pages, you'll get the nuts and bolts of travel in the provinces: when to come, the documentation you'll need, where to get more information, how to keep connected with the home office or family, on-the-ground resources, and more. These basics just might make the difference between a smooth trip and a bumpy one.

GETTING THERE
By Plane

Airports around Atlantic Canada offer access via scheduled flights. Halifax, Nova Scotia (YHZ), the region's major air hub, has frequent flights in and out of the region, as well as onward connections to local airports. Other major airports include Moncton, New Brunswick (YQM) and Charlottetown, Prince Edward Island (YYG). All offer direct flights to and from airports outside of the region.

The main air carriers serving Atlantic Canada are: **Air Canada** (www.aircanada.com; ☎ **888/247-2262**); its local commuter partner **Jazz** (www.flyjazz.ca), which is based in Halifax; **WestJet** (www.westjet.com; ☎ **888/937-8538**), which connects Halifax, Moncton, and Charlottetown with other airports in Canada; and **Porter Airlines** (www.flyporter.com; ☎ **888/619-8622**) which flies into Halifax and Moncton from Toronto. Several American carriers including **United** (www.united.com; ☎ **800/864-8331**) are also jumping into the Eastern Canada fray.

See the individual "Getting There" sections at the beginning of each chapter for more information on direct connections into specific cities.

By Car

Overland access to Atlantic Canada from the United States is through Maine. The most direct route to New Brunswick is to drive to Bangor (about 4½ hr. from Boston), then head east on Route 9 to Calais, Maine (about 2½ hr.). Here you can cross into St. Stephen, New Brunswick, and pick up Route 1 to Saint John and beyond. If you don't plan to stop until you hit Moncton or points east of Moncton, a slightly faster alternative is to continue northeast on the **Maine Turnpike**—which is the northernmost end of the Eastern Seaboard's famous Interstate 95—to Houlton, then cross the border and pick up the Trans-Canada Highway. Remember that the Turnpike is a toll road for a stretch (the toll is US$5 maximum one-way for a passenger car), although it becomes completely toll-free past exit 113 at Augusta.

New Brunswick can be accessed from other parts of Canada via Québec using the Trans-Canada Highway, which enters the province near Edmundston. Route 20 east from Montréal or Québec to Riviere-du-Loup links with Route 185, which becomes Route 2 at the border with New Brunswick; or the less-traveled route 132 enters New Brunswick at Campbellton.

By Ferry

A year-round ferry connects Saint John, New Brunswick (about a 4-hr. drive from either Bangor or Bar Harbor, Maine), with Nova Scotia; see "Getting Around," below for details. Reservations are advised during the peak summer season.

By Train

Inter-provincial rail service is now but a pale shadow of its former self. Prince Edward Island lacks rail service completely, as does southern New Brunswick (you can no longer travel by train to either Fredericton or Saint John).

There's just one train line: **VIA Rail** (www.viarail.ca; ☎ **888/842-7245**), the national rail carrier, which stops in a handful of towns along its single overnight route between Montréal and Halifax. The train runs six times daily (no Tues departures from either terminal). In New Brunswick, VIA trains stop at Campbellton, Charlo, Jacquet River, Petit Rocher, Bathurst, Miramichi, Rogersville, Moncton, and Sackville. In Nova Scotia, you can get on or off the train at Amherst, Springhill Junction, Truro, or Halifax. And that's it.

Fares for the trip depend on which class of seat you buy, from an economy seat (sleep sitting up) to various configurations of cabins. A non-discounted economy seat will run you about C$250 each way from Montréal to Halifax or back. Sleeping berths and private cabins are available at extra cost—the cheapest bed in a double-bunked cabin is about twice the cost of the no-bed fare—and VIA has even added a higher level of summer service on its overnight run (known as Sleeper Touring class) which includes better beds, presentations from an onboard guide, and a dome car. Discounts for those buying tickets in advance are sometimes possible.

The entire trip takes between 18 and 21 hours, depending on direction.

By Bus

Bus service into and out of this region tends to be slow and cumbersome. To get from New York to Halifax, for instance, you'd have to take one bus to Montréal (8–10 hr.), then connect to another bus line to Halifax (something like 18 hr.)—not my idea of a fun start to a vacation week.

Greyhound (www.greyhound.com; ☏ **800/231-2222**) offers service from diverse points around the United States to Montréal's bus station (☏ **514/843-4231**), where you can connect directly to Atlantic Canada–bound buses. Figure on spending 12 to 18 hours to get from Montréal to key cities in the eastern provinces; there is a 6am departure, for example, arriving in Halifax around midnight of the same day.

Acadian Lines (www.acadianbus.com; ☏ **800/567-5151**) offers service from Bangor, Maine, to New Brunswick several times weekly and reliable daily services within Nova Scotia, New Brunswick, and Prince Edward Island.

A few local transit companies pick up the ball from there, such as **Kings Transit** (www.kingstransit.ns.ca; ☏ **888/546-4442** or 902/678-7310), which can shuttle you cheaply among Wolfville, Kentville, and Digby.

GETTING AROUND

By Plane

There's a serious lack of competition for air routes in Eastern Canada, which can mean you'll pay high fares for even a short hop to or around the region. **Air Canada** (www.aircanada.com; ☏ **888/247-2262**) and its puddle-jumping subsidiary **Jazz** (www.flyjazz.ca) are often your only choices for both domestic and international flights. **WestJet** (www.westjet.com; ☏ **888/937-8538**) offers some other options.

Note that smaller airports throughout the region—such as Bathurst, Fredericton, Yarmouth, and Sydney—are starting to offer connections to the three main provincial hubs of Halifax, Moncton, and Charlottetown. E-mail or call the local tourism authority in advance about such connections if you're interested.

By Car

Atlantic Canada's road network is extensive and generally well maintained. But travelers expecting to find six-lane highways with high-speed on- and offramps will be in for a surprise. With few exceptions, the highway system here is on a far smaller scale. Even main arteries are nearly always just two lanes (one coming, one going), except on major routes connecting Fredericton and Saint John to Moncton, and then through to Halifax. The Trans-Canada Highway is the main road running through this region. It enters north of Edmundston, New Brunswick, and continues some 1,800km (1,120 miles) to St. John's, Newfoundland—taking a break at the Atlantic Ocean, of course. Numerous feeder roads connect to the Trans-Canada.

A few rules of the road: As in the United States and continental Europe, **drive on the right.** You may **make a right turn at a red light,** provided that you first stop fully and confirm that no one is coming from the left. (At some intersections, signs prohibit such a turn.) **Radar detectors are prohibited in all the Atlantic Provinces.** Drivers and all passengers are required to wear seat belts.

If you're arriving by plane, the usual suspects offer **car rentals** at major airports. Despite the number of rental outfits, however, it can be difficult to reserve a car during the short summer season, when demand soars. It's best to reserve ahead. Cars can be rented in any major center, most easily at airports. But be aware that it will be less expensive to pick up a car in town, than at an airport. Most major car rental firms are represented in the region. The best rates for rental can usually be obtained by booking ahead through a travel agent, the Internet or in tandem with air, train or accommodations. Rates depend on the season, type of car, and points of pickup and drop-off. Be sure to investigate car insurance carefully. You may be able to save substantial dollars by having rental cars included on your own car insurance or via your credit card coverage rather than buying it at a daily rate at the time of renting. Be sure to investigate carefully about **car-rental insurance** before setting out on your trip.

Remember that Canadian gas prices are higher than those in the U.S., though lower than they are in Europe. See "Gasoline" in "Fast Facts: The Maritimes" later in this chapter for more information.

By Ferry

There's an inter-provincial ferry that can considerably shorten the drive around the Bay of Fundy. The year-round ferry, known as the *Princess of Acadia,* links Saint John, New Brunswick, with Digby, Nova Scotia. The ferry sails once daily year-round, with two crossings per day during peak travel months and days. A peak season one-way fare (charged June–Oct) costs about C$41 for adults, C$26 for children age 6 to 13, C$5 per child age 5 and under, and C$31 for students and seniors; the car itself costs C$82 (more for trucks, vans, and buses), plus a C$20 fuel surcharge. Fares are a bit cheaper outside the peak travel months, and if you walk on and return within 30 days, there are also discounts available on the round-trip. Note that AAA and CAA members receive C$10 discounts on the car fare. Tariffs on this route haven't budged in several years; nevertheless, up-to-the-minute schedules and fares can be found at www.acadiaferry.com or by calling © **877/762-7245.**

A **second inter-provincial car ferry** links Prince Edward Island with Nova Scotia, though it doesn't save you time or money. You can also connect with Québec's Magdalen Islands by ferry from Souris in Prince Edward Island (www.ctma.ca), and with Newfoundland via a ferry from Sydney, Nova Scotia (www.marine-atlantic.ca).

By Train

Once again, I stress: There's just one train in Eastern Canada, **VIA Rail** (www.viarail. ca; © **888/842-7245**), which runs six times daily on an overnight route between Montréal and Halifax. You can theoretically connect between, say, Campbellton and Halifax in this way, though I've never met a casual tourist who did that. In New Brunswick, VIA trains stop at Campbellton, Charlo, Jacquet River, Petit Rocher, Bathurst, Miramichi, Rogersville, Moncton, and Sackville. In Nova Scotia, trains stop at Amherst, Springhill Junction, Truro, or Halifax. If you're serious about taking this train, see "Getting There," above, for more information, and consult the VIA website for fares and schedules.

By Bus

Decent bus service is offered between major cities and many smaller towns by **Acadian Lines.** For service between Nova Scotia, New Brunswick, and Prince Edward Island, contact Acadian at © **800/567-5151** or check the website at www.acadia bus.com.

TIPS ON ACCOMMODATIONS

Eastern Canada is a unique region, with a unique set of lodgings to match. You won't find many five-star hotels outside of the main cities, but rather a more homey hospitality—a patchwork of B&Bs, simple country inns, motels, and chain and business hotels. Here and there, genuine luxury resorts and inns can be found, serving amazing meals and offering top-tier rooms often furnished in antiques and Jacuzzis. Half of the adventure can be seeking out these treasures.

Here's a primer on the region's lodging situation.

Canada Select Ratings

One of the joys of booking travel to Eastern Canada is the useful ratings service supplied and constantly updated online (for free) by the Canadian government, a ratings system known as **Canada Select.**

Even better, you can view these ratings without leaving the comfort of your own home. Go to the website www.canadaselect.com to view their very complete listings and ratings.

It has to be said, however, that this system is *different* from Frommer's star-rating system, and completely unrelated to it. I have used my own judgment when assigning star ratings in this guide, without regard to the Canadian government's ratings.

Nevertheless, they are used by provincial visitor guides and thus provide a useful yardstick. The Canada Select system assigns a star value to each property, based on the various amenities supplied at a property (somewhat like the AAA's rating system for hotels and motels in North America).

The specific Canada Select rating system goes as follows:

o **One-star** properties are considered to offer "clean and well-maintained accommodations" and "the necessary facilities for an enjoyable stay." Inspectors check for and must find an adequately sized room, plus working window screens and coverings, closets or cupboards, linens, door locks, smoke detectors, and parking facilities.

o **Two stars** indicate "mid-range" properties. Everything here must be better than that at a one-star property: the mattresses, linens, window and wall coverings, carpets, lighting, furniture, and parking.

o **Three stars** indicate an "above-average" property with larger individual rooms, extra pieces of room furniture, coordinated decor, better-quality mattresses and linens, an alarm clock, and extra bath products in the bathrooms. All rooms in a three-star B&B must come with private bathrooms.

o **Four stars** indicate an "exceptional" property and services, with "superior quality throughout" the rooms, bathrooms, and common areas. These properties will usually have laundry services and lots of extra amenities.

o **Five stars** are reserved for properties that are "luxurious at a world standard," with "outstanding facilities, guest services, and amenities."

It needs to be said, though, that this rating system isn't perfect—nothing is, but it is a good guideline. There are a couple of points to be aware of: First, not all properties in Canada are members of Canada Select. (Properties have to pay a fee.) The majority join because it's tremendously useful as a marketing tool, so a Relais & Châteaux–affiliated property in New Brunswick, for example—a five-star experience by every possible measure—wouldn't join, because they don't need the marketing boost.

Second, it sometimes seems hotel inspectors are looking for inclusion (of breakfast, dinner, alarm clocks, parking lots, and so on) first, quality second. A place missing one thing on a long checklist might be demoted a star or two, even if it's great.

Types of Accommodations

Here are the various categories of lodgings you'll find in Eastern Canada, as defined and classified by Canada Select.

BED & BREAKFASTS Very common in Eastern Canada, the B&B (code: BB) must satisfy certain minimum requirements to be listed with Canada Select: inside entry to at least half the rooms, no more than three shared bathrooms, personalized service from the owner or innkeeper, and a three-item continental breakfast as a minimum. Further subcategories distinguish "bed and breakfast inns" (BBI), which must have five or more rooms; "tourist homes" (BB/TH), which aren't required to supply any breakfast at all; and "farm vacation" (FV) B&Bs, which must be located on fully operating farms. Everyone has dreamed of staying in a cute B&B on vacation, and indeed many of the places listed in this book fall into this category. They range from three-star experiences to places so simple they are assigned no stars at all. These places are adequate sleeps in the right location.

COTTAGES There are numerous cottages for rent in Canada's eastern provinces, at all price levels, and these can be one of the very best ways to see the region, especially for a family. You save money because you can cook, and the cottages are usually set in a lovely natural setting (beside the sea, overlooking fields or a golf course, and so on). And, a big plus for parents, there is always the option of putting the kids to bed and having some comfortable private time for Mom and Dad.

On the downside, they can vary wildly in quality and change details (owners, phone numbers, open status) from year to year. The three Maritime provinces each provide detailed lists of cottages in their visitor guides—so contact the provincial tourist offices in the places you're going for much more info, pictures, and listings. Another good place to get a look at cottages is on their websites, which usually include photographs.

HOTELS & MOTELS In practice, these vary so much that one hardly knows where to begin. Check our rankings closely. Also be aware that, at some point, you might end up in a chain hotel that's boring as bread. It happens, especially in smaller cities and towns, when the few good options (those cute B&Bs are often pretty small) are all filled up. Bring a book and your laptop; you'll survive, because chain hotels do at least deliver basic services—a gym, an Internet connection, a breakfast room—that rural country inns and B&Bs often can't provide.

INNS According to Canada Select, inns (code: I) must have "inside access" for at least 50% of the rooms, private bathrooms, and provide "personalized hospitality." The owners or innkeepers must live separately from the guest section nd they must serve a continental or full breakfast, with a minimum of three items, | , dinner. There are plenty of inns in the eastern provinces, but I'd quibble with the rankings assigned to some by the ratings board. Experience will reveal that at least some of them are aging and fading. Again, check the Frommer's ratings throughout this book for my choices.

RESORTS   According to Canada Select, a "resort" (code: R) must have four or more rooms in a main building, a full-service dining room, and some form of recreational facility (sports equipment, a pool, a spa, a fitness club—something). Resorts are destination properties and can include resort hotels, spas, ranches, condo hotels, and lodges, with rooms or housekeeping units.

Once again, there's sometimes a gap between appearance and reality. I've seen many a place in Eastern Canada describe itself as a "resort," when in fact it was anything but. Read reviews carefully before booking.

YOUTH HOSTELS   There are very few youth hostels in Eastern Canada, but those that are here are generally pretty decent, especially the urban hotels. Just a few are listed in this guidebook, because the quality can vary tremendously. If you don't mind the communal atmosphere and possibly doing a few chores before checkout, budget-conscious travelers should give them a look. Note that youth hostels once imposed an age limit on their guests (usually 25 or 26), but they no longer do in all except a few European countries.

The central office for "official" hostels in Canada is in Ottawa. Contact **Hostelling International-Canada** (© **613/237-7884**) by mail at 205 Catherine Street, Ste. 400, Ottawa, ON K2P 1C3, or check its website at www.hihostels.ca.

There are also some very good "independent" hostels, with no affiliation at all, in places like Digby.

UNIVERSITY DORMITORIES   In summer, when Canada's universities and colleges are (mostly) on break, many institutions open up their dorm rooms and communal spaces to traveling families for daily or weekly rentals. These rooms are almost uniformly spartan, inexpensive, and you often get the use of a private or shared kitchen in the deal. Dorm rooms are especially prevalent in Halifax and Charlottetown, but you can find them in other cities in Eastern Canada as well.

HOUSE RENTALS   Renting a house or condo apartment is an option in the Maritimes, though it's far, far easier to rent a cottage. Once again, check with the **tourist offices** of these provinces to get a sense about the situation, or check out HomeAway at www.homeaway.com and their vacation rentals by owner.

Another trick is to scour the listings of the **top realtors** in a given area. They often rent prime homes that are still on the market on a short-term basis—and sometimes "short-term" can be as short as 1 week.

CAMPGROUNDS & CAMPING CABINS   Campgrounds are easy to find throughout the region, both private and government-run in provincial and national parks. Many, such as KOAs, offer camping cabins. Rustic (they provide a roof, walls, and basic beds but no linens), they keep you dry and sometimes warm. You need your own sleeping bags and pillows. Great options if you like the outdoor experience but don't like tenting, and a good way to save money.

FAST FACTS: THE MARITIMES

Area Codes   The area code for New Brunswick is 506. The area code for Nova Scotia and Prince Edward Island is 902.

Business Hours   Bank, government, and business hours are generally 9am to 5pm in winter and, for some, 8am to 4pm in summer, Monday to Friday. Retail shops are generally open 10am to 10pm, every day except holidays; however, regulations differ from province to province, community, or time of the year, so check locally. Some retail shops, especially seasonal operations, may be open shorter hours.

Car Rental   See "Getting Around: By Car," earlier in this chapter.

Cellphones   See "Mobile Phones" later in this section.

Crime   See "Safety" later in this section.

Customs   International visitors can expect at least a probing question or two at the border or airport. Normal baggage and personal possessions should be no problem, but plants, animals, and weapons are among the items that may be prohibited or require additional documents before they're allowed in. For specific information about Canadian rules, check with the **Canada Border Services Agency** (www.cbsa-asfc.gc.ca; ℂ **506/636-5064** from outside the country or 800/461-9999 within Canada). Search for "bsf5082" to get a full list of visitor information.

Tobacco and alcoholic beverages face strict import restrictions: Individuals 18 years or older are allowed to bring in 200 cigarettes, 50 cigars, or 200 grams of tobacco; and only one of the following amounts of alcohol: 1.14 liters of liquor, 1.5 liters of wine, or 24 cans or bottles of beer. Additional amounts face hefty taxes. Possession of a car radar detector is prohibited, whether or not it is connected. Police officers can confiscate it and fines may run as high as C$1,000. A car driven into Canada can stay for the duration allowed the visitor, which is up to 6 months unless the visitor has arranged permission for a longer stay. Visitors can temporarily bring recreational vehicles, such as snowmobiles, boats, and trailers, as well as outboard motors, for personal use. If you do not declare goods or falsely declare them, they can be seized *along with the vehicle in which you brought them.*

For information on what you're allowed to bring home, contact one of the following agencies:

U.S. Citizens: U.S. Customs & Border Protection (CBP), 1300 Pennsylvania Ave., NW, Washington, DC 20229 (www.cbp.gov; (ℂ **877/287-8667**).

U.K. Citizens: HM Customs & Excise, Crownhill Court, Tailyour Road, Plymouth, PL6 5BZ (www.hmre.gov.uk; ℂ **0845/010-9000,** or 020/8929-0152 from outside the U.K.).

Australian Citizens: Australian Customs Service, Customs House, 5 Constitution Ave., Canberra City, ACT 2601 (www.customs.gov.au; ℂ **1300/363-263,** or 612/6275-6666 from outside Australia).

New Zealand Citizens: New Zealand Customs, the Customhouse, 17–21 Whitmore St., Box 2218, Wellington, 6140 (www.customs.govt.nz; ℂ **0800/428-786** or 04/473-6099).

If you're traveling with expensive items, such as laptops or musical equipment, consider registering them before you leave your country to avoid challenges at the border on your return.

Doctors   Walk-in clinics are found in most communities, except small villages. If you have an emergency, check the Yellow Pages in the telephone book for the hospital or clinic near to you, and its hours of operation. See "Health" below for more information.

Drinking Laws   The legal drinking age in Nova Scotia, New Brunswick, and Prince Edward Island (the minimum age at which a person is allowed to buy and/or drink alcohol) is 19. Liquor (including beer) can only be purchased at government-operated Liquor Commission stores or producing distillers or wineries. For a listing of locations go to www.mainbrace.ca.

Drinking and driving laws are tough, and enforced. Don't drink and drive. Also do not carry open containers of alcohol in your car or on your person unless in an area where drinking alcohol is permitted. National and Provincial Parks have alcohol regulations. Check when entering the park.

Visitors are allowed to bring small quantities of alcohol into Canada without paying duty or taxes. Requirements depend on your province of entry. It must accompany you, and you must be legal drinking age (19). Generally speaking you may bring: 1.5 liters (50 U.S. oz.) wine or wine coolers over 0.5 percent alcohol; or 1.14 liters (38 U.S. oz.) liquor; or total 1.14 liters (38 U.S. oz.) of wine and liquor; or 24×355 milliliter (12-oz.) cans or bottles of beer or ale, including beer coolers over 0.5 percent alcohol. You may bring more, but will have to pay customs and duty as required by the appropriate province before entering Canada. For information call the **Canadian Association of Liquor Jurisdictions** at ✆ **416/780-1851**.

Driving Rules See "Getting Around" earlier in this chapter.

Drugstores & Pharmacies Chain drugstores and independent pharmacies are located throughout Atlantic Canada. Stores in larger cities and towns are likely to be open later than those in more remote villages. One of the larger national chains is **Shoppers Drug Mart** (www.shoppersdrugmart.ca), which has a store locator on its website.

Electricity All Canadian hotels, inns, and private homes use the same electrical current as the United States: 110–115 volts, 60 cycles. If you're traveling from the U.S., you won't need adapters for your plugs. Coming from anywhere else, you probably will.

Embassies & Consulates All foreign embassies are located in Ottawa, Ontario, as follows:

Australian High Commission, Ste. 710–50 O'Connor St., Ottawa, Ontario K1P 6L2, www.embassy.gov.au, ✆ **613/236-0841**.

Embassy of Ireland, Ste. 1105, 130 Albert St., Ottawa, Ontario K1P 5G4, www.embassy ofireland.ca, ✆ **613/233-6281**.

New Zealand High Commission, Ste. 727, 99 Bank St., Ottawa, Ontario K1P 6G3, www.nzembassy.com/canada, ✆ **613/238-5991**.

United Kingdom, British High Commission, 80 Elgin St., Ottawa, Ontario K1P 5K7, http://ukincanada.fco.gov.uk, ✆ **613/237-1530**.

Embassy of the United States of America, 490 Sussex Dr., Ottawa, Ontario K1N 1G8, ✆ **613/238-5335**. **U.S. Consulate General Halifax**, Ste. 904, Purdy's Wharf Tower II, 1969 Upper Water St., Halifax, Nova Scotia B3J 3R7, http://canada.usembassy.gov, ✆ **902/429-2480**.

Emergencies The emergency number for Eastern Canada is ✆ **911** throughout.

Family Travel Atlantic Canada is simply a great place to take the kids: It's safe, clean, and sprinkled with just enough amusements and outdoor jaunts to keep them engaged. The provinces vary, though, in their ability to entertain the young 'uns.

Prince Edward Island is the best destination for young girls, simply due to the proliferation of attractions related to *Anne of Green Gables,* miles of sandy beaches, and lighthouses to explore. **New Brunswick** abounds with easy adventuring (golfing, biking, kayaking, big-tide sightseeing, and so on), living historic villages, and it throws in a handful of amusement parks and museums for good measure. **Nova Scotia** holds great appeal for the 6-and-up set: dinosaurs and fossils, forts with wonderful programs (check out Fortress Louisbourg), and one of the best interactive museum programs, with locations around the province, which is simply wonderful for kids.

To locate accommodations, restaurants, and attractions that are particularly kid friendly, refer to the "Kids" icon throughout this guide.

Gasoline Gas stations are basically the same as in the U.S., but gasoline is sold by the liter, not by the gallon. (3.8L equal 1 U.S. gal.). Gas prices in Newfoundland and Labrador fluctuate, as they do everywhere else in the world; as of press time, 1 liter cost about C$1.20 in St. John's and up to C$1.50 in more remote regions of the province.

Health Canada is one of the safest, cleanest countries in the world; as such, traveling in Eastern Canada doesn't pose any special health threats. Poisonous snakes? Sharks? Tropical diseases? Not here. And the food and water are very clean and safe to consume. Of course, you should still prepare for every eventuality anyway.

Health Care Canada's healthcare system is excellent; you shouldn't ever have trouble finding English-speaking medical help, unless you're in very remote areas of, for example, Northern New Brunswick (away from the coastal towns) or wilderness Cape Breton. It is advisable to always obtain good travel insurance to cover the time you are away from home. **Travel Health Online** (www.tripprep.com), sponsored by a consortium of travel medicine practitioners, can offer helpful advice on traveling abroad. The group maintains a relationship with one physician in the eastern provinces, Dr. Frank Lo in Halifax. In addition, the **International Society of Travel Medicine** (www.istm.org) lists one affiliated travel clinic on PEI and another in Moncton, New Brunswick.

Insurance Canadians are covered when traveling within Canada. However, most U.S. health plans (including Medicare and Medicaid) do *not* provide coverage for travel to Canada, and the ones that do often require you to pay for services upfront and reimburse you only after you return home. Those from other countries need to check out the situation in their country well before leaving home.

As a safety net, you may want to buy **travel medical insurance,** particularly if you're traveling to a remote or high-risk area where emergency evacuation might be necessary. Very few health insurance plans pay for medical evacuation back to the U.S. (which can cost US$10,000 and up), but a number of companies offer medical evacuation services anywhere in the world. If you're ever hospitalized more than 150 miles from home, **MedjetAssist** (www.medjetassistance.com; ✆ **800/527-7478**) will pick you up and fly you to the hospital of your choice virtually anywhere in the world in a medically equipped and staffed aircraft 24 hours a day, 7 days a week. Annual memberships are US$250 for an individual, US$385 for a family; you can also purchase shorter-term memberships starting at about US$100.

Pharmacies are easy to find in Eastern Canada (see above). Still, if you suffer from a chronic illness, consult your doctor before your departure. Pack **prescription medications** in your carry-on luggage, and carry them in their original containers, with pharmacy labels—otherwise they won't make it through airport security. Carry the generic name of prescription medicines, in case a local pharmacist is unfamiliar with the brand name. It is wise to make a list of ALL medications and carry it with you at all times. Ask your pharmacy for a printout.

Internet & Wi-Fi Cities like Halifax and Charlottetown are rife with Internet cafes; anywhere else, it's catch-as-catch-can—but many towns in Eastern Canada now sport at least one cybercafe. It might double as the town laundry/coffee shop, but it'll be there somewhere. So ask.

Most airports have **Internet kiosks** that provide basic Web access for a per-minute fee that's usually higher than cybercafe prices. Many **public and university libraries** in Canada offer Internet access free or for a small charge—you might have to surrender a piece of ID first. Most **youth hostels** in Canada have at least one computer with Internet access, though there is just a thimbleful of hostels in the Maritimes—Halifax has one. But avoid hotel business centers unless you're desperate; you'll usually pay exorbitant hourly rates.

More and more hotels, resorts, campgrounds, airports, cafes, retailers, and even entire cities are going **Wi-Fi,** becoming "hotspots" that offer free high-speed Wi-Fi access or charge a small fee for usage. Sometimes an entire community will be blanketed by coverage—the city of **Fredericton,** New Brunswick, for instance, has won national awards for its free citywide Wi-Fi network—but that's rare.

A hotel in Eastern Canada is virtually guaranteed to offer Wi-Fi access; however, it can be very expensive at the larger corporate hotels (typically C$10 a day—which can end at midnight, rather than for a 24-hr. period, which could result in a C$20 charge if you don't read the fine print); a motel, inn, or B&B in the region is about 70% likely to have it; coffee shops offer Wi-Fi in ever-increasing numbers. Keep in mind that you'll often have to pay for the privilege, though: Wi-Fi is not always free. It's a good idea to **search for Wi-Fi hotspots** ahead of time—there are various websites and mobile phone applications that can do this for you.

Language   English is spoken throughout the region. In some areas of all three provinces, Acadian French is also spoken.

Legal Aid   Legal Aid offices located across Canada can be sourced at www.canlaw.com/legalaid/aidoffice or contact the following:

Legal Information Society of Nova Scotia, 5523 B Young St., Halifax, Nova Scotia, B3K 1Z7, www.legalinfo.org, ✆ **800/665-9779** or 902/455-3135.

Legal Aid New Brunswick, 2-403 Regent St., Fredericton, New Brunswick E3B 3X6, ✆ **506/451-1424.**

Community Legal Information Association of Prince Edward Island, P.O. Box 1207, 1st Floor Sullivan Building, Fitzroy St., Charlottetown, Prince Edward Island, www.cliapei.ca, ✆ **800/240-9798** or 902/892-0853.

LGBT Travelers   Canada as a whole is considered extremely friendly to gay travelers. Eastern Canada varies from place to place in the warmth of the welcome, but the cities are uniformly accepting.

Halifax doesn't have any one especially "gay" district, but **GayHalifax** (http://gay.hfxns.org) is a good online starting point to help you find out what's going on locally with activists. **Destination Halifax** (www.destinationhalifax.com/rainbow) is the best online guide to the city's gay events that I've yet seen.

Mail   Canada Post offers a reliable international postal service. Postage for letters or postcards within Canada is approximately C60¢, to the United States C$1.05, and international C$1.75. You can determine costs with a rate calculator at www.canadapost.ca. Always include postal or zip codes on any mail being sent. Postage stamps and mailboxes are readily available throughout the Maritime Provinces. If you require fast shipment of parcels or letter packets, FedEx and other courier services are available in most towns and cities. Check the phone book. Some office supply stores and hotels offer pickup points for couriers.

Medical Requirements   Unless you're arriving from an area known to be suffering from an epidemic (such as cholera or yellow fever), inoculations or vaccinations are not required for entry into Canada.

Mobile Phones   Yes, foreign cellphones work in Canada. However, depending on your phone plan, you may have to pay roaming and long-distance charges that can push call costs up to very expensive. Some large U.S. carriers offer tack on Canadian calling plans that reduce these charges while making calls from within Canada. Check with your carrier about switching on to one such plan for the duration of your trip—without any penalties for switching it back off after you get back home, making sure they understand that you will be calling back to the U.S. from Canada and making calls within Canada.

You should be able to make and receive calls in all the populated areas of Eastern Canada, assuming your cellphone works on a GSM (Global System for Mobile Communications) system or you have a world-capable multiband phone. In the U.S., T-Mobile and AT&T Wireless use the quasi-universal GSM system; Sprint and Verizon don't. All European and most Australian phones come GSM-ready. GSM phones function with a removable plastic SIM card, encoded with your phone number and account information.

FYI, Canada has three national wireless providers, Bell Mobility, Rogers Wireless, and Telus Mobility. Rogers is GSM. Bell and Telus use CDMA technology.

To use the phone in Canada, simply call your wireless carrier before leaving home and ask if "international roaming" needs to be activated on your account and the cost. Again, per-minute charges can be high, even if you do subscribe to some form of extended calling plan or international add-on plan that includes Canadian minutes.

Buying a disposable Canadian cellphone is another option, and might be economically attractive if you can locate an inexpensive prepaid phone system. Stop by a Wal-Mart or cellphone shop and ask about the cheapest package that provides the service you need; you'll probably pay less than C$100 for a phone and a starter calling card. Local calls might be as low as C10¢ or C20¢ per minute.

All Canadian cellphones should work in the Atlantic provinces, although some of the "discount" brands with smaller coverage areas may only work in major centers. While you will not incur roaming charges if you are traveling out of province, long distance charges may apply. These provinces are thinly populated in some regions and as a result cell towers, especially Rogers, can be few and far between. You may not be able to use your cellphone everywhere; even driving the Trans-Canada Highway, you can pop in and out of service. In the major cities, you will always be reliably connected; in the smaller towns, most of the time; and, in the wilderness of the big national and provincial parks, probably only in hotspots or not at all. Definitely ask park wardens about cell coverage before you venture into the backcountry.

If you have access to the Web while traveling, you might consider a broadband-based telephone service (in technical terms, **Voice over Internet Protocol,** or **VoIP**) such as **Skype** (www.skype.com) or **Vonage** (www.vonage.com), which allows you to make free international calls if you use their services from your smart phone or laptop.

Money & Costs   Frommer's lists prices in the local currency. Smart travelers watch the exchange rates and buy money for their destination when advantageous.

THE VALUE OF THE CANADIAN DOLLAR VS. OTHER POPULAR CURRENCIES

C$	A$	€	NZ$	£	US$
1.00	0.95	0.70	1.20	0.65	1.00

Frommer's lists exact prices in the local currency. The currency conversions quoted above were correct at press time. However, rates fluctuate, so before departing, consult a currency exchange website such as **www.oanda.com/convert/classic** or **www.xe.com/ucc** to check up-to-the-minute rates.

Cost-wise, the eastern provinces of Canada are **incredibly affordable**—among the most affordable such places in North America. You'll pay normal prices for food and gas, because those things are generally imported to the provinces, but hotel and transit rates are middling to lower than average. And shopping is a downright bargain.

Canadian currency, like U.S. currency, is denominated in **dollars and cents,** though there are some differences. Canada has no C$1 bill, for example. Instead, Canadians use a C$1 coin (called a *loonie* because it depicts a loon) and a C$2 coin (sometimes called a *toonie*).

You'll **avoid lines at ATMs** and airports in Eastern Canada by exchanging some money before you leave home. You can exchange money at your local American Express or Thomas Cook office, or at your bank. Exchange enough petty cash to cover airport incidentals, tipping, and transportation to your hotel before you leave home, or withdraw money upon arrival at an airport ATM.

WHAT THINGS COST IN THE MARITIMES

	C$
Taxi to/from Charlottetown airport to downtown	10.00
or to/from Halifax airport to downtown	50.00
Bus fare in Halifax	3.25
Cup of coffee	2.50
Pint of beer	7.00
Moderate hotel room	100.00–150.00
Comfortable bed-and-breakfast	70.00–100.00
Takeout fish and chips	12.00
Expensive 3-course dinner without wine	65.00–85.00

If you're driving into Canada, you needn't worry about stocking up on Canadian dollars before or immediately upon entry into Canada. That's because **U.S. currency is widely accepted** here, especially in border towns, and you'll often see signs at cash registers announcing current exchange rates. These are not always the best rates, however, so it behooves you to visit an ATM or cash some traveler's checks as soon as you're able.

The easiest and best way to get cash right away in Eastern Canada is from an **ATM,** sometimes referred to as an ABM, "automated bank machine." They're widely available in most towns and cities. ATMs often offer the best exchange rates in Canada—avoid exchanging money at commercial exchange bureaus and hotels, which usually have the highest transaction fees. If your card uses the **Cirrus** (www.mastercard.com) or **PLUS** (www.visa.com) networks, you'll be able to find ATMs throughout Eastern Canada that connect to your bank.

Remember that **many banks impose a fee** every time you use a card at another bank's ATM, and that fee can be higher for international transactions (up to US$5 or more) than for domestic ones. Members of the Global ATM Alliance usually charge *no* transaction fees for cash withdrawals at fellow Alliance member ATMs; these include Bank of America in the U.S. and Scotiabank in Eastern Canada, as well as BNP Paribas, Barclays, Deutsche Bank 24, and Westpac. So, if you have a BoA account, seek out Scotiabank ATMs.

Finally, **credit cards** are one last safe way to get or spend money. They provide a convenient record of your expenses and generally offer relatively good exchange rates. You can even withdraw cash advances from your credit cards at banks or ATMs (provided you remember your PIN), though high fees can make these credit card cash advances a pricey way to get cash. Keep in mind that you'll pay interest from the moment of the cash advance withdrawal, even if you pay your monthly bills on time. Also, note that many banks now assess a 1% to 3% "transaction fee" on all credit card charges you incur abroad.

Credit cards that are more or less universally accepted in Eastern Canada include Visa, MasterCard, and American Express. Diners Club and Discover cards are accepted by a few merchants, but not many. Interac or debit cards are almost as widely accepted as cash.

One good habit to get into is to call your credit card company before you leave and advise them of your destination and dates of travel. It may save an embarrassing and upsetting delay in transactions while the credit card company checks for possible thefts. Remember to bring some cash, in any case: Many small establishments still accept no credit.

Multicultural Travelers All travelers are welcomed in the Maritime provinces, although many languages are not spoken unless you have arranged for a translator. English and some French is spoken, and most destinations popular with Japanese visitors have signage, and/or staff who speak Japanese.

Newspapers & Magazines Along with local newspapers, Canada's national newspaper, the *Globe and Mail*, is readily accessible, as are magazines. For foreign newspapers, check public or university libraries or news stands in larger communities.

Packing Dress style in Eastern Canada is basically casual unless you are attending a formal event. Summer days can be hot, but it cools nicely in the evenings. In winter you will need winter footwear, winter coats, hats, and gloves.

Passports It is no longer possible to enter Canada and return to the U.S. by showing a government-issued photo ID (such as a driver's license) and proof of U.S. citizenship (such as a birth or naturalization certificate). The **Western Hemisphere Travel Initiative (WHTI)**, which took full effect in 2009, requires all U.S. citizens returning to the U.S. from Canada to have a U.S. passport (this includes children 17 and under). In other words, if you are a U.S. citizen traveling to Canada by air, sea, or land, you must have a valid U.S. passport or a new passport card (see www.getyouhome.gov for details) in order to get back into the U.S.

You'll find current entry information on the website of the U.S. State Department at **www.travel.state.gov** and on the **Canada Border Services Agency** website, **www.cbsa-asfc.gc.ca**.

See www.frommers.com/tips for information on how to obtain a passport. See "Embassies & Consulates," above, for whom to contact if you lose yours while traveling in the U.S. and Canada. For other information, please contact the following agencies:

For Residents of Australia Contact the **Australian Passport Office** at www.passports. gov.au or ✆ **131-232.**

For Residents of Ireland Contact the **Passport Office** at www.dfa.ie or ✆ **01/ 671-1633**.

For Residents of New Zealand Contact the **Passport Office** at www.passports.govt. nz or ✆ **0800/225-050** in New Zealand, or 04/463-9360.

For Residents of the United Kingdom Visit your nearest passport office, major post office, or travel agency or contact **Identity and Passport Service** by searching its website at www.homeoffice.gov.uk or by calling ✆ **0300/222-0000.**

For Residents of the United States To find your regional passport office, either check the U.S. Department of State website at www.travel.state.gov, or call the **National Passport Information Center** toll-free number (✆ **877/487-2778**) for automated information.

Petrol Please see "Gasoline" earlier in this chapter.

Police Large communities usually have their own police forces in Canada, while smaller communities and rural areas are policed by the RCMP (Royal Canadian Mounted Police–who only ride horses on ceremonial occasions). Dialing 911 will connect you with the appropriate police force in the event of an emergency.

Safety The towns and cities of Atlantic Canada are small, well policed, and generally safe. Partygoers and those who have over-imbibed may occasionally be annoying or even a bit threatening, especially late on weekend nights in downtown neighborhoods, but serious crime is extremely rare in Eastern Canada.

Nonetheless, whenever you're traveling in an unfamiliar place in this region, stay alert, be aware of your immediate surroundings, and take precautions, such as locking your car and hotel room and not walking alone in dark, unpopulated urban areas late at night. Try not to drive late at night when there's likely to be no one else out on the road if you run into trouble. And **carry a cellphone** at all times if you have one; coverage in Eastern Canada certainly isn't complete, but it is improving year by year.

The emergency number for Eastern Canada is ✆ **911** throughout.

Senior Travel Few countries are as attentive to the needs of seniors as Canada. Discounts are extended to people 60 and over for everything ranging from public transportation to museum and movie admissions. Even many hotels, tour operators, and restaurants offer discounts, so don't be bashful about inquiring, but always carry some kind of identification that shows your date of birth. (It's always best to inquire before checking in or ordering.) This discount varies widely; in practice, the gap between senior prices and full price seems to be narrowing in recent years. But ask anyway.

Members of the **AARP** (www.aarp.org; ✆ **888/687-2277**) get discounts when traveling to or in Eastern Canada on hotels, airfares, and car rentals. AARP offers members a wide range of benefits, including *AARP The Magazine* and a monthly newsletter. Anyone over 50 can join. **CARP**, the Canadian Association of Retired Persons (www.carp.ca; ✆ **888/363-2279**) has chapters in Prince Edward Island, Nova Scotia, and New Brunswick, and a similar range of benefits.

Elderhostel now calls its programs **Road Scholar** (www.roadscholar.org; ✆ **800/454-5768**), which encompasses worldwide educational adventures and study programs for those aged 55 and over. They manage several great tours of Atlantic Canada, including a Nova Scotia–PEI combo (10 days). As a bonus, you can view the complete tour itinerary—including the actual inns and hotels you'll be staying in—online before laying down any cash.

Single Travel   Many reputable tour companies offer singles-only trips, and some of them dip into the Maritimes. **Singles Travel International** (www.singlestravelintl.com; ✆ **877/765-6874**) offers singles-only escorted tours to faraway places like London, Alaska, Fiji, and the Greek Islands; in past years, its fall foliage cruise has touched down in Halifax.

The popular outfitter **Backroads** (www.backroads.com; ✆ **800/462-2848**) offers active-travel trips to destinations worldwide, including several hiking, cycling, and kayak tours in Nova Scotia and a fun bike tour of Prince Edward Island.

One of the best bets for singles is to enroll in a program such as the culinary or artisan educational sessions or learning vacations (see "Tours" in chapter 2) that bring you together with like-minded folk. Check out the arts, music, and performing arts for example, or college or university offerings.

Remember that on some package vacations to Canada, as a single traveler you might be hit with the dreaded "single supplement" to the base price. To avoid it, agree to room with other single travelers or find a compatible roommate before you go from a specialized roommate-locator agency.

Smoking   All three Maritime provinces ban smoking in public places and workplaces. Basically, smokers are relegated to the outdoors, well away from entranceways. As well, many hotels rooms are designated nonsmoking. If you smoke, check when reserving or checking in to ensure you get a smoking room, otherwise you may face surcharges if you light up.

Taxes   Sales tax is added onto most purchases and services. In Prince Edward Island the federal GST of 5% is added, then a 10% provincial sales tax (PST) is added. PST is not charged on clothing or footwear (sports or protective equipment and accessories are not exempt). In Nova Scotia an HST (harmonized sales tax) of 15% is added. In New Brunswick an HST of 13% is added.

Telephones   Though they're used less and less, pay phones are still scattered throughout Atlantic Canada and are self-explanatory. Local calls cost from C25¢ to C50¢. Calls made to the United States or elsewhere abroad on a pay phone can be very pricey; bring a calling card, and check in advance to be sure it works in Canada and what the per-minute rates will be to the U.S. or other countries. You can also ask locally at drugstores, grocery, and convenience stores for prepaid calling cards, which usually offer a much better rate for calling long distance than feeding coins into a phone. (There might be a "setup" or per-call fee hidden in the cost of such cards, so read the fine print.)

The United States and Canada are on the same long-distance system. To make a long-distance call between the United States and Canada (in either direction), simply dial ℭ **1** first, then the area code and number. Callers to other countries will need to check the country code in the phone book or with the long distance operator.

Remember that numbers beginning with **800, 888** and **866** in Canada are toll-free—so some of these numbers won't work if they're dialed from outside Canada. Just the same, some toll-free numbers in the U.S. won't work if they're dialed from Canada.

Time　The three provinces in the Maritimes are in the Atlantic Time Zone. Change your clocks when crossing the border from the United States or Québec. Daylight saving time begins at 2am local time on the second Sunday in March when clocks are turned ahead 1 hour. Clocks are turned back at the end of daylight saving time on the first Sunday in November.

Tipping　In hotels, tip **bellhops** at least C$1 per bag (C$2–C$3 if you have a lot of luggage) and tip the **chamber staff** C$1 to C$2 per day (more if you've left a big mess for him or her to clean up). Tip the **doorman** or **concierge** only if he or she has provided you with some specific service (for example, calling a cab for you or obtaining difficult-to-get theater tickets). Tip the **valet-parking attendant** C$1 every time you get your car.

In restaurants, bars, and nightclubs, tip **service staff** and **bartenders** 15% to 20% of the check, tip **checkroom attendants** C$1 per garment, and tip **valet-parking attendants** C$1 per vehicle.

As for other service personnel, tip **cabdrivers** 15% of the fare; tip **skycaps** at airports at least C$1 per bag (C$2–C$3 if you have a lot of luggage); and tip **hairdressers** and **barbers** 15% to 20%.

For help with tip calculations, currency conversions, and more, download our convenient Travel Tools app for your mobile device. Go to www.frommers.com/go/mobile, and click on the Travel Tools icon.

Toilets　Washrooms are generally very clean and readily available. You won't find public washrooms on the street very often, but they are in malls, large retail stores, and government buildings. If you're stuck, a coffee shop or fast-food restaurant is your best bet.

Travelers with Limited Mobility　Canada has made tremendous efforts toward eliminating barriers to mobility for its citizens and, by extension, its tourist visitors. City pavements feature curb cuts for wheelchair travel, and larger hotels and airports sport wheelchair-accessible washrooms. A growing number of restaurants and tourist attractions are now designed for wheelchair accessibility as well, although room for improvement remains. National and provincial parks are almost always accessible, at least to a degree.

The **Canadian Paraplegic Association** (www.canparaplegic.org) runs a helpful website and also maintains an office in each of the three Maritime provinces. In New Brunswick, call ℭ **506/462-9555;** in Nova Scotia, call ℭ **902/423-1277;** and in Prince Edward Island, call ℭ **902/626-9523.**

Travelers with disabilities headed for Nova Scotia can also ask locally about accessible transportation and recreational opportunities by contacting the **Nova Scotia League for Equal Opportunities** (www.novascotialeo.org; ℭ **866/696-7536** or 902/455-6942). The organization maintains a useful network of contacts throughout the province.

Some travel agencies offer customized tours and itineraries for travelers with disabilities. One of the best is **Accessible Journeys** (www.disabilitytravel.com; ℭ **800/846-4537** or 610/521-0339), which can help you find a 10-day, wheelchair-accessible cruise touching Halifax and Saint John, for example.

Avis Rent a Car (www.avis.com/access; ℭ **888/879-4273**) has a good "Avis Access" program that offers services for customers with special travel needs. These include specially outfitted vehicles with swivel seats, spinner knobs, panoramic mirrors, and hand controls; mobility scooter rentals; and accessible bus service. Be sure to reserve well in advance.

Visas American travelers to Canada do not require visas and neither do residents of many other countries, including citizens of most European countries, Australia, New Zealand, Japan, Mexico, and some present and former British territories in the Caribbean—this includes anyone holding a green card in the U.S. or anyone who is a British overseas citizen of the U.K. Needless to say, bring your identification or the relevant paperwork on your trip. To be sure about whether you will need a visa or not, consult the Canadian government's up-to-date listing of countries whose residents do need one at **www.cic.gc.ca/english/visit/visas.asp**.

Visitor Information It's well worth a toll-free call or postcard in advance of your trip to stock up on the free literature and maps that provincial authorities liberally bestow upon those considering a vacation in their province. Here's how to reach the official tourism folks who dispense these goodies:

Nova Scotia Department of Tourism, Culture & Heritage, World Trade Centre, 6th Floor, 1800 Argyle St. (P.O. Box 456) Halifax, NS B3J 2R5. www.novascotia.com; ℰ **800/565-0000** or 902/425-5781.

New Brunswick Department of Tourism & Parks, P.O. Box 12345, Campbellton, NB E3N 3T6. http://tourismnewbrunswick.ca; ℰ **800/561-0123.**

Tourism PEI, P.O. Box 2000, Charlottetown, PEI C1A 7N8. www.tourismpei.com; ℰ **800/463-4734** or 902/368-4444.

All three provinces staff helpful **visitor centers** at key access points, including the main roadways running into the provinces and in their major cities. Expect cordial staff and exceptionally well-stocked racks overflowing with menus, brochures, and booklets. Excellent **road maps** are also available from all three provincial tourism authorities—ask at the welcome centers. These maps are free.

Staff at these centers provide a surplus of information on local attractions, and they can also fill you in on what's happening anywhere else in the province so that you can plan a few days in advance. If the staffers don't have the information you need at their fingertips, they'll often make phone calls and track it down for you.

All three provinces also publish free, magazine-size **travel guides** crammed with essential information on hotels, inns, campgrounds, and attractions. They set an international standard for high-quality information (and size), are excellent and unfailingly helpful. You can also go online to get information in advance. Here are a few places to start clicking:

o Nova Scotia's official website is a great whirlwind tour of accommodations and tourism sites; you can even download a bit of local music. It can be found at **www.novascotia.com**.

o Nova Scotia Provincial Parks' website provides basic, up-to-date information about its many excellent parks at **www.parks.gov.ns.ca**.

o The official New Brunswick tourism site offers a great place to start: **www.tourismnewbrunswick.ca**.

o The official Prince Edward Island tourism information resource can be found at both **www.gentleisland.com** and **www.peiplay.com**.

o Finally, for information about travels in the region's national parks, a good first stop is the Parks Canada official website at **www.pc.gc.ca**.

Water Water for consumption is monitored and safe throughout the Maritimes.

Wi-Fi See "Internet & Wi-Fi" earlier in this chapter.

Women Travelers This destination is popular with women travelers who appreciate the safety and ease of travel. A caution about being careful where you go late at night is the same as would be offered anywhere. Common sense and attention to your surroundings is always wise.

AIRLINE WEBSITES

Air Canada
www.aircanada.com

Air Saint Pierre
www.airsaintpierre.com

American Airlines
www.aa.com

British Airways
www.british-airways.com

Cubana Airlines
www.cubana.cu

Delta Air Lines
www.delta.com

Icelandair
www.icelandair.com

Porter Airlines
www.flyporter.com

Sunwing Airlines
www.flysunwing.com

Thomas Cook
flytomascook.com

United Airlines
www.united.com

US Airways
www.usairways.com

WestJet
www.westjet.com

Index

See also Accommodations and
Restaurant indexes, below.

General Index

GENERAL INDEX

273

Accommodations— Nova Scotia